T0235735

Lecture Notes in Computer Science 11995

More information about this series at http://www.springer.com/series/7409

Jan Mazal · Adriano Fagiolini ·
Petr Vasik (Eds.)

Modelling and Simulation for Autonomous Systems

6th International Conference, MESAS 2019
Palermo, Italy, October 29–31, 2019
Revised Selected Papers

 Springer

Editors
Jan Mazal 🄳
NATO Modelling and Simulation
Centre of Excellence
Rome, Italy

Adriano Fagiolini 🄳
MIRPA Lab
University of Palermo
Palermo, Italy

Petr Vasik 🄳
Faculty of Mechanical Engineering
Brno University of Technology
Brno, Czech Republic

ISSN 0302-9743   ISSN 1611-3349   (electronic)
Lecture Notes in Computer Science
ISBN 978-3-030-43889-0   ISBN 978-3-030-43890-6   (eBook)
https://doi.org/10.1007/978-3-030-43890-6

LNCS Sublibrary: SL3 – Information Systems and Applications, incl. Internet/Web, and HCI

This Springer imprint is published by the registered company Springer Nature Switzerland AG
The registered company address is: Gewerbestrasse 11, 6330 Cham, Switzerland

Preface

This volume contains selected papers presented at the conference on Modelling and Simulation for Autonomous Systems (MESAS 2019), held during October 29–31, 2019, in Palermo, Italy. The initial idea to launch the MESAS project was introduced by the NATO Modelling and Simulation Centre of Excellence in 2013, with intent to bring together the Modelling and Simulation and the Autonomous Systems/Robotic communities and to collect new ideas for concept development and experimentation in this domain. Since then, this event gathers together—in keynote, regular, poster, and forward thinking sessions—fully recognized experts from different technical communities in military, academia, and industry. The main topical parts of the 2019 edition of MESAS was "Future Challenges of Advanced M&S Technology," "M&S of Intelligent Systems - AI, R&D and Application," and "AxS in Context of Future Warfare and Security Environment (Concepts, Applications, Training, Interoperability, etc.)." The community of interest submitted 53 papers for consideration. Each submission was reviewed by three Technical Committee members or selected independent reviewers. The committee, in light of the review process outcome, decided to accept 37 papers to be presented (in seven sessions) and 22 full papers and 13 short papers were accepted to be included in the conference proceedings.

December 2019   Jan Mazal

MESAS 2019 Logo

MESAS 2019 Organizer

NATO Modelling and Simulation Centre of Excellence
(NATO M&S COE)

The NATO M&S COE is a recognized international military organization activated by the North Atlantic Council in 2012, and does not fall under the NATO Command Structure. Partnering nations provide funding and personnel for the centre through a memorandum of understanding. The Czech Republic, Italy, and the United States are the contributing nations, as of this publication. The NATO M&S COE supports NATO transformation by improving the networking of NATO and nationally owned M&S systems, promoting cooperation between nations and organizations through the sharing of M&S information, and serving as an international source of expertise.

The NATO M&S COE seeks to be a leading world-class organization, providing the best military expertise in modelling and simulation technology, methodologies, and the development of M&S professionals. Its state-of-the-art facilities can support a wide range of M&S activities including but not limited to: education and training of NATO M&S professionals on M&S concepts and technology with hands-on courses that expose students to the latest simulation software currently used across the alliance; concept development and experimentation using a wide array of software capability and network connections to test and evaluate military doctrinal concepts as well as new simulation interoperability verification; and the same network connectivity that enables the COE to become the focal point for NATO's future distributed simulation environment and services.

https://www.mscoe.org/

Organization

General Chairs

Adriano Fagiolini   University of Palermo, Italy
Stefan Pickl   Universität der Bundeswehr, Germany
Agostino Bruzzone   University of Genoa, Italy
Alexandr Štefek   University of Defence, Czech Republic

Program Committee Chair

Petr Stodola   University of Defence, Czech Republic

Program Committee

Ozkan Atan   University of Van Yüzüncü Yil, Turkey
Ronald C. Arkin   Georgia Institute of Technology, USA
Richard Balogh   Slovak University of Technology in Bratislava,
                                 Slovakia
Marco Biagini   NATO M&S COE, Rome, Italy
Antonio Bicchi   University of Pisa, Italy
Dalibor Biolek   University of Defence, Czech Republic
Agostino Bruzzone   University of Genoa, Italy
Erdal Cayirci   University of Stavanger, Norway
Fabio Corona   Modelling and Simulation Centre of Excellence, Italy
Andrea D'Ambrogio   University of Rome Tor Vergata, Roma, Italy
Frederic Dalorso   NATO ACT Autonomy Program, USA
Riccardo Di Matteo   University of Genoa, Italy
Radek Doskočil   University of Defence, Czech Republic
Jan Drozd   University of Defence, Czech Republic
Michal Dub   University of Defence, Czech Republic
Jan Faigl   Czech Technical University in Prague, Czech Republic
Jan Farlik   University of Defence, Czech Republic
Pavel Foltin   University of Defence, Czech Republic
Petr Frantis   University of Defence, Czech Republic
Giulio Franzinetti   Lio Tech Limited, UK
Corrado Guarino Lo Bianco   University of Parma, Italy
Karel Hajek   University of Defence, Czech Republic
Kamila Hasilova   University of Defence, Czech Republic
Václav Hlaváč   Czech Technical University in Prague, Czech Republic
Jan Hodicky   University of Defence, Czech Republic
Jam Holub   FEE CTU Prague, Czech Republic

Jaroslav Hrdina	Brno University of Technology, Czech Republic
Thomas C. Irwin	Joint Force Development, DoD, USA
Shafagh Jafer	Embry-Riddle Aeronautical University, USA
Sebastian Jahnen	Universität der Bundeswehr, Germany
Jason Jones	NATO M&S COE, Rome, Italy
Lukáš Kopečný	Brno University of Technology, Czech Republic
Piotr Kosiuczenko	Military University of Technology in Warsaw, Poland
Tomas Krajnik	Czech Technical University, Czech Republic
Tobias Kuhn	NATO M&S COE, Rome, Italy
Miroslav Kulich	CTU Prague, Czech Republic
Václav Křivánek	University of Defence, Czech Republic
Jan Leuchter	University of Defence, Czech Republic
Pavel Manas	University of Defence, Czech Republic
Marina Massei	University of Genoa, Italy
Jan Mazal	NATO M&S COE, Rome, Italy
Vladimir Mostyn	VSB-TUO, Czech Republic
Pierpaolo Murrieri	Selex ES – a Finmeccanica company, Italy
Andrzej Najgebauer	Military University of Technology, Poland
Jan Nohel	University of Defense, Czech Republic
Petr Novak	VSB-TUO, Czech Republic
Josef Prochazka	Univesity of Defence, Czech Republic
Lucia Pallottino	University of Pisa, Italy
Stefan Pickl	Universität der Bundeswehr, Germany
Vaclav Prenosil	Masaryk University, Czech Republic
Libor Preucil	CTU Prague, Czech Republic
Dalibor Procházka	University of Defence, Czech Republic
Paolo Proietti	MIMOS, Italy
Milan Rollo	Czech Technical University in Prague, Czech Republic
Martin Saska	Czech Technical University in Prague, Czech Republic
Marc Schmitt	Universität der Bundeswehr, Germany
Vaclav Skala	University of West Bohemia, Czech Republic
Marcin Sosnowski	Jan Dlugosz University in Czestochowa, Poland
Julie M. Stark	Office of Naval Research Global, USA
Petr Stodola	University of Defence, Czech Republic
Peter Stüetz	Universität der Bundeswehr München, Germany
Andreas Tolk	The MITRE Corporation, USA
Petr Vasik	University of Technology, Czech Republic
Jiří Vokřínek	Czech Technical University in Prague, Czech Republic
Premysl Volf	Czech Technical University in Prague, Czech Republic
Ludek Zalud	Brno University of Technology, Czech Republic
Fumin Zhang	Georgia Institute of Technology, USA
Radomír Ščurek	VSB-TUO, Czech Republic

NATO M&S COE Director

Michele Turi   NATO M&S COE, Rome, Italy

MESAS 2019 Event Director

Jason Jones   NATO M&S COE, Rome, Italy

MESAS 2019 Event Manager and Proceedings Chair

Jan Mazal   NATO M&S COE, Rome, Italy

MESAS 2019 Organizing Committee

Fulvio Morghese   NATO M&S COE, Rome, Italy
Maurizio Miele   NATO M&S COE, Rome, Italy

Contents

Future Challenges of Advanced M&S Technology

AxS in Context of Future Warfare and Security Environment (Concepts, Applications, Training, Interoperability, etc.)

M&S of Intelligent Systems - AI, R&D and Application

Aerial Reconnaissance and Ground Robot Terrain Learning in Traversal Cost Assessment

Miloš Prágr$^{(\boxtimes)}$ [iD], Petr Váňa[iD], and Jan Faigl[iD]

Faculty of Electrical Engineering, Czech Technical University in Prague,
Technicka 2, 166 27 Prague, Czech Republic
{pragrmi1,vanapet1,faiglj}@fel.cvut.cz
https://comrob.fel.cvut.cz

Abstract. In this paper, we report on the developed system for assessment of ground unit terrain traversal cost using aerial reconnaissance of the expected mission environment. The system combines an aerial vehicle with ground robot terrain learning in the traversal cost modeling utilized in the mission planning for ground units. The aerial vehicle is deployed to capture visual data used to build a terrain model that is then used for the extraction of the terrain features of the expected operational area of the ground units. Based on the previous traversal experience of the ground units in similar environments, the learned model of the traversal cost is employed to predict the traversal cost of the new expected operational area to plan a cost-efficient path to visit the desired locations of interest. The particular modules of the system are demonstrated in an experimental scenario combining the deployment of an unmanned aerial vehicle with a multi-legged walking robot used for learning the traversal cost model.

1 Introduction

Mobile robots deployed in outdoor environments can encounter hard-to-traverse areas which may hinder their motion efficiency and thus impede their assigned missions. Therefore, the traversability of the encountered terrains should be taken into account during mission planning to avoid parts of the environment with difficult terrains. Such terrain evaluation systems may entice the robot to avoid certain terrain types which have been learned from human labels [2], evaluate terrain geometry to avoid rough areas [18], or tradeoff the robot safety with the predicted execution time [3].

In [13], the traversal cost learning has been proposed based on the proprioceptive traversal cost experienced by the robot that is combined with the terrain appearance and geometry captured by the robot. A deployment of the terrain traversal cost learning and cost prediction has been reported within a path planning scenario [14] and an autonomous exploration mission [12]. On the other hand, mission planning can take advantage of the overhead imagery of the operational area, e.g., using an Unmanned Aerial Vehicle (UAV). The authors of [8]

© Springer Nature Switzerland AG 2020
J. Mazal et al. (Eds.): MESAS 2019, LNCS 11995, pp. 3–10, 2020.
https://doi.org/10.1007/978-3-030-43890-6_1

use a convolutional neural network on the RGB aerial imagery to classify terrains from the Estonian Land Board database. In [16], HSV locale-specific overhead features are used to predict LADAR-based features characterizing ground unit traversability. Kohonen's Self-organizing Maps [9] are used in [4] to identify potential invasion, unauthorized changes of land, and deforestation. Finally, overhead imagery has also been deployed in various disaster scenarios. The authors of [15] develop a UAV to map landslides; and in [17], a road network-based feature is used to localize aerial platforms over areas altered by earthquakes where previously available landmarks may be missing.

In this paper, we consider overhead imagery to facilitate energy-efficient multi-goal path planning for ground units represented by a small hexapod walking robot operating in an outdoor environment. A UAV is utilized to capture the outdoor field environment, and the RGB overhead imagery is coupled with the proprioceptive experience of the small hexapod walking robot. The Locally Weighted Projection Regression (LWPR) [19] is used to predict energy-based traversal cost from the overhead data. The traversal cost model is then coupled with the Traveling Salesman Problem (TSP) solver to find the energy-efficient multi-goal path to visits all the assigned goals.

The rest of the paper is organized as follows. The problem of multi-goal path planning from aerial imagery is presented in Sect. 2. The proposed methodology for prediction of ground unit traversal cost from overhead imagery and its use in multi-goal path planning is presented in Sect. 3. The experimental deployment scenario with the aerial imagery and ground robot proprioception dataset are described in Sect. 4. Finally, the paper is concluded in Sect. 5.

2   Multi-goal Path Planning from Aerial Imagery

The overhead imagery is utilized to facilitate energy-efficient multi-goal path planning for a ground unit, which is represented by a small hexapod walking robot shown in Fig. 1a. The robot is requested to visit a set of goal locations and return to its starting position that is the multi-goal path planning problem that can be formulated as the TSP [1]. The TSP is a well-studied problem formulation with several existing approaches [5]; however, we need to determine the individual costs of traveling from one goal location to another location. In this work, we consider the traversal cost assessment based on the learned terrain model as follows.

The prior experience with traversing various terrains is employed to select a path that minimizes the overall energy exertion. The environment is represented as a grid which corresponds to the overhead RGB image of the mission location, such as the area shown in Fig. 1b.

The robot proprioceptive experience is represented by the robot power consumption measurements, where the instantaneous power consumption [10] is

$$P_{in} = V \cdot I \quad [\text{W}], \tag{1}$$

where V is the current battery voltage, and I is the instantaneous current measurement sampled with 200 Hz. Due to the sampling, we can represent the time

(a) Hexapod walking robot   (b) RGB overhead image

Fig. 1. The (a) hexapod walking robot and (b) overhead image of the mission area.

interval T as a sequence of n time stamps $T = (t_1, \ldots, t_n)$. The energy consumption over T can be then computed as

$$E(T) = \sum_{i=2}^{n} (t_i - t_{i-1}) \frac{P_{in}(t_{i-1}) + P_{in}(t_i)}{2} \quad [\text{J}], \tag{2}$$

where t_i and t_{i-1} represent time stamps of two consecutive power consumption measurements. Finally, the robot traversal cost experience over the time interval T is the power consumption per distance traveled over the duration of T and can be defined as

$$c(T) = \frac{E(T)}{d(T)} \quad [\text{Jm}^{-1}], \tag{3}$$

where $d(T)$ is the distance traveled by the robot over the interval T.

In the presented results, we solve the instances of the TSP by the LKH solver [6] since it is known to be a fast heuristic providing a solution close to the optimum. However, in comparison to optimal solvers, the asymptotic time complexity of the LKH solver can be bounded by $\mathcal{O}(n^{2.2})$, which is sufficient even for quick updates of mission plans with tens of goal locations.

The TSP solver utilizes the distance matrix D where each element $D_{i,j}$ represents the energy exertion needed to travel from the location i to the location j. Therefore, the needed energy is determined as the path planning problem to find a path P^* from the corresponding grid cell n_g to the desired cell n_g' with the minimal energy exertion $E(P^*)$ as

$$P^* = \operatorname{argmin}_P E(P) = \operatorname{argmin}_P \sum_{i=1}^{|P|-1} E(n_i, n_{i+1}) \text{ with } n_1 = n_g, n_{|P|} = n_g' \tag{4}$$

where the path P is as a sequence of grid cells $P = (n_1, ..., n_{|P|})$, $|P|$ is the number of cells of the path P, and $E(n_i, n_j)$ is the energy to traverse from the grid cell n_i to n_j in its 8-neighborhood that is computed as

$$E(n_i, n_j) = \|(n_i, n_j)\| c_{model}(n_i, n_j) \quad [\text{J}], \tag{5}$$

where $\|(n_i, n_j)\|$ is the Euclidean distance between n_i and n_j; and $c_{model}(n_i, n_j)$ is the traversal cost prediction to traverse from n_i to n_j. The cost learning and prediction is further detailed in the following section.

3   Proposed Method

In this section, we describe how the overhead imagery is used to learn the model of the traversal cost that is utilized in the robot energy-efficient path planning according to (5). First, the overhead image of the mission environment is transformed into feature descriptors of the terrain by applying the Gaussian blur filter with $\Sigma = \lambda I$, where the parameter $\lambda = 5$ is selected with regards to the overhead image resolution. Thus, a particular terrain appearance descriptor $\boldsymbol{d}_t = (r, g, b)$ is defined as the RGB colors at the terrain's respective coordinates (pixels) in the blurred image. Then, such a particular terrain appearance descriptor is utilized either for the traversal cost learning; or traversal cost assessment. For the cost learning, the terrain descriptor is paired with the robot experience to learn the traversal cost model. For the cost assessment, the descriptor of a priory untraversed terrain is used with the model to predict the traversal cost, and thus the energy exertion over such terrain.

The experienced traversal cost is computed according to (3) for 10 s long intervals, which roughly span the gait cycle duration of the utilized hexapod walking robot. The intervals are then manually paired with the robot trajectory in the overhead image. Thus, each interval is assigned a terrain descriptor $\boldsymbol{d}_t$, which is combined with the experienced cost c to create the experience descriptor $\boldsymbol{d}_c = (r, g, b, c)$. The traversal cost model is learned by the LWPR algorithm [19] from a random permutation of the training set that consists of the terrain descriptors accompanied by the recorded traversal cost. The learning is repeated 10 times. The LWPR is parametrized with the initial distance metric $\mathbf{D}_{init} = 10\mathbf{I}$ and the distance metric learning rate $\alpha_{init} = 10$.

A priory unknown traversal cost c^* for a particular terrain descriptor d_t can be then predicted as

$$c^* = c_{LWPR}(\boldsymbol{d}_t). \tag{6}$$

Further, the traversal cost prediction $c_{model}(n_i, n_j)$ to traverse from the grid cell n_i to its neighbor n_j is defined as the mean of the LWPR predictions at the two respective grid cells

$$c_{model}(n_i, n_j) = \frac{c_{LWPR}(\boldsymbol{d}_t(n_i)) + c_{LWPR}(\boldsymbol{d}_t(n_j))}{2}, \tag{7}$$

where $d_t(n)$ is the terrain descriptor corresponding to the grid cell n.

4   Results

The proposed approach has been experimentally verified in the outdoor environment shown in Fig. 1b. The resolution of the used overhead image is 960×544 pixels. The Python bindings of the LWPR implementation [11] have been utilized to compute the LWPR models, and the available implementation of the LKH [7] has been used to solve instances of the TSP. The hexapod walking robot has traversed four different terrains; see Fig. 2. Every terrain has been traversed in at least three trials, each few gait cycles long. The *concrete* and *gravel* terrains are relatively easy to traverse, and the robot exhibits the lowest traversal cost. The *grass* is harder to traverse, and the cost is high. Finally, when traversing the *vegetation*, the robot is almost stuck and moves very slowly. Therefore, the traversal cost over the *vegetation* is the highest. In total, the learning set comprises 1094 traversal cost measurements paired with terrain descriptors. On average, it takes is 2.31 s (the wall time determined as the mean of 10 trials) to learn the LWPR model using the Intel Core i5-4460 CPU with 16 GB memory. The mean time to predict the traversal costs for the whole 960 × 544 pixel overhead image is 1.82 s.

(a) Concrete   (b) Gravel

(c) Grass   (d) Vegetation

Fig. 2. The hexapod walking robot traversing various terrains during the experimental deployment.

The approach is tested in three scenarios over the same mission area to demonstrate solutions with a different number of goal locations. In *Scenario 1*, the robot needs to plan a visit of 10 locations, which are mostly selected near, but not necessarily on, areas labeled as easily traversable according to human expertise. In *Scenario 2*, 10 points are spaced more evenly over the mission area.

Finally, 42 locations need to be visited in *Scenario 3*. The LKH solutions for *Scenarios 1*, *2*, and *3* are computed in 0.12 s, 0.12 s, and 0.25 s, respectively.

The traversal cost predictions and the paths computed for the individual scenarios are projected onto the overhead image, see Figs. 3, 4, and 5. Notice, even though the same learning set is used in each scenario, each time the traversal cost model is relearned with a different random permutation of the dataset to show an effect of the traversal cost learning which depends not only on the available learning data but also on the learning procedure itself. Thus, the predicted traversal costs slightly differ in the individual scenarios; however, the overall course of the planned path follows the rough distinction between the hard and easy to traverse terrains.

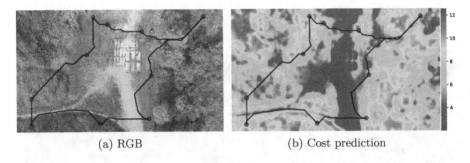

(a) RGB   (b) Cost prediction

Fig. 3. The planned path in *Scenario 1* projected onto the overhead image.

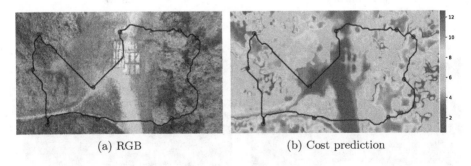

(a) RGB   (b) Cost prediction

Fig. 4. The planned path in the *Scenario 2* projected onto the overhead image.

In *Scenario 1* and *Scenario 2*, the computed paths often follow the concrete and gravel terrains, as these are the most energetically efficient terrain types. However, in some instances, the robot may choose to plan over the rougher terrain if such a path is significantly shorter despite higher traversal cost. In *Scenario 3*, the effect of traversal cost is much less prevalent because the higher density of points forces the robot to visit virtually every available terrain type. Regardless, even in this case, the path seems to avoid the rough areas to a lesser extent.

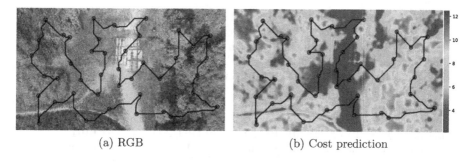

(a) RGB   (b) Cost prediction

Fig. 5. The planned path in the *Scenario 3* projected onto the overhead image.

5 Conclusion

In this paper, overhead imagery is combined with traversal cost learning to predict energy-based traversal cost of the multi-goal path in an outdoor mission with a hexapod walking robot. The traversal cost model that predicts the energy exerted per meter from RGB features in overhead imagery is learned using the LWPR algorithm. The proposed system is experimentally verified in an outdoor scenario using a small UAV and hexapod walking robot. The herein presented results support the feasibility of the proposed approach and suggest that the approach has been deployed successfully. In our future work, we aim to extend the presented approach to online learning using real-time communication between the ground and aerial vehicles.

Acknowledgement. The presented work has been supported under the OP VVV funded project CZ.02.1.01/0.0/0.0/16_019/0000765 "Research Center for Informatics". The support under grant No. SGS19/176/OHK3/3T/13 to Miloš Prágr and Petr Váňa is also gratefully acknowledged.

References

1. Alatartsev, S., Stellmacher, S., Ortmeier, F.: Robotic task sequencing problem: a survey. J. Intell. Robot. Syst. **80**(2), 279–298 (2015). https://doi.org/10.1007/s10846-015-0190-6
2. Belter, D., Wietrzykowski, J., Skrzypczyński, P.: Employing natural terrain semantics in motion planning for a multi-legged robot. J. Intell. Rob. Syst. **93**(3), 723–743 (2018). https://doi.org/10.1007/s10846-018-0865-x
3. Brunner, M., Brüggemann, B., Schulz, D.: Rough terrain motion planning for actuated, tracked robots. In: Filipe, J., Fred, A. (eds.) ICAART 2013. CCIS, vol. 449, pp. 40–61. Springer, Heidelberg (2014). https://doi.org/10.1007/978-3-662-44440-5_3
4. Felizardo, L.F., Mota, R.L., Shiguemori, E.H., Neves, M.T., Ramos, A.B., Mora-Camino, F.: Using ANN and UAV for terrain surveillance. In: International Conference on Hybrid Intelligent Systems (HIS), pp. 1–5 (2014). https://doi.org/10.1109/HIS.2013.6920414

5. Gutin, G., Punnen, A.P. (eds.): The Traveling Salesman Problem and Its Variations. Springer, Boston (2007). https://doi.org/10.1007/b101971
6. Helsgaun, K.: An effective implementation of the Lin-Kernighan traveling salesman heuristic. Eur. J. Oper. Res. **126**(1), 106–130 (2000)
7. Helsgaun, K.: LKH solver 2.0.9. http://www.akira.ruc.dk/~keld/research/LKH. Accessed 29 Aug 2019
8. Hudjakov, R., Tamre, M.: Aerial imagery terrain classification for long-range autonomous navigation. In: International Symposium on Optomechatronic Technologies, pp. 88–91 (2009). https://doi.org/10.1109/ISOT.2009.5326104
9. Kohonen, T.: The self-organizing map. Proc. IEEE **78**(9), 1464–1480 (1990). https://doi.org/10.1109/5.58325
10. Kottege, N., Parkinson, C., Moghadam, P., Elfes, A., Singh, S.P.N.: Energetics-informed hexapod gait transitions across terrains. In: IEEE International Conference on Robotics and Automation (ICRA), pp. 5140–5147. IEEE (2015). https://doi.org/10.1109/ICRA.2015.7139915
11. LWPR library (2007). https://github.com/jdlangs/lwpr. Accessed 28 May 2019
12. Prágr, M., Čížek, P., Bayer, J., Faigl, J.: Online incremental learning of the terrain traversal cost in autonomous exploration. In: Robotics: Science and Systems (RSS) (2019). https://doi.org/10.15607/RSS.2019.XV.040
13. Prágr, M., Čížek, P., Faigl, J.: Cost of transport estimation for legged robot based on terrain features inference from aerial scan. In: IEEE/RSJ International Conference on Intelligent Robots and Systems (IROS), pp. 1745–1750 (2018). https://doi.org/10.1109/IROS.2018.8593374
14. Prágr, M., Čížek, P., Faigl, J.: Incremental learning of traversability cost for aerial reconnaissance support to ground units. In: Mazal, J. (ed.) MESAS 2018. LNCS, vol. 11472, pp. 412–421. Springer, Cham (2019). https://doi.org/10.1007/978-3-030-14984-0_30
15. Rossi, G., Tanteri, L., Tofani, V., Vannocci, P., Moretti, S., Casagli, N.: Multitemporal UAV surveys for landslide mapping and characterization. Landslides **15**(5), 1045–1052 (2018). https://doi.org/10.1007/s10346-018-0978-0
16. Sofman, B., Lin, E., Bagnell, J.A., Cole, J., Vandapel, N., Stentz, A.: Improving robot navigation through self-supervised online learning. J. Field Robot. **23**(11–12), 1059–1075 (2006). https://doi.org/10.1002/rob.20169
17. Soleimani, B., Ashtiani, M.Z., Soleimani, B.H., Moradi, H.: A Disaster invariant feature for localization. In: IEEE/RSJ International Conference on Intelligent Robots and Systems (IROS), pp. 1096–1101 (2010). https://doi.org/10.1109/IROS.2010.5651930
18. Stelzer, A., Hirschmüller, H., Görner, M.: Stereo-vision-based navigation of a six-legged walking robot in unknown rough terrain. Int. J. Robot. Res. **31**(4), 381–402 (2012). https://doi.org/10.1177/0278364911435161
19. Vijayakumar, S., Schaal, S.: Locally weighted projection regression: an o(n) algorithm for incremental real time learning in high dimensional space. In: International Conference on International Conference on Machine Learning (ICML), pp. 1079–1086 (2000)

Combined PSO Methods for UAVs Swarm Modelling and Simulation

Stanisław Skrzypecki[✉], Zbigniew Tarapata, and Dariusz Pierzchała

Cybernetics Faculty, Military University of Technology, Warsaw, Poland
{stanislaw.skrzypecki,zbigniew.tarapata,
dariusz.pierzchala}@wat.edu.pl

Abstract. In this paper selected methods used for Unmanned Aerial Vehicles (UAVs) swarm simulation are presented. Proposed approach is based on Particle Swarm Optimization algorithm applied for a search problem in a large-scale terrain with enhancements like collision avoidance, leadership or formation arrangement mechanisms. The uniqueness of proposed work relies on appliance these mechanisms (separately or in combined way) to the PSO algorithm, whereas they have not been designed in the presented manner. Moreover, the mechanisms are meant to keep the PSO algorithm idea and its simplicity.

The UAVs swarm simulation is performed in original distributed simulation environment (built completely from the scratch) with the alternative communication provided by DIS or HLA protocols. The environment consists of a constructive component (responsible for multiagent and multiresolution modelling) for UAVs behaviours simulation and the VBS3 virtual simulator handling 3D visualizations and another objects control.

Keywords: UAVs swarm · PSO algorithm · Autonomous systems · Collision avoidance · Leadership · Formation arrangement · Distributed simulation

1 Introduction

The technical parameters of Unmanned Aerial Vehicle (UAV) and spectrum of usage are still significantly improving. Development of UAVs has led to a concept of drone swarm – the system, composed of many UAVs, acting jointly to achieve a specified goal. The UAVs swarm has growth on the concept of swarm intelligence term introduced in a context of cellular robotic systems in 1989 by Beni and Wang [1] and the swarm robotics systems (SRS). Consequently, worth to mention is the year 2005 when the American Office of the Secretary of Defense issued "Unmanned Aircraft Systems Roadmap: 2005–2030". This technical report contains UAVs development plan to reach goal which is fully autonomous swarms of aircrafts [12]. The simulations of drone swarm have demonstrated

© Springer Nature Switzerland AG 2020
J. Mazal et al. (Eds.): MESAS 2019, LNCS 11995, pp. 11–25, 2020.
https://doi.org/10.1007/978-3-030-43890-6_2

very high effectiveness of this solution [10] and these concepts are also close to realisation in real life – it has been showed in the recent years' projects LOCUST[1] and PERDIX.[2]

One of many other algorithms which might be adopted to SRS and further on UAVs swarms is Particle Swarm Optimisation (PSO) [15]. PSO developed in 1995 by Kennedy and Eberhart [5, 7] was meant for solving global optimisation problems. However, in years many other modifications and adaptions were introduced. Pugh and Martinoli presented the earliest multi robot search algorithm based on the principles of PSO [14], considering the stationary single target case. They use a one-to-one mapping between particles in the PSO swarm and robots, with modifications to handle real world constraints. These include obstacles as well as limitations on movement and communication ranges. Another PSO modification shows its adaption to dynamic and more complex environment in the odour source localization scenario [6]. The other algorithms modifications were Species-based PSO (SPSO) [9] and Niching PSO (NichePSO) [2] – they use subswarms to locate multiple optimal solutions for multi-modal optimisation problems. MR PSO using multi-swarm idea was used for finding a known number of stationary targets within an indoor environment [3]. The clustering PSO algorithm (CPSO) presented in [17] was aimed at addressing dynamic optimisation problems where locating and tracking multiple changing optima over time is important.

The enhancements proposed in the paper (like collision avoidance, leadership or formation arrangement mechanism) are not the most ideas to date. However these improvements have been presented in different manner for PSO and to use them separately or in combined way. Moreover, the mechanism are designed to keep the PSO algorithm idea and its simplicity. Collision avoidance for PSO was used by Pugh and Martinoli [14] with Breitenberg algorithm or in MR PSO by Derr and Manic with rule-based mechanism [3]. As an arrangement of formation in PSO can be regarded CPSO where the particles were assigned to different promising subregions, so the number of subswarms were adaptively adjusted [17]. Whereas, the leadership mechanism was presented by Zhou et al. in PSO-L [18] basing on two steps: stability analysis and convergence condition or in practical solution by Kownacki and Ołdziej [8] – where the swarm using flocking algorithm were following externally controlled leader.

The paper is organized as follows. Section 2 presents modified PSO algorithm and their enhancements like collision avoidance, leadership or formation arrangement mechanisms applied separately and in combined way. In Sect. 3 the programmable UAVs swarm modelling and simulation environment used to experiments was described. It includes the original DisSim concept and introduction to the simulation engine. Section 4 presents experiments for combined PSO methods in DisSim based simulator applied for signal sources search problem in a large-scale terrain presented in the previous work. Section 5 includes short paper summary with conclusions.

---

[1] Project LOCUST (Low-Cost UAV Swarming Technology) – the group of drones launched in 2016 from the ground launchers (up to 30), each aircraft is capable to execute self-conducting programmed actions [20].

[2] Project PERDIX – micro-drone swarm consisted of 103 Perdix drones launched in 2017 from three F/A-18 Super Hornets fighters and demonstrated advanced swarm behaviours such as collective decision-making, adaptive formation flying, and self-healing [19]; Perdix drone was initially developed at the MIT University in 2010-2011 [21].

2   Combined PSO Methods

The basis of PSO is to solve optimization problems, however, as we mentioned earlier, it can be used in multi robot search algorithm including UAVs. The PSO relies on computing the next position for each particle in all steps of simulation based on current position and velocity vector. This velocity vector (understood as position vector change in time unit) consists of three summands (and defining the influence of individual summands coefficient) defined as the weight of inertia, cognitive and collective (social) summand (coefficient).

The presented enhancements are not based on the original PSO but its modified version presented in the previous work [16] with the global neighbourhood and including maximum speed and search area restrictions such as maximal remembered signal value resetting for given aircraft and for all aircrafts in case of source being detected. Moreover, the particles' start position is not random – it is determined in one place.

In the further sections the basic formulas are used as follows:

x^i_t – position of the i-th particle (here: UAV) in the current step,

x^i_{t+1} – position of the i-th particle (here: UAV) in the next step,

v^i_{t+1} – particle velocity vector in the next step (notice: understood as position vector change in time unit),

x^i_{pbest} – the best position found by the i-th particle,

x_{gbest} – the best position found by a selected set of neighbours,

$c_{inertia}$ – weight of inertia coefficient,

$c_{cognitive}$ – cognitive coefficient,

c_{social} – social (collective) coefficient,

$r_1, \dots, r_n$ – random values from a uniform distribution U(0, 1),

v_{max} – maximum length of velocity vector,

$\Upsilon(\vec{v})$ – function to scale vector $\vec{v}$ if the length is greater than v_{max}

The $\Upsilon(\vec{v})$ function is used to provide more control for weight of summands with particular coefficients and to ensure the output velocity would not exceed the maximum length:

$$\Upsilon(\vec{v}) = \begin{cases} \frac{\vec{v}}{\|\vec{v}\|} v_{max}, & if \ \|\vec{v}\| > v_{max} \\ \vec{v}, & otherwise \end{cases} \tag{1}$$

The basic formulas for the new velocity (2) and the position (3) for the i-th particle in the step $t + 1$ are as follows:

$$v^i_{t+1} = \Upsilon\left(c_{inertia} v^i_t + c_{cognitive} r_1 \Upsilon\left(x^i_{pbest} - x^i_t\right) + c_{social} r_2 \Upsilon\left(x_{gbest} - x^i_t\right)\right) \tag{2}$$

$$x^i_{t+1} = x^i_t + v^i_{t+1} \tag{3}$$

The (2) and (3) equations are the base for further modifications. The enhancements are introduced as another summands (and coefficients) or another equation.

2.1 Leadership

PSO algorithm assumes each of particles is the same. Nevertheless, in case of use this algorithm for UAVs we can imagine that some aircrafts are marked as more important than others. These special particles may be some sort of leaders which should be followed by the others. The leader for each particle might be established in its neighborhood relation[3]. Moreover, such UAVs leaders may be controlled (entirely or in part as needed) by the external operator which allows to control such a swarm.

The leadership mechanism of PSO is based on introduction of another summand. The formula for a position for the i-th particle in the step $t + 1$ is unchanged (3), but for a new velocity is as follows:

$$
v_{t+1}^i = \Upsilon\left(c_{inertia}v_t^i + c_{cognitive}r_1\Upsilon\left(x_{pbest}^i - x_t^i\right) + c_{social}r_2\Upsilon\left(x_{gbest} - x_t^i\right)\right.
$$
$$
\left. + c_{leader}r_3\Upsilon\left(x_{leader}^i - x_t^i\right)\right) \tag{4}
$$

where:

x_{leader}^i — position of leader, established for the i-th particle,

c_{leader} — leader coefficient

The (4) equation can also be used for leader particle, but in that case it is the same as (2) equation (because $x_{leader}^i = x_t^i$).

2.2 Formations

Another presented enhancement of PSO algorithm for UAVs appliance is formations mechanism. A formation is defined as the expected particle position relative to reference point in its neighborhood relation. Such a reference point should be dynamic – it may be a position of one specified particle. The reference point may also be an average position calculated for many particles, but the solution with high formation coefficient value may have negative influence on dynamic manner of this point.

The formations mechanism in PSO is based on introduction of another summand and the formation vector which allows to specify expected position for particle relative to reference point. The formula for position for the i-th particle in the step $t + 1$ is the same (3), but for the new velocity (5) is as follows:

$$
v_{t+1}^i = \Upsilon\left(c_{inertia}v_t^i + c_{cognitive}r_1\Upsilon\left(x_{pbest}^i - x_t^i\right) + c_{social}r_2\Upsilon\left(x_{gbest} - x_t^i\right)\right.
$$
$$
\left. + c_{formation}r_3\Upsilon\left(x_{reference}^i + \Delta x^i - x_t^i\right)\right) \tag{5}
$$

where:

---

[3] This paper is not focused on neighborhood relations, because for the presented formulas it is not important. In further work the neighborhood relation will be defined as global (all the UAVs are in neighborhood) or determined (UAVs are in fixed size groups specified in advance).

$x^i_{reference}$ – position of reference point established for the i-th particle,

Δx^i – formation vector for the i-th particle,

$c_{formation}$ – formation coefficient

The (5) equation is more general state of (4) equations, It could be used for leadership mechanism if reference point would be position of leader and the formations vectors would be the zero vectors.

2.3 Simple Collision Avoidance

The particles in PSO is assumed to be as small as possible what cause the collisions between them are not considered. Nevertheless, treating UAVs as particles seems not to be good idea because in case of collisions the losses would cause large outlay and inefficiency of solution. The presented approach is different from both Breitenberg algorithm [14] and rule-based algorithms because collision avoidance is included in the same formula for the new velocity and influenced by distances between particles in a parameter called "range collision avoidance".

The collision avoidance mechanism of PSO is based on introduction of another summand with range collision avoidance parameter (7), influence of distances between particles coefficient and vectors between these particles. The formula for position for the i-th particle in the step $t + 1$ is the same (3) but for the new velocity (6) is as follows:

$$v^i_{t+1} = \Upsilon\left(c_{inertia}v^i_t + c_{cognitive}r_1\Upsilon\left(x^i_{pbest} - x^i_t\right) + c_{social}r_2\Upsilon\left(x_{gbest} - x^i_t\right)\right.$$
$$\left. + c_{collision}\Upsilon\left(\sum_{j=0}^{n} d_\alpha\left(x^i_t, x^j_t\right)\right)\right) \tag{6}$$

$$d_\alpha(x_A, x_B) = \begin{cases} \left(1 - \sqrt[\alpha]{\frac{\|x_A - x_B\|}{r_{max}}}\right)\frac{x_A - x_B}{\|x_A - x_B\|}v_{max}, & if\ 0 < \|x_A - x_B\| < r_{max} \\ 0, otherwise \end{cases} \tag{7}$$

where:

$c_{collision}$ – collision avoidance coefficient

$d_\alpha(x_A, x_B)$ – formula to obtain collision avoidance vector basing on particles positions x_A and x_B,

α – weight of collision avoidance vector component,

n – number of particles,

r_{max} – max. range to avoid collisions

2.4 Predicted Collision Avoidance

The simple collision avoidance is based on current positions of particles, wherever it could be improved by making computations on particles positions expected in the next step using formulas without collision avoidance (e.g. Eqs. (2) and (3)). Then, this outcome is revised by other formulas regarding distances between predicted particles' positions. These formulas for position with collision avoidance for the new velocity (8), the position (9) for the i-th particle in the step $t + 1$ are as follows:

$$v_{t+1}'^i = \Upsilon\left(v_{t+1}^i + c_{collision}\Upsilon\left(\sum_{j=0}^{n} d_\alpha\left(x_t^i, x_t^j\right)\right)\right) \tag{8}$$

$$x_{t+1}'^i = x_t'^i + v_{t+1}'^i \tag{9}$$

where:

$x_{t+1}'^i$ – "collision avoidance" position of the i-th particle in the next step,
$v_{t+1}'^i$ – "collision avoidance" velocity of the i-th particle in the next step

The predicted collision avoidance formulas seem to be more accurate regarding prediction of the next step position without collision avoidance, although it requires one more step to calculate and share this prediction. Such solution may be harder to implement in UAV swarm, because it would require more communication among aircrafts.

2.5 Combinations

Simple Collision Avoidance with Leadership
The simple collision avoidance with leadership mechanism includes combination of summands from Eqs. (4) and (6) with influence of distances between particles coefficient from Eq. (7). The formula for a position for the i-th particle in the step $t + 1$ is still unchanged (3) but for the new velocity (10) is as follows:

$$v_{t+1}^i = \Upsilon\left(c_{inertia}v_t^i + c_{cognitive}r_1\Upsilon\left(x_{pbest}^i - x_t^i\right) + c_{social}r_2\Upsilon\left(x_{gbest} - x_t^i\right)\right.$$
$$\left. + c_{leader}r_3\Upsilon\left(x_{leader}^i - x_t^i\right) + c_{collision}\Upsilon\left(\sum_{j=0}^{n} d_\alpha\left(x_t^i, x_t^j\right)\right)\right) \tag{10}$$

Simple Collision Avoidance with Formations
The simple collision avoidance with formations mechanism includes combination of summands from Eqs. (5) and (6) with influence of distances between particles coefficient from Eq. (7). The formula for position for the i-th particle in the step $t + 1$ is still unchanged (3) but for the new velocity (10) is as follows:

$$v_{t+1}^i = \Upsilon\left(c_{inertia}v_t^i + c_{cognitive}r_1\Upsilon\left(x_{pbest}^i - x_t^i\right) + c_{social}r_2\Upsilon\left(x_{gbest} - x_t^i\right)\right.$$
$$\left. + c_{formation}r_3\Upsilon\left(x_{reference}^i + \Delta x^i - x_t^i\right) + c_{collision}\Upsilon\left(\sum_{j=0}^{n} d_\alpha\left(x_t^i, x_t^j\right)\right)\right) \tag{11}$$

Predicted Collision Avoidance with Leadership

The predicted collision avoidance with leadership mechanism is still based on equations from Sect. 2.4 (8), (9), however, to predict particles position x_t^i without collision avoidance should be used Eqs. (5) and (3).

Predicted Collision Avoidance with Formations

The predicted collision avoidance with formations mechanism as previous is based on equations from Sect. 2.4 (8), (9), however, to predict particles position x_t^i without collision avoidance should be used Eqs. (6) and (3).

3 UAVs Swarm Simulation Environment

The UAVs swarm simulation is performed in the original distributed simulation environment based on DisSim package with the alternative communication provided by DIS or HLA protocols. The environment consists of a constructive component (responsible for multiagent and multiresolution modelling) for UAVs behaviours simulation and the VBS3 virtual simulator handling 3D visualisations and another objects control.

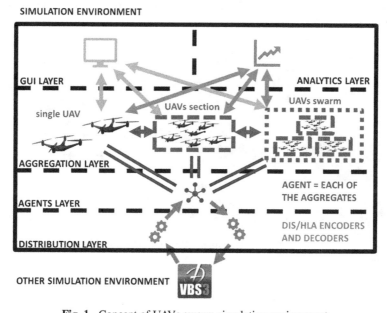

Fig. 1. Concept of UAVs swarm simulation environment

The constructive component is a simulation engine implemented in Java and based on discrete event-driven simulation (DES) techniques, multiagent systems and multiresolution modelling. It is also prepared to achieve interoperability with the VBS3 simulator. The DisSim supports sequentially events (*BasicSimStateChange*) realisation planned for many simulation objects (*BasicSimEntity*) and stored in a shared event calendar (*BasicSimCalendar*). The software offers a dynamic configuration of objects system (plug-in system), a number of auxiliary classes for generating pseudo-random numbers, monitoring and gathering variable states as well as calculation of statistics on accumulated time series [4, 11]. The DisSim package has been enhanced to include: (a) distributed protocols DIS and HLA; (b) multiagent systems; (c) multiresolution modelling [13]. These enhancements made it possible to build programmable environment for constructive simulation allowing studies on behaviors, movements and groups models of UAVs [16].

The architecture concept for the environment (shown in Fig. 1.) is based on the layer structure. The components of each layer have been designed based on interfaces and abstract classes that provide the modularity and extensibility of the solution. Each simulation object is a simulation agent and can be aggregated at any resolution level at the same simulation time. The prepared agent mechanisms allow the exchange of simulation events (so-called statechanges) with DIS or HLA plugins. These plugins are responsible for further messages exchange. The following layers are responsible for different functions: (a) GUI layer – simulation management and 2D visualisations; (b) the analytical layer – gathering measures and statistic calculations; (c) the aggregation layer – multiresolution of UAVs simulation; (d) agents layer – multi-agent approach, behaviour modelling; (e) distribution layer – cooperation with other simulators. Picture in Fig. 2. presents the cooperation of the two simulators: VBS 3 on the left and DisSim based simulation on the right.

Fig. 2. The state of two cooperating simulators: VBS 3 on the left and DisSim based simulation on the right picture

4   Simulation Experiments

Taking into consideration presented enhancements of Particle Swarm Optimization algorithm, they were implemented in DisSim based constructive component of simulation environment. In the experiments we applied it for a search problem and multicriteria optimization function already presented in the previous work [16]. To recall, the problem is to find as many terrestrial signal sources as possible in the shortest possible time in large-scale area with UAVs usage in specified maximum exploration time. The strength of the signal decreases with the distance from source according to the specified function. The source is mark as detected by UAV when the distance from the centre of source is within UAV sensor range. Moreover, aircrafts start a flight from one point with a specific initial speed and the maximum flight speed. However, the modifications applied in current paper are that UAVs do not start in one time but sequentially in some interval and aircrafts collisions are relevant.

To recall the applied multicriteria optimization function it is based on two criteria: the number of found sources and the exploration time. The first criterion is maximized and the second one is minimized. To determine one solution in the objective function a weighted sum method with weights of 0.5 for each of two summands is used. The first summand is the quotient of the number of found sources and number of signal sources. The second summand is the ratio of the time remaining to maximum exploration time, which is and maximum exploration time. In this manner the objective function is maximized in the value range [0, 1].

All the experiments are performed with PSO algorithm with maximum speed and search area restrictions modified with maximal remembered signal value resetting for given aircraft (x^i_{pbest}) and maximal remembered signal value for all aircrafts (x_{gbest} in their neighborhood relation) in case of source being detected. Such modifications also has been presented in the previous work [16].

Table 1. Default simulation parameters for evaluation in the Sect. 4.

Parameter	Value
Signal sources	4
UAVs number	60
Neighbourhood	Sections
Maximum exploration time [s]	1000
Signal range [m]	80
Range of aircraft sensors [m]	5
Maximum speed [m/s]	8
Search area [m × m × m]	600 × 400 × 100
Aircraft start interval [s]	1
$c_{inertia}$	1,3
$c_{cognitive}$	0,3
c_{social}	0,3
c_{leader}	0,4
$c_{formations}$	2
$c_{collision}$ (for simple)	1,8
$c_{collision}$ (for predicted)	1,3
α	2
r_{max}	26
Collisions damages	Enabled

The default model parameters for simulations executed in further sections are presented in Table 1. In the next sections it is directly stated whether some parameters are changed.

4.1 Collision Avoidance Mechanism Experiments

Table 2. presents results obtained with collisions causing UAVs damages and not. The collision avoidance mechanisms is not applied which is presented in col. I and II. Whereas col. III and IV consists results for respectively simple and predicted collisions avoiding mechanism. It can be noticed that in simulation with disabled collision damages (col. I) the exploration time is shorter and optimisation function has greater values than in column (col. II), it has also much more collisions detected value as should be expected, because as simulation advance the number of UAVs decreases. As could be foreseen the collision avoiding mechanism simulations (col. III and IV) result in much less collisions between aircrafts than these in col. I and II and the predicted collision mechanism has the best values. Moreover, they have even shorter exploration time and optimisation function has greater values than without this mechanism. The explanation could be that collision avoidance increases spaces within aircrafts which causes that aircrafts do not explore the same area.

Table 2. Experiments results with global neighbourhood for collision avoidance mechanism (50 simulations executions with 60 UAVs for each column).

Column	I	II	III	IV
Damages	Disabled	Enabled	Enabled	Enabled
Collision avoidance	None	None	Simple	Predicted
expl. time (avg.) [s]	193,20	211,19	152,80	156,58
expl. time (st. dev.) [s]	48,19	61,07	43,38	35,28
expl. time (max.) [s]	359	407	272	256
found signal sources (avg.)	4	4	4	4
found signal sources (st. dev.)	0	0	0	0
found signal sources (min.)	4	4	4	4
opt. func. (avg.)	0,9000	0,8900	0,9236	0,9217
opt. func. (st. dev.)	0,0200	0,0300	0,0217	0,0176
opt. func. (max.)	0,9500	0,9500	0,9560	0,9535
collisions (avg.)	36,61	9,02	0,22	0,06
collisions (st. dev.)	21,13	4,01	0,50	0,24
collisions (max.)	132	19	2	1

4.2   Combined Leadership Mechanism

Figure 3. presents results of experiments with the leadership mechanism. The UAVs are divided into sections in advance – the first starting aircraft in a section is the leader. The neighborhood relation for the global best position x_{gbest} is within a section. It can be seen in the figure that aircrafts follow the leaders of sections. The formula, presented for leadership mechanism, provides possibility to steer the leader influence with the leader coefficient. If it is greater the particles are heading into leader position more accurately. However, the reasonable adjusted leader coefficient still provides the basic PSO functions. Moreover, the mechanism may be used to force UAVs to explore terrain in sections (pairs, triples, etc.) providing redundancy in case of loss of aircrafts. It can be also used to improve group of UAVs management by smaller amount of operators controlling only leaders of swarm. The leadership mechanism can also be enabled and disabled depending on the necessity.

Experiments results obtained in 50 simulation trials for leadership mechanism with and without collision avoidance are presented in Table 3. Comparing the exploration times and optimization function values to these from Table 2 without leadership mechanism we can see they are worse and in case of col. II they were even experiments with only one found signal source. However, here are the results with section neighborhood and there with global neighborhood. Moreover, on these state of researches much more attention is paid to ensure this mechanism to work, which was completed. The further researches, e.g. with variate section size, may have other results. Considering, the collisions number it can be seen that conclusions may be also similar: disabled aircrafts damages cause high collisions number and with next columns the values are decreasing. The avoiding collision mechanism not only prevents damages, but also improves result of exploration time and optimization function.

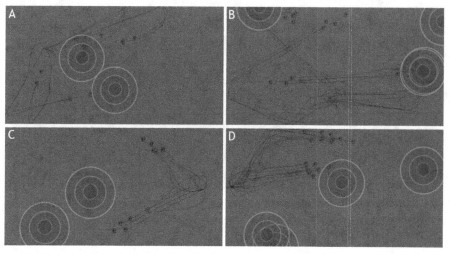

Fig. 3. UAVs simulation for leadership mechanism with various section number and sizes: (A) 4 × 2 (B) 4 × 4 (C) 2 × 5 (D) 2 × 10.

Table 3. Experiments results for leadership mechanism with 12 sections consisted of 5 aircrafts (50 simulations executions for each column).

Column	I	II	III	IV
Damages	Disabled	Enabled	Enabled	Enabled
Collision avoidance	None	None	Simple	Predicted
expl. time (avg.) [s]	268,50	488,98	210,84	217,56
expl. time (st. dev.) [s]	91,06	276,30	80,50	80,77
expl. time (max.) [s]	598	1000	562	581
found signal sources (avg.)	4	3,8	4	4
found signal sources (st. dev.)	0	0,6	0	0
found signal sources (min.)	4	1	4	4
opt. func. (avg.)	0,8658	0,7305	0,8946	0,8912
opt. func. (st. dev.)	0,0455	0,1936	0,0402	0,0404
opt. func. (max.)	0,9400	0,9285	0,9475	0,9460
collisions (avg.)	328,88	17,74	0,46	0,24
collisions (st. dev.)	222,19	4,27	0,67	0,47

4.3 Combined Formations Mechanism

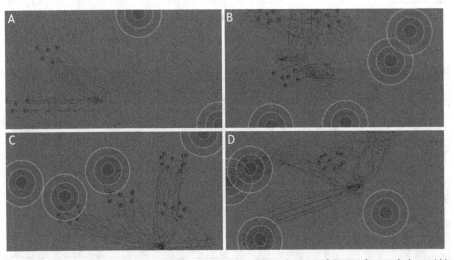

Fig. 4. UAVs simulation for formations mechanism with various section number and sizes: (A) 2×5 (B) 3×6 (C) 4×8 (D) 2×10.

Figure 4 presents experiments results with the formations mechanism. Like in the previous mechanism the UAV are divided in sections in advance – the first starting aircraft in section has role of reference point in the center of section, the other aircrafts are surrounding this reference around. The neighborhood relation to determine x_{gbest} is within section. In case of this mechanism to ensure that UAVs would follow theirs place in formation the formation coefficient is much higher than inertia coefficient or leadership coefficient in the previous mechanism.

Table 4. Experiments results for formations mechanism with 12 sections consisted of 5 aircrafts (50 simulations executions with 60 UAVs for each column).

Column	I	II	III	IV
Damages	Disabled	Enabled	Enabled	Enabled
Collision avoidance	None	None	Simple	Predicted
expl. time (avg.) [s]	203,58	247,28	332,68	274,68
expl. time (st. dev.) [s]	76,12	158,37	181,94	166,41
expl. time (max.) [s]	447	845	919	966
found signal sources (avg.)	4	4	4	4
found signal sources (st. dev.)	0	0	0	0
found signal sources (min.)	4	4	4	4
opt. func. (avg.)	0,8982	0,8764	0,8337	0,8627
opt. func. (st. dev.)	0,0381	0,0792	0,0910	0,0832
opt. func. (max.)	0,9645	0,9620	0,9520	0,949
collisions (avg.)	10,36	4,60	0,60	0,5
collisions (st. dev.)	7,06	3,55	0,77	0,67

The formations mechanism simulation experiments results (from 50 trials) are presented in Table 4. The conclusion of comparison between them and Table 2 may be the same as conclusions of such comparison for leadership mechanism. Nevertheless, when we compare the exploration times and optimisation function values in col. I and II to these in col. III and IV it can be seen that it is the first time when collision avoidance mechanism have worse results. The answer to this question will be consideration of further researches, but probably aircrafts in sections' formations have to close distance comparing to the max. range to avoid collisions parameter value (r_{max}). However, the collision numbers, like in the previous experiments, were significantly decreased.

5   Conclusion

The paper presents leadership, formations and collision avoidance mechanism implemented into the PSO algorithm for UAVs swarm usage in a new manner. Moreover, these mechanisms can be combined in one solution, e.g. leadership with sections consisted with few aircrafts and simple or expected collision avoidance. Moreover, it is important that mechanisms are designed to keep the PSO algorithm idea and its simplicity.

The leaderships and formations mechanisms introduce methods for management of the UAV swarm where the PSO in its basic version do not provide. They can be used to improve control of groups of aircrafts by not so many operators. Operators may control only leaders or reference points and thereby other aircrafts follow them respectively. It can be also imagined that such mechanisms are enabled and disabled depending on the necessity. Another idea of usage such mechanisms is to search some terrain in small sections (pairs, triples, fours, etc. and in some formation or not) to provide redundancy in case of some aircraft loose.

The experiments for the simple and predicted collision avoidance mechanisms shows efficiency of proposed methods. However, mechanisms do not prevent every collision between aircrafts, but number of them is significantly decreased (even average 0,06 collision per one execution of 60 UAVs simulation). The reason of such result will be the subject of further work, but preliminary explanation is that specific mutual position between UAVs and other PSO summand (inertia, cognitive, leadership and formations) neutralize collision avoidance summand impact. Moreover, the modifications of collision coefficients and other model parameters values can result in smaller destroyed UAVs amount (but also can weaken other enhancements). Nevertheless, it should be noticed that these days cost of UAVs is greatly decreases (e.g. many components can be made with 3D printers like in PERDIX project [21]) so some aircraft loses do not disqualify the approach to be employed in specific real setups.

The other interesting result of collision avoidance mechanisms experiments is that exploration time and optimisation function are better than without collision avoidance simulations (excluding results of experiments in case if combined formations mechanism, which requires another revision). The reason for that is because the aircrafts do not explore the same area, but they are dispersed to avoid collisions. Moreover, the predicted collision avoidance mechanism is characterised with the better results of collisions number than the simple one.

The presented combined mechanisms are on relatively early state of researches and there is still necessity to conduct further researches: to increase number of measurements of each experiment, to check greater variates of parameters values, its properly adjustments and dependences between them or to analyse relationships and sections sizes in different solutions. Moreover, collision avoidance mechanisms can be generalised to avoid crashes also with other objects (not only between aircrafts as presented). To the enhancements it can be also introduced some noise and other external factors like firing. The interesting ideas are to prepare presented PSO formulas in relative position system without knowing global position or to integrate maximum accelerate value and maximum movement radius of aircraft into basic equations.

References

1. Beni, G., Wang, J.: Swarm intelligence in cellular robotic systems. In: Proceedings of NATO Advanced Workshop on Robots and Biological Systems (1989)
2. Brits, R., Engelbrecht, A.P., Bergh, F.V.D.: A niching particle swarm optimizer. In: Proceedings of the Conference on Simulated Evolution and Learning, pp. 692–696 (2002)
3. Derr K., Manic M.: Multi-robot, multi-target particle swarm optimization search in noisy wireless environments. In: 2nd Conference on Human System Interactions, HSI 2009, pp. 81–86 (2009)

4. Dyk, M., Najgebauer, A., Pierzchała, D.: SenseSim: an agent-based and discrete event simulator for wireless sensor networks and the Internet of Things. In: Proceedings of 2015 IEEE 2nd World Forum on Internet of Things (WF-IoT) (2015). ISBN 9781509003655

5. Eberhart, R., Kennedy, J.: A new optimizer using particle swarm theory. In: Proceedings of the Sixth International Symposium on Micro Machine and Human Science, MHS 1995, pp. 39–43 (1955)

6. Jatmiko, W., Sekiyama, K., Fukuda, T.: A PSO-based mobile sensor network for odour source localization in dynamic environment: theory, simulation and measurement. In: IEEE Congress on Evolutionary Computation, CEC 2006, pp. 1036–1043 (2006)

7. Kennedy, J., Eberhart, R.: Particle swarm optimization. In: Proceedings of IEEE International Conference on Neural Networks, vol. 4, pp. 1942–1948 (1995)

8. Kownacki, C., Ołdziej, D.: Flocking algorithm for fixed-wing unmanned aerial vehicles. In: Bordeneuve-Guibé, J., Drouin, A., Roos, C. (eds.) Advances in Aerospace Guidance, Navigation and Control, pp. 415–431. Springer, Cham (2015). https://doi.org/10.1007/978-3-319-17518-8_24

9. Li, X.: Adaptively choosing neighbourhood bests using species in a particle swarm optimizer for multimodal function optimization. In: Deb, K. (ed.) GECCO 2004. LNCS, vol. 3102, pp. 105–116. Springer, Heidelberg (2004). https://doi.org/10.1007/978-3-540-24854-5_10

10. Munoz, M.F.: Agent-Based Simulation and Analysis of a Defensive UAV Swarm Against an Enemy UAV Swarm. Naval Postgraduate School, Monterey (2011)

11. Najgebauer, A., et al.: The qualitative and quantitative support method for capability based planning of armed forces development. In: Nguyen, N.T., Trawiński, B., Kosala, R. (eds.) ACIIDS 2015. LNCS (LNAI), vol. 9012, pp. 212–223. Springer, Cham (2015). https://doi.org/10.1007/978-3-319-15705-4_21

12. Office of the Secretary of Defense, Unmanned Aircraft Systems Roadmap: 2005–2030. Technical report, Department of Defense (2005)

13. Pierzchała, D., Skrzypecki, S.: Multi-agent and multi-resolution distributed simulation DisSim – VBS. In: Simulation in Research and Development (in Polish: Symulacja w badaniach i rozwoju), vol. 7, no. 1–2/2016, pp. 25–34 (2016)

14. Pugh, J., Martinoli, A.: Inspiring and modeling multi-robot search with particle swarm optimization. In: Swarm Intelligence Symposium, SIS 2007, pp. 332–339. IEEE (2007)

15. Senanayake, M., Senthooran, I., Barca, J.C., Chung, H., Kamruzzaman, J., Murshed, M.: Search and tracking algorithms for swarms of robots: a survey. In: Robotics and Autonomous Systems, vol. 75, Part B, pp. 422–434 (2016)

16. Skrzypecki, S., Pierzchała, D., Tarapata, Z.: Distributed simulation environment of unmanned aerial systems for a search problem. In: Mazal, J. (ed.) MESAS 2018. LNCS, vol. 11472, pp. 65–81. Springer, Cham (2019). https://doi.org/10.1007/978-3-030-14984-0_6

17. Yang, S., Li, C.: A clustering particle swarm optimizer for locating and tracking multiple optima in dynamic environments. IEEE Trans. Evol. Comput. 14(6), 959–974 (2010)

18. Zhou, L., Shi, Y., Li, Y., Zhang, W.: Parameter selection, analysis and evaluation of an improved particle swarm optimizer with leadership. Artif. Intell. Rev. 34(4), 343–367 (2010)

19. DroneBase - Drones and the Future of Entertainment. https://blog.dronebase.com/2017/07/10/drones-and-the-future-of-entertainment/. Accessed 21 Sep 2019

20. LOCUST: Autonomous, Swarming UAVs Fly into the Future. http://www.navy.mil/submit/display.asp?story_id=86558. Accessed 21 Sep 2019

21. Project Perdix | Beaver Works. https://beaverworks.ll.mit.edu/CMS/bw/projectperdixcapstone/. Accessed 21 Sep 2019

Kinematic Model of a Specific Robotic Manipulator

Jana Vechetová[(✉)]

Faculty of Mechanical Engineering, Brno University of Technology, Brno, Czechia
161790@vutbr.cz

Abstract. This paper presents a model of a specific nontrivial robotic manipulator used in practice for example for material handling. The main goal is to build a model of forward and inverse kinematics, using classical methods and differential geometry. Thus, this model is mahtematically precise. The kinematics of the robotic manipulator is also solved and visualized in MATLAB for better clarity. The acquired knowledge will be used to compare this precise kinematic model with other models that are obtained by other less explored methods.

Keywords: Forward kinematics · Inverse kinematics · Robotic manipulator

1 Introduction

In industry, robotic manipulators are widely used to manipulate various products. Today, there is an effort to model these manipulators by other more efficient methods (using geometric algebra, quaternions, ...), which deal with the singular positions of the manipulator or are computationally less demanding. However, a model constructed using classical methods can be used to verify the properties of the other models of manipulator. Note that results presented here can be used in the analysis of planar mechanisms [4,6].

The main part of this paper is based on a method that comes from [9]. Let us briefly introduce important terms that will be used in the following text.

We describe the model of the manipulator as a set of joints which connect a set of rigid links. Therefore we can say that we deal with the rigid motion which is precisely defined in [9]. An important notion is a twist which we classify as an infinitesimal version of a rigid motion which also provides a description of the instantaneous velocity of a rigid body in terms of its linear and angular components.

We also define a wrench as a single force applied along a line, combined with a torque about that same line. An important fact is that any system of forces acting on a rigid body can be replaced by this wrench.

If we describe an arbitrary object as a subset O of $\mathbb{R}^3$, then a rigid motion of an object is defined as a continuous family of mappings $g(t) : O \to \mathbb{R}^3$ which

© Springer Nature Switzerland AG 2020
J. Mazal et al. (Eds.): MESAS 2019, LNCS 11995, pp. 26–38, 2020.
https://doi.org/10.1007/978-3-030-43890-6_3

describes how every point of the body moves as a function of time, relative to some fixed Cartesian coordinate frame. It means that if we move the object along a continuous path, we can say that $g(t)$ maps the initial coordinates of a point on the body to the coordinates of the same point at time t. An important fact is that rigid body transformation preserves length and also the cross product.

1.1 Rigid Motion

As we already noted, rigid motion preserves distance between points. It means that the distance between any two particles of the moving object remains fixed all the time. Moreover, we can say that rigid displacement consists of rotation and translation of the object.

We represent the configuration of a rigid body by attaching a Cartesian coordinate frame to some point on the rigid body and keeping track of the motion of this body coordinate frame relative to a fixed frame. The motion of the individual particles in the body can then be retrieved from the motion of the body frame and the motion of the point of attachment of the frame to the body.

If we continue in this vein, we choose any point of the body and observe the coordinates of point relative to some known frame. Hence we get a curve $p(t) \in \mathbb{R}^3, t \in [0, T]$, for the trajectory of the whole body.

One can see that pure translational motion is simple to describe (see [9]). Therefore let us analyze only the rotation in more detail.

We call a set Q a configuration space for a system if every element $x \in Q$ corresponds to a valid configuration of the system and also every configuration of the system can be identified with a unique element of Q. Then we can say that every configuration of a rigid body that can rotate can be identified with a unique $R \in SO(3)$, where the space of rotation matrices in $\mathbb{R}^{3 \times 3}$ is defined as

$$SO(3) = \{R \in \mathbb{R}^{3 \times 3} : RR^T = I, \det R = 1\}.$$

Then we understand the rotation group $SO(3)$ as the configuration space of the system and a trajectory of the system is a curve $R(t) \in SO(3)$ for $t \in [0, T]$, where T is the final time. In the following text we use the fact, that rotation matrices can be composed.

If we continue with rotation, we can introduce the exponential coordinates for rotation. It becomes from the fact, that we need to rotate the link of a robot about a fixed axis. Let $\omega = (\omega(1), \omega(2), \omega(3)) \in \mathbb{R}^3$ be a unit vector which specifies the direction of rotation and let $\varphi \in \mathbb{R}$ be the angle of rotation in radians. Then we can write $R \in SO(3)$ as a function of ω and φ.

To compute the matrix exponential we get a Rodrigues' formula in the following form:

$$e^{\widehat{\omega}\varphi} = I + \widehat{\omega}\sin\varphi + \widehat{\omega}^2(1 - \cos\varphi), \quad \text{where } \widehat{\omega} = \begin{pmatrix} 0 & -\omega(3) & \omega(2) \\ \omega(3) & 0 & -\omega(1) \\ -\omega(2) & \omega(1) & 0 \end{pmatrix} \quad (1)$$

From literature (for example [9]), we know that every rotation matrix can be represented as the matrix exponential of some skew-symmetric matrix. It is important to note that the exponential map generates the rotation corresponding to the rotation about the axis ω by a specified amount φ.

Even though we focused mainly on rotations, rigid body motion consists of rotation and translation as we already mentioned. Finally, we can say that the action of the rigid transformation on a point can be characterized as

$$g(q) = p + Rq,$$

where p is the translation, R the rotation and q the point of the rigid body.

1.2   Homogeneous Representation

Now we represent the transformation of point and vectors by rigid transformations in terms of matrices and vectors in $\mathbb{R}^4$. We define a homogeneous coordinates of q as the following vector $\bar{q} \in \mathbb{R}^4$, then the origin O has the following form $\bar{O}$ and any vector v, as a difference of points, has a zero in the last position

$$\bar{q} = \begin{pmatrix} q_1 \\ q_2 \\ q_3 \\ 1 \end{pmatrix}, \qquad \bar{O} = \begin{pmatrix} 0 \\ 0 \\ 0 \\ 1 \end{pmatrix}, \qquad \bar{v} = \begin{pmatrix} v_1 \\ v_2 \\ v_3 \\ 0 \end{pmatrix}.$$

Then, in general, we have a homogeneous representation of $g = (p, R) \in SE(3)$

$$\bar{g} = \begin{pmatrix} R & p \\ 0 & 1 \end{pmatrix}, \tag{2}$$

where $SE(3) = SO(3) \times \mathbb{R}^3$ is a special Euclidean group.

1.3   Exponential Coordinates for Rigid Motion and Twists

We define a twist as an arbitrary element of the following group

$$se(3) = \{(v, \widehat{\omega}) : v \in \mathbb{R}^3, \widehat{\omega} \in so(3)\}.$$

In homogeneous coordinates, we write an element from this group as

$$\widehat{\xi} = \begin{pmatrix} \widehat{\omega} & v \\ 0 & 0 \end{pmatrix} \in \mathbb{R}^{4 \times 4},$$

where $v = -\omega \times q$. Keep in mind that $\widehat{\xi}$ can be understood as a generalization of the skew-symmetric matrix $\widehat{\omega} \in so(3)$.

Therefore the exponential of a twist can be interpreted as a mapping from initial to final configurations of the rigid body. An important fact is that the exponetial map of the twist is surjective, i.e. every rigid transformation g can be written as the exponential of some twist $e^{\widehat{\xi}\varphi} \in se(3)$.

$$e^{\widehat{\xi}\varphi} = \begin{pmatrix} I & v\varphi \\ 0 & 1 \end{pmatrix} \qquad \omega = 0 \tag{3}$$

$$e^{\widehat{\xi}\varphi} = \begin{pmatrix} e^{\widehat{\omega}\varphi} & (I - e^{\widehat{\omega}\varphi})(\omega \times v) + \omega\omega^T v\varphi \\ 0 & 1 \end{pmatrix} \qquad \omega \neq 0 \qquad (4)$$

We can say that every rigid body motion can be realized by a rotation about an axis combined with a translation parallel to that axis.

2   Model of the Manipulator

As previously stated, our manipulator consists of a set of rigid links and a set of joints. Generally speaking, we can meet three types of joints – revolute, prismatic and planar. Each type of the joint corresponds to a subgroup of the special Euclidean group $SE(3)$.

Let us introduce a model of IRB 4400 which is showed in Fig. 1. The manipulator consists of five joints j_0, j_1, j_2, j_3, j_4 and four links $l_{01}, l_{12}, l_{23}, l_{34}$, where each link l_{ik} connects joints j_i and j_k.

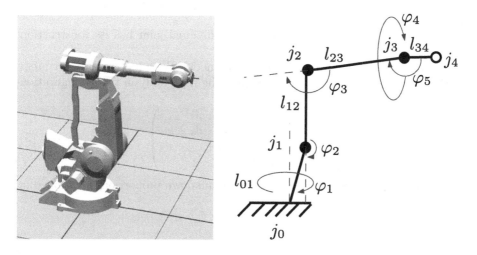

Fig. 1. IRB 4400

To characterize the position of one link relative to the other one we define five angles $\varphi_1, \varphi_2, \ldots, \varphi_5$ which also characterize rotation of a given joint.

3   Forward Kinematics

The forward kinematics of a manipulator determines the configuration of the end-effector (for us it is a tool or a gripper) given the relative configurations of each pair of adjacent links of the mechanism.

Our mechanism is a manipulator with five degrees of freedom.

We have two coordinate frames for our manipulator. The first is a *base frame* S, which is attached to a point on the manipulator which is stationary with respect to the first link l_{01}. And the second is the *tool frame* T, which is attached to the end-effector of the robot. Then the forward kinematics is represented by a mapping $g_{st}(t) : Q \to SE(3)$ which describes the relationship between the base frame S and the tool frame T.

We can say that if ξ is a twist, then the rigid motion associated with rotationg and translating along the axis of the twist is given by

$$g_{ab}(\varphi) = e^{\hat{\xi}\varphi} g_{ab}(0).$$

It is important to say that if ξ corresponds to a revolute joint, then $\varphi \in \mathbb{S}^1$ measures the angle of rotation about the axis.

Let us analyze each joint and link individually. We can say that for our case all joints are revolute with some restrictions. For example moving the second joint leave the orientation of the l_{23} link. In other words, changing the angle φ_2 in the positive direction causes, in the same time, moving φ_3 in the opposite direction with the same size of angle.

It is also important to note that each individual joint has its construction constrains which limit the range of each joint.

Let us begin to construct the kinematic model. We have a reference configuration of the manipulator for $\varphi = 0$, then the rigid body in this configuration is $g_{st}(0)$.

$$g_{st}(0) = \begin{pmatrix} 1 & 0 & 0 & 0 \\ 0 & 1 & 0 & d_1 + d_4 + l_{34} \\ 0 & 0 & 1 & d_2 + l_{12} + d_3 \\ 0 & 0 & 0 & 1 \end{pmatrix} \tag{5}$$

The following Fig. 2 explains the meaning of unknown proportions mentioned in the Eq. (5).

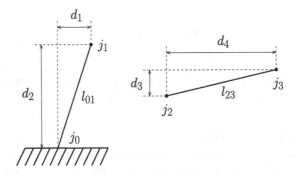

Fig. 2. Details of proportions

In order to continue, we need to introduce, how to characterize the i-th revolute joint. Let us recall that w_i is the unit vector of the direction of axis of rotation, q_i is the axis point and v_i is a unit vector pointing to the direction of translation. Then the revolute joint is

$$\xi_i = \begin{pmatrix} -w_i \times q_i \\ w_i \end{pmatrix}.$$

Let us also recall that the forward kinematics map can be seen as a product of exponentials by

$$g_{st}(\varphi) = e^{\hat{\xi}_1 \varphi_1} e^{\hat{\xi}_2 \varphi_2} \dots e^{\hat{\xi}_n \varphi_n} g_{st}(0) \tag{6}$$

Next part presents an overview of the characteristic parameters of our manipulator. We have the following vectors of the direction of axis of rotation:

$$w_1 = \begin{pmatrix} 0 \\ 0 \\ 1 \end{pmatrix}, \quad w_2 = w_3 = w_5 = \begin{pmatrix} -1 \\ 0 \\ 0 \end{pmatrix}, \quad w_4 = \begin{pmatrix} 0 \\ -1 \\ 0 \end{pmatrix}.$$

Another necessary part is to determine the points on these axes:

$$q_1 = j_0 = \begin{pmatrix} 0 \\ 0 \\ 0 \end{pmatrix}, \quad q_2 = j_1 = \begin{pmatrix} 0 \\ d_1 \\ d_2 \end{pmatrix}, \quad q_3 = j_2 = \begin{pmatrix} 0 \\ d_1 \\ d_2 + l_{12} \end{pmatrix}, \quad q_4 = q_5 = j_3 = \begin{pmatrix} 0 \\ d_1 + d_4 \\ d_2 + l_{12} + d_3 \end{pmatrix}.$$

After a detailed analysis of the axes of rotation we can define individual twists. The first comes from the following computation:

$$\xi_1 = \begin{pmatrix} -w_1 \times q_1 \\ w_1 \end{pmatrix} = \begin{pmatrix} -(0,0,1) \times (0,0,0) \\ 0 \\ 0 \\ 1 \end{pmatrix} = \begin{pmatrix} 0 \\ 0 \\ 0 \\ 0 \\ 0 \\ 1 \end{pmatrix}.$$

And the same method gives us the results of the rest of the twists:

$$\xi_2 = \begin{pmatrix} 0 \\ -d_2 \\ d_1 \\ -1 \\ 0 \\ 0 \end{pmatrix}, \quad \xi_3 = \begin{pmatrix} 0 \\ -d_2 - l_{12} \\ d_1 \\ -1 \\ 0 \\ 0 \end{pmatrix}, \quad \xi_4 = \begin{pmatrix} d_2 + l_{12} + d_3 \\ 0 \\ 0 \\ 0 \\ -1 \\ 0 \end{pmatrix}, \quad \xi_5 = \begin{pmatrix} 0 \\ -d_2 - l_{12} - d_3 \\ d_1 + d_4 \\ -1 \\ 0 \\ 0 \end{pmatrix}.$$

Using the Eq. (1) and computing it for the first joint we can see the matrix representing the rotation along the z-axis by

$$e^{\hat{\omega}_1 \varphi_1} = \begin{pmatrix} 1 & 0 & 0 \\ 0 & 1 & 0 \\ 0 & 0 & 1 \end{pmatrix} + \begin{pmatrix} 0 & -1 & 0 \\ 1 & 0 & 0 \\ 0 & 0 & 0 \end{pmatrix} \cdot \sin \varphi_1 + \begin{pmatrix} 0 & -1 & 0 \\ 1 & 0 & 0 \\ 0 & 0 & 0 \end{pmatrix} \cdot \begin{pmatrix} 0 & -1 & 0 \\ 1 & 0 & 0 \\ 0 & 0 & 0 \end{pmatrix} \cdot (1 - \cos \varphi_1) = \begin{pmatrix} \cos \varphi_1 & -\sin \varphi_1 & 0 \\ \sin \varphi_1 & \cos \varphi_1 & 0 \\ 0 & 0 & 1 \end{pmatrix}.$$

After using the homogeneous representation, we present the result of the exponential for the first joint by

$$e^{\widehat{\xi}_1\varphi_1} = \begin{pmatrix} \cos\varphi_1 & -\sin\varphi_1 & 0 & 0 \\ \sin\varphi_1 & \cos\varphi_1 & 0 & 0 \\ 0 & 0 & 1 & 0 \\ 0 & 0 & 0 & 1 \end{pmatrix}. \tag{7}$$

With the same computation we can achieve the result for the rest of joints:

$$e^{\widehat{\xi}_2\varphi_2} = \begin{pmatrix} 1 & 0 & 0 & 0 \\ 0 & \cos\varphi_2 & \sin\varphi_2 & d_1(1-\cos\varphi_2) - d_2\sin\varphi_2 \\ 0 & -\sin\varphi_2 & \cos\varphi_2 & d_1\sin\varphi_2 + d_2(1-\cos\varphi_2) \\ 0 & 0 & 0 & 1 \end{pmatrix}, \tag{8}$$

$$e^{\widehat{\xi}_3\varphi_3} = \begin{pmatrix} 1 & 0 & 0 & 0 \\ 0 & \cos\varphi_3 & \sin\varphi_3 & d_1(1-\cos\varphi_3) - (d_2+l_{12})\sin\varphi_3 \\ 0 & -\sin\varphi_3 & \cos\varphi_3 & d_1\sin\varphi_3 + (d_2+l_{12})(1-\cos\varphi_3) \\ 0 & 0 & 0 & 1 \end{pmatrix}, \tag{9}$$

$$e^{\widehat{\xi}_4\varphi_4} = \begin{pmatrix} \cos\varphi_4 & 0 & -\sin\varphi_4 & (d_2+l_{12}+d_3)\sin\varphi_4 \\ 0 & 1 & 0 & 0 \\ \sin\varphi_4 & 0 & \cos\varphi_4 & (d_2+l_{12}+d_3)(1-\cos\varphi_4) \\ 0 & 0 & 0 & 1 \end{pmatrix}, \tag{10}$$

$$e^{\widehat{\xi}_5\varphi_5} = \begin{pmatrix} 1 & 0 & 0 & 0 \\ 0 & \cos\varphi_5 & \sin\varphi_5 & (d_1+d_4)(1-\cos\varphi_5) - (d_2+l_{12}+d_3)\sin\varphi_5 \\ 0 & -\sin\varphi_5 & \cos\varphi_5 & (d_1+d_4)\sin\varphi_5 - (d_2+l_{12}+d_3)(1-\cos\varphi_5) \\ 0 & 0 & 0 & 1 \end{pmatrix}. \tag{11}$$

From Eqs. (7)–(11) and (5) it follows that the kinematics is given by the Eq. (6) as a multiplication of the exponentials. Therefore the final result of this multiplication show us the position and orientation of the gripper in the following form

$$g_{st}(\varphi) = \begin{pmatrix} R(\varphi) & p(\varphi) \\ 0 & 1 \end{pmatrix},$$

where each column of the rotation matrix $R(\varphi)$ represents the orientation of the gripper, while $p(\varphi)$ characterize the position of the gripper.

Let us introduce some basic results of the forward kinematics visualized in MATLAB. In Fig. 3 we can see the initial position of the manipulator.

The kinematics is characterized by the orientation of each joint. It means that we can see the result of the change angle in the following picture. Therefore the shape of the manipulator for $\varphi_1 = \frac{\pi}{6}$ (other φ_i are zero) is shown in the Fig. 4, where the initial state is characterized by black points and the current position of the manipulator is illustrated by red points.

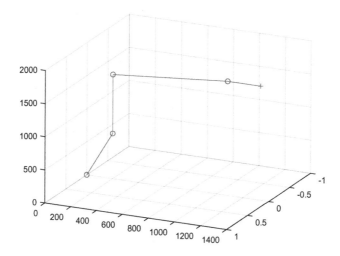

Fig. 3. MATLAB simulation – initial position of the manipulator

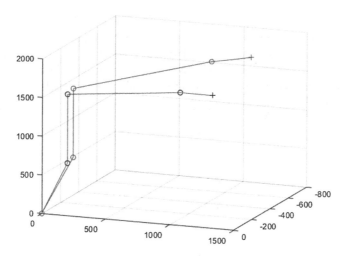

Fig. 4. MATLAB simulation for $\varphi_1 = \frac{\pi}{6}$ (Color figure online)

As we previously reported, we need to consider the fact that changing the angle φ_2 also causes the change of φ_3. This fact is due to the construction of the manipulator. In other words the value $\varphi_2 = \frac{\pi}{6}$ means that the value of $\varphi_3 = -\varphi_2 = -\frac{\pi}{6}$. This result is again shown in Fig. 5.

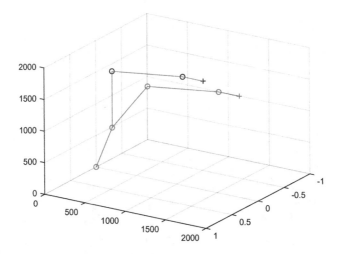

Fig. 5. MATLAB simulation for $\varphi_2 = \frac{\pi}{6}$

The last step in this procedure is to combinate different changes of the joints. We expect that each joint has a restriction caused by the construction of the manipulator. These limitations play a big role in the inverse kinematics. In this section, we are limited by using only reachable values of the angles. Therefore we illustrate one of the possible state. In Fig. 6 we can see a shape of the manipulator with the angles $\varphi_1 = -\frac{\pi}{6}$, $\varphi_2 = \frac{\pi}{6}$ and $\varphi_5 = \frac{\pi}{6}$.

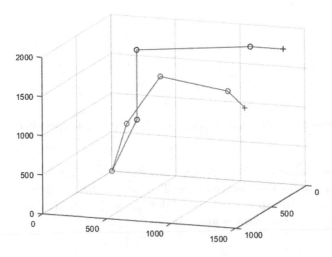

Fig. 6. MATLAB simulation for $\varphi_1 = -\frac{\pi}{6}$, $\varphi_2 = \frac{\pi}{6}$ and $\varphi_5 = \frac{\pi}{6}$

4   Inverse Kinematics

Now let us introduce a method which is used to construct the inverse kinematic model of the mechanism. The main idea is that we have a final position of the gripper and we need to analyze the position and the shape of the body of the mechanism according to the known position. We present one of the classic method to solve our problem by using Denavit-Hartenberg parametrization. For the inverse kinematics concept based on more algebraic background, one can see paper [5].

From the previous text, we know that the kinematics are given by Eq. (6) by multiplying the exponentials. For the inverse kinematics our aim is to solve this equation for $\varphi_1, \varphi_2, \ldots, \varphi_5$ and for given $g_d \in SE(3)$, where g_d is the desired configuration of the tool frame. It means that we look for some configuration of the system which corresponds to the desired position of the tool. However, we expect that this kind of problem can have more that one solution for this system.

4.1   Denavit-Hartenberg Parameters

Denavit-Hartenberg parameters (D-H) are the four parameters (φ, α, a, D) associated with a particular convention for attaching reference frames to the links of a robot manipulator. We have a base frame S and the tool frame T then we can say that the coordinates of the twists corresponding to each joint of the manipulator provide a complete parametrization of the kinematics of the manipulator. But more usual in robotics is the use of D-H parameters which we obtain by applying a set of rules (can be found in [2,3,12]), which specify the position and orientation of frames L_i attached to each link of the robot and then constructing the homogeneous transformations between frames denoted by $g_{l_{i-1}l_i}$.

To solve the system (6) let us use the Denavit-Hartenberg parametrization to characterize the system and relations between the individual parts of the manipulator.

In general, we can rewrite the kinematics in the Eq. (6) in terms of Denavit-Hartenberg parametrization as the following equation:

$$g_{st}(\varphi) = g_{l_0l_1}(\varphi_1)g_{l_1l_2}(\varphi_2)g_{l_2l_3}(\varphi_3)g_{l_3l_4}(\varphi_4)g_{l_4l_5}(\varphi_5)g_{l_5t} \tag{12}$$

By proper choice of link frames, we characterize each $g_{l_{i-1}l_i}$ as a matrix:

$$g_{l_{i-1}l_i} = \begin{pmatrix} \cos\varphi_i & -\sin\varphi_i\cos\alpha_i & \sin\varphi_i\sin\alpha_i & a_i\cos\varphi_i \\ \sin\varphi_i & \cos\varphi_i\cos\alpha_i & -\cos\varphi_i\sin\alpha_i & a_i\sin\varphi_i \\ 0 & \sin\alpha_i & \cos\alpha_i & D_i \\ 0 & 0 & 0 & 1 \end{pmatrix} \tag{13}$$

Let us compute the result using the D-H parameters which are listed in the following Table 1, where parameters d_i and l_{jk} are given from the construction of the mechanism and which can be seen in Figs. 1 and 2.

Table 1. Denavit-Hartenberg parameters for our manipulator

i	φ_i (rad)	α_i (rad)	a_i (mm)	D_i (mm)
1	φ_1	$-\frac{\pi}{2}$	$d_1 = 200$	0
2	φ_2	0	$l_{12} = 890$	$d_2 = 680$
3	φ_3	0	$d_3 = 150$	0
4	φ_4	$\frac{\pi}{2}$	0	$d_4 = 880$
5	φ_5	0	0	$l_{34} = 254$

According to the Table 1 and the form of the matrix in Eq. (13) we can quantify every matrix representing the relation between every two parts of the manipulator.

Here we present the overview of these matrices:

$$g_{l_0 l_1} = \begin{pmatrix} \cos\varphi_1 & 0 & \sin\varphi_1 & d_1 \cos\varphi_1 \\ \sin\varphi_1 & 0 & -\cos\varphi_1 & d_1 \sin\varphi_1 \\ 0 & 1 & 0 & 0 \\ 0 & 0 & 0 & 1 \end{pmatrix}, \text{where } d_1 = 200 \text{ mm},$$

$$g_{l_1 l_2} = \begin{pmatrix} \cos\varphi_2 & -\sin\varphi_2 & 0 & l_{12} \cos\varphi_2 \\ \sin\varphi_2 & \cos\varphi_2 & 0 & l_{12} \sin\varphi_2 \\ 0 & 0 & 1 & d_2 \\ 0 & 0 & 0 & 1 \end{pmatrix}, \text{where } d_2 = 680 \text{ mm and } l_{12} = 890 \text{ mm},$$

$$g_{l_2 l_3} = \begin{pmatrix} \cos\varphi_3 & -\sin\varphi_3 & 0 & d_3 \cos\varphi_3 \\ \sin\varphi_3 & \cos\varphi_3 & 0 & d_3 \sin\varphi_3 \\ 0 & 0 & 1 & 0 \\ 0 & 0 & 0 & 1 \end{pmatrix}, \text{where } d_3 = 150 \text{ mm},$$

$$g_{l_3 l_4} = \begin{pmatrix} \cos\varphi_4 & 0 & \sin\varphi_4 & 0 \\ \sin\varphi_4 & 0 & -\cos\varphi_4 & 0 \\ 0 & 1 & 0 & d_4 \\ 0 & 0 & 0 & 1 \end{pmatrix}, \text{where } d_4 = 880 \text{ mm},$$

$$g_{l_4 l_5} = \begin{pmatrix} \cos\varphi_5 & -\sin\varphi_5 & 0 & 0 \\ \sin\varphi_5 & \cos\varphi_5 & 0 & 0 \\ 0 & 0 & 1 & l_{34} \\ 0 & 0 & 0 & 1 \end{pmatrix}, \text{where } l_{34} = 254 \text{ mm}.$$

It is also necessary to define the initial position of the gripper. Therefore we present the matrix $g_{l_5 t}$ as

$$g_{l_5 t} = \begin{pmatrix} 1 & 0 & 0 & 0 \\ 0 & 1 & 0 & d_1 + d_4 + l_{34} \\ 0 & 0 & 1 & d_2 + l_{12} + d_3 \\ 0 & 0 & 0 & 1 \end{pmatrix}$$

Computation of the homogeneous transformation matrix M that connects the tool frame and the base frame is given by substituting these matrices into the Eq. (6).

From the forward kinematics we have a position and orientation of the gripper and then we get the system of 12 equations. If we consider instances from [12] we are able to solve this system analytically (using atan2 function) for some special manipulators, for the rest we need to use numerical methods shown in [3].

If we slightly simplify our manipulator (for example we do not consider the connection of the second and third joint) we are able to solve the system of equations, otherwise we use numerical methods presented in [3].

Using MATLAB and Maple we have solved these system for the inverse kinematics, therefore we introduce some results visually.

To place the gripper in the position $(x, y, z) = (0, 1600, 900)$, the algorithm of inverse kinematics returns the angle $\varphi_2 = 0.4736$ rad and $\varphi_3 = 0.1816$ rad. We can see the result in Fig. 7

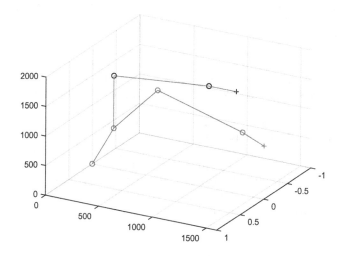

Fig. 7. MATLAB simulation of inverse kinematics ($x = 0, y = 1600, z = 900$)

5   Conclusion

This paper discusses forward and inverse kinematics of an industrial manipulator, which is one of the basic. The description of kinematics is complicated by the fact that the axes of rotation of the individual following arms are located out of the axes of the previous ones, hence we classify the mechanism as a special one. However, the simplified kinematic model has been assembled and tested in MATLAB. One of the reason is that its properties can be compared with models based on the use of other methods such as geometric algebras and quaternions [4,5].

Acknowledgement. The author was supported by a grant no. FV 19-06.

References

1. Corke, P.I.: A robotics toolbox for MATLAB. IEEE Robot. Autom. Mag. **3**, 24–32 (1996)
2. Denavit, J., Hartenberg, R.S.: A kinematic notation for lower-pair mechanisms based on matrices. ASME J. Appl. Mech. **22**, 215–221 (1955)
3. Grepl, R.: Kinematics and Dynamics of Mechatronic Systems. Akademicke nakladatelstvi CERM, Brno (2007)
4. Hrdina, J., Návrat, A., Vašík, P.: Control of 3-link robotic snake based on conformal geometric algebra. Adv. Appl. Clifford Algebras **26**(3), 1069–1080 (2015). https://doi.org/10.1007/s00006-015-0621-2
5. Hrdina, J., Návrat, A., Vašík, P.: Notes on planar inverse kinematics based on geometric algebra. Adv. Appl. Clifford Algebras **28**(3), 1–14 (2018). https://doi.org/10.1007/s00006-018-0890-7
6. Hrdina, J., Zalabova, L.: Local geometric control of a certain mechanism with the growth vector (4,7). J. Dyn. Control Syst. (2019, in press). https://doi.org/10.1007/s10883-019-09460-7
7. Iliukin, V.N., Mitkovskii, K.B., Bizyanova, D.A., Akopyan, A.A.: The modeling of inverse kinematics for 5 DOF manipulator. Procedia Eng. **176**, 498–505 (2016)
8. Liljebäck, P., Pettersen, K.Y., Stavdahl, O., Gravdahl, J.T.: Snake Robots, Modelling, Mechatronics, and Control. Springer, London (2013). https://doi.org/10.1007/978-1-4471-2996-7
9. Murray, R.M., Zexiang, L., Sastry, S.S.: A Mathematical Introduction to Robotic Manipulation. CRC Press, Boca Raton (1994)
10. Sciavicco, L., Siciliano, B., Sciavicco, B.: Modelling and Control of Robot Manipulators. Springer, New York (2000). https://doi.org/10.1007/978-1-4471-0449-0
11. Selig, J.M.: Geometric Fundamentals of Robotics. Monographs in Computer Science. Springer, New York (2004). https://doi.org/10.1007/b138859
12. Siciliano, B., Khatib, O.: Springer Handbook of Robotics. Springer, Heidelberg (2008). https://doi.org/10.1007/978-3-540-30301-5

Low-Cost RGB-D-SLAM Experimental Results for Real Building Interior Mapping

Jean Motsch[1], Yves Bergeon[1], and Václav Křivánek[2(✉)]

[1] CREC St-Cyr, Écoles de Saint-Cyr Coëtquidan, Guer, France
jean.motsch@st-cyr.terre-net.defense.gouv.fr
[2] University of Defence in Brno, Brno, Czech Republic
vaclav.krivanek@unob.cz

Abstract. Robot navigation inside a building relies on efficient localization of the device for motion planning. Mapping is also to be considered, and, along with high-end and costly solutions, low-cost devices prove to be useful. Therefore, this article presents well known low-cost solutions, with a methodology tailored for the mapping of a complex building floor. It takes care of the limitations of the sensor with some post-processing added to obtain beautiful point cloud as results of the experiments. Data acquired during an intensive campaign of measures by a trainee are presented. Finally, the analysis of the results shows the impact of the point cloud's size and the storage needed.

Keywords: Mapping · Localization · Kinect · SLAM · Visual SLAM · RGD-SLAM · Point cloud · Indoor navigation

1 Introduction

Indoor maps are often used in indoor robot navigation. Such maps allow planning the displacements of a robot efficiently, even in a very cluttered environment.

To fulfill this requirement, mapping systems use a combination of depth sensors (ultrasound, LiDAR, infrared) and adapted algorithms. When considering the building cost of the mapping system, the sensor and the amount of computing power are to be carefully chosen. For example, LiDAR (1D, 2D or 3D) are very efficient and accurate devices, but their cost is in the high-end range. On the other hand are located ultrasound or infrared devices, but with lower capabilities. In between, structured light devices, like the Microsoft Kinect family, offer a nice tradeoff between cost and performances.

In this context, this article deals with experiments made using a low-cost mapping solution used to complete description of the interior of a real building. It is structured as follows. Section 2 presents in details the low-cost mapping system used, while Sect. 3 gives more information when the interior of the building is taken into consideration. Section 4 shows some results obtained and makes some comments. Finally, conclusion and tracks for future work are proposed in Sect. 5.

© Springer Nature Switzerland AG 2020
J. Mazal et al. (Eds.): MESAS 2019, LNCS 11995, pp. 39–49, 2020.
https://doi.org/10.1007/978-3-030-43890-6_4

2   Low-Cost Mapping

A block-diagram description of the mapping process is given in Fig. 1. The following work was already experienced in [2], where the system configuration uses a low-cost 3D sensor and a low computing power desktop computer. Furthermore, the system must be simple enough to be operated by an intern. The situation is like the one described in [3] and [12].

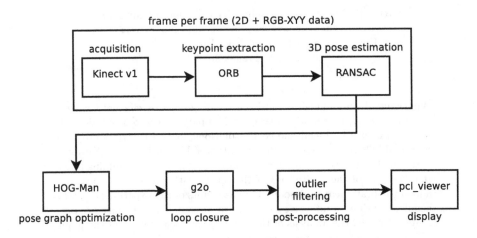

Fig. 1. System overview

2.1   The SLAM Loop

The mapping is performed during the motion of a 3D sensor in the interior of a building. As one has to follow the trajectory of the 3D sensor, the most used method is to perform localization and mapping simultaneously, also known as SLAM methods (Simultaneous Localization And Mapping). SLAM relies on a kind of "chicken-and-egg" problem, as shown in the Fig. 2. An Expectation Minimization (EM) algorithm, iterating two steps, solves the problem:

– computing the environment's map,
– estimating the sensor/robot localization.

Typical solutions for this problem rely on statistical tools [14], like Kalman filters or Monte-Carlo methods (as particle filters), in a Bayesian framework.

This section describes a very low-cost system to perform the interior mapping of a building.

2.2   The Sensor: Microsoft Kinect for Windows v1

Microsoft's project Natal introduced a line of motion sensing input devices, originally for the Xbox 360 gaming console. The Kinect for Windows v1, depicted

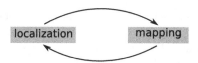

Fig. 2. The SLAM loop

in Fig. 3 was powered by a proprietary chipset developed by PrimeSense. Even if no longer supported by Microsoft, this Kinect has the following characteristics as a low-cost 3D sensor:

- RGB: 640 × 480 pixels (VGA) at 30 Hz,
- Depth: 320 × 240 at 30 Hz,
- Range: 1.2–3.5 m,
- Field of view: 57° (horizontal) × 43° (vertical),
- Data: RGB (pixel) XYZ (position)

2.3 The Localization Algorithm: RGB-D-SLAM

RGB-D-SLAM (v2) [4] is a SLAM solution dedicated for RGB-D cameras. It allows to quickly acquire colored 3D models of objects and indoor scenes, typically with a hand-held Kinect-style camera. It uses visual features to detect the points of interest used in the matching step. Those points are computed using either SURF (Speeded-Up Robust Features), SIFT (Scale-Invariant Feature Transform), or ORB (Oriented Fast and Rotate Brief) [9]. The results are key-points, localized in 2D (and their real 3D counterparts), and a summary of their vicinity. A RANSAC (Random Sampling and Consensus) algorithm is then used to estimate the 3D transformation between subsequent frames robustly.

This part of the processing is the most demanding in terms of processing power. When available, GPGPU (General Processing on Graphical Processing Unit) is used to compute the key-points, thus reducing the processing time.

To achieve embedded processing, the current image is matched only versus a subset of previous images. Subsequently, it constructs a graph whose nodes correspond to camera views (or *poses*) and whose edges correspond to the estimated 3D transformations.

Fig. 3. Microsoft Kinect for Windows v1

The graph is then optimized with HOG-Man (Hierarchical Optimization for Pose Graphs on Manifolds) to reduce the accumulated pose errors. Results take the form of a pose graph with a colored point cloud.

RGB-D-SLAM is currently running on top of ROS (Robot Operating System) on a Ubuntu box (14.04). The PC configuration is a low-end one: Pentium CPU, 4 GB of RAM and an entry-level graphics card, somewhat a little better than integrated graphics. Figure 4 shows a typical RGB-D-SLAM session. On top is the 3D point cloud with the camera trajectory displayed. The windows on the bottom, from left to right, show the RGB image, the depth map, the points of interest, and the matching points.

Fig. 4. RGB-D-SLAM v2 at work on ubuntu 14.04

2.4 The Closing: g2o Algorithm

When it comes to mapping, the probability of having the device in the same position multiple times is high. In this case, loop-closure filtering is needed to remove drifts in the map built during the process. That step is taken into account using the Generic Graph Optimization algorithm (g2o) as described in [11].

2.5 The Representation: 3D Point Cloud

Once obtained, maps can be represented using different methods, suitable for various applications. For example, occupancy grids, as Octomap [8], are well suited for navigation purposes. On the other hand, 3D clouds of points are more useful for 3D visualization. It will be the case in our experimental work.

3   Application to the Mapping of the Interior of a Building

3.1   Overview

When describing a building, several tools can be used. For new buildings, 3D CAD models may be available with an excellent level of details. For older buildings, elevation maps and blueprints are usually available. Those descriptions, while looking detailed and quite exhaustive, show the lack of two properties. Firstly, they are design documents, *i.e.* there may be subtle discrepancies between what was planned and what was built. Secondly, these documents show empty buildings, without considering furniture and everything that comes with a living interior. In that situation, it appears to be interesting to provide a "real-life" interior mapping of a building, including furniture and the clutter induced by living occupants. This 3D map also provides the height of objects that helps robot's navigation, under table for example. In this domain, previous work from [5] presents maps computed using both blueprints and 3D measures.

The chosen experiment was to map the first floor of our research center. An old blueprint is shown in Fig. 5. There are several offices, some lab facilities, and one large hall with a glass ceiling over 4 m height. Also, some offices have glass walls so that one office is visible from the adjacent offices. This floor is quite complex to map and will be a challenging test case for this study. The blueprint is at a very raw resolution, without scale and can't be used to assess the accuracy of our experimental results.

3.2   Caveats

As can be seen in Fig. 5, the size of the first floor makes it difficult to do the mapping in one shot. To deal with this size, the mapping is performed one office after the other.

As the acquisition algorithm has already been exposed, one has just to take care of these limitations on the 3D sensor, the PrimeSense chip of the Kinect for Windows v1. The Kinect uses an infrared light pattern that has been showed to be inaccurate when there is direct sun daylight in the scene. To avoid this limitation, measures must be made with curtains closed or without direct illumination. Also, the effective range of the Kinect is limited, therefore it's somewhat challenging to have right measures and pertinent data in a large hall. Moreover, when there is a lot of windows (ceiling, walls), the Kinect will see through them. As one office map must not contain data about adjacent offices, some post-processing might be necessary. Finally, to associate multiple maps, one *absolute* or *reference* pose has to be set. Then, for every room, the initial pose has to be carefully measured with respect to the *absolute* pose. In the experiments, the Kinect camera always begins its mapping being on the floor and looking in the same direction. In such situations, the pose is just given by a 2D translation.

Some precautions can be dealt with during the measurement process. Some have to be enforced by performing some post-processing as described in the following sections.

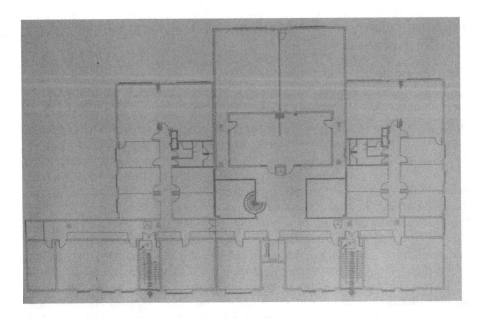

Fig. 5. Blueprint of the first floor of the building (no scale available)

3.3 Post-processing

A 3D point cloud represents every room (office, lab, corridor). As already mentioned, some post-processing is necessary. It is performed using the Point Cloud Library (PCL)[1] algorithms described in [13].

Outliers Filtering. As each room can be seen as a rectangular cuboid (a *shoebox*), points are to be restricted inside that box. Due to the glass walls, some points belong to adjacent rooms. In order to remove them, the *pass-through* algorithm is used with approximate dimensions of the room. Figure 6 shows one example of the filtering of a point cloud.

Point Cloud Sub-sampling. When displaying the point cloud, the large number of points makes it a difficult task for low-end computers with limited graphic processing power. One way to deal with this hardware limitation without introducing distortion and artefacts relies on cloud sub-sampling using a *Voxel Grid*. This can be seen as a set of tiny 3D boxes in space put over the input point cloud data. Then, in each *voxel*, a 3D box, all the points will be approximated, or *down-sampled*, with their centroid. This approach is a bit slower than approximating them with the center of the voxel, but it represents the underlying surface more accurately.

---

[1] pointcloud.org.

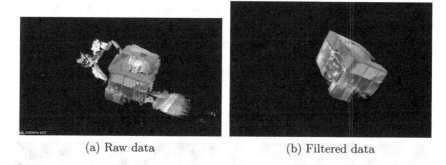

(a) Raw data   (b) Filtered data

Fig. 6. Outliers filtering

It is important to note that this sub-sampling is only performed for display reason. Every map is fully used, and only the outliers have been filtered.

Map Stitching. The merge of several maps (or point cloud) is performed using simple 2D translations performed on all the clouds except one. Figure 7 shows an example of the point cloud obtained when two adjacent offices are stitched together.

Fig. 7. A map stitched for two offices

4   Experimental Results

The experiments were pursued to map the first floor of the research center labs completely. Every room was mapped except the hall (patio) that is too tall and with a glass ceiling. Figure 8 presents the global map obtained for the first floor from the side view. Figure 9 shows the same result from a different point of view that can be compared to Fig. 5. It can also be observed that some rooms are missing. These are *technical rooms* which have no importance for navigation between labs. As already stated, without a ground truth, the accuracy of the obtained results can't be evaluated. [10] shows some accuracy evaluation in experiments similar to this work.

Fig. 8. Global map from side view

The conducted experiment showed an essential aspect that needs to be evaluated. When it comes to memory, the amount of data obtained through the Kinect and RGB-D-SLAM is huge. Table 1 shows the size and storage used for every single point cloud. The total size of the map/point cloud is about **350 millions points** while the storage needed exceed **5 500 MB**. The point cloud can only be rendered using a high-end graphics card with sufficient processing power. As already mentioned in Sect. 3.3, a Voxel Grid is an excellent way to display the point cloud after sub-sampling, usually at $2 \times 2 \times 2cm^3$ resolution.

This tremendous amount of memory is explained by the way the Kinect provides its data. In our case, every point in the point cloud needs 16 bytes of data to be represented[2].

It also explains that the processing time, to filter outliers or to down-sample the point cloud, is not negligible at all on computers with low processing power. That also means that such a map will be difficult to manipulate on an embedded system.

---

[2] http://wiki.ros.org/openni_launch/Tutorials/BagRecordingPlayback.

Fig. 9. Global map from the top view. The map has been sub-sampled to be manipulated and displayed.

Table 1. Point cloud size' and storage use

Room	Number of points (million)	Storage (MB)
Corridor	22.6	361
Corridor 2	11.7	187
Office 1	24.8	397
Office 2	17.0	271
Office 3	17.0	271
Office 4	21.3	342
Office 5	21.4	342
Office 6	26.0	417
Office 7	19.6	314
Office 8	17.5	280
Office 9	13.5	216
Office 10	16.3	262
Office 11	9.7	155
Office 12	18.2	292
Office 13	12.8	204
Lecture room	25.2	403
Lab 1	18.9	302
Lab 2	16.8	269
Lab 3	16.1	257

5   Conclusion and Future Work

This article showed an example of a real-case use of a 3D SLAM method to map the interior of a building. A low-cost sensor, the Kinect, associated with a robust RGB-D-SLAM algorithm, appears to be an excellent combination to perform this task.

Nevertheless, care has to be taken of some pitfalls related to the sensor or the mapping method. In particular, while a low-cost sensing device might be used, as a high-level of processing power is needed, a powerful back-end computer is to be used to process the data. Indeed, the graphic card has to be chosen carefully.

As a result of the experiment, a large point cloud representing the map of the first floor is now available. The size of this map requires to simplify this data to make it usable by embedded devices.

Future work will focus on two tracks. The first one will be to extract an elevation map from the point cloud. That means finding the floor, the ceiling, and the walls in a very cluttered environment. The second track is to use the available data to do planning and navigation for UGV and UAV collaborative maneuvers, as described in [1,6,7].

References

1. Bergeon, Y.T., Doskočil, R., Křivánek, V., Motsch, J., Štefek, A.: UAV assisted landing on moving UGV. In: 2015 International Conference on Military Technologies (ICMT), pp. 1–5, May 2015. https://doi.org/10.1109/MILTECHS.2015.7153646
2. Bergeon, Y.T., Hadda, I., Křivánek, V., Motsch, J., Štefek, A.: Low cost 3d mapping for indoor navigation. In: 2015 International Conference on Military Technologies (ICMT), pp. 1–5 (2015). https://doi.org/10.1109/MILTECHS.2015.7153749
3. Bergeon, Y.T., Křivánek, V., Motsch, J.: Proactive teaching of mechatronics in master courses - project case study. IFAC-PapersOnLine 49(6), 291–296 (2016)
4. Endres, F., Hess, J., Engelhard, N., Sturm, J., Cremers, D., Burgard, W.: An evaluation of the RGB-D SLAM system. In: Proceedings of the IEEE International Conference on Robotics and Automation (ICRA), St. Paul, Minnesota, USA, May 2012
5. Faramondi, L., Inderst, F., Panzieri, S., Pascucci, F.: Hybrid map building for personal indoor navigation systems. In: 2014 IEEE/ASME International Conference on Advanced Intelligent Mechatronics, pp. 646–651, July 2014. https://doi.org/10.1109/AIM.2014.6878152
6. Hodicky, J.: HLA as an experimental backbone for autonomous system integration into operational field. In: Hodicky, J. (ed.) MESAS 2014. LNCS, vol. 8906, pp. 121–126. Springer, Cham (2014). https://doi.org/10.1007/978-3-319-13823-7_11
7. Hodicky, J.: Standards to support military autonomous system life cycle. In: Březina, T., Jabłoński, R. (eds.) MECHATRONICS 2017. AISC, vol. 644, pp. 671–678. Springer, Cham (2018). https://doi.org/10.1007/978-3-319-65960-2_83
8. Hornung, A., Wurm, K.M., Bennewitz, M., Stachniss, C., Burgard, W.: Octomap: an efficient probabilistic 3d mapping framework based on octrees. Auton. Robots 34(3), 189–206 (2013). https://doi.org/10.1007/s10514-012-9321-0

9. Karami, E., Shehata, M., Prasad, S.: Image matching using SIFT, SURF, BRIEF and ORB: Performance comparison for distorted images. In: IEEE Newfoundland and Labrador Section Conference, November 2015

10. Khoshelham, K., Elberink, S.O.: Accuracy and resolution of kinect depth data for indoor mapping applications. Sensors **12**(2), 1437–1454 (2012). https://doi.org/10.3390/s120201437. https://www.mdpi.com/1424-8220/12/2/1437

11. Kuemmerle, R., Grisetti, G., Strasdat, H., Konolige, K., Burgard, W.: g2o: a general framework for graph optimization. In: Proceedings of the IEEE International Conference on Robotics and Automation (ICRA). pp. 3607–3613. Shanghai, China, May 2011. https://doi.org/10.1109/ICRA.2011.5979949

12. de La Bourdonnaye, A., Doskočil, R., Křivánek, V., Štefek, A.: Practical experience with distance measurement based on the single visual camera. Adv. Mil. Technol. **7**(2), 49–56 (2012)

13. Rusu, R.B., Cousins, S.: 3D is here: Point Cloud Library (PCL). In: IEEE International Conference on Robotics and Automation (ICRA), Shanghai, China, 9–13 May 2011

14. Thrun, S., Burgard, W., Fox, D.: Probabilistic Robotics. Intelligent Robotics and Autonomous Agents. The MIT Press, Cambridge (2005)

Deep Learning Algorithms for Vehicle Detection on UAV Platforms: First Investigations on the Effects of Synthetic Training

Michael Krump[⊠], Martin Ruß, and Peter Stütz

Institute of Flight Systems, Bundeswehr University Munich, Neubiberg, Germany
{michael.krump,martin.russ,peter.stuetz}@unibw.de

Abstract. Vehicle detection on aerial imagery taken with UAVs (unmanned aerial vehicles) plays an important role in many fields of application, such as traffic monitoring, surveillance or defense and rescue missions. Deep learning based object detectors are often used to overcome the resulting detection challenges. The generation of training data under different conditions and with the necessary variance is difficult and costly in real life. Therefore, virtual simulation environments are meanwhile often applied for this purpose. Our current research interests focus on the difference in performance, also called reality gap, of trainable vehicle detectors between both domains and the influence of differently designed training data. A general method for automatic image annotation with the required bounding boxes is described. In the first part of the investigations the training behavior of YOLOv3 on the natural UAVDT data set is analyzed and examined to what extent algorithms trained with natural images can be evaluated in the simulation. Finally, it is shown which performance can be achieved by exclusively synthetic training and how the performance can be improved by synthetic extension of the natural training set.

Keywords: YOLO · UAV · Aerial vehicle detection · UAVDT · Synthetic training data · CNN · Presagis · Virtual simulation · Reality gap

1 Introduction

Sensor payload systems are an important component of unmanned flight systems, since automated environmental perception and sensor data processing in real time is necessary to enable autonomous UAV missions. Computer-based data processing algorithms are therefore used to evaluate and process the sensor derived information. UAV based aerial imagery poses special challenges, as due to the different flight altitudes and flight situations the objects may differ in size, shape, orientation and background [1, 2]. In addition, various environmental and lighting conditions occur during detection, the vehicles are blurred by vibration and motion blur, and many fine, disturbing structures and objects are present in the images. Due to their high detection accuracy and the increasing generalization capability, deep convolutional neural networks (CNN) have recently been used more and more for vehicle detection on aerial images [2–10]. The subsequent

© Springer Nature Switzerland AG 2020
J. Mazal et al. (Eds.): MESAS 2019, LNCS 11995, pp. 50–70, 2020.
https://doi.org/10.1007/978-3-030-43890-6_5

performance of these methods is influenced to a large extent by the availability and quantity of suitable test and training data sets. In the field of airborne sensor technology, however, the generation of relevant data normally requires complex and cost-intensive flight missions, which are also limited by legal restrictions. In addition, only a fraction of the possible scenario variance and the environmental effects occurring during later use is captured. This might lead to detectors with low robustness against fluctuating environmental conditions.

A promising approach to avoid this problem is the use of virtual simulation environments to generate a database with synthetic sensor images. Natural images denote real-life sensor data, while computer-rendered data are referred to as synthetic images. These can cost-effectively and efficiently consider a multitude of atmospheric and sensory effects and thus represent a possibility to extend existing natural training data, increase their robustness or replace them completely. Furthermore, virtual environments offer the possibility to generate image information and highly accurate annotations as ground truth for supervised learning methods.

2   Object of Research

The basic question is to what extent and by which design features the synthetically generated image data can achieve functional realism. Functional realism refers to the accuracy of the simulation that provides all the visual information or features required for the respective algorithm [11]. Conversely, this leads to the same algorithm performance in both domains. This paper should investigate to what extent performance differences of trainable vehicle detectors occur for different combinations of synthetic and natural training and test data, visualized in Fig. 1. The UAVDT data set [1] serves as the basis for the natural image data, the synthetic image material is generated with the Presagis M&S Suite [12] and the YOLOv3 framework [13] is used for vehicle detection. Section 3 gives an overview of the state of the art in this field before Sect. 4 describes the structure of the synthetic data set generated for the investigations.

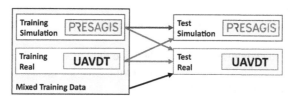

Fig. 1. Visualization of the different natural and synthetic training and test combinations considered in this paper.

The following research questions will be examined in this paper and the results are presented in Sect. 5:

(a)   What effects does learning rate and learning rate scheduling have on natural training and test data?

(b) Can existing real-world trained algorithms be applied to synthetic data and is it therefore possible to evaluate individual influences on detection performance in the simulation?
(c) What are the consequences of an exclusive training with synthetic data and is a transferability to natural test data possible?
(d) Can a hybrid approach with mixed training data increase detection performance and generalization capability?

3 State of the Art: Datasets, Simulation Testbed and Algorithms

The following is an overview of the state of the art in the field of vehicle detection on aerial photographs of UAVs. In the first part, publicly available and already annotated data sets are listed and compared. In the second part, the used virtual simulation environment is discussed, which serves as testbed for generating the synthetic dataset. Finally, different groups of detection algorithms will be considered together with application examples from the literature and it is explained why the YOLOv3 deep-learning framework is used for our further investigations with natural and synthetic data material.

3.1 Natural Datasets for UAV Vehicle Detection

As explained in the previous chapter, the training and evaluation of deep-learning based vehicle detectors for UAV aerial imagery poses new challenges to the underlying data sets [9]:

(a) Scale diversity: Due to the different flight altitudes of UAVs a wide range of object sizes must be covered, especially small objects with a small amount of information due to the low number of covered pixels.
(b) Perspective: While at high altitudes objects are usually viewed from a bird's eye view, at low altitudes, especially in combination with gimbals, much flatter viewing angles can occur.
(c) Multidirectional: In contrast to traffic monitoring, all object orientations can occur due to the flight movements of the UAV.
(d) High background complexity: Due to the wide field of view and the varying application scenarios, a large variety of backgrounds must be included, as these have a strong influence on object recognition.

Table 1 therefore provides a brief overview of the currently available and labelled data sets in the field of vehicle detection with UAVs. These are mostly designed for special applications and are often used as benchmarks to compare different algorithms.

Many data sets are designed for vehicle detection on satellite images and therefore show no variation of the viewing angle and the object size. UA-DETRAC includes these variations but is designed for traffic monitoring perspective. CARPK is suitable for vehicle counting on parking areas and DOTA is one of the few data sets containing oriented bounding boxes. CARPK, VisDrone2018-car and UAVDT are currently the

Table 1. Overview of UAV data sets and their properties. BB: Bounding Boxes, GSD: Ground Sample Distance (cm per pixel), VA: Variation of Viewing Angels, FL: Variation of Flight Altitudes/Object Size, Env: Variation of Environmental Conditions, ✔: yes, ✘: no, ◯: partially

	Year	Images	BB	Classes	GSD	VA	FA	Env	Resolution
VEDAI [14]	2015	1250	2950	9	12.5	✘	✘	✘	512, 1024
OIRDS [15]	2009	908	1800	4	15.2	◯	◯	✘	256–640
COWC [16]	2016	53	90963	5	15	✘	✘	✘	2K–19K
DOTA [17]	2018	2806	188282	15	div.	✘	✔	✘	~4000
DLR 3 K [18]	2015	20	5892	2	13	✘	✘	✘	5616 × 3744
Stanford Drone Dataset [19]	2016	929499	19000	6	?	✘	✘	✘	1400 × 1904
UA-DETRAC [20]	2018	140K	1.21M	4	div.	✔	✔	✔	960 × 540
CarPK [21]	2017	1448	89K	1	?	◯	◯	◯	1280 × 720
VisDrone [22]	2018	10209	54200	10	div.	✔	✔	✔	2000 × 1500
UAVDT [1]	2018	40K	800K	3	div.	✔	✔	✔	1024 × 540

most challenging large-scale drone-based datasets [8]. Due to the large number of images and the significant variations in flight altitude, viewing angle and environment (daylight, night, fog), we will use the UAVDT data set for the investigations presented here. Figure 2 shows two annotated example images from the dataset.

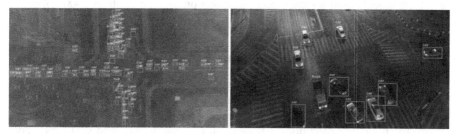

Fig. 2. Annotated sample images from the UAVDT data set [1] at different flight altitudes, environmental conditions and from different perspectives. The areas that were ignored during the annotation process are marked in red. (Color figure online)

3.2 Presagis M&S Suite for Training and Testing in Synthetic Environments

Virtual simulation environments are used to generate synthetic training data and to test algorithms trained with natural images under certain conditions in the simulation. The simulation toolbox should therefore fulfill several requirements:

(a) Physically based sensor simulation with realistic representation of different times of day and seasons
(b) Simulation and control of meteorological effects such as rain, fog, cloudiness and shadows
(c) Ability to overlay the rendered image with adjustable sensor effects, such as noise, image blur or color distortion
(d) Access to the setting parameters via a graphical user interface and via a programming interface (API)

For our investigations the Presagis M&S Suite [12] was used, because it fulfils the required framework conditions and offers a module-based tool chain with separate programs for modeling, terrain generation and visualization respectively sensor simulation. The atmospheric damping simulation is done with MOSART (MOderate Spectral Atmospheric Radiance and Transmittance) and radiation, convection and evaporation are considered.

For our experiments a test flight area on the campus of the Bundeswehr University Munich was modeled in Common Database (CDB) [23] format. Figures 3 and 5 shows some example images from this database. The modelling is based on a georeferenced aerial photograph of the terrain with a resolution of 20 cm per pixel (cpp), which is superimposed over an elevation layer. In order to avoid interferences caused by unlabeled vehicles, all vehicles that do not originate from the simulation were carefully retouched in advance. The CDB contains also additional layers for light points, surface features and materials. The material layer serves on the one hand for the infrared simulation, but also for the superposition of the aerial image serving as a basis with fine structures and textures for e.g. roads and grass areas. The last layer finally contains the modelled three-dimensional buildings and 3D tree models to reproduce the vegetation. The vehicle models used for the detection consist on average of about 3000 polygons and are dynamically placed at runtime.

3.3 Algorithms for UAV Vehicle Detection

At the top level, all detection algorithms can be divided into two groups. The first group does not require training data and is largely based on image processing methods like background or street segmentation and low-level features, such as colors, edges or geometric boundary conditions. Cheng et al. [24] use background subtraction and registration methods to detect dynamic vehicles and Azevedo et al. [25] use median-based background subtraction and Binary Large Object (BLOB) analysis of the foreground to identify candidates for vehicle positions. However, both methods are limited to the detection of moving objects. Zheng et al. [26] describe a combination of morphological operations to detect candidate vehicles from highway aerial images. Choi et al. [27] generated possible regions of interest (ROI) using a mean-shift clustering algorithm and subsequent fusion of geometric conditions, which are then verified with the log-polar shape descriptor. Hinz et al. [28] used a blob detector to detect vehicles on orthogonally recorded sensor data from a long-wave infrared camera. In [29] a Template Matching (TM) algorithm is presented in combination with a geometrically deformable model and previous extraction of the road network. However, most of these algorithms are limited to simple scenarios and are not robust to rotations or perspective distortions. The second group uses methods of supervised learning and therefore requires training data to learn the recognition and classification of relevant features. This group can be further split into shallow-learning based and deep-learning based methods based on CNNs.

Shallow-learning based methods use various high-level features, such as Haar-like feature, histogram of oriented gradients (HOG), local binary pattern (LBP) or scale-invariant feature transform (SIFT) and the corresponding descriptors for feature generation followed by a classifier like Support Vector Machine (SVM) or a cascade of classifiers (CC) to split into vehicle and non-vehicle categories. Xu et al. [30] presented a concept that bypasses the sensitivity to rotations by transforming the road segments into a certain normal direction and then performs a hybrid detection with Viola-Jones or linear SVM with HOG features. Moranduzzo et al. [31] for example used SIFT in combination with an SVM to classify the detected points of interest. Later they present an approach [32], which starts with selecting the asphalt areas, then computes two sets of HOG features for vertical and horizontal direction and finally yield a detection after the computation of a similarity measure, using a catalog of vehicles as a reference.

Deep learning based methods generate meaningful features in the first part of the network using convolutional layers, which are then classified in the rear part of the network. Within this group, a distinction is made between 2-stage detectors, such as Faster R-CNN or R-FCN, and 1-stage detectors, such as YOLO or SSD. While the first group generates possible ROIs with a specific region proposal network (RPN) and classifies them in the second stage, the second group combines these steps and thus achieves lower detection times. The disadvantage of these deep networks is on the one hand the increased training duration and on the other hand the large amount of annotated data required. In [33] the authors demonstrated the applicability of Fast R-CNN and Faster R-CNN for vehicle detection in aerial images from the DLR 3K and VEDAI datasets and tuned the performance for small object detection by adapting the anchor boxes of the RPN. Xu et al. [4] showed that Faster R-CNN is robust to illumination changes, in-plane rotation and also insensitive to the detection load, which shows the great potential for e.g. parking lot car detection. While in [6, 9, 10] it is shown that the different versions of YOLO are generally very well suited for vehicle detection on UAV aerial photographs, Benjdira et al. [7] showed that YOLOv3 outperforms Faster R-CNN in sensitivity and processing time, although they are comparable in precision metric. With an input image resolution of 608×608 pixels, YOLOv3 achieves a processing time of 51 ms (equivalent to almost 20 Hz) [13] and thus fulfils the real-time requirements of UAV systems. Another advantage is that the framework does not require any separately determined proposals and can therefore be trained end-to-end. The main reason why the YOLO framework was used for the investigations with synthetic training data presented here is the proven high generalization capability between different domains and image types. In [34] and [35] YOLO's design is shown to be more robust than other CNNs in abstracting between different domains such as photos, paintings and art styles.

Functionality and Special Features of YOLOv3. YOLOv3 is a 1-stage fully convolutional neural network belonging to a specific kind of object detectors called *single shot detectors*, which try posing object detection as a regression problem [13, 34, 36, 37]. In the first step, the input image is divided into a grid with $N \times N$ cells. For each cell that contains the center of one of the ground truths bounding boxes the network predicts a regression on the bounding box position and dimension namely relative to the grid position and the anchor size. Anchor boxes correspond to a kind of template bounding boxes. YOLOv3 uses a total of nine anchor boxes, which are calculated by k-means clustering from the used data set. Darknet-53 network with 53 layers pretrained on the ImageNet dataset is used for feature extraction. The prediction of only one type of class per grid cell leads to poorer detection of small and densely distributed objects. To avoid this disadvantage, Darknet-53 extracts the features from feature maps with three different scaling levels and assigns the three corresponding anchor boxes to each level. Non-Maximum Suppression (NMS) applied at the end of the network causes the reduction of highly overlapping bounding boxes so that only the bounding box with the highest object confidence remains.

4   Generation and Analysis of the Synthetic Data Set

Training and evaluation of algorithms in synthetic environments seems to become more and more popular. In the following, we will therefore describe the procedure for the automated generation of ground truth. Subsequently, the structure of the synthetic training data set will be analyzed.

4.1   Bounding Box and Ground Truth Generation for Synthetic Environments

Since the accuracy of the annotations has a large influence on the performance of the algorithms and the comparability in the evaluation [38], highly accurate and reproducible bounding boxes are required. Since these are not provided by all virtual simulation environments, this paper describes a general method to extend simulation environments with this functionality.

Fig. 3. Visualization of the calculated 3D hull of the object and the resulting bounding box after transformation into image coordinates

Johnson-Roberson et al. [39] have presented a method that reads the communication of the game engine with the graphics hardware and generates bounding boxes from it. Using the stencil buffer content, a semantic differentiation of the object classes is performed, before a differentiation of the individual objects takes place with the help of the depth buffer. Similar to [40], our method uses data directly from the simulation environment, but is also suitable for programs that only provide the object center point and the object size and do not support occlusion culling.

After the culling and rendering process, a list of objects that were in the last time step in the Field of View (FOV) of the camera is read out. This list contains the center positions of the objects in world coordinates and the corresponding object dimensions. Since the simulation does not support occlusion culling, a virtual laser beam is aligned to the object center. By reading out the intersection points with objects, possible obstacles leading to occlusions can be detected and the distance to the object can be determined. The object center point in world coordinates and the object dimensions are then read out for each visible vehicle using the programming interface. From this, the corner points of the three-dimensional box enveloping the vehicle can be determined. Since this is relative to the orientation of the world coordinate system, the 3D box must then be rotated according to the object orientation. With the help of the camera matrix, which must be recalculated in each simulation step, the three-dimensional corner points of the box can be converted from the world coordinate system into two-dimensional screen coordinates. A minimal enclosing rectangle from the resulting 8 points forms an accurate and reproducible bounding box. The center, width and height of the box are stored for each frame as ground truth in the annotation file. For the analysis of individual influencing factors, this file contains additional information about the vehicle object, such as color, orientation, background material and distance. In addition, general information about the simulation, such as flight altitude or viewing angle, the environment, such as time of day and visibility, and the render settings, such as shadow quality, resolution and noise level, are stored.

This method enables us to generate completely annotated image data with variable parameters in one step.

4.2 Image Generation Scheme, Parameter Distribution and Explorative Data Analysis

According to the recommendations in Sect. 3.1 for the generation of UAV based data sets for vehicle detection, the procedure with which we have created our synthetic training and test data sets is described in Fig. 4.

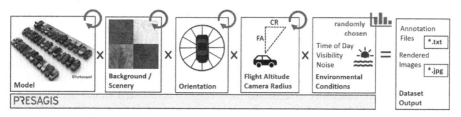

Fig. 4. Scheme for generating a training data set in simulation with predefined or random variation of individual parameters

In order to cover as many later object states as possible during training, the vehicle model, the scenery, the object orientation, the flight altitude and the camera radius are individually changed in predefined values in nested loops. To increase variation, each image from this set additionally contains different and randomly selected values for the parameters time of day, visibility and noise, equally distributed between certain limits (see Fig. 6). Figure 5 gives an overview of the effects of the individual simulation parameters. In both the training and test sets, it is iterated over a set of 38 available 3D car models (extended to 80 models by re-coloring), with one additional run without a vehicle model to ensure that a certain proportion of the images in the data set do not contain a vehicle.

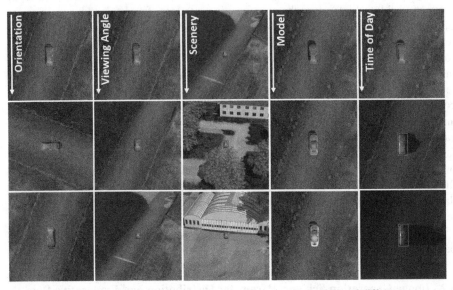

Fig. 5. Extract from the synthetic training data set. The separated effects of different parameter settings are visible in the individual columns.

The training set comprises 6 different sceneries, which were chosen so that both the background (light and dark grass and asphalt with and without road markings) and the surroundings (country road, large car park, industrial area) vary. Figure 6 visualizes the distribution of the used parameters. The object orientation was changed in 30-degree steps. Four flight altitudes of 15, 30, 50 and 90 m were selected. In order to get additional different viewing angles, the camera radius differs between 0, 20, 40 and 80 m. This generates a total of 93312 images. The time of day in each image is chosen randomly between 6 pm and 6 am, based on the position of the sun on September 1. The fog intensity or visibility is also randomly determined from equally distributed values between 300 and 30000 m. In addition, white noise, which however only influences the brightness value, is additive superimposed with weightings between 0 and 0.15. Although the values for the viewing angle and object distance attributes are not uniformly distributed due to this type of data generation and our choice of the discrete values for the other parameters, they still reasonably cover the relevant range (see Fig. 6).

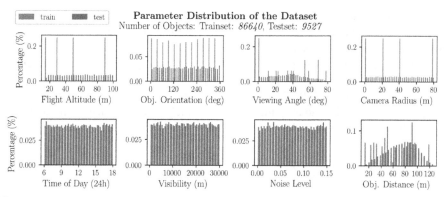

Fig. 6. Analysis of the distribution of different simulation and object parameters in the synthetic training and test data set. The training set contains 86640 bounding boxes for 93312 images, the test set 9527 bounding boxes for 9719 images.

The test data set contains four different scenarios at different positions than the training data set to avoid identical screen pairs in both sets. A further difference is that object orientation, flight altitude and camera radius do not have certain discrete values as before but are selected randomly within certain limits in order to examine the generalization capability for other object views. The resulting values for the viewing angle are distributed relatively homogeneously over the relevant area and decrease slightly for values above 40 degrees. The distance to the test object shows a clear accumulation of values at 80 m. At altitudes of up to 100 m, both characteristics correspond to the usual distribution of values in natural aerial images. The test data set contains a total of 9719 images.

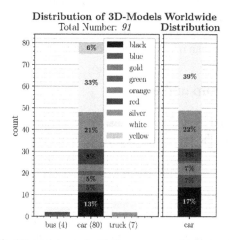

Fig. 7. Distribution of the 3D models used with the corresponding color distribution. On the right side the worldwide distribution of the vehicle colors is shown for comparison.

For the first investigations, in training and test set there is a maximum of one vehicle per image, but its position within the image is random. The rendered images have a resolution of *1024 × 540* pixels.

In order to ensure general applicability of the synthetically trained detector, the color distribution of the set of 38 3D models has been adjusted to the worldwide distribution of car colors [41] (see Fig. 7). This resulted in a total number of 80 car models. Since too few models were available for the "bus" and "truck" classes to make representative statements, we will only consider the "car" vehicle class in the following investigations.

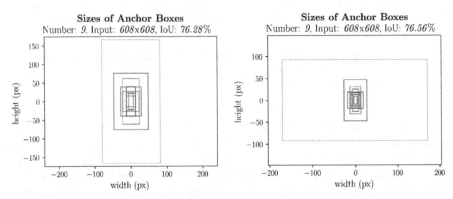

Fig. 8. Graphical visualization and corresponding IoU of the nine Anchor Boxes calculated with the k-means clustering algorithm. *Left*: Our synthetic training data set, *Right*: UAVDT data set

Figure 8 visualizes the nine calculated anchor boxes for the UAVDT and our synthetic dataset for an input resolution of *608 × 608*. In both cases the templates achieve a very good coverage of the actual bounding boxes with an Intersection over Union (IoU, see Sect. 5.1) of approx. 78%. Except for the largest box, both plots show a similar distribution in aspect ratios but differ in size, suggesting that vehicles in the UAVDT dataset tend to be smaller than in our synthetic dataset.

5   Experimental Setup and Results

In the following the metrics and training parameters used are briefly described and afterwards the results of the training of YOLOv3 with the UAVDT and the synthetic data set are presented.

5.1 Metrics for Evaluation

For the evaluation of the detection task, we use the definition of the Average Precision (AP) metric, which has also been used for the Pascal VOC Challenge since 2010 [38, 42]. AP corresponds to the area under the interpolated precision-recall (PR) curve for a specific Intersection over Union (IoU) threshold. IoU is a measure for the localization accuracy and describes the overlap ratio between a predicted bounding box BB_p and a ground truth bounding box BB_{gt}, above which a detection is regarded as True Positive (TP).

$$IoU = \frac{\text{area}(BB_p \cap BB_{gt})}{\text{area}(BB_p \cup BB_{gt})} \tag{1}$$

Precision measures the detector's ability to detect only relevant objects and describes the proportion of correct detections to all detections.

$$\text{Precision } p = \frac{\text{TP}}{\text{TP} + \text{FP}}, \qquad \text{FP: False Positive} \tag{2}$$

Recall measures the detector's ability to detect all ground truth objects and describes the proportion of correct detections to all ground truth bounding boxes that occur.

$$\text{Recall } r = \frac{\text{TP}}{\text{TP} + \text{FN}}, \qquad \text{FN: False Negative} \tag{3}$$

The PR-curve visualizes the relationship between Precision and Recall for different reliability levels and therefore provides a good overview of the general performance of the detector. AP reduces the interpolated PR-curve $p_{interp}(r)$ to a single value and is therefore well suited for comparing multiple detectors or monitoring learning progress.

$$AP = \int_0^1 p_{interp}(r)dr, \qquad p_{interp}(r) = \max_{\tilde{r} \geq r} p(\tilde{r})$$

5.2 Training

The YOLOv3 weights pre-trained on the ImageNet are used as a starting point for fine tuning on the data sets we are looking at. Fine Tuning is a kind of transfer learning where the robust feature extraction filters learned on large general data sets are transferred to the user's own detection tasks. This increases generalizability when training with smaller, more specific own data sets and at the same time reduces the training duration. Each training process starts with a warm-up phase of 1000 iterations, in which the pre-trained weights of the convolution layers in the front part of the network are transferred to the rear part, which is responsible for the classification of the new objects. The influence of different initial learning rates and different methods of learning rate scheduling was investigated. The other training parameters were largely taken from the YOLOv3 con-figuration file for the Pascal VOC data set. A batch size of 64 with a subdivision of 16 was used. The input image size was 608 × 608. The momentum was set to 0.9 and the decay to 0.0005. We used the internal data augmentation methods with variation values of 1.5 for saturation and exposure and 0.1 for hue. For each training set the appropriate anchor boxes were calculated and replaced in the configuration file. Detections with a reliability value below 0.005 were not considered for evaluation. Although this cuts off the PR curve to a certain degree at high recall values, therefore reduces the AP to a certain degree and must be considered when comparing different AP values, it is neces-sary to keep the calculation time of the evaluation within a manageable range. For the Non-Maximum Suppression the standard IoU threshold of 0.45 was used.

5.3 Natural Training Data and Influence of the Learning Rate

The first step was to investigate the performance of YOLOv3 for different learning rate curves in the natural image material of the UAVDT data set. Figure 9 visualizes the training behavior for the Pascal VOC configurations file. The learning rate after the warm-up phase is 0.001, before it is finally reduced step by step to one tenth after 40000 and 45000 iterations. This corresponds to a slow training with a low initial learning rate over 125 epochs. The AP value of the test set varies between 0.56 and 0.64, but shows no typical decrease at higher iterations, which would indicate overfitting.

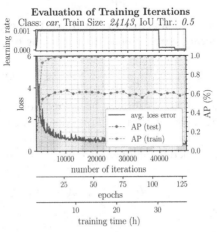

Fig. 9. Evaluation of training behavior over 50000 iterations using the natural UAVDT training set and the standard Pascal VOC configuration file for an IoU threshold of 0.5

Due to the relatively fast convergence of the detection power and the loss error, the behavior at a higher initial learning rate lr_{init} and an exponential learning rate scheduling was subsequently considered. In this case, the current learning rate lr_{act} is calculated for each iteration step according to the following formula:

$$lr_{act} = lr_{init} \cdot \gamma^x, \qquad x: \text{current iteration step}, \gamma: \text{base} \qquad (4)$$

Figure 10 shows the behavior for an initial learning rate of 0.004 and exponential decreases of varying magnitude. Despite a significantly lower number of iterations, the same performance was achieved in training and test set. Probably due to the four times higher initial learning rate, a slight decrease of the AP on the test set and thus beginning overfitting can be detected with increasing training duration. The AP of the test set shows significantly fewer fluctuations due to the exponential learning rate scheduling, which significantly improves the selection of the appropriate training duration. For this reason and because no influence could be determined for the different values for γ, a training with $\gamma = 0.9993$ is carried out for the following examinations.

As a result it can be stated that with this setup ($lr_{init} = 0.004$ and $\gamma = 0.9993$) a comparatively fast and at the same time stable learning process can be achieved for the natural data set considered here.

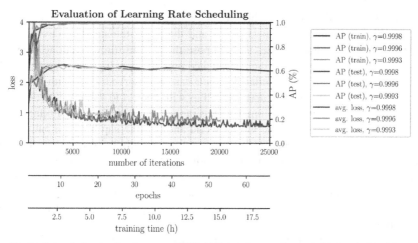

Fig. 10. Training behavior for the natural UAVDT training set for an IoU threshold of 0.5 when using an exponential learning rate scheduling with an initial learning rate of 0.004 and different values for the base γ

5.4 Performance on Synthetic Test Data for Natural Training

In this section the evaluation of detectors trained with natural images and existing algorithms on synthetic test material is considered. This enables the precise and reproducible analysis of individual influencing factors and testing under certain environmental conditions that are difficult to achieve in reality.

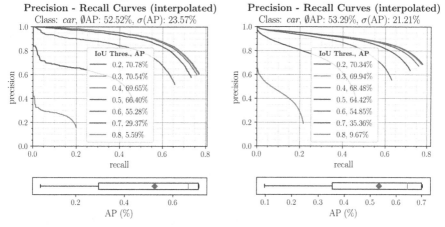

Fig. 11. PR curves for different IoU thresholds with average and standard deviation of AP and corresponding box plot diagram for training with natural UAVDT training set (4500 iterations, γ = 0.9993). Detection power on our synthetic test set (Left) and on the UAVDT (Right)

Figure 11 shows the detection performance on synthetic (*Left*) and natural (*Right*) test data when training with natural UAVDT training data set. The spreading of the curves and the AP at different IoU thresholds is a measure for the localization accuracy of the detector. The higher the mean value and the lower the standard deviation the better the detected bounding boxes superimpose the ground truth. Accurate detectors are characterized by the fact that the AP reached only drops at high IoU thresholds. In simulation and reality, a very similar behavior can be observed, both with respect to the change and the shape of the curve as well as with respect to the absolute detection performance. This suggests that similar effects in the natural world have similar effects on recognition performance in the virtual world and that the gap between natural and virtual in this direction is small. This result corresponds with the research results from the field of ground-based deep learning algorithms. Carrillo et al. [43] proved that a hyper parameter optimization of algorithms trained with natural images is possible in the virtual world with regard to learning rate and training duration. Also Gaidon et al. [40] showed that algorithms pretrained on natural data behave similar in natural and virtual worlds.

Overall, this indicates that an evaluation of detectors trained with natural images on virtual data is justified and a transferability from reality to simulation is possible. To what extent this is true for individual effects must be further investigated with corresponding image pairs.

5.5 Training with the Virtual Training Data Set

In the following, the performance during training with the synthetic data set described in Sect. 4.2 is examined.

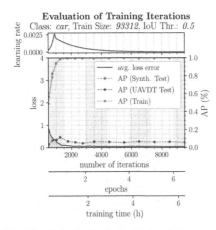
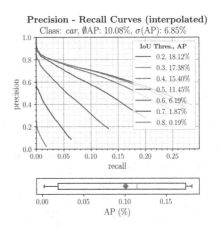

Fig. 12. *Left*: Evaluation of the training process for training with synthetic data and AP values of the evaluation on the synthetic test set and the UAVDT test set including the domains day and fog (without night) ($lr_{init} = 0.004$, $\gamma = 0.9993$). $lr_{init} = 0.001$ was also examined but showed no significant differences. *Right*: Detection performance of the synthetically trained YOLOv3 on the natural UAVDT test set (without images of the domain night) after 1250 training iterations. (Color figure online)

Figure 12 (*Left*) shows that the average loss error decreases very quickly to values around 0.08, in contrast to values around 0.8 using natural training data. This suggests that only a small model with few features has been learned, which is very well adapted to the given domain, but has learned too few general features to have a good generalization capability. The green curve shows that the model achieves a very good detection quality with AP values above 98% on the simulated test data. This shows that despite the discrete object views during training described in Sect. 4.2, it is possible to generalize to all different views in the test phase. From this it can be concluded that also with natural training data the distance between the occurring object views should not be larger than in the synthetic training set presented by us. The reasons for the high performance on synthetic data are on the one hand the reduced interference effects and the lower complexity of the data, with at the same time more pronounced features and on the other hand the use of the same 3D models for training and testing due to the limited number of models.

Figure 12 (*Left*) also shows the performance of the detector trained in the simulation on the natural UAVDT test data. In order to obtain representative results, only the test data of the day and fog categories were used, since the car headlights visible in the night category have not yet been simulated in the vehicle models used. First, it should be noted that the performance in this configuration is significantly lower, indicating that the gap from simulation to reality is significantly greater than in the other direction. This means that in the training setup used not all features necessary for detection in reality were available or learned, but the other way around they were. A clear overfitting to the synthetic data can already be seen starting at approx. 1500 iterations. Figure 12 (*Right*) shows the corresponding PR curves and the AP values. The large spread of the curves compared to the natural training indicates a reduced localization accuracy. At an IoU threshold of 0.3, which according to [44] is visually indistinguishable from a threshold of 0.5 for a human observer, an AP of 17.4% was achieved. This value can certainly be seen as a starting point for further investigations, as e.g. the Faster-RCNN detector trained with the natural UAVDT training set also only reaches an AP of 22.3%, but for a higher IoU threshold and probably on average for all vehicle classes (bus, car, truck) [1].

Table 2. Comparison between the UAVDT dataset and the synthetically generated dataset with respect to the occurring object numbers and image properties

	Training		Test		Ø Objects per image	Number of vehicle models
	Images	BB	Images	BB		
UAVDT	24143	394633	16592	361055	16.3	2700
Synth. dataset	93312	86640	9720	9527	0.93	38 (80 after recoloring)

Transferability in general can depend on many factors, such as the simulation environment used, the modeling quality, the data set compilation or the algorithm itself. Table 2 shows some relevant differences in our case that can contribute to the virtual reality gap. On the one hand, the natural training set has a significantly larger number of

BBs both overall and especially per image. Secondly, the number and variance of the different vehicle instances with 2700 in the UAVDT data set is significantly higher than with 80 3D car models used in the simulation. In addition, as shown in Sect. 4.2, the objects of the UAVDT data set are on average smaller than in the simulated data set, which can also worsen the detection performance by using the wrong initial anchor boxes during detection. Since the UAVDT data set consists mainly of images of urban main roads, the bounding boxes often contain road markings that are insufficiently reproduced in the simulation. Another reason may be that effects such as motion blur or camera distortion have not been considered when creating the synthetic data set. Further investigations must show which of these effects have an influence on the reality gap. Also in [40] and [43] the detection quality was lower with only training with synthetic data than with training with natural data, whereas in [40] the best results were achieved with virtual pretraining and natural fine tuning.

Overall, it was shown that in the simulation it is possible to generalize to all occurring object views despite discrete viewing angles during the training. Pure synthetic training with the setup used here is not yet sufficient to achieve results on independent natural data that are comparably good than with natural training data.

5.6   Training with Mixed Data Set

In this section, the performance for a mixed training set of natural and simulated data is considered. All natural training data of the UAVDT data set are used and extended with a certain amount of synthetic data.

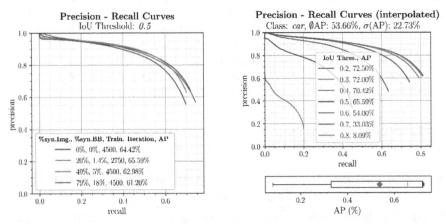

Fig. 13. *Left:* Comparison of the PR curves for different proportions of synthetic image material in the training data set. The UAVDT training set was included completely. Additionally, the proportion of synthetic bounding boxes, the training iteration and the AP are given. *Right:* Behavior of the training data set with 20% synthetic data (=green line on the left plot) for different IoU thresholds for comparison with Fig. 11 (Color figure online)

Figure 13 (*Left*) shows the resulting PR curves for synthetic proportions of 0%, 20%, 49% and 79% of the total training data set. By extending the training set with synthetic data, the achieved AP could be increased by almost 1.2% points at a IoU Threshold of 0.5 and a synthetic proportion of 20%. This improvement is mainly attributable to the higher recall values achieved and thus to a slight increase in generalization capability. This means that more vehicles tend to be recognized as such, while the precision remains unchanged compared to natural training over the entire curve. For too high proportions of simulated data, however, a deterioration in performance can also be observed, which is probably due to the overfitting to the synthetic data described in Sect. 5.5. Figure 13 shows for comparison with Fig. 11 the PR curves for different IoU thresholds for a synthetic proportion of 20%. It turns out that the lower the IoU threshold, the higher the improvement. At a threshold of 0.2, the AP improvement is almost 2.2% points. Also, in Sect. 5.5 and Fig. 13 (*Right*) a strong decrease of detection performance was observed when using synthetic training and natural test data for higher IoU thresholds. This indicates that the bounding box regression learned from the ideal synthetic annotations yields worse results with natural manually generated ground truth, since the inaccuracies are not mapped during training and the detector is trying to predict the ideal bounding box. This must be taken into account in the evaluation and speaks for the use of lower IoU thresholds in these cases [38].

Therefore, a hybrid approach with mixed training data can significantly improve the generalization ability and thus the detection performance if the IoU threshold is chosen appropriately and if the percentage does not exceed a certain percentage.

6 Conclusion and Future Work

In this paper we investigated the training behavior of deep neural networks for vehicle detection on aerial imagery in synthetic simulation environments and on natural data sets. An overview of the available natural and annotated data sets in this area is given and the UAVDT dataset was selected for the investigations because it contains a large number of images with significant variations. Due to its high generalization capability between different domains, the YOLOv3 algorithm is used for the detection task. Furthermore, we presented a general method to create ideal bounding boxes as ground truth annotations within virtual simulation environments. A scheme is described to generate a virtual training data set with a variety of viewing angles and random variations in time of day, fog density and noise. The training of the YOLOv3 framework on the natural UAVDT data set led to an AP of 64.4% for the class "car" when using the corresponding test set. Different learning rate scheduling methods were investigated and it was shown that with an exponential decrease of the learning rate a stable training behavior can be achieved with a simultaneously low training duration. The algorithm trained with natural images showed a similar behavior on the synthetic test set, which suggests that synthetic environments are well suited for the evaluation of existing algorithms. It has been shown that synthetic training with discrete values for object orientation and viewing angle allows the detector to generalize to all object views in the subsequent synthetic test set. The used gradations can be helpful when generating natural data sets. Exclusively synthetic training and testing on the natural UAVDT test set leads to a lower detection performance than natural training due to several possible factors. However, extending the natural training set with 20%.synthetic images can improve AP by more than two percentage points. It also turned out that using manually annotated ground truth, the IoU threshold can be set lower in order to avoid disturbing effects of inaccurate annotations on the evaluation.

In future work, the possible influencing factors that limit the transferability of synthetically trained algorithms to natural test data will be investigated. The main focus is on increasing the number of sceneries and vehicles in the synthetic training set and a higher variation of vehicle types by using more 3D models.

References

1. Du, D., et al.: The unmanned aerial vehicle benchmark: object detection and tracking. In: Ferrari, V., Hebert, M., Sminchisescu, C., Weiss, Y. (eds.) ECCV 2018. LNCS, vol. 11214, pp. 375–391. Springer, Cham (2018). https://doi.org/10.1007/978-3-030-01249-6_23
2. Li, Q., Mou, L., Xu, Q., Zhang, Y., Zhu, X.X.: R^3-Net: a deep network for multi-oriented vehicle detection in aerial images and videos. IEEE Geosci. Remote Sens. Soc., 1–14 (2019)
3. Radovic, M., Adarkwa, O., Wang, Q.: Object recognition in aerial images using convolutional neural networks. J. Imaging 3(2), 21 (2017)
4. Xu, Y., Yu, G., Wang, Y., Wu, X., Ma, Y.: Car detection from low-altitude UAV imagery with the faster R-CNN. J. Adv. Transp. **2017**, 1–10 (2017)
5. Tayara, H., Soo, K.G., Chong, K.T.: Vehicle detection and counting in high-resolution aerial images using convolutional regression neural network. IEEE Access **6**, 2220–2230 (2017)
6. Tang, T., Deng, Z., Zhou, S., Lei, L., Zou, H.: Fast vehicle detection in UAV images. In: RSIP 2017 - International Workshop on Remote Sensing with Intelligent Processing, Proceedings, pp. 1–5 (2017)
7. Benjdira, B., Khursheed, T., Koubaa, A., Ammar, A., Ouni, K.: Car detection using unmanned aerial vehicles: comparison between faster R-CNN and YOLOv3. In: 1st International Conference on Unmanned Vehicle Systems-Oman, UVS 2019, pp. 1–6 (2019)
8. Li, W., Li, H., Wu, Q., Chen, X., Ngan, K.N.: Simultaneously detecting and counting dense vehicles from drone images. IEEE Trans. Ind. Electron. **66**(12), 9651–9662 (2019)
9. Lu, J., et al.: A vehicle detection method for aerial image based on YOLO. J. Comput. Commun. **06**, 98–107 (2018)
10. Lechgar, H., Bekkar, H., Rhinane, H.: Detection of cities vehicle fleet using YOLO V2 and aerial images. Int. Arch. Photogramm. Remote Sens. Spat. Inf. Sci. ISPRS Arch. **42**, 121–126 (2019)
11. Ferwerda, J.A.: Three varieties of realism in computer graphics. In: Rogowitz, B.E., Pappas, T.N. (eds.) Proceedings SPIE Human Vision and Electronic (2003)
12. Presagis - COTS Modelling and Simulation Software. https://www.presagis.com/en/. https://www.presagis.com/en/page/academic-programs/
13. Redmon, J., Farhadi, A.: YOLOv3: An Incremental Improvement (2018)
14. Razakarivony, S., Jurie, F.: Vehicle detection in aerial imagery: a small target detection benchmark. J. Vis. Commun. Image Represent. **34**, 187–203 (2015)
15. Tanner, F., et al.: Overhead imagery research data set - an annotated data library & tools to aid in the development of computer vision algorithms. In: Proceedings - Applied Imagery Pattern Recognition Workshop, pp. 1–8 (2009). https://doi.org/10.1109/AIPR.2009.5466304
16. Mundhenk, T.N., Konjevod, G., Sakla, W.A., Boakye, K.: A large contextual dataset for classification, detection and counting of cars with deep learning. In: Leibe, B., Matas, J., Sebe, N., Welling, M. (eds.) ECCV 2016. LNCS, vol. 9907, pp. 785–800. Springer, Cham (2016). https://doi.org/10.1007/978-3-319-46487-9_48 .

17. Xia, G.S., et al.: DOTA: a large-scale dataset for object detection in aerial images. In: Proceedings of the IEEE Conference on Computer Vision and Pattern Recognition, pp. 3974–3983 (2018)
18. Liu, K., Mattyus, G.: Fast multiclass vehicle detection on aerial images. IEEE Geosci. Remote Sens. Lett. **12**, 1938–1942 (2015)
19. Robicquet, A., Sadeghian, A., Alahi, A., Savarese, S.: Learning social etiquette: human trajectory understanding in crowded scenes. In: Leibe, B., Matas, J., Sebe, N., Welling, M. (eds.) ECCV 2016. LNCS, vol. 9912, pp. 549–565. Springer, Cham (2016). https://doi.org/10.1007/978-3-319-46484-8_33
20. Lyu, S., et al.: UA-DETRAC 2018: report of AVSS2018 IWT4S challenge on advanced traffic monitoring. In: Proceedings of the AVSS 2018 - 2018 15th IEEE International Conference on Advanced Video and Signal Based Surveillance (2019)
21. Hsieh, M.R., Lin, Y.L., Hsu, W.H.: Drone-based object counting by spatially regularized regional proposal network. In: Proceedings of the IEEE International Conference on Computer Vision, pp. 4165–4173 (2017)
22. Zhu, P., Wen, L., Du, D., Bian, X., Ling, H.: VisDrone-VDT2018: the vision meets drone video detection and tracking challenge results, vol. 11206, pp. 1–23 (2018)
23. OGC (OpenGeoSpatial): Common Database Standard. https://www.opengeospatial.org/standards/cdb
24. Cheng, P., Zhou, G., Zheng, Z.: Detecting and counting vehicles from small low-cost UAV images. In: American Society for Photogrammetry and Remote Sensing Annual Conference 2009, ASPRS 2009, vol. 1, pp. 138–144 (2009)
25. Azevedo, C.L., Cardoso, J.L., Ben-Akiva, M., Costeira, J.P., Marques, M.: Automatic vehicle trajectory extraction by aerial remote sensing. Procedia Soc. Behav. Sci. **111**, 849–858 (2014)
26. Zheng, Z., Wang, X., Zhou, G., Jiang, L.: Vehicle detection based on morphology from highway aerial images. In: International Geoscience and Remote Sensing Symposium, pp. 5997–6000 (2012)
27. Choi, J., Yang, Y.: Vehicle detection from aerial images using local shape information. Adv. Image Video Technol. **5414**, 227–236 (2009)
28. Hinz, S., Stilla, U.: Car detection in aerial thermal images by local and global evidence accumulation. Pattern Recognit. Lett. **27**, 308–315 (2006)
29. Niu, X.: A semi-automatic framework for highway extraction and vehicle detection based on a geometric deformable model. ISPRS J. Photogramm. Remote Sens. **61**, 170–186 (2006)
30. Xu, Y., Yu, G., Wang, Y., Wu, X., Ma, Y.: A hybrid vehicle detection method based on Viola-Jones and HOG + SVM from UAV images. Sensors (Switzerland) **16**, 1325 (2016)
31. Moranduzzo, T., Melgani, F.: Automatic car counting method for unmanned aerial vehicle images. IEEE Trans. Geosci. Remote Sens. **52**, 1635–1647 (2014)
32. Moranduzzo, T., Melgani, F.: Detecting cars in UAV images with a catalog-based approach. IEEE Trans. Geosci. Remote Sens. **52**, 6356–6367 (2014)
33. Sommer, L.W., Schuchert, T., Beyerer, J.: Fast deep vehicle detection in aerial images. In: Proceedings of the 2017 IEEE Winter Conference on Applications of Computer Vision, WACV 2017, pp. 311–319 (2017)
34. Redmon, J., Divvala, S., Girshick, R., Farhadi, A.: You Only Look Once: Unified, Real-Time Object Detection (2015)
35. Westlake, N., Cai, H., Hall, P.: Detecting people in artwork with CNNs. In: Hua, G., Jégou, H. (eds.) ECCV 2016. LNCS, vol. 9913, pp. 825–841. Springer, Cham (2016). https://doi.org/10.1007/978-3-319-46604-0_57
36. Zafar, I., Tzanidou, G., Burton, R., Patel, N., Araujo, L.: Hands-On Convolutional Neural Networks with TensorFlow: Solve Computer Vision Problems with Modeling in TensorFlow and Python. Packt Publishing, Birmingham (2018)

37. Redmon, J., Farhadi, A.: YOLO9000: better, faster, stronger. In: CVPR 2017, pp. 7263–7271 (2016)
38. Everingham, M., Van Gool, L., Williams, C.K.I., Winn, J., Zisserman, A.: The pascal visual object classes (VOC) challenge. Int. J. Comput. Vis. **88**, 303–338 (2010)
39. Johnson-Roberson, M., Barto, C., Mehta, R., Sridhar, S.N., Vasudevan, R.: Driving in the matrix: can virtual worlds replace human-generated annotations for real world tasks? In: IEEE International Conference on Robotics and Automation (ICRA), pp. 746–753 (2017)
40. Gaidon, A., Wang, Q., Cabon, Y., Vig, E.: Virtual worlds as proxy for multi-object tracking analysis. In: Proceedings of the IEEE Computer Society Conference on Computer Vision and Pattern Recognition, pp. 4340–4349 (2016)
41. PPG Industries, Inc.: 2018 Global Color Trend Popularity. https://news.ppg.com/automotive-color-trends. Accessed 01 Aug 2019
42. Salton, G., McGill, M.: Introduction to Modern Information Retrieval. McGraw-Hill, Inc., New York (1986)
43. Carrillo, J., Davis, J., Osorio, J., Goodin, C., Durst, J.: High-fidelity physics-based modeling and simulation for training and testing convolutional neural networks for UGV systems (in review). In: Modelling and Simulation for Autonomous Systems, MESAS 2019 (2019)
44. Russakovsky, O., Li, L.-J., Fei-Fei, L.: Best of both worlds: human-machine collaboration for object annotation. In: 2015 IEEE Conference on Computer Vision and Pattern Recognition (CVPR), pp. 2121–2131. IEEE (2015)

Building a Generic Simulation Model for Analyzing the Feasibility of Multi-Robot Task Allocation (MRTA) Problems

Savaş Öztürk[1]([✉]) [ID] and Ahmet Emin Kuzucuoğlu[2] [ID]

[1] Software Testing and Quality Evaluation Laboratory, TUBITAK BILGEM, Gebze, Turkey
savas.ozturk@tubitak.gov.tr
[2] Electrical and Electronics Engineering Department, Marmara University, İstanbul, Turkey
kuzucuoglu@marmara.edu.tr

Abstract. Multi-Robot Task Allocation (MRTA) will gain much importance by the rise of autonomous vehicles and the Internet of Things (IoT) where several agents coordinate and work for a common goal. Due to their distributed nature, hardware complexity and environmental constraints, constructing and testing multi-robot systems may be expensive, dangerous and time-consuming. MRTA includes sub-problems such as coordination strategy, bid valuation, path planning, terrain complexity, robot design, path optimization, and overall optimization. There is a need for building a generic MRTA model to experiment with these numerous combinations in a controlled and automated fashion. This paper presents the structure of the MRTA generic simulation model which is designed to search for the optimal combination of MRTA taxonomy elements. An MRTA Simulation Tool (MRTASim) is designed to adapt the generic model to specific cases and to run simulations for real-life scenarios. Decision-makers can build their own MRTA models and they can be sure for the feasibility of large distributed and collaborated systems before initiating huge investments.

Keywords: Multi-Robot Task Allocation · MRTA simulation · Path planning · Multi-agents · Java Agent DEvelopment Framework (JADE)

1 Introduction

Rise of autonomous vehicles and the Internet of Things (IoT) has raised importance on collective and coordinative task execution [1–7]. Multi-Robot Task Allocation (MRTA) focuses on effectively assigning tasks to robots, i.e. m task to n robots. Assignments could be made by a centralized, intelligent decision-maker but in the case of failure of that entity, all the calculations could be sent to the wastebasket. Furthermore, calculation durations may be extended as the number of robots and/or tasks are higher. MRTA applications aim robustness, performance, and economy. MRTA solutions can be used at every problem that deals with distributed decision-making.

Building, deploying and testing a multi-robot system for a specific case can be costly, dangerous and time-consuming. Simulating the desired system enables executing

© Springer Nature Switzerland AG 2020
J. Mazal et al. (Eds.): MESAS 2019, LNCS 11995, pp. 71–87, 2020.
https://doi.org/10.1007/978-3-030-43890-6_6

numerous trials and tests without spending time and money, even it's extremely safe. There exist some software systems for easily building simulation models. Most of them focus on visual representation and dynamic features. MRTA differs from other robotic issues at problem characteristics; for example; moving on a rugged place, acceleration, and deceleration, gripping an object sensitively, learning from examples and giving smart answers, lifting heavy objects without consuming energy are not main tackles of MRTA. Instead, MRTA mostly deals with auctions and inter-robot communication, path planning, obstacle avoidance, optimization, and localization. Also, MRTA studies contain lots of various processes and algorithms, which combination of varieties fits to the intended use must be examined. This study uses the MRTA taxonomy from the authors' previous study and introduces an agent-based MRTA simulation software called MRTASim [5, 8]. The software enables experimentation of the elements of the taxonomy to achieve an optimal solution for a given "collect objects" mission.

MRTASim tool is powered by the flexibility of Java Agent Development Environment (JADE) and it differs from other general-purpose robot simulation tools such as Webots, Gazebo, MORSE and CoppeliaSim in domain specificity, interoperability and practicality [9]. The main objective of this study is to provide an experimental framework for single task-single robot-time extended assignment (ST-SR-TA) type MRTA problems.

The second section describes the aforementioned taxonomy briefly with examples. The third section gives details about agent-based software design. In the fourth section, case studies and benefits of the simulation on that are shown by experiments and results.

2 Simulation of Multi-Robot Task Allocation

2.1 Related Work

When multiple robots or agents are employed to accomplish a group of tasks, there arises "which robots will overtake which tasks and in which order?" problem [10]. The solution to this problem can be handled depending on the objective of the system i.e. in the shortest time, traversing the shortest path, with minimum energy consumption, by using least robots, etc. Assigning the most adequate tasks to the robots is simply called "multi-robot task allocation (MRTA)". Multi-robot task allocation is the problem of matching m tasks with n robots to decrease overall cost and execution time. Gerkey and Mataric classified MRTA problems in three axes [10]:

- single-task (ST) robots vs. multi-task (MT) robots: Robots are classified according to their capability of executing one or more tasks at the same time.
- single-robot (SR) tasks vs. multi-robot (MR) tasks: Some tasks are handled only one robot and some tasks require more than one robot to be done.
- instantaneous assignment (IA) vs. time-extended assignment (TA): Some problems are planned to be executed instantly and some problems additionally require future schedules.

Korsah et al. [11] extends the taxonomy of Gerkey & Mataric and adds the degree of interdependence which is classified as below:

- No Dependency (ND): "no dependency on any other tasks or agents in the system"
- In-Schedule Dependency (ID): "dependency on other tasks or agents"
- Cross-Schedule Dependency (XD): "dependency on its own and other agents' schedules"
- Complex dependencies (CD): Similar to XD, an agent also deals with other agents' sub-tasks.

The object collection problem is similar to multiple TSP (mTSP) problem and such problems are classified as ID [SR-ST-TA] [11]. Khamis et al. [12] summarize recent MRTA work and they focus on resolving task complexity, increasing performance, increasing reliability and simplicity in design. Depending on these survey studies, it can be seen that most of the MRTA work include but they are not restricted to traversing, path planning, task formation, object detecting, and tracking. Some issues are given less importance and they require further research such as dynamic allocation, heavily constrained allocation, and heterogeneous allocation.

According to Khamis et al. [12], although there exists a great number of MRTA algorithms reported in the literature, the topic has been given less attention. One of the objectives of this study is to represent the possibility of creating a generic MRTA model by little effort. MRTASim provides lots of instant algorithms and techniques to be integrated and tested in easily.

2.2 MRTA Simulation Model

In the light of the practical implementation of many MRTA simulations, we formed the taxonomy represented in Fig. 1. This taxonomy is used to build a generic MRTA simulation model and MRTASim tool. The tool enables the user to select MRTA characteristics from its Graphical User Interface (GUI). Giving all the details about MRTA taxonomy is out of this paper's scope, so prominent features are summarized below.

Role Assignment for Auctions. Recent MRTA studies are mostly focused on auction-based or market-based approaches and they benefit from economic principles at sharing goods [3, 13–15]. A robot has a task set to execute and it may transfer tasks to another robot which is more suitable to perform those tasks. Robots represent salesmen (sellers) or costumers (buyers) whereas tasks represent goods shared. "Seller" robot's cost at completing a task must be higher than "Buyer"'s. It will have an additional virtual profit as well. Otherwise, trade system can't limit redundant shares and this leads to chaos. Usually, a central agent (or robot) leads the task announcement, bid collection and bid evaluation jobs. These tasks can be carried out by one of the robots as well. Roles must be defined and assigned clearly to prevent overlapping and synchronization failure. Robots may concurrently be employed as "buyer" and "seller", or preferably one of them may be "seller" and others may be "buyer"'s. The method of choosing a "seller" at an auction round will be effective on load balance and hence on overall system performance. If a robot which has many tasks to do must transfer some of its tasks to idle or less-loaded robots.

Selection of Trade Tasks. Once a robot is employed as a "Seller", selection of trade tasks becomes the proceeding problem. Each task that the robot owns has a reward value and robot can choose according to the reward. Another approach can be the optimal way that the robot makes calculations as if one or more tasks are sold. This takes time but it is guaranteed that the best solution is achieved. A robot may ask itself "Which task's exclusion makes the maximum path length decrease?". The calculation of TSP length might be employed at this point. In some cases, selling a group of tasks is preferred to increase the profit. The combinatorial approach should be avoided to define the best task set to be traded.

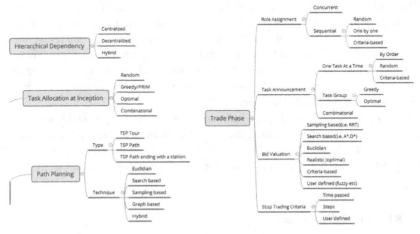

Fig. 1. MRTA problems taxonomy at four main branches.

Path Planning. Path planning is merely a part of robot motion planning such as trajectory planning and path finding and it has become one of the most studied topics of MRTA [6, 16]. Each of them gains specific importance depending on the problem. For example, when an aircraft approaches to an airport, it uses trajectory planning is used instead of path finding. In some cases, path planning, path finding and trajectory planning may be combined. As an example, Stodola proposed an optimal route planner for unmanned air vehicles which is an example of combining path planning and trajectory planning [17]. When it comes to path planning, optimization at path length and traverse time come to the fore. Path planning is the planning of the whole way from point A to point B, including visiting defined path points. If the robot returns to the start point at the end, then it is called a "tour". If point B is one of the pre-defined return points, we call it "path ending with a station". The main aim of the path planning is reaching point B in (a) in the shortest time (b) traversing the shortest way. There are well-known algorithms to calculate the distance between point A and point B depending on terrain characteristics, and/or expected resolution. Sampling-based methods like Rapidly Exploring Random Trees (RRT) [18], search-based methods like D*-Lite [19] or graph-based methods like Transition Points Method (TPM) [8] are widely used techniques of their classes. For example, Dias experimented RRT method at a warehouse terrain [15]. RRT is not likely to be a suitable way for orthogonal terrains as Fig. 2 shows. Because of its random nature, the robot reaches the task by using two different paths, furthermore, for the both ways, paths are longer than generated by other path planning techniques.

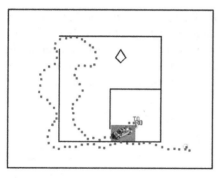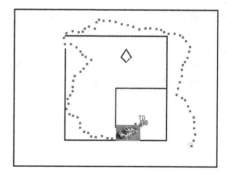

Fig. 2. Path finding by using generated vertexes of rapidly exploring random trees (RRT).

D*Lite, which is an enhanced and fast version of well-known A*, requires matrix-type information about the terrain that higher resolution increases the solution time. As an alternative, graph-based methods can be used.

Bid Valuation. Hybrid MRTA techniques are mostly based on trading between robots. Robots bid for a task after calculating a bid value. Location, current workload, the energy level of the robot, the priority of the task, obstacles, air conditions, and emergency cases may affect the bid calculation method. The utility is the benefit if the robot accomplishes a task. In some cases, a robot is rewarded when it completes a task. In this case utility (a.k.a bid) is calculated as (1). A robot doesn't bid for a task if the reward is equal to or less than cost.

$$Utility = \max(reward - cost, 0) \tag{1}$$

In this study, at TSP based approaches, bid valuation is calculated according to the TSP path length of the robot. If a robot is a seller, its cost becomes reward value and calculated as in (2) and if the robot is buyer cost is as in (3) where tsp_{len} is the TSP path length of robot's current schedule, tsp_{exc} is TSP path length if robot sells task, tsp_{inc} TSP path length if robot adds task to its current tasks. More tasks mean more load, to this end, to obtain task balance between robots, the penalty function is added as represented at (4).

$$reward = tsp_{len} - tsp_{exc} + penalty \tag{2}$$

$$cost = tsp_{inc} - tsp_{len} + penalty \tag{3}$$

$$penalty = tsp_{len} \times 0.2 \tag{4}$$

If bid valuation is not based on TSP, then cost value is the distance of robot to the task. The distance can be calculated by path planning methods. A 3% profit is added to the cost to prevent redundant shares.

Task Ordering. If the robot has more than one task to do, ordering tasks may be a challenging problem. For navigation tasks, the best way is to make task orders according to the Travelling Salesman Problem (TSP) solution. TSP is an NP-Hard Problem and if the number of cities is high, calculation time will be a great bottleneck. So it would be reasonable to prevent robots from gaining too many tasks at a time by limiting robot task capacity and making task allocations iterative. Figure 3 shows the task execution of four robots for two types of traversing; TSP path and TSP tour. It can be seen that TSP path and TSP tour task ordering solutions for the same task set may be different.

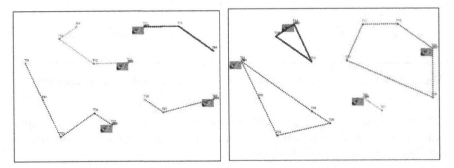

Fig. 3. Task ordering for TSP path and TSP tour (15 tasks, 4 robots)

3 Design and Implementation of MRTA Simulation

3.1 The Need for an MRTA Simulation Tool

Building an MRTA-based system involves in many challenges such as path planning, pricing, role assignment and so on. A combination of these concepts should be examined deeply. Selected terrain, robot specifications, task characteristics, robot, and task formation should be taken into account and experimental validation of deployment must be performed. Several simulation runs might help to select the best options for a selected problem. For example, path planning solutions may differ when the terrain is set as a 3-dimensional area instead of an orthogonal area. Or cost function used at the decision of selling a task to another robot may be optimized after running the simulation several times. Setting a huge number of simulation parameters and functions may be an exhaustive way of experimentation. There are several advantages of tool support for selecting predefined parameters and options via a user friendly interface:

- Defining simulation scenarios by a GUI tool is easy and fast.
- Scenarios can be run with several alternative parameters and this process can be automated.
- Using predefined options enables creating reliable scenarios by excluding human errors.
- Scenarios and simulation logs could be held separately for further investigation.
- Integrating and testing a new concept would be easier.

Experimentation in synthetic environments is a low-cost solution for investigating potential integration of autonomous systems into the operational field [20, 21]. Several tools and frameworks are advised to be used as multi-robot systems experimentation. The most known and used tools are listed below:

Player/Stage/Gazebo: Player is a networked interface to robots and sensors. Stage and Gazebo are Player-friendly multiple-robot simulators. They allow rapid prototyping and experiments with realistic robot devices. Various sensors and actuators are provided. The software runs on most UNIX-like OS's, and some parts also work on Windows [22].

Webots: Webots is an open source robot simulator that provides a complete development environment to model, program and simulate robots. It has features like rapid prototyping from scratch, libraries of robots, sensors, actuators, and objects, importing & exporting CAD models. Webots supports multi-platform development [23].

MORSE: MORSE is a generic simulator for academic robotics. It focuses on realistic 3D simulation of small to large environments, indoor or outdoor, with one to tenths of autonomous robots. MORSE comes with a set of *standard sensors, actuators* and *robotic bases*. New ones can easily be added [24].

CoppeliaSim: CoppeliaSim is the new name of V-REP Project. V-REP is a general purpose robot simulator with integrated development environment. Sensors, mechanisms, robots and whole systems can be modelled and simulated in various ways. It enables fast prototyping and verification, controller development, hardware control, simulation of factory automation systems, safety monitoring and product presentation [25].

All these tools are general purpose and require a lot of work to simulate MRTA scenarios. They focus on physical modelling, control mechanisms, sensors and actuators more than specific behaviors of coordinating robots.

In this study, a simulation software package that enables automation of MRTA experiments in order to determine the best configuration for a specific intended use is developed. The main advantages of introduced tool package are listed below:

- Most of the MRTA characteristics are selected by GUI without coding.
- Centralized, decentralized and hybrid task allocation
- Several path planning approaches (D*-Lite, RRT, TPM)
- Several shortest way (TSP) solution approaches (Tour, path, path ending with a specific terminal)
- Automated execution of predefined scenarios accordingly
- Preprocessing for graph creation when the number of edges and nodes are high
- Visual demonstration of the robot path history
- Simulation speed up to 2x, 4x, and 8x

The package consists of two modules: (a) Terrain Editor (b) MRTASim

3.2 Terrain Editor

Terrain Editor is the tool for editing the simulation world in a simple way. This study focuses especially on robot surveillance tasks, so the world is designed according to terrains available for indoor and outdoor navigation. Obstacles, walls and other objects can be practically created by a user-friendly interface. Initial positions of robots and tasks can be defined as well. A map or figure can be set as a background image. Coordinates and other characteristics of the objects are written to configuration files. The most important advantages of Terrain Editor are creating a graph (edges and vertices) according to defined terrain and calculating the shortest distances between all the vertices using Dijkstra's shortest path algorithm as a preprocessing. Figure 4 represents the map of Istanbul (Grand) Airport and automatically generated edges (yellow lines) and vertices (red dots). If the path planning method is chosen as graph-based at the simulation, the software uses the pre-calculated distance values for fast processing. Terrain Editor reads the scenario information from a folder named as scenario's id, and scenarios can be cloned easily by copying and pasting scenario folder. The complexity of the graph will be tailored according to the user requirements. Figure 4 shows a detailed terrain including 4692 vertices.

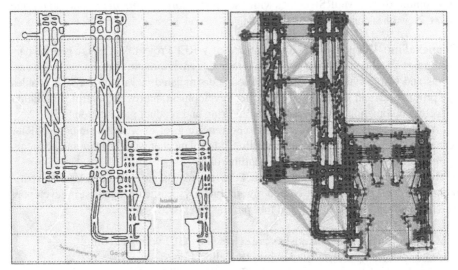

Fig. 4. (a) Istanbul (Grand) Airport terrain including runways, taxiways, junctions and apron sketched by user (b) graph including vertices and edges generated automatically (Color figure online)

3.3 MRTASim

An agent-based simulation is used for systems with agents who can autonomously make a decision considering other agents' decisions. MRTASim is a comprehensive agent-based simulation tool for planning, executing and logging MRTA simulations. Robots, Auctioneer (a central planner), Terrain and Simulation Manager are designed as agents. Java Agent-based Development Environment (JADE) is used to build simulation models of these agents. JADE simplifies the implementation of multi-agent systems through a middle-ware that complies with the FIPA specifications and through a set of graphical tools that support the debugging and deployment phases [9]. By using JADE, all MRTASim agents can be distributed to several machines. JADE is a suitable tool for imitating robot-like entities, it provides the flexibility of what a Java program can do.

MRTASim uses the messaging system and behaviors of JADE frequently. It is quite easy to send and receive messages. Messages are queued in a message list and executed by order. JADE encapsulates developer from the complexity of communication; there is no need for expertise at TCP-IP or sockets.

JADE behaviors are easily developed as well. JADE isolates developers from parallel programming and threading issues by bringing behaviors into use. Examples to some JADE behavior are One-shot, Cyclic, Ticker, Waker, Simple, Sequential, and Parallel. The only requirement to use behaviors efficiently is to build a feasible schedule. Activity design is an important phase of agent development. Agents can be initiated manually by executing its code, or dynamically by calling from another agent. JADE agents are FIPA-compliant, to this end, these agents provide interoperability. It is possible to join a JADE agent container using not only computers but also mobile phones or tablets from any geographical location that has an internet connection.

Four types of agents have been developed for this study:

Robot Agent
Robot Agent behaves like an autonomous real robot. It senses, decides and actuates. Obstacle sensing and avoidance have not been implemented yet, but robots are sensible to battery level and task announcements. For example, when the battery level is low, it cannot bid to any tasks, it looks for a suitable charge station and goes to charge. Robot Agent is informed about the map of the simulation world including walls, other robots, and obstacles. Unlike other agents, more than one robot agent can be employed.

Auctioneer Agent
Auctioneer Agent has a planner role. It is informed about all the tasks, charge stations and robots. When a robot is added to the system, Robot sends acknowledgment message to Auctioneer Agent to introduce itself. Auctioneer Agent is also responsible to help robots to find suitable charge station, to perform a centralized optimal assignment and to inform graphical user interface agent. AuctioneerAgent is disabled when distributed task allocation mode is on.

Terrain Agent
Terrain Agent shows the terrain, tasks, and robots on a graphical user interface. Robots send their momentary information (location, budget, battery level, completed tasks, charge count) with messages where Auctioneer Agent sends task and charge station information.

SimManager Agent
As its name implies, SimManager Agent is responsible for managing other agents' life cycles. SimManager Agent has a GUI which enables the user to set simulation parameters shown in Fig. 5a. Some preprocess calculations such as automatic station locating are handled if needed. If the automatic mode is on all the agents are started and killed automatically by the order and timing of SimManager Agent. Some information is read from configuration files.

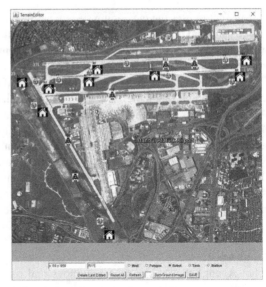

Fig. 5. (a) MRTASim model and scenario definition window. (b) TerrainEditor window

4 Experiments

In order to show the functionality of MRTASim tool, a step-by-step scenario building process is told in this chapter. In the first step, there are 15 tasks and one robot in an obstacle-free orthogonal space Figs. 6 and 7. A task is assumed as completed when one of the robots is reached and an amount of time is spent after that (it is for i.e. gripping the object). At each proceeding step, a new problem is introduced and the scenario is updated accordingly.

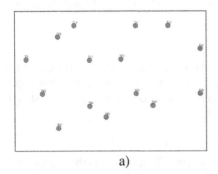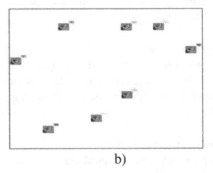

a)   b)

Fig. 6. Initial locations of (a) 15 tasks and (b) 8 robots for EmptyRoom, ArtGallery and Island terrains.

Tasks: The selected task set is based on data used for the TSP problem. To this end, it could be possible to verify that our shortest path plan algorithm is working. Each city is assumed as a task that only one of the robots has to visit once.

Robots: At the first step, one robot is charged for visiting all the 15 tasks. As the number of robots gradually increases, the task load of each robot and hence the number of cities for visiting and average task completion time will be decreased. On the opposite side, more robots mean more maintaining and deployment effort.

Obstacles: Obstacles between robots and tasks add a great amount of complexity in finding the right way with limited information. The first group of experiments does not deal with obstacles by assuming each robot has the skill of seeing all the items in the terrain and it can deliver an offer for all the tasks defined. In the second group of experiments, some walls are settled to monitor robot behaviors at looking for the tasks. MRTASim enables setting the robot's vision and service area. The service area is assumed as the field that robots can sense and access. Sometimes, a robot is assumed to sense everywhere on the terrain, and sometimes robots are assigned rectangular or circular shaped service areas. In both cases, robots are informed about tasks, other robots and obstacles in the neighborhood.

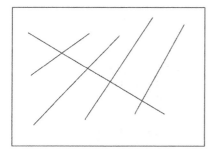 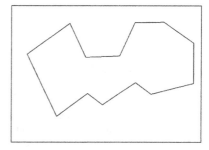

Fig. 7. Sample simple terrains (a) Art gallery (b) Island.

Table 1 lists the parameters of an MRTA simulation which can be set by GUI or set in the code. As seen in the table, there may be 2^n options to test if a combinatorial approach is preferred where n is the total number of all possible parameter inputs. We think that the user could choose an optimistic way to find the most feasible simulation parameters. For example, if there is no obstacle, comparing pathfinding methods is not useful. If there are lots of tasks that the robots have and robot loads are similar, trading is time-wasting, the optimal centralized allocation will help alone.

Experiment #1: Path Planning Comparison at Maze

We will demonstrate the path planning technique comparison on Maze terrain to compare several path planning techniques. In the beginning, there is one robot at the right-bottom of the terrain, it is out of the maze. At the heart of the maze, there exists a single task to visit, the robot calculates a path to arrive at that task by using four path planning techniques separately. As seen in Fig. 8, looking to computation time versus traverse length (cost/performance ratio), the best solution seems Dijkstra-type path planning if graph nodes can be generated for a given terrain. Preprocessing by calculating the shortest ways between the nodes will help for the fastest solution.

Table 1. MRTASim experiment parameters.

Property	Alternatives	Default	Can be set by
Terrain	Can be defined by TerrainEditor	Alphabetically first item	GUI
#Robots, #tasks	Read by config files, can be set by the user	Read by config files	GUI
Hierarchical dependency	Centralized/Trade/Agile	Centralized	GUI
Initial task allocation method	Greedy/Optimal/PRIM/Random	Optimal	GUI
Path planning method	TPM/D*Lite/RRT/TSP based	D*-Lite	
Robot service area	All-Terrain/Rectangular/Circular	All-Terrain: Each robot can bid any task in the terrain, communicational and spatial constraints are ignored	GUI
TSP mode	Tsp tour/Tsp path	TSP path: Robot stays stationary at the last reached task	GUI
Visit duration	Set by typing the duration amount in milliseconds	120 ms. – Each robot spends a constant time at each task visit (for example for gripping, cleaning, sweeping, etc.)	GUI
Robot capacity	Set by typing a number	40 – This is the upper limit of a robot's task capacity at a moment	GUI
Robot max. speed	Set by typing a number	20 km/h	GUI
Role assignment	Criteria based: Seller is selected according to several rules. Each robot calculates the path change when removing any task from its task list. If any robot fails at selling any task, it can't be a candidate for selling for the next tour		Code
Stop trading (Trade exit) criteria	User-defined: If three successive trade attempts fail or all robots fail to the trade at its turn respectively, trade process is over		Code
Bid valuation cost function	A cost function is calculated according to the formulas mentioned		Code

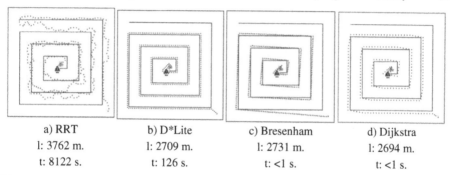

a) RRT	b) D*Lite	c) Bresenham	d) Dijkstra
l: 3762 m.	l: 2709 m.	l: 2731 m.	l: 2694 m.
t: 8122 s.	t: 126 s.	t: <1 s.	t: <1 s.

Fig. 8. Path planning techniques compared on Maze terrain (terrain dimensions: 350 m. × 350 m., l: traversed path length, t: path planning calculation duration at the processor)

Experiment #2: Centralized versus Trade Comparison at EmptyRoom

EmptyRoom terrain is an obstacle-free environment that robots can interact with all other robots and they can calculate the distance to any of other robots and tasks. Robots calculate distances by a simple Euclidian formula. The main objective is to investigate hierarchical dependency and initial task allocation. Traverse path lengths and total durations are shown in Table 2. For this case, it can be said that if we want to make traverse paths shorter, we had better choose Optimal initial task allocation plus trade option. To complete the tasks in a shorter time, initial task allocation alone seems a better option. Especially employing more robots makes a significant effect as reducing the completion time seven times lower (2200 ms. To 281 ms.) and the traverse path to half (2210 mt. to 360 mt.) when compared to one robot employed.

Table 2. Experiment results of EmptyRoom scenarios.

	Traverse path length (m.)			Total (calculation + traversing) duration (sec.)		
	Greedy	Optimal	Optimal + Trade	Greedy	Optimal	Optimal + Trade
1 robot	2210	2210	2210	2200	2200	2200
2 robots	2125	2125	2125	1166	1168	1170
4 robots	2089	2192	1679	723	592	727
8 robots	1001	1179	960	415	281	441

Experiment #3: Multi-Robot Path Planning at Art Gallery and Island

Art gallery problem is used for demonstrating that the security system of the gallery has the ability of monitoring all the precious stones and artwork at the same time, in other words, this problem is for testing the accessibility of all the terrain by a search algorithm. Empty Room terrain is revised to liken it to an art gallery by adding some walls. This terrain is to force robots creating efficient and fast path planning. Island terrain is similar to Art Gallery; except there is a section in the middle which robots can't enter. robots are wanted to bid for tasks that they can't find a path directly, so this scenario is especially

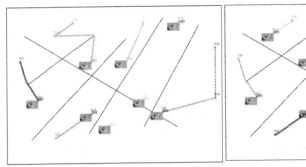

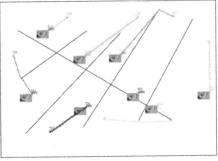

a) Art Gallery, 15 tasks, 8 robots, Greedy, D*-Lite, l: 1305 m. t: 1158 s.

b) Art Gallery, 15 tasks, 8 robots, Optimal, TPM, l: 1577 m. t: 313 s.

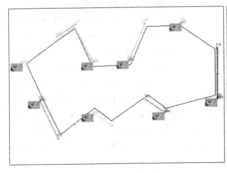

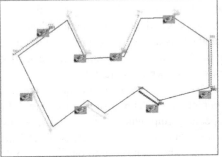

c) Island, 15 tasks, 8 robots, Greedy, D*-Lite, l: 1071 m. t: 702 s.

d) Island, 15 tasks, 8 robots, Optimal, TPM, l: 1079 m. t: 280 s.

Fig. 9. Screenshots from completed runs of ArtGallery and Island scenarios (terrain dimensions: 846 m. × 594 m., l: traversed path length, t: time passed while all tasks are being completed).

Table 3. Experiment results of EmptyRoom scenarios. GD: Greedy/D*-Lite, OD: Optimal/D*-Lite, OTD: Optimal-Trade/D*-Lite, GT: Greedy/TPM, OT: Optimal/TPM, OTT: Optimal-Trade/TPM

	Traverse path (m.)						Total duration (s.)					
	GD	OD	OTD	GT	OT	OTT	GD	OD	OTD	GT	OT	OTT
1 robot	–	–	–	3352	–	–	–	–	–	2405	–	
2 robots	5171	4049	4049	4050	4049	**3601**	1659	1498	1844	1392	1393	**1351**
4 robots	2616	2559	2559	2616	2559	**2281**	1376	1111	1326	817	**625**	758
8 robots	**1305**	1577	1580	**1305**	1577	**1320**	1158	1012	1468	440	**313**	459

for comparing path planning techniques such as graph-based and search-based. For the Art Gallery scenario, results show that tasks are completed in 4 times more time when D*-Lite selected as bid valuation method and initial allocation method as greedy even though more way is traversed. Figure 9 represents a selected situation (8 robots) that depicts this comparison both for Art Gallery and Island scenarios. It is seen that trading brings no significant advantage to these scenarios (Table 3).

Experiment #4: Big Scale Feasibility Analysis at Istanbul Ataturk Airport

One of the most efficient benefits of MRTASim tool rises at the optimization of the Multi-Depot Travelling Salesman Path Problem (MD-TSPP) [15]. MRTASim is employed at studying FOD (Foreign Object Debris) clearance mission at the airports. There is a need for safer, faster and cheaper ways to remove foreign objects from the airport runways. Airport management has an idea of using a multi-robot system to do this automatically. Decision-makers wonder whether they can do this without closing the airport and harming no one. MRTASim helps decision-makers at this point by modeling the airport runways, modeling FOD events and running numerous scenarios automatically to achieve the best case [5]. MRTASim had additional features at this work such as localized allocation, heat map based preprocessing, and automation. Any airport structure (runways, apron, taxiways, conjunctions) can be modeled by Terrain Editor tool and MRTA problems for several scenarios (i.e. land vehicle vs. air vehicle, centralized task allocation vs. autonomous task allocation, greedy task allocation vs. optimal task allocation, returning to base vs. remaining stationary, etc.) can be compared in terms of performance and efficiency (Fig. 10).

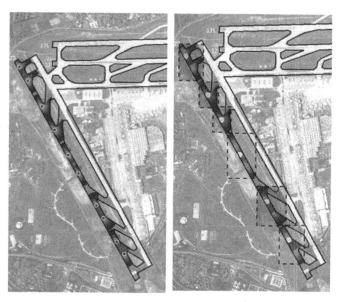

Fig. 10. Screenshots from Istanbul Ataturk Airport preprocessing.

5 Conclusion

Deploying, testing and maintaining multi-robot systems can be unsafe, expensive, time-consuming and challenging that simulation helps decision-makers to find an optimal solution before building the system. This work focuses on the simulation of MRTA problems which have a great number of questions to be solved such as hierarchical dependency, path planning, auctioning and bid valuation, communication, terrain specificity, hardware constraints to performance, etc. Besides, the effects of the number of tasks and task distribution, the number of robots and robot formations should be examined and this requires numerous tests for a combination of each option. MRTASim is developed to enable users building his/her own MRTA model and test it with lots of simulation runs in an automated way. This study represents the taxonomy to build a generic MRTA model and some examples of simulation runs. Experiments and cost analysis have clearly shown that MRTASim will enable a safer, faster and cheaper method for feasibility analysis of risky operations like FOD removal when compared to the traditional human-operated way. Future work will be based on extending MRTASim capabilities according to novel approaches and setting all the features from a graphical user interface such as setting bid valuation equations.

Acknowledgements. The authors would like to thank Scientific and Technological Research Council of Turkey (TUBITAK in Turkish) for funding this study, Clifton G.M. Presser, Rene Grothmann and William Fiset for sharing their TSP Java code, Konstantinos A. Nedas for sharing his Hungarian Algorithm Java code, and Daniel Beard for sharing his DStarLite Java Pathfinding code.

References

1. Ray, P.P.: Internet of robotic things: concept, technologies, and challenges. IEEE Access **4**, 9489–9500 (2016)
2. Rizk, Y., Awad, M., Tunstel, E.W.: Cooperative heterogeneous multi-robot systems: a survey. ACM Comput. Surv. **52**(2) (2019). Article no. 29
3. Ferri, G., Munafo, A., Tesei, A., LePage, K.: A market-based task allocation framework for autonomous underwater surveillance networks. In: OCEANS 2017 - Aberdeen, Aberdeen, pp. 1–10 (2017). https://doi.org/10.1109/oceanse.2017.8084769
4. Khalil, E.A., Ozdemir, S., Attea, B.A.: A new task allocation protocol for extending stability and operational periods in internet of things. IEEE Internet Things J. **6**(4), 7225–7231 (2019)
5. Öztürk, S., Kuzucuoğlu, A.E.: Multi-robot coordination approach for autonomous runway foreign object debris (FOD) clearance. Robot. Auton. Syst. **75**, 244–259 (2016)
6. Yao, W., Wan, N., Qi, N.: Hierarchical path generation for distributed mission planning of UAVs. In: IEEE 55th Conference on Decision and Control (CDC), Las Vegas, NV, pp. 1681–1686 (2016)
7. Das, G.P., McGinnity, T.M., Coleman, S.A., Behera, L.: A distributed task allocation algorithm for a multi-robot system in healthcare facilities. J. Intell. Rob. Syst. **80**(1), 33–58 (2014). https://doi.org/10.1007/s10846-014-0154-2
8. Öztürk, S., Kuzucuoğlu, A.E.: Optimal bid valuation using path finding for multi-robot task allocation. J. Intell. Manuf. **26**(5), 1049–1062 (2014). https://doi.org/10.1007/s10845-014-0909-4

9. Bellifemine, F.L., Caire, G., Greenwood, D.: Developing Multi-Agent Systems with JADE. Wiley, Hoboken (2007). ISBN 978-0-470-05747-6

10. Gerkey, B.P., Mataric, M.J.: A formal analysis and taxonomy of task allocation in multi-robot systems. J. Robot. Res. **23**(9), 939–954 (2004)

11. Korsah, G.A., Stentz, A., Dias, M.B.: A comprehensive taxonomy for multi-robot task allocation. Int. J. Robot. Res. **32**(12), 1495–1512 (2013)

12. Khamis, A., Hussein, A., Elmogy, A.: Multi-robot task allocation: a review of the state-of-the-art. In: Koubâa, A., Martínez-de Dios, J.R. (eds.) Cooperative Robots and Sensor Networks 2015. SCI, vol. 604, pp. 31–51. Springer, Cham (2015). https://doi.org/10.1007/978-3-319-18299-5_2

13. Zlot, R., Stentz, A., Dias, M.B., Thayer, S.: Multi-robot exploration controlled by a market economy. In: Proceedings of ICRA 2002, Washington, D.C., USA, pp. 3016–3023 (2002)

14. Oh, G., Kim, Y., Ahn, J., Choi, H.-L.: Market-based task assignment for cooperative timing missions in dynamic environments. J. Intell. Rob. Syst. **87**(1), 97–123 (2017). https://doi.org/10.1007/s10846-017-0493-x

15. Dias, M.B.: TraderBots: a new paradigm for robust and efficient multirobot coordination in dynamic environments. Ph.D. dissertation, Carnegie Mellon University (2004)

16. Pereyra, E., Araguás, G., Kulich, M.: Path planning for a formation of mobile robots with split and merge. In: Mazal, J. (ed.) MESAS 2017. LNCS, vol. 10756, pp. 59–71. Springer, Cham (2018). https://doi.org/10.1007/978-3-319-76072-8_4

17. Stodola, P.: Route optimization for cooperative aerial reconnaissance. In: Mazal, J. (ed.) MESAS 2017. LNCS, vol. 10756, pp. 83–91. Springer, Cham (2018). https://doi.org/10.1007/978-3-319-76072-8_6

18. LaValle, S.M.: Rapidly-exploring random trees: a new tool for path planning. In: TR 98-11, Computer Science Department, Iowa State University, October (1998)

19. Koenig, S., Likhachev, M.: D* Lite. In: Proceedings of the AAAI Conference of Artificial Intelligence (AAAI), pp. 476–483 (2002)

20. Hodicky, J.: HLA as an experimental backbone for autonomous system integration into operational field. In: Hodicky, J. (ed.) MESAS 2014. LNCS, vol. 8906, pp. 121–126. Springer, Cham (2014). https://doi.org/10.1007/978-3-319-13823-7_11

21. Hodicky, J.: Standards to support military autonomous system life cycle. In: Březina, T., Jabłoński, R. (eds.) MECHATRONICS 2017. AISC, vol. 644, pp. 671–678. Springer, Cham (2018). https://doi.org/10.1007/978-3-319-65960-2_83

22. Gerkey, B., Vaughan, R.T., Howard, A.: The player/stage project: tools for multi-robot and distributed sensor systems. In: Proceedings of the International Conference on Advanced Robotics (ICAR 2003), Coimbra, Portugal, 30 June–3 July 2003, pp. 317–323 (2003)

23. https://cyberbotics.com/#features

24. https://www.openrobots.org/morse/doc/latest/what_is_morse.html

25. http://www.coppeliarobotics.com/

Remark on Volumetric Errors
in Kinematic Chain of MCV 754 Quick

Jiří Novák[✉]

Institute of Mathematics, Faculty of Mechanical Engineering,
Brno University of Technology, Technická 2896/2, 61669 Brno, Czech Republic
`Jiri.Novak2@vutbr.cz`
`https://www.vutbr.cz/`

Abstract. In this article we assemble kinematic machine chains using homogeneous matrices and we get error vector DX, DY, DZ. At the same time we are working with error vector obtained using standard software tools by multilateration method. We compare the resulting values of both approaches and we are discussing.

Keywords: Volumetric precision · Multilateration · Milling machine · CNC

1 Introduction

Nowadays we usually use numerical control machine tools and other manufacturing machines and systems based on them (CNC, CAD, CAM). The technical development brings about requirements for greater accuracy of production. It is possible to increase this accuracy by refining the production of parts of manufacturing machines. This solution would be very costly.

There is another possibility to increase the final accuracy of the manufacturing machine. We can use a regular manufacturing machine and determine its accuracy by measuring its errors. After that, we change the setting of the machine to reduce the errors. There are some methods which implement this approach. We call them software compensations. For example: backlash, positioning error compensation, deflection compensation, perpendicularity compensation and volumetric compensation of the manufacturing machines [1].

2 Multilateration

Position error of a tool in workspace is determined as a difference between its nominal value, which is specified by the control software, and the actual position in which the tool is actually located. We can use various devices to determine the real position of the machine tool. There are for example laser tracers, laser trackers, ballbars or interferometers [2–5].

© Springer Nature Switzerland AG 2020
J. Mazal et al. (Eds.): MESAS 2019, LNCS 11995, pp. 88–96, 2020.
https://doi.org/10.1007/978-3-030-43890-6_7

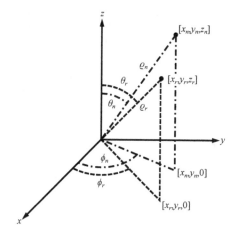

Fig. 1. Tool error of move to specified position

In this case, laser tracer (LT) was used. LT provides the position of the measured point in spherical coordinates, i.e. by the distance (radial component) and two angle components. The accuracy of the angle components is lower than the radial component. This fact disproportionately decreases the total accuracy of the measurement and increases the error of the measured tool's real position, which is possible to determine (Fig. 1).

This deficiency can be eliminated using the following method. This method consists in using three (or more) LTs to measure each single tool position. We will consider the measured distance from each LT measurement and we will omit the angular coordinates. We will get the resulting coordinate of the measured point as the intersection of three spheres, each having a centre in one of the LT, and a radius equal to the measured distance of the measured point from the LT [6].

The accuracy of this method of measuring a point's coordinates is extremely dependent on the accuracy with which we are able to determine the position of the LT. For this reason, the position of the individual LT is determined by repeated measurements. Then it is calculated by using the least squares method, thus achieving the desired maximum accuracy. This idea is called multilateration.

The advantage is that for both steps, i.e. determining the exact position of the LT's by the least squares method and for the subsequent calculation of the tool position from LT positions and measured distances, one and the same measurement can be used, thus significantly reducing the practical demands of this approach (Fig. 2).

3   Measuring on Milling Machine

Our data for this article were obtained by monitoring of a tool (milling cutter substitute) moving in the workspace of the MCV 754 Quick machine tool (see Fig. 3).

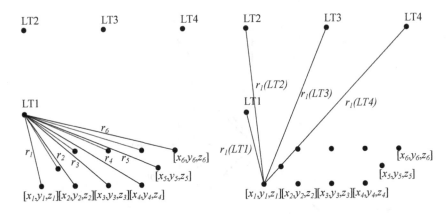

Fig. 2. Multilateration: first (left side) and second (right side) steps

The workspace range of our vertical machine-tool has the length of 754 mm, width of 500 mm and height of 550 mm. The clamping surface has the length of 1000 mm, width of 500 mm and maximum load of 400 kg.

This milling centre has three axis, 21 parameters of geometric errors can be described. For each axis there are three parameters describing translations and three parameters describing rotations. Moreover, there are tree parameters describing perpendicularity accuracy between each pair of axes.

The meaning of the errors described in the figure is the:

EXX (EYY EZZ) accuracy of move to position in axis x (or y or z)
EYX (EZX)   error of straightness y (or z) in direction of axis x
EXY (EZY)   error of straightness x (or z) in direction of axis y
EXZ (EYZ)   error of straightness x (or y) in direction of axis z
EAX EBX ECX   rotation diversion of axis x
EAY EBY ECY   rotation diversion of axis y
EAZ EBZ ECZ   rotation diversion of axis z
A0Z B0Z C0Y   perpendicularity errors between pairs of axis

Measuring was carried out by Etalon LaserTRACER. This measuring equipment uses light interference – the main component is a laser interferometer with nanometer resolution.

4 Kinematic Chain

We can compute a point's position considering the influence of geometric errors in three-axis machine tool workspace by so-called kinematic chain

$$\mathbf{T_1 E_1 T_2 E_2 T_3 E_3} \tag{1}$$

where $\mathbf{T_1}, \mathbf{T_2}, \mathbf{T_3}$ are translation matrices and $\mathbf{E_1}, \mathbf{E_2}, \mathbf{E_3}$ are error matrices.

Fig. 3. MCV 754 Quick machine tool

Translation matrices are:

$$\mathbf{T_1} = \begin{bmatrix} 1 & 0 & 0 & x \\ 0 & 1 & 0 & 0 \\ 0 & 0 & 1 & 0 \\ 0 & 0 & 0 & 1 \end{bmatrix}; \mathbf{T_2} = \begin{bmatrix} 1 & 0 & 0 & 0 \\ 0 & 1 & 0 & y \\ 0 & 0 & 1 & 0 \\ 0 & 0 & 0 & 1 \end{bmatrix}; \mathbf{T_3} = \begin{bmatrix} 1 & 0 & 0 & 0 \\ 0 & 1 & 0 & 0 \\ 0 & 0 & 1 & z \\ 0 & 0 & 0 & 1 \end{bmatrix} \tag{2}$$

Error matrices:

$$\mathbf{E_1} = \begin{bmatrix} 1 & -ECX & EBX & EXX \\ ECX & 1 & -EAX & EYX \\ -EBX & EAX & 1 & EZX \\ 0 & 0 & 0 & 1 \end{bmatrix}; \tag{3}$$

$$\mathbf{E_2} = \begin{bmatrix} 1 & -ECY & EBY & EXY \\ ECY & 1 & -EAY & EYY \\ -EBY & EAY & 1 & EZY \\ 0 & 0 & 0 & 1 \end{bmatrix}; \tag{4}$$

$$\mathbf{E_2} = \begin{bmatrix} 1 & -ECZ & EBZ & EXZ \\ ECZ & 1 & -EAZ & EYZ \\ -EBZ & EAZ & 1 & EZZ \\ 0 & 0 & 0 & 1 \end{bmatrix} \tag{5}$$

It is possible to neglect the error terms which do not affect the prescribed accuracy. This approach is given by matrices over the dual numbers [7,8] (Fig. 4).

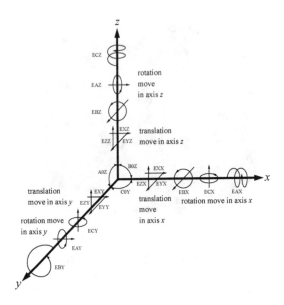

Fig. 4. Geometric errors of 3-axis machine-tool

5 Comparison

The data we will compare were obtained in two ways. The first data package contains compensation tables with the measured position errors compensations (Table 1). This compensation tables are obtained by proprietary software using Monte Carlo Method. The second data package was obtained from kinematic chain using volumetric precision (Figs. 5, 6, 7, 8, 9).

To maintain the same orientation of both data sets, the data from kinematic chain was processed by following transformations: errors DY's obtained using kinematic chain are multiplied by -1 and similar errors DZ's are subtracted by 0.01. We got triplets of graphs by this transformation, which are presented in next. We try to compare pairs of lines in our graphs by counting average square of difference between this lines. This comparison is in Table 2.

Table 1. Comparison of difference between our two data sets. In table are average absolute value of difference between position errors DX (resp. DY or DZ) obtained using kinematic chain and same position errors obtained from comparison tables.

x	z	DX	DY	DZ
0	0	0.0130	0.0032	9.0764×10^{-4}
0	50	0.0100	0.0032	6.6649×10^{-4}
50	50	0.0101	0.0033	7.4057×10^{-4}
50	0	0.0131	0.0032	9.9919×10^{-4}

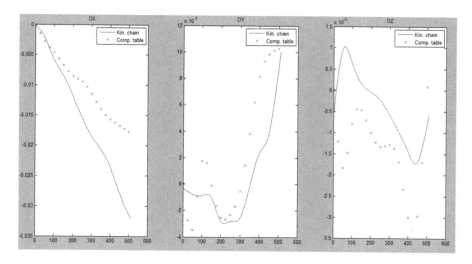

Fig. 5. Graphs of dependence errors DX (left), DY (center) and DZ (right) on (milling tool) movement along the axis y for constant coordinates x = 0 and z = 0. Meaning of symbols: solid line presents data from kinematic chain, crosses data from comparison tables

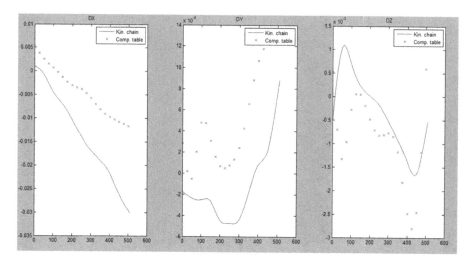

Fig. 6. Graphs of dependence errors DX (left), DY (center) and DZ (right) on (milling tool) movement along the axis y for constant coordinates x = 0 and z = 50. Meaning of symbols: solid line presents data from kinematic chain, crosses data from comparison tables

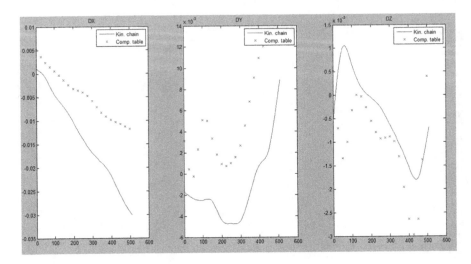

Fig. 7. Graphs of dependence errors DX (left), DY (center) and DZ (right) on (milling tool) movement along the axis y for constant coordinates x = 50 and z = 50. Meaning of symbols: solid line presents data from kinematic chain, crosses data from comparison tables

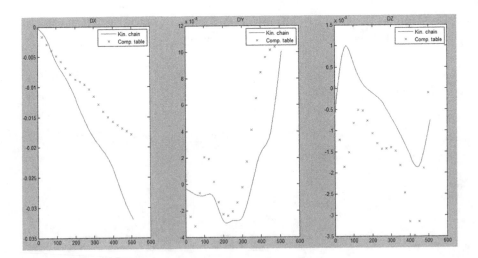

Fig. 8. Graphs of dependence errors DX (left), DY (center) and DZ (right) on (milling tool) movement along the axis y for constant coordinates x = 50 and z = 0. Meaning of symbols: solid line presents data from kinematic chain, crosses data from comparison tables

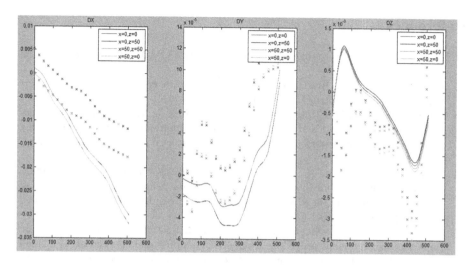

Fig. 9. Graphs of dependence errors DX (left), DY (center) and DZ (right) on (milling tool) movement along the axis y for constant coordinates x and z. Meaning of colors: $x = 0$, $z = 0$ is red, $x = 0$, $z = 50$ is blue, $x = 50$, $z = 0$ is cyan, $x = 50$, $z = 50$ is green. Meaning of symbols: solid line presents data from kinematic chain, crosses data from comparison tables (Color figure online)

Table 2. Comparison of difference between our two data sets. In table are average square of difference between position errors DX (resp. DY or DZ) obtained using kinematic chain and same position errors obtained from comparison tables.

x	z	DX	DY	DZ
0	0	4.5026×10^{-4}	3.6174×10^{-5}	2.7626×10^{-6}
0	50	2.8159×10^{-4}	3.9884×10^{-5}	1.8837×10^{-6}
50	50	2.8298×10^{-4}	4.1114×10^{-5}	2.2270×10^{-6}
50	0	4.5287×10^{-4}	3.7130×10^{-5}	3.2169×10^{-6}

6   Conclusion

The presented work is focused on comparison two approaches of determination of error position of points in the work space of a three-axis vertical milling machining centre. In the first case, compensation tables from LT was used. This data was compare with result given by kinematic chain. The difference between the corresponding position obtained by kinematic chain and compensation software TRAC CAL have shift character across individual axis.

Acknowledgement. The research was supported by a grant no. FSI-S-17-4464.

References

1. Marek, Jiří., et al.: Konstrukce CNC obráběcích strojů IV.0. MM publishing, Praha (2018). [in Czech]
2. Holub, M., Blecha, P., Bradac, F., Kana, R.: Volumetric compensation of three-axis vertical machining centre. MM Sci. J. **1**, 677–681 (2015)
3. Wiroj Sudathama, W., Matsumotoa, H., Takahashib, S., Takamasua, K.: Verification of the positioning accuracy of industrial coordinate measuring machine using optical-comb pulsed interferometer with a rough metal ball target. Precis. Eng. **41**, 63–67 (2015)
4. Moustafa, S., Gerwien, N., Haertig, F., Wendt, K.: Comparison of error mapping techniques for coordinate measuring machines using the plate method and laser tracer technique. In: XIX IMEKO World Congress: Fundamental and Applied Metrology, pp. 2457–2461 (2009)
5. Linares, J.-M., Chaves-Jacob, J., Schwenke, H., Longstaff, A., Fletcher, S., et al.: Impact of measurement procedure when error mapping and compensating a small CNC machine using a multilateration laser interferometer. Precis. Eng. **38**, 578–588 (2014). Elsevier
6. Aguado, S., Santolaria, J., Samper, D., Aguilar, J.J.: Study of self-calibration and multilateration in machine tool volumetric verification for laser tracker error reduction. Proc. Inst. Mech. Eng. Part B: J. Eng. Manuf. **228**(7), 659–672 (2014)
7. Holub, M., Hrdina, J., Vašík, P., Vetiška, J.: Three-axes error modeling based on second order dual numbers. J. Math. Ind. **5**(2), 1–11 (2015)
8. Hrdina, J., Vašík, P., Holub, M.: Dual numbers arithmentic in multiaxis machine error modeling. MM Sci. J. **2017**(1), 1769–1772 (2017)
9. Hrdina, J., Vašík, P.: Dual numbers approach in multiaxis machines error modeling. J. Appl. Math. (2014)
10. Holub, M., Jankových, R., Andrš, O., Kolíbal, Z.: Capability assessment of CNC machining centres as measuring devices. Meas: J. Int. Meas. Confederation **118**, 52–60 (2018)

Terrain Learning Using Time Series of Ground Unit Traversal Cost

Miloš Prágr[✉][iD] and Jan Faigl[iD]

Faculty of Electrical Engineering, Czech Technical University in Prague,
Technicka 2, 166 27 Prague, Czech Republic
{pragrmi1,faiglj}@fel.cvut.cz
https://comrob.fel.cvut.cz

Abstract. In this paper, we concern learning of terrain types based on the traversal experience observed by a hexapod walking robot. The addressed problem is motivated by the navigation of unmanned ground vehicles in long-term autonomous missions in a priory unknown environments such as extraterrestrial exploration. In such deployments, the robotic vehicle needs to learn hard to traverse terrains to improve its autonomous performance and avoid possibly dangerous areas. We propose to utilize Growing Neural Gas for terrain learning to capture the robot experience with traversing the terrain and thus learn a classifier of individual terrain types. The classifier is learned using a real time-series dataset collected by a hexapod walking robot traversing various terrain types. The learned model can be utilized to predict the traversal cost of newly observed terrains to support decisions on where to navigate next.

1 Introduction

Traversal of different terrains is one of the main concerns for unmanned ground vehicles in long-term deployments such as data gathering, environment monitoring, search-and-rescue, or exploration missions. For example, the Mars rover Spirit got stuck in soft sand despite being navigated with human oversight [2]. Ground robot system deployments range from terrain classification approaches that use human terrain type labels [1,22] or distinguish non-traversable obstacles [13]; to self-supervised systems that autonomously learn terrain type classifiers [8]. Alternatively, the terrain traversability might be computed directly as a function of terrain appearance and geometry [24], measure robot performance [12], or evaluate the foothold configuration of a multi-legged robot [15].

Our particular research on terrain traversability is focused on deployments without a priory learning of the traversal costs, and we aim to support instant deployments of online learned models. In [20,21], we develop a robotic system that incrementally learns to predict power consumption-based traversal costs that are experienced by the robots over various traversed terrains. Besides, in [19], we deploy a robotic system that incorporates fully autonomous spatial exploration of the terrain with a simultaneous exploration of the underlying traversal cost model of the traversed terrains, such that the learned cost

© Springer Nature Switzerland AG 2020
J. Mazal et al. (Eds.): MESAS 2019, LNCS 11995, pp. 97–107, 2020.
https://doi.org/10.1007/978-3-030-43890-6_8

model is instantaneously utilized in autonomous navigation to avoid costly terrains. Moreover, we investigate self-organizing neural network approaches in terrain classification and traversal cost prediction [4,5,18], namely variants of the Growing Neural Gas (GNG) [7], Self-Organizing Map (SOM) [11], and Improved Self-Organizing Incremental Neural Network (ISOINN) [23]. Although the previous results provide particular solutions experimentally verified in a series of deployments, they are limited to aggregated cost data that are driven by a spatial grid-based representation of the operational environment. However, the traversal cost is computed from a sequence of measurements. Therefore, the cost prediction can be based on direct employment of the input time series of the considered proprioceptive, but also exteroceptive measurements. Thus, in this paper, we report on our further research on terrain learning explicitly based on time series.

Time series data are already employed in many domains ranging from medicine [14,26] through handwriting [25] and gestures [17] to classification of physical activities [27]. Recently, machine learning approaches such as Support vector machines [9] and Deep convolutional neural networks [27] has been employed in time series classification. From the existing approaches, One-nearest-neighbor (1-NN) is a simple yet popular approach. When it is utilized with time-series data, the 1-NN can calculate the distance between time series measurements using the Dynamic Time Warping (DTW) [16], although the authors of [10] report in favor of the Euclidean distance. In [25], a semi-supervised 1-NN time series classifier is presented, and the authors of [26] demonstrate the speedup of 1-NN using numerous reduction. A combination of the k-NN with Growing Neural Gas (GNG) is presented in [17] to classify multi-channel time series.

In this paper, we report on the deployment of the GNG-based 1-NN terrain classifier that is learned using a time series dataset, and the proposed approach is compared to the baseline non-time series setup. Moreover, the learned classifier is employed in the prediction of the energy-based traversal cost. Finally, we investigate the representation of the robot proprioception as an aggregated cost computed over time series segments. In this case, the influence of the subsampling rates is investigated, and we report the computational efficiency of the proposed concise representation.

The paper is organized as follows. In Sect. 2, the utilized terrain traversal dataset is described in the context of the terrain classification and traversal cost prediction problems. The used GNG algorithm is described in Sect. 3, while Sect. 4 reports on the achieved results. The concluding remarks are in Sect. 5.

2   Time-Series Dataset and the Terrain Learning Problem

We address learning of terrain type classifiers using a dataset of terrain feature descriptors and multi-legged robot proprioceptive signals. The dataset is organized as time series sampled with 10 Hz. The time series is cut in 10 s long segments, where each segment represents a single locomotion gait cycle of the robot.

Hence, there are 101 data points in each segment. The segments are reported with 1 Hz to account for the different possible offsets with regards to the gait cycle. Furthermore, the baseline non-time series approach is represented as non-time series data points, where each non-time series data point corresponds to one time series segment.

Each data point (regardless of whether it is a part of the segment or a standalone, not time series point) comprises descriptors of the terrain shape and appearance coupled with the proprioceptive measurements of the robot power consumption. The terrain descriptors are based on the previous work [20], and each terrain descriptor characterizes the area of 0.2 m radius around the ground projection of the robot's body center of mass. The shape descriptors are determined from the eigenvalues of the covariance matrix of the surface points in the area as (f_5, f_6, f_7) presented in [13]. The appearance descriptors are the ab channel means of the Lab color space representation of the surface points in the area.

The instantaneous power consumption [12] signal is determined as

$$P_{in} = V \cdot I \quad [\text{W}], \tag{1}$$

where V is the battery voltage and I is the instantaneous current measurement, which is sampled with 10 Hz. Besides the raw power consumption signal, the aggregated traversal cost c is determined as the total energy consumed over the given interval. The aggregated cost c over the interval between two consecutive power measurements is computed using the trapezoid integration rule

$$c(t_i, t_{i-1}) = (t_i - t_{i-1}) \frac{P_{in}(t_{i-1}) + P_{in}(t_i)}{2} \quad [\text{J}], \tag{2}$$

where t_i and t_{i-1} are the corresponding sampling times, and $P_{in}(t_i)$ and $P_{in}(t_{i-1})$ are the respective power consumption measurements. Given the additive nature of the integration, it holds that

$$c(t_{i+1}, t_{i-1}) = c(t_{i+1}, t_i) + c(t_i, t_{i-1}) \quad [\text{J}]. \tag{3}$$

Therefore, the traversal cost $c(T)$ over a segment T with 101 power measurements sampled with 10 Hz is defined as

$$c(T) = \sum_{i=1}^{100} c(t_{i+1}, t_i) | \{t_i\}_{i=1}^{101} \in T \quad [\text{J}]. \tag{4}$$

In the considered dataset, we can distinguish two types of time series segments or non-time series points. The first type includes the time series segments T_{ts} with power measurements replaced by the aggregate traversal cost, which may be sampled at a lower frequency. Since each two subsampled points at t'_{j+1}, t'_j correspond to $k + 1$ points $(t_i, ..., t_{i+k})$ in the raw 10 Hz time series, where $t'_{j+1} - t'_j = t_{i+k} - t_i$, the cost for the interval (t'_{j+1}, t'_j) between the points in T_{ts} is computed using (2) and (3) as

$$c(t'_{j+1}, t'_j) = \sum_{l=i}^{i+k-1} c(t_{l+1}, t_l) \quad [\text{J}]. \tag{5}$$

 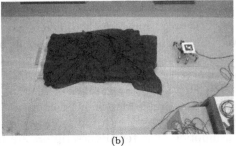

(a)   (b)

Fig. 1. (a) The utilized hexapod walking robot on the *cubes* terrain with *turf* terrain in the background; (b) and the overhead view of *cubes covered with black* terrain.

Therefore, the cost of the segment T_{ts} is the sum

$$c(T_{ts}) = \sum_{j=1}^{|T_{ts}|-1} c(t'_{j+1}, t'_j) | \{t_j\}_{j=1}^{|T_{ts}|} \in T_{ts} \quad [\text{J}], \tag{6}$$

where $|T_{ts}|$ is the number of points in the subsampled time series. The second type is the non-time series data points, which represent the robot power consumption as the mean over the 10 s segment T_{point}

$$\hat{P}(T_{point}) = \frac{1}{101} \sum_{i=1}^{101} P_{in}(t_i) | \{t_i\}_{i=1}^{101} \in T_{point} \quad [\text{W}], \tag{7}$$

and the aggregate cost over the 10 s long segment is thus approximated as

$$c(T_{point}) = 10\hat{P}(T_{point}) \quad [\text{J}]. \tag{8}$$

The latter type has been utilized in our previous research reported in [4,20], and therefore, it is considered as the baseline approach.

The time-series dataset is collected by the small battery-powered hexapod walking robot shown in Fig. 1a that is controlled by adaptive locomotion control [3] capable of crawling rough terrains. The robot is guided over a set of human-labeled terrains that can be categorized as *flat* office ground, artificial *turf*-like carpet, *black* fabric, and wooden *cubes* of uneven height and slope. Two further terrain types are created as *cubes covered with turf* and *cubes covered with black* fabric, see Fig. 1b. Thus, each time series segment or its corresponding non-time series point T is accompanied by a human terrain label. The performance of the terrain classifier C can be determined as the number of correct classifications further denoted as correctness:

$$correctness(\mathcal{T}, \mathcal{C}) = \frac{1}{|\mathcal{T}|} \sum_{T \in \mathcal{T}} \begin{cases} 1 & \text{if} \quad classify(T, \mathcal{C}) = label(T) \\ 0 & \text{otherwise} \end{cases} 100\%, \tag{9}$$

where $\mathcal{T}$ is the test set of time series segments T with hidden labels $label(T)$. The traversal cost predictor $\mathcal{I}$ is evaluated with regards to the RMSE

$$RMSE(\mathcal{T}, \mathcal{I}) = \sqrt{\frac{\sum_{T_{terrain} \in \mathcal{T}} (predict(T_{terrain}, \mathcal{I}) - c(T))^2}{|\mathcal{T}|}}, \qquad (10)$$

where the terrain descriptor segment $T_{terrain}$ is the queried time series segment T stripped of the proprioceptive measurements; and $c(T)$ is its ground truth traversal cost computed computed over the testing data using (4).

The dataset is organized into six sequences called trails, where each trail corresponds to one terrain. The individual segments or non-time series points in each trail are ordered as the robot has experienced them. Therefore, the dataset mimics the order of data in incremental learning. The learning set is created as the first two-thirds of each trail, and the last third is reserved for testing with regards to (9) and (10).

3   Time Series Learning Growing Neural Gas

A Growing Neural Gas (GNG) scheme [7] is employed to learn a classifier of terrain traversal time series segments. The baseline non-time series classifiers are also learned using this scheme, i.e., they are considered to be time series with one point. For the sake of brevity, the herein presented description of the GNG is limited to the use of the GNG in the classification scheme, which is summarized in Algorithm 1. We kindly refer the reader to [7] or [6] for a detailed description of the GNG algorithm.

The herein reported results are based on the Online Semi-Supervised Multi-Channel Growing Neural Gas (OSSMGNG) [17]. Similarly to the OSSMGNG, the proposed approach utilizes separate GNG structures learned for each of the particular classes. However, the dataset presented in Sect. 2 comprises time series segments with a fixed size, and there is no need to map unknown dimensions as in [17]. Thus, we employ the Euclidean $L2$-norm to compute the distance between the time series segments, because unlike the therein used DTW scheme, the Euclidean norm can be computed in $\mathcal{O}(d)$, where d is the data dimensionality. In the case when some of the dimensions of the segment are missing, i.e., during the inference, the distance is computed using only the known dimensions.

The GNG is updated in supervised way, i.e., the time series segment is accompanied by the terrain label, and the respective class network is updated with $\epsilon_{winner} = 0.1$, $\epsilon_{neighbor} = 0.01$, $\alpha_{split} = 0.5$, $\alpha_{error} = 0.99$, $a_{max} = 50$, and $\lambda = 30$, see **Supervised Update** procedure in Algorithm 1. Unlabeled segments are classified by finding the class of its nearest neighbor among nodes from all the GNGs (**Classify** procedure in Algorithm 1).

Finally, the learned classifier is used to infer missing dimensions of the segment $T_{terrain}$ using the 1-NN approach as follows. First, $T_{terrain}$ is classified; then, the nearest neuron within the respective GNG class is found, and the missing dimensions are determined from its reference vector. Further, the mechanism is used to predict the traversal costs over the observed terrain by inferring

---

Algorithm 1: Time series learning Growing neural gas

▶ **Supervised Update** $(T, label, \mathcal{G})$

Input: T – time series segment, $label$ – segment label, $\mathcal{G}$ - set of GNG models
for the individual terrain classes

1 $G \leftarrow \mathcal{G}[label]$ `// Select the respective GNG model for` $label$.
2 update(G, T) `// Update` G `using the time series segment measurement` T.

▶ **Classify** $(T, \mathcal{G})$

Input: T – time series segment, $\mathcal{G}$ - set of GNG models for the individual
terrain classes

1 $\mathcal{N} \leftarrow$ all_neurons$(\mathcal{G})$ `// Get all neurons in all GNG models.`
2 $neighbor \leftarrow$ nearest$(\mathcal{N}, T)$ `// Find 1-NN neuron to` T `among` $\mathcal{N}$.
3 **return** $label(neighbor)$ `// Report the label of the neighbor's GNG.`

▶ **Inference** $(T_{terrain}, \mathcal{G})$

Input: $T_{terrain}$ – time series segment stripped of cost measurements, $\mathcal{G}$ - set of
GNG models for the individual terrain classes

1 $label \leftarrow$ classify$(T_{terrain}, \mathcal{G})$ `// Label` $T_{terrain}$ `ignoring power dimension.`
2 $neighbor \leftarrow$ nearest$(\mathcal{G}[label], T_{terrain})$ `// Find nearest neuron in` $label$ `GNG.`
3 **return** $cost(neighbor)$ `// Report the missing cost dimension of` $neighbor$.

---

the missing aggregate cost dimension and then applying (6) or (8), respectively,
to compute the cost. The procedure is denoted **Inference** in Algorithm 1.

4   Results

We report on the achieved results on time series segment classification and traversal cost inference using the time series segment dataset described in Sect. 2. Two particular setups are considered as follows: 10 s segments with the aggregate costs denoted according to the number of subsampled points as *time series* 100, 50, 25, or 5, i.e., the segments are subsampled with 10, 5, 2.5, and 0.5 Hz, respectively; and the baseline non-time series setup with the mean power over the 10 s period is denoted *mean value*. In the following parts, we report on the terrain classification, cost prediction, and a short discussion of the results.

4.1   Terrain Classification

The classification correctness computed according to (9) is reported in Table 1. The best classification is achieved using the *time series* segments with 25 points and the respective confusion matrix is presented in Table 2. The *time series* segment with 5 points and the baseline non-time series *mean value* setup provide the worst performance among the evaluated classifiers. However, even the worst classifiers may achieve satisfiable performance over specific terrains. For example, *time series* with 5 points is the most precise classifier of *cubes covered with turf*.

Table 1. Classification correctness

Human Label	Mean value	Time series with # pts			
	(Baseline)	5	25	50	100
flat	63.60%	58.45%	84.19%	75.73%	71.69%
cubes	52.83%	51.34%	57.61%	57.91%	57.31%
cubes covered with black	75.21%	67.64%	79.83%	80.25%	78.99%
black	87.18%	84.37%	90.00%	93.43%	92.50%
turf	76.44%	85.09%	98.07%	98.55%	98.07%
cubes covered with turf	57.65%	81.08%	61.26%	60.36%	58.55%
All	69.47%	69.33%	78.97%	78.30%	76.81%

Table 2. Classification confusion matrix for the segments with the *time series* subsampled to 25 points

Human Label	Predicted Label					
	flat	*cubes covered with black*	*cubes*	*black*	*turf*	*cubes covered with turf*
flat	229	0	32	11	0	0
cubes	24	193	114	4	0	0
cubes covered with black	39	2	190	7	0	0
black	32	0	0	288	0	0
turf	0	0	0	0	204	4
cubes covered with turf	0	0	0	1	43	68

Overall, the most of the confusion between the individual terrains appear to be between the visually similar terrains such as *turf* and *cubes covered with turf*, or between the terrains that might exhibit similar shape property or proprioceptive experience. In Fig. 2, the terrain classification is projected onto the selected terrains. Notably, a portion of the terrains that are considered hard to traverse based on human expertise is classified as *flat*, suggesting that the human labels may not be consistent with the robot proprioceptive experience.

4.2   Traversal Cost Prediction

The performance of the traversal cost prediction evaluated using RMSE computed according to (10) is reported in Table 3. The results are similar to the classification since the *time series* with 25 points provides the best prediction, and the *time series* with 5 points provides the worst performance. It is interesting to note that except *flat*, the highest RMSE is over the terrain types *black* and *cubes covered with black* with the relatively high classification correctness as reported in Table 1.

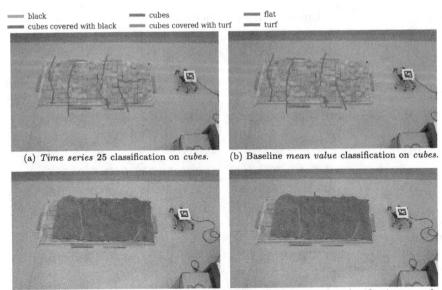

black   cubes   flat
cubes covered with black   cubes covered with turf   turf

(a) *Time series* 25 classification on *cubes*.   (b) Baseline *mean value* classification on *cubes*.

(c) *Time series* 25 classification on *cubes covered* (d) Baseline *mean value* classification on *cubes with turf*.   *covered with turf*.

Fig. 2. Terrain classification projected over the selected terrains.

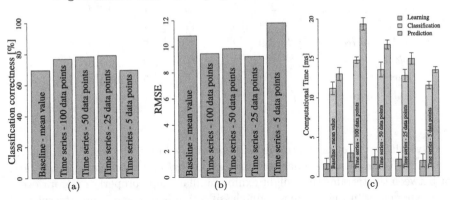

Fig. 3. Overall results for the (a) classification correctness, (b) RMSE of the traversal cost prediction, and (c) the measured execution wall time per one time series segment or non-time series data point using the Intel i5-4460 CPU, 16 GB memory, where the reported values are means of 10 runs.

4.3 Discussion

The results, aggregated in Figs. 3a and 3b, suggest that the *time series* segments subsampled with 25 points learn better classifiers and predictors than both the most dense *time series* with 100 points and the baseline non-time series *mean values*. According to the wall execution times reported in Fig. 3c, the subsampled

Table 3. Traversal cost prediction RMSE

Human Label	Mean value	Time series with # pts			
	(Baseline)	5	25	50	100
flat	14.43	14.96	11.63	12.65	10.78
cubes	7.91	8.02	7.90	8.36	8.47
cubes covered with black	12.06	10.77	7.89	9.18	8.42
black	12.68	16.47	11.78	12.09	12.70
turf	5.12	4.95	4.79	5.07	4.78
cubes covered with turf	6.44	5.62	6.19	6.22	5.89
All	10.82	11.77	9.21	9.83	9.46

time series are less computationally demanding than the *time series* with 100 points, but they are more demanding than the baseline non-time series *mean values*.

Finally, the reported confusion between the individual terrains in Table 2, and the high RMSE in Table 3 suggest that each terrain label may comprise multiple different robot proprioceptive experience. Therefore, human labels might not be sufficiently descriptive; they are downright misleading. The found observations thus support the results previously reported in [4].

5   Conclusion

In this paper, we investigate the time series representation of the hexapod walking robot terrain traversal dataset. A Growing Neural Gas (GNG) schema is used to classify the traversed terrains and predict energy-based traversal cost. The baseline non-time series setup is outperformed by the proposed time series of terrain descriptors and robot proprioception characterized as the aggregate traversal cost when it is subsampled with at least 2.5 Hz. Overall, the time series subsampled with 2.5 Hz learn the best classifiers and cost predictors among the evaluated classifiers. Moreover, they provide better computational efficiency than time series sampled with higher frequencies, albeit the baseline non-time series method is the fastest one. Finally, the herein presented results also support the previous conclusion that human terrain labels might be misleading when reasoning about the robot traversal experience.

Acknowledgments. The presented work has been supported under the OP VVV funded project CZ.02.1.01/0.0/0.0/16_019/0000765 "Research Center for Informatics". The support under grant No. SGS19/176/OHK3/3T/13 to Miloš Prágr is also gratefully acknowledged.

References

1. Belter, D., Wietrzykowski, J., Skrzypczyński, P.: Employing natural terrain semantics in motion planning for a multi-legged robot. J. Intel. Rob. Syst. **93**(3), 723–743 (2018). https://doi.org/10.1007/s10846-018-0865-x
2. Brown, D., Webster, G.: Now a stationary research platform, NASA's mars rover spirit starts a new chapter in red planet scientific studies. NASA Press Release (2010)
3. Faigl, J., Čížek, P.: Adaptive locomotion control of hexapod walking robot for traversing rough terrains with position feedback only. Rob. Auton. Syst. **116**, 136–147 (2019). https://doi.org/10.1016/j.robot.2019.03.008
4. Faigl, J., Prágr, M.: On unsupervised learning of traversal cost and terrain types identification using self-organizing maps. In: International Conference on Artificial Neural Networks (ICANN), pp. 654–668 (2019). https://doi.org/10.1007/978-3-030-30487-4_50
5. Faigl, J., Prágr, M.: Incremental traversability assessment learning using growing neural gas algorithm. In: Advances in Self-Organizing Maps, Learning Vector Quantization, Clustering and Data Visualization, pp. 166–176 (2020). https://doi.org/10.1007/978-3-030-19642-4_17
6. Fišer, D., Faigl, J., Kulich, M.: Growing neural gas efficiently. Neurocomputing **104**, 72–82 (2013). https://doi.org/10.1016/j.neucom.2012.10.004
7. Fritzke, B.: A growing neural gas network learns topologies. In: Neural Information Processing Systems (NIPS), pp. 625–632. MIT Press (1994)
8. Giguere, P., Dudek, G.: Clustering sensor data for terrain identification using a windowless algorithm. In: Robotics: Science and Systems (RSS). Robotics: Science and Systems Foundation (2008). https://doi.org/10.15607/RSS.2008.IV.004
9. Kampouraki, A., Manis, G., Nikou, C.: Heartbeat time series classification with support vector machines. IEEE Trans. Inf. Technol. Biomed. **13**(4), 512–518 (2009). https://doi.org/10.1109/TITB.2008.2003323
10. Keogh, E., Kasetty, S.: On the need for time series data mining benchmarks: a survey and empirical demonstration. Data Min. Knowl. Disc. **7**(4), 349–371 (2003). https://doi.org/10.1023/A:1024988512476
11. Kohonen, T.: Self-organizing Maps. Springer, Heidelberg (2001). https://doi.org/10.1007/978-3-642-56927-2
12. Kottege, N., Parkinson, C., Moghadam, P., Elfes, A., Singh, S.P.N.: Energetics-informed hexapod gait transitions across terrains. In: IEEE International Conference on Robotics and Automation (ICRA), pp. 5140–5147 (2015). https://doi.org/10.1109/ICRA.2015.7139915
13. Kragh, M., et al.: Object detection and terrain classification in agricultural fields using 3D lidar data. ICVS 2015. LNCS, vol. 9163, pp. 188–197. Springer, Cham (2015). https://doi.org/10.1007/978-3-319-20904-3_18
14. Lines, J., Davis, L.M., Hills, J., Bagnall, A.: A shapelet transform for time series classification. In: International Conference on Knowledge Discovery and Data Mining (SIGKDD), pp. 289–297. ACM (2012). https://doi.org/10.1145/2339530.2339579
15. McGhee, R.B., Frank, A.A.: On the stability properties of quadruped creeping gaits. Math. Biosci. **3**, 331–351 (1968). https://doi.org/10.1016/0025-5564(68)90090-4
16. Müller, M., et al.: Dynamic time warping. Information Retrieval for Music and Motion, pp. 69–84. Springer, Heidelberg (2007). https://doi.org/10.1007/978-3-540-74048-3_4

17. Nooralishahi, P., Seera, M., Loo, C.K.: Online semi-supervised multi-channel time series classifier based on growing neural gas. Neural Comput. Appl. **28**(11), 3491–3505 (2016). https://doi.org/10.1007/s00521-016-2247-2

18. Prágr, M., Faigl, J.: Benchmarking incremental regressors in traversal cost assessment. In: International Conference on Artificial Neural Networks (ICANN), pp. 685–697 (2019). https://doi.org/10.1007/978-3-030-30487-4_52

19. Prágr, M., Čížek, P., Bayer, J., Faigl, J.: Online incremental learning of the terrain traversal cost in autonomous exploration. In: Robotics: Science and Systems (RSS), vol. 15 (2019). https://doi.org/10.15607/RSS.2019.XV.040

20. Prágr, M., Čížek, P., Faigl, J.: Cost of transport estimation for legged robot based on terrain features inference from aerial scan. In: IEEE/RSJ International Conference on Intelligent Robots and Systems (IROS), pp. 1745–1750. IEEE (2018). https://doi.org/10.1109/IROS.2018.8593374

21. Prágr, M., Čížek, P., Faigl, J.: Incremental learning of traversability cost for aerial reconnaissance support to ground units. In: Mazal, J. (ed.) MESAS 2018. LNCS, vol. 11472, pp. 412–421. Springer, Cham (2019). https://doi.org/10.1007/978-3-030-14984-0_30

22. Rothrock, B., Kennedy, R., Cunningham, C., Papon, J., Heverly, M., Ono, M.: SPOC: deep learning-based terrain classification for mars rover missions. In: AIAA SPACE 2016. American Institute of Aeronautics and Astronautics (2016). https://doi.org/10.2514/6.2016-5539

23. Shen, F., Yu, H., Sakurai, K., Hasegawa, O.: An incremental online semi-supervised active learning algorithm based on self-organizing incremental neural network. Neural Comput. Appl. **20**(7), 1061–1074 (2011). https://doi.org/10.1007/s00521-010-0428-y

24. Stelzer, A., Hirschmüller, H., Görner, M.: Stereo-vision-based navigation of a six-legged walking robot in unknown rough terrain. Int. J. Robot. Res. **31**(4), 381–402 (2012). https://doi.org/10.1177/0278364911435161

25. Wei, L., Keogh, E.: Semi-supervised time series classification. In: International Conference on Knowledge Discovery and Data Mining (SIGKDD), pp. 748–753. ACM (2006). https://doi.org/10.1145/1150402.1150498

26. Xi, X., Keogh, E., Shelton, C., Wei, L., Ratanamahatana, C.A.: Fast time series classification using numerosity reduction. In: International Conference on Machine Learning (ICML), pp. 1033–1040. ACM (2006). https://doi.org/10.1145/1143844.1143974

27. Zheng, Y., et al.: Time series classification using multi-channels deep convolutional neural networks. WAIM 2014. LNCS, vol. 8485, pp. 298–310. Springer, Cham (2014). https://doi.org/10.1007/978-3-319-08010-9_33

Simulation of the Guidance and Control Systems for Underactuated Vessels

Silvia Donnarumma[✉], Massimo Figari, Michele Martelli, and Raphael Zaccone

Department of Electrical, Electronics and Telecommunication Engineering and Naval Architecture (DITEN), University of Genoa, 16145 Genoa, Italy
donnarumma@dime.unige.it, {massimo.figari,michele.martelli, raphael.zaccone}@unige.it

Abstract. Intelligent and/or autonomous vehicle technologies are rapidly growing to meet the needs of marine safety and transport efficiency. One of the requirements to manage autonomous vehicles includes the integration between route planning and automatic motion control. In the authors' opinion, the latter could be sketched in three different layers: obstacle detection, planning and actuation. Moreover, the three layers should be able to interact in real-time. Dealing with such a challenging task, one of the best techniques to develop and test the logic is the use of the time-domain simulation. In the present work, a simulation model, integrating a path planning algorithm in the presence of obstacles with a track keeping controller, is developed. The path planning is based on a modified version of the Rapidly-exploring Random Tree (RRT*) algorithm. The track keeping is based on the Line-of-Sight (LOS) waypoints navigation for underactuated vessels. To achieve more reliable results, a detailed ship simulation model is used as a benchmark. Different scenarios and navigation modes are successfully tested, and the results are presented and analysed.

Keywords: Autonomous vessels · Simulation · Track keeping · Collision avoidance

1 Introduction

Modern ships are attracting attention by the research community owing to the increased on-board electronic devices and computational resources, likewise recently occurred for autonomous vehicles such as cars, planes, helicopters, and trains [1].

Technological breakthroughs arising from dynamic positioning applications have shown that it is possible to operate a vessel autonomously in a restricted area, under the supervision of on-board personnel, [2, 3]. Simultaneously, on-shore, the goals subsequently achieved with automotive applications have brought benefits to the driving comfort of vehicles. Similarly, the autonomous industry is now able to provide navigation support that can suggest the best instructions to the commander to cross crowded

© Springer Nature Switzerland AG 2020
J. Mazal et al. (Eds.): MESAS 2019, LNCS 11995, pp. 108–119, 2020.
https://doi.org/10.1007/978-3-030-43890-6_9

navigation areas or to take charge of the management of the vehicle under his supervision. The possibility of integrating these solutions into the navigation system under standard conditions, thanks to the available technological support, would allow masters to have a system capable of solving instantly very complex optimization problems. Safe navigation and obstacle avoidance are some of the most relevant challenges on which research on autonomous ships is based.

Nowadays, attention on crew training and emergency procedures are milestones for reducing the risk of accidents at sea. Standards regulating navigation in crowed areas are reported in COLREGS [4], but the success of the manoeuvres depends on both environmental and human factors. The collision avoidance has always been a crucial topic in the marine scientific community, the work by Skjong [6] presents a differential formulation of the collision avoidance problem, together with an algorithm to compute the solution by numeric integration. Most of the marine applications are based on classic heuristic algorithms, such as genetic algorithms (GA) [7–9]. Hasegawa in [10] presents a different approach based on potential field methods. More recently, the rapidly-exploring random tree (RRT) algorithm, and its optimizing version RRT* have been studied into details. RRT algorithm has been introduced by LaValle & Kuffner [11], who analyze its performances on various applications. In particular, [12] compares RRT to dynamic programming in planning feasible (non-optimal) trajectories. The effectiveness of these algorithms is analyzed in [5], together with reference herein, and a new "ad hoc" path planning methodology is proposed. The core of the presented algorithm is indeed to use the computational power available in every ICT device to help the bridge operators in potentially dangerous situations, without taking any action, yet acting as a virtual bridge assistant that suggests the correct manoeuvre.

On the other hand, developing new control systems able to steer vessels under the supervision of the commander is the subject of marine engineering research since the early 1900s, [13]. As previously mentioned, the coupling of the strong results coming from the automotive industry together with the great results for station keeping, sparked the interest of the sector in the possibility of providing devices able to both suggest or actuate command directly. Such devices can limit stress in some short term demanding operations or, maybe even more, long term standard operations. For such a reason, guidance systems have been developed together with the increasing diffusion of inertial navigation systems [14]. As proposed in [15], and reference herein, guidance is, indeed, of crucial importance for autonomous ships and demands for the use of different motion models [16–19]. A well-known approach is based on selecting a sequence of waypoints and constructs the desired path as the sum of the successive straight lines and [20] provides solutions able to achieve smoothing transitions between waypoint by relaxing the turning problem. In [15, 21] authors show results from guidance and control systems designed to be robustly integrated into a complex controller orchestra able to steer an underactuated vessel from blue to narrow water.

This paper aims to present results from the methodologies implemented in order to improve ship safety, preventing grounding and collision and, at the same time, to support navigation. Indeed, the presented simulation platform was initially developed trying to solve two independent problems: the evaluation of the best evasive route and the development of a control system able to allow an under-actuated vehicle to maintain a predetermined trajectory.

In the present case study results from the integration of the, already implemented, collision avoidance together with the, already tested, path following are presented in a unique simulation platform. In particular, the presented work deals with a vessel, fitted with standard propulsion configuration (two propellers with rudders and a bow thruster). The simulator adopted for the integration with the whole controller is a multi-physics platform, able to represent the dynamics of a ship in three degrees of freedom, taking into account for the entire propulsion system together with automation. Detailed information of each sub-module can be found in [22, 23].

2   Simulation Platform

In this section, the motion controller structure is presented. In particular, Fig. 1 shows a flow-chart of the system. Analyzing the diagram from the top there are the inputs provided by the commander: the waypoints that identify the desired manoeuvre. At each time the collision avoidance system checks for possible obstacles. If no collision is possible, the waypoints are directly sent to the navigation system that translates the waypoints into heading requirements to ensure the vessel can regain course within a certain user-defined length, [5]. Otherwise, the system calculates an evasive manoeuvre that provides for the subsequent return into the course by generating new waypoints that are sent to the guidance system. On the bottom of the figure, the controller converts the course requirements signals into rudder angles and bow-thruster commands, in accordance with [15].

Then, the purpose of a marine automatic collision avoidance system is to detect the obstacles, plan and, perhaps, actuate the evasive manoeuvre. A detection system is able to identify the presence of obstacles in the environment and rapidly update the path by providing a set of waypoints to safely guide the ship through the target, following COLREG. The planned manoeuvre is represented in the following form:

$$P_k = (x_k, y_k), \qquad k = 0, \ldots, N \qquad (1)$$

where P_k is the kth waypoint, and $0, N$ represent the start and the target point, respectively. The motion planning system takes into account the manoeuvring capabilities of the ship, in order to provide a feasible evasive path.

The guidance system is based on the well-known *line-of-sight* algorithm, modified in accordance with [15]. Indeed, the proposed controller deals with 2 degrees of freedom and use propellers and rudders in autopilot mode with the possibility of also activating the bow thruster in a *drift-free track* condition. A proportional-integral-derivative (PID) controller has been synthesized similar to the one proposed in [21] fed with tracking error:

$$e_\psi = \psi - \psi_{des} \qquad (2)$$

where ψ is the actual vessel heading and ψ_{des} is the desired heading.

Eventually, the switching or concurrent use of bow-thruster and rudders for course keeping is subject to a left-over speed law that allows propulsion to be used in high-efficiency conditions.

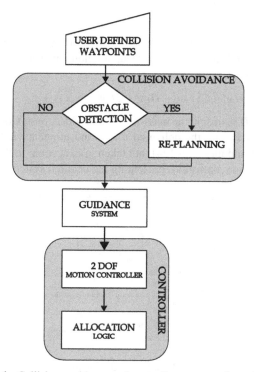

Fig. 1. Collision avoidance and controller structure flow-chart.

2.1 Ship Modeling

In this section, the several models used to identify the dynamic behaviour of all the main ship subsystem are reported.

2.1.1 Kinematics

Let $\boldsymbol{\eta} := [x, y, \psi]^T \in \mathbb{R}^3$ be the array expressing the position and orientation of the vessel with respect to the Earth-Fixed Frame, and let $\boldsymbol{v} := [u, v, r]^T \in \mathbb{R}^3$ be the array containing the linear and angular velocity components with respect to the Body-Fixed basis. The kinematic relation between $\boldsymbol{\eta}$ and $\boldsymbol{v}$ is given by the following expressions [20]:

$$\dot{\boldsymbol{\eta}} = \boldsymbol{R}(\psi)\boldsymbol{v}, \qquad \boldsymbol{R}(\psi) = \begin{pmatrix} \cos\psi & -\sin\psi & 0 \\ \sin\psi & \cos\psi & 0 \\ 0 & 0 & 1 \end{pmatrix} \qquad (3)$$

2.1.2 Dynamics

The notation $\tau := [X, Y, N]^T \in \mathbb{R}^3$ is introduced for the array containing the components of longitudinal and lateral forces and their resultant moment. The ship motion equations are:

$$M\dot{v} + C(v)v + D_0 v + D(v)v = \tau_D + \tau_E \tag{4}$$

Where M, C and D represent the mass-inertia and added mass, Coriolis and damping matrices respectively. τ_D are the delivered forces and moments and τ_E represent the environmental forces and moments [24], not taken in to account in this case.

The whole simulation platform representing the detailed system is shown in Fig. 2.

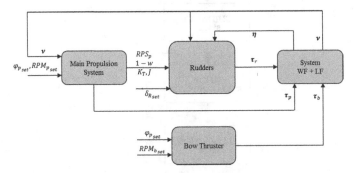

Fig. 2. Detailed simulation model

The main elements of the propulsion plant are two main engines, two gearboxes, two controllable pitch propellers and one controllable pitch bow-thruster. The ship is equipped with two independent shaft lines, the main elements of the propulsion plant are two main engines, two gearboxes, and two controllable pitch propellers, the simulation blocks that identify one shaft line is reported in Fig. 3. One controllable pitch bow-thruster and two rudders constitute the manoeuvring devices.

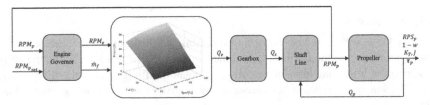

Fig. 3. Propulsion plant model

2.1.3 Engine

The engine governor computes the fuel flow requirement on the basis of the propeller speed error. It is a PI controller with the following law:

$$\dot{m}^r_f = K_{P_{RPM}} e_{RPM} + \int_0^t K_{I_{RPM}} e_{RPM}(\xi)d\xi \tag{5}$$

Where $e_{RPM} = \frac{100}{N_{MAX}}(N_e^r - RN_s^r)$ is the error from the setpoint coming from the controller and $K_{P_{RPM}}$ and $K_{I_{RPM}}$ are the constant coefficients of the regulator. Then, the fuel flow is saturated in accordance with the maximum engine torque limits:

$$\dot{m}_f = \begin{cases} \dot{m}_f^r & \dot{m}_f^r < \dot{m}_f^{(max)} \\ \dot{m}_f^{(max)} & otherwise \end{cases} \tag{6}$$

2.1.4 Shaft Line

Equation (7) describes the shaft line dynamics:

$$\frac{d\omega}{dt} = \frac{Q_E(t) - Q_p(t) - Q_f(t)}{I_e + I_g + I_s + I_p} \tag{7}$$

where $I_e + I_g + I_s + I_p$ represent the engine, gear, shaft and propeller rotational inertia; Q_E, Q_P and Q_f are the engine, propeller and frictional torque, respectively. In order to catch the asymmetric behaviour of a twin-screw ship, the dynamics of the two shaft lines have been implemented separately.

2.1.5 Propeller

In literature, several numerical methods based, for instance, on the potential approach or R.A.N.S.E. solvers, have been proposed to predict propeller hydrodynamic loads. Unfortunately, due to their long computational time, these methods are not suitable to be applied in the context of a time-domain simulator like the one described in the present work. Therefore, the hydrodynamic forces, both for propeller and bow thruster, have been evaluated through a quasi-steady-state methodology based on the propeller open water tests. These tests provide an open water diagram, which allows the evaluation of the thrust coefficient K_T and torque coefficient K_Q.

For controllable pitch propellers, these coefficients depend on the advance coefficient J and from the blade angle φ:

$$K_T = \frac{T}{\rho n^2 D^4}, \quad K_Q = \frac{Q}{\rho n^2 D^5} \tag{8}$$

2.1.6 Rudder

For the same reasons as before, also in this case the rudder forces have been evaluated through a quasi-static-methodology, using lift and drag coefficients C_L and C_D. In addition, the complex interaction between rudder and propeller has been taken into account using the approach described in [25].

2.2 RRT* Algorithm

This section presents a brief overview of the RRT algorithm application to ship motion control. RRT [11] is a space-exploring algorithm that generates a tree of feasible paths, that explore the space trying to reach all the feasible configurations from a starting point. RRT can take into account holonomic and non-holonomic constraints.

The algorithm builds a tree that is composed of a set of nodes and a set of edges E, growing it for a fixed number of iterations. First, the algorithm generates a new random position in the domain, then finds the node that is nearest to it.

A new node is then generated in accordance with the constraints, moving by a fixed step from the nearest node in the direction of the new random position.

The RRT algorithm does not perform any optimization neither computes any cost or return function, i.e. it does not provide any ranking criterion for the solutions, in favour of the computation speed. A heuristic variant of the RRT, named RRT*, is based on the RRT algorithm, has some additional steps in order to heuristically drive the tree growth to minimize a cost function. In particular, two separate actions, both aiming to locally drive the growth through optimality, take place before the new node is added, to select his parent and child nodes in accordance to the cost function.

The selection of a proper cost function allows, thus controlling the trajectories generated by the algorithm [5]. Note that, unlike in the RRT, an increase in the number of iterations in RRT* leads to better solutions.

In the proposed approach, constraints are set to generate collision free trajectories respecting the kinematic limits of the ship [26]. In particular, the trajectories are required to keep a minimum distance from the obstacles and the other ships: the threshold distance needs to be properly selected, and should also take into account the uncertainties coming from the obstacle localization system, as well as the possible overshoots from the waypoints due to the motion control and actuation. Further details and a potential implementation of COLREGs can be found in [27].

2.3 Motion Control

As briefly introduced in Sect. 1, the motion control is based on two independent controllers that provide for both the vessel heading and the speed. In such a way, the sway and the yaw are controlled, based on the algorithm known as line-of-sight approach, with the *drift-free track* while the surge is indirectly controlled through the *speed-pilot*. The integrated controller orchestra is detailed in [15].

In particular, both the controller structures are PID type and the coefficient synthesis has been carried out by using optimization algorithms based on linear matrix inequalities (LMI) technique, [21].

3 Simulation Results

This section compares results from the simulations of the proposed navigation system with and without the collision avoidance system. Such simulations also take into account the presence of moderate environmental disturbances by the action of a wind coming from the east with an average speed of 10 knots. In Figs. 4 and 6 the blue curves represent the trajectory of the ship navigating autonomously via the blue markers, while the red curve represents an obstacle that heads over to the trajectory of the ship at a constant speed. In Figs. 5 and 7 the blue curve represents the distance of the ship from the obstacle and the red dashed curve is the safety distance. All the quantities shown are dimensionless in ship lengths.

As can be seen in Fig. 4, the autonomous navigation system crosses all the required waypoints without taking into account the presence of other units in the surrounding environment. In Fig. 5, the distance from the obstacle overlaps the limits reaching zero. Figure 6 shows the effects of collision avoidance. In fact, the system replaces the user-defined requirements with the appropriate commands able to avoid the collision and, actually, by handling the path planning of the vehicle during the obstacle overing. Eventually, user-defined waypoints back into the navigation system after the obstacle has been overcome. Indeed, the ship remains to its original course. In this case, it can be seen in Fig. 7 that the distance from the obstacle remains, for the entire manoeuvre, within the safety domain.

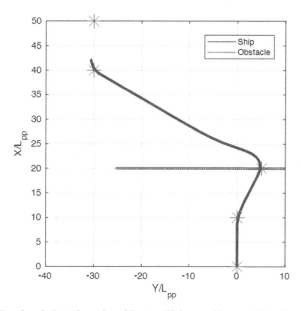

Fig. 4. Vessel and obstacle paths without collision avoidance. (Color figure online)

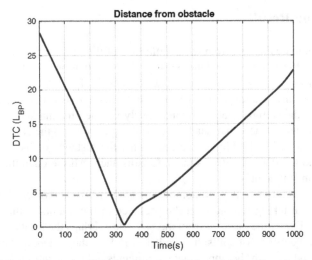

Fig. 5. Vessel distance from the obstacle when the collision avoidance is not active. (Color figure online)

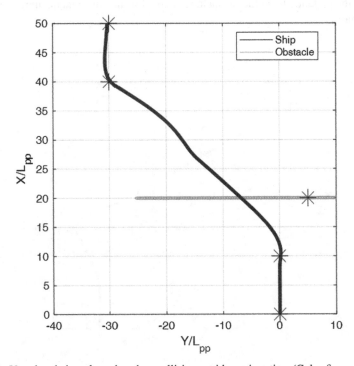

Fig. 6. Vessel and obstacle paths when collision avoidance is active. (Color figure online)

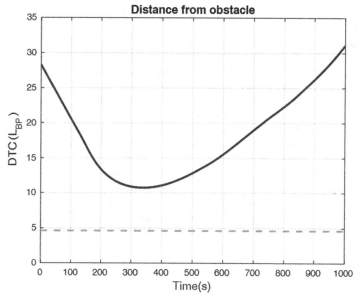

Fig. 7. Vessel distance from the obstacle when the collision avoidance is active. (Color figure online)

4 Conclusions

The integration of a collision avoidance logic together with a guidance system able to allows safe autonomous navigation has been described, and results are critically compared. At this stage the proposed avoidance methodology can deal in real-time in case of complex scenarios, taking into account for environmental disturbances, albeit limited. Optimization problems are suitable in terms of computational time for the relatively slow ship dynamics and longe distances. The novelty with respect to references can be evaluated in the automatic return to the original course, without human actions. Moreover, the robustness of each sub-system of the proposed structure has been validated in both stand-alone and orchestral mode by giving a large multi-purpose domain to the system. Indeed, the user can act in each part of the structure by using the outputs of each block as suggestions, and without diverging the algorithms. Further research will concern the validation of the model in more complex scenarios and the integration in the algorithm of information about the environmental disturbances will be crucial part of the path replanning.

References

1. Stateczny, A., Burdziakowski, P.: Universal autonomous control and management system for multipurpose unmanned surface vessel. Pol. Marit. Res. **26**, 30–39 (2018)
2. Faÿ, H.: Dynamic Positioning Systems: Principles, Design, and Applications. OPHRYS (1990)

3. Sorensen, A.J.: A survey of dynamic positioning control systems. Annu. Rev. Control **35**, 123–136 (2011)
4. COLREGS - International Regulations for Preventing Collisions at Sea
5. Zaccone, R., Martelli, M.: A random sampling based algorithm for ship path planning with obstacles. In: Proceedings of the International Ship Control Systems Symposium (iSCSS), 2–4 October 2018. http://doi.org/10.24868/issn.2631-8741.2018.018
6. Skjong, R., Mjelde, K.M.: Optimal evasive manoeuvre for a ship in an environment of fixed installations and other ships. Model. Ident. Control **3**, 211–222 (1982)
7. Ito, M., Zhnng, F., Yoshida, N.: Collision avoidance control of the ship with a genetic algorithm. In: Proceedings of the 1999 IEEE International Conference on Control Applications, vol. 2, pp. 1791–1796. IEEE (1999)
8. Smierzchalski, R., Michalewicz, Z.: Modelling of ship trajectory in collision situations by an evolutionary algorithm. IEEE Trans. Evol. Comput. **4**(3), 227–241 (2000)
9. Alvarez, A., Caiti, A., Onken, R.: Evolutionary path planning for autonomous underwater vehicles in a variable ocean. IEEE J. Oceanic Eng. **29**(2), 418–429 (2004)
10. Hasegawa, K., Fukuto, J., Miyake, R., Yamazaki, M.: An intelligent ship handling simulator with automatic collision avoidance function of target ships. In: Proceedings of INSLC 2017 (2012)
11. LaValle, S.M., Kuffner Jr., J.J.: Rapidly-exploring random trees: progress and prospects. In: 4th Workshop on the Algorithmic Foundations of Robotics; Algorithmic and Computational Robotics, New Directions, Hanover, NH, pp. 293–308 (2000)
12. LaValle, S.M.: From dynamic programming to RRTs: algorithmic design of feasible trajectories. In: Bicchi, A., Prattichizzo, D., Christensen, H.I. (eds.) Control Problems in Robotics, pp. 19–37. Springer, Heidelberg (2003). https://doi.org/10.1007/3-540-36224-X_2
13. "Now – The Automatic Pilot" Popular Science Monthly, February 1930, p. 22
14. Draper, C.: Control, navigation, and guidance. IEEE Control Syst. Mag. **1**, 4–17 (1981)
15. Alessandri, A., Donnarumma, S., Martelli, M., Vignolo, S.: Motion control for autonomous navigation in blue and narrow waters using switched controllers. J. Mar. Sci. Eng. JSME **7**(6). https://doi.org/10.3390/jmse7060196
16. Rauch, H.E.: Autonomous control reconfiguration. IEEE Control Syst. Mag. **15**, 37–48 (1995)
17. Lekkas, A., Fossen, T.: Integral LOS path following for curved paths based on a monotone vubic Hermite spline parametrization. IEEE Trans. Control Syst. Technol. **22**, 2287–2301 (2014)
18. Fossen, T., Pettersen, K.: On uniform semiglobal exponential stability (USGES) of proportional line-of-sight guidance laws. Automatica **50**, 2912–2917 (2014)
19. Paliotta, C., Lefeber, E., Pettersen, K.Y., Pinto, J., Costa, M.: de Figueiredo Borges de Sousa, J.T.: Trajectory tracking and path following for underactuated marine vehicles. IEEE Trans. Control Syst. Technol. **27**(4), 1423–1437 (2019)
20. Fossen, T.: Marine Control Systems. Marine Cybernetics, Trondheim (2002)
21. Alessandri, A., et al.: System control design of autopilot and speed pilot for a patrol vessel by using LMIs. In: Soares, C.G., Dejhalla, R., Pavletić, D. (eds.) Proceedings 16th International Congress of the International Maritime Association of the Mediterranean. CRC Press, pp. 577–584 (2015)
22. Alessandri, A., et al.: Dynamic positioning system of a vessel with conventional propulsion configuration: Modeling and simulation (2015) Maritime Technology and Engineering - Proceedings of MARTECH 2014: 2nd International Conference on Maritime Technology and Engineering, pp. 725–734
23. Donnarumma, S., Martelli, M., Vignolo, S.: Numerical models for ship dynamic positioning MARINE 2015 - Computational Methods in Marine Engineering VI, pp. 1078–1088 (2015)
24. Martelli, M.: Marine Propulsion Simulation, pp. 1–104. De Gruyter open (2015)

25. Martelli, M., Viviani, M., Altosole, M., Figari, M., Vignolo, S.: Numerical modelling of propulsion, control and ship motions in 6 degrees of freedom. In: Proceedings of the Institution of Mechanical Engineers, Part M: Journal of Engineering for the Maritime Environment, vol. 228, pp. 373–397, November 2014
26. Zaccone, R., Martelli, M.: A collision avoidance algorithm for ship guidance applications. J. Marine Eng. Technol. **19**, 62–75 (2019)
27. Zaccone, R., Martelli, M., Figari, M.: A colreg-compliant ship collision avoidance algorithm. In: 18th European Control Conference, ECC 2019, art. no. 8796207, pp. 2530–2535 (2019)

Automatic Take Off and Landing for UAS Flying in Turbulent Air - An EKF Based Procedure

Caterina Grillo$^{(\boxtimes)}$ and Fernando Montano

Engineering Department, Università degli Studi di Palermo, Viale delle Scienze al Parco d'Orleans, Bld. 8, 90128 Palermo, Italy
caterina.grillo@unipa.it

Abstract. An innovative use of the Extended Kalman Filter (EKF) is proposed to perform automatic take off and landing by the rejection of disturbances due to turbulence.

By using two simultaneously working Extended Kalman Filters, a procedure is implemented: the first filter, by using measurements gathered in turbulent air, estimates wind components; the second one, by using the estimated disturbances, obtains command laws that are able to reject disturbances.

The fundamental innovation of such a procedure consists in the fact that the covariance matrices of process (Q) and measurement (R) noise are not treated as filter design parameters. In this way determined optimal values of the aforementioned matrices lead to robust control laws.

At any moment, during the estimation process, the EKF employs the optimal values of Q and R. To determine these ones, adequate constrains, related to flight path characteristics, are inserted into the algorithm.

In particular, to determine wind components, the constrains are imposed to elevation, altitude and longitudinal position; whereas, to determine control actions, the constrains are imposed to an adequate performance index obtained by using measurements gathered by a small set of sensors (IMU, air data boom and a low rate GPS) in turbulent air.

Keywords: Extended Kalman Filter · Automatic take off/landing · Adaptive control laws

1 Introduction

Over the last two decades, many research activities have been performed in the field of guidance, navigation and control (GNC) of unmanned aircraft.

In the field of navigation, Benzerrouk et al. [1] develop an adaptive system based on different fading techniques to solve the problem of data fusion in denied environments. Different algorithms are proposed and compared, based on the most recent approaches in non-linear filtering during interferences caused by multiple sources or by signal degradation. Both Extended Kalman Filter (EKF) and the last developed Cubature based Kalman Filter (CKF) are implemented to estimate the navigation flight states for UAV.

© Springer Nature Switzerland AG 2020
J. Mazal et al. (Eds.): MESAS 2019, LNCS 11995, pp. 120–129, 2020.
https://doi.org/10.1007/978-3-030-43890-6_10

Despite of the wide set of research papers into the field of GNC for UAVs, estimation of wind components, usually performed for manned aircraft, is not taken into account for these vehicles.

However, because of their low airspeed, light weight and limited power, the performances and stability characteristics of UAS are strongly influenced by external disturbances. The problem is more important during take-off and landing phases because airspeed is very low. Therefore it is mandatory to determine wind components in order to design the flight control system for fully autonomous (from take-off to landing) UAS.

Usually, to eliminate wind effects, the ground speed instead of air speed is employed. In this field, Nelson et al. [2] demonstrate robustness to wind disturbances of vector field guidance.

Brezoescu et al. [3] perform on-line estimation of steady wind and use obtained estimates in path-following.

Liu et al. [4] design a disturbance observer to estimate external winds.

Disturbance Observer Based Control (DOBC) is a very reliable technique for disturbance rejection and it is used in Smith et al. [5].

In [6], to perform a precise path following taking into account the strong effects of turbulence on the planned flight paths of UAVs, authors propose an innovative application of the EKF that simultaneously determines the wind components and the control actions able to reject their effects.

In [7] authors estimate wind components with an innovative metrics for tuning EKF.

In present paper authors, upgrading previous procedure [6, 7], carry out an optimization algorithm to perform a fully autonomous take-off or landing procedure in turbulent air. Such optimization procedure automatically affords to determine both the Process Noise Covariance matrix (Q) and the Measurement Noise Covariance matrix (R).

By using the proposed optimization technique, the Q matrix depends on either the desired flight path or the turbulence characteristics. In fact at any moment, during the estimation process, the EKF employs the optimal values of Q. To determine these ones, adequate constrains, that are related to flight path characteristics, are inserted into the algorithm.

In particular, to determine wind components, the constrains are imposed to elevation, altitude and longitudinal position; whereas, to determine control actions, the constrains are imposed to a performance index.

Since two EKFs are simultaneously employed. The first one, by using instrumental measurements gathered in turbulent air, estimates disturbances. The obtained wind velocity components are inserted into the second EKF. The measurements of the second filter are the desired take-off/landing flight path. The augmented state of such a filter contains the control displacements. In this way, the filter is forced to estimate the unknown displacements of the controls that are necessary to fly the desired flight path.

2 Proposed Procedure

As stated previously, the aim of present work is to permit a fully autonomous UAS to perform a precise take-off or landing path in turbulent air.

The Fig. 1 shows the schematic block of the outlined procedure.

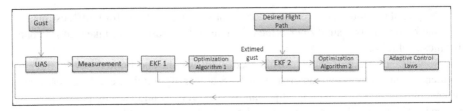

Fig. 1. Schematic block of the proposed procedure

According to Fig. 1 the following steps form the proposed on-line procedure:

1. Estimation of disturbances via a first EKF (wind components determination);
2. Insertion of the estimated wind components into the predictor of a second EKF;
3. Estimation, by using the second EKF, of control positions;
4. Application of the determined control action to the aircraft.

2.1 First EKF: Estimation of Disturbances

An EKF has been tuned up to determine the wind components.

An accurate non-linear mathematical model of the aircraft flying in turbulent air constitute the predictor of such a filter. The classical rigid body equations of motion in body axes have been used [8] by inserting Eq. (1) into the aerodynamic forces and moments.

$$
\begin{aligned}
m\dot{u} &= -mqw - mg\,\sin\vartheta + F_x \\
m\dot{w} &= +mqu - mg\,\cos\vartheta + F_z \\
I_y\dot{q} &= M \\
\dot{\vartheta} &= q + q_g \\
\dot{x} &= u\,\cos\vartheta + w\,\sin\vartheta \\
\dot{h} &= u\,\sin\vartheta - w\,\cos\vartheta
\end{aligned}
\tag{1}
$$

where:

$$
F_x = \tfrac{1}{2}\rho V^2 S C_x
$$

$$
F_z = \tfrac{1}{2}\rho V^2 S C_z
$$

$$
M = \tfrac{1}{2}\rho V^2 S C_m c
\tag{2.1}
$$

$$
T = \tfrac{1}{2}\rho V^2 S C_T
$$

Into (2.1)

$$
\begin{aligned}
C_x &= C_L\,\sin\alpha - C_D\,\cos\alpha + C_T \\
C_z &= -C_L\,\cos\alpha - C_D\,\sin\alpha
\end{aligned}
\tag{2.2}
$$

Into (2.2), aerodynamic coefficients are expressed by:

$$C_L = C_{L_\alpha}\alpha + C_{L_{\dot\alpha}}\dot\alpha\frac{c}{2V_0} + C_{L_q}q\frac{c}{2V_0} + C_{L_\delta}\delta_e$$

$$C_D = C_{D_0} + 0.001625C_L^3 + 0.30061C_L^2 + 0.007446C_L$$

$$C_m = C_{m_0} + C_{m_\alpha}\alpha + C_{m_{\dot\alpha}}\dot\alpha\frac{c}{2V_0} + C_{m_q}q\frac{c}{2V_0} + C_{m_\delta}\delta_e \qquad (2.3)$$

$$C_T = C_{T_V}\frac{V-V_0}{V_0} + C_{T_\delta}\delta_{th}$$

$$C_{T_V} = -3C_{T_e} + C_{T_e}\frac{V_e}{\eta_e}\left(\frac{\partial\eta}{\partial V}\right)_e$$

Because of, as it is well known, the wind components modifies aerodynamic forces and moments the airspeed (V), the angle of attack (α) and the pitch rate q have to be expressed by:

$$V = \sqrt{(u+u_g)^2 + (w+w_g)^2}$$

$$\alpha = atan\frac{w+w_g}{u+u_g}$$

$$q = q + q_q$$

with - (u_g, w_g, q_g) unknown wind components in body axes.

Equation (1) have been modified by inserting the wind components into the aerodynamic forces and moments using Eqs. (2.1, 2.2 and 2.3).

The six aircraft state variables in body axes and the three wind components form the state of the system:

$$X = \left[u, w, q, \vartheta, x_E, h, u_g, w_g, q_g\right]^T \qquad (3)$$

where, ϑ is the elevation angle, x_E and h are the spatial coordinate of the centre of mass and its altitude.

To estimate the disturbance the following equations are inserted into the predictor:

$$\dot u_g = 0$$
$$\dot w_g = 0 \qquad (4)$$
$$\dot q_g = 0$$

The corrector of such a filter employs a set of measurements gathered in turbulent air.

The selected measurement data set is:

$$Z = [V, q, \vartheta, x_E, h]^T$$

Because of no hypothesis has been made about wind dynamics (Eq. (4)) the filter is forced to estimate disturbances by using measurements.

As previous stated, to tune the EKF, an optimization procedure has been implemented. The optimization process is based on the control of prediction errors. Since wind components modifies both flight path and attitude, constrains have been imposed on errors of pitch angle, horizontal displacement and height [7].

Selected constrains have been chosen with the aim of using wind data in the design of a flight control system. Therefore, to perform a precise take-off/landing flight path, it is necessary high precision in attitude determination.

It is important to note that to apply the proposed procedure [7], to estimate wind components simply the initial value of the covariance matrices of initial condition $(\overline{\overline{P}}_0)$, process noise $(\overline{\overline{Q}}_0)$ and measurement noise $(\overline{\overline{R}}_0)$ have to be selected.

Obtained values of $\overline{\overline{Q}}$ and $\overline{\overline{R}}$ are optimal values because they are obtained by the minimization of the covariance matrix of the state estimation error $(\overline{\overline{P}}_k)$.

It is noticeable that, according to the imposed constrains, optimal values of the covariance matrices are linked to: aircraft parameters, wind characteristics and aircraft flight path.

Finally the tuning is fully autonomous and the procedure requires low computational power.

2.2 Second EKF: Estimation of Control Actions

By using Eqs. (2.1, 2.2 and 2.3), at any time the estimated wind components, are inserted into the predictor of the second EKF.

The predictor is constituted by the same UAS non-linear mathematical model of the first predictor but, in this case, aerodynamic coefficient in Eq. 2.3 are expressed as follow:

$$C_L = C_{L_\alpha}\alpha + C_{L_{\dot\alpha}}\dot\alpha\frac{c}{2V_0} + C_{L_q}q\frac{c}{2V_0} + C_{L_\delta}\delta_e + \boldsymbol{C_{L_\delta}\Delta\delta_e}$$

$$C_D = C_{D_0} + 0.001625C_L^3 + 0.30061C_L^2 + 0.007446C_L$$

$$C_m = C_{m_0} + C_{m_\alpha}\alpha + C_{m_{\dot\alpha}}\dot\alpha\frac{c}{2V_0} + C_{m_q}q\frac{c}{2V_0} + C_{m_\delta}\delta_e + \boldsymbol{C_{m_\delta}\Delta\delta_e} \qquad (5)$$

$$C_T = C_{T_V}\frac{V-V_0}{V_0} + C_{T_\delta}\delta_{th} + \boldsymbol{C_{T_\delta}\Delta\delta_{th}}$$

$$C_{T_V} = -3C_{T_e} + C_{T_e}\frac{V_e}{\eta_e}\left(\frac{\partial\eta}{\partial V}\right)_e$$

where $\Delta\delta_e$ and $\Delta\delta_{th}$ are responsible of wind rejection.

To estimate the disturbance rejection the following equations are inserted into the predictor:

$$\Delta\dot\delta_e = 0$$
$$\Delta\dot\delta_{th} = 0 \qquad (6)$$

The corrector of such a filter uses, as measurements, the desired values of the characteristic variables of the take-off/landing path:

$$Z_d = [V, q, \vartheta, x_E, h]^T$$

To determine Q matrix elements, an optimization algorithm has been carried out. Such a procedure is based on a cost function J that is calculated starting from residuals $\left(r_k = z_k - h\left(\hat{x}_{\bar{k}}, 0\right)\right)$ [9].

The selected cost function has the following expression:

$$J_k = a \cdot r_{V_k} + b \cdot r_{q_k} + c \cdot r_{\vartheta_k} + d \cdot r_{x_k} + e \cdot r_{z_k} + f \cdot V_{z_k} \tag{7}$$

where:

a, b, c, d, e, f are coefficients linked to variable dimensions
$r_V, r_q, r_\vartheta, r_x, r_z$ are variable residuals
V_z is the vertical speed
The imposed constrain is:

$$J \leq J_{MAX} \tag{8}$$

The value J_{MAX} of performance index is computed with the maximum imposed variable errors.

When Eq. (8) is not verified, the algorithm modifies Q matrix elements.

By employing the proposed methodology, the EKF determines the control vector $[\Delta\delta_e \Delta\delta_{th}]^T$.

In such a way the aircraft unknown augmented state vector is:

$$X = [u, w, q, \vartheta, x, h, \Delta\delta_e, \Delta\delta_{th}]^T$$

Therefore eight differential equations represents the non-linear mathematical model in turbulent air.

The proposed procedure, by using the above designed cost function J, determine the Q matrix. In particular, when Eq. (8) is not verified, it has been imposed that Q elements are equal to residuals by the following expressions:

$$
\begin{aligned}
Q_u &= r_{V_k} * 100 \\
Q_w &= r_{V_k} \\
Q_q &= r_{q_k} \\
Q_\vartheta &= r_{\vartheta_k} * 10 \\
Q_x &= r_{x_k} \\
Q_z &= r_{z_k} * 100 \\
Q_{\Delta\delta_e} &= \left(r_{V_k} + r_{\vartheta_k}\right) * 10^{-3} \\
Q_{\Delta\delta_{th}} &= V_{z_k} * 10^{-3}
\end{aligned}
\tag{9}
$$

The cost function J is calculated at every time step. Even if initial Q matrix values are wrong, proposed procedure correct these ones until the imposed constrain (8) is verified. Obtained Q values are optimal for the automatic take-off and/or landing in turbulent air.

3 Results

The procedure has been applied on an UAS that is a 1:5 scale model of the ultra-light aircraft N3-PUP [6, 7].

In Tables 1 and 2 are reported geometrical characteristics and fundamental performances of the studied UAS.

Table 1. UAS model geometrical characteristics

	Value
Mean chord **c**	0.24 m
Wing span **b**	1.86 m
Wing area **S**	0.4464 m^2
Mass **W/g**	2.5 kg
Inertia moment **I$_y$**	0.1080 kg m^2
Maximum power	27.56 kg m/sec

Table 2. UAS fundamental performances

	Value
V$_{ms}$	7.08 m/sec
V$_{max, OF}$	27 m/ses
V$_{cruise}$	23.6305 m/sec

Figure 2 shows the desired take-off path.

In Fig. 3 is reported a comparison between desired take-off flight path and disturbed one. It is possible to note that in the disturbed path the UAS will reach an altitude that is more than 2 times the desired one.

By employing the optimization algorithm, the flight path become red line of the Fig. 4. In the same figure are reported the desired take-off flight path and disturbed one.

As it is shown, simulations demonstrate that the disturbance rejection is performed efficiently. Obtained results demonstrate an almost complete rejection of the gust effects on the take-off path. The altitude error, starting from almost 200 m in the disturbed path, is reduced to about 50 m.

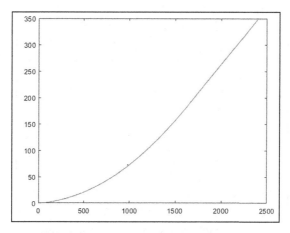

Fig. 2. Desired take-off path (Measurement set)

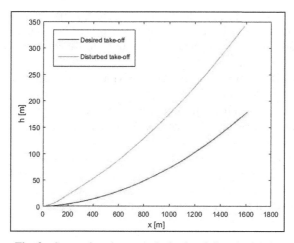

Fig. 3. Comparison between desired and disturbed paths

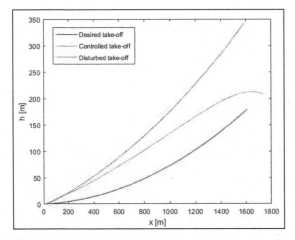

Fig. 4. Desired VS Disturbed VS Controlled take-off paths

4   Concluding Remarks

The proposed procedure permits to perform a fully autonomous take-off/landing procedure and it may be considered as the first step for a fully autonomous mission.

It is particularly suited for UAS because requires low computational power and it can be simple to implement on-board.

The proposed algorithm permits to exceed previous limit constituted by the trial and error procedure for filter tuning.

In fact proposed procedure, using appropriate imposed constrains, permits to calculate automatically elements inside Process Noise Covariance matrix and Measurement Noise Covariance matrix.

It is necessary remark that proposed algorithm is robust, in fact it estimates control displacements for gust rejection.

Further development of the present paper is the extension of the proposed method to the six DoF model of aircraft and the on-board implementation.

References

1. Benzerrouk, H., Salhi, H., Nebylov, A.: Non-Gaussian sensor fusion analysis with "Gaussian mixture and adaptive" based cubature Kalman filtering for unmanned aerial vehicle. Int. Rev. Aerosp. Eng. (IREASE) **6**(6), 264–277 (2013)
2. Nelson, D., Barber, D., McLain, T., Beard, R.: Vector fields path following for miniature air vehicles. IEEE Trans. Rob. **23**(3), 519–529 (2007)
3. Brezoescu, A., Espinoza, T., Castillo, P., Lozano, R.: Adaptive trajectory following for a fixed-wing UAV in presence of crosswind. J. Intell. Robot Syst. **69**, 257–271 (2013)
4. Liu, C., McAree, O., Chen, W.-H.: Path following control for small fixed-wing unmanned aerial vehicles under wind disturbances. Int. J. Robust Nonlinear Control **23**, 1682–1698 (2013)
5. Smith, J., Su, J., Liu, C., Chen, W.-H.: Disturbance observer based control with anti-windup applied to a small fixed-wing UAV for disturbance rejection. J. Intell. Robot Syst. **88**, 329–346 (2017). https://doi.org/10.1007/s10846-017-0534-5

6. Grillo, C., Montano, F.: An EKF based method for path following in turbulent air. Int. Rev. Aerosp. Eng. **10**(1), 1–6 (2017)
7. Grillo, C., Montano, F.: Wind component estimation for UAS flying in turbulent air. Aerosp. Sci. Technol. **93**, 105317 (2019)
8. Etkin, B.: Dynamics of Atmospheric Flight. Whiley, New York (1972)
9. Welch, G., Bishop, G.: An introduction to the Kalman filter (TR 95041). Department of Computer Science, University of North Carolina at Chapel Hill (2004)

Simulating UAS-Based Radiation Mapping on a Building Surface

Tomas Lazna$^{(\boxtimes)}$, Petr Gabrlik, Tomas Jilek, and Frantisek Burian

Central European Institute of Technology, Brno University of Technology,
Purkynova 123, 612 00 Brno, Czech Republic
{tomas.lazna,petr.gabrlik,tomas.jilek,frantisek.burian}@ceitec.vutbr.cz

Abstract. This paper discusses the mapping of ionizing radiation on building surfaces by using an unmanned aircraft system (UAS). The mapping task itself is important for the decommissioning of various nuclear facilities, for example, fuel processing sites or nuclear waste storage areas. The surface map can inform relevant authorities about the strength and distribution of radioactive sources inside an investigated building. The UAS is employed for the given purpose thanks to its many advantages, such as low price and the possibility of approaching a surface closely; moreover, the applied technique enables the user to create a 3D model of the target via such means as aerial photogrammetry. We set up an approximate model of a real building within our university campus, capturing the inner structures and subdividing the examined area into partial sectors, or groups, according to the construction materials; this criterion is relevant for simulating radiation propagation. The choice of the actual study location allows future experimental verification of the proposed methods; moreover, we can work with authentic photogrammetric products obtained during previous flights. In the project, two surface mapping methods are designed and tested on the simulated scenario, which assumes several radiation sources inside the building. One of the techniques simply assigns the measured value to the nearest point of the photogrammetric building model, while the other considers also rough information on the position of the sources to estimate the surface intensity more precisely. For better interpretation, the scattered data points are interpolated. Finally, the results of both approaches are compared with the computed reference map.

Keywords: Radiation mapping · Simulation · UAS · Aerial photogrammetry

1 Introduction

Radiation mapping is a measurement task that yields knowledge of radiation distribution in space and time. The overall method and its variants find application in various areas of human activity, such as geophysical survey, response to nuclear accidents, searching for lost (stolen) sources, or general radiation protection.

© Springer Nature Switzerland AG 2020
J. Mazal et al. (Eds.): MESAS 2019, LNCS 11995, pp. 130–147, 2020.
https://doi.org/10.1007/978-3-030-43890-6_11

In view of available options, the conservative approach involves helicopter-based systems; however, as ionizing radiation poses health risks, unmanned operation has become widely preferred. Unmanned aircraft systems (UASs) are essentially usable in the same manner as human-operated craft, albeit with the advantage of a lower price and the possibility of reaching spaces inaccessible to piloted helicopters. After the Fukuschima Dai-ichi Nuclear Power Plant disaster, both an autonomous unmanned helicopter [1] and a UAS [2] were applied to map the consequences, i.e., the radiation contamination. UAS-based mapping has also been utilized in uranium mines [3] to provide, above all, data to secure the radiation protection of tourists. The localization of radionuclides via a teleoperated UAS is studied in [4].

This paper focuses on the radiation mapping of building; in other words, the authors' aim is to measure the radiation intensity on the surfaces. The acquired data find use in multiple scenarios, as follows: First, the building can be employed in industrial or medical procedures that require the storage and handling of radiation sources; such operations include, for example, non-destructive testing. If performed in an urban area, the mapping should respect public safety. Second, the building should be checked for possible leaks, especially if used as a radioactive processing or storage facility. In this context, it is important to regularly check the containers' condition. Third, a building may be chosen as a hiding place by perpetrators of various crimes, including illegal disposing or theft of radiation sources; in such circumstances, the method facilitates confirming the presence and eventually estimating the location of the items inside the structure. Finally, the building itself can be made of contaminated materials. The application of UASs in the described tasks is beneficial due to the possibility of approaching the surfaces closely and within a fine grid; consequently, operators are able to compile precise surface maps.

Within the central aim of the study, we are demonstrating the capabilities of UAS-based surface mapping, employing of radiation measurement simulation. The actual location, however, is a real building on Brno University of Technology campus, represented by a 3D model. The presented methods are designed to be applicable to actually measured data too. Our team has previous experience with simulating ionizing radiation: The results presented in [5] have been exploited to extend the capabilities of a multi-robot system for the localization of radioactive sources, as shown in [6].

The paper comprises several parts, organized in the following manner: Sect. 2 provides a survey of methods to simulate radiation measurements in the vicinity of the examined building; the surface mapping algorithms are introduced in Sect. 3; Sect. 4 compiles the achieved results, and these are summarized and discussed in Sect. 5.

2 Simulation of Measured Radiation Data

The goal of this section is to generate radiation intensity data as if they were measured by a UAS flying around a building containing radiation sources.

Such simulation must comprise a 3D model including the individual materials because these exhibit different attenuation and affect the radiation propagation significantly. Based on the intersection of radiation rays with the materials, the radiation intensity can be computed for each UAS position and radiation source.

2.1 Radiation Theory

Within the scope of the paper, ionizing radiation emitted by radioactive isotope (radionuclide) sources is considered. In most cases, radionuclides decay in the alpha or beta modes, yielding heavy or light charged particles, respectively. Sometimes the new isotope remains in the excited state, and its transition to the base energy is accompanied by the emission of a gamma particle (a high-energy photon). As the charged particles interact with the environment more frequently, they have low penetrability and are unlikely to leave a building; thus, we focus exclusively on the gamma radiation.

A gamma radiation source is characterized by an activity [Bq] which expresses the number of disintegration cycles per second; one or more energy levels of emitted photons [keV]; and, for each of these levels, a corresponding yield of photons [%], which defines the portion of emissions per disintegration cycle. Note that radioactive decay is a stochastic process and the activity represents merely a mean value. The radiation intensity can be represented by, for example, a photon flux of low practical importance; it then appears preferable to characterize the intensity by its effect on matter, a task where the dose rate [$Gy \cdot h^{-1}$] embodies the basic quantity that characterizes the increment of the absorbed dose (energy deposited in matter by ionizing radiation per unit mass). For a specific radioisotope having activity A, the dose rate $\dot{D}_1$ at 1 m away from the source is given by equation [7]:

$$\dot{D}_1 = \frac{\Gamma \cdot A}{3.7 \cdot 10^6} \tag{1}$$

where Γ denotes the exposure rate constant [$R \cdot cm^2 \cdot mCi^{-1} \cdot h^{-1}$] which describes both the energy and the yield of emitted photons.

The propagation of radiation in space is affected by the traveled distance and the materials it passes through. The intensity is inversely proportional to the square of the distance (inverse square law). In a material, the radiation decays exponentially, at a rate determined by the linear attenuation coefficient μ, which is material-specific and depends on the radiation energy. When passing through multiple substances, the total attenuation is not defined by their arrangement but rather the overall thickness of each material, d. The propagation of single-energy radiation can be expressed by the following equation:

$$I = I_0 \frac{\exp\left(-\sum_{i=1}^{n} \mu_i d_i\right)}{\left(\sum_{i=1}^{n} d_i\right)^2} \tag{2}$$

where I_0 is the initial intensity.

Ultimately, the photon flux reaches a detection system. The sensitivity of the detectors is dependent on the incident radiation energy and other factors, such as temperature. Moreover, the detection process itself is stochastic. Let us assume that the detector has been adequately calibrated for the building mapping task and is able to provide correct dose rate values in a specified operation range. Then, to simplify the model, the stochastic character of both the radioactive decay and the detection is included in the computation of the dose rate $1\,\mathrm{m}$ away from the source: the relevant value is a random number drawn from the Poisson distribution, with the mean value given by Eq. 1. Due to practical issues, the Poisson distribution is approximated by the normal one: $\mathcal{P}(\lambda) \sim \mathcal{N}(\lambda; \lambda)$. The distribution remains valid for positive integers; thus, dose rate values are handled in $\mathrm{nGy} \cdot \mathrm{h}^{-1}$.

The radiation emitted by the studied sources does not constitute the only instance of the effect being detected, as it is necessary to consider also the radiation background consisting of two main components, namely, terrestrial and cosmic radiation. While the former is made up by radionuclides naturally occurring in the environment (in particular, uranium and its decay products, such as thorium and radium), the latter originates from stars in the outer space. Again, the background level is not a constant value due to the stochastic character of the ionizing radiation sources and detection. We decided to model the level by using Poisson's noise with the mean value $\dot{D}_{Bg}$ provided by, for example, the Safecast project [8].

Given R sources, the dose rate measured by a UAS-based simulated detector can be computed as

$$\dot{D} = \sum_{r=1}^{R} \frac{(x \leftarrow \mathcal{P}(\dot{D}_{1r})) \cdot \exp\left(-\sum_{i=1}^{n} \mu_{ri} d_{ri}\right)}{\left(\sum_{i=1}^{n} d_{ri}\right)^2} + (y \leftarrow \mathcal{P}(\dot{D}_{Bg})) \qquad (3)$$

2.2 Building Model

The three-dimensional model of a building is an essential element for the simulation of ionizing radiation propagation. Such a model involving individual construction materials and elements can be obtained in multiple ways. The most reliable approach is to utilize the construction documentation, which, besides the dimensions and materials, may include also an actual digital 3D model. Another option, chosen by the authors of this paper, is to create the model independently. As we selected a real building situated at Brno University of Technology, we could employ UAS-based photogrammetry for the 3D reconstruction. The aerial image data were already previously acquired by a DJI Phantom 3 Advanced UAS and processed in the Agisoft Metashape Professional photogrammetric software (Fig. 1). Since, for the georeferencing, we employed position data from a low-accuracy onboard global navigation satellite system (GNSS) receiver, the expected absolute model accuracy should be in the order of meters, as proposed by other relevant articles [9,10]. Such an accuracy, and the average image ground resolution of 1.0 centimeter per pixel, are sufficient with respect to the discussed application.

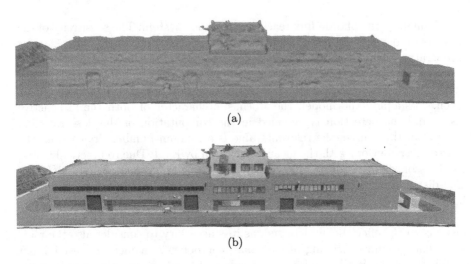

(a)

(b)

Fig. 1. The UAS photogrammetry-based 3D model of the actual building (triangle mesh (a), textured mesh (b)).

The photogrammetry technique reconstructs outer surfaces only; however, there are also automatic methods, utilized mainly in geographic information systems (GIS), which estimate building shapes based on a digital elevation model (DEM, photogrammetric or laser scanning product) [11]; such techniques are nevertheless unable to reconstruct inner structures either. For this reason, we used both the aforementioned photogrammetry-based model, represented by a point cloud or a triangular mesh, and the information stemming from the actual survey as the basis for the manual digitization process. A coarse model including the inner structures and distinguishing several basic construction materials was assembled in SketchUp Make 2017. To perform the simulation discussed in this paper, we considered only the left part of the building illustrated in Fig. 1.

The resulting model, presented in Fig. 2, involves four construction elements represented by different materials; the components are the walls, roof, doors, and windows. Even though the real building is obviously much more complex, the above-listed elements are copiously present and have different attenuation parameters.

To keep the model adequately straightforward, each construction element is represented by a single material. The walls are modeled by using bricks, with the attenuation coefficient provided in [12]. The referenced article [13] outlines the window glass parameters employed herein (note that zero concentration of CdO is chosen). In the doors and roof, the attenuation is caused especially by plates of aluminium or iron, respectively. These objects are therefore perceived as a combination of metal and thermal isolation where the latter component is neglected; relevant parameters of the elements can be found in [14]. The idea is to illustrate the difference between the building materials rather than to use precise coefficients. Finally, the parameters of the air are listed in [14], too.

Fig. 2. A coarse digital representation of the left part of the actual building, comprising major construction elements and materials. The corresponding items are walls (green), roof (red), windows (blue), and doors (orange). (Color figure online)

Table 1. The construction elements and materials in the digitized building model.

Element	Material	Width [m]	μ [cm^{-1}] at 662 keV
Wall	Brick	0.3	0.0567
Roof	Iron (3%)	0.3	$0.582 \cdot 0.03$
	Therm. isolation (97%)		
Door	Aluminum (10%)	0.04	$0.203 \cdot 0.1$
	Therm. isolation (90%)		
Window	Glass	0.01	0.127
Environment	Air (20 °C)	—	$9.33 \cdot 10^{-5}$

In the aforementioned references, the mass attenuation coefficients are specified; in order to convert these to the linear coefficients, we have to use multiplication by the density of the relevant material: $\mu = \rho \cdot \mu_m$. Attenuation values for the energy of 662 keV were chosen because they correspond to the selected radiation sources (Sect. 2.4). The elements and material details are summarized within Table 1.

In terms of further processing, it is vital that every model element has been closed (for example, every rectangle must have six faces) and the individual elements are not overlaid. Finally, the building model is exported as four STL files, one for each material. This format describes the geometry by utilizing a triangle mesh, with each triangle defined by the coordinates of the three vertices.

2.3 Analysis of the Material Structures in a Ray Trajectory

Simulating potentially measurable gamma radiation values by using an onboard UAS sensor requires us to know the positions of the source and the UAS as well as the total effective thickness of each material intersected by a gamma ray. The structures of the materials in the gamma ray trajectory can be obtained by analyzing the sequence of the gamma ray intersections with the outer surfaces

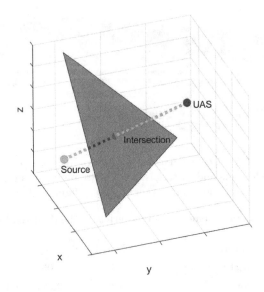

Fig. 3. A gamma ray intersection with a triangle.

of the objects defined by the triangle mesh. It is required to find the triangles that the gamma ray intersects and also the distances between the intersections and the source (Fig. 3).

Representing the building as multiple separate closed objects allows us to analyze the effective thickness of all materials in the gamma ray trajectory progressing from the gamma radiation source to the measurement spot. The thickness of all intersected materials is estimated out of intersections sorted by distances between the gamma radiation source and the gamma ray intersection with the triangle that is a part of the outer surface of some object. The ray-and-triangle intersection is solved via the algorithm by Moller and Trumbore [15].

In the initial phase, the estimation algorithm detects the first material penetrated by the gamma ray; at the next stage, the sorted gamma ray - triangle intersections are analyzed to estimate the type of material located in front of every surface on which an intersection is detected. This approach requires consistent models of portions of the building; to facilitate valid material estimation, the partial models must not overlap. If the UAS is positioned outside the overall model, the material of the environment (typically air) is added to the estimated structure as the last material in the gamma ray trajectory.

All thicknesses of one and the same material in the estimated structure are summed to yield the total material thickness for every material crossed by a gamma ray. The total gamma radiation attenuation is computed from the partial attenuations caused by all types of intersected materials, with the estimated total thickness as described by Eq. 3.

2.4   Experimental Setup

The presented research considers one scenario composed as follows: the building model introduced in Sect. 2.2; the UAS trajectory defining the positions where the radiation is measured; and several radiation sources inside the building.

The simulated UAS flight was designed with respect to the flight characteristics of real unmanned aircraft. Considering our application, where the UAS is intended to fly as close to the building surface as possible, the only option is to employ multi-rotor aircraft enabling all-direction movement and hovering. The minimum safe distance from the surface depends mainly on the navigation system accuracy, an this ranges within the order of meters in the case of consumer-grade GNSS receivers. Accordingly, the designed trajectory is three meters away from the building at any moment. Close ground flying, if necessary, can be performed by an unmanned ground vehicle (UGV) [16].

The flight speed of $2\,m \cdot s^{-1}$, the realistic value chosen for the simulation, leads to the measuring interval of 2 m, considering the sampling period of one second. To homogeneously cover the building surface with a $2 \times 2\,m$ grid, an identical interval was set as the distance between the individual flight lines. As a consequence of the setting, the trajectory consists of five layers around the building facade and one layer above the roof. The situation is illustrated in Fig. 4.

A scenario is assumed that involves stolen and hidden radioactive nuclides; these are separated into multiple crates or boxes, as if they were transported from different locations. The setup involves 9 identical unshielded sources in a regular square grid having the area and height above ground level of $6.6\,m^2$ and 0.5 m, respectively (Fig. 4). A rather common radioisotope, namely, Caesium-137, was selected for the purpose (it finds application in, for example, radiotherapy or gamma-ray well-logging devices); the photons are emitted with an energy equal to 662 keV and a yield of 85.1% [17], corresponding to the exposure rate constant of $3.43\,R \cdot cm^2 \cdot mCi^{-1} \cdot h^{-1}$ [18]. The total activity of the sources equals 400 MBq, a value selected with respect to the possibility of detecting increased radiation levels outside the building. The average background radiation level at the location amounts to $110\,nGy \cdot h^{-1}$.

3   Radiation Mapping Methods

This section explains how to process data either simulated or actually measured in the vicinity of the building. The goal is to acquire a smooth picture of the radiation intensity distribution at the surfaces. Two methods to convert 'air' data points to 'surface' ones are suggested; these points are then interpolated to form the map.

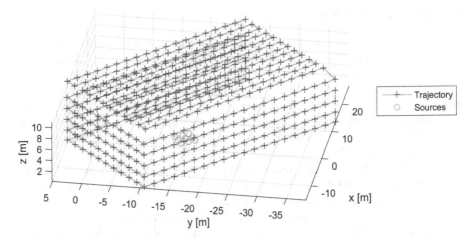

Fig. 4. The UAS trajectory covering a space three meters away from the building surface. The waypoints (blue crosses) correspond to the positions where the radiation is to be measured; nine radiation sources are located inside the building. (Color figure online)

3.1   Radiation Mapping Method 1

This approach is rather straightforward, as it consists in assigning the dose rate value of a point to its perpendicular projection on the relevant surface (either a wall or a roof). To find the projection analytically, the data points would have to be divided into subsets and provided with corresponding directional information. Instead, simplification is performed, and we assume that the projection equals the nearest element of a point cloud representing the building model. At lower altitudes, the nearest points are located on the ground, and therefore only points exhibiting a height greater than the threshold are selected for the processing. Due to the uneven density of the previously acquired point cloud, especially in its vertical parts (walls), the assumption is not generally valid, and there is the possibility of assigning multiple values to the same point; in any such case, the values are averaged.

The accuracy of this approach apparently decreases with increasing distance from the studied object. The main benefits include the method's simplicity and, above all, ability to evaluate the results given by the procedure described below.

3.2   Radiation Mapping Method 2

The technique addresses issues linked to data acquisition at spots relatively remote from the surfaces via estimating the original point where the radiation is generated. Such a point does not physically embody a specific radiation source, because our scenario contains multiple radioisotopes; rather than that, the spot represents a 'center of radiation' (analogy with a center of mass). Knowing the center's position can help compensate errors induced by the measurement geometry if the sources are organized in a compact formation.

The estimation itself is based on an initial guess improved by the Gauss-Newton algorithm exploited in solving non-linear least squares problems. Four parameters of the center are sought: the coordinates x, y, z, and the emitted dose rate $\dot{D}_1$. The method iteratively minimizes the error function represented by the sum of residuals $\sum_{m=1}^{M} r_m$ via using a Jacobian matrix $\boldsymbol{J}$ of partial derivatives of the residual function

$$r_m = \dot{D}_m - \dot{D}_{EstBg} - \frac{\dot{D}_1}{(x_m - x)^2 + (y_m - y)^2 + (z_m - z)^2}, \tag{4}$$

where the triplet (x_m, y_m, z_m) denotes the point's coordinates, $\dot{D}_m$ represents the measured dose rate, and $\dot{D}_{EstBg}$ is the estimated radiation background level. The influence of the attenuation is omitted, as the material and structural description of the building is generally unavailable (in this paper, the model finds use solely in the simulation of measurements). Note that the background needs to be subtracted, as we cannot neglected it when comparing the measured values. The parameter vector $\boldsymbol{\theta} = (x, y, z, \dot{D}_1)$ is updated in each step via

$$\boldsymbol{\theta}_{k+1} = \boldsymbol{\theta}_k - (\boldsymbol{J}^{\mathsf{T}}\boldsymbol{J})^{-1}\boldsymbol{J}^{\mathsf{T}}\boldsymbol{r}(\boldsymbol{\theta}_k) \tag{5}$$

The proposed model includes only a single virtual source; thus, the result is not overly sensitive to the initial guess. In this context, for example, we may choose coordinates in the center of the building, with the emitted dose rate being equal to the maximum value present in the dataset. Relevant details on the Gauss-Newton method are comprised within a dedicated chapter of [19], and a functional application to a similar problem is characterized in [20].

After estimating the center of radiation, we chose two effects to be compensated. First, a measurement point is generally farther from the sources than its corresponding counterpart, namely, a surface point; thus, the actual dose rate value present on the surface is greater than the measured one. Second, the growing altitude difference between the sources and a measurement point is accompanied by an increasing distance of the perpendicular projection from the actual ray intersection (Fig. 5a); this effect then causes a height shift of the map. To solve the problem, we propose lowering the measurement altitudes prior to the actual search for the nearest point and also adjusting the dose rate with the ratio of the square distances.

If only the point cloud is relied on, the height difference of a measurement point and its corresponding ray intersection cannot be found accurately. Instead, the average value for each flight level is estimated, and all relevant points are shifted evenly. The estimation exploits the similarity of the triangles (Fig. 5b).

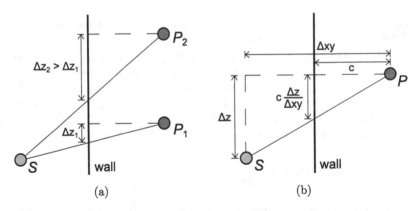

Fig. 5. The height shift effect (a), and the related compensation (b); the S stands for the source position, and the blue points P_i represent the measurement positions. The height shift expresses the distance Δz_i between the perpendicular projection of a point P_i and the spot where the rays emitted by a source actually intersect the surface. (Color figure online)

After finding the point (x_s, y_s, z_s) nearest to the adjusted measurement point (x_m, y_m, z_m) with the dose rate $\dot{D}_m$, we compute the surface dose rate as:

$$\dot{D}_s = \dot{D}_m \frac{(x_m - x)^2 + (y_m - y)^2 + (z_m - z)^2}{(x_s - x)^2 + (y_s - y)^2 + (z_s - z)^2}. \tag{6}$$

3.3   Data Interpolation

Both of the described methods yield a set of points with assigned dose rate values, denotable as nodes. To build a dense surface map, the values in the vacant points between the nodes need to be interpolated. Being vacant, all elements of the point cloud having the minimal distance to the nodes lower that 2 m are selected; the threshold exploits the measurement grid spacing. The interpolation is performed via the MATLAB's `scatteredInterpolant`, which utilizes the Delaunay triangulation [21].

The resulting interpolated map is also employed to evaluate the methods' accuracy. First, a reference map is built by computing the theoretical values in a regular 0.5 m grid on the surface, omitting the stochasticity and the radiation background. Then, to each reference point, the nearest point cloud element is assigned. Finally, the sum of absolute differences between the values of corresponding points that exist in both the studied and the reference datasets is computed as the evaluation criterion.

4   Results

The section describes the results obtained from the measurement simulation and mapping methods within the applied building model; in this context, the radiation sources and a real amount of measurements performable by the on-board radiation sensor are characterized too. To compare the results of different mapping approaches, we simulated the reference data on the outer surface of the building. All the simulations are processed in MathWorks MATLAB, with the operating times measured on a PC comprising an Intel Core i7-2700K processor.

4.1   Simulated Radiation Data

The modeled parts of the building, whose outer surface is decomposed into a triangle mesh, and the simulated data acquisition positions are shown in Fig. 6. For clarity, we visualize only the gamma rays from the first radiation source; the simulation, however, is carried out for all of the sources. Applying the algorithm for material structure estimation in the gamma ray trajectory (described in Sect. 2.3) to all data acquisition and radiation source positions, we yield the total attenuation of the gamma radiation from every source related to every data acquisition position. The result of the material structure analysis for the first radiation source and all positions where the data are acquired is shown in Fig. 7. Apparently, the material of the environment (air) is the most significant material structure component as regards the total thickness. The simulation comprises 9 radiation sources and 479 data acquisition points. The triangle mesh describing the building consists of 320 triangles in total (walls: 200; roof: 12; doors: 36; windows: 72). The material structure analysis lasts approximately 30 s. The reference dataset is acquired via simulated measurement at points homogeneously distributed on the outer surface of the building; this dataset includes 5,411 points, and the simulation takes approximately 6 min. The simulated measurements carried out by utilizing the on-board radiation sensor are visualized in Fig. 8. The computed reference map set into the building point cloud that exploits the simulated radiation measurements on the outer surface of the building is shown in Fig. 9a. The relevant simulation times equal 0.04 s and 0.23 s, respectively.

4.2   Radiation Mapping

Both of the described radiation mapping methods were supplied with one and the same simulated dataset, and they also exhibited an identical total computation time, namely, 5.5 s (surface mapping: 3 s; interpolation: 2.5 s). The results are introduced as components of the photogrammetric model, Fig. 9b and c. The radiation center was estimated at the position displayed in Fig. 10; the distance between the middle source and the center equals 0.37 m. The algorithm was run with the background dose rate of $80\,\mathrm{nGy \cdot h^{-1}}$, showing that the method yields more ·accurate results when the background is underestimated. In the interpolated maps, the doors on the longer wall can be clearly seen, whereas those on the shorter one are significantly less sharp; this difference is due to

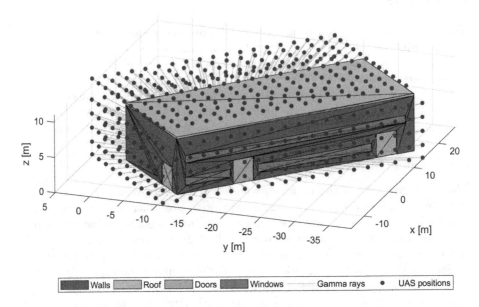

Fig. 6. The modeled parts of the building; simulated data acquisition points; and gamma rays from the first radiation source.

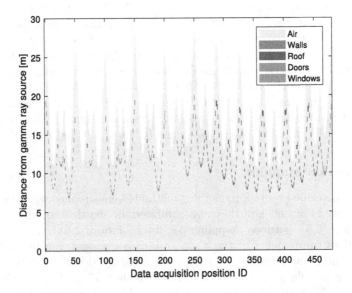

Fig. 7. The estimated material structures in the gamma ray trajectory, related to the first gamma source.

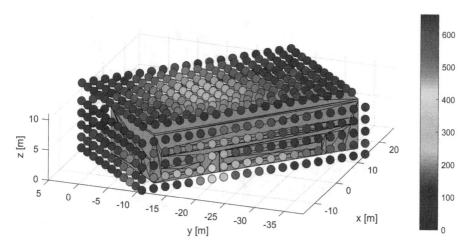

Fig. 8. The simulated values (the dose rate in $nGy \cdot h^{-1}$) measurable by an on-board radiation sensor.

Table 2. The radiation mapping methods compared with the reference.

	Sum of errors $[nGy \cdot h^{-1}]$	Minimum $[nGy \cdot h^{-1}]$	Maximum $[nGy \cdot h^{-1}]$	Mean $[nGy \cdot h^{-1}]$	Stand. dev. $[nGy \cdot h^{-1}]$
Reference	-	0	635	79	97
Method 1	$4.81 \cdot 10^5$	96	408	161	50
Method 2	$2.92 \cdot 10^5$	6	629	114	90

the doors' specific distances from the sources. The windows are also partially recognizable in the maps, as we can see horizontal stripes of an increased dose rate where the glass is. Note that the intensity values assigned to the roof by method 2 were greater than those quoted in the reference map; this discrepancy stems from the roof's strong attenuation, which cannot be considered by the designed algorithm.

A relevant numerical comparison with the reference is outlined in Table 2; in addition to a sum of errors, the statistical parameters of all three datasets (namely, the minimum, maximum, mean, and standard deviations) are offered, allowing the reader to assess the similarity.

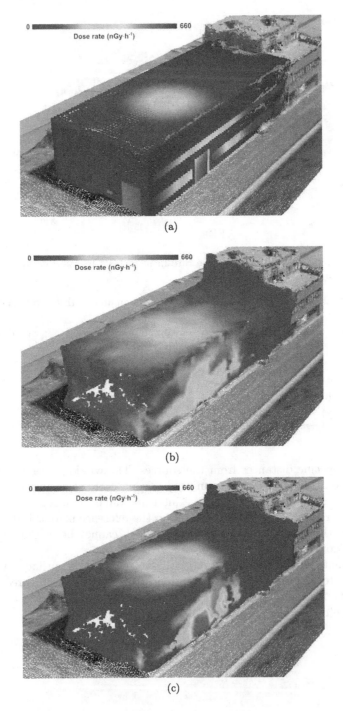

Fig. 9. The reference surface radiation map (a), and the results of the mapping methods 1 (b) and 2 (c).

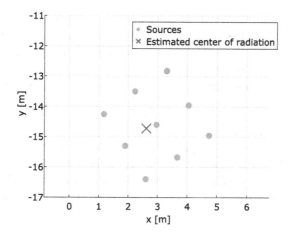

Fig. 10. Estimated center of radiation; the height difference relative to sources equals 0.09 m.

5 Conclusion

The primary aim of the paper consisted in presenting and comparing various methods for radiation intensity mapping on urban surfaces. The analysis was performed by utilizing simulated radiation data corresponding to a realistic scenario including a UAS flight around the actual building examined. The assembled functional model, together with the ray–triangle intersection method, allowed us to analyze the individual ray trajectories and to assess the influence of diverse construction materials. For the simulation, equations describing radiation propagation in narrow beam geometry were used, although, in fact, the scenario involved broad beam geometry. Such simplification was possible because the distance of both sources and the UAS from the attenuators (obstacles, including walls) was relatively high compared to the materials' thickness and, also, the radiation was monoenergetic.

Both of the proposed and investigated mapping methods directly relate the UAS-measured radiation intensities to the actual building surface model, which can be acquired via, for example, aerial photogrammetry. We believe this approach accentuates the context between the model and radiation levels. The mapping method 1 is very intuitive and straightforward; however, it offers only a low level of detail, as various effects are neglected, including the actual distance from the surface or the source's position. The more complex method 2 considers the measurement geometry, namely, the mutual position of the sources and data acquisition points. Although the intensity values vary and, at a particular moment, do not represent the actual local dose rate, the results are significantly better in terms of both the details' reconstruction and the objective assessments. The assembled radiation layer clearly displays the construction elements, for instance, doors, and exhibits a 40% lower sum of errors from the reference model compared to the method 1. Notably, if stolen and hidden sources were sought, the algorithm would deliver their location in a relatively accurate manner, without the necessity to enter the building. The overall results, however, were achieved within a rather simplified scenario; it is thus probable that in a more specific case the method 2 would not yield such convincing outcomes.

This study still allows ample room for further improvements and extensions. In this sense, we intend to focus on other, more realistic experimental setups to compare relevant mapping results. Such scenarios may then include different types of sources, activities, layouts, or flight trajectories. In the future, the simulation method could require improvements where additional real-world effects are to be comprehended; however, we do not plan to employ the Monte Carlo N-Particle Transport Code (MCNP) [22], which, despite being a highly accurate simulation tool, is not an easily accessible solution. Further in this context, the developed algorithms will be refined experimentally.

Acknowledgments. This work was supported by the European Regional Development Fund under the project Robotics 4 Industry 4.0 (reg. no. CZ.02.1.01/ 0.0/0.0/15_003/0000470).

References

1. Sanada, Y., Torii, T.: Aerial radiation monitoring around the Fukushima Dai-ichi nuclear power plant using an unmanned helicopter. J. Environ. Radioact. **139**, 294–299 (2015)
2. Martin, P.G., Payton, O.D., Fardoulis, J.S., Richards, D.A., Yamashiki, Y., Scott, T.B.: Low altitude unmanned aerial vehicle for characterising remediation effectiveness following the FDNPP accident. J. Environ. Radioact. **151**, 58–63 (2016)
3. Martin, P.G., Payton, O.D., Fardoulis, J.S., Richards, D.A., Scott, T.B.: The use of unmanned aerial systems for the mapping of legacy uranium mines. J. Environ. Radioact. **143**, 135–140 (2015)
4. Aleotti, J., et al.: Detection of nuclear sources by UAV teleoperation using a visuo-haptic augmented reality interface. Sensors **17**(10), 2234 (2017)
5. Gabrlik, P., Lazna, T.: Simulation of gamma radiation mapping using an unmanned aerial system. In: 15th IFAC Conference on Programmable Devices and Embedded Systems PDeS 2018, pp. 256–262. Elsevier (2018)
6. Lazna, T., Gabrlik, P., Jilek, T., Zalud, L.: Cooperation between an unmanned aerial vehicle and an unmanned ground vehicle in highly accurate localization of gamma radiation hotspots. Int. J. Adv. Robot. Syst. **15**(1), 1–16 (2018)
7. Knoll, G.F.: Radiation Detection and Measurement. Wiley, Hoboken (2010)
8. Brown, A., Franken, P., Bonner, S., Dolezal, N., Moross, J.: Safecast: successful citizen-science for radiation measurement and communication after Fukushima. J. Radiol. Prot. **36**(2), S82–S101 (2016)
9. Stöcker, C., Nex, F., Koeva, M., Gerke, M.: Quality assessment of combined IMU/GNSS data for direct georeferencing in the context of UAV-based mapping. In: International Conference on Unmanned Aerial Vehicles in Geomatics, Bonn, Germany, pp. 151–157 (2017)
10. Lo, C.F., et al.: The direct georeferencing application and performance analysis of UAV Helicopter in GCP-free area. In: International Conference on Unmanned Aerial Vehicles in Geomatics, Toronto, Canada, pp. 151–157 (2015)

11. Lafarge, F., Descombes, X., Zerubia, J., Pierrot-Deseilligny, M.: Building reconstruction from a single DEM. In: 2008 IEEE Conference on Computer Vision and Pattern Recognition, Anchorage, AK, USA, pp. 1–8 (2008)
12. Salinas, I.C.P., Conti, C.C., Lopes, R.T.: Effective density and mass attenuation coefficient for building material in Brazil. Appl. Radiat. Isotopes. **64**, 13–18 (2006)
13. Ahmed, G.S.M., Mahmoud, A.S., Salem, S.M., Abou-Elnasr, T.Z.: Study of gamma-ray attenuation coefficients of some glasses containing CdO. Am. J. Phys. Appl. **3**(4), 112–120 (2015)
14. Hubbell, J.H., Seltzer, S.M.: Tables of X-Ray Mass Attenuation Coefficients and Mass Energy-Absorption Coefficients. National Institute of Standards and Technology, Gaithersburg, Maryland (2004)
15. Moller, T., Trumbore, B.: Fast, minimum storage ray-triangle intersection. J. Graph. Tools. **2**(1), 21–28 (1997)
16. Nejdl, L., et al.: Remote-controlled robotic platform for electrochemical determination of water contaminated by heavy metal ions. Int. J. Electrochem. Sci. **10**(4), 3635–3643 (2015)
17. Be, M.M., et al.: Monographie BIPM-5 - Table of Radionuclides, vol. 3. Bureau International des Poids et Mesures, Sevres (2006)
18. Smith, D.S., Stabin, M.G.: Exposure rate constants and lead shielding values For over 1,100 radionuclides. Health Phys. **102**(3), 271–291 (2012)
19. Deuflhard, P.: Least squares problems: gauss-newton methods. In: Newton Methods for Nonlinear Problems, Springer Series in Computational Mathematics, pp. 173–231. Springer, Heidelberg (2011). https://doi.org/10.1007/978-3-642-23899-4_4
20. Lazna, T.: Optimizing the localization of gamma radiation point sources using a UGV. In: 2018 ELEKTRO. IEEE (2018)
21. Amidror, I.: Scattered data interpolation methods for electronic imaging systems: a survey. J. Electron. Imaging **11**(2), 157–176 (2002)
22. Goorley, T., et al.: Features of MCNP6. In: SNA + MC 2013 - Joint International Conference on Supercomputing in Nuclear Applications + Monte Carlo. EDP Sciences, Les Ulis, France (2014)

Inverse Kinematics for the Industrial Robot IRB4400 Based on Conformal Geometric Algebra

Radek Tichý[⊠]

Faculty of Mechanical Engineering, Brno University of Technology, Brno, Czechia
Radek.Tichy@vutbr.cz

Abstract. We present a solution to the inverse kinematics problem of 5 DoF IRB4400 industrial serial robot arm based on conformal geometric algebra. The algorithm relies on the intersections of geometric primitives such as lines, circles, planes and spheres. This approach provides clear geometric intuition about the problem. In the solution we analytically describe the way how to find the final position of each joint and based on these positions we also determine the joint parameters (i.e. the angles) including the orientation according to the robot's construction.

Keywords: Conformal geometric algebra · Inverse kinematics · IRB4400

1 Introduction

Geometric algebra (GA) has recently become a rapidly spreading tool for efficient solution to problems with geometric nature. Mathematically, GA is a Clifford algebra with an embedding of a Euclidean space and two additional operations, see [1–3] for mathematical background and introduction to computations. As a result, both Euclidean objects and transformations are represented by elements of a single algebra. Consequently, the Euclidean transformations are performed just by algebra operations. Such geometrically oriented approach finds applications in many engineering areas, such as computer graphics [4,5], computer vision [6] and mechanics [7,8].

Within this paper we describe a way of finding a solution to the inverse kinematics of 4-link industrial robot ABB IRB4400 with 5 degrees of freedom. For classical inverse kinematics models based on Euler's angles or differential geometry see e.g. [9,10]. In our solution we use conformal geometric algebra (CGA) which is a Clifford algebra with signature $(4, 1)$ denoted as $\mathbb{G}_{4,1}$. Geometric primitives intrinsic to CGA are spheres which may be represented by an algebra element. Note that a point is a zero radius sphere, a point pair is a sphere S^0, lines and planes are spheres S^1 and S^2 with infinite radii. Apart from Euclidean (rotations, translations) and several more transformations (dilations, scaling) we can also determine intersections of objects very simply, which makes CGA a convenient tool for inverse kinematics calculation.

© Springer Nature Switzerland AG 2020
J. Mazal et al. (Eds.): MESAS 2019, LNCS 11995, pp. 148–161, 2020.
https://doi.org/10.1007/978-3-030-43890-6_12

2   Conformal Geometric Algebra - CGA

Let us note that the properties and definitions of conformal geometric algebras can be found in e.g. [3, 11]. For modelling a 3D robot it is sufficient to work with a vector space $\mathbb{R}^{4,1}$ equipped with the scalar product of signature $(4, 1)$. The corresponding Clifford algebra $Cl(4, 1)$ has the vector basis $\{e_1, e_2, e_3, e_+, e_-\}$ and the algebra operation called *geometric (Clifford) product* satisfies

$$\mathbf{a}^2 = Q(\mathbf{a}), \quad \forall \mathbf{a} \in \mathbb{R}^{4,1} \subset Cl(4, 1), \tag{1}$$

where $Q(\cdot)$ is the quadratic form of the scalar product. The associative and distributive algebra $Cl(4, 1)$ as a span of the set $\{e_1, e_2, e_3, e_+, e_-\}$ is determined by the following identities:

$$e_1^2 = e_2^2 = e_3^2 = e_+^2 = 1, \ e_-^2 = -1,$$
$$e_i e_j = -e_j e_i, \ i \neq j, \ i, j \in \{1, 2, 3, +, -\} \tag{2}$$

Note that we get $2^5 = 32$-dimensional vector space.

From the view of geometry it is more convenient to work with a different basis of $Cl(4, 1)$. Consider a basis $\{e_0, e_1, e_2, e_3, e_\infty\} \in \mathbb{R}^{4,1}$ with the corresponding quadratic form given by matrix

$$Q = \begin{pmatrix} 0 & 0 & -1 \\ 0 & 1_{3\times3} & 0 \\ -1 & 0 & 0 \end{pmatrix}, \tag{3}$$

where $1_{3\times3}$ is an identity 3×3 matrix. Note that in the terms of a canonical basis we have

$$e_0 = \frac{1}{2}(e_- - e_+), \quad e_\infty = e_- + e_+, \tag{4}$$

where e_0 and e_∞ play the role of the origin and the infinity, respectively. From the geometric product two further operations can be derived: *inner product* and *outer product (wedge)*. Generally, the wedge of two basis blades E_i and E_j, with $k = gr(E_i)$, $l = gr(E_j)$ is defined as

$$E_i \wedge E_j := \langle E_i E_j \rangle_{k+l} \tag{5}$$

and the inner product is defined as

$$E_i \cdot E_j := \begin{cases} \langle E_i E_j \rangle_{|k-l|}, & i, j > 0, \\ 0, & i = 0 \text{ and/or } j = 0, \end{cases} \tag{6}$$

where $gr(E)$ denotes a grade of the basis blade E and $\langle \ \rangle_k$ denotes the grade projection into grade k. We call such the algebra *conformal geometric algebra* (CGA) and denote $\mathbb{G}_{4,1}$. Wedge basis of CGA is displayed in Table 1.

With the setting described above, we are given an embedding $C : \mathbb{R}^3 \to \mathbb{K}^4 \subset \mathbb{R}^{4,1}$ ($\mathbb{K}^4$ is the null cone) defined as

$$C(\mathbf{x}) = \mathbf{x} + \frac{1}{2}\mathbf{x}^2 e_\infty + e_0, \tag{7}$$

Table 1. Wedge basis of CGA

Scalars	1
Vectors	$e_1, e_2, e_3, e_0, e_\infty$
2–blades	$e_1 \wedge e_2, e_1 \wedge e_3, e_1 \wedge e_0, e_1 \wedge e_\infty, e_2 \wedge e_3,$ $e_2 \wedge e_0, e_2 \wedge e_\infty, e_3 \wedge e_0, e_3 \wedge e_\infty, e_0 \wedge e_\infty$
3–blades	$e_1 \wedge e_2 \wedge e_3, e_1 \wedge e_2 \wedge e_0, e_1 \wedge e_2 \wedge e_\infty, e_1 \wedge e_3 \wedge e_0,$ $e_1 \wedge e_3 \wedge e_\infty, e_1 \wedge e_0 \wedge e_\infty, e_2 \wedge e_3 \wedge e_0, e_2 \wedge e_3 \wedge e_\infty,$ $e_2 \wedge e_0 \wedge e_\infty, e_3 \wedge e_0 \wedge e_\infty$
4–blades	$e_1 \wedge e_2 \wedge e_3 \wedge e_0, e_1 \wedge e_2 \wedge e_3 \wedge e_\infty, e_1 \wedge e_2 \wedge e_0 \wedge e_\infty,$ $e_1 \wedge e_3 \wedge e_0 \wedge e_\infty, e_2 \wedge e_3 \wedge e_0 \wedge e_\infty$
Pseudoscalar	$I = e_1 \wedge e_2 \wedge e_3 \wedge e_0 \wedge e_\infty$

which is a CGA representation of a point. Other Euclidean objects can also be represented in this algebra. Let $\mathcal{A} \subseteq \mathbb{R}^3$ be a particular Euclidean object. Then $\mathcal{A}$ is represented by $A \in \mathbb{G}_{4,1}$ such that

$$\mathbf{x} \in \mathcal{A} \Leftrightarrow C(\mathbf{x}) \cdot A = 0 \tag{8}$$

and it is called IPNS (inner product representation). Dually $\mathcal{A}$ can be represented by A^* satisfying

$$\mathbf{x} \in \mathcal{A} \Leftrightarrow C(\mathbf{x}) \wedge A^* = 0, \tag{9}$$

which is called OPNS (outer product representation). Note that the duality is obtained by multiplying by an inverse of the pseudoscalar which in this particular algebra is $I^{-1} = -I$, i.e. $A^* = -AI$. The Euclidean objects and their representations are listed in Table 2. In OPNS the objects are constructed with the help of points P_i lie on them. In IPNS a sphere is represented by its center point P and its radius r. A plane is represented by its normal vector $\mathbf{n}$ and distance to the origin d. Other objects, i.e. a circle, a line and a point pair, are constructed with the help of the wedge product of certain objects. In this sense the wedge product of objects in IPNS represents their intersection, e.g. an intersection of two spheres is a circle, an intersection of two planes is a line, etc. The extraction

Table 2. Euclidean objects and their IPNS and OPNS representation.

Entity	IPNS	OPNS
Point	$P = \mathbf{x} + \frac{1}{2}\mathbf{x}^2 e_\infty + e_0$	
Sphere	$S = P - \frac{1}{2}r^2 e_\infty$	$S^* = P_1 \wedge P_2 \wedge P_3 \wedge P_4$
Plane	$\tau = \mathbf{n} + d e_\infty$	$\tau^* = P_1 \wedge P_2 \wedge P_3 \wedge e_\infty$
Circle	$Z = S_1 \wedge S_2$	$Z^* = P_1 \wedge P_2 \wedge P_3$
Line	$L = \pi_1 \wedge \pi_2$	$L^* = P_1 \wedge P_2 \wedge e_\infty$
Point pair	$Pp = S_1 \wedge S_2 \wedge S_3$	$Pp^* = P_1 \wedge P_2$

of the parameters from a multivector representing a certain Euclidean object is possible [11]. For instance two points of a point pair Pp can be extracted as

$$P_{1,2} = \frac{\pm\sqrt{Pp^* \cdot Pp^*} + Pp^*}{-e_\infty \cdot Pp^*}. \tag{10}$$

In CGA the Euclidean transformations are represented by certain algebra elements called versors. Any transformation represented by a versor V of the element O (any object from Table 2) is realized by conjugation

$$O \to VO\tilde{V}, \tag{11}$$

where $\tilde{V}$ is the reverse and versors satisfy $V\tilde{V} = 1$. For instance, the translation in the direction $t = t_1e_1 + t_2e_2 + t_3e_3$ is represented by the translator

$$T = e^{-\frac{1}{2}te_\infty} = 1 - \frac{1}{2}te_\infty. \tag{12}$$

The rotation around the normalized axis L by an angle ϕ is represented by the rotor

$$R = e^{-\frac{1}{2}\phi L} = \cos\frac{\phi}{2} - L\sin\frac{\phi}{2}. \tag{13}$$

Let o_1, o_2 denote the IPNS of two planes or two lines. The angle α between these objects is computed as

$$\alpha = \arccos\frac{o_1^* \cdot o_2^*}{|o_1^*||o_2^*|}. \tag{14}$$

3   Manipulator Description

A manipulator or a serial robot arm is a robotic device composed of various number of links which connect motorised joints. In our case the links are denoted as l_{01}, l_{12}, l_{23} and l_{34} and joints are denoted as $j_0, \ldots j_4$, where j_4 is the endpoint which does not affect the manipulator kinematics, see Fig. 1. Denote that all the joints are revolute and their setting is given by the values of angles $\varphi_1, \ldots \varphi_5$ as indicated in Fig. 1. The construction of the ABB IRB4400 manipulator can be seen in Fig. 1, in the second picture. Angle φ_1 rotates the whole manipulator around the vertical axis through origin. φ_2 is an angle between link l_{12} and the vertical axis and φ_3 is an angle between link l_{23} and the axis through joints j_2, j_3 in initial configuration as denoted in the picture. Note that without change of φ_3 the link l_{23} preserves its orientation if φ_2 is changed. Therefore rotation in φ_2 acts as a translation to the effector point. The rotation in φ_4 affects the axis of rotation φ_5 and finally φ_5 denotes the angle between links l_{23}, l_{34}. Let us note that angle $\varphi_i, i = 1, \ldots, 5$ actually represents an impulse given to a particular joint, i.e. φ_i is the angle (orientation is included) which the particular link is rotated about from its initial configuration pictured in Fig. 1. The initial configuration is then expressed as $a_0 = (\varphi_1, \varphi_2, \varphi_3, \varphi_4, \varphi_5) = (0, 0, 0, 0, 0)$, i.e. the manipulator is in the position displayed in Fig. 1 and no angle is changed.

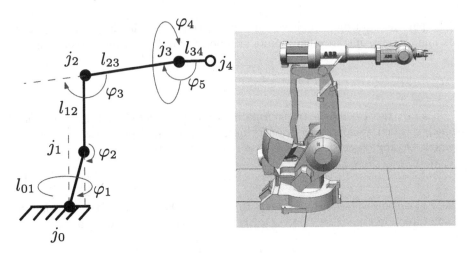

Fig. 1. Manipulator model description

4   Inverse Kinematic Model

In the inverse kinematics of IRB4400 we are given the final position of the effector, i.e. the joint j_4, and an orientation of the gripper, i.e. an orientation of the link l_{34}. The task is to find all joint angles, i.e. a final configuration. CGA approach leads to an analytical solution of this problem. For better explanation we also propose pictures of computing the model with a particular input data.

4.1   Finding the Final Positions of the Joints

The joints are represented as CGA points

$$J_i = C(j_i), \quad i = 0, \cdots, 4. \tag{15}$$

The input position of the effector is given by Euclidean vector $\bar{j}_4$ represented as

$$\bar{J}_4 = C(\bar{j}_4) \tag{16}$$

and the orientation of the gripper by v. The orientation can be represented by a line through $\bar{J}_4$ parallel to the vector v. Define a point $P = C(j_4 + v)$, then the representation of the input orientation is given by

$$L_3^* = \bar{J}_4 \wedge P \wedge e_\infty. \tag{17}$$

Before we will step into the computation of the remaining joints, let us recall that the position of the base joint J_0 does not change, therefore

$$\bar{J}_0 = J_0 = e_0. \tag{18}$$

At first we compute $\bar{J}_3$ with help of the intersection of the line L_3 and a sphere with center $\bar{J}_4$ and radius l_{34}

$$S_3 = \bar{J}_4 - \frac{1}{2}l_{34}^2 e_\infty. \tag{19}$$

The intersection denotes the point pair Pp_3 and the corresponding point $\bar{J}_3$ with respect to the orientation of the gripper is extracted (see Fig. 2):

$$Pp_3 = S_3 \wedge L_3, \tag{20}$$

$$\bar{J}_3 = \frac{-\sqrt{Pp_3^* \cdot Pp_3^*} + Pp_3^*}{-e_\infty \cdot Pp_3^*}. \tag{21}$$

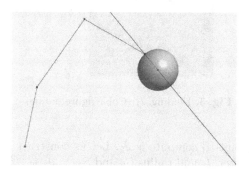

Fig. 2. Finding $\bar{J}_3$

The next joint we will compute is $\bar{J}_1$. From the construction of the manipulator, we can notice that the rotation φ_1 allows the joint J_1 to move along the circle Z_1 indicated in Fig. 3 by a blue circle and given as follows: Let $S_1 = C(J_{1z}e_3) - \frac{1}{2}(J_{1x})^2 e_\infty$ be a sphere with its center at the point with J_{1z} z-coordinate (other coordinates are equal to zero) and radius J_{1x}, where J_{1x}, J_{1z} are Euclidean $\{x, z\}$-coordinates of the joint J_1, respectively. We define a plane through J_1 parallel to the plane xy as $\tau_1 = e_3 + J_{1z}e_\infty$. Then the circle of a possible motion of J_1 is given as the intersection of these objects:

$$Z_1 = S_1 \wedge \tau_1. \tag{22}$$

Another observation is that the joints J_0, J_1, J_2, J_3 always lie in a common plane perpendicular to xy. Thus we consider the plane

$$\tau_{12}^* = \bar{J}_3 \wedge L_0^*, \tag{23}$$

where L_0^* is the OPNS representation of the line perpendicular to xy plane through the origin. The intersection of τ_{12} and Z_1 is a pointpair indicating two final possible positions of J_1. From the inner construction of the robot we determine the correct point (see Fig. 3):

$$Pp_1 = Z_1 \wedge \tau_{12}, \tag{24}$$

$$\bar{J}_1 = \frac{+\sqrt{Pp_1^* \cdot Pp_1^*} + Pp_1^*}{-e_\infty \cdot Pp_1^*}. \tag{25}$$

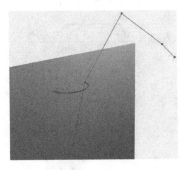

Fig. 3. Finding $\bar{J}_1$ (Color figure online)

The remaining joint to compute is $\bar{J}_2$. Let us construct two spheres, $S_{12} = \bar{J}_1 - \frac{1}{2}l_{12}^2 e_\infty$ with center $\bar{J}_1$ and radius l_{12} and $S_{23} = \bar{J}_3 - \frac{1}{2}l_{23}^2 e_\infty$ with center $\bar{J}_3$ and radius l_{23}. The intersection of these spheres is a circle

$$Z_2 = S_{12} \wedge S_{23}, \tag{26}$$

see the left picture in Fig. 4. The joint $\bar{J}_2$ is one of the points of the pointpair given as the intersection of the circle Z_2 and the plane τ_{12}

$$Pp_2 = Z_2 \wedge \tau_{12}. \tag{27}$$

Again from the construction of the robot the correct point is the one representing the lower value of φ_2, hence according to the right picture in Fig. 4

$$\bar{J}_2 = \frac{+\sqrt{Pp_2^* \cdot Pp_2^*} + Pp_2^*}{-e_\infty \cdot Pp_2^*}. \tag{28}$$

4.2   Computing the Joint Angles

Having the initial and the final positions of the joints, as we can see in Fig. 5, we can compute the final configuration of the manipulator, i.e. the joint angles $\varphi_1, \ldots, \varphi_5$. Let us recall that in the way of restrictions on the angles we consider

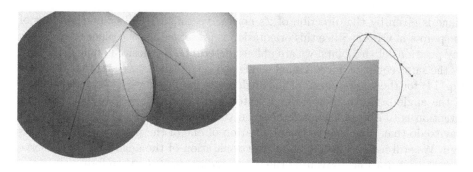

Fig. 4. Finding $\bar{J}_2$

Table 3. The simplified restrictions on the angles of the model.

Angle	φ_1	φ_2	φ_3	φ_4	φ_5
Range	$(-165, 165)$	$(-70, 95)$	$(-30, 155)$	$(-180, 180)$	$(0, 180)$

a simplified model of the manipulator. For the actual model ranges of some of the angles are dependent on each other. The ranges of all angles for our simplified model are given in Table 3 and we do not consider any dependency between angles. The positive orientations of the angles are denoted by arrows in Fig. 1.

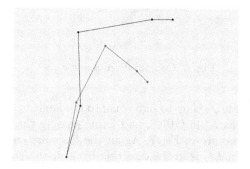

Fig. 5. Initial positions of joints - black, final positions of joints - red (Color figure online)

Angle φ_1: The angle φ_1 can be expressed as the angle between the plane passes through the points $\bar{J}_0, \bar{J}_1, \bar{J}_2$, which is precisely plane τ_{12} from Eq. (23), and a plane passes through J_0, J_1, J_2

$$\rho_{12}^* = J_0 \wedge J_1 \wedge J_2 \wedge e_\infty, \tag{29}$$

see Fig. 6. Now the caution must be taken when we use the Eq. (14). We have to realize that in CGA every object has its orientation. The orientation of the plane is given by the direction of its normal vector in IPNS or by the order of the points in OPNS. Since this orientation is preserved for the planes ρ_{12}, τ_{12} for any positions of the joints, we are able to determine the desired angle up to sign by the same equation for any final configuration. At first we claim that if we use Eq. (14) for the computation of the angle between planes we get the supplement of the angle between their normal vectors. In Fig. 6 it is clearly seen that our intention is to obtain the angle between the normal vectors of the planes. One way to do that is to change the orientation of one of the planes by changing its sign. We still have to decide about the orientation of the angle. We can observe that the orientation is given by the x, y coordinates of $\bar{J}_1$, therefore

$$\varphi_1 = k_1 \arccos \frac{-\tau_{12}^* \cdot \rho_{12}^*}{|\tau_{12}^*||\rho_{12}^*|}, \tag{30}$$

where $k_1 = 1$ if the projection of $\bar{J}_1$ into xy plane lies in q_1 or q_2 and $k_1 = -1$ if the same projection lies in q_3 or q_4, q_i is i-th quadrant of xy plane.

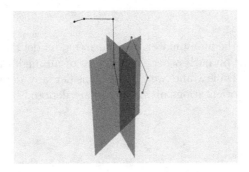

Fig. 6. Computation of angle φ_1

Angle φ_2: The angle φ_2 is up to sign equal to the angle between a vertical line through $\bar{J}_1$, denoted as L_v^* in OPNS, and a line passing through $\bar{J}_1, \bar{J}_2$ denoted as L_{12}^*, see the left picture in Fig. 7. Again the lines are constructed in a way that the orientation of L_{12}^* is in the direction from $\bar{J}_1$ to $\bar{J}_2$ and the orientation of L_v^* is in upward direction, then

$$\varphi_2 = k_2 \arccos \frac{L_v^* \cdot L_{12}^*}{|L_v^*||L_{12}^*|}. \tag{31}$$

The sign of the angle can be determined according to the mutual position of the projections of $\bar{J}_1$ and $\bar{J}_2$ into xy plane. Particularly $k_2 = 1$ if the projection of $\bar{J}_2$ lies in the same quadrant as the projection of $\bar{J}_1$ further from the origin and $k_2 = -1$ in any other case, see the right picture in Fig. 7.

Angle φ_3: Let us construct a vertical line through origin $L_0 = e_1 \wedge e_3$. We can define a rotor corresponding to the rotation given by φ_1:

$$R_1 = \cos(\frac{\varphi_1}{2}) - L_0 \sin(\frac{\varphi_1}{2}). \tag{32}$$

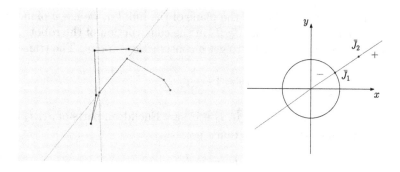

Fig. 7. Computation of angle φ_2

We consider two lines, $L_{23}^* = J_2 \wedge J_3 \wedge e_\infty$ which represents the link l_{23} in the initial position and $L_{\bar{2}\bar{3}}^* = \bar{J}_2 \wedge \bar{J}_3 \wedge e_\infty$ representing the same link in the final position. With help of R_1 we can rotate $L_{\bar{2}\bar{3}}$ about φ_1 in reversed orientation as

$$L_{\bar{2}\bar{3}rot} = \tilde{R}_1 L_{\bar{2}\bar{3}} R_1. \tag{33}$$

The lines $L_{23}, L_{\bar{2}\bar{3}rot}$ lie in a common plane and the angle between them is up to sign equal to φ_3, therefore

$$\varphi_3 = k_3 \arccos \frac{L_{23}^* \cdot L_{\bar{2}\bar{3}rot}^*}{|L_{23}^*||L_{\bar{2}\bar{3}rot}^*|}. \tag{34}$$

Similarly as for the previous angles $k_3 = \pm 1$. As we mentioned before, the direction of the link l_{23} is not dependent on the transformations φ_1, φ_2. Let $\bar{J}_{3z}, \bar{J}_{2z}$ be z-coordinates of $\bar{J}_3, \bar{J}_2$, respectively, then $k_3 = 1$ if $\bar{J}_{3z} - \bar{J}_{2z} < d_3$ and $k_3 = -1$ if $\bar{J}_{3z} - \bar{J}_{2z} > d_3$, where d_3 is the difference between z-coordinates of J_3, J_2 in the initial positions.

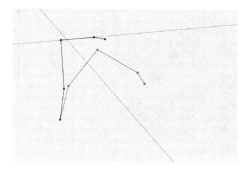

Fig. 8. Computation of angle φ_3

Angle φ_4: In the case of the angle φ_4 we follow the construction of the manipulator as indicated in the right picture of Fig. 1. Instead of the plane passes through $\bar{J}_2, \bar{J}_3, \bar{J}_4$ which is the plane of the link l_{23}, we use a plane of the shoulder that connects the joints $\bar{J}_2, \bar{J}_3$ in the construction of the robot. At first we translate the joint $\bar{J}_2$ in order to get a construction's point. The translator is

$$T_2 = 1 - \frac{1}{2}t_2 e_\infty, \tag{35}$$

where $t_2 = \frac{(\bar{j}_2 - \bar{j}_1)}{|\bar{j}_2 - \bar{j}_1|} d_3$. Recall that $\bar{j}_1, \bar{j}_2 \in \mathbb{R}^3$ are Euclidean parts of $\bar{J}_1, \bar{J}_2$ respectively. Then we have the construction's point

$$\bar{J}_{2c} = T_2 \bar{J}_2 \tilde{T}_2 \tag{36}$$

and finally we can describe two planes (see the left picture in Fig. 9)

$$\tau_c^* = \bar{J}_{2c} \wedge \bar{J}_3 \wedge \bar{J}_4 \wedge e_\infty, \tag{37}$$

$$\tau_{\bar{1}2\bar{3}}^* = \bar{J}_1 \wedge \bar{J}_2 \wedge \bar{J}_3 \wedge e_\infty. \tag{38}$$

As in the case of angle φ_1 to compute the angle between the planes which is up to a sign equal to φ_4, we want the planes in the initial configuration to have opposite orientations to each other. For that reason the angle is computed as

$$\varphi_1 = k_4 \arccos \frac{-\tau_c^* \cdot \tau_{\bar{1}2\bar{3}}^*}{|\tau_c^*||\tau_{\bar{1}2\bar{3}}^*|}. \tag{39}$$

The orientation is determined with help of the normal vector of the plane $\tau_{\bar{1}2\bar{3}}$, or more precisely the projection of this vector n_{xy} into xy plane, and v_{34} which is the same projection of the vector with start point $\bar{J}_3$ and end point $\bar{J}_4$. Then $k_4 = 1$ if $n_{xy} \cdot v_{34} > 0$ (the angle between vectors is acute) and $k = -1$ if $n_{xy} \cdot v_{34} < 0$ (obtuse angle). The right picture in Fig. 9 displays a situation where the sign of φ_4 is negative.

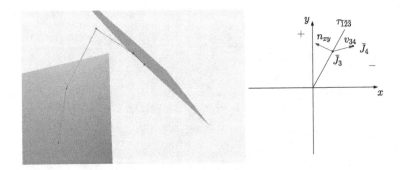

Fig. 9. Computation of angle φ_4

Angle φ_5: With help of the point $\bar{J}_{2c}$ given by Eq. (36) we can define a line

$$L_c^* = \bar{J}_{2c} \wedge \bar{J}_3 \wedge e_\infty \tag{40}$$

that represents a shoulder of the robot. Next we have a line of the gripper passing through $\bar{J}_3, \bar{J}_4$

$$L_{\bar{34}}^* = \bar{J}_3 \wedge \bar{J}_4 \wedge e_\infty. \tag{41}$$

Then φ_5 is equal to the angle between these two lines

$$\varphi_5 = \arccos \frac{L_c^* \cdot L_{\bar{34}}^*}{|L_c^*||L_{\bar{34}}^*|}. \tag{42}$$

Due to a restriction on the range of φ_5, we only consider the positive sign of the angle.

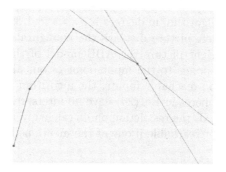

Fig. 10. Computation of angle φ_5

4.3 Experiment

The inverse kinematics model was programmed and tested in Python. The computation was done with help of module Clifford (by H. Hadfield) and for the visualisation we used module Pyganja (by H. Hadfield) and Ganja (by Steven De Keninck). From Clifford module we import tools for CGA algebra by commands:

```
from clifford.g3c import *
from clifford.tools.g3c import *
```

Then we are able to work with CGA objects within python language in very intuitive and efficient way. As an example we show a code where two points are created with help of function 'up' which conformalizes a Euclidean vector in order to obtain a CGA point. Then the OPNS of the line passes through these points is created and its IPNS is computed by dual operator:

```
P1 = up(0)
P2 = up(e1+e2+e3)
L_opns = P1^P2^einf
L_ipns = L_opns.dual()
```

where the output row by row is

$$-(0.5\char`^e4) + (0.5\char`^e5)$$
$$(1.0\char`^e1) + (1.0\char`^e2) + (1.0\char`^e3) + (1.0\char`^e4) + (2.0\char`^e5)$$
$$(1.0\char`^e145) + (1.0\char`^e245) + (1.0\char`^e345)$$
$$-(1.0\char`^e12) + (1.0\char`^e13) - (1.0\char`^e23)$$

In this manner the algorithm for inverse kinematics described above was programmed. We tested the functionality of the code for many different inputs, i.e. an orientation and a point we want to reach. For the inputs that are reachable by the manipulator, our algorithm produced the same results as ABB Robot studio. In our example the input end point in millimetres is $[1200, 1150, 730]$ and the orientation of the gripper is given by vector $(1, 0, -1)$. The final configuration computed by the algorithm in degrees is $a_f = (48.4, 39.8, 40.3, -66.0, 35.4)$, see Fig. 11 where the left picture displays the configuration computed by our algorithm and in the right picture the ABB model of the same configuration whose end point corresponds to the input point of our algorithm is displayed. Let us note that for non-reachable inputs, the algorithm fails either at finding point $\bar{J}_2$ because the spheres in Eq. (26) have no intersection or an angle in the final configuration exceeds the restriction on its range given by Table 3. Thus for our model a point is not reachable if one of the mentioned situations occurs.

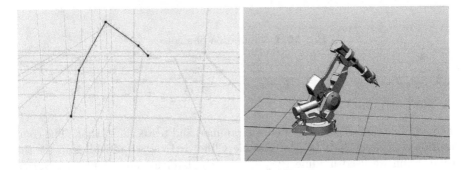

Fig. 11. Comparison of the result with ABB Robot studio.

5   Conclusion

We proposed a CGA-based algorithm that solves the inverse kinematics problem for a specific serial robot arm ABB IRB440. The solution is based on intersections of the spheres as natural geometric primitives in CGA which keeps the geometric insight and requires knowledge specific robot's geometry only. We also solved the problem of a choice of suitable intersections among all possibilities and, furthermore, managed to determine the sign of the angles respecting the construction conditions. The algorithm was tested for different inputs over the whole workspace and compared with simulations in ABB Robot Studio. Our outputs were accurate to satisfy machine precision.

Let us note that the problem of inverse kinematics based on geometric algebra was discussed in [12] for planar 2-link robot or in [13] for a robot with different geometry. In our solution we presented the obstacles of the geometry of IRB4400 that we successfully overcame. With the development of new software tools for geometric algebra codes optimization, e.g. Gaalop [11] and its modification for python called Gajit [14], the algorithms based on geometric algebra could be implemented to industrial solutions in the future.

Acknowledgements. The author was supported by solution grand FV19-04 science Fund of the FME 2019 at Brno University of Technology.

References

1. Dorst, L., Fontijne, D., Mann, S.: Geometric Algebra for Computer Science: An Object-Oriented Approach to Geometry. Morgan Kaufmann, Burlington (2007)
2. Lounesto, P.: Clifford Algebras and Spinors. Cambridge University Press, Cambridge (2006)
3. Perwass, C.: Geometric Algebra with Applications in Engineering. Springer-Verlag, Heidelberg (2009). https://doi.org/10.1007/978-3-540-89068-3
4. Hrdina, J., Návrat, A., Vašík, P.: GAC application to corner detection based on eccentricity. In: Gavrilova, M., Chang, J., Thalmann, N.M., Hitzer, E., Ishikawa, H. (eds.) CGI 2019. LNCS, vol. 11542, pp. 571–577. Springer, Cham (2019). https://doi.org/10.1007/978-3-030-22514-8_57
5. Hrdina, J., Matoušek, R., Tichý, R.: Colour image segmentation by region growing based on conformal geometric algebra. In: Gavrilova, M., Chang, J., Thalmann, N.M., Hitzer, E., Ishikawa, H. (eds.) CGI 2019. LNCS, vol. 11542, pp. 564–570. Springer, Cham (2019). https://doi.org/10.1007/978-3-030-22514-8_56
6. Stodola, M.: Monocular kinematics based on geometric algebras. In: Mazal, J. (ed.) MESAS 2018. LNCS, vol. 11472, pp. 121–129. Springer, Cham (2019). https://doi.org/10.1007/978-3-030-14984-0_10
7. Corrochano, E.B.: Geometric Computing for Perception Action Systems. Springer, Heidelberg (2012). https://doi.org/10.1007/978-1-4613-0177-6
8. Hrdina, J., Návrat, A., Vašík, P., Matoušek, R.: CGA-based robotic snake control. Adv. Appl. Clifford Algebras **27**(1), 621–632 (2016). https://doi.org/10.1007/s00006-016-0695-5
9. Aristidou, A., Lasenby, J., Chrysanthou, Y., Shamir, A.: Inverse kinematics techniques in computer graphics: a survey. Comput. Graph. Forum **37**, 35–58 (2017)
10. Murray, R.M., Li, Z., Sastry, S.S.: A Mathematical Introduction to Robotic Manipulation. CRC Press, Boca Raton (2017)
11. Hildenbrand, D.: Foundations of Geometric Algebra Computing. Springer, Berlin Heidelberg (2013). https://doi.org/10.1007/978-3-642-31794-1
12. Hrdina, J., Návrat, A., Vašík, P.: Notes on planar inverse kinematics based on geometric algebra. Adv. Appl. Clifford Algebras **28**(3), 1–14 (2018). https://doi.org/10.1007/s00006-018-0890-7
13. Kleppe, A.L., Egeland, O.: Inverse kinematics for industrial robots using conformal geometric algebra. Model. Ident. Control Norw. Res. Bull. **37**, 63–75 (2016)
14. Hadfield, H., Hildenbrand, D., Arsenovic, A.: Gajit: symbolic optimisation and JIT compilation of geometric algebra in Python with GAALOP and Numba. In: Gavrilova, M., Chang, J., Thalmann, N.M., Hitzer, E., Ishikawa, H. (eds.) CGI 2019. LNCS, vol. 11542, pp. 499–510. Springer, Cham (2019). https://doi.org/10.1007/978-3-030-22514-8_50

Design of an Active-Reliable Grasping Mechanism for Autonomous Unmanned Aerial Vehicles

Ashwin Suresh Nedungadi and Martin Saska[✉]

Multi-Robot Systems, Czech Technical University, Prague, Czech Republic
{nedunash,martin.saska}@fel.cvut.cz
http://mrs.felk.cvut.cz/

Abstract. This paper presents a novel design of an active grasping mechanism for autonomous Unmanned Aerial Vehicles (UAVs) aimed to carry ferromagnetic objects in assembly tasks. The proposed design uses electromagnets along with a combination of sensors to provide fast and reliable feedback. The designed gripper with its control system is aimed to be fully autonomous and will be employed in a task in the Mohamed Bin Zayed International Robotics Challenge (MBZIRC) 2020 competition where a group of autonomous UAVs cooperatively build a wall. The design is optimized for the Tarot 650 drone platform and for outdoor operation, while taking into consideration robustness of performance and resilience to aerial maneuvers. We describe the design of the gripper, the overall system and the approach used to obtain the feedback from the sensors which is crucial for robust aerial grasping and for high level planning of the assembly task. Various outdoor experiments were conducted on fabricated bricks to verify the proposed approach and to demonstrate the ability of the system to autonomously build a wall.

Keywords: Unmanned Aerial Vehicles · Multi-rotor systems · Aerial grasping · Aerial manipulation · Active gripper · Feedback estimation

1 Introduction

Multi-Rotor or Unmanned Aerial Vehicles (UAVs) with on-board equipment are ideal platforms for autonomous navigation and exploration tasks such as Inspection [1], Mapping [2,3], Exploration [4], Search & Rescue [5] and Transport [6–8] due to their small size, low cost, ability to hover on the spot and the variety of configurations in which they can be built.

With the growing number of applications for UAVs, they are also used in tasks where interaction and manipulation with the environment [9] is necessary which creates an increasing demand for the development of grasping mechanisms that can lift and manipulate objects.

The required grippers have to be reliable and be able to lift a variety of payloads while staying light-weight and consuming low-power to be used onboard UAVs.

© Springer Nature Switzerland AG 2020
J. Mazal et al. (Eds.): MESAS 2019, LNCS 11995, pp. 162–179, 2020.
https://doi.org/10.1007/978-3-030-43890-6_13

Although there has been recent interest in developing such grasping mechanisms for UAVs, there haven't been much research done in developing electromagnetic grasping solutions due to the worry of power consumption and weight. With the development of low-power electromagnets with heavy payload capabilities, it is more viable and reliable to create electromagnetic grasping solutions due to the simplicity, scalability and future scope offered by them.

1.1   State of the Art

Available solutions of aerial grasping mechanisms include work done by RISC laboratory at King Abdullah university of science and technology [10] where a passive magnetic gripper with an impulse release mechanism and push-button feedback was developed. While this sort of gripper provides a low-power passive solution, the grasping capabilities provided by permanent magnets are inferior compared to an electromagnet. Furthermore, the release mechanism that relies on servos to separate the grasped object is bulky and adds another layer of unnecessary complexity. A scaled up version of this concept is also presented in the work [11] developed by the KAIST team for MBZIRC 2017. The system integrates 2 camera modules required for grasping and uses 13 neodymium magnets and 4 servomotors to forcefully separate an object from the gripper.

Another popular solution for gripper design utilizes electro-permanent magnets (EPMs), due to their low-power consumption, payload capabilities and the ability to magnetize and demagnetize the electro-permanent magnet as required with the use of external circuits.

Such a solution was also utilized by our team [12] and various others [13,14] using the OpenGrab EPM V3 from nicadrone[1].

A custom version of such a mechanism is also presented in an earlier work by ETH Zurich [15] which has the ability to grasp objects with curved surfaces and utilizes alnico and neodymium magnets.

Although electro-permanent solutions are popular candidates for aerial grasping and manipulation tasks, they come with disadvantages. They are expensive, do not scale well with mass, have low grasping capabilities and require an active control circuit to magnetize and demagnetize the magnet. Furthermore, there is a need for firm contact with the object in order to magnetize and grasp the object successfully.

As experienced by our team [12] and others [13,14] during the last MBZIRC 2017 competition, the magnet can also break if used with heavy force and the circuitry can burn out if the command signal is sent multiple times resulting in many gripper failures and an overall low success rate [13].

The teams also found that the EPM solution provided to be too weak in outdoor conditions where gripper failure was even caused due to the thick layer of paint on the objects in the competition [12–14].

A unique idea for aerial grasping using a self sealing suction mechanism is presented and tested in the work [16]. Although the possibility of using suction

---

[1] https://nicadrone.com/products/epm-v3.

for aerial grasping proves to be a great solution for non-magnetic object grasping and grasping of items with small curvature, the disadvantage of having a big enough compressor for sufficient volume flow [16] on the UAV combined with its complexity made it a clearly unsuitable candidate for our task.

While the above mentioned aerial grasping solutions are not as robust, simple or heavy payload compatible, our solution is designed for ferrous payloads and provides reliable feedback using multiple sensors on whether an object is successfully grasped or not. Moreover, electromagnets provide the solid advantage of scalability to the system, being cheap and can be hot swapped on the field to accommodate heavier or lighter payloads or in case of failure.

The mechanical design of our gripper is developed with reliability and operation in outdoor desert conditions in mind while being able to lift objects weighing up to 4 kg.

1.2 Motivation and Preliminaries

The primary motivation of this work comes from our participation in an upcoming robotics competition in the United Arab Emirates that will be held in March of 2020 (MBZIRC 2020)[2] which consists of solving various challenges using autonomous robots. The proposed system is targeted for Challenge II where a group of three UAVs cooperatively detect and retrieve various ferrous bricks of different sizes and colors to assemble them into a pre-defined structure. The proposed challenge will take place under a GPS denied outdoor environment in Abu Dhabi similar to the third challenge from MBZIRC 2017[3] where our team won the first place [12,17]. The gripper used for the previous competition consisted of an electro-permanent magnet OpenGrab EPM V3 end effector and a compression shaft which attaches to a 3D printed mounting frame on a ball joint described in our previous work [12]. However, due to the disadvantages of using EPM based grasping solutions mentioned in Sect. 1.1, we decided to propose an alternate gripper for the competition in 2020.

An important factor to consider while designing a grasping mechanism for UAVs is that the holding force of a ferrite magnet decreases by approximately 85% in shear if the gripper and the payload are not parallel to the ground [12]. This effectively reduced the holding force of the EPM [12] to approximately 2.25 kg even though the EPM used theoretically had 15 kg of holding force.

Moreover, the degrees of freedom provided by the gripper plays a role in if the UAV can successfully carry an object during flight as it has various forces acting on it, therefore a mechanism with at least 2 degrees of freedom and that can align itself parallel to the ground is required. It was also experienced that the thickness of the metal surface must be above 0.2 mm for reliable grasping. Anything less and the magnetic field produced by the magnet would not successfully attach to the object due to weak magnetic strength.

---

[2] https://www.mbzirc.com/challenge/2020.
[3] https://www.mbzirc.com/challenge/2017.

As the UAVs transporting the object will be in flight and will experience accelerations and have a downward force acting at all times due to the thrust generated by the propellers, it is crucial to design a gripper with enough holding force that can withstand all such disturbances in harsh outdoor conditions.

2   Hardware Architecture

The hardware components used for the MBZIRC competition are handpicked to meet the required criteria such as payload, reliable sensor data and computational power. The UAV frame chosen for the grasping task is the tarot 650 sport quad-copter with a carbon fiber body making it lightweight while satisfying the size requirements given for the MBZIRC 2020 competition.

The proposed UAV platform is a complex system with multiple onboard sensors and computational units shown in Fig. 1. The open-source nature of the system makes it ideal for rapid prototyping which in turn makes them perfect for competition scenarios and multi-robot system research.

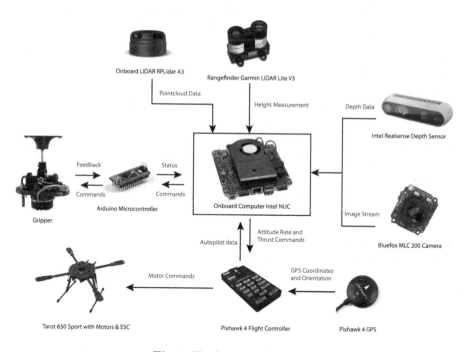

Fig. 1. Hardware architecture

The system is controlled at the lowest level by a Pixhawk 4 flight controller[4] with its own GPS that provides reliable coordinates and contains various sensors such as gyroscopes, accelerometers and magnetometers.

---

[4] https://docs.px4.io/v1.9.0/en/flight_controller/pixhawk4.html.

An Intel NUC-i7[5] onboard computer provides the necessary computational power required to solve the onboard image processing, signal processing, state estimation, feedback control, motion planning and UAV coordination tasks effectively. The communication between the computer and the Pixhawk controller is done with the MAVlink protocol and communication between the UAVs in a group is achieved with the help of the onboard WIFI module on the onboard NUC computer.

Two Bluefox MLC 200[6] cameras are used onboard the UAV, one running an optic flow [18] algorithm that provides odometry during navigation and the other fitted with a fisheye lens in the detection for brick grasping [19] while the onboard LIDAR is used for localization [12] of the UAV and mapping of the environment.

The Intel realsense depth camera[7] on the other hand, will be used conditionally should the task require it, for example in the case of assembly of the wall in challenge 2 or in challenge 3 where a group of UAVs must extinguish a series of fires in a simulated urban fire-fighting scenario.

While the onboard pixhawk controller provides barometric altitude readings, the UAV does not have any information about the distance to a detected brick or the ground from the pixhawk. This is solved by the garmin lite v3 rangefinder[8] which provides distance to ground readings in realtime.

Finally, the gripper communicates information about the feedback status with the onboard computer with the help of an arduino nano microcontroller running a custom serial protocol explained in the next section and can be controlled via the serial protocol for grasp and release of an object.

Serial Communication: The communication between the gripper and the onboard computer on the UAV is facilitated by a custom "MRS Serial" protocol.

Messages transmitted and received via this protocol consists of 8-bits following the rules of UART communication. The protocol is described in the Fig. 2.

Each character inside the box represents one 8 bit value. The first byte is always the character "b", this represents the start of a serial message and is converted into decimal notation during checksum.

The next byte written is the payload size. Payload of the message can range from 1 to 256 bytes long and the first byte of the payload is the message id, which is pre-defined and serves to differentiate between different messages of the

---

[5] https://www.intel.com/content/www/us/en/products/boards-kits/nuc/boards.html.

[6] https://www.matrix-vision.com/USB2.0-single-board-camera-mvbluefox-mlc.html?camera=mvBlueFOX-MLC200wG&selectInterface=Alle&selectMpixels=Alle&selectFps=Alle&selectSensor=Alle&selectColor=Alle&selectSize=Alle&selectShutter=Alle&selectModel=Alle&col=1&row=0.

[7] https://www.intelrealsense.com/stereo-depth/?utm_source=intelcom_website&utm_medium=button&utm_campaign=day-to-day&utm_content=D400_learn-more_button.

[8] https://buy.garmin.com/en-US/US/p/557294overview.

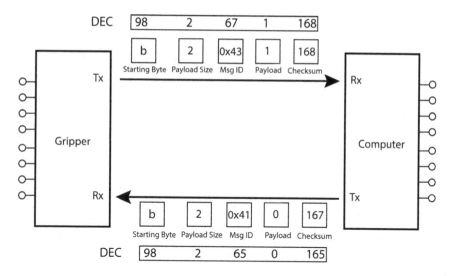

Fig. 2. Description of the serial protocol

same length. The message id is followed by the payload and finally, the checksum is calculated and compared at the receiving end. If the checksums do not match, the message is discarded.

3   System Software Pipeline

The software used for the UAVs utilizes the open-source Robot Operating System (ROS) running onboard the Intel NUC computer using which each task and sub-tasks can be split into smaller manageable structures in ROS (nodes). All software changes are rigorously tested in Gazebo simulator along with the firmware from Pixhawk as this provides a realistic test-bed for our systems minimizing crashes and increasing safety during field tests.

An overview of the system pipeline is illustrated in Fig. 3. The main core of the system consists of a state machine which is used to manage all sub-systems and asynchronously multiplexes between different sub-pipelines as required depending upon a particular task, which in our case corresponds to challenge II. The state machine is designed with the help of FlexBE (Python Library) and is fully integrated into the designed ROS system framework [17].

The state machine, in the first step is fed information from a brick placement scheduler which relays information about each brick object and its pre-defined parameters such as color, weight and priority. It also contains the order of how each brick must be placed in the wall as prescribed by a plan given to us before the challenge. The second step consists of the state machine performing various sweeps of the competition arena where individual bricks are detected, localized and the scheduler is updated accordingly.

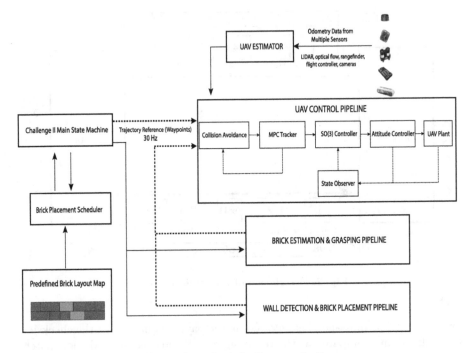

Fig. 3. Overview of software pipeline

The brick estimation and grasping sub-pipeline is illustrated in Fig. 4. As illustrated, the onboard color camera searches the competition arena while running a brick detection algorithm that uses color segmentation [19,20] and navigates during flight on an optical flow algorithm using a grey-scale camera [18]. Once a brick is detected and localized the coordinates of the brick on the ground is calculated and relayed to the brick estimation algorithm which generates the map containing the brick states. The brick estimator keeps track of all the detected bricks in the environment and deactivates or deletes a brick if the grasping is unsuccessful or if the brick is already assembled on the wall.

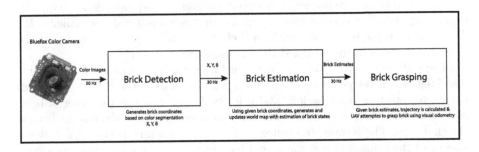

Fig. 4. Sub-pipeline for autonomous grasping

Once the brick is estimated and trajectory leading to a particular brick is known, the UAV goes to the given coordinates using waypoints and aligns itself horizontally above the estimated position of the brick. It then descends to a height of 1.5 m above the ground, once the UAV has reached the desired height and is aligned above the brick it tries to grasp the brick by turning on the gripper and descending gently onto the brick surface. If the brick is successfully grasped the gripper returns positive feedback and the UAV ascends to nominal height and flies to the wall-building area where each brick is assembled with the help of a ground robot according to the brick layout map using a realsense depth sensor and visual servoing.

If the UAV is unable to grasp the brick in 3 attempts, the state machine terminates the process with the outcome that grasping was unsuccessful.

On the low-level, the UAV is stabilized and controlled by the control pipeline [21] shown in Fig. 3. Automatic control of the UAVs relies on esti-mates of the states of the UAV model. The platform is equipped with multiple onboard sensors providing independent odometric data and fuses this informa-tion to obtain a single and smooth estimate of UAV pose which contains both horizontal and vertical position estimation and is an important criteria as the SO(3) state feedback is sensitive to noise.

The position controller uses the estimated state as feedback to follow the trajectories given to it by the trajectory planner.

4 Gripper Design

The proposed design of the gripper consists of an assembly of 4 major parts:

1. Electromagnet with switching circuit
2. A gripper housing with shaft and mounting attachment
3. A combination of hall sensor embedded in the magnet (Fig. 6) and inductive proximity sensor for feedback estimation of grasping.
4. Arduino microcontroller that processes raw data from the sensors, communi-cates with the on-board computer and also controls the switching circuit for the electromagnet.

4.1 Electromagnet and Switching Circuit

An industrial electromagnet with dimensions 49/21 mm^9 capable of lifting up-to 40 kg of payload provides the necessary magnetic strength for grasping. In the previous prototypes of the gripper, we have experimented with dual electromag-nets for grasping each that can lift up to 25 kg and it was found that a single 40 kg capable electromagnet performed better than dual smaller electromagnets. Our solution is supplied a constant 12 V DC for its operation and has a cus-tom built N-MOSFET switching circuit integrated with the Arduino that can

---

^{9} https://es.aliexpress.com/item/32817542468.html.

Fig. 5. Modeled CAD assembly of proposed gripper showing 1. Electromagnet, 2. Gripper housing, 3. Sensors used for feedback, 4. Arduino microcontroller

be toggled by the UAV's onboard computer using a rosservice call as needed. Although the electromagnet consumes 10 W, it is insignificant compared to the power drawn by the UAV's onboard computer (60 W) and motors (1000 W) from the 27000 mAh Li-Po Battery. And considering the magnets won't be turned on and in operation continuously throughout the flight, there is no reason to be concerned by the electromagnet's power consumption.

4.2   Gripper Housing and Mount

The gripper housing and mounting bracket was designed to be sturdy and have 2 degrees of freedom in the pitch and roll axis but not in the yaw as this is undesirable for precise aerial manipulation. The housing consists of a main mount where the sensors, magnet and microcontroller are fixed, an inner and outer ring structure with ball bearings to facilitate the movement along the two described axis and a shaft with a mounting bracket so it can be attached to the UAV with 4 screws. By the mechanical design of the gripper, the angle of rotation for the 2 axes are restricted to approximately 45°, this ensures that the grasped object does not fall down or swing too much and cause disturbance for the drone.

4.3   Feedback Sensors

Reliably estimating the feedback of a successful grasp is the most crucial task for autonomous grasping. Our solution integrates two different sensors for estimating feedback from the gripper which can be seen in Fig. 6.

(a) Side view of gripper showing proximity sensor and arduino microcontroller

(b) Front view with hall effect sensor embedded on electromagnet surface

Fig. 6. Realized gripper with on-board sensors and switching circuit

Magnetic Sensing with Hall-Effect Sensor: The sensor used is a linear hall-effect sensor[10] which senses the change in the magnetic field of the electromagnet when a ferromagnetic object is grasped. The electromagnet when powered, has a steady magnetic field provided there is no parasitic fields in its close vicinity. When a ferrous object is grasped, this magnetic field is reduced and this drop is directly proportional to the thickness of the ferrous surface. By using a hall-effect sensor near the electromagnet, we measure this drop in magnetic field when an object is grasped and the arduino microcontroller provides the feedback estimation to the drone. The drawback with using this technique is that the hall-sensor drifts and the sensor requires to be calibrated before each grasp. In such case the drone signals to the gripper before each grasp attempt and a short calibration is done where a threshold value is calculated as shown in Fig. 11. Then after the UAV has grasped the proposed object, the gripper checks if the current value from the sensor is less than the threshold and provides a True or False value for the feedback.

Distance Sensing with Inductive Proximity Sensor: The second sensor used is an off the shelf industrial proximity cylindrical sensor[11] with 8 mm diameter and 5 cm height. It is lightweight, noise immune and weighs around 13 g. It

---

[10] Honeywell SS49e Linear Hall Effect Sensorhttps://sensing.honeywell.com/SS49E-linear-and-angle-sensor-ics.

[11] LJ8A3-2-Z Inductive Proximity Sensor.

outputs a high analog value when there is no ferrous object near its proximity and switches to a lower analog signal when a ferrous object is bought near it. In the case that the object is very close to it, i.e. the gripper has something grasped it outputs a constant value of zero. Two different sensors with different sensing distances of 8 mm and 2 mm were tested and the smaller proximity sensor with the sensing distance of 2 mm was sufficient for our task as the sensor only required a one time position calibration with respect to the magnet and could be fixed in its place.

A direct comparison of the previous gripper used and the proposed gripper (Fig. 7) is provided in the Table 1.

Table 1. Comparison between the two gripping systems

Parameter	Previous gripper	Proposed gripper
Weight	250 g	400 g
Max theoretical payload	15 kg	40 kg
Max payload in shear	2.25 kg	6 kg
Max tested payload	500 g	4 kg
Feedback	Single	Multiple
Scalable	No	Yes
Joint	Ball joint with 3-DOF	Mechanical with 2-DOF

(a) 3 DOF EPM based gripper used for MBZIRC 2017

(b) Proposed gripper for MBZIRC 2020

Fig. 7. Comparison between the previous gripper used and the proposed gripper

4.4   Control Through ROS:

The microcontroller onboard the gripper communicates with ROS using the serial protocol described in Sect. 2, the node publishes the feedback estimate of the gripper along with some diagnostic data like the analog sensor readings and state of the gripper during flight for easier debugging and records it in a rosbag for later analysis (Fig. 8).

Any node can call a rosservice to toggle the gripper on and off using the services "grip" and "ungrip".

During the challenge, the state machine for grasping running on the onboard computer can receive the feedback estimation from the gripper node and perform the grasping autonomously.

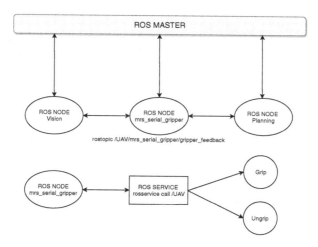

Fig. 8. ROS architecture

5   Feedback Estimation and Algorithm

Figure 9 describes the estimation algorithm running on the onboard arduino microcontroller. The raw data from the sensors are filtered after which the feedback is estimated as follows.

5.1   Hall Sensor

Before each grasping attempt, the hall sensor is calibrated and the threshold is determined. The UAV then attempts to grasp the object and if successfully grasped, the value from the hall sensor should drop below the calculated threshold. Hence the feedback status is updated and the UAV can proceed onto the next task. If the object would drop at any point in flight, the feedback status changes and the UAV will start searching again instead of wasting time going to the objective wall building area.

5.2   Proximity Sensor

The feedback from the proximity sensor consists of an analog high signal if there is no ferrous object in proximity and an analog low signal if there is any object in proximity. By presetting this distance between the object surface and the proximity sensor in a one time calibration, we can ensure that the proximity sensor is only triggered if the UAV successfully grasps an object.

The final feedback estimate consists of a fusion of each of the individual feedback estimates provided by the hall effect and proximity sensor. By fusing the

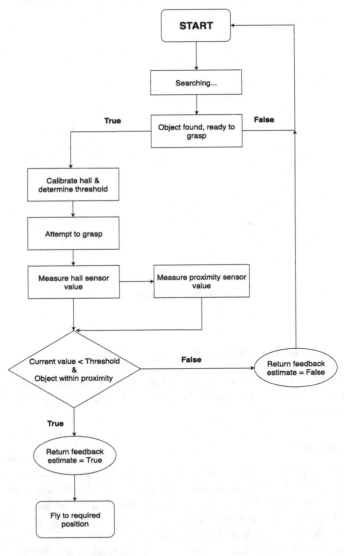

Fig. 9. Flowchart of estimation algorithm

different sensor outputs using two different sensing techniques, we can minimize false estimations.

6   Outdoor Experiments

We conducted a series of outdoor experiments where the UAVs with the wall building algorithm along with the gripper system was rigorously tested with fabricated bricks that consists of foam and metal sheets with the defined parameters in Table 2.

The test flight consisted of both manual and autonomous grasping tests. In both cases the flight time was measured to be approximately 12 min before the batteries had to be exchanged for a new one.

Table 2. Parameters of tested bricks

Brick color	Dimensions	Mass
Red	$0.30\,\text{m} \times 0.20\,\text{m} \times 0.20\,\text{m}$	1.2 kg
Green	$0.60\,\text{m} \times 0.20\,\text{m} \times 0.20\,\text{m}$	2.8 kg
Blue	$1.20\,\text{m} \times 0.20\,\text{m} \times 0.20\,\text{m}$	4.0 kg

(a) Grasped green brick

(b) Building wall structure

(c) UAV attempts to place brick in line

(d) Tested prototype with dual grasping

Fig. 10. Snaps from outdoor experiments where the complete system is tested under the challenge II scenario (Color figure online)

During test flights (Fig. 10), a mission planner in the form of a hierarchical state machine [17] running on the drone received and processed information of the sequence of bricks and then directed each drone to the relevant brick which is then recognized and validated by the onboard vision system. The gripper system was able to pick up, provide the right feedback and release all sizes of the ferrous bricks described in the challenge and the only limitation in payload was due to the maximum thrust produced by the drone.

In our case, the maximum payload tested was around 4 kg and the drone's maximum payload after the onboard instruments and battery pack was approximately 7 kg. Figure 11 shows the experimental data where the gripper grasped 4 different bricks during the test flight. The corresponding peaks and troughs in the hall sensor's output can be explained as follows:

1. When the magnet is first turned on the hall effect sensor's signal rises to a high value, this is the phase when the calibration is done. As this rise is not always the same and can drift depending on the parasitic fields around, the threshold is calculated before each individual grasping attempt.
2. When an object is grasped, the drop in magnetic field is noticeable and we can see the corresponding feedback estimation.

The feedback estimation from the proximity sensor is also shown in Fig. 11. The proximity sensor's value drops from a high analog value to zero when the gripper grasps a metal object and the feedback estimate changes accordingly.

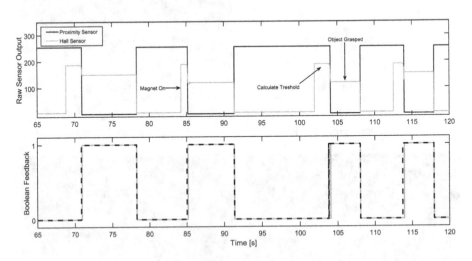

Fig. 11. Experimental data showing raw sensor output and final output produced by the feedback estimation algorithm in four different grasping attempts

During the autonomous grasping of bricks, the state machine generates "setpoints" or "waypoints" as positional data for the UAV to follow based on the brick estimates. The UAV then navigates to these set of points in the cartesian plane using it's own odometry data from optic flow.

The graph of the generated setpoints and actual UAV position from odometry during a grasping attempt and the positional control error is shown in Figs. 12 and 13.

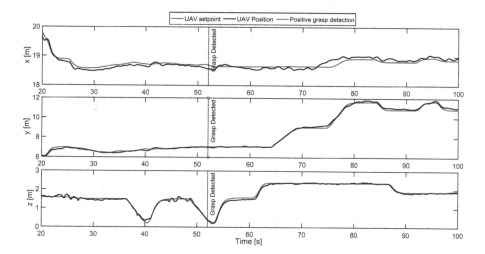

Fig. 12. Plot of uav setpoints and actual uav position during autonomous grasping

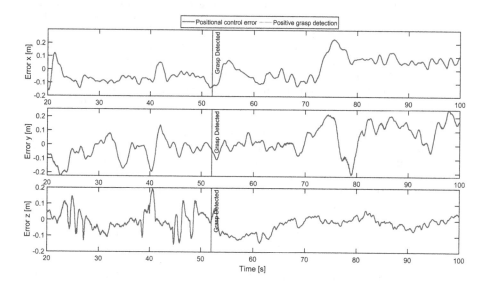

Fig. 13. Positional control error during autonomous grasping

7   Conclusion

In this work, we have detailed and proposed a novel yet simple mechanism that is both reliable and robust for aerial manipulation and grasping tasks. The overall system architecture, hardware design and the algorithm used to estimate feedback are described.

We have also discussed the advantages, disadvantages and challenges faced by using such technology onboard UAVs while expanding on our previous work and have performed several outdoor experiments with test objects to validate our proposal. The proposed concept outperforms current designs in terms of payload capabilities and has potential to be useful for various applications involving UAVs in the areas of drone delivery and disaster relief. The key challenges in the task included designing a tolerant mechanical housing, making sure that the system did not induce oscillations in the drone and that it could reliably give fast feedback continuously throughout the flight.

Acknowledgement. The presented work has been supported by the Czech Science Foundation (GAČR) under research project No. 17-16900Y. We also thank the Khalifa University of Science for funding our participation in the MBZIRC 2020. The support of the Grant Agency of the Czech Technical University in Prague under grant No. SGS17/187/OHK3/3T/13 is also gratefully acknowledged.

References

1. Loianno, G., Thomas, J., Kumar, V.: Cooperative localization and mapping of MAVs using RGB-D sensors. In: 2015 IEEE International Conference on Robotics and Automation (ICRA), pp. 4021–4028, May 2015
2. Chudoba, J., Kulich, M., Saska, M., Báča, T., Přeučil, L.: Exploration and mapping technique suited for visual-features based localization of MAVs. J. Intell. Robot. Syst. **84**(1), 351–369 (2016)
3. Ozaslan, T., Loianno, G., Keller, J., Taylor, C.J., Kumar, V.: Spatio-temporally smooth local mapping and state estimation inside generalized cylinders with micro aerial vehicles. IEEE Robot. Autom. Lett. **3**(4), 4209–4216 (2018)
4. Tomic, T., et al.: Toward a fully autonomous UAV: research platform for indoor and outdoor urban search and rescue. IEEE Robot. Autom. Mag. **19**(3), 46–56 (2012)
5. Michael, N., Shen, S., Mohta, K., Mulgaonkar, Y., Kumar, V.: Collaborative mapping of an earthquake-damaged building via ground and aerial robots. J. Field Robot. **29**(5), 832–841 (2012). https://onlinelibrary.wiley.com/doi/abs/10.1002/rob.21436
6. Ritz, R., D'Andrea, R.: Carrying a flexible payload with multiple flying vehicles. In: 2013 IEEE/RSJ International Conference on Intelligent Robots and Systems, pp. 3465–3471, November 2013
7. Michael, N., Fink, J., Kumar, V.: Cooperative manipulation and transportation with aerial robots. Auton. Robots **30**(1), 73–86 (2011). https://doi.org/10.1007/s10514-010-9205-0
8. Loianno, G., Kumar, V.: Cooperative transportation using small quadrotors using monocular vision and inertial sensing. IEEE RA-L Robot. Autom. Lett. **3**(2), 680–687 (2018)

9. Torre, A., Mengoli, D., Naldi, R., Forte, F., Macchelli, A., Marconi, L.: A prototype of aerial manipulator. In: 2012 IEEE/RSJ International Conference on Intelligent Robots and Systems, pp. 2653–2654, October 2012
10. Fiaz, U.A., Abdelkader, M., Shamma, J.S.: An intelligent gripper design for autonomous aerial transport with passive magnetic grasping and dual-impulsive release. In: 2018 IEEE/ASME International Conference on Advanced Intelligent Mechatronics (AIM), pp. 1027–1032, July 2018
11. Lee, J., Hyunchul Shim, D., Cho, S., Shin, H.: A mission management system for complex aerial logistics by multiple unmanned aerial vehicles in MBZIRC 2017. J. Field Robot. **36**(5), 919–939 (2019). https://onlinelibrary.wiley.com/doi/abs/10.1002/rob.21860
12. Loianno, G., et al.: Localization, grasping, and transportation of magnetic objects by a team of MAVs in challenging desert like environments. IEEE Robot. Autom. Lett. **3**(3), 1576–1583 (2018)
13. Bahnemann, R., Pantic, M., Popovic, M., Schindler, D.: The ETH-MAV team in the MBZ international robotics challenge. J. Field Robot. **36**(1), 78–103 (2019). https://onlinelibrary.wiley.com/doi/abs/10.1002/rob.21824
14. Castaño, A., Real, F., Ramón-Soria, P., Capitán, J.: Al-Robotics team: a cooperative multi-unmanned aerial vehicle approach for the Mohamed Bin Zayed International Robotic Challenge. J. Field Robot. **36**(1), 104–124 (2019). https://onlinelibrary.wiley.com/doi/abs/10.1002/rob.21810
15. Gawel, A., et al.: Aerial picking and delivery of magnetic objects with MAVs. In: 2017 IEEE International Conference on Robotics and Automation (ICRA), pp. 5746–5752 (2017)
16. Kessens, C.C., Thomas, J., Desai, J.P., Kumar, V.: Versatile aerial grasping using self-sealing suction. In: 2016 IEEE International Conference on Robotics and Automation (ICRA), pp. 3249–3254, May 2016
17. Spurny, V., et al.: Cooperative autonomous search, grasping and delivering in a treasure hunt scenario by a team of UAVs. J. Field Robot. **36**(1), 125–148 (2019)
18. Walter, V., Novák, T., Saska, M.: Self-localization of unmanned aerial vehicles based on optical flow in onboard camera images. In: Mazal, J. (ed.) MESAS 2017. LNCS, vol. 10756, pp. 106–132. Springer, Cham (2018). https://doi.org/10.1007/978-3-319-76072-8_8
19. Stepan, P., Krajnik, T., Petrlik, M., Saska, M.: Vision techniques for on-board detection, following, and mapping of moving targets. J. Field Robot. **36**(1), 252–269 (2019). https://onlinelibrary.wiley.com/doi/abs/10.1002/rob.21850
20. Baca, T., Stepan, P., Saska, M.: Autonomous landing on a moving car with unmanned aerial vehicle. In: The European Conference on Mobile Robotics (ECMR) (2017)
21. Baca, T., Hert, D., Loianno, G., Saska, M., Kumar, V.: Model predictive trajectory tracking and collision avoidance for reliable outdoor deployment of unmanned aerial vehicles. In: 2018 IEEE/RSJ International Conference on Intelligent Robots and Systems (IROS), pp. 6753–6760, October 2018

Multiple Carrier-Vehicle Travelling Salesman Problem

Tigran Fahradyan, Nicolas Bono Rossello$^{(\boxtimes)}$, and Emanuele Garone

Service d'Automatique et d'Analyse des Systèmes, Université Libre de
Bruxelles (ULB), Av. F.D. Roosevelt 50, CP 165/55, 1050 Brussels, Belgium
{tfahrady,nbonoros,egarone}@ulb.ac.be

Abstract. In this paper the Carrier-Vehicle Travelling Salesman Problem (CV-TSP) is extended to the case of 2 carriers and one small vehicle. The paper defines a minimum-time trajectory mission plan for the visit of a group of target points by the small vehicle. In this scenario, the main goal is to optimize the use of both carriers as a support of the vehicle. A Mixed-Integer Second Order Conic Programming (MISCOP) formulation is proposed for the case of a given order of visit. Additionally, the authors develop a fast heuristic which provides close to optimal results in a decent computational time. To end the paper several simulations are computed to show the effectiveness of the proposed solution.

1 Introduction

Over the past few years, the use of autonomous systems is experiencing a tremendous rise. As a result, the tasks and applications envisioned for this kind of systems are gaining in complexity and importance. Current rescue missions, logistics and transportation activities require such a wide range of capabilities -large autonomy, small size and maneuverability- that they cannot be provided by a single class of vehicle. Alternatively, the combination of different class platforms represents a more adequate solution to reach the specifications demanded [11].

While the coordination of several units of homogeneous vehicles has been widely developed and many complex applications are already established [2,3], the research work in heterogeneous systems is still at an early stage. In recent years, different research groups have studied the Traveling Salesman Problem applied to a team of heterogeneous vehicles. The Multi-Depot Heterogeneous Fleet Routing Vehicle Problem [16] considers the use of vehicles with different capacities and speeds to solve a routing problem. In [1], influenced by the current rise of drone applications, the last mile delivery problem is solved using a TSP approach for a group of drones while deployed by a truck with a fixed route.

Another recent contribution to this field is the Carrier-Vehicle Travelling Salesman Problem (CV-TSP) [7]. This variant of the TSP presents as a novelty the use of two different vehicles, a fast small vehicle and a slow carrier, which

This work has been supported by the European Commission under the Grant Agreement number 774571 (project PANTHEON- "Precision farming of hazelnut orchards").

are combined to perform different missions. The CV-TSP considers the scenario where a fast vehicle with limited endurance is transported and serviced by a slower carrier. The authors define a mathematical model of a carrier-vehicle system dynamics and the associated constraints. An optimal trajectory calculation connecting two points is provided, followed by a generalization of the problem to the visit of set of points obtaining a first sub-optimal solution. In [5], a first exact solution method for the CV-TSP was proposed. This problem, originally thought for rescue missions, rapidly demonstrated the applicability in other fields as logistics or transportation problems [12,13].

More recently, [4] extends the CV-TSP and proposes the case of 2 vehicles and one carrier. This extension of the original problem is motivated by cooperative search and reconnaissance missions in heterogeneous robot systems. Moreover, it can be easily proved that a larger group of heterogeneous vehicles for visiting a given set of target points will always result in a solution (i.e. total travel time) lower or equal than the one of a heterogeneous team of 2 vehicles. This work also provides a first non-linear formulation and good results using a deep learning approach.

In this paper we introduce a novel extension of the CV-TSP to the case of two carriers and one single vehicle, which is depicted in Fig. 1. In the described scenario, the small vehicle can choose indistinctly between both carriers to land and be serviced. Equivalently to [4], this variant always provides a faster mission time that the original case. It should be noticed that this complementary extension remains interesting as it includes a whole new group of additional applications. Such as the case of maritime monitoring, where we can find examples of single UAVs with multiple cruise bases [14] or mobile self powered carriers with a single UAV flying from one to another [9]. Another application example is encountered in the EU project PANTHEON "Precision farming of hazelnut orchards". In this case, the UAVs used for the orchard coverage have a limited autonomy and data storage. There, the coordination in movement between an aerial vehicle and larger ground robots to charge batteries and download data would increase the scalability of the concept to large-scale plantations [8].

The remainder of the paper is organized as follows. In Sect. 2 the problem is defined and an optimal mixed-integer formulation is proposed. In Sect. 3 a fast heuristic is presented for the case of large inputs. In Sect. 4 several numerical results are shown. In Sect. 5 we finish with some conclusions and future work.

2   Problem Statement

The system studied is composed of two different types of vehicles: carriers that are slow with a maximum speed V_c and unlimited endurance and small vehicles that are faster with $V_v \geq V_c$ but have a limited endurance $a \geq 0$. Both types of vehicles can cooperate such that the carriers can deploy, recover, and service the UAVs. Such a system composed by a single carrier and a single vehicle is defined in detail in [6].

Consider a mission where the carrier-vehicle system is composed of one fast vehicle and two carriers. The mission consists of the visit by the fast vehicle of an ordered set $Q = q_1, \ldots, q_n$ of target points in the 2D plane. The aim is to define the trajectories of the three vehicles such that the mission time completion is minimized.

As shown in [6], it is enough to define the position of the system at the take-off and landing points. Therefore, let us define $x_{to,i} \in \mathbb{R}^2$ as the take-off position for the target point i and $x_{l,i} \in \mathbb{R}^2$ its landing position. Regarding the carriers, it is worth to notice that $x_{to,i}$ is also the position of the carrier from which the vehicle takes off, while $y_{to,i} \in \mathbb{R}^2$ can be defined as the position of the other carrier at the exact same instant. Similarly, $x_{l,i}$ represents the position of the carrier on which the vehicle lands after visiting the i-th target points, while $y_{l,i} \in \mathbb{R}^2$ denotes the position of the other carrier. These variables allow to define the position of the whole carrier-vehicle system all along the mission.

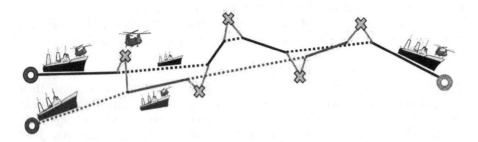

Fig. 1. Schematic of the multiple carrier-vehicle salesman problem in a maritime scenario.

The vehicle path for such a team presents two kind of time intervals. In the case of n target points, the time when the vehicle is on board of a carrier denoted by $t_i^{to,l}$, $i = 1, \ldots, n$ and when the vehicle is airborne denoted by $t_i^{to,l}$, $i = 1, \ldots, n+1$. Knowing that the vehicle flight time is limited by the endurance a, the following constraints must be satisfied:

$$0 \leq t_i^{to,l} \leq a \quad i = 1, \ldots, n \tag{1}$$

$$0 \leq t_i^{l,to} \quad i = 1, \ldots, n+1. \tag{2}$$

Each point visit is composed of two line segments: from vehicle take-off position $x_{to,i}$ to target point q_i and from target point to vehicle landing position $x_{l,i} \in \mathbb{R}^2$, with $i = 1, \ldots, n$. Assuming that the elapsed time at target point is null, the following constraint must be considered:

$$\|x_{to,i} - q_i\| + \|q_i - x_{l,i}\| \leq V_v t_i^{to,l} \quad i = 1, \ldots, n. \tag{3}$$

Between landing and takeoff instants, the vehicle must remain on one of the carriers. Therefore, during these periods it is considered as part of the carrier system, moving with a maximum speed V_c, following that:

$$\|x_{l,i-1} - x_{to,i}\| \leq V_c t_i^{l,to} \quad i = 1, \ldots, n+1 \tag{4}$$

$$\|y_{l,i-1} - y_{to,i}\| \leq V_c t_i^{l,to} \quad i = 1, \ldots, n \tag{5}$$

where $x_{l,0} = x_{c,0}$, $y_{l,0} = y_{c,0}$ and $x_{to,n+1} = x_f$.

In the case considered in this paper, after each takeoff, the vehicle can either return to the carrier or land on the other one. This behaviour is denoted by the binary decision variable α_i with $i = 1, \ldots, n$. This variable takes the value of 1 when the vehicle is landing on the same carrier, or 0 when it switches.

This behaviour can be denoted as follows

$$\alpha_i \in \{0, 1\} \quad i = 1, \ldots, n \tag{6}$$

$$\alpha_i \|x_{to,i} - x_{l,i}\| \leq V_c t_i^{to,l} \quad i = 1, \ldots, n \tag{7}$$

$$\alpha_i \|y_{to,i} - y_{l,i}\| \leq V_c t_i^{to,l} \quad i = 1, \ldots, n \tag{8}$$

$$(1 - \alpha_i) \|x_{to,i} - y_{l,i}\| \leq V_c t_i^{to,l} \quad i = 1, \ldots, n \tag{9}$$

$$(1 - \alpha_i) \|y_{to,i} - x_{l,i}\| \leq V_c t_i^{to,l} \quad i = 1, \ldots, n \tag{10}$$

Since the goal of the mission is to minimize the total travelling time, the solution is equivalent to the minimization of the sum of all time segments corresponding to the vehicle path phases. The optimization problem can be given in the form of Mixed Integer Non-linear Programming (MINLP) problem as

$$\underset{\alpha,x,y,t}{\text{minimize}} \quad \left(\sum_{i=1}^{n} t_i^{to,l} + \sum_{i=1}^{n+1} t_i^{l,to} \right) \tag{11}$$
$$\text{subject to} \quad (1) - (5), (6) - (10).$$

The non-linearity in constraints (7)–(10) makes the formulation complex to solve with current solvers. However, similar to what is done in [10], it is possible to rewrite constraints (7)–(10) as second order cone constraints, where the equivalent logical expression

$$(\alpha_i = 1) \Rightarrow \|x_{to,i} - x_{l,i}\| \leq V_c t_i^{to,l} \tag{12}$$

can be reformulated as

$$\|x_{to,i} - x_{l,i}\| \leq V_c t_i^{to,l} + (1 - \alpha_i)L \quad i = 1, \ldots, n. \tag{13}$$

Similarly, the other constraints can be rewritten as

$$\|y_{to,i} - y_{l,i}\| \leq V_c t_i^{to,l} + (1 - \alpha_i)L \quad i = 1, \ldots, n \tag{14}$$

$$\|x_{to,i} - y_{l,i}\| \leq V_c t_i^{to,l} + \alpha_i L \quad i = 1, \ldots, n \tag{15}$$

$$\|y_{to,i} - x_{l,i}\| \leq V_c t_i^{to,l} + \alpha_i L \quad i = 1, \ldots, n. \tag{16}$$

Therefore, the optimization problem is now given as follows

$$\underset{x}{\text{minimize}} \quad (\sum_{i=1}^{n} t_i^{to,l} + \sum_{i=1}^{n+1} t_i^{l,to}) \tag{17}$$
$$\text{subject to} \quad (1) - (5), (6), (13) - (16)$$

being a Mixed-Integer Second Order Conic Program (MISCOP) where L is a large enough real positive number. An example of a solution for 10 points is given in Fig. 2.

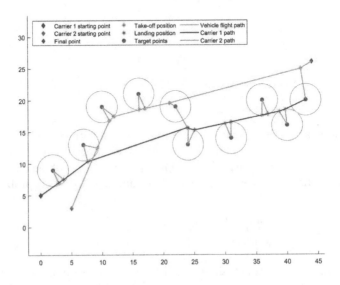

Fig. 2. Example of a mission of 10 points

The L parameter has to be large enough but a too large value would increase drastically the computational time [15]. Fortunately, this parameter has a physical meaning illustrated in Fig. 3 (for the case of $\alpha_i = 0$) in terms of distance between vehicles. Therefore, given the characteristics of the problem, it is possible to analytically determine the interval of L_{min} such that the constraints (13), (14), (15) and (16) hold true. Figure 3 shows a configuration of $x_{to,i}, x_{l,i}, y_{to,i}, y_{l,i}$ and the corresponding interval of L. L_1 and L_2 are, respectively, the minimum distances such that constraints (13) and (14) are no longer active. The green point $x_{L,2}$ corresponds to the worst case scenario in which the distance $\|x_{to,i} - x_{l,i}\|$ is maximal and equal to aV_v. It corresponds to the case in which $t_i^{to,l} = a$. Similarly, the point $y_{to,2}$ corresponds to the worst case scenario in which the distance $\|y_{to,i} - y_{l,i}\|$ is maximal and equal to $aV_v + 2aV_c$.

Therefore, the parameter L can be computed beforehand as

$$L_{min} = \max(a(V_v + V_c), \|x_{to,i} - y_{to,i}\| \quad i = 1, \ldots, n) \tag{18}$$

being convex problem easy to solve.

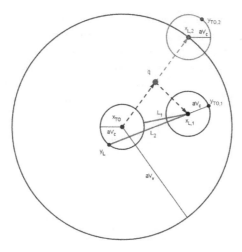

Fig. 3. Illustration of minimum distance L for the constraints (13) and (14). (Color figure online)

3 Proposed Heuristic

The mixed-integer formulation proposed in (17) provides an optimal solution, but given the NP-hard nature of the problem becomes computationally expensive for large inputs. Hence, in this section we propose a fast heuristic able to solve the problem with satisfactory results.

Given the integer relaxation of the constraint (6) as

$$0 \le \alpha_i \le 1 \quad i = 1, \ldots, n \tag{19}$$

the resulting formulation

$$\begin{aligned} \underset{x}{\text{minimize}} \quad & (\sum_{i=1}^{n} t_i^{to,l} + \sum_{i=1}^{n+1} t_i^{l,to}) \\ \text{subject to} \quad & (1) - (5), (13) - (16), (19) \end{aligned} \tag{20}$$

is a Second-Order Conic Programming (SOCP) problem, a kind of convex problem easy to solve. The presented heuristic takes this result as an input for a rounding algorithm. The main idea behind the heuristic lies in the fact that the solution from the relaxed problem (20) can be seen as a probability on the variable α to be chosen 1. Therefore the final trajectory calculation takes the values more likely to provide a better solution.

However, since $\alpha_i \in [0, 1]$, in constraints (13)–(16) the geometric meaning of parameter L is lost. The solution and computational time becomes sensitive to the value of L. Based on an empirical approach, the following formula was obtained:

$$L_{approx} = 1.6d^* (\frac{aV_v}{d^*} + 0.068)(0.88 - \frac{V_c}{V_v}) \tag{21}$$

where d^* is the average length separating successive target points. This expression allows, depending on the configuration parameters of the problem, to select a value of L that very likely provides a close to optimal solution. Being a first tentative to define an appropriate value of L, the heuristic considers a range of values of L with 20% and 40% deviation to avoid unexpected results.

The main steps of the heuristic are schematically represented as follows:

Given : $X = \{q,\ x_{0,c},\ y_{0,c},\ x_f,\ a,\ V_v,\ V_c\}$
Find : $x_{to,i}\ y_{to,i}\ x_{l,i}\ y_{l,i}\ \alpha$

1.   **Compute** L_{approx} with Eq. (21)
2. $L_{list} = L_{approx} \times [0.6, 0.8, 1, 1.2, 1.4]$
3.   **For each** L_i in L_{list}
4.   **Solve** relaxed SOCP problem (20)
5.   **get** α
6.   **round** α
7.   **Solve** original problem (11) with rounded α
8.   **get** f_i
8.   **end**
9. $f_{heuristic} = min(\{f_i, :\ i = 1, \ldots, 5\})$

4   Numerical Results

This section shows different numerical simulations in terms of computational time and optimality to compare the performance of the mixed-integer formulation and the proposed heuristic. A series of randomized simulations have been performed to compare the results with different points distributions. The simulations have been performed using MOSEK v9.0.89 for the convex problems and GUROBI solver for the mixed-integer problems, both in YALMIP environment.

Figure 4 represents the level of degradation Δ of the heuristic solution related to the optimal solution among 500 simulations. Due to the computing time of the mixed-integer program the simulations considered only a set of 9 visit points.

In Tables 1 and 2 the results from these simulations are detailed. It can be seen how the average degradation of the solution respect to the optimal value is only 2.47% and that 82% of the cases have less that 5% degradation.

A second comparison in terms of computational time was also carried out. Figure 5 represents the evolution of computational times with respect to the number of target points. The results show that the heuristic approach grows linearly with the number of target points meanwhile the mixed-integer solution drastically increase for more than 16 points.

These results support the clear advantage of the proposed heuristic when the number of points becomes larger. Additionally, it shows the good performance in terms of optimality.

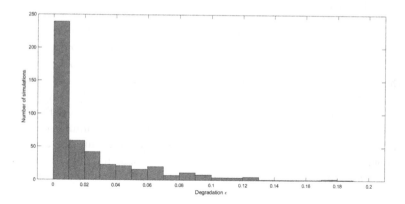

Fig. 4. Distribution of the level of degradation Δ in the simulations.

Table 1. Degradation of the heuristic result respect to the optimal.

No. of points	Avg deg.	Max deg.
9	2.47%	28.15%

Table 2. Results distribution regarding different degradation thresholds.

No. of points	<1%	<5%	<10%	<15%
9	53.8%	82.80%	95.20%	98.2%

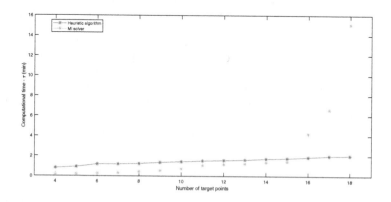

Fig. 5. Comparison of computational time evolution with respect to the number of target points.

5   Conclusion

This paper introduces a novel extension of the Carrier-Vehicle Travelling Salesman Problem considering the use of two carriers. The presented results show the advantages of the considered scenario and a proper way to formulate and solve the problem. The problem and constraints are defined in a way that allows to write it as Mixed-Integer Second Order Program (MISOCP) which provides optimal results. Additionally, a simple and fast heuristic is also defined, which is proved to have good results in terms of optimality and computational time.

The obtained results can be used for the planning of monitoring activities or similar logistic problems involving a team of two carriers and one vehicle. Future extensions could allow the faster vehicle to visit multiple points with a single takeoff.

References

1. Agatz, N., Bouman, P., Schmidt, M.: Optimization approaches for the traveling salesman problem with drone. Transp. Sci. **52**(4), 965–981 (2018). https://doi.org/10.1287/trsc.2017.0791.   http://pubsonline.informs.org/doi/10.1287/trsc.2017.0791
2. Bektas, T.: The multiple traveling salesman problem: an overview of formulations and solution procedures. Omega **34**(3), 209–219 (2006). https://doi.org/10.1016/j.omega.2004.10.004.   https://linkinghub.elsevier.com/retrieve/pii/S0305048304001550
3. Cattaruzza, D., Absi, N., Feillet, D.: Vehicle routing problems with multiple trips. Ann. Oper. Res. **271**(1), 127–159 (2018). https://doi.org/10.1007/s10479-018-2988-7
4. Chen, Y., Ren, S., Chen, Z., Chen, M., Wu, H.: Path planning for vehicle-borne system consisting of multi air–ground robots. Robotica, 1–19 (2019). https://doi.org/10.1017/S0263574719000808. https://www.cambridge.org/core/product/identifier/S0263574719000808/type/journal_article
5. Gambella, C., Lodi, A., Vigo, D.: Exact solutions for the carrier–vehicle traveling salesman problem. Transp. Sci. **52**(2), 320–330 (2018). https://doi.org/10.1287/trsc.2017.0771. http://pubsonline.informs.org/doi/10.1287/trsc.2017.0771
6. Garone, E., Naldi, R., Casavola, A.: Traveling salesman problem for a class of carrier-vehicle systems. J. Guid. Control Dyn. **34**(4), 1272–1276 (2011). https://doi.org/10.2514/1.50539. http://arc.aiaa.org/doi/10.2514/1.50539
7. Garone, E., Naldi, R., Casavola, A., Frazzoli, E.: Cooperative path planning for a class of carrier-vehicle systems. In: 2008 47th IEEE Conference on Decision and Control, Cancun, Mexico, pp. 2456–2462. IEEE (2008). https://doi.org/10.1109/CDC.2008.4739357. http://ieeexplore.ieee.org/lpdocs/epic03/wrapper.htm?arnumber=4739357
8. Gasparri, A., Ulivi, G., Bono Rossello, N., Garone, E.: The H2020 project Pantheon: precision farming of hazelnut orchards (extended abstract), Florence, Italy, September 2018
9. Jiang, J., Tao, J., Xin, G.: An unmanned aerial vehicle cluster network cruise system for monitor. In: E3S Web Conference, vol. 38, p. 01029 (2018). https://doi.org/10.1051/e3sconf/20183801029. https://www.e3s-conferences.org/10.1051/e3sconf/20183801029

10. Klauco, M., Blazek, S., Kvasnica, M., Fikar, M.: Mixed-integer SOCP formulation of the path planning problem for heterogeneous multi-vehicle systems. In: 2014 European Control Conference (ECC), Strasbourg, France, pp. 1474–1479. IEEE, June 2014. https://doi.org/10.1109/ECC.2014.6862400. http://ieeexplore.ieee.org/document/6862400/

11. Koç, C., Bektaş, T., Jabali, O., Laporte, G.: Thirty years of heterogeneous vehicle routing. Eur. J. Oper. Res. **249**(1), 1–21 (2016). https://doi.org/10.1016/j.ejor.2015.07.020. https://linkinghub.elsevier.com/retrieve/pii/S0377221715006530

12. Othman, M.S.b., Shurbevski, A., Karuno, Y., Nagamochi, H.: Routing of carrier-vehicle systems with dedicated last-stretch delivery vehicle and fixed carrier route. J. Inf. Process. **25**(0), 655–666 (2017). https://doi.org/10.2197/ipsjjip.25.655. https://www.jstage.jst.go.jp/article/ipsjjip/25/0/25_655/_article

13. Ren, S., Chen, Y., Xiong, L., Chen, Z., Chen, M.: Path planning for the marsupial double-UAVs system in air-ground collaborative application. In: 2018 37th Chinese Control Conference (CCC), Wuhan, pp. 5420–5425. IEEE, July 2018. https://doi.org/10.23919/ChiCC.2018.8483087. https://ieeexplore.ieee.org/document/8483087/

14. Wei, L., Li, Y.B., Xu, J.H., Luo, X.X.: Unmanned aerial vehicle maritime cruise base site selection strategy research in the Bohai Sea. In: AMM, vol. 724, pp. 378–382 (2015). https://doi.org/10.4028/www.scientific.net/AMM.724.378. https://www.scientific.net/AMM.724.378

15. Williams, H.P.: Model Building in Mathematical Programming, 5th edn., p. 433, March 2013

16. Yao, B., Yu, B., Hu, P., Gao, J., Zhang, M.: An improved particle swarm optimization for carton heterogeneous vehicle routing problem with a collection depot. Ann. Oper. Res. **242**(2), 303–320 (2015). https://doi.org/10.1007/s10479-015-1792-x

Speeded Up Elevation Map
for Exploration of Large-Scale
Subterranean Environments

Jan Bayer$^{(\boxtimes)}$ and Jan Faigl

Faculty of Electrical Engineering, Czech Technical University in Prague,
Technicka 2, 166 27 Prague, Czech Republic
{bayerja1,faiglj}@fel.cvut.cz
https://comrob.fel.cvut.cz

Abstract. In this paper, we address a problem of the exploration of
large-scale subterranean environments using autonomous ground mobile
robots. In particular, we focus on an efficient data representation of the
large-scale elevation map, where it is desirable to capture the shape of
the terrain to avoid areas not traversable by a robot. Subterranean environments such as mine tunnel systems can be in units of kilometers large,
but only a relatively small portion of the environment represents observable parts. Therefore, uniform grid-based elevation maps with resolution
in units of centimeters are not memory efficient, and more suitable are
hierarchical tree-based structures. However, hierarchical structures suffer
from the increased computational requirements of accessing particular
grid cells needed in determination of the navigational goals or evaluation of the terrain traversability in planning safe and cost-efficient paths.
We propose a speed-up technique to combine the benefits of uniform
grid-based and tree-based representations. The proposed elevation map
representation keeps the memory footprint low using tree structure but
enables fast access to the grid cells corresponding to the robot surroundings. The efficiency of the proposed data representation is demonstrated
in an experimental deployment of the autonomous exploration of outdoor
and subterranean environments.

1 Introduction

Mobile robots can be deployed in hard to access and dangerous areas to reduce
possible risks for humans, specifically in search and rescue missions in underground tunnels or collapsed buildings [17]. A human operator can teleoperate
robots, but a small communication range in underground tunnels limits operational radius. Therefore, autonomous exploration [26] is needed to search large
underground environments such as in the DARPA Subterranean Challenge [5],
where robots are requested to search for the artifacts such as survivors, extinguishers, drills machine, and cell phone, to name few.

© Springer Nature Switzerland AG 2020
J. Mazal et al. (Eds.): MESAS 2019, LNCS 11995, pp. 190–202, 2020.
https://doi.org/10.1007/978-3-030-43890-6_15

Since an underground environment like mines and caves forms a net of corridors that can be very large (in kilometers), it is desirable to use a memory-efficient map representation to cover the whole environment with sufficient resolution for traversability assessment. On the other hand, it is also desirable to keep the average access time to the map representation as low as possible because frequent access to the map is common for exploration algorithms. An example of exploration processes that access the environment map includes

- the insertion of the new measurements;
- traversability assessment;
- growing untraversable areas by the radius of the robot shape circumference;
- computation of the cost map;
- detection of possible goal locations;
- and path planning.

Therefore, efficient map representation can have a significant impact not only on the memory requirements but also on the computational requirements and the latency between the integration of new sensor measurements and a new decision.

Existing terrain models capable of covering large environments are based on a tree structure to save memory requirements such as OctoMap [12]. However, access time to the leaves of tree-like representations is slower than the access time to the uniform grid due to the necessity to search the tree for the leaves. For relatively large robots like Talon [19], or ClearPath Husky with sufficient payload capacity, it is possible to overcome the access time by increasing computational power and the required energy resources. However, for small robots like Micro Tactical Ground Robot (MTGR) [18] or walking hexapod robots [7] with limited payload, the computational resources are limited to small embedded computers. Therefore, computational efficiency might play a significant role in the operational time. Thus, we studied memory-efficient terrain model representation to capture large areas with sufficient precision for traversability assessment that also enables fast access to the terrain representation. The main contribution of the presented approach is considered in memory and computationally efficient data representation of the elevation map suitable for mobile robot exploration. The proposed solution is demonstrated on autonomous exploration with a small hexapod walking robot equipped with the relatively limited computational power of the onboard embedded computer. Besides, we report on experimental results from a practical deployment of the developed solution in the mine environment.

The rest of the paper is organized as follows. A brief overview of the related work is presented in Sect. 2. The developed map representation and the exploration framework are described in Sect. 3. The achieved results, including map captured during the exploration and evaluation of the computational requirements, are reported in Sect. 4. The concluding remarks and ideas for future work are in Sect. 5.

2   Related Work

The robotic exploration is a problem to create a model of the environment by a mobile robot. The frontier-based exploration introduced in [25] is a well-known approach for spatial robot exploration widely adapted by existing exploration approaches [1,22]. In frontier-based exploration, robots are navigated towards waypoints determined at the borders of known and unknown parts of the environment [11]. Besides, the navigation waypoints can also be determined using entropy [4], or the exploration can be driven by decreasing uncertainty of the terrain model being created, e.g., as reported in [21]. Nevertheless, the common property of the exploration approaches is frequent access to the data representation of the model being created [8]. Since, we are focused on the memory-efficient model representation, we consider relatively straightforward deployment of the frontier-based exploration [2] to demonstrate utilization of the model and impact of different memory representations (Fig. 1).

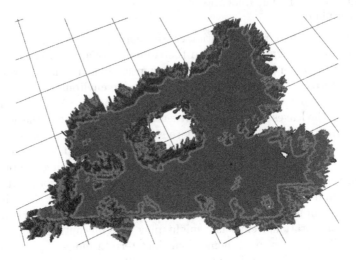

Fig. 1. Example of the elevation map with the resolution 7.5 cm. The grid at the background has cell size 5 m.

In robotic exploration, the traditional terrain model representation is the occupancy grid [6] that covers the space by a uniform grid, where each cell is associated with the probability that the space represented by the cell is occupied. The occupancy grid is a suitable model for flat terrains with easily distinguishable obstacles that are represented as cells with a high value of the occupancy probability. However, a subterranean environment is often not flat, since the shape of the terrain is usually uneven. The extension of the occupancy grid to full 3D representation is presented in [24], where the authors represent the map by a uniform 3D grid. The disadvantage of [24] is the memory ineffectiveness, which is addressed by tree-like structured map representation known as the OctoMap [12]. Since the OctoMap is based on the octree, the complexity of the access to the tree leaves can be bounded by $O(\log(n))$, where n is the number of tree nodes. Thus the access to the octree is significantly slower than the access time to the terrain model represented by the uniform grid, which has the constant access time $O(1)$.

If we assume only a single layer of the terrain, the elevation map [20] can be employed to model the shape of the terrain by estimating the height of the terrain at each cell of the grid. The advantage of the elevation map is its simplicity because cell heights can be stored in the 2D grid, which is more memory efficient than the 3D grid [24]. Due to the simpler structure [9], the access is also faster than for 3D maps stored in tree structures. Besides the uniform 2D grid, e.g., used in [20], the elevation map can also be stored in a tree structure (quadtree) similarly to the occupancy mapping technique described in [15]. Then, the elevation map becomes even more memory-efficient representation than 3D grids at the cost of the access time because of the tree-like structure.

The presented work is motivated by an outdoor exploration scenario with a small hexapod walking robot and a wheeled robot (see Fig. 3) in the Tunnel Circuit event of the DARPA Subterranean Challenge [5]. The selected deployment scenarios with long tunnels allow us to assume only a single terrain layer. Hence, the terrain model is based on the memory-efficient elevation map stored as a quadtree. The fast access to the tree-like structure is supported by the proposed caching mechanism that significantly reduces the access time. The developed memory representation is demonstrated within a complete exploration framework, where particular processes access to the terrain model. Therefore, the reported experimental results represent realistic computational requirements of the practical deployments in exploration missions.

3   Autonomous Exploration Framework

The proposed terrain model representation is integrated into the autonomous exploration system that consists of five main modules: *sensors and localization, mapping, exploration, path following*, and robot *controller*. The modules and their connections into the system architecture are visualized in Fig. 2. The exploration framework is developed in C++ using the ROS middleware [23].

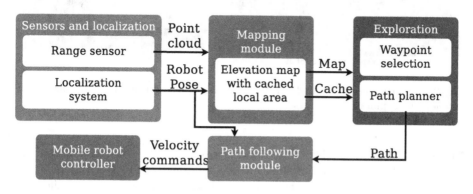

Fig. 2. Architecture of the developed autonomous exploration system.

The utilized *sensors* provide range measurements, and the *localization system* provides a pose of the robot that are both used by the *mapping* module to build the spatial model of the environment. The map is further used to determine possible goal locations to explore unknown parts of the environment. The next navigational goal is determined from the possible goal locations using the employed exploration strategy. The *path following* module ensures the robot follows the path planned to the selected navigational goal by steering the robot by the velocity. The individual modules are further described in the rest of this section to provide a complete overview of the utilized autonomous exploration system, and the proposed map representation is detailed in Sect. 3.1.

Sensors depend on the particular sensory system of the robot, but in this paper, we utilize two robotic platforms showed in Fig. 3 for the experimental verification of the proposed exploration system. The first is the hexapod walking robot that uses the RGB-D camera Intel RealSense D435 [13] as the source of range measurements. The localization of the hexapod walking robot is provided by the small embedded localization module, the Intel RealSense T265 [14], that runs onboard visual SLAM from the fisheye stereo camera enhanced by sensory fusion with the inertial measurement unit. The wheeled robot can carry a more massive payload, and therefore, a laser range finder is used to obtain 3D scans of the robot environment. The localization of the wheeled robot is based on the Iterative Closest Point algorithm [3] combined with odometry.

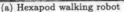

(a) Hexapod walking robot   (b) Wheeled robot

Fig. 3. Robotic platforms used for the experimental verification of the developed autonomous exploration system.

Mapping Module builds the elevation map from the captured point clouds synchronized with the estimated robot pose. Although the representation of the proposed map is a tree-like structure, we describe the map as the uniformly sampled grid to improve the clarity and readability of the processes dealing with the map. Thus, each map sample (i, j) represents a height h and height variance σ_h^2 of the corresponding terrain place. From incoming point clouds, points that do not belong to the top modeled surface of the terrain are filtered out.

The filtered point cloud is then fused with the elevation map using one dimensional Kalman filter [9].

The measurements of the terrain height z_k and its variance $\sigma^2_{z,k}$ from the new k-th input point cloud are fused with the corresponding heights with the map according to the equations

$$h_k = \frac{\sigma^2_{z,k} h_{k-1} + \sigma^2_{h,k-1} z_k}{\sigma^2_{z,k} + \sigma^2_{h,k-1}} \tag{1}$$

$$\sigma^2_{h,k} = \frac{\sigma^2_{z,k} \sigma^2_{h,k-1}}{\sigma^2_{z,k} + \sigma^2_{h,k-1}}. \tag{2}$$

Parts of the map which were not affected by the new measurements are considered *unknown*.

The proposed elevation map is further used for the traversability assessment based on the height difference of the neighboring cells as follows. If the local height difference $g_h(i,j)$ defined by (3) is higher than the threshold g_{max}, the cell is considered untraversable; otherwise, the cell is traversable. The value of g_{max} is estimated based on the kinematics of the particular robot. Since the planner plans the path for the center of the robot body, the physical dimensions of the robot are incorporated to the map by growing the untraversable cells by the radius of the robot shape circumference. Moreover, we generate the cost map to penalize robot states close to the untraversable cells by utilizing the distance transform [10]. The cost $d(i,j)$ of each cell is thus based on its distance to the closest untraversable cell, or it is labeled as unknown if measurement about the corresponding area is not available.

$$\begin{aligned} g_h(i,j) = \max(\{&|h(i,j) - h(i-1,j)|, \\ &|h(i,j) - h(i+1,j)|, \\ &|h(i,j) - h(i,j-1)|, \\ &|h(i,j) - h(i,j+1)|\}) \end{aligned} \tag{3}$$

Exploration Module determines the next navigational goal based on the identified frontiers [25]. The frontier cells are determined in the elevation map as traversable cells that are incident with unknown cells. The total number of frontier cells depends on the resolution of the map. In general, for a high-resolution map, the number of frontier cells can be large, and it would be computationally very intensive to select possible goal locations from all the frontier cells. Thus, we followed the approach [16] and employed the clustering of the frontier cells. The nearby frontier cells are clustered into similarly sized sets, and a single representative of each set (cluster) is determined as the possible goal location.

The next navigational goal is selected as the goal location with the lowest cost of the path from the current robot pose. The path is determined by the A* algorithm with the heuristic function computed as the Euclidean distance to the goal location. The travel cost between two neighboring nodes n and n' is computed as the distance on the eight-neighborhood (D8) that is increased by the cost $d(n)$ to penalize robot presence near the obstacles. $d(n)$ is non-negative cost decreasing with D_8 distance from the closest untraversable cell [10]. The selection of the next navigational goal is focused on the nearby area of the robot, i.e., we consider a limited planning horizon. Therefore, a possible goal location is considered unreachable if a path between the robot pose and the goal location is not found in less than 20 000 expansions of the A* algorithm.

The robot is then navigated along the path to the selected goal location by the *path following* module. A new goal location is determined if the current waypoint is reached or after $T_{exp} = 8$ s. The exploration terminates if there is not a reachable goal location.

Path Following Module ensures that the robot follows the path planned by the *exploration* module. The path is represented as a sequence of waypoint locations that are progressively processed. The forward and angular velocities for the robot controller are generated based on the distance and angular displacement of the recent waypoint of the path. The next waypoint from the sequence is processed if the robot gets less than 1 cm far from the recent waypoint.

3.1   Map Representation

Since we suppose exploration of the environment with tunnels, we represent the map by a **quadtree** structure, see Fig. 4, to reduce the memory requirements. The disadvantage of the tree-like representation is the access time to the tree leafs that can be bounded by $O(\log n)$, where n denotes the number of the map cells that depends on the size of the map, which is slower than the access time for the map represented by a uniform grid that can be bounded by $O(1)$. Complex access to the tree-like representation increase computational requirements, and for limited computational power, it slows down map processing. It is specifically distinctive when the elevation map is processed by multiple methods, which happens in the exploration mission during the integration of new measurements, obstacle growing, determination of frontier cells and goal locations, and also during path planning.

We propose to overcome the issue of the high complexity of repetitive access to the map by an additional data structure that works as a **cache**. We suppose that new measurements do not affect all the cells of the elevation map, but only cells that are close to the robot since the range of the sensors is limited. Hence, the proposed cache stores the references to all the quadtree leafs close to the robot. In Fig. 4, it can be seen that the cached area overlaps the area affected by measurements, which ensures the consistency of the area changed by the measurements with the rest of the map. The quadtree map representation enables us to represent the unknown space efficiently, while still, the operations like convolution can run almost as quickly as on the map stored in a uniform grid. The cost of maintaining the cache is its computation, which is needed when the new point cloud updates the map. The real impact of the proposed hybrid representation has been evaluated during real exploration missions, and the achieved results are reported in the following section.

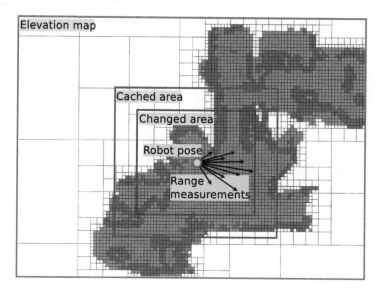

Fig. 4. Elevation map representation.

4   Results

We have designed two exploration experiments to show the speedup of the mapping due to the proposed cache, and demonstrate how the proposed memory-efficient solution represents a large-scale subterranean environment. The first experiment has been done using the small hexapod walking robot employed in the exploration of the outdoor rough grassy terrain. The second experiment reported is a deployment of the autonomous exploration in one trial during the Tunnel Circuit event of the DARPA Subterranean Challenge in August 2019, where the wheeled robot autonomously explored the entry part of the underground tunnel.

4.1   Exploration with Small Hexapod Walking Robot

During the experimental deployment of the exploration framework with the small hexapod walking robot in the scenario shown in Fig. 5, we have captured data from the onboard sensors using the ROS rosbag tool. The captured sensor data can be played back at the same frequencies as they were generated by the sensors, which enables us to benchmark mapping performance with and without the proposed cache using different computational environments. In particular, the evaluation of the mapping processes has been performed with two computers. The first computer is equipped with the Intel i5 3320M processor clocked at 2.6 GHz and 8 GB RAM. The second computer is small embedded computer Odroid-XU4 with Octa-core CPU Samsung Exynos 5422 (four A15 cores running at 2.0 GHz and four A7 cores running at 1.4 GHz), and 2 GB memory. Both computers

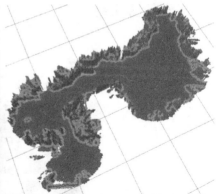

(a) Outdoor experimental setup   (b) Resulting elevation map with resolution 7.5 cm with the visualization grid of the size 5 m at the background

Fig. 5. Exploration experiment with the hexapod walking robot used as a benchmark for mapping process using different memory representations of the map.

have sufficient computational power for autonomous exploration with the hexapod walking robot. The computational times for the particular mapping steps (including insertion of new sensor measurements) are summarized in Tables 1 and 2. The input point clouds contain more than 60 000 measurements, and the depth camera produced the point clouds at the frequency 5 Hz. The robot traversed 46 m in 44 min during the experimental deployment. Although the results indicate that both computational platforms are sufficient for the exploration even without the proposed cache, the cache reduces the computational requirements about two times, which might further support the deployment of more sophisticated exploration strategies. Note that the power consumption of the computational environment with the Odroid-XU4 is about two times less than for the setup with the Intel i5.

Table 1. The mean computational time for mapping steps

Process name	Intel i5 CPU		Odroid-XU4	
	No cache	With cache	No cache	With cache
Cache update	0.0	5.2	0.0	9.9
Traversability assessment	17.5	1.8	30.5	3.2
Growing untraversable areas	19.1	1.8	32.4	4.7
Cost map building	17.4	5.8	34.6	22.3
Frontier detection and clustering	4.8	0.4	8.6	0.9
Total mapping time	76.1	32.0	146.4	76.7

All reported times are in milliseconds.

Table 2. Utilization of the computational resources

Mapping	Intel i5 CPU [%]	Odroid-XU4 [%]
Mapping without the cache	38	92
Mapping with the cache	18	52

4.2 Exploration of Subterranean Environment

The second experimental deployment is based on the exploration of the 130 m long mine entrance during the Tunnel Circuit event of the DARPA Subterranean Challenge, see Fig. 6. We have measured the size of the created elevation map, and compare it to the size of the uniform grid map needed to cover the same area. The resulting memory requirements summarized in Table 3 support that the developed memory representation of the terrain map is memory efficient. Even though the memory requirements per each cell are larger for the proposed representation (because of the quadtree structure) than for the uniform grid, the results show that the memory footprint of the proposed map representation with the uniform grid-like cache is still lower than for the uniform grid only.

(a) Wheeled robot is entering the tunnel

(b) Resulting elevation map with market robot trajectory

Fig. 6. Wheeled robot in the tunnel of the Safety research course during the Tunnel Circuit event of the DARPA Subterranean Challenge.

Table 3. Memory requirements of the map representation

Map representation	Map cell size [B]	Total map size [MB]
Grid based representation	9	58.0
Proposed quadtree representation	64	4.8

Note that the results in Table 3 are calculated for the 130 m long entrance to the mine, the total length of the tunnels in the mine is several kilometers.

5   Conclusion

In this paper, we report on the experimental results of the developed autonomous exploration system with the proposed memory representation of the elevation map. Although the proposed hybrid memory representation based on the quadtree tree with a uniform grid cache is straightforward and relatively easy to implement, it provides noticeable benefits in the reduced memory and computational resources. The presented results support the memory and computational efficiency of the developed solution and enable autonomous exploration using a relatively small robotic platform with limited computational resources. The exploration system has also been successfully deployed in the Tunnel Circuit of the DARPA Subterranean Challenge. In the future, we aim to generalize the idea of the memory representation for the full 3D map of the explored environment.

Acknowledgement. The presented work has been supported under the OP VVV funded project CZ.02.1.01/0.0/0.0/16_019/0000765 "Research Center for Informatics". The support under grant No. SGS19/176/OHK3/3T/13 to Jan Bayer is also gratefully acknowledged.

References

1. Amigoni, F., Banfi, J., Basilico, N.: Multirobot exploration of communication-restricted environments: a survey. IEEE Intell. Syst. **32**(6), 48–57 (2017). https://doi.org/10.1109/MIS.2017.4531226
2. Bayer, J., Faigl, J.: On autonomous spatial exploration with small hexapod walking robot using tracking camera Intel RealSense T265. In: European Conference on Mobile Robots (ECMR) (2019)
3. Besl, P.J., McKay, N.D.: A method for registration of 3-D shapes. IEEE Trans. Pattern Anal. Mach. Intell. **14**(2), 239–256 (1992). https://doi.org/10.1109/34.121791
4. Carrillo, H., Dames, P., Kumar, V., Castellanos, J.A.: Autonomous robotic exploration using occupancy grid maps and graph SLAM based on Shannon and Rényi entropy. In: IEEE International Conference on Robotics and Automation (ICRA), pp. 487–494 (2015). https://doi.org/10.1109/ICRA.2015.7139224
5. Chung, T.: DARPA Subterranean (SubT) Challenge. https://www.darpa.mil/program/darpa-subterranean-challenge. Accessed 12 July 2019

6. Elfes, A.: Using occupancy grids for mobile robot perception and navigation. Computer **22**(6), 46–57 (1989)
7. Faigl, J., Čížek, P.: Adaptive locomotion control of hexapod walking robot for traversing rough terrains with position feedback only. Robot. Auton. Syst. **116**, 136–147 (2019). https://doi.org/10.1016/j.robot.2019.03.008
8. Faigl, J., Kulich, M.: On benchmarking of frontier-based multi-robot exploration strategies. In: European Conference on Mobile Robots (ECMR), pp. 1–8 (2015). https://doi.org/10.1109/ECMR.2015.7324183
9. Fankhauser, P., Bloesch, M., Hutter, M.: Probabilistic terrain mapping for mobile robots with uncertain localization. IEEE Robot. Autom. Lett. **3**(4), 3019–3026 (2018). https://doi.org/10.1109/LRA.2018.2849506
10. Felzenszwalb, P.F., Huttenlocher, D.P.: Distance transforms of sampled functions. Theory Comput. **8**, 415–428 (2012)
11. Galceran, E., Carreras, M.: A survey on coverage path planning for robotics. Robot. Sci. Syst. (RSS) **61**(12), 1258–1276 (2013). https://doi.org/10.1016/j.robot.2013.09.004
12. Hornung, A., Wurm, K.M., Bennewitz, M., Stachniss, C., Burgard, W.: OctoMap: an efficient probabilistic 3D mapping framework based on octrees. Auton. Robots **34**(3), 189–206 (2013). https://doi.org/10.1007/s10514-012-9321-0
13. Intel RealSense Depth Camera D435. https://click.intel.com/intelr-realsensetm-depth-camera-d435.html. Accessed 4 Aug 2018
14. Intel RealSense Tracking Camera T265. https://click.intel.com/order-intel-realsense-tracking-camera-t265.html. Accessed 23 May 2019
15. Kraetzschmar, G.K., Gassull, G.P., Uhl, K.: Probabilistic quadtrees for variable-resolution mapping of large environments. IFAC Proc. vol. **37**(8), 675–680 (2004). https://doi.org/10.1016/S1474-6670(17)32056-6
16. Kulich, M., Faigl, J., Přeučil, L.: On distance utility in the exploration task. In: IEEE International Conference on Robotics and Automation (ICRA), pp. 4455–4460 (2011). https://doi.org/10.1109/ICRA.2011.5980221
17. Liu, Y., Nejat, G.: Robotic urban search and rescue: a survey from the control perspective. J. Intell. Robot. Syst. **72**(2), 147–165 (2013). https://doi.org/10.1007/s10846-013-9822-x
18. Micro tactical ground robot. http://www.robo-team.com/products/mtgr/. Accessed 11 July 2019
19. Peter Wells, D.D.: TALON: a universal unmanned ground vehicle platform, enabling the mission to be the focus. In: SPIE, vol. 5804 (2005). https://doi.org/10.1117/12.602887
20. Pfaff, P., Triebel, R., Burgard, W.: An efficient extension to elevation maps for outdoor terrain mapping and loop closing. Int. J. Robot. Res. **26**, 217–230 (2007). https://doi.org/10.1177/0278364906075165
21. Prágr, M., Čížek, P., Bayer, J., Faigl, J.: Online incremental learning of the terrain traversal cost in autonomous exploration. In: Robotics: Science and Systems (RSS) (2019). https://doi.org/10.15607/RSS.2019.XV.040
22. Quattrini Li, A., Cipolleschi, R., Giusto, M., Amigoni, F.: A semantically-informed multirobot system for exploration of relevant areas in search and rescue settings. Auton. Robots **40**(4), 581–597 (2015). https://doi.org/10.1007/s10514-015-9480-x
23. Quigley, M., et al.: ROS: an open-source robot operating system. In: ICRA Workshop on Open Source Software (2009)
24. Roth-Tabak, Y., Jain, R.: Building an environment model using depth information. Computer **22**(6), 85–90 (1989). https://doi.org/10.1109/2.30724

25. Yamauchi, B.: A frontier-based approach for autonomous exploration. In: IEEE International Symposium on Computational Intelligence in Robotics and Automation (CIRA), pp. 146–151 (1997). https://doi.org/10.1109/CIRA.1997.613851
26. Yanguas-Rojas, D., Mojica-Nava, E.: Exploration with heterogeneous robots networks for search and rescue. IFAC PapersOnLine **50**(1), 7935–7940 (2017). https://doi.org/10.1016/j.ifacol.2017.08.768

Modular Rover Design for Exploration and Analytical Tasks

Robert Pastor[(⊠)], Daniel Huczala, Aleš Vysocký, Petr Oščádal, Jakub Mlotek, Dominik Heczko, Zdeněk Zeman, and Petr Široký

Department of Robotics, Faculty of Mechanical Engineering, VSB–Technical University of Ostrava, 17. listopadu 2172/15, 708 00 Ostrava-Poruba, Czech Republic
{robert.pastor,daniel.huczala,ales.vysocky,petr.oscadal,jakub.mlotek,
dominik.heczko,zdenek.zeman,petr.siroky1}@vsb.cz
https://www.fs.vsb.cz/354

Abstract. Rovers and other unmanned ground vehicles (UGV) were a matter of space exploration or post-disaster reconnaissance. Rovers work in tough conditions where presence of a human is uncomfortable or dangerous. This results in main requirements for rover - durable chassis, stable communication for direct control or transfer of data and task-specific tools for experiments and measurements. In this article we propose solutions for fulfilling those requirements.

Keywords: Rover · Omni-directional move · Robot · Geology · Remote control

1 Introduction

Experimental rover K3P4 was developed by students for international competition European Rover Challenge 2019. Boundary conditions and task specifications for proposed design are based on rules of this competition. According to rules of the competition a wide range of problems must be solved to design this complex system. From the construction point of view the rover chassis must have lightweight design with ability of attachment of different task specific modules. The operator has no line of sight visual contact with the rover, the control is done remotely and only the data from cameras and sensors can be used in teleoperation. Path-planning and terrain mapping is a part of data processing from different sensors and computation based on fitness functions. As a student projects all the problems must be solved cost-efficiently with a limited budget.

There are four tasks to be performed by the rover:

- Maintenance Task
- Collection Task
- Science Task
- Traverse Task

J. Mazal et al. (Eds.): MESAS 2019, LNCS 11995, pp. 203–215, 2020.
https://doi.org/10.1007/978-3-030-43890-6_16

Goal of the Maintenance Task is simulation of remote operation with rover around a control panel. After localization of the panel with switches and socket plugs, individual devices are detected with image recognition algorithm and set to the requested state with manipulation arm. During Collection Task the rover is intended to find, pick up, store in the container and transport aluminum caches to the designated position. Science Task is focused on geological exploration. Collecting and analysing soil samples is performed in the target area. Surface soil is collected using the manipulator and deep samples are taken with a drill. In Traverse Task the robot has to perform a ride through set of way-points in an unknown terrain. Watching the images from cameras is restricted for the operator in this task and the rover must solve this task autonomously. An important goal is to use autonomous functions e.g. automatic approach with the arm to target location, autonomous ride, automatic storing of the samples to the containers.

Rules include general restrictions for the rover and conditions for performing different tasks. From general restrictions are the most important: no direct view of the rover from the operator's position, communication frequencies restriction, recommended weight limit up to 60 kg, maximum distance of the rover from the operator position is 100 m or speed limit of 0,5 m/s to ensure safety. Safety is a priority and stop button and light beacon is compulsory.

Extraterrestrial conditions are simulated with restriction of using GPS and other satellite based navigational systems. Surface of the competition environment called "Marsyard" consists of mixture of clay, sand and gravel in combination with rocks acting like obstacles. Depth map with points of interest is provided on the event.

2   Related Work

UGVs are used in extraterrestrial environment but also in the missions on the Ground. Reconnaissance missions are planned and simulated for a long time with taking into account also the transportation of the vehicle to the destination area and planned tasks [4,10]. There are also lower scale projects of vehicles with same purpose intended for competitions [12,14].

Providing geographical data and analysis of terrain in large areas is an important purpose of rovers [7]. The traversing ability is crucial and requires advanced solutions to overcome obstacles and rough terrain conditions. This leads to development of special suspension systems [5,13] and concepts of rover chassis [11] including locomotion subsystem with wheels, walking performed with legs or crawler type chassis with tracks.

Rovers can be equipped with extensions for geological analysis, manipulation device or other task specific equipment. To perform manipulation rover needs dexterous arm [9] which can carry tools [1] cameras and other sensors. The rover uses cameras for navigation and even for geological analysis [2] for the complex analysis of the target environment rover must be equipped with sufficient sensors [8]. There is a significant progress in development of extraterrestrial rovers intended for regolith sample analysis [15] bringing ideas for surface and deep sample collection and analysis.

3   Rover Design

Chassis of the rover was developed with the emphasis on the robustness and connectivity with modules. During competition different modules could be implemented for a specific task, for example see figures. (Fig. 1a and b). The suspension mechanism is based on our simulations where we compared different kinematics to decide which is the most suitable for given scale, speeds and terrains.

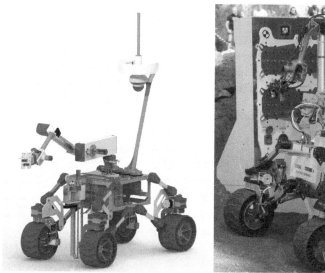

(a) Rover in geology task configuration   (b) Rover in manipulation configuration

Fig. 1. Different rover configurations

3.1   Simulations

The rover will be moving at relatively slow speeds. The maximum allowed speed at the European rover challenge is 0,5 m/s. Many current slow moving rover on space missions today are using 6 wheeled rocker-bogie suspension. Those rovers however are moving at a much slower speeds, for example the NASA Curiosity rover has a maximum speed of 0,038 m/s [3]. We wanted to determine if a rigid rocker bogie style suspension is suitable for speeds that are one or two orders of magnitude higher than those of current planetary rovers.

We were aiming to make a four wheel design. Dynamic simulations of the rover suspension kinematics were used to figure out whether a rocker suspension or an independent suspension performed better. The rocker system is a 4 wheeled version of a rocker-bogie suspension (Fig. 2a). There is a rocker on each side of the rover with a single pivot. Each rocker rigidly connects two wheels and a balancing lever. The center of the balancing lever is connected to the chassis, which causes the chassis pitch and roll angles to be the average of the two rockers. The independent suspension has all wheels suspended on parallelograms with springs and dampeners (Fig. 2b). The springs allow the parallelogram joints to move 40° down from a horizontal, fully compressed position. During the simulations we developed a third model. A combination of the previous two, referred to in this paper as "our design". Our design consists of parallelograms for each wheel, however instead of independent suspension, the bottom center joints are coupled and connected to a balancing lever, situated on the bottom of a chassis (Fig. 2c) (Fig. 3).

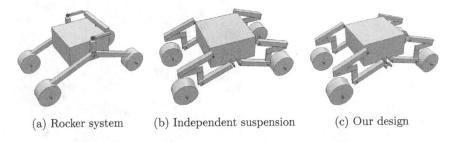

(a) Rocker system   (b) Independent suspension   (c) Our design

Fig. 2. Simulation models

Fig. 3. Simulated traverse in artificial terrain

The models were built in V-rep, a simulation software from Coppelia Robotics. The simulated environment consists of a heightfield, generated from a Perlin noise image, with the height differences of 0.5 m. Each simulation run was performed multiple times on different parts of this heightfield and then averaged, to get more universal results.

The first measurement looks at the systems' ability to keep the chassis in the same orientation (Fig. 4). Chassis angles of rotation with respect to the world coordinate frame is recorded and the result is calculated according to the formula (1).

$$S_\alpha = \frac{\sum_{i=1}^{n} |\alpha_i d_t|}{n} \tag{1}$$

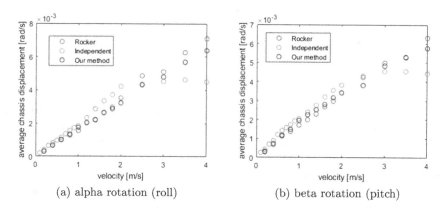

(a) alpha rotation (roll)   (b) beta rotation (pitch)

Fig. 4. Chassis stability

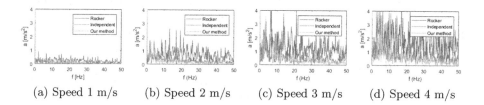

(a) Speed 1 m/s   (b) Speed 2 m/s   (c) Speed 3 m/s   (d) Speed 4 m/s

Fig. 5. Amplitude spectrum of chassis acceleration

The overall accelerations and vibrations were measured with an accelerometer inside the simulated chassis. The test was performed for four different velocities. The frequency spectrum (Fig. 5) shows the vibration amplitudes from 0 to 50 Hz. Figure 6 shows the average acceleration (gravity + vibrations) exerted on the rovers' chassis.

Our design performed better than the other two models in the simulations. Therefore we picked it for further development.

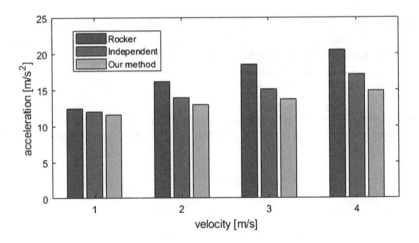

Fig. 6. Average acceleration exerted on the chassis

3.2 Chassis

In terms of manufacturing, the rover consists of aluminum alloy material and plastics. Connections are made with bolts and rivets. We often utilize 3D printing to reduce weight of the components that are not under a heavy stress and their dynamic deformations are not crucial. It allows us to utilize rapid prototyping methods. For example: the joints between parallelogram arms in the suspension are on their fourth iteration. The parts are manufactured from PLA, Nylon or ABS, on printers Prusa MK3S and Flashforge Inventor.

The undercarriage features a novel suspension system which is a second generation of parallelogram suspension system [6]. The kinematics are based on simulations from previous chapter. The mechanism has only one degree of freedom. Suspension on each side is connected with belt and both sides are connected with lever under the chassis. Every wheel is capable of steering and thanks to the parallelogram suspension, every steering axis is parallel to each other.

Vertical rotation axis of wheel is going through the middle of the wheel which is providing possibility of different steering principles for great maneuverability of the rover (Fig. 7). Double Ackermann steering geometry is used during longer crossing and center-point rotation for precise rover orientation. Wheel itself is mounted directly onto the worm gearbox output shaft via flange with clamp connection. Wheel is also equipped with a 3D printed airless rubber tire made from Stratasys FDM TPU 92A, which dampens shock and vibration while driving (Fig. 8).

3.3 Task Specific Modules

For manipulation with objects, samples and even for inspection has the rover attachable manipulator (Fig. 9b). This is a 5 degrees of freedom serial link manipulator with maximal payload 2 kg and maximal reach 1100 mm which can be

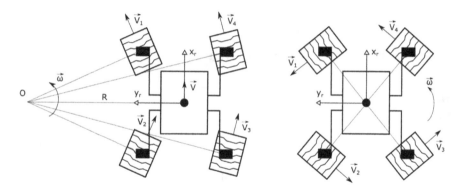

Fig. 7. Double Ackermann (left) and center-point (right) steering

(a) Adaptation to terrain   (b) Chassis concept

Fig. 8. Parallelogram suspension system

extended with end-effector. First rotational link allows the arm to reach objects on the ground next to the rover. The control of the manipulator is described in Subsect. 3.6.

The end-effectors are mostly 3D printed. In the middle of the grasping effectors a camera is placed and on the side of the effector there is an IR sensor measuring distance from objects. The jaw is mounted on a rack rail. Gears provide transmission from a rotating DC motor. There are three end-effectors used for the tasks except Traverse Task where no manipulation is required.

During the Science Task the soil samples are collected and analysed in four separately detachable container capsules (Fig. 10a). Each capsule is sealed and opens or closes on operator's demand. The samples are weight and temperature, humidity, and color of the soil is measured. Another sensor can provide value of particles per cubic meter for a specific gas (CO, LPG, CH_4, etc.) depending on its calibration. Every container is able to detect different gases. The soil is scooped by the end-effector with two shovels (Fig. 10b). They are driven by a motor strong enough to face even small rocks. Drill module is attached to the

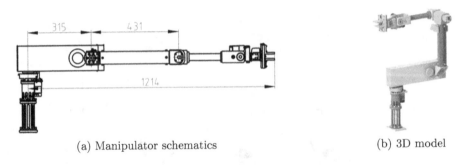

(a) Manipulator schematics   (b) 3D model

Fig. 9. Manipulation arm

side of the rover. It has a separate motor for the drilling and a separate motor for the lifting mechanism. Mechanism is divided into three main mechanical parts: parallelogram, drill guide-ways, and drill. Stroke of vertical movement is 340 mm. The sample is stored in the drill itself using detachable transparent tube. On side of this capsule is scale for easy detection of amount of soil in it. At the bottom there is a membrane for letting the soil to enter the capsule while preventing it from falling out at the same time.

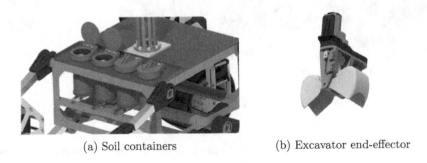

(a) Soil containers   (b) Excavator end-effector

Fig. 10. Soil analysis task modules

In Maintenance Task the operator drives the rover towards the control panel, while avoiding obstacles, which he can see through cameras. The image recognition system detects the position and orientation of the panel and its components. After approaching the panel the operator uses the arm to turn the knobs and switches to a designated position. As the last thing in the maintenance task, the operator grasps the high-power plug from the ground and insert it into a socket. End-effector uses parallel shaped grasps for switching. The middle is circle-shaped for picking-up a plug. The voltage is measured by nails on the side, connected to the voltmeter.

Collection Task requires the rover to detect the green aluminum caches in the field of view. Afterwards, the robot is driven to the first cache and after approaching the cache, the operator starts an automated sequence which lowers the arm towards the cache, picks it up and stores in the cache container module. The operator saves the current view from the cameras into an image file to document the operation. There are three caches in total and one of them is hidden in the terrain. A circle shaped grasp end-effector that can easily rotate around its axis is used. When a cache is picked-up no matter in which orientation, the gravity rolls the cache so it always points vertically downwards.

Traverse Task is specific when only raw data as odometry can be send to the operator from the rover, no camera image is allowed. However, a map with landmarks and waypoint coordinates are provided by the judges. Also, in the terrain there are points with tags that can server for determining the position of the rover. A small Intel T265 camera is installed to measure odometry. Other cameras deployed on the rover can detect the visual markers so two independent systems provide the position information for the operator.

3.4   Overview Subsystem

Rover is equipped with several sensors which provide the operator information about surrounding environment. Main camera is mounted to the communication mast and captures the rover from the top. It is a one of two HIKVISION MINI PTZ 4MPix zoomable cameras. This view provides the operator information about obstacles and objects around the rover and also current configuration of subsystems e.g. pose of the manipulator. Same camera is mounted to the bottom of the chassis and provides image of the ground. This is useful during sample collection and observation of objects collected with the manipulator from the ground.

Endoscope type camera is attached directly to the end-effector. With this camera operator can precisely move the arm to the reach position above the object of interest. Distance in the grasping direction is measured with the SHARP 2d120x infrared sensor.

Image from cameras can be directly transmitted to the operator station or processed in the NUC computer. Image processing is done using Cascade algorithm which provides convolutions over desired image with a set of filters. This is used for cache localization and detection of objects on the control panel during Maintenance Task.

3.5   Communication Subsystem

Communication is provided at 2.4 GHz frequency, the routers used are Mikrotik GrooveA 52HPn on the rover acting like a server and Mikrotik RB SXTG-2HnD with 60° sector antenna on the operator station acting like client. Client control station can be substituted with laptop or mobile phone. Omnidirectional antenna is placed on the communication mast above the rover. The communication is tested to be reliable over the distance of 600 m in good conditions (direct line of sight and low signal interference) (Fig. 11).

Fig. 11. Communication environment

3.6   Control of the Rover

The system is based on ROS framework. Master computer Intel NUC with support of Raspberry Pi 3 control board provide computation power to solve instructions for lower level controllers, image recognition tasks and communication. Individual motors are controlled through h-bridge drivers connected to Arduino control boards. The ROS platform runs on Linux-based software, we use Ubuntu 16.04 that supports ROS Kinetic version, and it simplifies the data exchange and control of the devices. For example the Rosserial package is used to communicate via USB between Arduinos and master computer. IP Camera Driver, Rosbridge Server and Web Video Server packages provide the image from HIKVISION IP cameras for the operator. There are many subprograms used in case of control that so the robot performs desired operation. Most of them we programmed in Python. The Rviz User Interface of the ROS can visualize many useful information of the whole system, e.g. images from cameras, joint states, odometry, sensors values. The ROS is made in a robust way, the packages work independently so if any of devices is not needed, it may be disconnected without any impact on the other parts of the system.

The situational awareness is vital for operating the rover in unknown environments. Therefore the operator has to be informed about the state of the rover at all times and with minimum delay. We achieve this with the view of multiple cameras and a live 3D model of the rover that shows the current state of all joints.

The operator can control the movement of the rover and the camera angles with the joystick. Or he can control the arm using an arm controller and its panel functions. The two monitors setup allows comfortable viewing of the robot state and functions. The right monitor shows an Rviz visualization, with the live 3D model of the robot and views from a mast camera and an undercarriage camera. The 3D model moves in the same way the real robot moves, it shows the position of the real arm on the rover and the position of the arm controller. The left monitor is our virtual dashboard. Written in HTML and JavaScript, it contains buttons and information for all necessary functions. The user can open and close soil containers, start the sampling drill, send the arm to a saved location, take an image with a camera and more. The image from the end-effector camera is showed in the middle of this dashboard. The whole operator's station is shown in figure (Fig. 12).

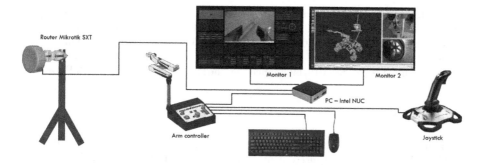

Fig. 12. Operator's control station

There are three modes of controlling the manipulator. The autonomous mode uses saved trajectories to drive the manipulator. The trajectories are composed of saved positions and moves in the joint space or Cartesian space, delays, end-effector commands, and sensor interrupts. Direct control mode uses analytical inverse kinematics approach and allows to drive the tool center point in desired directions with specified orientation. The last mode uses 1:2 scaled model of the robot's arm that the operator can hold and move to desired position. The rover's manipulator follows the movements of the controller and using forward kinematics it drives to the desired position. Inverse kinematics mode is precise, on the other hand forward kinematics with the scaled model works faster. The operator can choose which mode suits the best when a task has to be performed. However, autonomous mode provides the best results in case of speed and accuracy, but it can not be used always when the trajectory points must be defined before a task. Therefore, only the autonomous approach to the most used positions was used, e.g. home position, ground-contact position, above-containers positions.

4   Conclusions

In this paper we introduce basic concept of the rover which can solve different problems according to given tasks. The initial tests were performed in simulations where we compared our new design method for suspension kinematics with the two most used ones - rocker system and independent suspension. The results confirmed our assumption and proved the benefits of our method over the others in better stability and ability to mitigate vibrations. The main test was the competition itself, with its time constrains. The tests provided data for further development. Novel suspension system including advantages from parallelogram connection and self-levelling mechanism was proposed and will be a subject of the next research. Modular structure provided fast reconfiguration capability of the system and keeps the system extensible and up-gradable according to upcoming tasks. Usage of Robot Operating System (ROS) environment provides software robustness and reliability for such complex systems.

Acknowledgement. This work was sponsored among others by the Research Platform focused on Industry 4.0 and Robotics in Ostrava Agglomeration project, project number CZ.02.1.01/0.0/0.0/17_049/0008425 within the Operational Programme Research, Development and Education. This work has been also supported by specific research project SP2019/69 financed by the state budget of the Czech Republic.

References

1. Baumgartner, E.T., Bonitz, R.G., Melko, J.P., Shiraishi, L.R., Chris Leger, P.: The Mars Exploration Rover instrument positioning system. In: 2005 IEEE Aerospace Conference, pp. 1–19, March 2005. https://doi.org/10.1109/AERO.2005.1559295

2. Coates, A., et al.: The PanCam instrument for the ExoMars rover. Astrobiology **17**(6–7), 511–541 (2017). https://doi.org/10.1089/ast.2016.1548

3. Gannon, M.: See the curiosity rover's 1st year on mars in 2 minutes (video), August 2013. https://www.space.com/22226-mars-rover-curiosity-time-lapse-video.html

4. Kubota, T., Kunii, Y., Kuroda, Y., Working Group: Japanese lunar robotics exploration by co-operation with lander and rover. J. Earth Syst. Sci. **114**(6), 777–785 (2005). https://doi.org/10.1007/BF02715963

5. Kubota, T., Kuroda, Y., Kunii, Y., Nakatani, I.: Small, light-weight rover "micro5" for lunar exploration. Acta Astronaut. **52**(2), 447–453 (2003). https://doi.org/10.1016/S0094-5765(02)00187-X. Selected Proceedings of the 4th IAA International conference on L ow Cost Planetary Missions

6. Pastor, R., Vysocky, A., Siroky, P., Konecny, Z., Karnik, L.: Use of different simulation methods for design of experimental rover. MM Sci. J. **12**(2018), 2616–2620 (2018). https://doi.org/10.17973/mmsj.2018_12_2018102

7. Rekleitis, I.M., Dudek, G., Milios, E.E.: Multi-robot exploration of an unknown environment, efficiently reducing the odometry error. In: IJCAI, vol. 2, pp. 1340–1345 (1997)

8. Rice, M.S., et al.: Geologic overview of the Mars Science Laboratory rover mission at the Kimberley, Gale crater, Mars. J. Geophys. Res. Planets **122**(1), 2–20 (2017). https://doi.org/10.1002/2016JE005200

9. Rusconi, A., Magnani, P., Michaud, S., Gruener, G., Terrien, G., Merlo, A.: Dextrous lightweight arm for exploration (DELIAN). In: Advanced Space Technologies in Robotics and Automation (ASTRA), Noordwijk, The Netherlands (2015)

10. Schuster, M.J., et al.: Towards autonomous planetary exploration. J. Intell. Robot. Syst. **93**(3), 461–494 (2017). https://doi.org/10.1007/s10846-017-0680-9

11. Seeni, A., Schafer, B., Rebele, B., Tolyarenko, N.: Robot mobility concepts for extraterrestrial surface exploration. In: 2008 IEEE Aerospace Conference, pp. 1–14, March 2008. https://doi.org/10.1109/AERO.2008.4526237

12. Sigüenza, M., Guillen, D., Arroyo, D., Cuellar, F.: Mobile robots development: a case study from robotics competitions and course projects. In: 2017 IEEE XXIV International Conference on Electronics, Electrical Engineering and Computing (INTERCON), pp. 1–4, August 2017. https://doi.org/10.1109/INTERCON.2017.8079703

13. Wedler, A., et al.: LRU-lightweight rover unit. In: Proceedings of the 13th Symposium on Advanced Space Technologies in Robotics and Automation (ASTRA) (2015)

14. Zahir, E., et al.: 6 wheeled mars rover design for terrain traversing, equipment servicing, astronaut assistance and on-board testing. In: 2016 IEEE/SICE International Symposium on System Integration (SII), pp. 917–922, December 2016. https://doi.org/10.1109/SII.2016.7844117
15. Zhang, T., et al.: The progress of extraterrestrial regolith-sampling robots. Nat. Astron. **3**(6), 487 (2019)

Machine Learning-Based Open Framework for Multiresolution Multiagent Simulation

Dariusz Pierzchała[✉] and Przemysław Czuba[✉]

Cybernetics Faculty, Military University of Technology, Warsaw, Poland
{dariusz.pierzchala,przemyslaw.czuba}@wat.edu.pl

Abstract. M&S of systems, their dynamic structures and particularly the behaviour of internal component objects, should be performed at the level of detail which is adequate to the problem and modelling purpose defined. In the scenarios related to the complex world strictly one level is insufficient - there is necessary to build a multi-resolution model that represents structures and actions at different levels of detail. This is the main and direct reason for the application of the Multi-resolution Agent Model (MrAM) approach in the simulation with functions for a state's transformation (aggregation/disaggregation). It is common practice to implement methods of resolution adaptation in such a way that they are completely closed in the compiled program code. Meanwhile, the multiplicity of different possible scenarios regarding group and individual behaviours indicates that there are necessary software constructions enabling the end user to create both new, open models of behaviours and algorithms for aggregation/disaggregation of the state.

Moreover, the environment surrounding agents influences target states differently at different moments in time. The article proposes an approach to determining the consensus state of agents with the use of machine learning methods.

The consensus between agents according to the appropriate approach, depending on the conditions and state, will be a generalized method adaptable to the environment of agents. We propose the reinforcement learning model as a multiagent game in order to achieve HRE state and thus complete disaggregation.

To meet the requirements, the original Java-based framework for hybrid simulation (discrete, event-based and continuous) with the ability to model the object as an agent at multiple levels, automatic triggering of updates on all modelled levels, and Groovy-based scripts. The scripting technology is integrated with the standalone Java software and enables the implementation of behaviors and state transformations that are really open in scripts.

The article presents the proposed framework solution on the example of an autonomous system model composed of many cooperating objects. We share our experiences related to the extension of the "SymSG Border Tactics" simulation environment dedicated to CAX exercises in The Poland Border Guard.

Keywords: Hybrid simulation · Multiresolution agent-based modelling · Machine learning · Reinforcement Learning

© Springer Nature Switzerland AG 2020
J. Mazal et al. (Eds.): MESAS 2019, LNCS 11995, pp. 216–228, 2020.
https://doi.org/10.1007/978-3-030-43890-6_17

1 Introduction

Contemporary peacekeeping operations, being conducted by military, state security and emergency formations need effective and adequate simulation systems in order to properly train commanders and their subordinate personnel. The process of training is being constantly modified - these issues is especially important for the Polish since Poland's accession to the EU and to the Schengen Agreement. The dynamics of changes in requirements, operational and organizational conditions as well as external constraints are a reason to searching more effective and adequate training methods. As for now in Polish Border Guard, courses have been conducted without advanced simulation tools, causing time-consuming and cost-intensive trainings directly at border guard posts. The modern training methods with the use of variable resolution simulators in operational games will make the education much more realistic, complete and tailored to the current needs of both individual officers and staff. What is more, the majority of trainings will be possible to be conducted in one training centre without unnecessary hazardous but with wider access and significantly reduced costs.

The whole final result of the mentioned research [1] is the complete and technologically modern simulation environment "SymSG Border" dedicated to Computer Assisted Exercises (using originally developed simulation library DisSim) and to Virtual Reality based trainings. The system stays in line with the guidelines of FRONTEX, enabling cooperation with other EU institutions and compliant training systems. The main subject of paper's is the first component "SymSG Border Tactics" - the constructive simulator which serves as Command & Control subsystem. The proposed core framework delivers event-based programming concepts facilitating control flow inside interacting multiresolution simulation models, where a concept "resolution" is defined as a conceptual level at which an object (entity) is simulated. One simple object (like UAV) is a disaggregated high-resolution entity (HRE) while a group of objects states LRE (aggregate low-resolution entity). Such multiagent environments are often very dynamic thus disaggregation processes should be adaptable to deviations of environment conditions. The significant problem of MRM theory (addressed in the paper) is related to: how to properly fill out a state vector of a HRE/LRE object after state transformation between low and high resolution levels in a manner that complies with both the rules of formation control and reflecting to the environmental constraints. In the paper we propose an approach to disaggregation problem with use of Multi-Agent Reinforcement Learning (MARL) algorithm. Further, we have applied the reinforcement learning model as a "multi-agent game" to be "played" in order to achieve HRE state and thus complete disaggregation.

It is common practice to implement simulation algorithms in such a way that state changes are strictly closed in the compiled program code. Despite the fact that the implemented simulator already significantly supports the training process, there is an actual need for such solutions, thanks to which it will be easier to modify the algorithms of simulated objects' behaviour and without rebuilding a software code. This will allow to relatively quickly increase the range of available scenarios and build new behaviours of simulated objects regarding new simulation algorithms of refugees or smugglers as well as for simulated UAVs or SG guard troops.

The article is twofold - one thread concerns ML-based methods for MRM and the other one concerns Groovy scripting technology adopted for reinforcement learning and state transformations. We share our experiences deals with the original DisSim framework extended with hybrid simulation (discrete, event, continuous) and the ability to model the software agent at multiple resolution levels and automatic triggering of updates on all modelled levels. The Groovy scripts immersed in DisSim is integrated with Java classes and enables the implementation of behaviours, state transformations and key reinforcement learning functions as custom modification scripts.

2 Related Work

Multi-resolution modelling (MRM) is essential for exploratory analysis of complex adaptive Systems of Systems (SoS) design spaces because it is neither cognitively nor computationally possible to keep track of all relevant variables and causal relationships (Davis and Bigelow). A resolution might have many dimensions - a high resolution level corresponds to a low level of aggregation (high-resolution entity, HRE) and analogously – a low resolution level to a high level of aggregation (low-resolution entity, LRE), for instance in terms of entity's attributes. When the two or more entities on different levels of resolution interact with each other, the problem with consistency will always occur. Thus, the typical problems are related to (1) uncertain data utilised to calculate HRE/LRE object state variables regarding proper state transformation and consistency management functions and (2) formation control as the fundamental motion coordination problem in the multiagent systems where agents converge to predefined geometric shapes.

There's been many attempts to address the problems to date. In the section we shortly present selected methods that will serve as justification for more generalized and unified approach. In the work [2] the Attribute Dependency Graph is introduced for maintaining consistency and then estimation of cost of aggregation/disaggregation operations. Next work [3] concerns formal modelling of MRM supported by both state mapping functions and consistency correction methods. In [4] Authors propose a multi-criteria optimization task for UAV group to find sources of terrestrial signal in a given area. There were defined three algorithms to solve the problem: one exact algorithm and two heuristic algorithms basing on the PSO algorithm. There are described both agent-based model and practical software for modelling of UAV behaviours at diverse resolution levels. The novelty proposed in [5] considers an approach which combines a graph theory, HLA simulation standard, a special ontology and rough set formalisms into a synergistic approach. The Rough Set Theory facilitates discovering patterns hidden in data-based information, reasoning with incomplete information and classifying new cases. The ontology-based model gives possibilities to unify meaning of domain concept and relationship. It provides also the inference abilities to verify the instance data correctness according to consistency rules. Finally, the ontology make easier sharing knowledge about a domain and accomplishing semantic interoperability. Authors of [6] studied application of multi-agent methods in multiresolution simulation hence aggregation and disaggregation process. They proposed multiagent formation control protocol based on formation graph where nodes represent agents positions whilst the edges possible communication channels between matched pairs of agents. Every graph edge has additionally information about node desired position to each node it is connected to. Final formation agents' desired relative position in a formation is described by a consensus protocol for a static in time topology. Hence, we can interpret desired relative agents' positions as combination of desired positions of his predecessors. Although this approach gives good results for correctly defined formation graphs, it has few drawbacks. First, effectiveness of the method is closely related to definition of formation shape (Formation Graph). Poorly defined graph might result in an inefficient disaggregation or even makes it unfeasible - creation of graph which gives efficient result is not an easy task [7]. Further, a formation control protocol does not take into consideration the environmental (external) conditions are still altering. In a given moment in time, some formation shapes could be more preferable than others. Moreover, formation definition is based on a formation graph and there is only the finite number of shapes which can be defined. There is unfeasible to predefine shapes and match them for every situation that 'could' arise along with simulation flow.

Disaggregation outcomes depend on many conditions, especially related to an environment. That's why no simple, unified algorithm can take into consideration so many different variables and on that basis give desired outcome. Next feature is adaptability - multiagent environments are naturally very dynamic and disaggregation method should be adaptable to deviations in environment conditions. Further important reason is scalability - an algorithm should follow the increasing number of agents. Currently, we are observing more and more interesting research in machine learning technology. Some work related to this direction are reported – one of them is [8] where Authors propose a new state representation for deep multi-agent Reinforcement Learning. The agents are treated as samples and the empirical mean embedding is used as input for a decentralized policy.

Deep Reinforcement Learning is a very general paradigm (e.g. a toolkit OpenAI Gym). In its fundamental principle a robust and performant RL system should be great at any kind of task. Investigating this area, we can meet number of reinforcement learning methods which in their core uses Deep Neural Networks for approximation of optimal disaggregation policy. Taking into consideration lack of a sufficient set of data to identify hidden patterns in data, problems with an unsupervised learning and insufficient sets of examples with exemplary states for unsupervised learning we conclude that instead of building a very precise model of the agent a method is required that adapts the agent to the situation and the environment. In the paper we propose Deep Reinforcement Learning (DRL) approach for disaggregation problem - such a solution is supported by a number of mentioned reasons.

3   Adaptation of Reinforcement Learning

Reinforcement Learning (RL) offers a formal framework for solving sequential decision-making task. It could be described as the method to decide, from experience, the sequence of actions to perform in an uncertain (often stochastic) environment in order to achieve some goals [9]. RL problem could be stated as finding the best policy (course of actions) to perform inside environment by an agent capable of making decisions which optimizes given notion of cumulative rewards. RL is based on trial-and-error experience notion which makes an agent to learn new behaviours or modify current ones. Following paragraphs describe basic components and assumptions of Reinforcement Learning framework.

Figure 1 describes interaction between agent and an environment in RL setting.

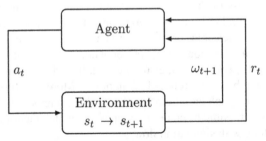

Fig. 1. Interaction between Agent and Environment inside RL framework. Environment is in state s_t at time t. Agent performs an action a_t at time t which causes an environment to transition to state s_{t+1}. As the response agent receives observation about environment ω_{t+1} at time $t + 1$ and reward r_t for the action he performed at time t.

3.1 Definitions

Markov decision process (MDP) is a way to formalize sequential decision-making task. Therefore, MDPs are naturally the basis of reinforcement learning problems. An MDP is a 5-tuple (S, A, T, R, γ) where [9]:

S is the state space,
A is the action space,
$T : S \times A \times S \rightarrow [0, 1]$ is the transition function (set of conditional transition probabilities between states),
$R : S \times A \times S \rightarrow R$ is the reward function, where R is a continuous set of possible rewards in a range $R_{max} \in \mathbb{R}^+ (e.g., [0, R_{max}])$,
$\gamma \in [0, 1)$ is the discount factor.

The system is fully observable in an MDP, which means that the observation ω_{t+1} is the same as the state of the environment: $s_t = \omega_t$. Probability of agent moving from state s_t to s_{t+1} is given by transition function $T(s_t, a_t, s_{t+1})$ and the reward is given by a bounded reward function $R(s_t, a_t, s_{t+1}) \in R$.

Every RL problem follows a Markov property which means that the future of the process does not depend on past observations (only the current one). At each time step agent performs an action, changes the environment state and receives reward.

Policy $\pi(s, a) \in \Pi$ is a function which maps specific state to probabilities of selecting each possible action from that state. Agent primary objective is to find a policy, that is a policy that maximises expected return[1] $V^\pi(s) : S \rightarrow \mathbb{R}$ (also called V-value function) for policy π. Finally, Q-value function $Q^\pi(s, a) : S \times A \rightarrow \mathbb{R}$ (sometimes called *action-value* function) for policy π. This function is particularly important because it tells for

---

[1] In this paper *return* and *reward* will be used interchangeably.

an agent following policy π, which action is best to take at any given state. Optimal Q-value function is defined as follows: $Q^*(s, a) = \max_{a \epsilon A} Q^\pi(s, a)$. Optimal policy can be directly obtained from $Q^*(s, a)$: $\pi^*(s) = \max_{a \epsilon A} Q^*(s, a)$. In other words, optimal policy is a course of action that agent needs to perform in order to maximize expected reward.

3.2 Reinforcement Learning Methods

One of the basic and most popular value-based method is Q-learning. In its core it uses lookup table of $Q(s, a)$ values with one entry for each state-action pair. In every time step Q-learning algorithm update $Q(s, a)$ values with use of Bellman equation [10]. We will not go into details here because this method is effective only for problems with small size of states and actions. For complex, continuous environments size of lookup table becomes unsustainable.

Deep Q-network (DQN) algorithm is the solution for this problem. In its architecture DQNs are just Deep Neural Networks. Introduced by authors in [11] DQN approximates $Q(s, a)$ values for every state-action pair and eventually network will approximate the optimal $Q^*(s, a)$.

This approach requires two heuristics to limit the instabilities [9]:

- Q-network weights are updated every $C \epsilon \mathbb{N}$ iterations,
- Algorithm uses Replay Memory technique [7] which stores last $N_{replay} \epsilon \mathbb{N}$ time steps. Network is being trained on set of tuples $<s, a, r, s'>$ called mini-batch selected randomly from the replay memory.

Unfortunately, due to distribution nature of multi-agent systems each agent updates its policy independently from other entities in environment. Therefore, environment from the point of view of single agent is not stationary any more. This is a violation of Markov assumptions required for convergent of Q-learning [14].

Policy gradient (PG) methods are another popular choice for different RL tasks [14]. On the contrary to Q-learning based methods, PG algorithms are directly adjusting the parameters of policy. Simple approaches to this method also give poor results in multi-agent settings.

Authors of [14] propose a Multi-Agent Actor Critic method which gives promising results in cooperative and competitive tasks (which are the two fundamental problems of MAS). In their algorithm agents based on local observation learn to reach shared objectives using communication channels as well as physical interactions.

In work of [13] a broad review and comparison of state-of-the-art multi-agent reinforcement methods is provided.

3.3 Disaggregation Method

In multiresolution multi-agent simulation, an agent can be viewed as Multi-resolution Entity (MRE). Transition between Low Resolution (LR) to High Resolution (HR) occurs during disaggregation process which is basically a mapping from LR state to HR state at time t.

In this paper we propose an idea of disaggregation method with use of Reinforcement Learning Method. In this context, reinforcement learning problem is the "multi-agent game" that needs to be played in order to achieve HRE state and thus complete disaggregation.

Let's assume we have access to trained Deep Neural Network (DNN) which approximates optimal policy for particular reinforcement learning problem (defined in terms of Markov Decision Process) and at time t arrives a disaggregation request to LRE. At start every HR agent has its state equal to LR state at time t. Environment where the game will be played by HR agents is the segment of simulation environment at time t. This means that if simulation environment is dynamic then disaggregation process steps can differ for various simulation states. When HRE and environment are initialized the game is played. At every timestep agents are choosing an action according to optimal policy approximated by DNN. Method input accepts current environment state (agent observation) as input and gives the best action to be played in return. Process stops when game is resolved or other condition is fulfilled. HR state after disaggregation is the same as game agents' final states. Sketch of described process is given in Fig. 2.

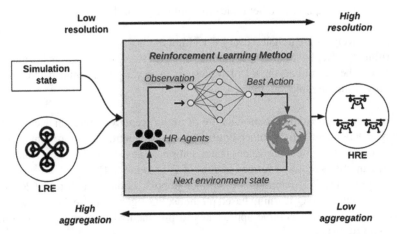

Fig. 2. Disaggregation process based on reinforcement learning method.

4   Multiagent Multiresolution Simulation Framework

We have constructed the Multiagent Multiresolution Simulation Framework that will implement disaggregation method described in previous section. Figure 3 shows conceptually an architecture related to this idea.

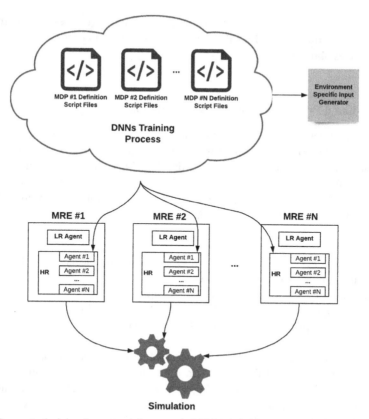

Fig. 3. Conceptual view of proposed framework: MDPs definitions script files, DNNs Training Process and Multi-resolution Entities (simulation agents).

4.1 Architecture

Proposed framework consists of following components:

- *MDPs definitions* – for each disaggregation method corresponds specific MDP with its procedure's implementations stored in separate script files. Each MDP is the description of particular reinforcement learning problem to be solved and hence disaggregation process;
- *DNN Training Process* – place where HR agents Deep Neural Networks are trained. This process starts before actual simulation and uses *Environment Specific Input Generator* for producing different environment conditions per every training episode. Training process is based on Memory Replay technique. This allows for online training also – during simulation experiences can be stored and then used for ad-hoc training (after or during simulation);
- *Multi-resolution Entity* – simulation entity which can be viewed on many resolution levels, each one constructed from agents;

- *Simulation* – actual simulation part - when Low Resolution receives a disaggregation signal during simulation, High Resolution Agents are using DNN with computed weights to establish new state.

4.2 Java-Based Framework for Hybrid Simulation

The majority of several assessments indicate constructive simulation methods as the most universal type of simulation. It is based on formal models of objects and their implementation in computer programs. We developed the original Java-based discrete simulation software package (named DisSim) [15] in order to facilitate creating constructive simulation software – both discrete and quasi-continuous as well as hybrid. DisSim is an object paradigm based package. The basic entity is an object 'o' with its attributes:

- $O = \{o = <id, c>\}$, $c \in C^O$, $id \in N$ - a set of simulated objects of 'c' class that are identified by an 'id' with a unique value;
- C^O - a non-empty set of classes of modelled objects;
- A_c - a non-empty set of attributes specified for the $c \in C^O$ object class;
- V_a^c - a set of acceptable values of the $a \in A_c$ attribute of the $c \in C^O$ objects class.

The C^O and A_c sets contain the numbers of modelled object classes and their attributes. At any time t of the simulation time each measurable feature of the system is represented by an ordered quadruple: $<o, a, v, t>$. The state of the modelled system $ST(t)$ will be the vector created by all attributes of all objects at the simulation time t. In the simulation $v \in V_a^c$ values of $a \in A_c$ attributes are determined as a result of the user-defined state change function. Consequently, along with the assumptions for each object there are defined: the state vector with attributes and either the events or periodically executed equations that change the values of attributes (and finally a state of the system). The term event 'e' from a finite set of events 'E' is understood as the algorithmic change in object's state which is scheduled for a specific simulation moment t.

The result of an implementation in Java of the above model are the DisSim subpackages of classes designed for:

- the package *simcore* – the classes for controlling the whole experiment: passage of simulation time, events ordering and changes of state (both discrete and quasi-continuous);
- the package *broker* – a message bus supporting messages exchange between simulation objects (two modes: publisher-subscriber and notifier-observer);
- the package *random* – a (pseudo)random number generator with a broad range of methods responsible for different probability distributions (including template for user defined empirical distribution function);
- the package *monitors* – monitoring, collecting and statistical analysis, both in the interior *Statistics* class and in *R* statistical package (very popular software environment for statistical computing and graphics) via dedicated interface.

Every $o \in O$ simulation object of the $c \in C^O$ class inherits from the abstract *BasicSimEntity* class. Its A_c attributes store the values of the state vector. Each event $e = <t, f_e^S>$ is a state change created in objects inherited from the generic *BasicSimStateChange* class. An event is the result of a f_e^S state change function implemented as the *transition()* method of the *BasicSimStateChange* class. The event class attributes include: scheduled execution time and priority of the status change (*runSimTime, priority*) and an optional time step (*repetitionPeriod*) for either a discrete with a fixed step or a quasi- continuous simulation. For the latter type of simulation a special repeatable event class *RKEvent* is dedicated. After each time step (stored in *repetitionPeriod*), the values of equations describing the system state are determined in the method *transition()*. The exact form of the equations has to be determined in *Function <RKFunctionParameters, List <Double>>* by the DisSim user. The *Function* is a realization of Java functional interface thus an user is expected to implement lambda expressions and method references. Additionally, an interpreter classes for Groovy scripts have been implemented. The integration between DisSim classes and Groovy scripts has been achieved on the base of GroovyScriptEngine and specialized methods to load scripts (GroovyScriptEngine(loadScriptByName(name)), and subsequently execute scripts' code with parameters (*getDeclaredMethod(method).invoke(scriptRef, args)*). For each object instance of *BasicSimStateChange* class new algorithm of the method *transition()* might be defined in a separated Groovy script file. Finally, codes from scripts will be loaded into the scripts' map in DisSim and launched by an interpreter during an execution of the *transition()* methods inside objects inherited from *BasicSimStateChange* and defined by the DisSim user.

During research for deep neural networks and Markov Decision Processes implementations open-source library *Deeplearning4j* based on Java language was used. It supports a wide range of neural networks configuration, provides reinforcement learning framework and has well developed documentation with examples.

Referring to the "SymSG Border Tactics" simulation software [1] it is tightly linked with DisSim classes which provide a set of abstractions used for object state changes implementations. The solution comes with significant amount of simulation models implementations - each element extends *BasicSimEntity* abstract class. One of the most advanced is *road blockade*, the another provides functionalities to work as *refugee*. State change *BasicSimStateChange* (one-shot or repeatable) and activities *BasicSimProcess* (sequence of events) are a base for *reactionToDangerousIncident*. Service activities such as controlling traffic objects are implemented extending the *BasicSimAction* abstract. In similarity to *BasicSimStateChange* there is a wrapper class containing shared functionalities – *BlockadeOfficerAction*. By means of the use of open Groovy scripts almost every action taken by simulation objects might be modified or even exchanged for another source code.

4.3 Multi-agent Reinforcement Learning

Agent training process is based on concrete Markov Decision Process definition which corresponds to adequate disaggregation method. Such definition is stored in separate script files where each one is responsible for different MDP function:

- *reset* – returns an environment to its initial state based on Low Resolution state and additional conditions (fetched from *Environment Specific Input Generator*);
- *observation* – returns current observation about environment to agent. It could be a vector of other agents and entities positions that agent perceived. Information could be partial as agent not always have view about whole environment state;
- *reward* – for each action performed inside environment agent receives individual reward which evaluates how well he performed. If agents want to accomplish a collaborative goal then sum of their rewards will be shared among them;
- *isDone* – evaluation function which checks if agent accomplished its goal. This is optional as each episode can end after specific number of time steps.

MDP interface contains all above methods. Their implementations are used inside prepared environment that could be identical as target simulation environment or it's chosen part. Until reinforcement learning method converges to optimal policy agents choose actions in-side environment based on current observation, move and perceive reward with next observation. Next, they memorize transition they made to be used in future training process.

Script Manager responsibility is to load supplied MDPs scripts when training process starts to memory and at select proper method implementation at algorithm run time. Internally Manager stores scripts as *key-value* pairs where key is a two-tuple: $<MDP_{ID}, METHOD_{NAME}>$ and *value* is the desired script.

Figure 4 presents pseudocode for the algorithm.

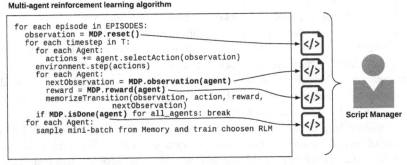

Multi-agent reinforcement learning algorithm

```
for each episode in EPISODES:
    observation = MDP.reset()
    for each timestep in T:
        for each Agent:
            actions += agent.selectAction(observation)
        environment.step(actions)
        for each Agent:
            nextObservation = MDP.observation(agent)
            reward = MDP.reward(agent)
            memorizeTransition(observation, action, reward,
                               nextObservation)
        if MDP.isDone(agent) for all_agents: break
    for each Agent:
        sample mini-batch from Memory and train choosen RLM
```

Script Manager

Fig. 4. Pseudocode sketch of algorithm for agent training process inside multi-agent environment.

5 Conclusion

In the paper we presented the main concepts which stand behind the software tool for modelling and simulation MRM with the reinforcement learning model as a multiagent game in order to achieve HRE state and thus complete disaggregation. Moreover, these original and adapted software packages can be combined in one solution with prospective high potential for research opportunities.

However, we focuses mostly on advantages (like generality and adaptability) we would like to hint a few drawbacks of the proposed approach: high difficulty of Multi-Agent Reinforcement Learning algorithm definition, need of computational resources, uneasy defining of right reward methods (an agent learnt behaviour is direct consequence of reward function) or necessity of tuning properties of algorithm.

In contrast to most of existing simulation tools our proposition has a capability to modify behaviours or activities by programming Groovy/Python scripts even after building a closed ready-to-use software. It is the technical advantage of the work we have been conducted. Our further goal is primarily to create a library with rich content of simulation models of MRE entities and behavior algorithms specified to different situations which face troops of Border Guard.

References

1. Chmielewski, M., Kukiełka, M., Frąszczak, D., Bugajewski, D.: The architectural software concepts implemented in distributed high resolution constructive simulation environment SymSG Border Tactics, supporting Polish Border Guard computer assisted exercises. In: 2017 Fourth International Conference on Mathematics and Computers in Sciences and in Industry (MCSI) (2017). https://doi.org/10.1109/MCSI.2017.50. ISBN 978-1-5386-2820-1
2. Natrajan, A., Reynolds, P.F., Srinivasan, S.: Guidelines for the Design of Multi-resolution Simulations. US DoD DMSO (1997)
3. Wei, S., Cai, B.G., Li, S.H., Liu, Z.G., Wang, J.: Multi-resolution simulation strategy and its simulation implementation of Train Control System. IEEE (2011). 978-1-4577-0574-8/11
4. Skrzypecki, S., Pierzchała, D., Tarapata, Z.: Distributed simulation environment of unmanned aerial systems for a search problem. In: Mazal, J. (ed.) MESAS 2018. LNCS, vol. 11472, pp. 65–81. Springer, Cham (2019). https://doi.org/10.1007/978-3-030-14984-0_6
5. Pierzchała, D.: Application of ontology and rough set theory to information sharing in multi-resolution combat M&S. In: Sobecki, J., Boonjing, V., Chittayasothorn, S. (eds.) Advanced Approaches to Intelligent Information and Database Systems. SCI, vol. 551, pp. 193–203. Springer, Cham (2014). https://doi.org/10.1007/978-3-319-05503-9_19
6. Pierzchała, D., Czuba, P.: Method of agents' state estimation in multiresolution multiagent simulation. Comput. Sci. Math. Model. **8**, 29–39 (2018). ISSN 2450-0054
7. Lin, Z., Francis, B., Maggiore, M.: Feasibility for formation stabilization of multiple unicycles. In: 2004 43rd IEEE Conference on Decision and Control (2004). https://doi.org/10.1109/CDC.2004.1428776. ISBN 0-7803-8682-5
8. Hüttenrauch, M., Šošic, A., Neumann, G.: Deep reinforcement learning for swarm systems. J. Mach. Learn. Res. **20**(54), 1–31 (2019)
9. François-Lavet, V., Henderson, P., Islam, R., Bellemare, M.G., Pineau, J.: An introduction to deep reinforcement learning. Found. Trends Mach. Learn. **11**(3–4), 219–354 (2018)
10. Bellman, R.E., Dreyfus, S.E.: Applied Dynamic Programming. Princeton University Press, Princeton (1962). ISBN 10: 0691079137
11. Mnih, V., et al.: Human-level control through deep reinforcement learning. Nature **518**(7540), 529–533 (2015)
12. Lin, L.-J.: Self-improving reactive agents based on reinforcement learning, planning and teaching. Mach. Learn. **8**(3–4), 293–321 (1992)
13. Nguyen, T.T., Nguyen, N.D., Nahavandi, S.: Deep reinforcement learning for multi-agent systems: a review of challenges, solutions and applications (2018)

14. Lowe, R., Wu, Y., Tamar, A., Harb, J., Abbeel, P., Mordatch, I.: Multi-Agent Actor-Critic for Mixed Cooperative-Competitive Environments (2017)
15. Pierzchała, D., Najgebauer, A.: Simulator for analysis cyber threats to RFID based system. In: MATEC Web Conference, vol. 210 (2018). https://doi.org/10.1051/matecconf/201821004022. Published online 05 October 2018

Future Challenges of Advanced M&S Technology

Model of Observation Posts Deployment in Tactical Decision Support System

Petr Stodola[✉], Jan Drozd, Jan Nohel, and Karel Michenka

University of Defence, Brno, Czech Republic
{petr.stodola,jan.drozd,jan.nohel,karel.michenka}@unob.cz

Abstract. This paper deals with the model of observation posts deployment in the area of operations. The goal of the model is to find optimal positions for a number of observation posts in order to observe as large area of interest as possible provided that the tactical requirements and conditions for the task at hand are kept. The first part of the paper presents the mathematical formulation of the model. Then, a stochastic algorithm based on the simulated annealing principle is proposed for the problem solution. Next part shows the application of the model which is implemented in the Tactical Decision Support System, the purpose of which is to aid commanders on the tactical level in their decision-making process. The last part shows results from experiments conducted on a set of benchmark problems which are based on the typical military scenarios.

Keywords: Observation post · Model · Deployment · Positioning · Area of interest · Simulated annealing · Experiments · Tactical Decision Support System

1 Introduction

Modern technologies have brought new perspectives and trends both in the military and civil domains in the last decades. Unmanned robotic systems have been used in military operations as well as in many civil applications. For example, Unmanned Aerial Systems (UASs) have been used in applications such as monitoring and inspection [1, 2], mapping [3], communication and networking [4], traffic monitoring [5], construction [6], and many others.

In the military, the trend is to use the robotic vehicles in connection with the decision support systems for tasks such as monitoring, reconnaissance, surveillance, searching for target objects, etc. These systems plan the operation in support of a commander. The goal is to plan and execute the operation optimally according to the selected optimization criterion. For example, these systems can plan the reconnaissance operation to explore the area of interest as fast as possible with UASs that are available.

At the University of Defence, the Tactical Decision Support System (TDSS) is being developed for the tactical level commanders of the Czech Army as a part of the Command, Control, Communication, Computer, Intelligence, Surveillance, and Reconnaissance (C4ISR) system. The main goal is to support commanders on the tactical level with their decision-making process.

J. Mazal et al. (Eds.): MESAS 2019, LNCS 11995, pp. 231–243, 2020.
https://doi.org/10.1007/978-3-030-43890-6_18

The TDSS consists of many models of military tactics. The commander can use one of the models to plan his/her task, if the model and the task are mutually compatible. The plan respects the current tactical situation and requirements, and provides the possible variants to fulfil the task along with the second-order effects [7]. The models implemented in the TDSS are e.g. models for planning logistics on the battlefield, planning reconnaissance or surveillance operations using multiple unmanned aerial or ground vehicles [8], at many others. More information about this topic is covered in [9–22].

This article deals with one of the models of the TDSS: Deployment of Observation Posts in the Area of Operations (DOPAO). The goal of this model is to plan the location(s) of observation post(s) in order to observe as large area of interest as possible while the key tactical requirements need to be met.

The paper is organized as follows. Section 2 presents the mathematical model. In Sect. 3, the problem solution is proposed based on the stochastic principles. Section 4 presents the model implementation in the TDSS. Section 5 shows the benchmark problems designed to verify the proposed solution. Finally, Sect. 6 concludes the paper and presents the future work of the authors.

2   Problem Formulation

Let $A_I \subset A$ be the area of interest to be observed as a part of the area of operations. This area is represented by a polygon with or without holes. Every point laying in the area of operations is defined by its elevation, which is altitude above the sea level. In the area, there may be a number of non-transparent objects and obstacles of some height. The uneven terrain and/or obstacles may occlude some portion of the area when observed from a static position.

Let $O = \{O_1, O_2, \ldots, O_N\}$ be a finite set of observation posts to be deployed in the area of operations where $N \geq 1$ is their number. From each observation post $O_i \in O$, a portion of the area of interest $A_i \subseteq A_I$ is observed. Every point, laying inside the area of interest with a visual line of sight (VLOS) between the observation post and this point, is marked as visible; otherwise it is marked as occluded. The total portion (coverage) of the area of interest, that is observed from at least one of the observation posts, is determined according to formula (1).

$$A_O = \bigcup_{i=1}^{N} A_i \quad \text{for all } O_i \in O \tag{1}$$

where

A_O is the area of interest observed from all posts,
A_i is the area of interest observed from post $O_i \in O$,
N is the number of observation posts deployed

Each observation post $O_i \in O$ is defined by the parameters as follows:

- Height of observer: the height above the terrain from which the area of interest is monitored.

- Height of target objects: minimum height of target objects inside the area of interest to be observed. Lower objects may not be detected.
- Visibility range: maximum range in which objects can be detected. It is a distance between the observation post and farthest point where objects can still be detected.

The principle of determining visibility from observation posts to points inside the area of interest is shown in a plane in Fig. 1. There is a cross-section of terrain, an observation post is placed on the left, an object to be observed located inside the area of interest on the right. The minimal object height may determine whether or not the object is visible from the observation post: object ② is visible, whereas object ① is not.

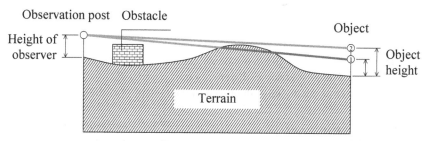

Fig. 1. Visibility from an observation post in a plane

Figure 2 presents the plan view of an example situation. There are two observation posts, the area of interest is bounded by a polygon of blue color. Green area is the total area observed from both posts ($A_O = A_1 \cup A_2$), red area is occluded.

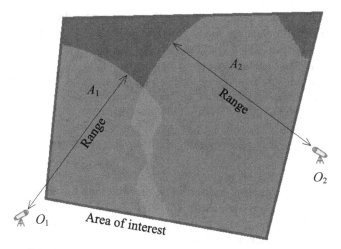

Fig. 2. Coverage of the area of interest (Color figure online)

Let $S \in A$ be a position of a superordinate unit in the area of operations. Let $C = \{C_1, C_2, \ldots\}$ be an infinite set of all points in the area of operations which can provide shelter for observation posts, typically edges of forest, vegetation or terrain obstacles. Let $R = \{R_1, R_2, \ldots\}$ be an infinite set of points in the area of operations which constitute possible escape routes.

Let $Eny = \{Eny_1, Eny_2, \ldots, Eny_M\}$ be a finite set of enemy units deployed in the area of operations where $M \geq 0$ is their number. Enemy units observe some portion of the area of operations based on their locations and parameters, which are the same as in case of observation posts (height of observer, height of objects, visibility range). The area observed by the enemy $A_{Eny} \subseteq A$ is a set of all points to which at least one enemy units has the VLOS – see formula (2)

$$A_{Eny} = \bigcup_{i=1}^{M} A_{Enyi} \quad \text{for all } Eny_i \in Eny \tag{2}$$

where

A_{Eny} is the area observed by all enemy units,
A_{Enyi} is the area of interest observed by enemy unit $Eny_i \in E$,
M is the number of enemy units deployed in the area of operations

The locations of observation posts are not known at the beginning. The objective of the DOPAO model is to maximize the portion of the area of interest observed from all posts according to formula (3).

$$maximize(|A_O|) \tag{3}$$

where $|A_O|$ is the size of the area of interest observed from all observation posts

There are some tactical requirements on observation posts limiting their possible locations in the area of operations. Basic requirements can be formulated as follows:

- Connection with the superordinate unit.
- Hidden establishing and abandoning the post, hidden observation process.
- Proximity of the escape route in case of emergency leave.
- Minimization of probability of disclosure by the enemy.

Individual requirements are ensured by the following principles (all constraints are optional):

- Posts must be placed within same maximum distance from the superordinate unit to ensure the communication – see constraint (4).
- Posts must be placed near an edge of forest, vegetation or some other terrain obstacles to ensure the hidden observation process – see constraint (5).
- Posts must be placed in some proximity of an escape route (road) to be able to leave in emergency – see constraint (6).
- Posts must not to be placed in the area observed by the enemy – see constraint (7).
- Posts must be placed outside the area of interest – see constraint (8).

$$|O_i - S| \leq D_{comm} \quad \text{for all } O_i \in O \tag{4}$$

$$\min(|O_i - C_1|, |O_i - C_2|, \ldots) \leq D_{shelter} \quad \text{for all } O_i \in O \text{ and } C_j \in C \tag{5}$$

$$\min(|O_i - R_1|, |O_i - R_2|, \ldots) \leq D_{escape} \quad \text{for all } O_i \in O \text{ and } R_j \in R \tag{6}$$

$$O_i \notin A_{Eny} \quad \text{for all } O_i \in O \tag{7}$$

$$O_i \notin A_I \quad \text{for all } O_i \in O \tag{8}$$

where

$O_i \in O$	is an observation post to be deployed,
S	is the superordinate unit deployed in the area of operations,
D_{comm}	is the maximum allowed distance between posts and superordinate,
$C_j \in C$	is a point which can provide a shelter for observation posts $O_i \in O$,
$D_{shelter}$	is the maximum allowed distance between posts and a shelter,
$R_j \in R$	is a point constituting a possible escape route to leave post $O_i \in O$,
D_{espace}	is the maximum allowed distance between posts and an escape route,
A_{Eny}	is the area observed by enemy units,
A_I	is the area of interest

3 Problem Solution

A stochastic algorithm based on the simulated annealing principles has been proposed to solution of the problem formulated in the previous section. A solution to the problem is represented by a vector of $2N$ independent variables where N is the number of observation posts to be positioned: $X = \{x_1, y_1, x_2, y_2, \ldots, x_N, y_N\}$, i.e. a position of each observation post $O_i \in O$ is given by two-dimensional coordinate x_i, y_i.

The algorithm in pseudocode is shown in Fig. 3. The key parameter of the algorithm is temperature T. Solution X is processed in successive loops (points 3 to 16), which differ by the value of temperature; the temperature is lowered from one loop to another until it reaches its minimum value T_{min} (which is a termination condition of the algorithm).

In each loop, a number of steps are repeated (points 5 to 15). The key process is the transformation of solution X to solution X' (point 6). This transformation consists in changing the value of:

- One randomly selected variable in solution X.
- All variables in solution X.
- Variables in solution X selected randomly with probability $p_{trasform}$.

Which option will be used depends of the setting. The selected variable(s) is(are) changed based on the current value of temperature T. In general, the higher the temperature, the bigger the change. Thus, at the beginning of the algorithm, the variable may be changed in its full domain, where towards the end of the optimization, only small changes are made. It has an effect of searching the full state space at the beginning, and tuning the solution at the end. The changes are made by a random number generator with the Gaussian distribution.

```
Observation Post Positions Optimization
  1. generate and evaluate a random solution X for N posts
  2. set T = Tmax
  3. while T > Tmin
     4. set k = r = e = 0
     5. while k < kmax and r < rmax and e < emax
        6. transform and evaluate solution X' from X
        7. if solution X' is feasible
           8. calculate the Metropolis criterion p(X → X')
           9. with probability p(X → X')
              10. replace solution X → X'
              11. set r = r + 1
        12. else
           13. set e = e + 1
        14. set k = k + 1
     15. save the best solution if found
  16. decrease T = T · α   (0 < α < 1)
  17. return the best solution found
```

Fig. 3. Optimization algorithm

It the transformed solution X' is feasible (point 7), i.e. it meets all selected requirements expressed by formulae (4) to (8), the new coverage of the area of interest A'_O is calculated and the original solution is replaced by the transformed solution (point 10) with the probability given by the Metropolis criterion (point 8) in formula (9). This criterion states that if the original solution is worse (it has smaller coverage), it is always replaced, otherwise it is replaced with the probability depending on the difference between both solutions and the current temperature. This principle helps the solution not to be stuck in a local optimum.

$$p(X \rightarrow X') = \begin{cases} 1 & \text{for } |A'_O| \geq |A_O| \\ e^{-\frac{|A_O|-|A'_O|}{T}} & \text{otherwise} \end{cases} \tag{9}$$

where

$p(X \rightarrow X')$	is the probability of replacing solution X by solution X',
$\lvert A_O \rvert$	is the size of the observed area of interest of solution X,
$\lvert A'_O \rvert$	is the size of the observed area of interest of solution X',
T	is the current temperature

Each loop (points 5 to 15), where the temperature does not change, is terminated when at least one of the following conditions is met:

- Number of transformations k exceeds the maximum value k_{max}.
- Number of replacements r exceeds the maximum value r_{max}.
- Number of infeasible solutions generated e exceeds the maximum value e_{max}.

4 Implementation

The DOAPO model and the proposed algorithm have been implemented into the Tactical Decision Support System (TDSS). This system works with the real geographic data and supports the basic elements and functions following from the model formulation, such as:

- Definition of the area of interest in the form of a polygon.
- Estimation of a terrain elevation in an arbitrary point inside the area of operations based on the Digital Elevation Model (DEM).
- Management of the database of topographic and other objects based on the Topographic Digital Data Model (TDDM). Each object is represented by a polygon with or without holes and its parameters (e.g. object height).
- Management of enemy units and their basic parameters.
- Calculation of the visibility from a number of points to a specified polygon, taking into account the occlusion effect caused by non-transparent objects.

Different objects of the TDDM model are used for different purposes:

- Non-transparent objects, such as buildings, forests and fences, as obstacles which may occlude of some portion of the area of interest.
- Objects, such as forest and vegetation strips, as possible shelters.
- Roads and communication infrastructure as possible escape routes.

In the implementation, infinite sets of points (e.g. A_O, C, R) or continuous variables (coordinates) are simplified to finite sets and discrete variables by rasterization. The coverage of the area of interest is computed in each square lying inside the area of interest independently. The size of the coverage $\lvert A_O \rvert$ is represented by a number of squares which have the VLOS from any observation post. The precision of the results can be influenced by setting the size of squares (rasterization step).

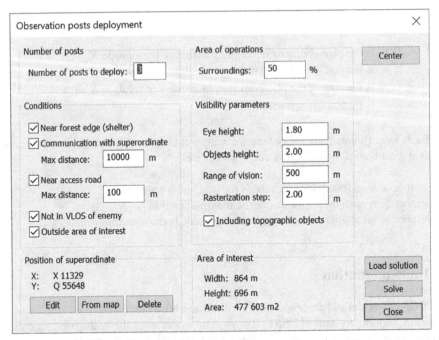

Fig. 4. Implementation of the DOPAO model in the TDSS

The main dialog of the DOPAO model is shown in Fig. 4. The number of observation posts to be deployed are specified in the upper-left corner. Below, the tactical requirements and conditions based on formulae (4) to (8) can be specified; each condition is optional. Basic visibility parameters (height of observer, height of objects, visibility range) can be set on the right, but must be the same for all observation posts. The rasterization step can be also specified. The visualization of results can be seen in Fig. 5. Locations of three optimization posts (A, B, C) were optimized. The area of interest is bounded by a blue line, green color represents the area observed from the posts, red color means unobserved area. The total coverage is 88.36%.

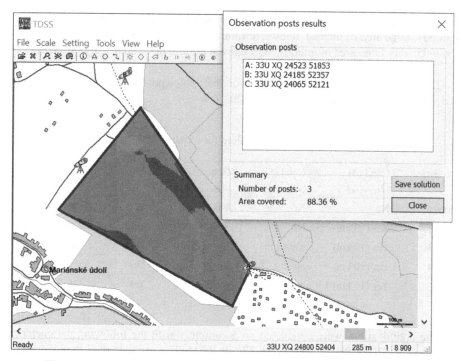

Fig. 5. Implementation of the DOPAO model in the TDSS (Color figure online)

5 Experiments and Results

Five scenarios have been designed as benchmark problems to verify the algorithm proposed for solution. Table 1 shows their basic parameters. The scenarios reflect the typical reconnaissance operations. Individual scenarios can be characterized as follows:

- dop01: small area of interest, flat terrain, no obstacles.
- dop02: small area of interest, slightly uneven terrain, no obstacles.

Table 1. Scenarios

Scenario	Area of interest			Observation posts	
	Width	Height	Area	Number	Range
dop01	483 m	399 m	177,597 m^2	1	400 m
dop02	523 m	523 m	118,084 m^2	3	500 m
dop03	789 m	789 m	405,789 m^2	6	500 m
dop04	1,071 m	1,799 m	1,459,594 m^2	10	300 m
dop05	3,096 m	1,626 m	3,323,185 m^2	30	500 m

- dop03: medium-sized area of interest, uneven terrain, high density of obstacles.
- dop04: large area of interest, uneven terrain, low density of obstacles.
- dop05: very large area of interest, very uneven terrain, medium density obstacles.

Table 2 presents conditions for locations of observation posts required in the scenarios as defined in Sect. 2 – see formulae (4) to (8).

Table 2. Conditions for scenarios

Scenario	Cond (4) (D_{comm})	Cond (5) $(D_{shelter})$	Cond (6) (D_{escape})	Cond (7)	Cond (8)
dop01	No	No	Yes (50 m)	Yes	No
dop02	Yes (10 km)	No	Yes (50 m)	Yes	Yes
dop03	Yes (10 km)	Yes (5 m)	Yes (100 m)	Yes	Yes
dop04	Yes (10 km)	No	Yes (100 m)	Yes	No
dop05	Yes (10 km)	No	No	Yes	No

The optimizations were conducted on a computer with the following parameters: Intel Core i7-7700 CPU @ 3600 GHz, 32 GB RAM. The parameters of the algorithm (see Fig. 3 in Sect. 3) were set as follows: $T_{max} = 100$, $T_{min} = 5$, $\alpha = 0.9$, $k = 500$, $r = 200$, $e = 500$, a single variable randomly selected was changed in a transformation. Rasterization step was set as follows: 2 m for scenarios dop01, dop02 and dop03, 4 m for scenario dop04 and 5 m for scenario dop05.

Table 3 shows the results of optimizations. The table records the total coverage (in percent) as well as the time needed for optimization (min:sec). The objective was to find the best solution for individual scenarios and conditions. In all cases, the coverage of the area is above 89% except for scenario dop03 where it is below 80%. The reason in this case is the high density of obstacles in the area of interest, and requirements that posts has to be near shelter (edge of forest) and outside the area of interest. Even so, the total coverage is more than 78%. The optimization time shows its dependence on the size of the area of interest and the number of observation posts to be deployed.

Table 3. Results

Scenario	Coverage	Optimization time
dop01	89.65%	0:13
dop02	93.60%	0:24
dop03	78.65%	0:52
dop04	95.81%	1:09
dop05	98.83%	4:38

The situation of scenario dop03 is illustrated in Fig. 6. On the left, an environment is shown, the coverage (78.65%) is on the right.

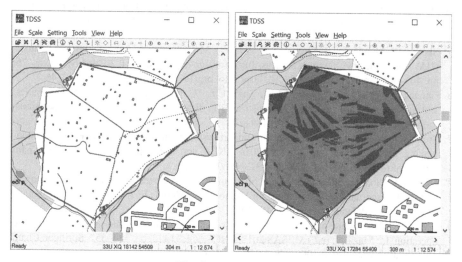

Fig. 6. Scenario dop03

6   Conclusions

In the paper, the DOPAO model (Deployment of Observation Posts in the Area of Operations) was formulated and the solution based on stochastic approach using simulation annealing principles was proposed. The implementation in the Tactical Decision Support System (TDSS) was introduced. A set of experiments were designed as benchmark problems. All scenarios reflect the parameters of typical reconnaissance operations. Various conditions and tactical requirements were set.

The results show that the algorithm is able to find high quality solutions even for scenarios with (a) hard limiting conditions (shelter, escape route), (b) complex environment (high density of obstacles, uneven terrain), and (c) high number of observation posts (30 in case of scenario dop05 which is 60 independent variables in a solution).

The future work of the authors will be aimed at statistical evaluation of the results on the proposed scenarios, assessment of the performance of the algorithm in regard to the tactical requirements and complexity of the environment, and comparison of results with other probabilistic approaches and methods (in simpler cases even with the optimal solution found using the brute force search).

References

1. Malandrino, F., Chiasserini, C.F., Casetti, C., Chiaraviglio, L., Senacheribbe, A.: Planning UAV activities for efficient user coverage in disaster areas. Ad Hoc Netw. **89**, 177–185 (2019)

2. Langhammer, J.: UAV Monitoring of Stream Restorations. Hydrology **6**(2), 29 (2019)
3. Räsänen, A., Virtanen, T.: Data and resolution requirements in mapping vegetation in spatially heterogeneous landscapes. Remote Sens. Environ. **230**, 111207 (2019)
4. Huang, H., Savkin, A.V.: A method for optimized deployment of unmanned aerial vehicles for maximum coverage and minimum interference in cellular networks. IEEE Trans. Ind. Inform. **15**(5), 2638–2647 (2018)
5. Škorput, P., Mandžuka, S., Gregurić, M., Vrančić, M.T.: Applying Unmanned Aerial Vehicles (UAV) in traffic investigation process. In: Karabegović, I. (ed.) NT 2019. LNNS, vol. 76, pp. 401–405. Springer, Cham (2020). https://doi.org/10.1007/978-3-030-18072-0_46
6. Chuang, C.C., Rau, J.Y., Lai, M.K., Shih, C.L.: Combining unmanned aerial vehicles, and internet protocol cameras to reconstruct 3-D disaster scenes during rescue operations. Prehospital Emerg. Care **23**(4), 479–484 (2019)
7. Stodola, P., Mazal, J.: Tactical decision support system to aid commanders in their decision-making. In: Hodicky, J. (ed.) MESAS 2016. LNCS, vol. 9991, pp. 396–406. Springer, Cham (2016). https://doi.org/10.1007/978-3-319-47605-6_32
8. Stodola, P., Nohel, J., Mazal, J.: Model of optimal maneuver used in tactical decision support system. In: International Conference on Methods and Models in Automation and Robotics, Miedzyzdroje, Poland, pp. 1240–1245 (2016)
9. Drozd, J.: Experiment of the tactical decision support system within company defensive operation. In: Mazal, J. (ed.) MESAS 2018. LNCS, vol. 11472, pp. 544–552. Springer, Cham (2019). https://doi.org/10.1007/978-3-030-14984-0_40
10. Stodola, P., Kozůbek, J., Drozd, J.: Using unmanned aerial systems in military operations for autonomous reconnaissance. In: Mazal, J. (ed.) MESAS 2018. LNCS, vol. 11472, pp. 514–529. Springer, Cham (2019). https://doi.org/10.1007/978-3-030-14984-0_38
11. Drozd, J., Stodola, P., Křišťálová, D., Kozůbek, J.: Experiments with the UAS reconnaissance model in the real environment. In: Mazal, J. (ed.) MESAS 2017. LNCS, vol. 10756, pp. 340–349. Springer, Cham (2018). https://doi.org/10.1007/978-3-319-76072-8_24
12. Rybanský, M., Dohnal, F., Hošková-Mayerová, Š., Svatoňová, H.: The impact of drainage on terrain UGV movement. In: IGRSM International Conference and Exhibition on Geospatial & Remote Sensing (IGRSM 2018). In: IOP Conference Series: Earth and Environmental Science, vol. 169 (2018)
13. Blaha, M., Šilinger, K.: Application support for topographical-geodetic issues for tactical and technical control of artillery fire. Int. J. Circuits Syst. Sign. Process. **12**, 48–57 (2018)
14. Mazal, J., Stodola, P., Procházka, D., Kutěj, L., Ščurek, R., Procházka, J.: Modelling of the UAV safety manoeuvre for the air insertion operations. In: Hodicky, J. (ed.) MESAS 2016. LNCS, vol. 9991, pp. 337–346. Springer, Cham (2016). https://doi.org/10.1007/978-3-319-47605-6_27
15. Mazal, J., Stodola, P., Hrabec, D., Kutěj, L., Podhorec, M., Křišťálová, D.: Mathematical modeling and optimization of the tactical entity defensive engagement. Int. J. Math. Models Methods Appl. Sci. **9**, 600–606 (2015)
16. Bruzzone, A.G., Procházka, J., Kutěj, L., Procházka, D., Kozůbek, J., Scurek, R.: Modelling and optimization of the air operational manoeuvre. In: Mazal, J. (ed.) MESAS 2018. LNCS, vol. 11472, pp. 43–53. Springer, Cham (2019). https://doi.org/10.1007/978-3-030-14984-0_4
17. Nohel, J.: Possibilities of raster mathematical algorithmic models utilization as an information support of military decision making process. In: Mazal, J. (ed.) MESAS 2018. LNCS, vol. 11472, pp. 553–565. Springer, Cham (2019). https://doi.org/10.1007/978-3-030-14984-0_41
18. Petrea, N., et al.: Experimental survey regarding the dangerous chemical compounds from military polygons that affect the military health and the environment. Rev. Chim. **69**(7), 1640–1644 (2018)

19. Hodicky, J.: Standards to support military autonomous system life cycle. In: Březina, T., Jabłoński, R. (eds.) MECHATRONICS 2017. AISC, vol. 644, pp. 671–678. Springer, Cham (2018). https://doi.org/10.1007/978-3-319-65960-2_83
20. Hodicky, J., Prochazka, D., Prochazka, J.: Training with and of autonomous system – modelling and simulation approach. In: Mazal, J. (ed.) MESAS 2017. LNCS, vol. 10756, pp. 383–391. Springer, Cham (2018). https://doi.org/10.1007/978-3-319-76072-8_27
21. Hodicky, J., Prochazka, D., Prochazka, J.: Automation in experimentation with constructive simulation. In: Mazal, J. (ed.) MESAS 2018. LNCS, vol. 11472, pp. 566–576. Springer, Cham (2019). https://doi.org/10.1007/978-3-030-14984-0_42
22. Pomazalová, N., Korecki, Z., Darkwah, S.A.: The new approaches in logistics services accomplishment. In: 5th European Conference on Innovation and Entrepreneurship. National and Kapodistrian University of Athens, pp. 453–460. Academic Publishing, Greece (2010)

The Weighted Core of Games Based on Tactical Decisions

Jaroslav Hrdina[1,2], Petr Vašík[1]([⊠]), Josef Procházka[1,2], Libor Kutěj[2], and Radomír Ščurek[3]

[1] Institute of Mathematics, Faculty of Mechanical Engineering, Brno University of Technology, Brno, Czech Republic
{hrdina,vasik}@fme.vutbr.cz
[2] University of Defence, Brno, Czech Republic
{josef.prochazka,libor.kutej}@unob.cz
[3] WSB Uniwersity Dabrówa Gornicza, Dabrówa Gornicza, Poland
radomir.scurek@gmail.com

Abstract. We modify the core axioms towards the so–called weighted solution. We also discuss the corresponding properties of Myerson value. We present a modification of axiomatic definition of solution on the set of games w.r.t. tree structure of the set of players. Significant properties of new solutions are discussed. The theory is motivated by tactical decisions in army and the notions are demonstrated on an example.

Keywords: Tree game · Tactical decision

1 Introduction

Let us suppose that a strategic game is defined in a normal form (N, v) where $N = \{1, ..., n\}$ is the set of players, $\{X_i\}$ denotes the set of strategies and $v : X_1 \times \cdots \times X_n \to \mathbb{R}$ is the pay-off function. Furthermore, suppose that here is an additional structure (hierarchy) among the subset of the set of players which is in the form of a tree. To define the proper game model, let us set the following notation. W.L.O.G. we suppose that there is a given order of the tree nodes in each level and that the nodes have either 0 or at least two direct successors. The root will be denoted by L^1. Suppose that there is K_1 direct successors of L^1 which will be denoted by L^{u_k}, where $u_k = (1, k)$ is a vector denoting the path from the root and $k \in \{1, 2, ..., K_1\}$. Using this notation for all levels $L_1, ..., L_l$ each with $K_1, ..., K_l$ elements, respectively, the node position on the level L_j is given uniquely (w.r.t. given order on each level) by the vector $u_k = (1, u_2, u_3, ..., u_{K_j-1}, k)$, where $k \in \{1, ..., K_j\}$. For instance, the coordinates of the square node in Fig. 1 are of the form $(1, 2, 2, 2)$ given that the order on each level starts from the left. Further, using the previous notation, we have that

$$\mathcal{L} = \dim u$$

© Springer Nature Switzerland AG 2020
J. Mazal et al. (Eds.): MESAS 2019, LNCS 11995, pp. 244–252, 2020.
https://doi.org/10.1007/978-3-030-43890-6_19

is the level order of the node with coordinates u (assuming that each node has at least two successors) and

$$\mathcal{D} = \dim\langle u_k \rangle + 1 \text{ for all } k$$

is the tree depth. Moreover, by a leaf on the l-th level we understand a node with coordinates $u = (1, u_2, u_3, ..., u_l)$ such that there is no node with coordinates $u + k$, $k \in \mathbb{N}$, where $u + k = (1, u_2, u_3, ..., u_l, k)$. These nodes are those without successors. In case that all the tree branches are of the same depth $\mathcal{D}$, the leaf can be defined as a node with coordinates u such that $\dim u = \mathcal{D}$. For the notation to be complete let us note that for $u = (1, u_2, u_3, ..., u_{l-1}, u_l)$ by $u - u_l$ we understand a vector $(1, u_2, u_3, ..., u_{l-1})$. In the sequel, we suppose the branch depth to be equal and denote it by $\mathcal{D}$.

Our aim is to evaluate the contribution of particular troops w.r.t. their coalitional potential. Thus the coalitional function should be evaluated on a tree T as a function $\sigma : 2^{L(T)} \to \mathbb{R}$, where $L(T)$ stands for the set of all leaves.

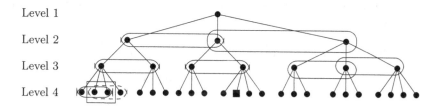

Fig. 1. Tree game with possible coalitions

In other words, we have the coalition pay–off function given on the leaves. If the tree structure should be preserved, we modify the function σ into the function $\hat{\sigma} : (2^{L(T)})_u \to \mathbb{R}$, where $L(T)$ is the set of all leaves and $(2^{L(T)})_u$ is a subset of $L(T)$ of leaves with coordinates $u + k$ for some $k \in \mathbb{N}$. In the sequel, we denote $\hat{\sigma}$ by σ as there is no confusion possible. To find out more about the games with hierarchy structure we refer to [8], to find the precise definitions of elementary notions see [10].

Example 1. The inspiration for previous definitions comes from military operations. Note that the tree setting corresponds to military hierarchy completely from the overall command (root) to the leaves (combat units). Let us suppose that a military operation is considered as a strategic game and the complete pay–off is given. Furthermore, the combat units (leaves) are of the same type and strength and at the same level (all branches of the tree have the same depth). Once the pay–off is redistributed among the units, e.g. by the Shapley or Myerson value, their importance within the operation is defined and the strategic decisions may be specified more precisely. Particularly, those units characterized by e.g. loyalty, devotion and reliability can be given the tasks with the least pay–off. Moreover, if the commander specifies the coalitions working on common task, it may happen that a single unit pay–off would be larger than if the predefined coalition is joined. Note that w.r.t. the army hierarchy the demand on coalitions to be made on the leaves with common predecessor and only within one level is reasonable. In particular, we suppose the application in arbitrary forces with a given hierarchy and with tasks with different value, see e.g. [1,2]. Our ambition is to support the operation command by providing additional criteria on existing systems, [3,4], especially with cooperative elements, [5]. To see one of possible scenario simulation see [6].

2 Myerson Value

We treat the game with incomplete coalition structure and therefore we shall use Myerson value rather than the Shapley value. Yet due to given hierarchy in the form of a tree we do not need the Myerson value in full generality but we introduce some related notions and discuss the simplifications in our particular application. Let $\Omega \subset 2^N$ such that $\emptyset \in \Omega$ be the set of admissible coalitions that respect the tree hierarchy. In the sequel, we demonstrate all notions on the following example:

$$\Omega = \{\{1\}, \{2\}, \{3\}, \{4\}, \{1,2\}, \{3,4\}, \{1,2,3\}\} \subset 2^{\{1,2,3,4\}}$$

The set Ω is called a basis of coalitional structure. We define the collection of supportable coalitions in the coalitional structure Ω by

$$N(\Omega) = \{S \in \Omega | \exists T, R \in \Omega \backslash \{\emptyset, S\} \text{ such that } S = T \cup R \text{ and } T \cap R = \emptyset\}.$$

In our case we obtain

$$N(\Omega) = \{\{1,2\}, \{2,4\}, \{1,2,3\}\}.$$

For our considerations it is crucial that if the coalition structure respects the tree form (in the sense of our definition) then $N(\Omega)$ is the set of all coalitions within all tree levels apart from the leaves level. The basis of Ω is now defined as a set of the non–supportable coalitions by

$$B(\Omega) = \Omega \backslash N(\Omega).$$

In our case we have
$$B(\Omega) = \{\{1\}, \{2\}, \{3\}, \{4\}\}$$

and even generally it is always the set of leaves, i.e. all one–element sets. In our class of examples the notions of the basis and leaf coincide. Now we can define the union stable cover of the coalitional structure Ω is the smallest collection $\bar{\Omega} \subset 2^N$ such that $\Omega \subset \bar{\Omega}$ and for all $S, T \in \bar{\Omega}$ with $S \cap T = \emptyset$ it holds that $S \cup T \in \bar{\Omega}$. Thus in our case $\bar{\Omega} = 2^{\{1,2,3,4\}}$ and generally in our class of games

$$\bar{\Omega} = 2^N.$$

This is clear because the basis is formed by one–element sets and therefore $\bar{\Omega}$ contains all subsets. Let $S \subset N$ be an arbitrary coalition. The family of Ω-components of S is defined by

$$C_\Omega(S) = \{T \in \bar{\Omega} | T \subset S \text{ and there is no } R \in \Omega : T \subsetneq R \subset S\}.$$

We demonstrate this notion on several generic possibilities:

$$C_\Omega(\{i\}) = \{\{i\}\}$$
$$C_\Omega(\{1,2\}) = \{\{1,2\}\}, \ldots$$
$$C_\Omega(\{1,3\}) = \{\{1,3\}, \{1\}, \{3\}\}, \ldots$$
$$C_\Omega(\{1,2,3\}) = \{\{1,2\}, \{3\}\}, \cdots$$
$$C_\Omega(\{1,2,3,4\}) = \{\{1,2,3,4\}\}.$$

Now it is clear that Ω–components of one–element set is formed by one–element sets, that of two–element sets by either $\{\{i,j,\}\}$ if $\{i,j,\} \in \Omega$ or $\{\{i,j,\}, \{i\}, \{j\}\}$ otherwise, for three–elements sets depends on the number of common predecessors etc. Altogether the analysis is rather straightforward. For example, the grand Ω-component $\hat{C}_\Omega = \cup C_\Omega(N) \subset N$ is then N. Finally let $\Omega \subset 2^N$ be a coalitional structure such that $\emptyset \in \Omega$ and let $v : 2^N \to \mathbb{R}$ by a pay–off function over coalitional structure. The Ω-restriction of the game v is given by

$$v_\Omega(S) = \sum_{T \in C_\Omega(S)} v(T).$$

Let $\mathcal{M}^N = \{\Omega | \Omega \subset 2^N\}$ be the collection of all coalitional structures on N. The Myerson value is a function $\mu_i : \mathcal{M}^N \to \mathbb{R}^N$ such that for every game v and every player $i \in N$ the Myerson value is the Shapley value of its -restriction, i.e.,

$$\mu_i(\Omega) = \varphi_i(\Omega).$$

Finally note that the properties of Mayerson value are Component-efficiency property, isolated player property and balanced pay–off property. I.e. for every global component $S \in C_\Omega(N)$ we have $\sum_{i \in S} \varphi_i = v(S)$, for every Ω-isolated player $i \in N \backslash \hat{C}_\Omega$ holds that $\mu_i = 0$ and for every support coalition $S \in B(\Omega)$ and for all players $i, j \in S$:

$$\varphi_i(\Omega) - \varphi_i(\tilde{\Omega}) = \varphi_j(\Omega) - \varphi_j(\tilde{\Omega}),$$

where $\tilde{\Omega} = \overline{B(\omega)\backslash\{S\}}$. Let us note that similarly to Shapley value, even Myerson value does not have to be contained in the core.

3   Axiomatic Definition of Solutions

In TU games by solution we usually understand the distribution of the pay–off (profit) among the participants, see [9,11]. Our case is different. We do not redistribute the profit but set a measure of a single player contribution for the whole team. Similarly to the classical case, the initial information is the added value of a player when he joins the coalition. This defines the unit's value which makes it possible to compare how useful is a distinguished unit. Let $\mathcal{U}$ be a set of players and let (N, v) be a game. Denote

$$X^*(N, v) = \{x \in \mathbb{R}^N | x(N) \leq v(N)\}$$

the set of feasible pay–off vectors. If Γ is a set of games, a solution σ on Γ is a function which associates with each game $(N, v) \in \Gamma$ a subset $\sigma(N, v)$ of $X^*(N, v)$. Note that σ may be characterized by a set of axioms which is our aim - to modify the axioms defining the solution to apply on our situation.

Note that often for a single TU game (N, v) the reasonable solution is defined as the core $\mathcal{C}(N, v)$ by

$$\mathcal{C}(N, v) = \{x \in X^*(N, v) | x(S) \geq v(S) \text{ for all } S \subseteq N\}.$$

On the set of games the core can be defined by axioms denoted as NE, IR, WRGP, and SUPA. Let us recall the definitions, [7].

Definition 1. *A solution σ on a set Γ of games satisfies nonemptiness (NE) if the following condition*

$$\sigma(N, v) \neq \emptyset \text{ for every } (N, v) \in \Gamma$$

holds.

Definition 2. *A solution σ on a set Γ of games is individually rational (IR) if it satisfies the following condition*

$$\text{if } (N, v) \in \Gamma \text{ and } x \in \sigma(N, v), \text{ then } x^i \geq v(\{i\}) \text{ for all } i \in N.$$

To recall the axiom WRGP we first have to establish the following notion.

Definition 3. *Let (N, v) be a game, $S \subset N, S \neq \emptyset$, and let $x \in X^*(N, v)$. The reduced game with the respect to S and x is the game $(S, v_{S,x})$ defined by*

$$v_{S,x}(T) = 0, \text{ if } T = \emptyset,$$
$$v_{S,x}(T) = v(N) - x(N \setminus S), \text{ if } T = S,$$
$$v_{S,x}(T) = \max_{Q \subset N-S} (v(T \cup Q) - x(Q)), \text{ otherwise.}$$

Remark 1. The reduced game $(S, v_{S,x})$ describes the following situation. Assume that all members of N agree that the members of $N \setminus S$ will get $x^{N \setminus S}$. Then, the members of S may get $v(N) - x(N \setminus S)$. Furthermore, suppose that the members of $N \setminus S$ continue to cooperate with the members of S. Then, for every $T \subsetneq S$ which is non–empty, the amount $v_{S,x}(T)$ is the (maximal) total pay–off that the coalition T expects to get. However, we notice that the expectations of different disjoint subcoalitions may not be compatible with each other, because they may require cooperation of the same subset of $N \setminus S$. Thus, $(S, v_{S,x})$ is not a game in the ordinary sense. It serves only to determine the distribution of $v_{S,x}$ to the members of S.

Now we can define.

Definition 4. *A solution σ on a set Γ of games has weak reduced game property (WRGP) if it satisfies the following condition*

$$if\ (N, v) \in \Gamma, S \subset N, 1 \leq |S| \leq 2,\ and\ x \in \sigma(N, v)$$
$$then\ (S, v_{S,x}) \in \Gamma\ and\ x^S \in \sigma(S, v_{S,x}),$$

where $(S, v_{S,x})$ is a reduced game.

Definition 5. *A solution σ on a set Γ of games is superaditive (SUPA) if*

$$\sigma(N, v_1) + \sigma(N, v_2) \subset \sigma(N, v_1 + v_2)$$

when $(N, v_1), (N, v_2)$ and $(N, v_1 + v_2)$ are in Γ.

Let us discuss which axioms are important for us. Clearly, it is SUPA because obviously different operations of branches can not generate bigger profit than the whole army. Also NE is valid as we have to find some solution. The axiom IR itself is not inevitable because some units can be "sacrificed" for the good of the whole and thus the individual rationality may be suppressed. Now we introduce new axiom that could suit our situation better.

Definition 6. *A solution σ on a set Γ of games is called α-level individually rational (α–IR) if it satisfies the following condition*

$$if\ (N, v) \in \Gamma\ and\ x \in \sigma(N, v),\ then\ x^i \geq \alpha v(\{i\})\ for\ all\ i \in N.$$

We distinguish two cases, first if $\alpha > 1$ and second if $\alpha < 1$. The first case reads that the individual demands of a particular unit are greater than it can get which might be interesting in some type of games. Nevertheless, the second case $\alpha < 1$ is much more interesting for us, where a single unit has to tolerate an individual loss for the good of the whole.

Next, the axiom WRGP makes sense, moreover even stronger RGP may be taken into account, [7].

Definition 7. *A solution σ on a set Γ of games has the reduced game property, RGP, if it satisfies the following condition: If $(N, v) \in \Gamma$, $S \subseteq N$, $S \neq \emptyset$, and $x \in \sigma(N, v)$, then $(S, v_{S,x}) \in \Gamma$ and $x^S \in \sigma(S, v_{S,x})$.*

Note that according to [7], RGP is a condition of self–consistency meaning that if (N, v) is a game and $x \in \sigma(N, v)$ then for every $S \subseteq N, S \neq \emptyset$ the proposal x^S solves $(S, v_{S,x})$ and, therefore, it is consistent with the expectations of the members of S as reflected by the reduced game $(S, v_{S,x})$.

For the purposes of this paper let us put this aside.

In the following we provide some qualitative analysis of solutions. It is well known that IR and WRGP imply PO, which stands for Pareto optimal and is defined as follows.

Definition 8. *A solution σ on a set Γ of games is Pareto optimal (PO) if it satisfies the following condition*

$$\text{if } \sigma(N, v) \subset X(N, v) = \{x \in \mathbb{R}^N | x(N) = v(N)\} \text{ for every } (N, v) \in \Gamma.$$

Let us focus on the case of α–IR solutions, where $\alpha < 1$. We prove the following properties.

Lemma 1. *Let σ be a solution on a set Γ of games. If σ satisfies PO and α-IR, where $0 < \alpha < 1$, then it does not satisfy WRGP.*

Proof. We consider a reduced game w.r.t. the subset $\{i\} \subset N$. If WRGP should be satisfied for $\sigma \in \Gamma$, then σ restricted onto the set of reduced games $(\{i\}, v_{\{i\},x})$ must satisfy PO and α-IR. On the other hand, if σ is PO then

$$v_{\{i\},x} = v(x) - x(N - \{i\}) = x(N) - x(N - \{i\}) = x^i,$$

i.e. $v_{\{i\},x} = x^i$. This is a contradiction to the fact that $(\{i\}, v_{\{i\},x})$ is α-IR.

Lemma 2. *Let σ be a solution on the set Γ of games. If σ satisfies WRGP and α-IR, where $0 < \alpha < 1$, then it does not satisfy PO.*

Proof. If σ satisfies WRGP and α-IR, then for the reduced game $(\{i\}, v_{\{i\},x})$ the following must hold:

$$v_{\{i\},x}(\{i\}) = v(x) - x(N - \{i\}) < \alpha x^i,$$

which means that

$$v(x) < \alpha x^i + x(N - \{i\}) < x(N)$$

and thus PO is not satisfied.

Let us modify the notion of a reduced game for a subset S such that $|S| \le 2$ as follows. If $|S| = 1$ we define

$$\bar{v}_{S,x}(\emptyset) = 0,$$

$$\bar{v}_{S,x}(\{i\}) = \frac{1}{\alpha}(v(N) - x(N \setminus S))$$

and if $|S| = 2$ we set

$$\bar{v}_{S,x}(\emptyset) = 0,$$
$$\bar{v}_{S,x}(S) = v(S) - x(N \setminus S),$$
$$\bar{v}_{S,x}(\{i\}) = \frac{1}{\alpha}\left(\max_{Q \subset N \setminus \{i\}} \{v(\{i\} \cup Q) - x(Q)\} \right), \text{ otherwise.}$$

Then the following modification of WRGP can be established.

Definition 9. *A solution σ on the set Γ of games has α–weak reduced game property α–WRGP if it satisfies the following condition*

if $(N, v) \in \Gamma, S \subset N, 1 \leq |S| \leq 2$, and $x \in \sigma(N, v)$

$$\text{then } (S, \bar{v}_{S,x}) \in \Gamma \text{ and } x^S \in \sigma(S, \bar{v}_{S,x}),$$

where $(S, \bar{v}_{S,x})$ is a reduced game defined as above.

Lemma 3. *Let σ be a solution on the set Γ of games. If σ satisfies α–IR and α–WGRP, the it also satisfies PO.*

Proof. Assume, on the contrary, that there exist $(N, v) \in \Gamma$ and $x \in \sigma(N, v)$ such that $x(N) < v(N)$. Let $i \in N$, by α–WRGP, $(\{i\}, \bar{v}_{\{i\},x}) \in \Gamma$ and $x^i \in \sigma(\{i\}, \bar{v}_{\{i\},x})$. By α–IR, $x^i \geq \alpha \bar{v}_{\{i\},x}(\{i\})$. On the other hand

$$\bar{v}_{\{i\},x}(\{i\}) = \frac{1}{\alpha}(v(N) - x(N - i)) > \frac{1}{\alpha}x^i.$$

Thus, the desired contradiction has been obtained.

Let us establish the following notion. By C^α we understand a set

$$C^\alpha = C^\alpha(N, v) = \{x \in X^*(N, v)| \; x(N) = v(N), \; x^i \geq \alpha v(\{i\})$$
$$\text{for all } i \in N \text{ and } x(S) \geq v(S) \text{ for } |S| > 1\}$$

Theorem 1. *Let σ be a solution on the set Γ of games. If σ satisfies α–IR and α–WRGP, then $\sigma(N, v) \subset C^\alpha(N, v)$ for every $(N, v) \in \Gamma$.*

Proof. Let $(N, v) \in \Gamma$ and $n = |N|$. If $n = 1$, then $\sigma(N, v) \subset C^\alpha(N, v)$ by α–IR. By Lemma above σ satisfies PO. Hence, if $n = 2$, then

$$\sigma(N, v) \subset \{x \in X^*(N, v)| \; x(S) = \bar{v}(S), \; x^i \geq \bar{v}(\{i\}) \text{ for all } i \in N\} = C^\alpha(N, v).$$

If $n \geq 3$ and $x \in \sigma(N, v)$. then α-WRGP implies that $x^S \in \sigma(S, \bar{v}_{S,x})$ for all $S \in 2^N$, so $x^S \in C^\alpha(S, v_{S,x})$ for every $S \in 2^N$. Let $T \subset N$ satisfy $\emptyset \neq T \neq N$. Choose $i \in T$ and $j \in N - T$, and let $S = \{i, j\}$. The fact that $x^S \in C^\alpha(S, v_{S,x})$ implies that

$$0 \geq \alpha \bar{v}_{S,x}(\{i\}) - x^i \geq v(T) - x(T).$$

Hence $x \in C(N, v)$.

Thus the axiomatic setting is established.

4   Conclusion

We modified the core axioms towards the so–called weighted solution and presented a modification of axiomatic definition of solution on the set of games w.r.t. tree structure of the set of players. We demonstrated all notions on an example of the set of players with a hierarchy given by the army structure. Significant properties of new solutions are discussed. The theory is motivated by tactical decisions in army. In the future, we will apply the notions on a larger set of players and more realistic structure. We expect novel suggestions to tactical decisions.

Acknowledgement. The research was supported by a grant no. FSI-S-17-4464.

References

1. Stodola, P., Drozd, J., Mazal, J., Hodický, J., Procházka, D.: Cooperative unmanned aerial system reconnaissance in a complex urban environment and uneven terrain. Sensors **19**(17), 1–16 (2019)
2. Mazal, J., Stodola, P., Procházka, D., Kutěj, L., Ščurek, R., Procházka, J.: Modelling of the UAV safety manoeuvre for the air insertion operations. In: Hodicky, J. (ed.) MESAS 2016. LNCS, vol. 9991, pp. 337–346. Springer, Cham (2016). https://doi.org/10.1007/978-3-319-47605-6_27
3. Stodola, P., Mazal, J.: Architecture of the Advanced Command and Control System, In: 6th International Conference on Military Technologies, ICMT 2017, Piscataway, NJ 08854–4141 USA: Institute of Electrical and Electronics Engineers Inc., pp. 340–343 (2017)
4. Stodola, P., Mazal, J.: Model of optimal cooperative reconnaissance and its solution using metaheuristic methods. Defence Sci. J. **67**(5), 529–535 (2017)
5. Hrabec, D., Mazal, J., Stodola, P.: Optimal manoeuvre for two cooperative military elements under uncertain enemy threat. Int. J. Oper. Res. **35**(2), 263–277 (2019)
6. David, W., et al.: Giving life to the map can save more lives Wildfire scenario with interoperable simulations, Adv. Cartogr. GIScience Int. Cartogr. Assoc., 1, 4 (2019). https://doi.org/10.5194/ica-adv-1-4-2019
7. Peleg, B., Sudhölter, P.: Introduction to the Theory of Cooperative Games. Theory and Decision Library C. Springer, Heidelberg (2007). https://doi.org/10.1007/978-3-540-72945-7
8. Gilles, P.R.: The Cooperative Game Theory of Networks and Hierarchies. Springer, Heidelberg (2010). https://doi.org/10.1007/978-3-642-05282-8
9. Owen, G.: Game Theory. W. B. Saunders, Philadelphia (1968)
10. Peters, H.: Game Theory - A Multi-Leveled Approach. Springer, Heidelberg (2008). https://doi.org/10.1007/978-3-540-69291-1
11. Webb, J.N.: Game Theory - Decisions, Interaction and Evolution. Springer, London (2007). https://doi.org/10.1007/978-1-84628-636-0

The Possibilities and Usage of Missile Path Mathematical Modelling for the Utilization in Future Autonomous Air Defense Systems Simulators

Josef Casar$^{(\boxtimes)}$ (ID) and Jan Farlik (ID)

University of Defence in Brno, Kounicova 65, 66210 Brno, Czech Republic
{josef.casar,jan.farlik}@unob.cz.com

Abstract. The missile guidance system is one of the most important component of a missile itself and it should be reflected also in a simulation environment. Therefore, the tactical simulators should contain as precise missile models as possible. Unfortunately, the most of contemporary simulators use just a very simplified mathematical models. To bring the simulation closer to the reality the model of each missile should work according to a specific guidance method containing a real guidance equations. The article focuses on the creation and implementation of specific missile characteristics into a tactical simulation environment and outlines its usage for the future simulator of an autonomous air defense system.

Keywords: Air defense · Missile · Model · Guidance · Simulation

1 Introduction

In almost any simulation, we can encounter the problem of selecting the appropriate level of detail. Depending on the purpose of using the simulator, there is a general effort to approach reality as much as possible while avoiding unnecessary calculations. When simulating SBAD units (or other types of troops) using tactical simulators, the situation is even more complicated. The reason is unavailability or security classification of the parameters of technical means that we want to simulate. In the area of SBAD, this fact is connected mainly with anti-aircraft missiles models.

When creating simulations designed to train operators of anti-aircraft systems or pilot training, it is highly desirable that the behavior of these models be as close to reality as possible. Most commercially available simulators, however, deal only with maximum range (long range and altitude) and if the target is within its limits, the simulator simply begin the engagement process. Usually, there is no solved mathematical model or flight path of the missile, which in most cases is simply approaching the target.

2 Missile Guidance Laws

Missile Guidance Law is a rule that defines the movement of a missile's movement to the position and movement of a target so that they engage one another. Depending on

© Springer Nature Switzerland AG 2020
J. Mazal et al. (Eds.): MESAS 2019, LNCS 11995, pp. 253–261, 2020.
https://doi.org/10.1007/978-3-030-43890-6_20

the guidance system used, guidance methods can be divided into two-point, three-point and autonomous guidance methods [1].

Two-point methods define the relationship of the direction of the missile velocity vector to the direction of the target in the form of a requirement for the angle of approach or the aiming angle. Typical representatives include [2, 3] Pursuit guidance, Line of Sight Guidance or Proportional navigation.

Three-point methods prescribe the relative position of the three points (target, missile, homing position) by linking the direction of the deliberate missile relative to the deliberate target. In general, these methods can be divided into a zero-angle approach and a non-zero-angle approach.

3 Mathematical Model

Creating an accurate mathematical model of a particular type of missile would require detailed knowledge of all parameters that are mostly unavailable. The mathematical model of the guidance method is based on mathematical equations describing the basic relations between the missile and the target (or guidance station). These equations are derived from the principle of operation and the definitions described in the previous chapter.

Despite the fact that the amount of literature dealing with missile guidance and simulation has increased considerably in recent years, this area is largely fragmented due to the lack of information. Given that the guidance methods used and other technical data are almost always secret (company secrets), it would be advisable to use at least a few well-known and available guidance methods and their principles and implement them in a tactical simulator environment.

Created models could serve not only for simulation of current anti-aircraft means, but also for development and simulation of new anti-aircraft systems. Simulation of the future anti-aircraft missile system could include mathematical models of the missiles used and their guidance methods so that they could be changed autonomously, if necessary, depending on current target information.

3.1 Model of Three Points LOS Guidance Method

As an example, the three points LOS guidance method was chosen, which prescribes zero angle of approach angle between the guidance station-missile LOS and the guidance station-target LOS, where all three points (guidance station, missile, target) lie on one straight line – guidance station-target LOS.

Guided Missile Kinematics. When solving kinematic tasks of missile movement, it is appropriate to use the earth's spherical coordinate system, shown in Fig. 1. The position of the missile in this system is determined by three spherical coordinates:

- radiusvector (direct distance) $\bar{r}$;
- a position angle ε, expressing the angle between the radiusvector $\bar{r}$ and the horizontal plane xz;

- azimuth ς, which is defined as the angle between the projection of the radiusvector $\bar{r}$ in the horizontal plane xz and the earth's axis x

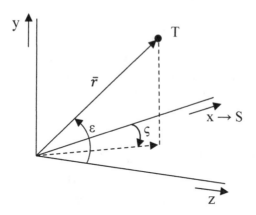

Fig. 1. Spherical system of Earth's coordinate axes.

The essence of the definition of the "three points LOS" method together with the geometric relations is graphically depicted in the projection to the xy plane in Fig. 2, which contains the following parameters: R - missile, T - target, $\bar{r}$ - missile radiusvector, $\overline{r_T}$ - target radiusvector, $\bar{v}$ - missile velocity, $\overline{v_T}$ - target velocity, ε - missile positioning angle, ε_T - target positioning angle, θ - missile velocity vector direction, θ_T - target velocity vector direction.

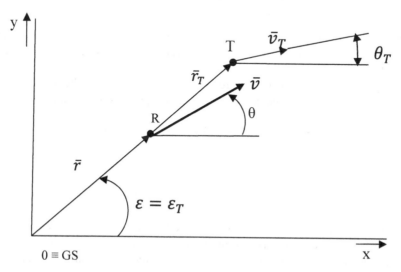

Fig. 2. Projection of geometric relations of the method to the xy plane.

Radiusvectors $\bar{r}$ and $\overline{r_T}$ determine the position of the center of gravity of the missile and targets relative to the coordinate system of the guidance station GS. The magnitude of the radiusvector, or position vector, in the Cartesian coordinate system in space is obtained from the following relation:

$$|\bar{r}| = \sqrt{x^2 + y^2 + z^2} \tag{1}$$

Other parameters necessary to calculate kinematic missile movement are the target height H_T, the horizontal distance of the target S_T and the course parameter of the target P_T, which are shown in Fig. 3.

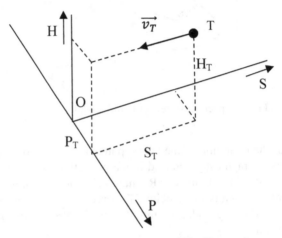

Fig. 3. Parametric rectangular system of Earth's coordinate axes.

Each vector kinematic equation corresponds to three scalar equations, expressing the relationships between the size of the vector components in the axes of the selected coordinate system. The scalar kinematic equations of the successive movement of the missile should be expressed in the direction of the axes of the spherical coordinate system. The transformation and adjustment of these equations is as follows:

$$\dot{r} = v \cos \Theta \cos(\psi - \Sigma) \cos \varepsilon + v \sin \Theta \sin \varepsilon \tag{2}$$

$$r\dot{\varepsilon} = -v \cos \Theta \cos(\psi - \Sigma) \sin \varepsilon + v \sin \Theta \cos \varepsilon \tag{3}$$

$$r \cos \varepsilon \dot{\Sigma} = v \cos \Theta \sin(\psi - \Sigma) \tag{4}$$

Mathematical Model of Guided Missiles in the MATLAB Program. When calculating in MATLAB, we must first determine the initial conditions of the missile and target. The following source code shows the entry of the initial inputs and target parameters (described graphically in previous figures).

```
g=9.81;
t=0;
dt=0.01;
ST=12000;
PT=0;
HT=1000;
vT=300;
thT=pi;
psT=0;
xT=ST;yT=PT;zT=HT;
rT=sqrt(xT^2+yT^2+zT^2);
rch=sqrt(xT^2+yT^2);
epsT=atan(zT/rch);
sigT=atan(yT/xT);
```

The modified kinematic equations of the missile represent the first integration step:

```
drT=vT*cos(thT)*cos(psT-sigT)*cos(epsT)+vT*sin(thT)
*sin(epsT);
depsT=-vT*cos(thT)*cos(psT-sigT)*sin(epsT)/rT+vT*sin(thT)
*cos(epsT)/rT;
dsigT=vT*cos(thT)*sin(psT-sigT)/(rT*cos(epsT));
```

As with the target, it is now necessary to indicate the initial parameters of the missile:

```
rM=0;          % missile radiusvector
drM=48;        % initial missile speed [m/s]
thM=epsM;      % direction of the missile radiusv.
psM=sigM;      % missile azimuth
vM=48;         % missile speed [m/s]
ax=60;         % missile acceleration [m/s^2]
yM=0;
```

Now we will use the *for* loop in which we perform a numerical solution of ordinary differential equations using the Euler method. At the same time, the preparation for the next integration step is in progress together with the preparation for the graphic outputs of the resulting solution. This procedure is illustrated and described in the following source code:

```
for i=1:100000

    t=t+dt;
%Spherical target coordinates
    rT=rT+drT*dt;
    epsT=epsT+depsT*dt;
    sigT=sigT+dsigT*dt;
%Spherical coordinates and velocity of the missile
    rM=rM+drM*dt;
```

```
    thM=epsT+asin(rM*depsT/vM);
    psM=sigT+asin(rM*dsigT/vM);
    vM=vM+ax*dt;                        %missile velocity

% Preparing for the next integration step
    depsT=-vT*cos(thT)*cos(psT-
sigT)*sin(epsT)/rT+vT*sin(thT)*cos(epsT)/rT;
    dsigT=vT*cos(thT)*sin(psT-sigT)/(rT*cos(epsT));
    drM=vM*cos(thM)*cos(psM-
sigT)*cos(epsT)+vM*sin(thM)*sin(epsT);

% Right-angled coordinates of the target and missile,
normal accelerations
    %ST - horizontal target distance [m]
    xT=xT-vT*dt;
    %SM - horizontal missile distance [m]
    xM=rM*cos(epsT)*cos(sigT);
    %PM - missile course parameter [m]
    yM=rM*cos(epsT)*sin(sigT);
    %HM - missile altitude [m]
    zM=rM*sin(epsT);

%Preparation for graphic output
    VM(i)=vM;
    XT(i)=xT;
    YT(i)=yT;
    ZT(i)=zT;
    XM(i)=xM;
    YM(i)=yM;
    ZM(i)=zM;
% calculation end when missile reach the target (maximum
10m distance between M and T)
    if sqrt((xT-xM)^2+(yT-yM)^2+(zT-zM)^2)<10
        break
      end
end
```

To plot the resulting solution in the space shown in Fig. 4, use plot3 as shown in the source code below.

```
figure
plot3(XM,YM,ZM,'r',XT,YT,ZT,'b','LineWidth',1.5);
grid;
```

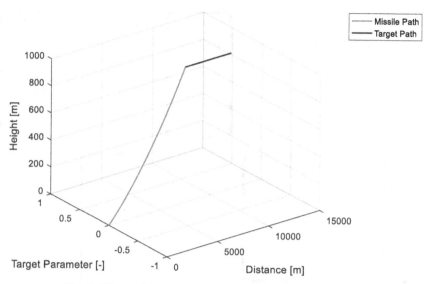

Fig. 4. The resulting movement of missiles and targets in space.

3.2 Model Implementation

Parameters important for the construction of the mathematical model and for the calculation of the flight path of the rocket may vary in different methods of guidance. It is for this reason that it is important to precisely define the inputs of specific methods, which are necessary for the calculations, as well as the resulting outputs determining the behavior and position of the rocket in space.

The information about the missile and the target is also related to the issue of the difficulty of the calculation. Depending on the level of detail, working with mathematical models may have very high processing power requirements (coordinate transformation between systems-on-board, spherical, parametric, etc.). A suitable solution here seems to be a calculation outside the simulator itself, so as not to overload it and possibly slow it down. Thus, if a tool containing individual models had, for example, a Distributed Interactive simulation (DIS) or High Level Architecture (HLA) interface, it would be possible to link it to most current tactical simulators and control the flight path of the missile just by exchanging its parameters (e.g. position).

The algorithm in Fig. 5 describes the process of selecting the optimal system in terms of target parameters (distance, type, etc.) and could also be applied to the future "Autonomous Anti-Aircraft Missile System".

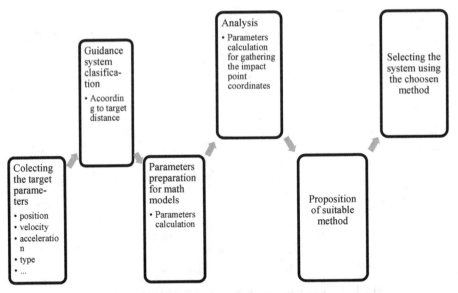

Fig. 5. Optimal method selection algorithm.

4 Conclusion

The above model is partially simplified and does not take into account, for example, friction and other environmental influences. Improvements could also be achieved by incorporating sub-characteristics affecting the missile's flight control system (missile rotation, autopilot, stabilization, ...) or a broader description of the guidance process dynamics (stability and accuracy description), which would again lead to more accurate results.

The operation of the anti-aircraft system itself depends, among other things, on the information obtained about the target. Given that the current positions and other flight parameters are constantly known in the simulator, it would be appropriate to delay the process of obtaining and transmitting this information in order to achieve a more realistic simulation.

Today, there is a constant effort for military simulators improvement (e.g. [4, 5]). In the future, the new autonomous simulator algorithms could serve not only for the training of the ground air defense forces, but also for the training of pilots and their improvement against the anti-aircraft missiles.

References

1. Yanushevsky, R.: Modern Missile Guidance, 2nd edn. Taylor & Francis Group, Boca Raton (2008). ISBN 1-4200-6226-3

2. Farlik, J., Stary, V., Casar, J.: Simplification of missile effective coverage zone in air defence simulations. In: Proceedings of the 2017 International Conference on Military Technologies (ICMT), ICMT 2017, pp. 733–737. Institute of Electrical and Electronics Engineers Inc., Piscataway (2017). ISBN 978-1-5386-1988-9
3. Siouris, G.M.: Missile Guidance and Control Systems. Springer, New York (2004). https://doi.org/10.1007/b97614. ISBN 03-870-0726-1. Accessed 10 July 2019
4. Hodicky, J., Prochazka, D.: Challenges in the implementation of Autonomous Systems into the battlefield. In: Proceedings of the 2017 International Conference on Military Technologies (ICMT), ICMT 2017, pp. 743–747. Institute of Electrical and Electronics Engineers Inc., Piscataway (2017). ISBN 978-1-5386-1988-9. https://doi.org/10.1109/miltechs.2017.7988855
5. Hodicky, J.: Modelling and simulation in the autonomous systems' domain – current status and way ahead. In: Hodicky, J. (ed.) MESAS 2015. LNCS, vol. 9055, pp. 17–23. Springer, Cham (2015). https://doi.org/10.1007/978-3-319-22383-4_2. ISSN 03029743. ISBN 978-331922382-7

Practical Comparison of Communication Technologies Suitable for Field Robotics

Matous Hybl[1,2]([⊠]), Tomas Jilek[1,2], and Ludek Zalud[1,2]

[1] DCI FEEC, Brno University of Technology, Brno, Czech Republic
xhyblm00@stud.feec.vutbr.cz, {tomas.jilek,ludek.zalud}@ceitec.vutbr.cz
[2] CEITEC, Brno University of Technology, Brno, Czech Republic
http://www.feec.vutbr.cz
http://www.ceitec.vutbr.cz

Abstract. The aim of this paper is to describe development of an evaluation system for practical comparison of wireless communication technologies used in field robotics. The evaluation system is capable of measuring data rate, drop rate and latency in both communication directions. The evaluation system closely simulates communication of a teleoperated field robot with its base station - which is a highly asymmetric communication link, because there is a high data rate video feed transmission from the robot to the base station.

This paper describes specifics of wireless communication links used in field robotics and considerations that need to be taken into account when developing such system. The wireless link evaluation system is described from hardware and software point of view.

Keywords: Field robotics · Wireless communication technology · Evaluation system · 802.11 · Mobile robot

1 Introduction and Motivation

Communication is one of the key areas in mobile and especially field robotics where intensive research needs to be conducted because success of teleoperated field robotics missions depends on stable, long range and low latency communication. The nature of field robotics missions determines that the communication link must be wireless which brings significant challenges concerned with latency and most importantly range.

This article describes an approach to building an evaluation tool for communication links used in field robotics. It is capable of measuring latency, loss rate, reordering and with suitable communication hardware also SNR and RSSI. The evaluation system works by simulating traffic that is usually present in teleoperated field robotics missions - there are control data transmitted from the operator to the robot and video feed with telemetry data transmitted in the opposite direction - from the robot to the operator. This way the results are better than with just measuring data rates with random data as the measurement

© Springer Nature Switzerland AG 2020
J. Mazal et al. (Eds.): MESAS 2019, LNCS 11995, pp. 262–273, 2020.
https://doi.org/10.1007/978-3-030-43890-6_21

process is an approximation of a real life mission. First version of this evaluation system was described in [1] where it was successfully tested while evaluating 2.4 GHz and 5 GHz 802.11 communication links.

The motivation behind development of such evaluation system was the ability of rapid testing of communication interfaces and therefore being able to deliver the best wireless communication performance in field robotics missions which are primary research goal of our research group. The main goal is to greatly improve communication link for our research group's Orpheus series robots [2–4].

2 Measuring Communication Link Properties

The goal of this section is to provide insight into requirements needed for implementation of the communication link evaluation system. First, specifics of communication in mobile robotics are described. Analysis of video feed communication model is done in order to closely simulate video feed traffic. For latency measurement time synchronization is required which is also described here.

2.1 Specifics of Communication in Field Robotics

Data traffic in teleoperated field robots consists of two types of UDP datagrams - video feed coming from the robot to the base station and control and telemetry data that are transmitted in both directions. A schematic diagram showing the traffic can be seen in the Fig. 1. As can be seen in the figure, the base station sends control data at frequency of about 30 Hz and the data has a length of about 80 B, while the robot sends video feed with data rate of approximately 800 kbps and telemetry data which are responses to the control data therefore have about the same frequency of 30 Hz but their length is about 120 B.

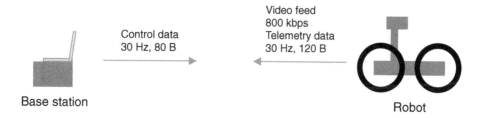

Fig. 1. A graphical representation of communication between the base station and the robot

2.2 Analysis of Video Feed Data

In order to closely simulate the video feed traffic the video feed must be captured and analyzed. The video feed consists of UDP datagrams that contain h.264 or h.265 encoded video. This codec effectively compresses small changes in the picture resulting in low data rate, while full frame changes such as moving with the camera result in high data rate. Therefore to accurately analyze the video feed, the camera needs to be moving during the capture to generate high data rate video feed. The data required to simulate the feed are timestamps and lengths of the datagrams.

The video feed was captured using Wireshark, which is a well-know tool for network traffic analysis, by applying a filter on the interface that is used to connect to the camera. The applied filter left out all datagrams whose source IP address was the address of the camera and whose destination IP address was the address of the computer. The measured data was then exported as a CSV.

Captured datagram information were then analyzed using MATLAB. First the CSV file was loaded to a matrix and then timestamps alongside with datagram lengths were extracted. The data can be seen in the Fig. 2. As can be seen the majority of captured datagrams have 1400 B length. A window with length of one second containing a lot of datagrams with 1400 B length (indicating high data rate) was selected. Datagrams contained in the selected second are shown in the Fig. 3.

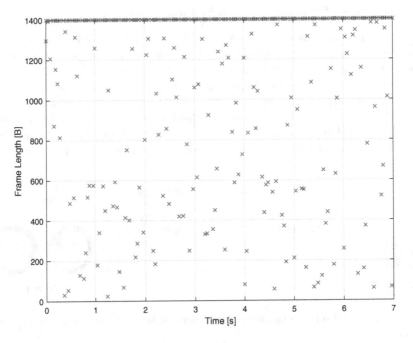

Fig. 2. Captured video feed datagram length in time

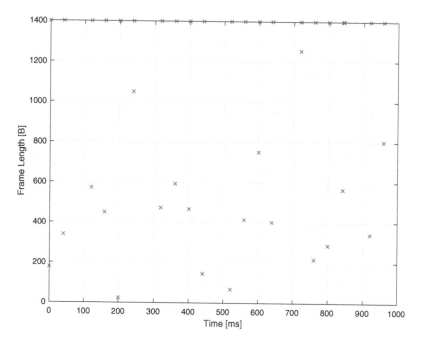

Fig. 3. Selected window of the the video feed datagram capture

The selected datagrams then needed to be transformed into data that could be used by the evaluation system. That means that timestamps in seconds needed to be transformed to milliseconds. Observing the timestamps in the raw data showed that the data is grouped into groups of four to eight datagrams, which are sent in bursts with period of 10 ms. This is useful for optimizing the evaluation system sending algorithm. Timestamps and datagram lengths were then exported so that they could be used in the evaluation system.

2.3 Time Synchronization

Latency measurement requires time synchronization between the two communication simulators, which can be achieved using PTP (precision time protocol - IEEE 1588) [5]. This protocol is capable of microsecond precision and on Linux it is implemented on Linux using the `ptpd` daemon. In case of this measurement system, `ptdp` was installed on both of the embedded computers used in the system. The robot simulating computer then serves as a master in the PTP, while the base simulating computer serves as a PTP slave. The slave automatically finds the master and adjusts time accordingly.

The previously described setup works only when the two parts of the evaluation system are present on the same network and the connection is done using a transparent radio bridge. In the case that there is not a transparent link and the two parts are on separate networks another parameter needs to be passed o the `ptpd` daemon command. The robot simulating part needs to be started with command `sudo ptpd -M -i eth0 -u BASE_STATION_SIMULATOR_ADDRESS` and the base station simulator with command `sudo ptpd -s -i eth0 -u ROBOT_SIMULATOR_ADDRESS`.

3   System for Evaluation of Communication Links

Our proposed and developed evaluation system for communication links works by closely simulating traffic generated by the robot and the base station, therefore provides accurate results and shows the behavior of the link.

There are two parts of the evaluation system - robot and base station simulator - which simulate traffic generated by the robot and the base station. These parts each consist of a Raspberry Pi running custom software. To control the evaluation system another program is used. The robot simulator is supposed to be mobile, therefore it was equipped with a rechargeable battery and a voltage regulator.

In order to achieve best results, the robot simulating part of the evaluation system has to be placed in certain height above the ground in order to improve radio waves propagation. For the experiments it was therefore placed on a cardboard box. The base simulating part of the measurement system was placed on a table in a designated spot. Both parts of the evaluation system can be seen during an experimental evaluation with MikroTik router based communication link in the figures below (Figs. 4 and 5).

Fig. 4. Base simulator hardware placed on a designated spot on a table

Fig. 5. Robot simulator hardware placed on a box used to maintain altitude

3.1   Communication Simulating Software

Communication simulating program was designed to simulate the communication model of the robot. The program uses scheduling implemented using epoll, that schedules sending and receiving of UDP datagrams to simulate traffic.

The program is meant to be run all the time. It always waits for an incoming TCP connection that begins the evaluation. Once the evaluation begins, datagrams are sent periodically and received datagrams are parsed and analyzed.

The evaluation runs for predetermined number of seconds and saves result of the evaluation for each second. After the evaluation is complete the resulting data are sent to the TCP connection that started the evaluation. A simple diagram showing communication between the programs is shown in the Fig. 6.

Implementation-wise there is only one program that can be switched to act as a robot simulator a base station simulator using command line arguments. The program is also capable of communication with MikroTik routers utilizing MikroTik API [6] in order to read RSSI and SNR values, address of the router is also specified using a command line argument.

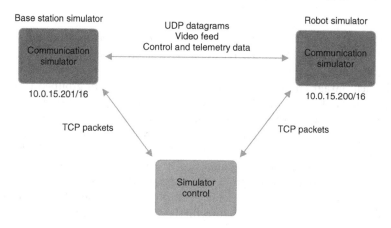

Fig. 6. Diagram showing communication between programs in the measurement system

Program binaries are installed on the Raspberry Pis using a Makefile generated by CMake. After installation the program can be launched by calling commsim -a BASE_STATION_SIMULATOR_ADDRESS -m MIKROTIK_ADDRESS or commsim -b -a ROBOT_SIMULATOR_ADDRESS -m MIKROTIK_ADDRESS depending on whether the program should simulate traffic from the robot or from the base station. The MIKROTIK_ADDRESS is an optional parameter and the -b parameter specifies that the simulation program should act as a base station simulator.

Simulating Control and Telemetry Traffic. Control and telemetry traffic consists of datagrams with average length of 80 bytes in the direction to robot and of 120 bytes in the direction from robot. Datagrams in both directions are sent with frequency of 30 Hz therefore need to be sent every 33 ms. Structure of datagrams sent by the evaluation system is shown in the Fig. 7. As can be seen in the figure, the first byte is a header with a predefined single byte constant 0x10 that can be used to ignore packets that are not sent by the evaluation system. Then number of the second of the evaluation is sent as a single byte to identify datagrams that are received after the second concludes. Single byte sequence number follows the second that is used to identify reordered datagrams and finally there are eight bytes containing timestamp in milliseconds since 1.1.1970 that is used to calculate the latency. The rest of the datagram is filled with pseudo random data.

Header	Second	SQN	Timestamp	Pseudo-random data
1 B	1 B	1 B	8 B	(required length - 11) B

Fig. 7. Structure of a packet used for simulating control and telemetry traffic

Simulating Video Feed Traffic. Video feed capture and analysis in the Sect. 2.2 showed that video feed datagrams are sent in batches irregularly and the sending loop can be optimized by running every 10 ms. First on the program launch datagram lengths obtained by the analysis are grouped to batches according to the timestamp. Then in every sending loop iteration the program checks if any datagrams should be sent and sends them if needed. Datagrams are then received and analyzed similarly to the control and telemetry datagrams.

The structure of the datagrams is similar to the one described in the Sect. 3.1. However, there are some minor changes to it. Firstly the header byte contains 0x20 constant. Secondly apart from sending second, millisecond is also sent in two bytes. In the evaluation of telemetry and control traffic, the millisecond is currently not sent but could be used to further improve drop rate and datagram reorder analysis. The datagram structure is shown in the Fig. 8.

Header	Second	Millisecond	SQN	Timestamp	Pseudo-random data
1 B	1 B	2 B	1 B	8 B	(required length - 13) B

Fig. 8. Structure of a datagram used for simulating video feed traffic

Measuring Latency. Synchronization of time described in the Sect. 2.3 alongside with timestamps being send in the datagram is used to measure latency between sending and receiving datagrams. The calculation then requires only to subtract time received in the datagram from current time in milliseconds. To avoid for integer overflow errors caused by imprecise time synchronization it is vital that the smaller time is always subtracted from the greater time. After calculation of latency, it is saved and maximal and minimal latency are calculated. When evaluation is completed in the second, average latency is computed according to the Eq. 1 as well as standard deviation of the latency according to the Eq. 2. Code used for latency computation is shown in the Listing 1.1.

$$\bar{t} = \frac{1}{N} \sum_{i=1}^{N} t_i \tag{1}$$

where $\bar{t}$ is average latency, t is vector of measured latencies and N is number of measured latencies

$$\sigma = \sqrt{\frac{1}{N-1}\sum_{i=1}^{N}(t_i - \bar{t})^2} \tag{2}$$

where $\bar{t}$ is average latency, t is vector of measured latencies and N is number of measured latencies

```
1  uint64_t time = millis();
2  uint64_t receivedTime = 0;
3  memcpy(&receivedTime, datagram.data + 5, 8)
4
5  uint64_t latency = 0;
6  if (time > receivedTime) {
7     latency = time - receivedTime;
8  } else {
9     latency = receivedTime - time;
10 }
11
12 if (latency > maxLatency) {
13    maxLatency = (uint16_t) latency;
14 }
15 if (latency < minLatency) {
16    minLatency = (uint16_t) latency;
17 }
18
19 latencies[latencyIndex] = (uint16_t) latency;
20 latencyIndex++;
```

Listing 1.1. Calculating latency

Measuring Datagram Reordering and Loss. There are two mechanisms used to detect delayed datagrams. Firstly, the second in which the datagrams were sent must be the same as the second in which they were received. If that is not the case, then the datagrams are counted. Also if sequence number of the received frame is lower than sequence number of previously received datagram, the datagram is counted. Algorithm used for delayed datagram detection is shown in the Listing 1.2.

```
1  uint8_t frameSecond = datagram.frame[1];
2
3  if (frameSecond != state.second) {
4     delayedPacketsFromLastSeconds++;
5     return;
6  }
```

```
7
8   if (newFrameNumber < lastReceivedFrameNumber) {
9     delayedPackets++;
10  } else {
11    lastReceivedFrameNumber = newFrameNumber;
12  }
```

Listing 1.2. Detecting delayed datagram

Lost datagrams are calculated from the number of sent datagrams that is hardcoded to the program by subtracting the number of received datagrams from the current second.

3.2 Evaluation System Control and Data Processing

Evaluation is started using the evaluation control program. The program first starts the measurement by sending a predefined TCP packet to the simulator programs and then waits until the simulator programs send data back over the TCP socket. Once the measurement results are sent from both of the simulators the results are saved in CSV format. An example of calling the program is csc -r ROBOT_SIMULATOR_ADDRESS -b BASE_STATION_SIMULATOR_ADDRESS -f OUTPUT_FILE. An example of the output file contents is shown in the Listing 1.3. Similarly to the communication simulation program the control program binary is installed using a Makefile generated by CMake.

```
1   robot
2   sentPackets,receivedPackets, ...
3   30,27,0,0,29.12,41.92,3,155,80,0,0,0,0,0,1000,0,-89,14
4   30,30,0,0,8.29,7.32,2,26,80,0,0,0,0,0,1000,0,-89,14
5   ...
6   base
7   sentPackets,receivedPackets, ...
8   30,25,0,0,24.5,22.95,0,77,0,70,0,0,41.76,37.45,
       3,152,-88,17
9   30,30,0,1,30.72,33.37,0,118,0,78,0,5,40.81,32.16,
       3,116,-88,17
10  ...
```

Listing 1.3. Example of measurement system output file contents

3.3 Processing the Measured Data

Results provided by the evaluation system need to be further processed to provide meaningful data for experiments. The processing is performed using a function programmed in MATLAB. In each measurement there are data from 30 s. The data are averaged and maximal values are selected. The script outputs results to a csv file.

4   Sample Results

The Figs. 9, 10 and 11 show sample data output from the evaluation system, more specifically comparison of data from two evaluations - of 2.4 GHz and 5 GHz 802.11 communication links. The evaluations were performed in four points with different distances and different numbers of obstacles.

The first figure - Fig. 9 shows comparison of average latencies. The second figure - Fig. 10 shows comparison of latency deviations. The third figure - Fig. 11 shows comparison of drop rates.

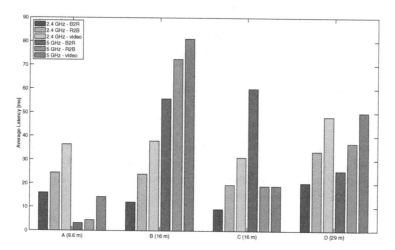

Fig. 9. Comparison of average latencies from evaluation of 2.4 GHz and 5 GHz 802.11 communication links

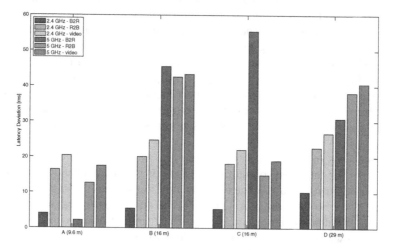

Fig. 10. Comparison of latency deviations from evaluation of 2.4 GHz and 5 GHz 802.11 communication links

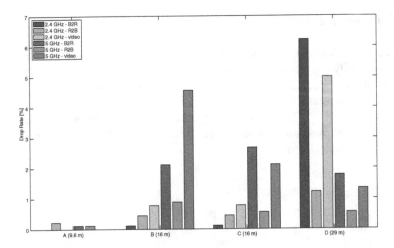

Fig. 11. Comparison of drop rates from evaluation of 2.4 GHz and 5 GHz 802.11 communication links

It can be seen that generally 5 GHz link performs worse than the 2.4 GHz one. There are some irregularities in the data that could most likely be avoided using repeated measurement and by measuring in areas where frequency spectrum on these frequencies is not used that much.

5   Further Work

There are a few ways of further enhancing the evaluation system. The most significant of them is adding a touch screen display to the robot simulator Raspberry Pi, thus adding a graphical user interface. This would bring significant simplification to the usage of the evaluation system as the need for an external computer starting the simulation would be eliminated. Another advantage would be the possibility to show the measured data in real time and measure again in case of any fatal error. Showing the data in real time also means that the results processing would be done directly on the Raspberry Pi, therefore eliminating the need for external scripts for data processing, but there would have to be a way to upload the results to an external storage, such as a file server or an USB flash drive.

Another way of improving the evaluation system would be allowing for onboard network interface configuration. This proposes significant challenge as improper configuration causes the entire evaluation system to become unusable. This could also be configurable using the aforementioned graphical user interface.

Another problem that needs to be solved is simulation of a moving vehicle because there will be more noise and the demodulation might be problematic.

6   Conclusion

The aim of this thesis was to provide an insight into how to develop an evaluation system for communication links in field robotics. Specifics of communication model in field robotics was examined alongside with video feed data. Based on these principles an example evaluation system was developed. The evaluation system is very simple but has many drawbacks, mostly caused by complicated setup and usage because there are many steps to be done before the evaluation itself starts. Many of these drawbacks will hopefully be solved by implementing the graphical user interface mentioned in the Sect. 5.

The evaluation system was tested in [1] where 2.4 GHz and 5 GHz 802.11 communication links were evaluated. Comparison of the two communication links proved that the 5 GHz link had lower range and higher latency. It was proven that the evaluation system works and it can be used for future comparisons of communication links and more importantly of their different configuration. The evaluation system targets not only 802.11 based systems but also any radio communication systems equipped with ethernet and TCP/IP stack (for example radios based on 433 MHz ISM frequencies). For comparison of the communication links it is also more important to tell which is better than to provide absolute values of measured data.

Acknowledgments. This work was supported by the European Regional Development Fund under the project Robotics 4 Industry 4.0 (reg. no. CZ.02.1.01/0.0/0.0/15_003/0000470) and the completion of this paper was made possible by the grant No. FEKT-S-17-4234 - "Industry 4.0 in automation and cybernetics" financially supported by the Internal science fund of Brno University of Technology.

References

1. Hybl, M.: Communication in Mobile Robotics. Brno University of Technology, Brno (2019)
2. Nejdl, L., et al.: Remote-controlled robotic platform for electrochemical determination of water contaminated by heavy metal ions. Int. J. Electrochem. Sci. **10**(4), 3635–3643 (2015)
3. Zalud, L.: ARGOS - system for heterogeneous mobile robot teleoperation. In: IEEE/RSJ International Conference on Intelligent Robots and Systems, pp. 211–216 (2006)
4. Zalud, L.: Orpheus – universal reconnaissance teleoperated robot. In: Nardi, D., Riedmiller, M., Sammut, C., Santos-Victor, J. (eds.) RoboCup 2004. LNCS (LNAI), vol. 3276, pp. 491–498. Springer, Heidelberg (2005). https://doi.org/10.1007/978-3-540-32256-6_44
5. Precision Time Protocol. http://www.ncbi.nlm.nih.gov
6. API In CPP. https://wiki.mikrotik.com/wiki/API_In_CPP

DARPA Subterranean Challenge: Multi-robotic Exploration of Underground Environments

Tomáš Rouček[1]([envelope]), Martin Pecka[1], Petr Čížek[1], Tomáš Petříček[1], Jan Bayer[1],
Vojtěch Šalanský[1], Daniel Heřt[1], Matěj Petrlík[1], Tomáš Báča[1],
Vojěch Spurný[1], François Pomerleau[2], Vladimír Kubelka[2], Jan Faigl[1],
Karel Zimmermann[1], Martin Saska[1], Tomáš Svoboda[1], and Tomáš Krajník[1]

[1] Faculty of Electrical Engineering, Czech Technical University, Prague, Czechia
`rouceto1@fel.cvut.cz`
[2] Université Laval, Quebec City, Canada

Abstract. The Subterranean Challenge (SubT) is a contest organised by the Defense Advanced Research Projects Agency (DARPA). The contest reflects the requirement of increasing safety and efficiency of underground search-and-rescue missions. In the SubT challenge, teams of mobile robots have to detect, localise and report positions of specific objects in an underground environment. This paper provides a description of the multi-robot heterogeneous exploration system of our CTU-CRAS team, which scored third place in the Tunnel Circuit round, surpassing the performance of all other non-DARPA-funded competitors. In addition to the description of the platforms, algorithms and strategies used, we also discuss the lessons-learned by participating at such contest.

1 Introduction

The recent developments in artificial intelligence, spatio-temporal mapping, sensing technologies, and computing resulted in rapid improvements in the ability of robots to act independently and to deal with unexpected situations [2]. However, similar to other fields of science, robotics research is currently facing a crisis of reproducibility, which has several causes. First is complexity: each robotic system comprises of a large number of individual submodules, which are often evaluated in isolation and their impact on the efficiency of the entire system is often neglected. The second reason is experimental costs: Performing a field experiment requires one to solve several technical and logistical issues, which are not scientifically appealing. Thus, evaluations are often based on datasets which do not reflect the complexity and unpredictability of real environments. The third reason is the evaluation criteria: failures of the methods are often assumed to be

The work is funded by the CSF project 17-27006Y STRoLL and OP VVV MEYS RCI project CZ.02.1.01/0.0/0.0/16_019/0000765.

J. Mazal et al. (Eds.): MESAS 2019, LNCS 11995, pp. 274–290, 2020.
https://doi.org/10.1007/978-3-030-43890-6_22

caused by technical issues, and the failed cases are not accounted for in experimental results. Therefore, the reliability and robustness of the methods are often not included in experimental evaluations, which typically focus on other aspects, like accuracy or computational complexity [7,13].

All of the aforementioned issues contribute to sub-optimal performance of robotic systems when deployed in real-world situations. To alleviate this problem, several experts have proposed comparing the performance of robotic systems by means of robotic contests, such as MIROSOT [35], Eurobot [20], RoboTour [10], RockIn [31] or MBZIRC [32]. Each of these contests aims at different abilities of the robots, and they evaluate the complete system performance in a limited number of experimental trials. Thus, in these contests, system reliability is more important than the performance of the individual modules (Fig. 1).

Fig. 1. Team of our ground and aerial robots deployed in the DARPA contest mine operated by the Federal Centre for Disease Control.

One of the long researched topics in the robotics community is autonomous exploration, where a robot is supposed to build a detailed spatial [4] or spatio-temporal [28] map of its operational environment. Apart from the mapping itself, exploration requires the robot to estimate its own position accurately, decide where to move to refine and complete its map, traverse difficult terrain, avoid dangerous situations, and recover from mapping or self-localisation errors. While the aforementioned problems were thoroughly studied separately, there are not many systems capable of performing exploration in a reliable manner without supporting infrastructure allowing for their supervision [28].

The ability to rapidly explore the operational environment is desirable especially in security and search-and-rescue scenarios, where the robots are supposed to create a map of the affected area and identify locations of potential victims or other relevant objects. It is assumed that knowledge provided by the robots, i.e., detailed maps of the environment, improves the safety and efficiency of search-and-rescue teams. Moreover, robots can provide information from non-accessible or otherwise dangerous areas, such as gas-filled tunnels, unstable ground, damaged structures, large crevices, or contaminated locations.

The robots for search-and-rescue missions are often teleoperated by radio, and their ability to act independently is limited to ensure efficiency and safety during the mission. However, large-scale underground disaster response scenarios with no prior communication infrastructure illustrated by the DARPA Subterranean Challenge require a certain level of autonomy since the connection with the robots might be lost. Thus, the robots deployed in these scenarios have to be able to act independently and autonomously in order to perform the exploration.

The DARPA SubT challenge aims to boost the development of reliable autonomous robotic exploration in adverse underground environments without any supporting infrastructure. The common practice in robotics research is to evaluate the individual capabilities of the robotic systems. But, during the contest, the performance of robotic teams is evaluated by their ability to quickly and accurately locate relevant objects in underground sites with a variable degree of complexity. Such evaluation puts the whole robotic system to the test.

In this paper, we describe the multi-robot system developed for the DARPA SubT challenge by the team CTU-CRAS of the Czech Technical University in Prague. The description contains details about the hardware of the robots, localization systems, mapping, navigation, as well as our approach to multi-robot coordination.

2 Related Work

Despite the advances in mapping and localisation, robotic exploration of hazardous environments in search-and-rescue scenarios is typically performed by means of teleoperation. However, limitations in bandwidth, data delays and outages, sensor noise, sensor deficiencies and adverse environmental factors impose a high cognitive load on the robot operator. This, along with the need for fast mission execution, imposes significant stress, which often results in performance deterioration and frequent errors with potentially serious consequences. All of these factors are multiplied if the operator has to supervise and direct multiple robots, see Fig. 2. These factors, along with the ones mentioned in Sect. 1, motivated the research in autonomous exploration of adverse environments, such as underground facilities.

One of the first reported attempts to acquire a 3D map of underground mines was reported in [33], followed by [9]. While these works were successful, they focused on 3D mapping itself, and it did not consider autonomous exploration or object detection. Rather, these mapping systems consisted of a sensor-equipped cart, which was guided through the mine by a human operator. After this pioneering effort, more authors addressed the same problem later on. Some of the efforts are summarized in [16], which compares the performance of different subterranean mapping methods. In [16], the authors conclude that the

Fig. 2. Setup of the operator station and signs of stress when supervising a team of robots with limited autonomous capabilities

sensor technologies, data processing algorithms and mapping methods are not ready to compose a reliable system for autonomous exploration. The importance of using robots in mine search and rescue operations was stressed in [18], who summarized the impact of mine accidents, and their experiences of using robots in underground search-and-rescue missions.

Since then, new sensors like 3D lidars, high-dynamic range cameras, as well as better localisation and mapping algorithms have emerged leading to new solutions to the problem. For example [37] propose to use a marsupial setup consisting of a "mother" and "baby" robot, which is released to map hard-to-access areas. The authors of [19] investigated the performance of different mapping strategies using a fast 3D laser scanner. However, the need for reliability still favors robust solutions, which can withstand explosions and fire [34] or can operate in flooded mines [15]. These often exploit installed infrastructure, like magnetic wires, ceiling lights or radio beacons [27], and use reactive behaviors for navigation. Still, the advances in 3D mapping, traversability analysis and autonomous navigation allowed for the design of systems that perform the exploration in an autonomous manner while reasoning about the mine structure [21]. Similar systems were reported to autonomously venture hundreds of meters into abandoned mines [14].

In this paper, we report on the hardware, software and communication design and performance of a multi robot system, which builds upon the experiences of the aforementioned works as well as lessons learned during projects aimed at robotic search and rescue missions [12].

3   Contest Specification

DARPAs Subterranean Challenge (SubT) is one of the contests organized by the Defense Advanced Research Projects Agency (DARPA) to test and push the limits of current technology. The SubT challenge is focused on exploration of unknown, large subterranean environments by teams of ground and aerial mobile robots. In particular, the task of the robotics teams is to actively search for people and other objects of interest. The efficiency of the team is assessed by the number of objects found and accuracy of their position estimation [6].

The contest occurs at several different underground courses with a structure unknown to the participating team. A typical course is expected to span over 8 km of length, and contain about 20 objects of interest. The contesting robots are expected to operate in adverse conditions such as fog, rubble, dripping water, or mud and they have to be able to traverse inclined, declined and constrained passages. A contest team can setup their control station close to the course entrance, but only the robots are allowed to enter the course itself. The organizers provide basic information of the type of course, and indicate which types of objects are to be located. After that, robots are sent inside and only one operator is permitted to supervise their status from the control station located at the course entrance. The robots are then required to locate the specified objects and report their positions to the supervising team. The team score increases each time a robot locates an object and reports its position within 5 m from its true position. However, the team score is decremented in case of a false positive detection or mislocalisation.

3.1   Contest Environment

The challenge is divided into four rounds, where the first three occur in specific environments ("Tunnels", "Urban" and "Caves"), with a different set of objects to be located. The "Tunnel" environment round occurs in a mine, the "Urban" in an underground parking lot or a subway station and "Caves" in naturally-formed caves. The final, fourth round will comprise of all three environments.

All environments are expected to have little or no GPS coverage and very limited range of radio communication. The absence of communication imposes strong requirements on the robots' ability to operate autonomously. The robots will have to autonomously locate the objects and return back to the control station to report their position.

Each environment brings its own challenges in terms of physical barriers and dynamics.

The "Tunnel" environment will comprise of long tunnels of similar width, with ground varying from dry concrete to debris, mud, shallow water and train tracks. Moreover, the robots are expected to encounter fog, smoke and dripping water.

The second, "Urban" track resembles urban underground areas, such as subway stations or basements. Thus, one can expect better lighting conditions, and open, large areas interconnected with narrow tunnels accompanied by stairs, ladders and inclines. We also expect perceptual problems caused by glossy, reflective surfaces, which pose a problem both for cameras and laser rangefinders.

The last type of environment – the "Caves" – is most likely going to be set in larger caverns with smaller constrained passages in between. This environment is going to be challenging due to the vastness of the caverns and difficult traversability of the terrain, which is expected to be non-even and slippery.

3.2   Artifacts and Scoring

The scoring of teams is performed for each run of each track. Points are earned for messages sent to the DARPA-provided interface – these messages contain identification of the detected object (artifact) along with its position. The score is increased if the correct type is reported within the correct error bound which is illustrated in Fig. 3. Each of the artifact types is specified by DARPA, providing the exact item appearance and a link where to obtain them. For the first track, there are several artifacts published comprising of: backpacks, fire extinguishers, small drills, human survivors (dressed up mannequins) and cell-phones Fig. 3. For the latter tracks, the robots might have to perform other tasks than purely object search, e.g. they might need to measure the presence of hazardous gasses or identify certain specific locations of the infrastructure (position of ingress etc).

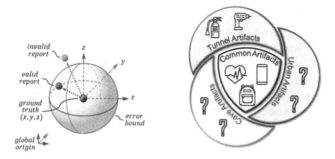

Fig. 3. (Left) Artifact detection error boundaries, (Right) DARPA-provided artifact types

3.3   Competition Timeline and Rounds

The competition is held from September 2018 until August 2021.

Between these dates, there are 3 competitions tracks followed by a final event, see Table 1. Apart from these tracks, there are two exercise events to provide an opportunity to further test the systems in close-to-real conditions. One was already held at April 2019 called STIX and the other one will probably occur on April 2021. In this paper, we will describe the results achieved during the STIX and Tunnel circuit rounds.

Table 1. Timeline of whole competition [6]

Event	Date
SubT Integration Exercise (STIX)	April 2019
Tunnel circuit	August 2019
Urban circuit	February 2020
Cave circuit	August 2020
Final exercise	April 2021
Final event	August 2021

4   Robots and Sensory Equipment

The team is comprised of two tracked and one wheeled UGV, two six-legged crawling robots and two quadrotor UAVs. The capabilities of the individual robots of the team are complementary. The tracked robots can traverse more difficult terrain, while the wheeled robot is faster. The crawling robots, which are rather slow, are capable of navigating in adverse terrain, through narrow tunnels and other spatially constrained areas. The quadrotor robots are not constrained by the terrain at all, but their operation time is short and they do not carry all the sensors of their ground counterparts because of their limited payload.

4.1   Wheeled Robot - Husky A200

The husky is a wheeled platform produced by Clearpath capable of speeds of up to 3 m/s, with a rugged chassis capable of withstanding and traversing mud, light rocks, and steep inclines. This platform is powered by lead-acid batteries capable of sustaining several hours of operation with payloads of up to 50 kg. The onboard sensors consist of a RoboSense 3D lidar with 30° × 360° field of view and range up to 200 m, which is the primary sensor for localization and mapping. To detect the objects of interest, the robot is equipped with five Bluefox RGB cameras positioned to achieve 360° field of view. To accommodate for the low light conditions, the cameras are running at 15 FPS and the robot is equipped with LED stripes attached to all sides of its body. Object detection itself is performed on an NVidia Jetson TX2 board, which achieves detection rates of around 2 frames per second. A NUC-i5 computer performs the calculations for localization, mapping and control.

Since the payload capacity far exceeds the weight of the sensory and computational equipment, the robot carries some extra devices. Currently, it is equipped with two eight-slot containers for communication relays. The robot can deploy the individual relays in order to keep a low-bandwidth communication link with the command station [5]. In the future, the robot will be fitted with docks for hexapods and UAVs, and deploy them at locations suitable for these platforms similar to [30].

Fig. 4. The husky platform after leaving a muddy mine. Note the Robosense 3D lidar on the top and the gray carousel between the wheels. The carousel stores and releases the communication modules described in Subsect. 4.5.

4.2   Tracked Robots - Absolem

The two tracked Absolem platforms produced by BlueBotics SA are designed to traverse terrain common in disaster sites. Their size and weight is slightly lower than the Husky robot, and while their payload capacity is sufficient to carry all the desired sensors, they would not be able to carry other robots. Each Absolem robot has two base tracks and four helper tracks (called flippers) which are controlled independently by a method based on [22, 23]. The primary sensor for navigation is a SICK LMS151 lidar attached to a pivot on the front of the robot. The pivot rotates along the robot's longitudinal axis, rotating the lidar's scanning plane so that the robot obtains a 3D point cloud of the environment in front of it. The 3D point cloud is processed by an embedded, Intel Core i7-based PC, which runs navigation, mapping, localization and exploration algorithms. Similar to the Husky robot, object detection is performed by a Jetson TX2 board, which processes images provided by the PointGrey Ladubyg3 omnicamera. Both Absolem robots are supposed to thoroughly search areas not accessible by the Husky robot. Since their sensory and computational capabilities are similar, the Absolem and Husky robots are using the same localization, mapping and exploration methods which will be described further on in Sect. 5.

4.3   Crawling Robots - Hexapods

The crawling robots are based on the six-legged PhantomX Mark II platform, which can carry over 2 kg of equipment. The robots can move with velocities of around 0.2 m/s, and their batteries allow for 1 h of autonomous operation. Both navigation and object detection is based on a rig composed of 10 W LED directional illumination, and two Intel Realsense cameras. The T265 camera, which performs visual SLAM onboard, provides the main computer with an estimate of its position, alleviating it from computationally costly localization algorithms [3]. The D435 RGBD camera provides data for map building, exploration and object detection, performed by an NVidia Jetson TX2 board. Due to their excellent terrain handling capabilities, these robots are supposed to explore areas inaccessible by the other ground robots [8]. However, their movement speed is rather low, so in future missions, they will be carried by and deployed by the Husky robot (Fig. 5).

Fig. 5. Absolem (back) and hexapod (front) platforms after a run in the mine

4.4   Aerial Robots - Quadrotors

The aerial robots are based on the F450 kit by DJI, controlled by the PixHawk board. Their primary sensor to perform localization and mapping is an RPLidar A3, which provides 16000 distance measurements per second in a 360° circle in one plane. The sensor range is 25 m, and its (adjustable) rotation rate is set to

10 RPS, which provides sufficient overview to safely move in narrow tunnels with speeds of up to 1 m/s. Laser-based localization is based on the Hector SLAM [11] package, which is supposed to work well in conditions that we anticipate in the contest environment [29]. For object detection, each UAV carries a Bluefox RGB camera with an LED illumination stripe. The detection itself is performed by a modified YOLOv2 CNN on the CPU of the onboard i7 NUC PC, which also performs localization and mapping. With this setup, the processing of one image takes approximately 2 s, which is just sufficient in order not to miss an object when flying at standard velocities. Both UAVs are setup to run the exploration process automatically after launch, so they can be deployed easily by any member of the team (Fig. 6).

Fig. 6. One drone platform entering the mine

4.5 Communication

As mentioned before, one of the limiting factors for search and rescue robots is the constrained radio communication in the winding underground tunnels. The lack of radio link with sufficient bandwidth not only prevents direct tele-operation, but also makes mission supervision and monitoring difficult. Ideally, robots should provide the mission supervisor with a live video feed and share the information about their environment with each other. This would require them to maintain a high-bandwidth radio link during the entire mission, which is unrealistic. While autonomously operating robots do not need to provide live video and sensor data streams, they still need to share their positions and report the locations of objects to the command station. This means that it is desirable to maintain a reliable, low-bandwidth radio link. To deal with these requirements, our system uses 3 different kinds of communications with different levels of reliability, bandwidth and usage.

Short-Range Link: WiFi. During the system setup and initial deployment, all robots and the command station are close to each other. Therefore, one can use standard, off-the-shelf WiFi, which has sufficient bandwidth to data-intensive sensor measurements and videos in real time. This is necessary during system setup, because one needs to verify functionality of the individual software modules. Moreover, the robots can use the WiFi to exchange the information they gathered about their environment and share their 3D maps.

Mid-range Link: Mobilicom. For mission monitoring and teleoperation, we use high-power, mesh-enabled communication systems produced by Mobilicom. While this system is able to transmit signals over large distances, the signal power drops significantly in cases where line of sight is not maintained. To deal with this issue, we coordinate the mission so that the robots which carry the mobilicom modules try to maintain line of sight. This allows them to re-transmit the signals from any of them to the base station, located at the mission control site. The system achieves about 1 Mbit throughput with the individual stations being 100 m apart from each other. This allows them to share low-quality video feeds for teleoperation, elevation maps to coordinate exploration, and pictures to confirm object detection. However, the size of the modules allows their use on the wheeled and tracked robots only, which limits the system range to ∼300 m.

Long-Range Link: Motes. To overcome the aforementioned limitation, we employ another communication system, which has a limited throughput sufficient to share the robot and object positions only. These "Mote" modules are small enough to be carried by all of our robots, The Husky robot, which is always deployed in the beginning of the exploration mission, carries up to 16 of these modules (see Fig. 4), and can drop them to create a network of relays, providing communication infrastructure for the other robots. While the bandwidth of this network is low, it is still sufficient to share the positions of the robots and artifacts amongst the team and transmit this data to the base station.

5   Software

While appropriate hardware is necessary to perform the challenge, the software influences the performance of the system in a significant way. To address the importance of the software solutions, DARPA also organized a "virtual track" where the teams provide software solutions only, and the contest occurs in realistic simulations of the deployment sites. As expected, most teams regularly test their software in simulation as part of the development process, as simulation of the systems is much less tedious compared to real-world testing. Moreover, simulation allows us to test the individual software modules in isolation as well as in a holistic manner. The software used on all of our robots had to solve the problems of localization, mapping, navigation, object detection and exploration. Moreover, the robots had to coordinate their exploration efforts.

5.1 Object Detection

The performance of the exploration system is evaluated in terms of its ability to detect and locate potential victims as well as objects that provide a cue of their location. Object detection is performed by every robot of our team by processing camera data by a neural network using a customized version of the YOLOv3 [25,26] object detector. If the robot has a 3D map of its surroundings, the bounding box provided by the YOLOv3 detector is projected into the 3D map. Then, the final position of the detected object is established by application of Kalman filtering over the detections that are temporally consistent. Only if the detection is certain, the robot sends position and RGB snapshot of the detected object. This prevents flooding of the communication network with image data, potentially preventing other robots from reporting the objects detected.

Since the rules explicitly prohibit training the neural network at the mine where the challenge occurs, we trained the YOLO on imagery gathered in other mines. Good performance of the detection method during the contest indicated a good ability of the neural network to generalize the training data.

5.2 Localization and Mapping

Apart from detecting objects of interest, one has to exactly determine their position. For that, a robot, which detects the object, has to know its own position with sufficient accuracy. The problem of self-localization, i.e. reliable estimation of the robot position, is tackled differently depending on the given platform. The wheeled and tracked robots are exploiting the richness of the 3D data provided by their 3d rangefinders. This allows them to combine their odometry with a 3D version of the iterative closest point method (ICP), which performs simultaneous localization and mapping (SLAM) [24]. The UAVs combine a Hector SLAM [11] method, based on their 2D lidars, with visual localization, based on the ORB-SLAM2 method [17] - both of the methods create a map of the environment as part of the ego-motion estimation process. Localization of the hexapods is based on the Intel T265 camera module which provides a position estimate based on a proprietary gray-scale visual-inertial SLAM algorithm. The robots are equipped with a secondary RGBD camera (Intel D435) which builds a 3D map [3], and uses the map to guide the robot to unexplored areas.

5.3 Navigation

The maps built in the previous steps are first transformed from full 3D to a 2.5D elevation map, which is subsequently analyzed for traversability. Then, a motion plan is generated and executed by running the A* pathfinding algorithm over the elevation map. To improve their ability to overcome adverse terrain, the tracked robots incorporate the information of their RGBD cameras and position their auxiliary tracks accordingly [22,23]. The UAVs implemented a guided random walk algorithm which forces the vehicle to go in a specified direction while avoiding obstacles on the way.

The method used proved to be universally applicable and it works well on our crawling, wheeled and tracked robots. As the aerial robots do not move on the ground, they plan their path to simply avoid obstacles detected by the 2D lidar.

5.4   Exploration

The ground robots are using two modes of exploration, which are both based on the frontier paradigm [36]. The tracked UGVs use frontiers generated by RGBD cameras since we established that we cannot reliably recognize objects at greater distances. Entropy of those frontiers is then calculated using position data from all of the robots, which causes the robots to prefer unvisited frontiers over those already seen by other robots or by itself.

However on the Husky platform the frontiers are extracted by the 3D lidar so that they appear at a greater distance from the platform, which is used to move towards them with the speed the Husky robot offers. The robot assesses the accessibility of all unexplored cells in the elevation map and marks them as possible frontiers, and then tries to move towards the position of the closest one.

5.5   Coordination

Coordination of the robots is done using the powerful data-link made available by the 4G Mobilicom mesh communicators in the tunnel. This allows the operator to guide the robots towards the locations of interest. Robots also share their positions to the rest of the robot crew using the low-bandwidth link established by the droppable "Motes" described in Subsect. 4.5. Sharing this information allows better coordination of the exploration efforts by avoiding exploration of areas already visited by other robots. Knowledge of other robot positions is also useful in detecting situations where a robot is stuck or lost.

5.6   Interface

Since in the rules of the competition allow only one human to communicate with the robots (including reporting artifacts and teleoperation), it was necessary to design a user-friendly interface for the robot team as well as for each of the larger robots. The large UGVs are streaming their data to a control PC at the operation base on which all of the information from each robot is displayed. Detections, positions, maps and other useful information can be shown to the operator so they can eventually guide the robots from adverse situations by full teleoperation, or by providing them with intermediate goals in the elevation map. On the other hand, UAVs only have a fully autonomous mode, and while they provide the positions of the detected objects, they don't allow the operator to interfere with their operation. The artifact detections reported by the ground and aerial robots are provided to the team supervisor via a secondary computer, who can then decide to accept or reject a given object detection.

6 Experiments and Deployments at Mines

So far, our robotic team was deployed at three experimental sites: "URC Josef" – a CTU experimental mine, "Edgar" Coal Mine in Idaho Springs and "NIOSH" mine facility near Pittsburgh.

The "Edgar" mine deployment, which was organized by DARPA, consisted of four independent exploration runs. During these runs, the robots were able to detect three objects at correct positions and report them to the fleet operator. However, due to the technical difficulties with inter-robot communication, only one of the aforementioned runs was performed autonomously. After the runs, we were invited to enter the mines in person, and the organizers pointed out difficult situations which we could encounter in the future runs, like a fog-generating machine, which filled the corridors with thick haze, or difficult-to-find objects, such as a cellphone located underneath a grilled floor.

The second round of experiments was conducted at "Josef" experimental mine owned by the Czech Technical University in Prague. These were focused on evaluations of the system robustness, dataset gathering, and verification of particular components and approaches. During these tests, we were capable of exploring substantial parts of the mine, going over gravel and uneven terrain, while detecting and localising objects. Moreover, we gradually improved the efficiency of our team, which was reflected in a decrease of the deployment and setup time as well as an increase of the run lengths and numbers of objects detected.

The final four experiments were conducted as part of the DARPA Subterranean "Tunnel" challenge. Two experiments were performed at the 'Safety research mine' and the other two at the 'Experimental mine' of the National Institute of Occupational Safety and Health (NIOSH). During the first run, our system suffered from radio interference from the emergency stop system, causing our robots to halt every few meters and prevented smooth operation. The problem was fixed in software and during the subsequent runs, we were able to find and locate five objects per trial. This score placed us one point behind the team CoStar, which was a joint team of researchers from MIT, JPL/NASA, Caltech and KAIST.

The most difficult problem encountered was the operator's cognitive load when coordinating several robots in the exploration mission. The second problem was related to a lack of perceptual capability to distinguish between shallow, passable puddles, and deeper pits filled with water. Other problems were related to communication – the fleet had to be carefully coordinated so that the robots closer to the base station acted as communication relays to ensure that the radio link to the most distant robot is maintained. On the other hand, the localisation, mapping and object detection algorithms all worked in a satisfactory manner.

7   Conclusion

In this paper, we described a multi-robot system for search and rescue operations in underground areas. The team consisted of three heavy-duty platforms with advances sensors and strong computational capabilities, two crawling robots and two aerial vehicles with limited payload and action radius. We provided basic information of the hardware, software, and communication methods, which should be sufficient to get a basic insight into our system workings.

The system described here was not implemented for the purposes of the contest. Rather, it is a result of the integration and refinement of several software components used in other scientific projects at the CTU's Center for Robotics and Autonomous Systems. The integration efforts started in December 2018, with some of the platforms (e.g. Husky and its sensors) arriving in May 2019, making it rather challenging to perform the integration and testing prior to the contest.

The performance of the system described was thoroughly tested during the contest, organised by the Defense Advanced Research Project Agency (DARPA). During the "Tunnel" round, where our robots were supposed to search for specific objects in abandoned mines, our team achieved third position out of 11 teams, and first place in the non-DARPA funded teams category [1].

For the future rounds, we will focus on improving the autonomous behaviors, implementation of coordination methods with restricted communication, reduction of the operator load and improved handling of hard terrain. Since the aforementioned issues are not only technical, we will approach them as scientific questions. Thus, participation in the DARPA contest will help us to identify new problems, which are worth being investigated.

References

1. Rolling, walking, flying, and floating, SubT challenge teams traverse the tunnel circuit, August 2019. https://www.darpa.mil/news-events/2019-08-22
2. Atkeson, C.G., et al.: Achieving reliable humanoid robot operations in the DARPA robotics challenge: team WPI-CMU's approach. In: Spenko, M., Buerger, S., Iagnemma, K. (eds.) The DARPA Robotics Challenge Finals: Humanoid Robots To The Rescue. STAR, vol. 121, pp. 271–307. Springer, Cham (2018). https://doi.org/10.1007/978-3-319-74666-1_8
3. Bayer, J., Faigl, J.: On autonomous spatial exploration with small hexapod walking robot using tracking camera intel RealSense T265. In: European Conference on Mobile Robots (ECMR) (2019)
4. Burgard, W., Moors, M., Fox, D., Simmons, R., Thrun, S.: Collaborative multi-robot exploration. In: ICRA, pp. 476–481 (2000)

5. Čížek, P., Faigl, J.: Dynamic building of wireless communication infrastructure in underground environments. In: Modelling and Simulation for Intelligent Systems (MESAS) (2019)
6. DARPA: Competition rules tunnel circuit, July 2019
7. Dillmann, R.: Ka 1.10 benchmarks for robotics research. European Robotics Network (EURON), IST-2000-26048 (2004)
8. Faigl, J., et al.: On localization and mapping with RGB-D sensor and hexapod walking robot in rough terrains. In: 2016 IEEE International Conference on Systems, Man, and Cybernetics (SMC), pp. 002273–002278. IEEE (2016)
9. Huber, D.F., Vandapel, N.: Automatic three-dimensional underground mine mapping. Int. J. Rob. Res. 25(1), 7–17 (2006)
10. Iša, J., Dlouhý, M.: Robotour-robotika.cz outdoor delivery challenge. In: Proceedings of the 1st Slovak-Austrian International Conference on Robotics in Education, Bratislava, Slovakia. Citeseer (2010)
11. Kohlbrecher, S., Von Stryk, O., Meyer, J., Klingauf, U.: A flexible and scalable slam system with full 3D motion estimation. In: 2011 IEEE International Symposium on Safety, Security, and Rescue Robotics, pp. 155–160. IEEE (2011)
12. Kruijff-Korbayová, I., et al.: TRADR project: long-term human-robot teaming for robot assisted disaster response. KI-Künstliche Intelligenz 29(2), 193–201 (2015)
13. Lier, F., et al.: Towards automated system and experiment reproduction in robotics. In: 2016 IEEE/RSJ International Conference on Intelligent Robots and Systems (IROS), pp. 3298–3305. IEEE (2016)
14. Losch, R., Grehl, S., Donner, M., Buhl, C., Jung, B.: Design of an autonomous robot for mapping, navigation, and manipulation in underground mines. In: IEEE/RSJ International Conference on Intelligent Robots and Systems (IROS). IEEE, October 2018
15. Maity, A., Majumder, S., Ray, D.N.: Amphibian subterranean robot for mine exploration. In: 2013 International Conference on Robotics, Biomimetics, Intelligent Computational Systems. IEEE (2013)
16. Morris, A., et al.: Recent developments in subterranean robotics. J. Field Rob. 23(1), 35–57 (2006)
17. Mur-Artal, R., Montiel, J.M.M., Tardós, J.D.: ORB-SLAM: a versatile and accurate monocular SLAM system. IEEE Trans. Rob. 31(5), 1147–1163 (2015). https://doi.org/10.1109/TRO.2015.2463671
18. Murphy, R.R., Kravitz, J., Stover, S.L., Shoureshi, R.: Mobile robots in mine rescue and recovery. IEEE Rob. Autom. Mag. 16(2), 91–103 (2009)
19. Neumann, T., Ferrein, A., Kallweit, S., Scholl, I.: Towards a mobile mapping robot for underground mines. In: Proceedings of the 2014 PRASA, RobMech and AfLaT International Joint Symposium, Cape Town, South Africa, pp. 27–28 (2014)
20. Obdrzalek, D.: Eurobot junior and starter-a comparison of two approaches for robotic contest organization. In: Robotics in Education, Bratislava (2010)
21. Oßwald, S., Bennewitz, M., Burgard, W., Stachniss, C.: Speeding-up robot exploration by exploiting background information. IEEE Rob. Autom. Lett. 1(2), 716–723 (2016)
22. Pecka, M., Šalanský, V., Zimmermann, K., Svoboda, T.: Autonomous flipper control with safety constraints. In: 2016 IEEE/RSJ International Conference on Intelligent Robots and Systems (IROS), pp. 2889–2894, October 2016. https://doi.org/10.1109/IROS.2016.7759447
23. Pecka, M., Zimmermann, K., Petrlík, M., Svoboda, T.: Data-driven policy transfer with imprecise perception simulation. IEEE Rob. Autom. Lett. 3(4), 3916–3921 (2018). https://doi.org/10.1109/LRA.2018.2857927

24. Pomerleau, F., Colas, F., Siegwart, R., Magnenat, S.: Comparing ICP variants on real-world data sets. Auton. Rob. **34**(3), 133–148 (2013). https://doi.org/10.1007/s10514-013-9327-2

25. Redmon, J., Divvala, S., Girshick, R., Farhadi, A.: You only look once: unified, real-time object detection. In: Proceedings of the IEEE Conference on Computer Vision and Pattern Recognition, pp. 779–788 (2016)

26. Redmon, J., Farhadi, A.: YOLOv3: an incremental improvement. arXiv preprint arXiv:1804.02767 (2018)

27. Rusu, S.R., Hayes, M.J.D., Marshall, J.A.: Localization in large-scale underground environments with RFID. In: 2011 24th Canadian Conference on Electrical and Computer Engineering (CCECE). IEEE, May 2011

28. Santos, J.M., Krajník, T., Fentanes, J.P., Duckett, T.: Lifelong information-driven exploration to complete and refine 4-D spatio-temporal maps. IEEE Rob. Autom. Lett. **1**(2), 684–691 (2016). https://doi.org/10.1109/LRA.2016.2516594

29. Santos, J.M., Portugal, D., Rocha, R.P.: An evaluation of 2D SLAM techniques available in robot operating system. In: 2013 IEEE International Symposium on Safety, Security, and Rescue Robotics (SSRR), pp. 1–6. IEEE (2013)

30. Saska, M., Krajník, T., Přeučil, L.: Cooperative μUAV-UGV autonomous indoor surveillance. In: International Multi-Conference on Systems, Signals & Devices, pp. 1–6. IEEE (2012)

31. Schneider, S., et al.: The RoCKIn@home challenge. In: 41st International Symposium on Robotics, ISR/Robotik 2014, pp. 1–7. VDE (2014)

32. Spurný, V., et al.: Cooperative autonomous search, grasping, and delivering in a treasure hunt scenario by a team of unmanned aerial vehicles. J. Field Rob. **36**(1), 125–148 (2018)

33. Thrun, S., et al.: A system for volumetric robotic mapping of abandoned mines. In: Proceedings of the IEEE International Conference on Robotics and Automation (ICRA) (2003)

34. Wang, W., Dong, W., Su, Y., Wu, D., Du, Z.: Development of search-and-rescue robots for underground coal mine applications. J. Field Rob. **31**(3), 386–407 (2014)

35. Wong, C.C., Wang, W.W., Lee, Y.L.: Soccer robot design for FIRA MiroSot league. In: IEEE International Conference on Mechatronics, ICM 2005, pp. 457–460. IEEE (2005)

36. Yamauchi, B.: A frontier-based approach for autonomous exploration. In: CIRA, vol. 97, p. 146 (1997)

37. Zhao, J., Liu, G., Liu, Y., Zhu, Y.: Research on the application of a marsupial robot for coal mine rescue. In: Xiong, C., Liu, H., Huang, Y., Xiong, Y. (eds.) ICIRA 2008. LNCS (LNAI), vol. 5315, pp. 1127–1136. Springer, Heidelberg (2008). https://doi.org/10.1007/978-3-540-88518-4_120

Utilization of Modeling and Simulation in the Design of Air Defense

Vlastimil Hujer ⓘ, Miroslav Kratky ⓘ, and Jan Farlik$^{(\boxtimes)}$ ⓘ

University of Defence in Brno, Kounicova 65, 66210 Brno, Czech Republic
{vlastimil.hujer,jan.farlik}@unob.cz.com

Abstract. A key feature of a military operation is its non-repeatability, with a results that can affect history. The success of a military operation depends on the ability and art of the commanders and their staffs to implement the decision-making process. Critical part of the decision-making process is the creation of variants of the activities of own troops based on variants of enemy activities and based on knowledge of the structure and behavior of the enemy. In the case of ground air defense, the variants (courses) of actions are primarily designed with respect to the anticipated air enemy in air defense clusters. Courses of actions can be mutually assessed based on the effectiveness and efficiency of air defense clusters. Nowadays, the creation of courses of actions is a time-consuming stage in the decision-making process, which depends on the knowledge, skills and experience of the commanders and staffs. War games used to evaluate courses of actions do not allow to assess all possible situations and responses. Modeling and simulation is an appropriate apparatus for evaluating variants of the air enemy's activities and based on such results it is possible to decide on the optimum battle configuration of own forces. The model of the enemy's activity structure, own troops, and environment will allow to simulate a large number of combat activities on both sides and assess the most appropriate option for own troops. Probabilistic methods such as the Monte Carlo method and its derivatives will allow the evaluation of the activity variants. The results of the use of probabilistic methods will then be used in the application of game theory and determination of optimal courses of actions, strategy in the sense of game theory, own forces. By programming the models, commanders and staffs will be given a tool to assess the effectiveness and efficiency of ground-based air defense clusters and will be able to make adequate decisions. This article brings a concept of such tool.

Keywords: Air defense · Model · Simulation · Decision

1 Introduction

Before their first deployment, military commanders and staffs shall be trained, exercised and practiced to acquire the necessary knowledge, skills and experience to plan and conduct military operations. As part of their individual training, they are trained in the field of military art, learning jointly with other commanders and staff during the training. They will consolidate the correct habits necessary for planning and leading forces in a

© Springer Nature Switzerland AG 2020
J. Mazal et al. (Eds.): MESAS 2019, LNCS 11995, pp. 291–298, 2020.
https://doi.org/10.1007/978-3-030-43890-6_23

military operation. During the exercises, they further verify the acquired knowledge, skills and gain initial experience. The situation will change for commanders at first deployment, when young commanders without experience of real military operations must apply their newly acquired knowledge, skills and experience.

Experience shows (e.g. [1]) that the knowledge and skills of staff work is generally sufficient, but confidence in the acquired information raises new questions when first deployed. These include, inter alia, confidence in the information received in the decision-making process as a fundamental process of staffing in military operations planning. The quality and credibility of information obtained by intelligence is verified by established procedures. Trust in the information generated in the decision-making process is based on the knowledge of the structure of the decision-making process and the knowledge of the methods used to process the information in such a process.

2   Conditions of Success of Military Operation

The success of a military operation depends on the ability and skill of the commanders and their staffs in the decision-making process. A commander in a stressful conflict situation is more sensitive (than other persons in peaceful conditions) to the understanding and transparency of the procedures for sorting, selecting and processing information. The information produced by procedures corresponding to human thinking is easier for the commander to accept, as they can easily change the sorting, selection and calculation parameters, knowing the significance of such changes. Another aspect enhancing commanders' confidence in the information gathering is the ability to assess all possible alternatives of the battlefield environment. The complexity of the information processing methods within the decision-making process has a major influence on the quality of decisions of individual commanders. Technological and scientific development offers the means and tools that make clear and timely decisions.

Military operations are an integral part of modern history and are currently, among other things, an instrument for the promotion and maintenance of peace. A key feature of a military operation is its unrepeatability consisting in a large number of variables affecting its outcome. The impact of military operation affect the history. A military operation is the interaction of two or more actors trying to achieve their goals. Such objectives are generally contradictory. The actors in the military operation are their own military forces and their allies, enemy forces, environments including terrain, weather and other natural influences. Among the actors are the population and the influence of globalization and public opinion.

A simplified idea of the military operation is shown in Fig. 1, which shows specifically the clash of the air enemy with ground air defense. In the figure, the red elements represent the air enemy, in this case helicopters, aircraft and evaluated airstrike avenues of approach, the blue elements indicate own forces and characteristics such as air defense systems range and radar range, as well as command and control system and defended object. The green elements represent the terrain, flora and fauna, the gray ones show the influence of weather and climate and the yellow pattern shows the area in which combat activities must not take place with regard, for example, to public opinion.

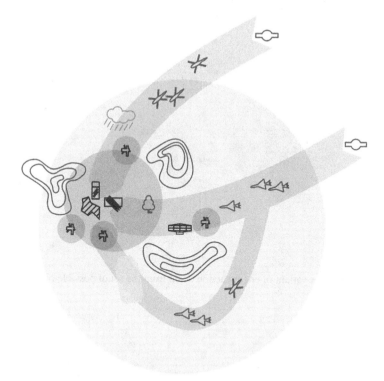

Fig. 1. Military operation idea chart (Color figure online)

3   Timely and Full Assessment of the Situation

Creating variants of the enemy's activity is not a trivial task and involves the application of information about the enemy's doctrines, acquired by current intelligence activities, the enemy's procedures, etc. Creating variants of the enemy's activities without the use of appropriate software is a time-consuming stage in the decision-making process. The difficulty of this stage also depends on the knowledge, skills and experience of the commanders and staffs.

The complexity of the variants of activities is shown in Fig. 2, which on closer examination shows a variant of the activities shown in Fig. 1.

Another time-consuming stage of the decision-making process is the evaluation of the variants of the activities of their own troops, which is carried out in the form of the so-called war game. Moreover, it is not possible to assess all possible situations and responses without a corresponding tool.

Figure 3 shows four variants of the possible development of a military operation depending on the selected variants of air enemy activities. In principle, an infinite number of such variants can be found. Properties of the real world such as suitable positioning for fire systems and radars, location of airports, terrain and weather limits the number of variants see below.

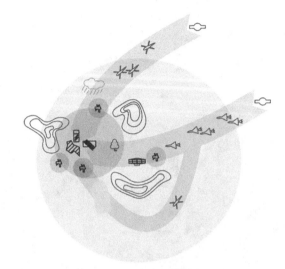

Fig. 2. Another variant of enemy action taken from the set of possible outcomes

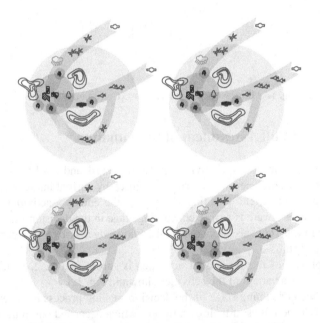

Fig. 3. Variants of activities of own troops depending on the variants of the enemy's activities.

4 Decision-Making Modelling

A variant of the operation as a description of the battlefield elements, see for example Fig. 1, represents its simplified model (modelling of such area was also deeply studied e.g. in [2], or [3]). The degree of simplification depends on the knowledge, skills and experience of the commanders and staff, the time available to carry out the decision-making process and, last but not least, the support of such a process with tools such as software (e.g. [4]). Too simplified model will produce distorted results, which may be unrealistic and may significantly affect the outcome of a military operation. Computer technology and its software create suitable means for realization of necessary calculations for comparison and selection of optimal variant of activity.

A variant of the activities of the troops is a sequence of activities of the troops in time and from the point of view of the planning of the military operation (decision-making process) also represents a scenario of the development of the military operation. A troop activity variant is a record of the initial status of the troops, followed by a description of the altered status of the troops at given times. The time points may be of the same length or distance may be given by another parameter, such as the duration of the shortest action from the previous time point under consideration, the moment of subsequent interaction of the two modeled elements, etc. deployment of troops in space. The variant of the activity is always related to the terrain, weather and other influences (population, fauna, flora, public opinion, etc.) - the environment at a given moment of time. A variant of the activity of its own troops is created for each moment in time following the created variant of the enemy's activity. In this sense, the variants of activities are variants of ground-to-air combat.

From the point of view of one selected side (opponent or own troops), a military operation can be limited to the conflict of two rival parties, with one rival party selected on one side and everything else on the other. It is easier to define this situation by describing the variants of the activities of the competing parties in response to possible variants of the activities of the other side depending on the evolution of the military operation environment. Such a procedure allows the description of military operations understandable even to inexperienced commanders.

The decision-making process is part of the staff work and serves the commanders and staffs to select the optimal variant of the troops under certain conditions. Although there are several variations to the military decision-making process, common steps can be observed. Upon receipt of an order from the commander, an initial clarification of the task resulting from the order shall be made, followed by an analysis of such task. The results of the analysis are used in the creation of variants of activities, which are then analyzed by the so-called war game, whose results are used to compare the individual variants of activities. The final steps of the decision-making process are the selection of a variant and the creation of an order or plan of a military operation. A critical part of the decision-making process is the creation of variants of the activities of their own troops, which are created on the basis of variants of the enemy's activities. The variants of the enemy's activities are based on the experience and knowledge of the structure and behavior of the enemy, based mainly on doctrines, combat use and tactics, taking into account other influences such as natural, population activity, public opinion, etc. There is not enough time to create more variants of activities. In addition, the quality of the variants produced depends on the knowledge, skills and experience of the staff, and varies in this sense. The activity variant is a description of the structure and activity of forces and its weapons, terrain, weather and evaluation of their influence on the activity of the troops.

5   Simulation of the Process of Designing the Battle Layout

The model of enemy activities, own troops and environment allows to simulate a large number of alternatives of individual variants of activities on both sides. In particular, the initial status of the variants defines and differentiates the individual variants of activities from each other. Theoretically, it is possible to create an infinite number of variations of activity, but the model and simulation are a simplification of the real system - a military operation that follows its internal rules. For example, the deployment of forces is not in real operation random and the activities of troops are governed by doctrines and correspond to the capabilities of real commanders and staffs (see Fig. 4, where purple circles represent the possible position of their own fire equipment and radar). The possible activities of the air enemy are shown in Fig. 2. For this reason, the number of variants of activities, especially the initial states, will be limited. Nevertheless, it will be significantly higher than in the decision-making process without software support, see Fig. 3. The number of unique initial states of activity variants is given by the number of acceptable variations (term from combinatorics) of forces and troops activity at any given time. Alternatives to an activity variant are a different sequence of activities based on the same initial status of the activity variant.

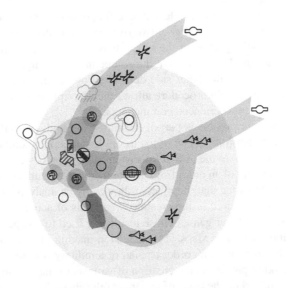

Fig. 4. Possible layout in the model of variants

The process of creating variants of activities is associated with the mutual numerical evaluation of enemy activities (Table 1 - I, II, III, ...) and own troops (A, B, C, ...), as well as taking into account the environment. Numerical evaluation of activity variants expresses the rate of weakening of the enemy (positive number) or own troops (negative number). This model leads to the use of probabilistic methods such as the Monte Carlo method and its derivatives to evaluate the variants of activity.

Thus obtained mutually evaluated variants of the activities of enemy and own troops F (X, Y) can be entered in the table, e.g. Table 1.

Table 1. Mutual comparison of variants

Own variants	Enemy variants		
	I	II	III
A	F(A, I)	F(A, II)	F(A, III)
B	F(B, I)	F(B, II)	F(B, III)
C	F(C, I)	F(C, II)	F(C, III)

Table 1 contains input information on the application of game theory and determination of the optimal variant of activity, strategy in terms of game theory, own forces. The result of such a game is not only information about which of the variants of the activities of their own troops brings the most benefit, but also information about the worst result we can achieve (Fig. 5).

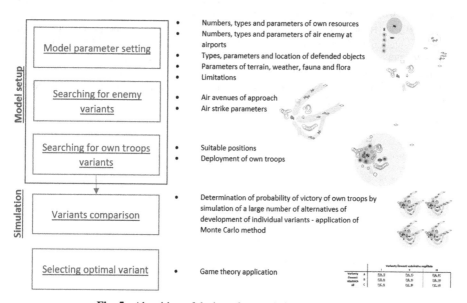

Fig. 5. Algorithm of design of ground air combat systems

6 Conclusion

It can be stated that by software implementation of the model and simulation, commanders and staffs will get a tool to evaluate the effectiveness and efficiency of ground-to-air combat and will be able to make timely decisions corresponding to the requirements of the situation. The advantage of such a model is its easy understanding of non-technical commanders and intuitiveness of the process of creating and evaluating variants, as well as selecting the optimal variant. Another strength of using modeling and simulation in the decision-making process is the possibility of implementing the knowledge, skills and experience of successful commanders into the model.

References

1. Hodicky, J., Prochazka, D.: Challenges in the implementation of autonomous systems into the battlefield. In: Proceedings of the 2017 International Conference on Military Technologies (ICMT), pp. 743–747. Institute of Electrical and Electronics Engineers Inc., Piscataway (2017). https://doi.org/10.1109/miltechs.2017.7988855. ISBN 978-1-5386-1988-9
2. Bruzzone, A.G., Procházka, J., Kutěj, L., Procházka, D., Kozůbek, J., Scurek, R.: Modelling and optimization of the air operational manoeuvre. In: Mazal, J. (ed.) MESAS 2018. LNCS, vol. 11472, pp. 43–53. Springer, Cham (2019). https://doi.org/10.1007/978-3-030-14984-0_4. ISSN 03029743, ISBN 978-303014983-3
3. Prochazka, D., Hodicky, J.: Modelling and simulation as a service and concept development and experimentation. In: Proceedings of the 2017 International Conference on Military Technologies (ICMT), pp. 721–727. Institute of Electrical and Electronics Engineers Inc., Piscataway (2017). ISBN 978-1-5386-1988-9
4. Frantis, P.: Visualization of common operational picture. WIT Trans. Eng. Sci., 347–354 (2014). ISSN 1743-3533. ISBN 9781845648534

Analysis and Optimization of the Resilience Enhancement Circle via Data Farming

Mario Dally[(✉)], Sebastian Jahnen[(✉)], Maximilian Moll, and Stefan Pickl

Fakultät für Informatik, Universität der Bundeswehr München, 85577 Neubiberg, Germany
{Mario.Dally,Sebastian.Jahnen,Maximilian.Moll,
Stefan.Pickl}@unibw.de

Abstract. The importance of communication networks increases with every new system and over the last 20 years these networks have become a critical infrastructure like the electricity network. Besides all cables and connections, the core of these networks are the information transfer systems with routers and switches. To guarantee the availability of these systems resilience is needed. The present paper evaluates possibilities to ensure resilience by the training for IT-Experts. For this purpose, typical errors and the way to fix these failures are inspected. A concept for combining the simulation of failures in systems and the mean time to restore (MTTR) was developed. Related to the information provided by the simulation, the concept was extended by details about the experts training level to specify the MTTR. Our approach is a possible way for providing information related to the field of training in context between experience and computer-generated information. Goal of our work is to enlarge the resilience of systems in critical infrastructures like communication networks by drawing conclusions about the IT-Experts training.

Keywords: OSI model · Optimized training schedules · Data Farming · Man versus computer · Computer networks · Resilient enhancement circle

1 Introduction

The term resilience became more and more important over the last twenty years. But what is it about? "Resilience" comes from the Latin etymology "resilire" which means to "rebound" and in material science it is about robustness and elasticity [1]. The concept of resilience has been studied in a large number of fields and lots of definitions have been created, e.g. *a system's ability to function before, during and after major disruptions through reliance upon multiple mobility options* [2] or the definition of resilience as a process [3]. In resilience engineering resilience describes the ability to recover from a problem brought by an error or failure instead of becoming tragic [4]. Troubleshooting is related to the ability of recovering in every system, because a failure has to be found, inspected, and repaired. The work of troubleshooting is determined through the combination of the inspected systems and people. This fact leads to the conclusion that troubleshooting is defined as socio-technical. Resilience in socio-technical systems has to be inspected from many different views [5]. One possible view is about the training

© Springer Nature Switzerland AG 2020
J. Mazal et al. (Eds.): MESAS 2019, LNCS 11995, pp. 299–305, 2020.
https://doi.org/10.1007/978-3-030-43890-6_24

level of the troubleshooting personnel. This paper deals with the training of IT-Experts for troubleshooting failures and errors in communication systems and its nodes, respectively. First, we will define some terms and connect them with the OSI Model and failures in networks. Secondly, we will simulate failures over a given time and inspect the recovering rate. This rate will be expanded by details about the training level of the IT-Experts and a new simulation model is build. The refined simulation model is the base for our concept and leads to conclusions about planning a training for IT-Experts.

2   Terms, Definitions, and Relations to the ISO/OSI Model

Large networks which are distributed over a huge distance, for example the internet, are called Wide Area Networks (WAN) [6]. These networks operate according to the ISO/OSI-Reference Model (ISO/IEC 14908-1:2012) and failures in networks can be assigned to the layers given by the model.

Failures represent all kinds of errors and malfunctions in networks, e.g. lost connections or routing errors. There is no detailed specification of failures in this paper, except an assignment of failures to the layers of the ISO/OSI-Reference Model. Since the simulations of this work are intended to illustrate our approach, the errors are schematically assigned to the model. Only the first three layers are considered, where the complexity of failures increase with every level. Concerning the impact of failure, we only consider the repair times without taking into account any topology or structure. Measurements are only done by the repair rate because our approach focused on the duration of recovering [7] related to the training level of IT-Experts.

The arrival rate of failures in this paper is defined with simple assumptions because for describing our approach it is sufficient. Therefore, the arrival rate of failures is not related to given or simulated network traffic [8]. Further the failures are not related to known vulnerabilities or from the perspective of an attacker [9].

As repair rate/Mean Time to Restore (MTTR) is a duration of time defined, which is related to the complexity of the given failure and the assignment to Layer of the OSI model (low complexity -> short period of time). As mentioned before no further specifications of the failures are made and nor the time to fix/repair these failures. Analyzing and defining these failures in the inspected network [10] could be part for a future work. The repair rate/MTTR is related directly to the training level of IT-Experts.

Training level of IT-Experts describes an assumption about the qualification of IT-Experts and is shown by a simple quantification on a scale from 1 to 10. The capability of repairing arriving failures is given with level 1. All levels differ from each other only by the needed time of repairing a failure. The scale provides a simulation parameter and is not yet put in any context of known qualifications or trainings.

3   Simulation-Based Analysis of the Performance Measure

The research of a possible behavior in communication networks before, after, and during failures has to start with the inspection of single nodes. This is the fact owned by the cascading of failures in complex networks [11]. Simulations give the opportunity to inspect the possible behavior of single nodes if failures happen. The simulations in this work are used to exemplify our approach and not to determine specific values.

3.1 Simulation with Fixed Values

The first step for building a simulation with failures and restore times is defining an arrival rate for failures, their classification, and the repair rate related to the classification. The training level of IT-Experts is represented as real value between 0 and 1, where 0 means no training at all and a value of 1 defines perfectly educated personnel. The occurrence of disruptions is represented by a Poisson process [12] characterized by the values in Table 1. Further, the simulation model uses exponentially distributed repair times whose expected values depend on the category and the corresponding training level. Their basic value, i.e. considering the training level to be 1, can also be found in Table 1.

In order to give a formalized description of the model let $k \in \{1, 2, 3\}$ be the failure category and $a_k \in (0, 1]$ the associated training level. We assume the repair time $t_r(k)$ of a failure of category k to be exponentially distributed with rate $\lambda_k \cdot a_k$, where λ_k is the basic rate of the category k. These definitions lead to the following considerations. If a person is not trained at all, i.e. $a_k \to 0$, the limit value of the expected repair rate $E(t_r(k)) = 1 / (\lambda_k \cdot a_k)$ is directed to infinity. If on the other hand the IT-expert is perfectly trained and $a_k = 1$, $t_r(k) \sim \exp(\lambda_k)$.

In a simulation run the failures of each category appear independently. This leads in a first step to a three-dimensional array containing the number of occurrences of failures. Secondly, the repair times are determined and summed up to a single value.

Table 1. Simulation values

OSI-layer	Category	Arrival rate	Expected repair times
1	Easy	1 per day	2 min
2	Medium	0.6 per day	15 min
3	Difficult	0.4 per day	60 min

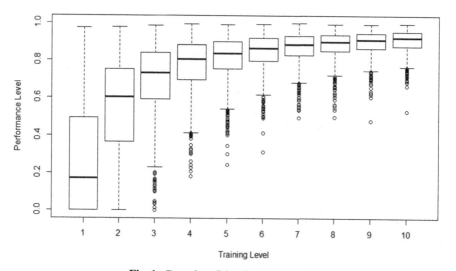

Fig. 1. Box plot of the simulation results

This single time value is divided by the considered time horizon of the simulation to get the percentage of time the simulated system is serviceable, a typical performance measure. The results of repeating these steps for a discrete division of the training level from 0.1 to 1 (scaled from 1 to 10) are represented in Fig. 1. The performance level of 1000 repetitions for each considered level is depicted as box plot.

3.2 Defining the Training Level

The used value for the training level in Sect. 3.1 is defined as a linear increasing integer without any relations. This assumption differs from reality and a way for defining the training level is needed. There is only one possibility to build relations for the training level, an inspection of the training schedule. For example, the schedule of an official Cisco training to achieve the CCNA[1] qualification in Routing & Switching embraces topics about at least the first three OSI layers. The duration of the course is designed with ten days. The main difference between official courses from commercial providers and the military training is about the reached aim. Motivation of military trainings is to drill and educate the students in way that the permanent security of the operation is guaranteed [13]. It is proven that the transmission of knowledge is not enough, especially in situations with a high level of stress. To reach that level of training, every learning process in the military has to be supported by repetitions [14].

This leads to the status quo, military trainings which covers the same topics as trainings from commercial providers take more time, because they include time for practice and repetition. Consequently, for increasing the training level of IT-Experts in military the decisive role is time.

The more difficult it is to troubleshoot a failure (e.g. higher category) the more time is needed in training to increase the training level in this category. Let's say a value 1 represents the training level after passing an existing military training for IT-Experts with a given schedule, reaching a higher training level in every category is the aim of optimize the training. For this purpose, the assumptions in Table 2 are made.

Table 2. Assumptions for increasing the training level

Category	Exercise time	Time to reach next level
Easy	2 days per course	Exercise time × 1.5
Medium	3 days per course	Exercise time × 1.75
Difficult	5 days per course	Exercise time × 2

3.3 Correlation Effects in Training

Defining and separating failure categories does not regard the correlation between the topics which are related to each category. For example, the Address Resolution Protocol

---

[1] CCNA; Cisco Certified Network Associate.

(ARP) which is mandatory in every IPv4 network is located between OSI Layer 2 and 3. Thus, an elemental and necessary question is about the interdependencies between failure categories or rather the connection between the topics and the training levels. Troubleshooting usually starts with a routine or a predefined process. This process is initiated with the inspection of known errors [15], beginning from easy to difficult, what is concurrent with starting at the first layer of OSI Model. Therefore, failures in one Layer can be caused by failures in another Layer [16], for instance an error at Layer 2 produces an error at Layer 3. On the basis of these correlations an increase of exercise and repetition time for troubleshooting OSI Layer 3 problems can also cause a higher training level in all underlying Layers.

This leads to a definition of the training level depending on the third category with the given values in Tables 1 and 2. A decreasing expected repair time for category three failures reduces the time of troubleshooting failures in category one and two, related to the shown correlations. As assumption for a new simulation the effect for decreasing the expected repair rate in category three has an implication of 50% in all underlying categories. Figure 2 shows the results of the new simulation.

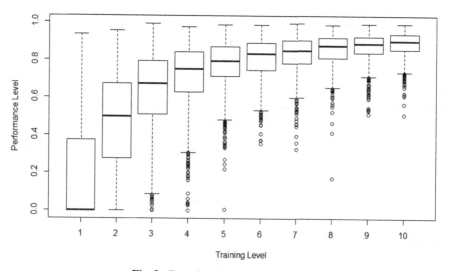

Fig. 2. Box plot of the new simulation

4   Simulations for Optimized Training Schedules: Data Farming

The simulation in Sect. 3.3 takes the correlation effect into account and leads to a training with five days extra per course to reach the next training level. Time is an important factor because every further day in training leads to one day more the student is missing in daily work.

The assumptions made in the simulation are just of theoretical nature and differ from real life settings because a training experience does not increase linear. Progress in training is a highly complex topic and defining quantitative values needs lot of research and experience.

The necessary experience is located in military schools and training facilities. A possible way for research approaches is to collect, compare, inspect, and discuss the many different experiences from students and teachers. The results of these studies could be the basis for further simulations, for example in the context of Data Farming. Data Farming is a popular tool for decision support in the NATO [17]. With the help of improved simulations, it is possible to produce more data whose analyzation is the key for the inspection and quantification of the needed values [18]. The gained knowledge helps to put the simulations about troubleshooting and training level closer to real-life settings. This enables to compare cost and benefit regards to duration of a training and transmitted knowledge (e.g. training level), what directly affects the training schedule.

5 Conclusion

The incidence and frequency of failures in networks, related with network traffic and attacks against the infrastructure is a highly examined research field. Results of this research contribute to achieve the aimed resilience. Our approach tries to add an additional view to reach this goal.

The paper describes a possibility for building a simulation to enlarge the resilience of systems, considering the training for IT-Experts. Resilience can be described as a multi-faced capability which is addressed by multiple ways, for example training [19]. First a simple simulation with theoretical assumptions was build. Small adaptations in this simulation, assumptions about correlation effects in training, showed initial impacts. Defining the values in the simulation and put them into real life settings is the next evaluation step of research. This needs the combination of experience and simulations (e.g. Data Farming & Big Data Analysis) combined with an inspection of human factors [20]. Adapted values can redefine and enable the starting simulation to be part of a bigger system simulation, e.g. a tactical network topology (TNT) [21], in a Resilience Enhancement Circle [22]. As part of system simulation, our concept with the simulation approach could enlarge the resilience of the system as element of the resilience engineering.

References

1. Laprie, J.-C.: From dependability to resilience. In: 38th IEEE/IFIP International Conference on Dependable Systems and Networks, pp. 8–9 (2008)
2. Amdal, J.R., Swigart, S.L.: Resilient Transportation Systems in a Post-Disaster Environment: A Case Study of Opportunities Realized and Missed in the Greater New Orleans Region (2010)
3. Southwick, S.M., Bonanno, G.A., Masten, A.S., Panter-Brick, C., Yehuda, R.: Resilience definitions, theory, and challenges: interdisciplinary perspectives. Eur. J. Psychotraumatol. 5(1), 1–14 (2014)
4. Westrum, R.: A typology of resilience situations. In: Woods, D.D. (ed.) Resilience Engineering, pp. 67–78. CRC Press, Boca Raton (2017)
5. Woods, D.D.: Four concepts for resilience and the implications for the future of resilience engineering. Reliab. Eng. Syst. Saf. 141, 5–9 (2015)
6. Schulte, W.: WAN - Wide Area Network: Einführung in die Technik und Protokolle. VDE VERLAG GmbH, Berlin (2014)

7. Barker, K., Ramirez-Marquez, J.E., Rocco, C.M.: Resilience-based network component importance measures. Reliab. Eng. Syst. Saf. **117**, 89–97 (2013)
8. Paxson, V., Floyd, S.: Wide area traffic: the failure of Poisson modeling. IEEE/ACM Trans. Netw. **3**(3), 226–244 (1995)
9. Faramondi, L., et al.: Network structural vulnerability: a multiobjective attacker perspective. IEEE Trans. Syst. Man Cybern. Syst. **49**, 2036–2049 (2018)
10. Gill, P., Jain, N., Nagappan, N.: Understanding network failures in data centers: measurement, analysis, and implications. ACM SIGCOMM Comput. Commun. Rev. **41**(4), 350–361 (2011)
11. Crucitti, P., Latora, V., Marchiori, M.: Model for cascading failures in complex networks. Phys. Rev. E **69**(4), 045104 (2004)
12. Law, A.M., Kelton, W.D.: Simulation Modeling and Analysis, 3rd edn. McGraw-Hill, New York (2000)
13. Novaco, R.W., Cook, T.M., Sarason, I.G.: Military recruit training. In: Meichenbaum, D., Jaremko, M.E. (eds.) Stress Reduction and Prevention, pp. 377–418. Springer, Boston (1989). https://doi.org/10.1007/978-1-4899-0408-9_12
14. Metzig, W., Schuster, M.: Lernen zu lernen, 9th edn. Springer, Heidelberg (2016). https://doi.org/10.1007/978-3-662-48897-3
15. Dhamdhere, A., Teixeira, R., Dovrolis, C., Diot, C.: NetDiagnoser: troubleshooting network unreachabilities using end-to-end probes and routing data. In: Co-NEXT 2010 Proceedings of the 6th International Conference, pp. 18–30. ACM, New York (2010)
16. Wang, H.J., et al.: Automatic misconfiguration troubleshooting with peer pressure. In: OSDI 2004: 6th Symposium on Operating Systems Design and Implementation, pp. 245–257. USENIX Association, San Francisco (2004)
17. Kallfass, D., Schlaak, T.: NATO MSG-088 case study results to demonstrate the benefit of using data farming for military decision support. In: Proceedings of the Winter Simulation Conference, pp. 221–233. WSC, Berlin (2012)
18. Bein, W., Pickl, S., Tao, F.: Data analytics and optimization for decision support. Bus. Inf. Syst. Eng. **61**(3), 255–256 (2019)
19. Madni, A., Jackson, S.: Towards a conceptual framework for resilience engineering. IEEE Syst. J. **3**, 181–191 (2009)
20. Karwowski, W.: Ergonomics and human factors: the paradigms for science, engineering, design, technology and management of human-compatible systems. Ergonomics **48**(5), 436–463 (2005)
21. Bordetsky, A., Netzer, D.: TNT testbed for self-organizing tactical networking and collaboration. Naval Postgraduate School, Monterey, CA (2009)
22. Panteli, M., Mancarella, P.: The grid: stronger, bigger, smarter?: presenting a conceptual framework of power system resilience. IEEE Power Energy Mag. **13**, 58–66 (2015)

Virtual Reality and Autonomous Systems to Enhance Underwater Situational and Spatial Awareness

Alberto Tremori[(✉)], Arnau Carrera Viñas, David Solarna, Pilar Caamaño Sobrino, and Sasha B. Godfrey

NATO STO Centre for Maritime Research and Experimentation (CMRE),
Viale San Bartolomeo 400, La Spezia, Italy
{Alberto.Tremori,Arnau.Carrera,David.Solarna,Pilar.Caamano,
Sasha.Godfrey}@cmre.nato.int

Abstract. This paper presents a virtual/augmented reality (VR/AR) framework to enhance the situational and spatial awareness at tactical level in the underwater domain. Technology supporting operations in this challenging environment has been scarcely explored in the literature. Consequently, a detailed study has been carried out in order to identify all the steps necessary to transform underwater data into formats suitable for the representation in VR/AR environments. In this context, an application for enhancing the situational and, more precisely, the spatial awareness in the maritime domain has been drafted and proposed.

Keywords: Modelling and simulation · Autonomous systems · Virtual reality · Augmented reality · Situational awareness

1 Introduction

The concept of situational awareness comprises the ability to perceive elements in the environment, comprehend their meaning and be able to project their status in the near future. Similarly, spatial awareness refers to the cognizance of a precise environment and of a precise situation that an operator is supposed to possess while performing a specific activity.

Enhancing situational and spatial awareness is particularly difficult when working with autonomous systems in the underwater environment. Indeed, there exist a "cultural barrier" between the operational community and the adoption of autonomous systems. Another limitation is the difficulty of the operators in representing and interpreting the acoustic data that is usually available from underwater operations. Therefore, the authors believe that a considerable effort is needed this far to improve the awareness in such domain.

To improve the human awareness in preparing, supervising and analysing underwater missions performed by autonomous vehicles, CMRE is proposing the integration of underwater data collected by autonomous systems into a virtual environment. This approach is intended to introduce the concept of augmented virtual reality. In this synthetic

J. Mazal et al. (Eds.): MESAS 2019, LNCS 11995, pp. 306–316, 2020.
https://doi.org/10.1007/978-3-030-43890-6_25

environment, real data collected by different sensors and, possibly, at different times, is provided to the operator within a multi-layer, three-dimensional model of the mission area. The operator is able to visualize and operate in such a virtual environment augmented by multiple layers of information, such as indicators of the estimated quality of information, input from processing algorithms (e.g. anomaly detection), and representation of the environmental characteristics (e.g. currents and temperatures). This approach is designed to support conventional augmented reality applications, such as augmenting the information on the cameras of remotely operated vehicles (ROV).

Examples of application comprise Mine Counter Measure missions, familiar to CMRE, as well new areas of research such as countering underwater IED (Improvised Explosive Device). Operators will be supported by the augmented virtual reality environment during the post-mission analysis, after the mission area has been surveyed by underwater vehicles. The operator first localizes possible targets and then identifies the ones requiring further exploration, recognizing possible targets. In both cases, the mission environment is provided to the operator in a user-friendly format, with three-dimensional models of the objects present in the scene, facilitating data visualization and interpretation and supporting in pursuing the mission objectives.

The paper is organized as follows: Sect. 2 presents a general background on the usage of VR/AR for enhancing situational and spatial awareness; Sect. 3 proposes a VR/AR framework introducing the necessary phases to transform the raw data and integrate them into the VR/AR environment; Sect. 4 describes a use-case example for the designed framework; Sect. 5 draws conclusions and introduces the future challenges related to the proposed architecture.

2 Background on VR/AR Reality Applications for Situational Awareness

This section contains the result of a literature review on state-of-the-art works on using augmented reality and virtual reality techniques to support the enhancement of situational awareness in the maritime domain, especially by decreasing the latency in information comprehension.

The US DoD definition of situational awareness is the ability to "perceive elements in the environment, comprehend their meaning and project their status in the near future" [1, 2]. Acquiring precise situational awareness is paramount for the decision making process. Indeed, the amount of information and data presented to the decision maker can hamper such process. In fact, new warfare scenarios are characterised by an increasing volume of information and by a concurrent reduction of time available to make decisions. These two factors increase the risk of incorrect decision making due to information overload [3].

Multiple experiments, both in the industrial and research environments, have shown the potential of adopting AR and VR for visualising data gathered within multi-asset missions. This approach has also proven valuable to increase users' interaction with the remote mission environment.

In the military domain there are two areas in which VR/AR applications are currently developed [1]:

- Conducting operations: visualisation of plans, asset information, communication network on site, and geography/oceanography data.
- Planning: augmentation of reconnaissance or intelligence information on maps for collaboration and shared awareness between planners both outside and inside the operation area.
- Training and education: creation of a virtual and safe world where user are immersed and provided with a way to gain valuable experience of dangerous or life threating environments from the safety of a training room.

What is the maturity level of this fast-evolving technology? Today, VR/AR military research is devoted to increase the understanding of this technology and demonstrate how it can be adopted for future defence applications. Demonstrations showed that the VR/AR technology is able to shape the decision-making process. The interest of the military community in VR/AR is underlined by their inclusion in programs such as the Multinational Capability Development Campaign (MCDC) [4], an ongoing NATO initiative or the Plan Jericho, which is devoted to implement future high tech solutions in the Royal Australian Air Force [5]. Another example of such applications at national level is provided by the Army of the Czech Republic [6].

The first extensive experiments on conducting operations supported by virtual and augmented reality were conducted by NASA in the late 1990's. Their investigation began in the context of zero-gravity simulations, where control architectures based on virtual reality interfaces were deployed to control tethered vehicles operating underwater [7, 8]. This NASA research evolved over the years and, nowadays, the experimental control station is capable of receiving position telemetry and rendering the vehicle simulated estimated pose in a 3D environment, augmenting video streams and status information [9, 10].

The experiments conducted by NASA paved the way for the investigation of VR/AR applications in other domains. Underwater augmented reality has been successfully applied, especially at tactical level, for remotely operated vehicles and human divers. In those applications, communication uses umbilical tethers and, thanks to the available bandwidth, may rely mainly on optical sensors information. Operations are generally conducted on off-shore installations, where the target is well known, and a continuous 3D view of the vehicle/operator position and orientation in the environment is needed to operate safely [11]. To provide the users with enhanced situational awareness, the virtual environment is used to display reality "as clear as possible", instead of "as real as possible", augmenting the cognitive capabilities of the operator, whose sensing capabilities are hampered by the severe environment.

Diver applications are still at prototype level; the most mature one, to the best of the authors' knowledge, is developed by the US Navy and consists in integrating virtual-environmental data or task-related information on the divers' mask to improve visual cues and increase the understanding of the surroundings. In more detail, such information is aimed at reducing the mental workload of the diver and consists of orientation and position data, navigation aids (arrows pointing to the target, the track of the paths to follow), the 3D model and the simulation of the tasks to be performed [12, 13].

When considering autonomous underwater vehicles (AUVs), the human operator's role shifts from a perceptual/motor-control task to monitoring, reasoning, judging, and tasking. To address these challenges, innovative control stations for maritime vehicles, like NEPTUS [14] or SeeTrack [15], allow visualising incoming real-time data collected by the assets into a virtual mission environment. In particular, multi-mission data collected by different sensors can be combined into a single integrated tactical picture.

VR/AR is also used to generate collaborative working and visualisation environments to support military planning in joint command and control situations. Virtual collaborative desks (VCDs) are platforms designed for knowledge sharing, team collaboration, and decision making. This application proved itself useful for the development of shared situational awareness and common operational pictures [16]. Those virtual environments enable the creation of distributed teams able to operate without a static spatial reference frame across organisations [17]. The adoption of such solutions for command and control (C2) during coalition operations gives rise to context-dependent information release issues. Information exchange policies should be embedded in the C2 systems shared by the coalition, enforcing constraints for information release, data shaping, and policy obligations. A successful attempt in this sense has been done by Carvalho and Ford in the design of NextVC2 [18] proposing a shared virtual reality-based C2 system implementing XACML (eXtensible Access Control Markup Language). This allows users to share the same virtual space, while the individual situational awareness is built up on the specific information filtered according to the user profile.

It is also worth mentioning a few researches on adaptive (also known as intelligent) interfaces. These interfaces embed data mining and machine learning algorithms to discover relevant information, enhance the level of autonomy, and support the operator's decision making process. Adaptive interfaces are designed to improve users speed, accuracy, awareness, coordination, and to reduce their workload [19]. Relevant applications in the autonomous vehicles domain include: (i) providing the users with visual indicators of task relevance and risk while performing the mission [19]; (ii) mapping data into user-defined decision impact values, generating decision surfaces superimposed on the geographical map of the scenario [20]; and (iii) implementing intelligent agents (IA) for decision making [21].

In the military domain, this research topic is developed for instance by the Australian Department of Defence, which is developing a machine learning-based simulation capability coupled with C2 systems to reduce the cognitive burden on human operators producing recommendations, alerts, and constraints, as well as providing autonomy on low level tasks [22]. Moreover, the Czech Army has studied and proposed an architecture to include virtual reality hardware devices in their command, control, communications and intelligence (C3I) current capabilities [23].

3 Tactical VR/AR for Underwater Situational and Spatial Awareness

This paper proposes a VR/AR framework for maritime situational and spatial awareness designed to support the analysis of the mission data collected during underwater operations. The underwater environment is mainly sensed using acoustic sensors, since electromagnetic waves are significantly affected by water absorption. Acoustic sensors facilitate operations at longer ranges and allow working in turbid conditions, at the price of dramatically reducing the available bandwidth [24] and providing, in general, noisy data of lower resolution and more difficult to interpret. The proposed framework aims at enhancing the spatial and situational awareness fusing the collected data into 3D-representable models to visualised using VR/AR in a multi-layer framework.

The proposed approach (see Fig. 1) is supposed to receive multiple inputs coming from different types of sensor. Such data is transformed into point clouds or other 3D-representable formats and merged into a common reference system. Finally, the single point clouds are fused together, filtered, and transformed into a mesh. The final mesh and all the extracted information are provided to the visualisation module through a predefined data structure. Hence, the operator may display the reconstructed scenario augmented with the additional information taking advantage of the visualisation engine and the VR/AR.

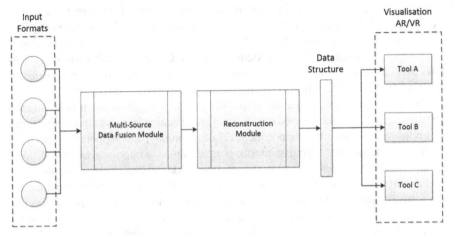

Fig. 1. High-level flowchart of the proposed approach

As it can be appreciated from the flowchart, the proposed methodology is independent from the type of input data, aiming at interfacing with all the sensors available to the user. Indeed, in the requirement definition phase, the user specifies the type of data to be integrated in the VR/AR framework. Hence, a format-specific module is designed to extract point clouds, or other 3D-representable information, from that specific raw data. Figure 2 shows the most common types of acoustic sensors, which can be classified as: (i) imagining sonars, measuring the reflectivity of the seafloor (side-scan sonar and forward-looking sonar); and (ii) sonar delivering range measurements (echo sounder, profiling sonar or multibeam echo sounder) [24].

Different solutions exist to convert all such data sources to 3D objects. For imagining sonars we can find examples like [28], which uses data from a side-looking sonar, and [29, 30] using a forward-looking sonar. Conversely, for range sonar we can highlight examples like [31] or [32].

Following the pipeline, the point clouds extracted from the input data (Fig. 3, phase 1) are filtered to reduce noise and fused in a common reference system (Fig. 3, phase 2). The resulting point cloud, containing 3D information of multiple data, is interpolated

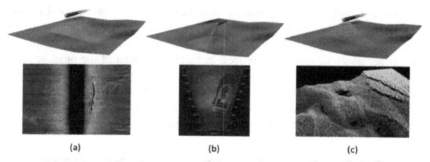

Fig. 2. Different types of sonar, with details on the acquisition geometry and the resulting data: (a) a side-scan sonar system with the acoustic images generated by the two side looks; (b) a forward-looking sonar system with an example of the resulting 2D image; and (c) a multibeam echosounder with the corresponding point cloud. The images are from [25, 26], and [27].

and refined to obtain a smoother surface (Fig. 3, phase 3). Different techniques (e.g., [33–35] and [36]) exist to transform the unorganized point cloud information into a surface providing a comprehensible visual representation (Fig. 4).

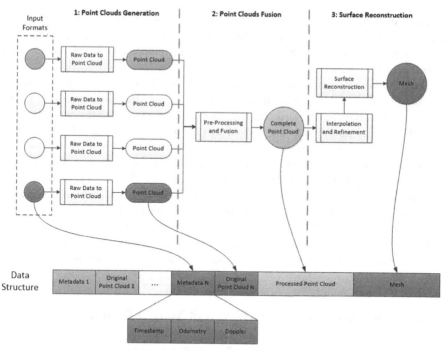

Fig. 3. Flowchart of the proposed approach displaying details in the "Multi-Source Data Fusion Module", "Reconstruction Modules", and on the data structure to interface with the visualization tool.

It is worth noting that the algorithm is designed to store the raw input data, meta-data, all the intermediate results obtained through the processing chain, and the final reconstructed surface into a data structure. This structure is designed for all the cases where it is necessary to access and process not a single output of the pipeline but the whole information, either the original data or the results. It is the case for example of the tactical use case of next section, where the reconstructed seafloor is augmented with additional pieces of information, for example the result of a change detection application, and presented to a Mine Countermeasure (MCM) operator.

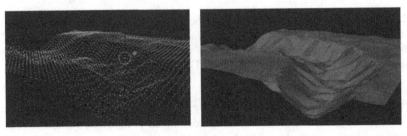

Fig. 4. Example of surface reconstruction from a point cloud. The images are from [37].

In this context, the user of the VR/AR may decide to enrich the visualised scene with additional information (e.g., segmentation, classification, cinematic characterization, environmental data, etc.). To fulfil this need, the data structure contains a set of features generated by such user-specific processing.

Once the information is transferred to the VR/AR, the user will be able to select different visualisation modalities from the graphical user interface according to the features contained in the data structure (e.g., colour the changes with respect to the past, shade the objects according to the probability of error, highlight possible threats, add cinematic-related information etc.).

The integration of the 3D models into the VR/AR framework may be performed by different applications (e.g., Unity3D, Unreal Engine, OpenGL, etc.). The high interoperability between the proposed pipeline and the possible visualisation tools is achieved thanks to the transmission of a fixed data structure through a tool-specific interface. The data structure is filled with the extracted information while the input data is processed through the pipeline. According to the user requirements, it may be possible to develop a custom interface able to transform and provide the data structure to any visualisation tool.

4   An Example of Usage for MCM and M-IED Scenarios

This section will briefly describe a case-specific implementation, where VR/AR capabilities will support the operations performed during an MCM mission, or during counter-IED (C-IED) operations in the context of port protection.

VR/AR, according to the authors, is supposed to be used during post-mission analysis, where the operator will be able to navigate in the reconstructed environment, visualise different types of information according to the current needs, and take decisions with such an awareness that traditional systems do not provide.

For the two scenarios, we assume the input data to be collected by high-frequency multibeam echosounders, able to provide high-resolution range measurements. This assumption is consistent with the work done at CMRE, where this type of sensor is mounted on MCM-specific vehicles and it is used to collect data during missions. The generation of point clouds from multibeam data (Fig. 5, phase 1) requires less effort with respect to other cases, where the sensors do not provide distance information but only reflectivity measurements (non-interferometric SAS, FLS, etc.).

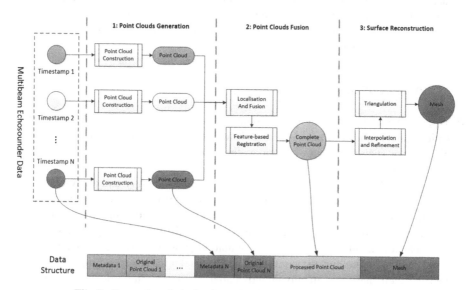

Fig. 5. Processing chain for the MCM or IED specific methodology.

The second phase of the pipeline (Fig. 5, phase 2) integrates multiple data into the same reference system. This will be accomplished in possibly two steps. First, a localization procedure will be used to geo-reference the resulting points by combining the range measurements with the metadata coming from the vehicle. The localisation allows defining a common reference system for each point cloud. Second, registration techniques may be used to refine the results and reduce the impact of possible localisation errors. Implementations of registration techniques, such as the iterative closest point algorithm and the SIFT feature-based registration, will be provided by the PCL library [30].

The reconstruction of a surface from the resulting point cloud (Fig. 5, phase 3) will be performed using a triangulation procedure. Different implementations are provided by the PCL library. However, before being triangulated, the points are interpolated and refined so as to possibly obtain a smoother surface. In addition, procedures working directly on the mesh may be used to further enhance the final surface. Among other, within the PCL library it is possible to apply Laplacian smoothing, which makes the cells better shaped and distributes the vertices more evenly.

Finally, as depicted at the bottom of Fig. 5, the entire set of input data and the results of all the steps of the processing chain will be collected in a data structure. The data structure will be sent to the visualisation tool, which will use the information to provide the operator with a VR/AR environment. Leveraging on the complete information contained in such a structure, the operator will be able not only to visualise the reconstructed seafloor with possibly reconstructed targets, but also to use the available metadata to augment the information being presented.

An example is the possibility for the operator to access historical data and, taking advantage of the timestamps contained in the data structures, visualise the result of change detection algorithms. While processing the data collected during a particular mission, the operator may compare the reconstructed seafloor with the reconstructions output from previous missions. Indeed, the multiple sources of information will be overlaid in the same virtual environment.

5   Conclusions and Way Ahead

This paper focuses on the on-going investigation about the adoption of VR/AR to enhance situational and spatial awareness in the underwater domain, with a specific focus on the application of such techniques to support the visualization and detection of potential threats on the seafloor.

A state of the art has been accomplished in order to identify and analyse existing works. Leveraging on the collected information, the M&S CMRE team has identified an application where VR and AR may bring added value to support operations, to train operators and, last but least, to overcome an existing cultural gap between the operational community and the adoption of autonomous systems in those environment that are challenging to human operators. The proposal aims at supporting operators by increasing their maritime situational and spatial awareness. In particular, this will be achieved by providing the operator with underwater data in a user-friendly format and by collecting the available information (e.g., vehicle-related information, uncertainty, etc.) in a unique framework.

The CMRE M&S team is studying a processing pipeline necessary to propose VR/AR applications based on raw underwater sensor data collected by autonomous systems. Such an innovative framework is expected to have an impact in supporting the analysis of the data collected during underwater missions. In particular, the identification of threats in an MCM or M-IED scenarios was used as use case for the proposed approach.

CMRE will continue working on the development of the proposed framework. At the end of the first quarter of the 2020, the CMRE should deliver and demonstrate a prototype for concept development in a harbour protection M-IED scenario.

Acknowledgements. The researches described in this paper have been funded by Allied Command Transformation in the PARC project and by the NATO Head Quarter Defence Against Terrorism Programme of Work (DAT POW).

References

1. Riley, J., Endsley, M., Bolstad, C., Cuevas, H.: Collaborative planning and situation awareness in army command and control. Ergonomics **49**(12–13), 1139–1153 (2006)
2. Papasin, R., et al.: Intelligent virtual station. In: 7th International Symposium (2003)
3. Zocco, A., De Paolis, L.: Augmented command and control table to support network-centric operations. Def. Sci. J. **65**(1), 39 (2015)
4. NATO C2 Centre for Excellence: MCDC 2017-18 - Information Age Command and Control Concepts. https://wss.apan.org/s/MCDCpub/MCDC1718/MCDC_201718_Public_Shared_Documents/MCDC_17-18_Project_Fact_Sheets/MCDC_17-18_InfoAgeC2_Project.pdf. Accessed 24 Jan 2018
5. VR Scout: The Australian Air Force is Now Testing the Microsoft HoloLens. https://vrscout.com/news/the-australian-air-force-is-now-testing-the-microsoft-hololens. Accessed 23 Jan 2017
6. Františ, P., Hodický, J.: Virtual reality in presentation layer of C3I system. In: MODSIM05 - International Congress on Modelling and Simulation: Advances and Applications for Management and Decision Making, Proceedings, pp. 3045–3050 (2005)
7. Fleischer, S., Rock, S., Lee, M.: Underwater vehicle control from a virtual environment interface. In: Symposium on Interactive 3D Graphics, Monterey, CA, USA, April 1995
8. Piguet, L., Hine, B., Hontalas, P., Fong, T., Nygren, E.: The virtual environment vehicle interface: a dynamic, distributed and flexible virtual environment. In: IMAGINA 1996: New Frontiers of CyberExistence (1996)
9. Stoll, E., Wilde, M., Pong, C.: Using virtual reality for human-assisted in-space robotic assembly. In: World Congress on Engineering and Computer Science (2009)
10. Bualat, M.: Astrobee Space Station Robotic Free Flyer. NASA. https://ntrs.nasa.gov/archive/nasa/casi.ntrs.nasa.gov/20160009763.pdf. Accessed 28 July 2016
11. Lin, Q., Kuo, C.: Assisting the teleoperation of an unmanned underwater vehicle using a synthetic subsea scenario. Presence **8**(5), 520–530 (1999)
12. US DoD: Eyes in the Dark: Navy Dive Helmet Display Emerges as Game-Changer. https://www.defense.gov/News/Article/Article/873877/eyes-in-the-dark-navy-dive-helmet-display-emerges-as-game-changer/. Accessed 27 July 2016
13. Morales, R., Keitler, P., Maier, P., Klinker, G.: An underwater augmented reality system for commercial diving operations. In: OCEANS, Biloxi, MS, USA. IEEE (2009)
14. LSTS: NEPTUS Command and Control Software. https://lsts.fe.up.pt/toolchain/neptus
15. SeeByte: SeaTrack V4. http://www.seebyte.com/military/seetrack-military/
16. Louvieris, P., Collins, C., Mashanovich, N.: Investigating the use and effectiveness of virtual collaboration desks for collaborative military planning. In: 42nd Hawaii International Conference on System Sciences, HICSS 2009 (2009)
17. Duklis, P.: The Joint Reserve Component Virtual Information Operations organization (JRVIO); Cyber Warriors Just a Click Away, Carlisle Barracks, PA, U.S. (2006)
18. Carvalho, M., Ford, R.: NextVC2—a next generation virtual world command and control. In: Military Communications Conference, MIILCOM, pp. 1–6 (2012)
19. Roldan, J., Peña-Tapia, E., Martín-Barrio, A., Olivares-Méndez, M., Del Cerro, J., Barrientos, A.: Multi-robot interfaces and operator situational awareness: study of the impact of immersion and prediction. Sensors **17**(8), 1720 (2017)
20. Smallman, H.S., Rieth, C.A.: ADVICE: decision support for complex geospatial decision making tasks. In: Lackey, S., Chen, J. (eds.) VAMR 2017. LNCS, vol. 10280, pp. 453–465. Springer, Cham (2017). https://doi.org/10.1007/978-3-319-57987-0_37
21. Hou, M., Kobierski, R., Herdman, C.: Design and evaluation of intelligent adaptive operator interfaces for the control of multiple UAVs. In: NATO RTO HFM 135 Symposium, Biarizze, France (2006)

22. Machine Learning & Recommender Systems for C2 of Autonomous Vehicles. https://www.dst.defence.gov.au/sites/default/files/events/documents/ISTAS-2016_Machine_Learning_Recommender_Systems_Glenn-Moy.pdf

23. Františ, P., Hodický, J.: Virtual reality in presentation layer of C3I system. In: MODSIM05 - International Congress on Modelling and Simulation: Advances and Applications for Management and Decision Making, Melbourne, Australia, pp. 3045–3050 (2005)

24. Urick, R.: Principles of Underwater Sound, 3rd edn. Peninsula Publishing, Newport Beach (2013)

25. Hurtós, N.: Forward-looking sonar mosaicing for underwater environments. Universitat de Girona, Girona, Spain (2014)

26. https://noaacoastsurvey.wordpress.com/tag/side-scan-sonar/

27. https://www.idaholidar.org/blog/2015/04/14/nsf-grant-to-develop-lidar-tools/

28. Coiras, E., Groen, J.: 3D target shape from SAS images based on a deformable mesh. In: Proceedings of the 3rd International Conference and Exhibition on Underwater Acoustic Measurements: Technologies and Result, Nafplion, Greece (2009)

29. Guerneve, T., Petillot, Y.: Underwater 3D reconstruction using BlueView imaging sonar. In: IEEE Oceans, Genova, Italy (2005)

30. Trucco, A., Curletto, S.: Extraction of 3D information from sonar image sequences. IEEE Trans. Syst. Man Cybern. Part B (Cybern.) **33**(4), 687–699 (2003)

31. Kulawiak, M., Lubniewski, Z.: 3D imaging of underwater objects using multi-beam data. Hydroacustic **17**, 123–128 (2014)

32. Machado, D., Furfaro, T., Dugelay, S.: Micro-bathymetry data acquisition for 3D reconstruction of objects on the sea floor. In: OCEANS 2017, Aberdeen, UK (2017)

33. Hoppe, H., DeRose, T., Duchamp, T., McDonald, J.: Surface reconstruction from unorganized points. In: Proceedings of the 19th Annual Conference on Computer Graphics and Interactive Techniques, New York, NW, USA (1992)

34. Kazhdan, M., Bolitho, M., Hoppe, H.: Poisson surface reconstruction. In: Proceedings of the Fourth Eurographics Symposium on Geometry Processing, Aire-la-Ville, Switzerland (2006)

35. Amenta, N., Choi, S., Dey, T.K., Leekha, N.: A simple algorithm for homeomorphic surface reconstruction. In: Proceedings of the Sixteenth Annual Symposium on Computational Geometry, New York, NY, USA (2000)

36. Cohen-Steiner, D., Da, F.: A Greed Delaunay-based surface reconstruction algorithm. Visual Comput. Int. J. Comput. Graphics **20**(1), 4–16 (2004). https://doi.org/10.1007/s00371-003-0217-z

37. https://github.com/domlysz/BlenderGIS/wiki/Make-terrain-mesh-with-Delaunay-triangulation

Smartness and Autonomy for Shipboard Power Systems Reconfiguration

Massimo Cossentino, Salvatore Lopes, Giovanni Renda, Luca Sabatucci[✉],
and Flavia Zaffora

National Research Council of Italy (CNR), Istituto di Calcolo e Reti ad Alte
Prestazioni (ICAR), Via U. La Malfa, 153, Palermo, Italy
{massimo.cossentino,salvatore.lopes,giovanni.renda,
luca.sabatucci,flavia.zaffora}@icar.cnr.it
http://www.ecos.pa.icar.cnr.it

Abstract. Smart Ships represent the next generation of ships that use ICT to connect all the devices on board for integrated monitoring and safety management. In such a context, the Shipboard Power System (SPS) is critical to the survival and safety of the ship because many accidents are due to electrical failures. The SPS reconfiguration consists of a variation of the electrical topology to supply energy to critical services successfully. The proposed reconfiguration procedure uses an autonomous and mission-oriented approach, and it employs a generic-purpose self-adaptive Fault Management System.

It delivers a set of possible runtime solutions that properly consider the current ship mission and operating scenario while dealing with multiple failures.

Solutions, achieving a partial reconfiguration of the system, are considered when a full recovery strategy is not available according to the current ship conditions.

1 Introduction

Today, ships transport about 80% of the world's commodities, and this trend continues to rise in the next years. Most commercial ships run on diesel oil, and they produce sulfur and nitrogen oxides, CO2, soot particles and fine dust as exhaust gases. According to the International Maritime Organization, maritime transport produces one billion tons of CO2 each year; that is, it is responsible for almost 2.5% of total greenhouse gas emissions.

The exhaust gases have substantial consequences for people and the environment. There is an international commitment for reducing ship emissions, using fuel with less sulfur and special filters or alternative energy sources such as liquefied natural gas (LNG), hydrogen, or electric energy.

Recently, many ships use diesel-electric transmission system. Diesel generator produces electricity that drives not only electric engines but also almost all the on-board equipment such as the lighting systems, air conditioning, and all the

© Springer Nature Switzerland AG 2020
J. Mazal et al. (Eds.): MESAS 2019, LNCS 11995, pp. 317–333, 2020.
https://doi.org/10.1007/978-3-030-43890-6_26

devices for the ship's normal operations. These ships can save up to 20% of fuel in operating condition, and all the machinery suffers a lower number of faults.

Consequently, the management and control of the ship power system (disregarding the way electricity is produced) is a crucial factor for efficiency and, above all, safety (power system reliability, fault-safeness). New technologies, like the Internet of Things (IoT), is going to be extensively used in new generation ships. Therefore it becomes essential to develop ICT powerful tools for optimizing not only fuel/energy consumption but also for restoring safe operation conditions after an electrical fault or accident.

The component that governs the inner life of a ship is the Shipboard Power System (SPS) that supplies power to critical systems like navigation, communication, and combat operations. During normal operation conditions, once a mission is settled, faults and failures in the shipboard power system can occur, and reconfiguration is needed. Such a process consists of a variation of the electrical topology to successfully restore energy to critical services by selecting the loads that are necessary to accomplish the mission. Sometimes reconfiguration occurs under hard constraints: available power is not sufficient to feed all the loads; it could be the case to consider partial solutions.

Moreover, recent accidents have shown the real importance of a timely response in restoring the electrical power, to pursue survivability and navigation safety for the passengers, the crew, and the ship.

Run-time reconfiguration implies the close integration of the electric part (together with monitoring/control devices) with the software control part with reasoning attitudes. The overall system should be able to take decisions and to adapt according to different scenarios.

Such a system frames as a Smart Cyber-Physical System (CPS) with autonomous behavior and the capability to provide timely response and safe reconfiguration solutions. It is also important to underline the role of the human. The crew may both participate in the reconfiguration, and the commander is in charge of supervising the reconfiguration enactment.

This paper articulates as follows: Sect. 2 explores the problem of developing a smart and autonomous SPS reconfiguration; Sect. 3 presents the software architecture conceived for the purpose. Afterward, Sect. 4 presents the testbed we developed for evaluating the proposed approach. Finally, in Sect. 5, we discuss the challenges for future works and the implementation of the experiment on a larger scale.

2   The Problem

The Shipboard Power Systems (SPS) is the electrical spine running through a ship that governs almost all of its parts. This electrical skeleton supplies power to loads, explicitly classified in non-vital, semi-vital, and vital [2]. Vital loads are so defined because they are non-sheddable loads that directly affect the survivability of the ship, while the non-vital ones may be shed to prevent a total loss of ship's electrical power, or for protection purposes.

This categorization may change due to a change of the mission or if some unprevented event occurs so that some previously vital load turns into semi-vital or non-vital (and vice-versa).

The purpose of the paper is to present how to face the issue of adaptation and reconfiguration methods for Shipboard Power Systems. The reconfiguration procedure is driven by the 'control system' that communicates with all the generators and loads to keep the continuity of service during reconfiguration operations. To successfully reconfigure the SPS, the proposed CPS should fulfill the following requirements:

- smartness, i.e., the system should show a reasoning aptitude (agent-oriented paradigm);
- adaptivity, that means the system can efficiently adapt to environmental changes;
- distribution: the system is heterogeneous and its (physical and software) components are located in different places;
- real-time: the system is able to promptly perceive environment events.

Notably, three qualities are strictly compulsory:

Autonomy: The property of autonomy yields to define components that are not necessarily activated by humans. Autonomy is an essential property of those systems (such as ambient intelligence and cyber-physical system) that must be able to manage themself to address their goals. Autonomous agents may carry out actions in an automated manner when certain conditions hold. Moreover, multi-agents systems provide a flexible instrument to decompose a complex system into a set of autonomous entities. They also offer a new metaphor in which computing is something that happens by and through communication [12].

Smartness: Smart reconfiguration methodologies are a challenging task that needs complex coordination between electrical power and protective functions. This feature must preserve human intervention, that is always the final decision-maker. The smartness quality implies the use of some reasoning method. A concrete contribution comes from the adoption of goal-driven methodologies and the BDI paradigm [15] in which Belief, Desire, and Intention are inspired to the human cognition.

Adaptation: As Russell Ackoff says [1], "a system is adaptive if, when there is a change in its environmental and/or internal state reducing its efficiency in pursuing some of its goals, it reacts or responds by changing its state or that of the environment to increase its efficiency in pursuing that goal". Agent-oriented architectures support adaptation because the entities could communicate with each other and react to the modified state of the environment [27]. In the maritime domain, faults are malfunctions of some devices in the electrical circuit and the ship's mission is composed of goals, each of them represents the necessity to supply power to a specific load.

Qureshi et al. [14] classifies the self-adaptation systems in four main groups:

1. Type I - Systems with anticipated reactions: they have one single plan developed at design-time.
2. Type II - Systems with many strategies to be applied at run-time: the strategies are employed following the monitoring of the environment.
3. Type III - Systems with dynamic goals: the knowledge they base on is uncertain, they change their goals and functionalities according to the changing environment.
4. Type IV - Self-inspecting and self-modifying systems: alike biological systems, they continuously adapt where no other refinements are possible.

Recently we have conducted an extensive survey of approaches to SPS [24], discovering most of the reconfiguration algorithm adopts adaptation of type I and II. The strategy, shown in this paper, can be placed in the third group, trying to develop the better features performed by a goal-oriented [9,22], runtime adaptive systems [18,20], using a multi-agent system and a multi-paradigm approach [8].

The proposed approach embraces a series of possible scenarios, goals, and decisions based on functional and non-functional requirements [19]. Goals can be prescriptive and correspond to functional requirements [22] when related to onboard operations, or they can be soft if they are goals that can be partially fulfilled [9]. The adoption of goals allows to obtain a description of the expected behavior in terms of loads that must be powered [6]. The hierarchy of goals and subgoals is here managed by the setting of a Mission, that relates loads priority with goals and human decision. The reconfiguration system is compliant to the set mission and to the varying importance of goals according to the failures occurred. A failure is the trigger for the adaptive system to enact the reconfiguration. The degree of autonomy in the decision process often measures the ability of the system to take decisions about its behaviour: the level of abstraction used in the decision process has a great impact on the mechanisms for the adaptation [10]. Feedback loop then is a key concept for automatic processes in self-adaptive system [3], especially for the final human control, because it improves reliability and robustness of the system itself [6].

The next section presents an architecture supporting autonomy, smartness and adaptation for shipboard power systems reconfiguration.

3   An Architecture for Autonomous and Smart Systems

This section illustrates the proposed solution, based on a middleware for building self-adaptive systems, and on Matlab/Simulink for physical simulations of the resulting configuration.

3.1   The Three Levels of Autonomy

Autonomy is a paramount aspect of complex adaptive systems in which some design decisions move towards run-time when the state of the system and its environment are defined. Such category of systems emphasizes the need for explicitly designing the architecture as a feedback loop [3]. Indeed, the feedback loop (or closed loop) is a generic mechanism for grounding autonomic reasoning and decision making (about the action to be executed) on the observation of the context.

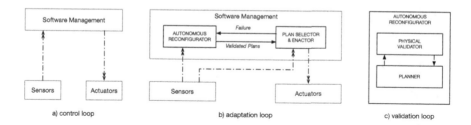

Fig. 1. Abstract view of the three kind of feedback loops

In order to realize the intended autonomy and the capability of the system to react to changes in the environment as well as the goal or the system performance, we introduced three different feedback loops that will be described in the following.

(a) **The Control Loop**: it realizes the close relationship between hardware (with Sensors, and Actuators) and software (with the Management function). Cyber-Physical Systems (CPSs) are complex systems characterized by a closed-loop interaction between physical and computational entities, as shown in Fig. 1a. The overall system is instrumented with software monitors of hardware sensors, and with software reconfiguration actions enacted by hardware actuators. Sensors provide raw measurements from the hardware, and actuators are related to control the electric layer functionalities. Sensors and actuators are related by a control and decision component (the software Management), which implements the dynamic adaptation policy or strategy.

(b) **The Adaptation Loop**: it realizes the SPS self-repairing system (Fig. 1b). As a consequence of a failure, the Autonomous Reconfigurator generates a set of solutions (reconfiguration plans) by composing primitive actions to address the current ship's Mission. A mission is a description of the relation between the operating context and the degree of priority to be assigned to the system goals[1]. During the execution of one of these plans, errors and failures may happen, thus leading the Reconfigurator to modify its job and to produce different solutions. The reconfiguration of power flows in the electrical circuit is defined as a state search problem. The primitive actions are, mainly, tied up to the switchers that may be used to change the configuration. Other actions are task delegations towards human operators onboard (crew). Plan failures may happen due to hardware and software malfunctioning.

---

[1] Goals are classified by different priority depending on the specific context. Thus, the reconfiguration system always prefers to address higher priority goals.

(c) **The Validation loop**: it ensures the physical reliability of the generated plans for reconfiguring the circuit (Fig. 1c). It consists of two collaborating layers: the Planner, that works at a conceptual model, and the Physical Validator which adopts a more precise physical model. At the conceptual level, the electrical topology is modeled as a set of first-order logic rules, like:

```
generator(mg1).
...
switcher(sw_1).
...
load(load1).
...
on(load1):- closed(sw_1), up(n10).
up(n10):- up(n1).
up(n10):- up(n11), closed(swp1).
...
up(n11):- closed(swp1), up(n10).
...
```

The model grounds on a simple ontology in which node, load, generator, and switcher are terms for describing electrical elements, up and down (powered/not powered) are the properties of a node, and open/closed are the properties of a switcher. Connections between the nodes in the circuit render as 'premises-conclusion' sentences. The previous slice of code asserts that circuit is made of a set of elements (generators, switches and loads). Then it asserts the fact that load L1 is connected to node 10 via the switcher sw_1. It receives power when the node is up, and the corresponding switch is closed. Node 10, in turn, receives energy from two nodes: node 1 and node 11 via the switcher swp1. Each connection rule also has a reciprocal rule. Therefore it is necessary to specify also that node 11 is connected to node 10 via the same switch swp1. Whereas the conceptual model is suitable for fast planning, it lacks many details that exist in the real circuit. For this reason, a Physical Validator is instrumented with a Matlab/Simulink model of the same circuit. It is responsible for verifying the correct functioning of the generated solution, thus avoiding phenomena like generators overload. This way, only the solutions that pass this check are available for the execution.

3.2 The Overall Architecture for Smart Management

In the rest of the section, we discuss the main components of the proposed architecture [8] for shipboard power system reconfiguration (see Fig. 2). It is characterized by three distinctive features: (1) it is a cyber-physical system, (2) it adopts complex decision making algorithms, and (3) it encompass the human in the loop.

The core component is the **Proactive Means-End Reasoning** [18] that is responsible for iteratively producing reconfiguration solutions to repair electrical failures. This module works at the conceptual level, and it adopts the following elements.

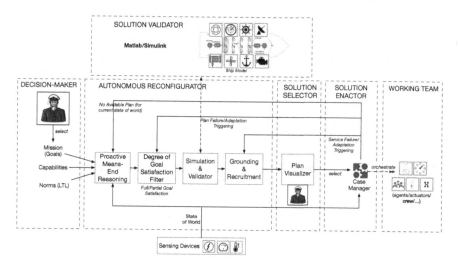

Fig. 2. The detailed architecture of the proposed fault management system

The *State of World* is the description of the perceived state of the electrical circuit, including the state of switchers and ammeters. It is implemented as an agent's belief, i.e., a set of non-contradictory predicates that are believed to be true.

The *Goal* is a desired state of the world the system wants to achieve [22]. In this domain, a goal could describe which loads should be supplied. As an example, let us consider an electric system composed of 3 loads (bulb lights), two generators providing input power to the system and three on/off switches to control the flow of power reaching the loads. A goal could express the on/off condition of each load. In the framework, a goal is expressed via linear temporal logic (LTL) [17], and it is a run-time element, i.e., it is injected into the system at run-time (and therefore it is not known apriori by agents), and it may change during the course of the execution. Goals are collected in the form of a Mission, that associates each goal with a level of priority. Together with goals, LTL can be used to specify behavioral norms that must be taken in considerations during the plan generation.

The *Capability* describes an action that is available in the domain for modifying the state of the world [20]. The ability to pilot the circuit switchers is encoded as system capabilities. Every agent in the system knows its capabilities and how (and when) to use them.

The planning algorithm explores the space of reconfiguration solutions by composing different sequences of capabilities, starting from the last known state of the world, to address as many as possible goals in the current mission.

The second component of the architecture is the **Degree of Goal Satisfaction Filter**. It adopts a heuristic for ordering the generated solutions according to which extent they address the mission's goals.

Let us take the goal "the navigation system, the communication system, and the radar system should be powered". In case of severe malfunctioning, when the main generators are off, the auxiliary generators are switched on. Let us suppose they can not produce enough power for the three components to work correctly. For such a reason, the system should produce plans for partially restoring the energy on board, even if not all goals are fully satisfied.

The heuristic considers two factors: (1) a domain-independent factor that is the distance from the full goal satisfaction, (2) a domain-dependent factor that is the quality of solution according to physical measures.

Distance from the full goal satisfaction. Many different ways may be conceived to measure this distance. We studied an analogy, where we consider each sub-condition specified in the goal as a piece of an electric circuit, more specifically as a resistor [9]. The value of this resistor is either close to 0 (short circuit) if the condition holds or be a great value (labeled R_{max}) if the condition is far to be addressed.

The *quality of solution (according to physical measures)* considers: the priority assigned to shaded loads, over/under usage of the generators, and the kind of employed generators (main vs. auxiliary) [23]. This metric is used to compare solutions with the same degree of goal satisfaction. In future works, it also considers the presence of human actions in the solution.

Simulation and Validation. Cyber-physical systems are often safety-critical: in such cases, software embedded in devices has the capability of both helping people and killing people. It is necessary to provide adequate confidence that their behavior conforms to established requirements [16]. Whereas assurance is typically performed at design and development time, in our architecture, the behavior is generated at run-time; therefore, it yields a run-time verification [5]. To this aim, the architecture comprises a Simulation and Validation module that operates to check physical details that may be concealed in the conceptual model for planning. Indeed, each generated plan is simulated through this module to become available and executable. The module exploits an instance of Matlab (with Simulink) in which the electrical circuit is modeled. Therefore, a Matlab script sets up the initial conditions and simulates each single actions. The objective is verifying that physical values (voltage and current) remain within given thresholds along with the whole plan execution. Another objective of the simulation is to extract other QoS values that can not be calculated in the conceptual model, for instance, the exact percentage of power produced by each generator to enable optimal utilization of each source and to avoid overloading it.

Grounding and Recruitment. The basic approach for executing the generated plan is to employ a multi-agent system in which each agent represents one electric component in the power system layer. Multi-agent systems allow the natural distribution of the code across logical and physical nodes. In our architecture, we introduce a hierarchical control and decomposition of functionalities. This introduces a necessary level of coordination, but, at the same time, ensures to strengthen the overall robustness. The *Grounding and Recruitment* component is responsible for the phase of agent recruitment to make the solution concrete and executable. Further details are in [21].

Plan Visualizer. The *Plan Visualizer* is a presentation component that has the responsibility to enable the human decision-maker to select the preferred reconfiguration strategy to be enacted. The presentation exploits a graphical representation of the circuit to highlight switch operations and final load configuration (see Fig. 3).

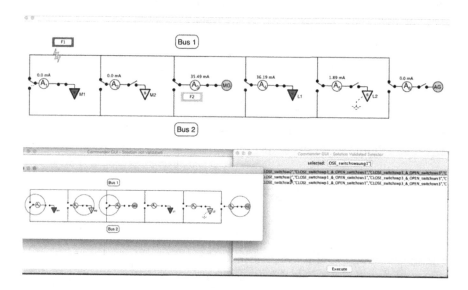

Fig. 3. The GUI for selecting one of the validated solutions

Case Manager. The hierarchical group of agents is responsible for granting the execution of the selected plan. The *Case Manager* works like a distributed workflow management system. It is enriched with execution supervision and management of errors and failures. For further details, please refer to [7].

4   Experimental Evaluation

In a broader sense, smart ships are vessels that are able to sail and operate by themselves. There are two broad categories of smart ships: unmanned ships and autonomous ships. Unmanned vessels are remotely piloted by an operator on a control center. Autonomous ships should be equipped with a computer system that can monitor all the running services onboard and take decisions to optimize sailing operations. While it is unlikely that the human contribution to the ship control could be eliminated, it is reasonable to foresee that the crew size would be dramatically reduced. In that way, shipping companies could reduce personnel expenses and leave more space for goods. Moreover, there is also a safety concern since around 70 to 80% of marine accidents at sea are a result of human error, often because of a not enough skilled crew.

However, the vision of a fully autonomous vessel may be addressed incrementally, where some degrees of smartness can be introduced on board to help the crew to manage the complexity of navigation tasks. In this paper, we focus on the shipboard power sub-system of a vessel.

A common configuration of a shipboard power system presents two power buses where all electric devices or sub-systems are connected (Fig. 4).

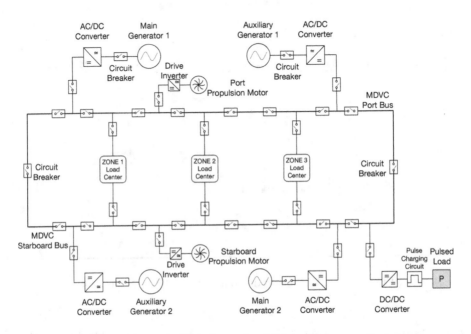

Fig. 4. The typical topology of a shipboard power system

In our experiment, we used a real scaled model to prove our approach. The next section reports a detailed description of the logic model and the physical implementation.

Although that could seem a simplification of the real vessel SPS complexity, it constitutes a good testbed for demonstrating the goodness of the proposed approach. All the basic components of an electric power system are included in the logic model and implemented with small scale devices. This model could be further detailed using a hierarchical representation of services and loads. In this way, the model can be as detailed as it is necessary to be. A single load representing an aggregation of several loads or sub-systems can be disaggregated with the real characterization of every single load or sub-system. A more detailed model is just useful for more in-depth control of single loads, but it does not affect the way loads are managed or the operating strategies for resolving eventual electric power loss.

4.1 Specification of the Proposed Testbed

To validate the proposed approach, we developed a testbed that represents a simplified model of DC-powered AEV. Figure 5 reports the electrical schema of the considered exemplary vessel. It is a dual bus power system with two electric engines, two simple loads and two generators: a main generator that is able to feed the entire list of loads and an auxiliary generator who can only feed one engine (M1, for instance, in Fig. 5) and one resistive load (L1, for instance, in Fig. 5).

In the following, we report details of the realized prototype. It is the result of the overlapping of three different layers: *(i)* the ship's load layer representing the electric circuit of a simple AEV, *(ii)* the ship's monitoring and control layer that is responsible for collecting data about the power system status, and *(iii)* the fault level, intertwined with the load one, that is devoted to simulating fault occurrences.

The Ship's Load Layer. The ship layer embodies a dual bus electric system feeding 6 zones (see Fig. 5). Two zones regard the two electric engines (M1 and M2), two zones contain the two resistor loads (L1 and L2), and finally, power is provided by generators in the two remaining zones: one main generator (MG) and an auxiliary one (AG) that is usually switched off. Each zone may be powered by either one of the two buses thanks to a two-way switch. A breaker may isolate each zone. This configuration allows studying a few different scenarios. For instance, *standard navigation*, in which the two engines and the load L1 are vital while the load L2 is semi-vital. Conversely, during the *emergency navigation*, one engine (M1) and one load (L1) are vital, the engine M2 is semi-vital, and the load L2 is non-vital. Other scenarios may be considered, as well. Power generators are dimensioned to allow some interesting situations to happen: main generator (MG) is able to power all the ship's loads at the same time, while the auxiliary generator (AG) can only feed one engine and one of the two resistor loads (L1 and L2 have the same specifications). It is worth noting that in normal conditions, efficiency reasons suggest using generators in a range that is known a priori (usually around 80–90% of the maximum amount of power). Generators may be overloaded, usually for a specific percentage of the maximum power and a predetermined amount of time. The proposed approach is able to do that when absolutely necessary.

The Ship's Monitoring and Control Layer. The monitoring and control layer is responsible for reading relevant electric (and environmental) data in order to allow for the construction of the current system state. This is fundamental for evaluating the performance and deduce some decay that may be the precursor of a fault, as well as the state is used to detect the fault when it occurs. Monitoring is usually performed by electric and environmental sensors connected to a data network. Control actions are performed by commuting breakers/switches in order to connect loads to different buses and to switch on/off loads and generators.

The Fault Layer. The testbed triggered studying the reaction of the proposed approach to SPS when three different types of fault happen:

- Interruption of current flow either in a bus or in a wire connecting the bus to the zone (two-way switches). This causes the interruption of current flow in a portion of the circuit and may affect one or more loads/generators. It may even isolate a portion of the circuit. If the interruption involves vital elements for the current ship's mission, the reconfiguration strategy aims to find an alternate way to provide sufficient power to the affected loads.
- Load/Engine out of work. This fault differently impacts the solution strategy according to the relevance of the damaged element in the current ship's mission. If it is vital, mission goals cannot fully be achieved. The system must consider partial solutions by powering other vital and semi-vital loads.
- Generator out of work. This is one of the more severe faults since it limits the amount of available power, and therefore, it reduces the overall capability of the system to sustain other faults. The reconfiguration strategy has to select which loads (according to their level of priority for the current ship's mission) may be powered by the remaining generators, and then it has to find a way to convey power to them.

We are not currently studying situations where faults are in the sensors (providing wrong measures or not measures at all) and in the switches/breakers.
Fault scenarios may also be categorized according to their time frame of occurrence as it follows:

1. Single fault: a fault occurring in a not predetermined time in a specific part of the system as described above. The system is supposed to be correctly running before a single fault. The detection of the fault triggers the reconfiguration to bring back the system to full functionality. This case is studied in many contributions from literature [4,11,26,28]. However, often, the focus is on the optimal usage of power produced by generators.
2. Multiple faults: two or more concurrent faults happening in a not predetermined time in one or more parts of the system. This may be the case of extensive damage coming from a collision, an explosion, the hit of a projectile. In the literature, this situation is not very frequently studied. Some samples are [13,25]. This scenario is one of the most significant ones because of the hazard to the survivability of the ship.
3. Cascade Faults: two or more faults happening at different times. Two different sub-cases may be considered as well: each new fault happens when the (partial or full) recovery has achieved, one or more new faults happen when the reconfiguration process is still ongoing. While the first sub-case may be considered as a reiteration of the single fault case (but that may be a decay in system's performance after the first fault), the latter situation is the most challenging one since it delays the solution, increasing its complexity.

The proposed SPS reconfiguration system is able to deal with all of the above listed types of faults. Of course, it cannot ensure full recovery of the ship's functionality (that may not be possible according to some fault conditions), nor it ensures the optimization of generators usage, conversely, it aims to quickly redirect power to loads that are vital for the current ship mission.

A typical solution offered by the system consists of redirecting the power to a bus when the other is damaged. This could even solve the problem of isolated portions of the system, if a generator is present in each of the separated parts. Of course, in so doing, the proposed solutions should also consider the available power and therefore, the list of loads to be powered is compiled in order not to overload the connected generator. A fundamental role in this part is played by a detailed electrical simulation of the system under fault conditions that is performed by using a Matlab model.

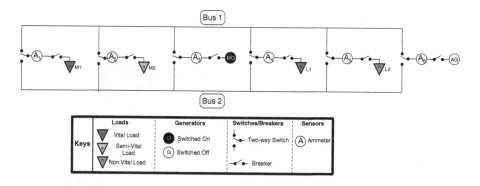

Fig. 5. The logic electric schema of the simulated AEV

4.2   Testbed Implementation Details

The realized testbed (see Fig. 6) employs two RaspberryPi microcomputers for collecting electrical data; such data is used for deducing the system state that is provided to the main computer (a workstation) hosting the system simulations and the autonomous reconfigurator (see Subsect. 3.2). Control actions prescribed by the reconfiguration process are enacted by another RaspberryPi microcomputer that controls relays playing the role of circuit switches and breakers. All the computing nodes are connected in a network, and the different actors/agents deployed in them continuously communicate and cooperate in pursuing their goals.

Generators are realized by using an ATX power source, and therefore they could be theoretically considered ideal power sources (the available power is much more than the needed one). Power limits of real generators are simulated by disconnecting the source when necessary.

The two power buses are realized by connection bars connecting cables from zones. This indeed introduces a simplification since the bus behavior is nearer to that of an ideal bus rather than that of a real power bus where losses of power and drops of voltages may occur. For the scope of this testbed, such a simplification may not be considered relevant.

The ships' load layer operates at 3.3 V while relays (the ship's control layer) are controlled using a 5 V source. A set of INA219 current sensors is used to realize the ship's monitoring layer; they read the values of current in the 6 zones (including generators).

The testbed includes two resistive loads (with a LED lamp to monitor their status) and two electric engines. Most of the faults are simulated by interrupting a wire (usually using a relay), in one of the loads (L2) we simulated a current dispersion that generates an increase in the load power request by introducing another resistive load in parallel to L2. This load may be activated (thus simulating the fault) with another relay.

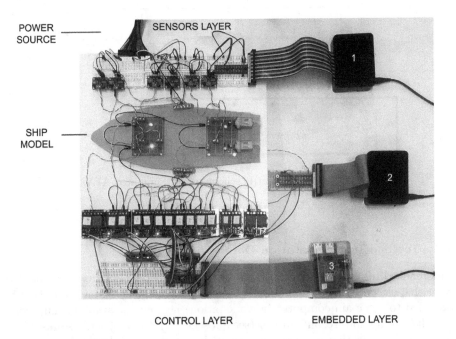

Fig. 6. The realised testbed with 3 RaspberryPi, relays, resistive loads and electric motors

4.3   Limits of the Proposed Testbed

The current version of our testbed is affected by some limits; first of all, it represents a small size circuit. Besides what can be thought, this does not facilitate the job for our autonomous reconfigurator since in a small circuit there are less available alternate paths for current and therefore the reconfigurator has no alternatives than finding all of them (and it is possible to verify them by hand). The scalability of the proposed approach may not be verified by using this testbed nor it was intended to be, since from the beginning, it was intended as a proof-of-concept system, and therefore it aimed to demonstrate the goodness of the approach in a real (even small) system that could be easily monitored by the human to verify the results proposed by the reconfigurator.

Some other minor limits come from specific electric choices like the adoption of a low voltage power system, a bread-board mounting for a portion of the circuit and commercial-grade components that may have relevant tolerance. Again these may be considered as minor factors not affecting the validation of the approach proposed in this work. In fact, this allows testing the cooperation among the different entities (actors/agents) employed in the solution and the effective interaction with the hardware level and in particular with the ship's monitoring and control layer.

5 Conclusions and Future Works

Smart vessels are now becoming a reality in both civil and military fields. While smartness has a direct impact on almost every aspect of the design, construction, and operation of the ship, we can note that nowadays autonomy mainly affects a few subsystems like the navigation one.

The shipboard power system (SPS) is one of the most sensitive subsystems of the vessel since its performance affects almost every other system. Faults in SPS are among the most relevant causes of loss of control and accidents.

In the proposed approach we developed a solution for the runtime reconfiguration of the SPS in case of single or multiple faults that is at the same time smart and autonomous. It dynamically considers the status of the system and computes different solutions (even partial solutions) that are proposed to the human stakeholder for final decision. We also developed a testbed for performing extensive testing and evaluation of our approach.

In the future we are working to extend the proposed method with the capability to deal with partial goal satisfaction also with temporal constraints. Other future extensions will give a larger role to the human for carrying on repairs whose effect on the solution will be properly taken into account by the proposed reconfigurator.

References

1. Ackoff, R.L.: Towards a system of systems concepts. Manage. Sci. **17**(11), 661–671 (1971)
2. Bose, S., Pal, S., Natarajan, B., Scoglio, C.M., Das, S., Schulz, N.N.: Analysis of optimal reconfiguration of shipboard power systems. IEEE Trans. Power Syst. **27**(1), 189–197 (2011)

3. Brun, Y., et al.: Engineering self-adaptive systems through feedback loops. In: Cheng, B.H.C., de Lemos, R., Giese, H., Inverardi, P., Magee, J. (eds.) Software Engineering for Self-Adaptive Systems. LNCS, vol. 5525, pp. 48–70. Springer, Heidelberg (2009). https://doi.org/10.1007/978-3-642-02161-9_3

4. Butler-Purry, K.: Multi-agent technology for self-healing shipboard power systems. In: Proceedings of the 13th International Conference on Intelligent Systems Application to Power Systems. IEEE (2005). 5–pp.

5. Cheng, B.H.C., et al.: Using models at runtime to address assurance for self-adaptive systems. In: Bencomo, N., France, R., Cheng, B.H.C., Aßmann, U. (eds.) Models@run.time. LNCS, vol. 8378, pp. 101–136. Springer, Cham (2014). https://doi.org/10.1007/978-3-319-08915-7_4

6. Cheng, B.H.C., et al.: Software engineering for self-adaptive systems: a research roadmap. In: Cheng, B.H.C., de Lemos, R., Giese, H., Inverardi, P., Magee, J. (eds.) Software Engineering for Self-Adaptive Systems. LNCS, vol. 5525, pp. 1–26. Springer, Heidelberg (2009). https://doi.org/10.1007/978-3-642-02161-9_1

7. Cossentino, M., Lodato, C., Lopes, S., Sabatucci, L.: MUSA: a middleware for user-driven service adaptation. In: Proceedings of the 16th Workshop "From Objects to Agents", Naples, Italy, 17–19 June 2015

8. Cossentino, M., Lopes, S., Renda, G., Sabatucci, L., Zaffora, F.: A metamodel of a multi-paradigm approach to smart cyber-physical systems development. In: Proceedings of the 20th Workshop "From Objects to Agents", Parma, Italy, 26–28 June (2019)

9. Cossentino, M., Sabatucci, L., Lopes, S.: Partial and full goal satisfaction in the MUSA middleware. In: Slavkovik, M. (ed.) EUMAS 2018. LNCS (LNAI), vol. 11450, pp. 15–29. Springer, Cham (2019). https://doi.org/10.1007/978-3-030-14174-5_2

10. de Lemos, R., et al.: Software engineering for self-adaptive systems: a second research roadmap. In: de Lemos, R., Giese, H., Müller, H.A., Shaw, M. (eds.) Software Engineering for Self-Adaptive Systems II. LNCS, vol. 7475, pp. 1–32. Springer, Heidelberg (2013). https://doi.org/10.1007/978-3-642-35813-5_1

11. Feliachi, A., Schoder, K., Ganesh, S., Lai, H.J.: Distributed control agents approach to energy management in electric shipboard power system. In: 2006 IEEE Power Engineering Society General Meeting. IEEE (2006). 6–pp.

12. Luck, M., McBurney, P., Shehory, O., Willmott, S.: Agent technology: computing as interaction (a roadmap for agent based computing). University of Southampton (2005)

13. Ouyang, L., Li, Y., Tan, Y., Xiao, J., Cao, Y.: Reconfiguration optimization of DC zonal distribution network of shipboard power system. In: 2016 IEEE Transportation Electrification Conference and Expo, Asia-Pacific (ITEC Asia-Pacific), pp. 444–448. IEEE (2016)

14. Qureshi, N.A., Perini, A., Ernst, N.A., Mylopoulos, J.: Towards a continuous requirements engineering framework for self-adaptive systems. In: 2010 First International Workshop on Requirements@ Run. Time, pp. 9–16. IEEE (2010)

15. Rao, A.S., Georgeff, M.P., et al.: BDI agents: from theory to practice. In: ICMAS, vol. 95, pp. 312–319 (1995)

16. Rushby, J.: Software verification and system assurance. In: 2009 Seventh IEEE International Conference on Software Engineering and Formal Methods, pp. 3–10. IEEE (2009)

17. Rybakov, V.: Linear temporal logic with until and next, logical consecutions. Ann. Pure Appl. Log. **155**(1), 32–45 (2008)

18. Sabatucci, L., Cossentino, M.: From means-end analysis to proactive means-end reasoning. In: Proceedings of the 10th International Symposium on Software Engineering for Adaptive and Self-Managing Systems, pp. 2–12. IEEE Press (2015)
19. Sabatucci, L., Lodato, C., Lopes, S., Cossentino, M.: Towards self-adaptation and evolution in business process. In: AIBP@ AI* IA, pp. 1–10. Citeseer (2013)
20. Sabatucci, L., Lodato, C., Lopes, S., Cossentino, M.: Highly customizable service composition and orchestration. In: Dustdar, S., Leymann, F., Villari, M. (eds.) ESOCC 2015. LNCS, vol. 9306, pp. 156–170. Springer, Cham (2015). https://doi.org/10.1007/978-3-319-24072-5_11
21. Sabatucci, L., Lopes, S., Cossentino, M.: MUSA 2.0: a distributed and scalable middleware for user-driven service adaptation. In: De Pietro, G., Gallo, L., Howlett, R.J., Jain, L.C. (eds.) KES-IIMSS 2017. SIST, vol. 76, pp. 492–501. Springer, Cham (2018). https://doi.org/10.1007/978-3-319-59480-4_49
22. Sabatucci, L., Ribino, P., Lodato, C., Lopes, S., Cossentino, M.: GoalSPEC: a goal specification language supporting adaptivity and evolution. In: Cossentino, M., El Fallah Seghrouchni, A., Winikoff, M. (eds.) EMAS 2013. LNCS (LNAI), vol. 8245, pp. 235–254. Springer, Heidelberg (2013). https://doi.org/10.1007/978-3-642-45343-4_13
23. Sabatucci, L., Cossentino, M., De Simone, G., Lopes, S.: Self-reconfiguration of shipboard power systems. In: Proceedings of the 3rd eCAS Workshop on Engineering Collective Adaptive Systems, Trento, Italy. IEEE (2018)
24. Sabatucci, L., De Simone, G., Cossentino, M.: Shipboard power system reconfiguration - a self-adaptation exemplar. In: Proceedings of the 4th International Workshop on Software Engineering for Smart Cyber-Physical Systems (SEsCPS 2018), Gothenburg, Sweden (2018)
25. Shariatzadeh, F., Kumar, N., Srivastava, A.K.: Optimal control algorithms for reconfiguration of shipboard microgrid distribution system using intelligent techniques. IEEE Trans. Ind. Appl. **53**(1), 474–482 (2016)
26. Solanki, J.M., Schulz, N.N., Gao, W.: Reconfiguration for restoration of power systems using a multi-agent system. In: Proceedings of the 37th Annual North American Power Symposium, pp. 390–395 (2005)
27. Weiß, G.: Adaptation and learning in multi-agent systems: some remarks and a bibliography. In: Weiß, G., Sen, S. (eds.) IJCAI 1995. LNCS, vol. 1042, pp. 1–21. Springer, Heidelberg (1996). https://doi.org/10.1007/3-540-60923-7_16
28. Xue, W., Fu, Y.: A two-step method for reconfiguration of shipboard power system. In: 2011 IEEE Electric Ship Technologies Symposium, pp. 167–172. IEEE (2011)

AxS in Context of Future Warfare and Security Environment (Concepts, Applications, Training, Interoperability, etc.)

AI-Powered Lethal Autonomous Weapon Systems in Defence Transformation. Impact and Challenges

Walter David[1]([✉]), Paolo Pappalepore[2], Alexandra Stefanova[3], and Brindusa Andreea Sarbu[4]

[1] Italian Army Education Training and Doctrine Command, 00143 Rome, Italy
walter.david@esercito.difesa.it
[2] Italian Air Force HQs, 00185 Rome, Italy
paolo.pappalepore@aeronautica.difesa.it
[3] United Drone Community, 1000 Sofia, Bulgaria
astefanova@udc.bg
[4] First District Court, 040095 Bucharest, Romania
andreea.sarbu@just.ro

Abstract. Robotics and artificial intelligence (AI) are changing business, and transforming defense and warfare. In particular, the paper addresses the challenges from the easy availability of AI resources to be applied to drones that are already an asymmetric threat, and the issues concerning the *Lethal Autonomous Weapons Systems (LAWS)* that promise military advantages like the reduction of deployed soldiers, loss of civilians, damage of infrastructures, and the rapid support to decision-making. Autonomous systems can also help in disaster and humanitarian operations. However, the deployment of systems that are more and more autonomous from humans poses multidimensional challenges for their certification, compliance with ethics and international humanitarian law and present risks to security. Mechanisms for the mitigation of their proliferation to malicious non-state actors and a *meaningful human control* should be implemented. War gaming in a theoretical, risk-safe environment can assess the threats and impact of robotic weapons on future defense planning and operations. From the example of the lessons learned in the automotive industry, simulation can be applied to digital twin models of the AI system and the environment to train and test under unexpected and extreme conditions, unanticipated hardware and software failure situations and in complex dynamic operational contexts including interaction with civilian entities.

Keywords: Robotics · Artificial intelligence · Autonomous systems · Lethal Autonomous Weapon Systems · Assessment · Risks · Modelling and simulation

1 Introduction

The *Fourth Industrial Revolution* is changing business and everyday life with artificial intelligence, robotics, big data, quantum computing, nanotechnology, biotechnology,

© Springer Nature Switzerland AG 2020
J. Mazal et al. (Eds.): MESAS 2019, LNCS 11995, pp. 337–350, 2020.
https://doi.org/10.1007/978-3-030-43890-6_27

internet of things, 3D printers and autonomous systems (AS), merging together the physical, digital and biological domains, combining hardware, software, and biology into complex *cyber-physical systems* [1].

Unmanned and autonomous multi-domain systems (UAxS) are more and more common in civilian environments [2–4] but disruptive technologies are also leading the transformation of defense. After the invention of the gun powder and nuclear weapons, UAxS are considered to drive the *Third Warfare Revolution* [5], with increasing autonomy [6] from their human operators. In fact, some weapons can already operate with a high level of autonomy, like for example the Super aEgis II sentry turret and the Samsung SGR-A1 semi-autonomous sentry gun [7].

But while UAxS are a capability for military forces, they are also a growing threat to critical infrastructures and urban sensitive sites. Micro, mini and small drones can fly very low, mostly undetected by civilian aviation and air defense radar systems while solutions for their detection, identification, and neutralization are very complex, making them a cheap and effective weapon in asymmetric warfare.

Decision-making in crisis requires updated situational awareness, with information that must be continuously updated from ground based and aerial sources including unmanned systems' sensors [8]. By combining drones and artificial intelligence (AI) technologies, the information captured from sensors is transmitted and the content analyzed [9]. These systems are able to *perceive* their surroundings and to choose a course of action (COA). Rapidly decreasing prices of drones already allow small municipalities and rescue teams to afford them [9]. Drones are used for last mile logistics, e.g. for speedy delivery of medicines to remote villages [10]. In humanitarian missions, drones can map different areas, help prevent and monitor crisis and support responders' efforts to find people in need and locate threats.

2 Methodological Approach

The idea behind this paper comes from authors' participation to Italian Defense organized workshops focused on defense transformation, with thematic in-depth study on disruptive technologies, with the active participation of representatives from defense, services, academia, research and industry involved in the processes of innovation and technologic development. In facts, authors have been involved in a series of initiatives including workshops supported by brainstorming, techniques of alternative analysis, lead discussion, devoted to investigate the impact and implications of artificial intelligence (AI) and the man-machine interaction/integration, with a particular focus on the implications that novel systems will have for the military sector.

Aim of this article is to contribute to knowledge and promote discussion on the impact and challenges of AI and robotics on security. Due to authors' sound juridical background, the characteristics of the autonomous weapon systems and the challenges that they are already posing from the ethical, legal perspectives are presented.

In this study, tests' results were impressive. United Drone Community (UDC) proved how, at very low cost, with internet access it is possible to assemble a device like the very light (25 g) *Mini SeeK3R*, equipped with low quality camera (640 × 480 px) and transmitter, able to connect with a neural network, detect and recognize over 100 objects and people (see Fig. 1). Such cheap, small, drones are not covered by European Union regulation (250 g is the minimum weight) and can execute certain operations undetected, potentially compromising privacy and security.

Fig. 1. United Drone micro drone following moving object

Another UDC device, the *Stinger*, has been equipped with tools for penetration (pen) testing of computer networks, running radio frequency interception. It demonstrates that it is easy to exploit online datasets like Arxiv, Github, Paddle, Keras, MXnet, etc., and then to act almost autonomously in a particular environment [9].

Italian Army author is taking part to experimentation conducted at the School of Infantry of the small Unmanned Ground Vehicle (UGV) *VIPER 2 MIL* (see Fig. 2) prototype built by Ingegneria dei Sistemi (IDS) that could be deployed in support of infantry teams, equipped with a variety of payloads, to improve the surveillance, reconnaissance, monitoring and inspection capacity of areas considered *at risk*, like in urban

Fig. 2. The *VIPER 2 MIL* prototype

buildings, narrow spaces and tunnels, providing *real-time* information gathered from cameras operating both in the visible and infrared spectrum or from CBRN sensors.

3   Autonomy and Decision-Making

John Boyd's *Observe Orient Decide Act (OODA)* (see Fig. 3) decision–making model is very useful when rapid decisions are required, in combat or business. Autonomous systems (AS) emulate human cognitive skills and depending on the context, they can adapt their behaviors. The Level of Autonomy (LOA) is an important parameter of the behavior of the AS and of its interaction with the (human) controllers.

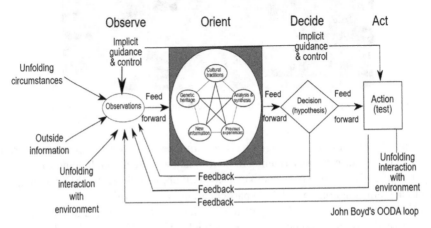

Fig. 3. The OODA loop

NASA established an interesting scale of autonomy for Unmanned Aerial Systems (UAS) based on eight LOAs for each OODA category (see Table 1).

The *Observe* column deals with data collection and filtering, the *Orient* column refers to options from analysis, prediction and integration, the *Decide* column to decision-making according with the available options, and the *Act* column to how autonomously the UAS can act. In levels 1–2, the human is primary, in levels 3–5 the system operates with human interaction, in levels 6–8, the system operates independently of the human who can get limited information [11].

Advances in AI are driven by *machine learning* systems exploiting *neural networks* organized in levels that contain artificial neurons, and are facilitated by the growing computing power and the availability of big deals of examples for their training.

Machine learning systems depend on the data used to train the algorithms. Most *deep learning* systems (e.g., convolutional neural networks) use data as input for extracting the features required for solving a problem [12].

In *reinforcement learning* systems (see Fig. 4) an agent performs actions that modify the environment, causing changes from a state to another and when it gets positive results, it receives a reward. The algorithm uses past experience acquired through interactions

Table 1. Scale of autonomy for UAS versus OODA (Source: Proud et al. [11])

Level	Observe	Orient	Decide	Act
8	The computer gathers, filters, and prioritizes data without displaying any information to the human	The computer predicts, interprets, and integrates data into a result which is not displayed to the human	The computer performs ranking tasks. The computer performs final ranking, but does not display results to the human	Computer executes automatically and does not allow any human interaction
7	The computer gathers, filters, and prioritizes data without displaying any information to the human. Though, a "program functioning" flag is displayed	The computer analyzes, predicts, interprets, and integrates data into a result which is only displayed to the human if result fits programmed context (context dependant summaries)	The computer performs ranking tasks. The computer performs final ranking and displays a reduced set of ranked options without displaying "why" decisions were made to the human	Computer executes automatically and only informs the human if required by context. It allows for override ability after execution. Human is shadow for contingencies
6	The computer gathers, filters, and prioritizes information displayed to the human	The computer overlays predictions with analysis and interprets the data. The human is shown all results	The computer performs ranking tasks and displays a reduced set of ranked options while displaying "why" decisions were made to the human	Computer executes automatically, informs the human, and allows for override ability after execution. Human is shadow for contingencies
5	The computer is responsible for gathering the information for the human, but it only displays non-prioritized, filtered information	The computer overlays predictions with analysis and interprets the data. The human shadows the interpretation for contingencies	The computer performs ranking tasks. All results, including "why" decisions were made, are displayed to the human	Computer allows the human a context-dependant restricted time to veto before execution. Human shadows for contingencies
4	The computer is responsible for gathering the information for the human and for displaying all information, but it highlights the non-prioritized, relevant information for the user	The computer analyzes the data and makes predictions, though the human is responsible for interpretation of the data	Both human and computer perform ranking tasks, the results from the computer are considered prime	Computer allows the human a pre-programmed restricted time to veto before execution. Human shadows for contingencies
3	The computer is responsible for gathering and displaying unfiltered, unprioritized information for the human. The human stilt is the prime monitor for all information	Computer is the prime source of analysis and predictions, with human shadow for contingencies. The human is responsible for interpretation of the data	Both human and computer perform ranking tasks, the results from the human are considered prime	Computer executes decision after human approval. Human shadows for contingencies
2	Human is the prime source for gathering and monitoring all data, with computer shadow for emergencies	Human is the prime source of analysis and predictions, with computer shadow for contingencies. The human is responsible for interpretation of the data	The human performs all ranking tasks, but the computer can be used as a tool for assistance	Human is the prime source of execution, with computer shadow for contingencies
1	Human is the only source for gathering and monitoring (defined as filtering, prioritizing and understanding) all data	Human is responsible for analyzing all data, making predictions, and interpretation of the data	The computer does not assist in or perform ranking tasks. Human must do it all	Human alone can execute decision

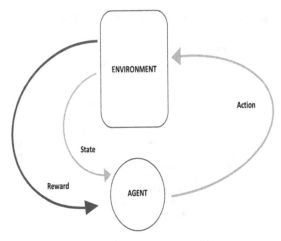

Fig. 4. Reinforcement learning model

with the environment to learn an optimal behaviour (*action*) to carry out a specific task and maximise the sum of the rewards.

YOLO (You Only Look Once) is a state of the art, *real-time* object detection system, able to process images at 30 FPS [13] by applying a single neural network to the image, dividing the image into regions, predicting the bounding boxes (see Fig. 5) and the probabilities for each region. Bounding boxes are weighted by the predicted probabilities. For example, one can run the detector

./darknet detect cfg/yolov3.cfg yolov3.weights data/dog.jpg

that will give an output like:

truth_thresh: Using default '1.000000'
Loading weights from yolov3.weights...Done!

Fig. 5. Real-time object detection with YOLO

data/dog.jpg: Predicted in 0.029329 s.
dog: 99%
truck: 93%
bicycle: 99%

The *real-time* detection can be run also from a webcam, by compiling Darknet with CUDA and OpenCV [14], then running the command:

./darknet detector demo cfg/coco.data cfg/yolov3.cfg yolov3.weights

4 Autonomous Systems Impact on the Defence

Simulation techniques as text-mining, morphological analysis, scenario building, Delphi, structured brainstorming, multi-criteria analysis, crowdsourcing, and wargaming can be applied to evaluate the potential disruptiveness of a technology, the military benefits of future weapons, and the implications for defense.

A conceptual experiment was conducted with NATO *Disruptive Technology Assessment Game (DTAG)* [15, 16] analytical, table–top seminar simulation in a theoretical, low-risk environment [17]. The DTAG process applied to a *Future Operating Environment* that will be more and more *Confused Congested Contested Connected* and *Constrained* (see Fig. 6) includes:

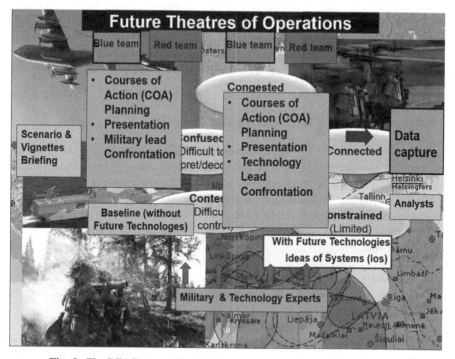

Fig. 6. The DTAG game process in a future operating environment scenario

- The identification of future technologies, using as a standardized description, Ideas of Systems (IoS) cards;
- The wargaming with Blue and Red teams of military and technology experts developing their plans. For each scenario vignette there is a first confrontation without, and a second one with the use of selected IoS cards. Wargame facilitates discussions for evaluation of new technologies' strengths and weakness;
- The analysis to assess what systems/technologies have a truly disruptive effect. Data are captured during the game using a computerized tool and notes.

In effect, UAxS are widely expected to transform defense. As an example, swarms of Unmanned Aerial Systems (UAS) have been assessed with regard to their impact on operations. A *Doctrine Organization Training Materiel Leadership Facilities Personnel Interoperability (DOTMLFPI)* perspective has been included to provide indications on the impact on defense planning [18].

Small UAS, often deployed in swarms, are a real threat to both civil and military sites and are proliferating with affordable hardware and products designed for the development of deep neural networks. Due to their size, countermeasures require a multiple domain (electromagnetic, acoustic, electro-optic) approach. Destruction of flying drones in cities requires *soft kill* techniques, with assets manned by trained operators, making defense more complex and costs much higher than the attack.

Robotic weapons promise significant military advantages [19], they would act as force multipliers, extending warfighters' reach by selectively striking targets, for example, terrorists. Fewer *boots on the ground* could be deployed. The integration of multiple sources information would provide better intelligence and situational awareness [6] while the accurate concentration of force on the selected targets could reduce the civilian (and also combatants') casualties and the damage of critical infrastructures, buildings and private properties.

5   Ethical and Legal Issues, Risks for Security

Drones perform reconnaissance but still an operator decides about strikes [5]. However, soon multiple systems able to identify and attack targets automatically through object and facial recognition algorithms could be supervised by just a human.

The United Nations Office for Disarmament Affairs (UNODA), in the *Perspectives on Lethal Autonomous Weapon Systems, 2017* [20], defined a *Lethal Autonomous Weapon System (LAWS)* as any weapon system with autonomy in its critical functions, that is a weapon system able to:

- **select** (*search for, detect, identify, track or select*)
- **attack** (*use force against, neutralize, damage or destroy*) **targets without human** intervention.

Already in 1942, Isaac Asimov introduced ethics in robotics, with his *Three Laws of Robotics* (plus an additional later zeroth law) but today robots span from the vacuum cleaners to the industrial production machines and even to the surgery robots made from DNA and proteins [21].

According to the *doctrine of the moral equality*, combatants, regardless their side pr if they are fighting a just war, are moral agents who continuously exercise their choice and responsibility [22] and are under obligations of the International Humanitarian Laws (IHL) on the conduct of hostilities.

Autonomous weapons are not specifically regulated by IHL [23, 24]; in particular, they do not comply with the following principles:

- **Distinction.** The parties must at all times distinguish between military objectives and civilian objects, civilians, active combatants, and those *hors de combat*;
- **Proportionality in attack.** It is prohibited to launch an attack which may be expected to cause incidental loss or injury to civilians, damage to civilian objects and would be excessive in relation to the anticipated direct military advantage;
- **Precautions in attack.** Constant care must be taken in the conduct of operations to spare civilians and civilian objects. All feasible precautions must be taken to avoid/minimize loss and injury to civilians and damage to civilian objects.

Therefore, autonomous weapons should have the ability to identify and recognize complex targets like active combatants from civilians in evolving and confused contexts, often in urban areas, understand the situation from formal mathematical models and evaluate if the possible courses of actions (COA) adhere to IHL.

However, so far autonomous systems do not have the common sense reasoning required by the 1949 Geneva Convention, and there is no IHL definition of what is a *civilian,* easy to be translated into software code for making a distinction or proportionality decisions about the use of lethal force [23, 24].

When things would go wrong, despite would be difficult to identify who is liable (the commander, the manufacturer, the designer, the mission planner?) under the law of state responsibility, a state could be held liable for IHL violations from the use of robots [22, 23]. Communications links between command and control (C2) systems and UAxS are vulnerable, a virus could infect an UAS swarm. Malfunctioning or hacked systems could attack wrong targets or fire on civilians.

EU Parliament resolution of 27th of February 2014 prohibits the development, production and use of autonomous weapons that allow attacks to be launched without human intervention, while EU Council resolution of 15th of November 2016 states that autonomous weapons must be governed by IHL and other international laws [20]. UN Convention on Certain Weapons (CCWUN) Group of Government Experts (GGE) focused on nations' development of systems, IHL and human control. However, more urgent is the risk of LAWS proliferation to *malicious armed non-state actors (ANSA)* that could acquire robotic weapons and do not consider themselves constrained by any moral or legal rules [23, 24].

6 Simulation for Systems Which Can Learn

Trust is critical, for humans to work with adaptive non-deterministic systems working at high levels of autonomy [2, 3] and requires new approaches. In fact, due to the potential for catastrophic consequences and higher costs of error in military applications, AI training data sets should perfectly represent the real operational data.

Training data for military AI systems need a higher level of Test and Evaluation, Verification and Validation (TEV&V) than in commercial sectors but it is useful to consider lessons learned and standards from systems already performing safety-critical tasks, as industrial robots, flight autopilots and in particular, automated and self-driving trains and vehicles.

These technologies already deal with issues concerning the human control and supervision, human-machine interaction in emergency, deactivation, predictability and reliability [25]. Self-driving cars are subject to the International Organization for Standardization (ISO) and the Society of Automotive Engineers (SAE) standards [25] that may help for supporting the drafting of robotic weapons standards.

Simulation plays the key role in rapid analysis of scenarios as it is the only safe, risk-free methodology able to develop and to conduct tests in a virtual debugging environment. Trust in AI algorithms can come from explanations for the way the outputs are produced [25].

Modelling creates a live digital twin model of the real world. Missions may be tested in many iterations, for assessing the systems' behavior and effectiveness [26]; limits of autonomous vehicles can be explored to identify failures under unanticipated extreme weather or road traffic conditions, rare but catastrophic hardware and software faults and the dynamic evolution of a complex future operating environment that include urban and peri-urban areas [27].

Assessment of AI decision-making requires a mix of *live, virtual, and constructive (LVC)* simulation at different scales. Unmanned Autonomous Systems (UAxS) can be defined in Commercial of the Shelf (COTS) simulator MASA SWORD which allows defining units, equipment, sensors, weapon systems, ammunition types and many more aspects, the better defined, the more accurate will be the simulation's results.

In SWORD it is possible to define which actions the UAxS is able to perform at what speed or to compose a swarm of military robots (See Fig. 7).

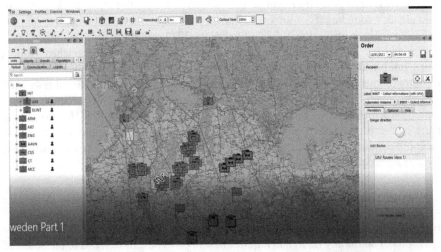

Fig. 7. In SWORD an UAV started to collect information identifying enemy

These units can be given missions which will interact with the terrain, sensor capabilities, weapon systems etc., obviously respecting the doctrine, to be executed and have an impact on the course of action (COA). A special SWORD module allows the users to analyze and improve planning of the COA and to experiment with doctrine and other elements that might have an impact on the outcomes of a conflict. This module is also meant to improving the results from war gaming experiments. MASA AI engine DirectAI, with the right datasets, provides accurate outcomes of conflicts.

New AI technologies are now emerging in the gaming industry for optimal strategy generation. It would be a huge step forward and provide an advantage over the enemy if this approach could also be used for military planning. These promising new tools, combined with simulation and digital solutions, could enable the military decision maker to *accelerate mission planning* and present an *optimal and accurate visualisation of the situation* in the field and its likely evolution.

The rapid production of accurate COA in decision process, enabled by such new technologies would give a real strategic superiority and would limit risk of being overtaken by enemies who already start to use such technologies. In fact, military operations often happen in contexts where facts may be difficult to discern (the *fog of war*). As already mentioned, the *future operating environment* will be even more *confused, congested, connected, contested and constrained*.

Recent AI advances imply that such tools are now feasible, specifically in the field of *deep reinforcement learning* which provides the ability to win at strategy games, like Go and more recently StarCraft. AI coupled with learning functions is nowadays almost unrivalled by human. Such technologies implemented in constructive simulation are going to enhance the reliability of decision-making.

7 Conclusions and Possible Solutions

In conclusion, this paper presents the outcomes from the brainstorming, analysis workshops in the military innovation sector about the transformation that disruptive technologies are going to cause to defense, driven by artificial intelligence (AI) and robotics.

A micro drone has been created and it shows how easy is for everyone to connect with a neural networks, detect and recognize objects and people. Small UAxS are already a threat, in particular as hybrid warfare tools. Convergence and affordability of drone and AI technologies already present risks for security.

Authors suggest that towards the future development of AI, autonomous systems (AS) will support humans in their choice of the optimal COA. In fact, in time-critical settings, due to growing (big) data available, humans will need support from machines providing intelligence from multiple sources, actionable decision-making information [28], and effective automation of operational planning. Man-machine teams exploiting improved human-machine interfaces would blend human and AI capabilities [29].

On the other hand, the deployment of AS as robotic weapons promise significant military advantages [19], like the requirement for fewer *boots on the ground* and the reduction of casualties and damages; systems able to identify (through object and facial recognition algorithms) and attack targets automatically could eventually be supervised by a human (*man on the loop*). However, autonomous weapons pose ethical issues and do not comply with IHL [23], in particular, with the principles of *distinction. proportionality, precautions in attack*.

This issue is of vital interest for the defense sector, in a situation of considerable international turbulence [19]; this paper highlights the requirement for a multi-dimensional approach.

From the security perspective, in order to mitigate the risk of transfer for LAWS and their critical components to malicious actors, it will be necessary to implement a transparent export controls regime, for example through the Wassenaar Arrangement platform that maintains the list of dual-use goods and technologies [29].

From the legal perspective, the *principles of humanity* and the *dictates of the public conscience* are mentioned in article 1(2) of Additional Protocol I and in the preamble of Additional Protocol II to the Geneva Conventions, known as the *Martens Clause*. A *meaningful human control* or *appropriate levels of human judgement* must be retained over weapon systems and the use of force, with the human able to intervene in *real-time* [25, 30].

Finally, it is illustrated how, from the factual and operational perspective, core components of human control include system's predictability and reliability in its intended or expected circumstances of use [20]. Research will focus on building system gradually evolving their codes of conduct to make decisions based on Rules of Engagement (ROE) and laws [5, 31, 32], requiring a considerable advancement in AI and computational power [21, 33], and protection from cyber-attacks [21, 34].

Trust is critical, for humans to work with AS [35, 36], Machine learning systems depend on the data used to train the algorithms therefore training data sets for military applications should be perfectly representative of the real operational data.

Standards for autonomous weapon systems must be designed to ensure they can be used with minimal risk of unintended and unexpected consequences and should be at least as stringent as those for civilian applications like in the automated and self-driving cars industry [25].

In fact, due to the potential for catastrophic consequences and higher costs of errors in military operations [25], military AI systems need a higher level of Test and Evaluation, Verification and Validation (TEV&V) than systems for the commercial sector and require the application of war gaming and modelling and simulation techniques, including a mix of *live, virtual and constructive* tools [27].

From the lessons learned of simulation in the automotive industry, digital twin models of the system and the environment could be applied in order to stress the AI under rare conditions and unexpected failure situations. AI should be trained and tested in crucial aspects of operational planning and decision-making using realistic scenarios that include models of civilians, wounded combatants, humanitarian actors, weather, road traffic conditions, natural disasters and complex targets in environments such as megacities and urban areas with high population density.

References

1. Schwab, K.: The executive chairman of the World Economic Forum, in Foreign Affairs (2015)
2. Hodicky, J.: Autonomous systems operationalization gaps overcome by modelling and simulation. In: Hodicky, J. (ed.) MESAS 2016. LNCS, vol. 9991, pp. 40–47. Springer, Cham (2016). https://doi.org/10.1007/978-3-319-47605-6_4
3. Hodicky, J., Prochazka, D., Prochazka, J.: Automation in experimentation with constructive simulation. In: Mazal, J. (ed.) MESAS 2018. LNCS, vol. 11472, pp. 566–576. Springer, Cham (2019). https://doi.org/10.1007/978-3-030-14984-0_42
4. Hodický, J., Procházka, D.: Challenges in the implementation of autonomous systems into the battlefield. In: Proceedings of the 2017 International Conference on Military Technologies (ICMT), pp. 743–747. Institute of Electrical and Electronics Engineers Inc., Piscataway (2017). https://doi.org/10.1109/miltechs.2017.7988855. ISBN 978-1-5386-1988-9
5. Walsh, T.: Regulating the Third Revolution in Warfare, Australian Institute of International Affairs. https://www.internationalaffairs.org.au/australianoutlook/2062-the-world-that-ai-made/. Accessed 21 Oct 2019
6. Rabkin, J., Yoo, J.: Disruptive Technologies to Upend Rules of War. http://www.nationaldefensemagazine.org/articles/2017/10/31/disruptive-technologies-to-upend-rules-of-war. Accessed 23 May 2019
7. Parkin, S.: Killer Robots: the soldiers that never sleep (2018). http://www.bbc.com/future/story/20150715-killer-robots-the-soldiers-that-never-sleep. Accessed 24 May 2019
8. David, W., et al.: Giving life to the map can save more lives. Wildfire scenario with interoperable simulations. Advances in Cartography and GIScience of the International Cartographic Association, 1, 4 (2019). https://doi.org/10.5194/ica-adv-1-4-2019
9. Stefanova, A., Puliyski, A.: AI-Drones: accessibility versus security. In: Proceedings of the 7th Crisis Management and Disaster Response Interagency Conference, CMDR COE, Sofia, June 2019 (2019). https://www.cmdrcoe.org/menu.php?m_id=8&f_id=1423. Accessed 21 Oct 2019
10. Meier, P.: Our strategy on cargo drone projects for public health. https://blog.werobotics.org/2019/07/08/our-strategy-on-cargo-drone-projects-for-public-health. Accessed 03 Nov 2019
11. Proud, R.W., Hart, J.J., Mrozinski, R.B.: Methods for determining the level of autonomy to design into a human spaceflight vehicle: A function specific approach. NASA Johnson Space Center, Houston, TX (2003)
12. Maltoni, D.: http://bias.csr.unibo.it/maltoni/ml/DispensePDF/2_ML_Fondamenti.pdf. Accessed 28 Nov 2019
13. Github: https://github.com/Garima13a/YOLO-Object-Detection. Accessed 21 Oct 2019
14. Pjreddie: https://pjreddie.com/darknet/yolo/. Accessed 21 Oct 2019
15. NATO Assessment of Possible Disruptive Technologies for Defence and Security, AC/323(SAS-062) TP/258, NATO RTO, February 2010 (2010)
16. NATO Disruptive Technology Assessment Game – Evolution and Validation, AC/323(SAS-082) TP/427, NATO RTO, April 2012 (2012)
17. Kindvall, G., Lindberg, A., Trané, C., Westman, J.: Exploring Future Technology Development, FOI-R–4196—SE, June 2017 (2017). ISSN 1650-1942
18. FFI-NOTAT Eksternnotat 16/00336 Emerging Technology Concepts and Defence Planning in the Nordic Countries, 1 February 2016 (2016)
19. Pappalepore, P.: Presentation: Implicazioni legali dell'utilizzo di mezzi autonomi dotati di intelligenza artificiale come sistemi d'arma. In: Workshop "La Trasformazione in ambito Difesa", Rome, 21–22 November 2018 (2018)
20. Chertoff, P.: Perils of Lethal Autonomous Weapons Systems Proliferation: Preventing Non-State Acquisition (2018). http://www.css.ethz.ch/en/services/digital-library/articles/article.html/a4f0de69-1e0b-401e-871d-1956fa9063d3. Accessed 23 Nov 2019

21. Anderson, M.R.: After 75 years, Isaac Asimov's Three Laws of Robotics need Updating, 17 March 2017 (2017). http://theconversation.com/after-75-years-isaac-asimovs-three-laws-of-robotics-need-updating-74501. Accessed 29 May 2019

22. Bazargan, S.: Moral Equality of Combatants, 01 February 2013 (2013). https://doi.org/10.1002/9781444367072.wbiee343

23. Davison, N.: A legal perspective: Autonomous Weapons **UNODA Occasional Papers, No. 30** on Systems under International Humanitarian Law (2017). Accessed 30 Aug 2019

24. Sharkey, E.N.: The evitability of autonomous robot warfare. Int. Rev. Red Cross **94**(886) (2012). https://www.icrc.org/en/international-review/article/evitability-autonomous-robot-warfare

25. International Committee of the Red Cross (ICRC): Autonomy, Artificial Intelligence and Robotics: Technical aspects of Human Control, Geneva, August 2019 (2019)

26. Schultz, A.C., Grefenstette, J.J., De Jong, K.A.: Test and evaluation by genetic algorithms. IEEE Expert **8**(5), 9–14 (1993)

27. TaaS: Digital Twins: Testing Autonomous Vehicles in a Virtual World, Transportation as a Service (TaaS) Magazine, December 2018 (2018)

28. Air Force Research Institute: Technology Horizons A Vision for Air Force Science and Technology 2010-30 Air Force Research Institute,155 North Twining Street, Maxwell AFB, AL, 36112-6026 (2011)

29. David, W., Pappalepore, P., Rozalinova, E., Sarbu, B.A.: The rise of the robotic weapon systems in armed conflicts. In: Proceedings of the 7th Crisis Management and Disaster Response Interagency Conference, Sofia, Bulgaria, June 2019 (2019)

30. United Nations: Recommendations to the 2016 Review Conference submitted by the Chairperson of the Informal Meeting of Experts, para. 2 (b) (2016)

31. Pomazalová, N., Korecki, Z., Darkwah, A.S.: The new approaches in logistics services accomplishment. In: Proceedings of the 5th European Conference on Innovation and Entrepreneurship, National and Kapodistrian University of Athens, Greece on 16–17 September 2010, pp. 453–460. Academic Publishing (2010). ISBN 978-1-906638-75-7

32. Foltin, P., Vlkovský, M., Mazal, J., Husák, J., Brunclík, M.: Discrete event simulation in future military logistics applications and aspects. In: Mazal, J. (ed.) MESAS 2017. LNCS, vol. 10756, pp. 410–421. Springer, Cham (2018). https://doi.org/10.1007/978-3-319-76072-8_30

33. Foltin, P., Gontarczyk, M., Świderski, A., Zelkowski, J.: Evaluation model of the companies operating within logistic network. Arch. Transp. **32**(4), 21–34 (2015). ISSN 0866-9546

34. Brunclík, M., Vogal, L., Foltin, P.: Computer modelling and simulation of the supply chain in military operation. In: Proceedings of the 18th International Scientific Conference - Business Logistics in Modern Management, pp. 671–682. Josip Juraj Strossmayer University of Osijek, Faculty of Economics in Osijek, Osijek, Chorvatsko (2018). ISSN 1849-5931

35. Mazal, J., Stodola, P., Procházka, D., Kutěj, L., Ščurek, R., Procházka, J.: Modelling of the UAV safety manoeuvre for the air insertion operations. In: Hodicky, J. (ed.) MESAS 2016. LNCS, vol. 9991, pp. 337–346. Springer, Cham (2016). https://doi.org/10.1007/978-3-319-47605-6_27

36. Stodola, P., Mazal, J.: Architecture of the advanced command and control system. In: 6th International Conference on Military Technologies, ICMT 2017, pp. 340–343. Institute of Electrical and Electronics Engineers Inc., Piscataway, NJ 08854-4141 USA (2017). ISBN 978-1-5386-1988-9

Aspects of Air Defence Units C2 System Modelling and Simulation

Vadim Stary[(⊠)] [ID] and Jan Farlik [ID]

University of Defence in Brno, Kounicova 65, 662 10 Brno, Czech Republic
{vadim.stary,jan.farlik}@unob.cz

Abstract. The article is focused on the area of modelling and simulation of the Surface Based Air Defence (SBAD) units, especially on issues of Command and Control (C2) and Tactical Battle Management Functions (TBMF) in the simulator environment. The article describes the general overview of the C2 and TBMF of the SBAD units, presents the state of art in today's tactical simulators (PRESAGIS simulation SW) and suggests the possible way of implementation to reach the model and simulation corresponding with the real world entities.

Keywords: Air Defence · Modelling · Simulation · Command and Control

1 Introduction

Modelling and simulation of military units, structures and procedures are one of the most useful tools for the tactical planning, training and development of different types of military entities [1]. SBAD unit with its C2 system, structure and procedures represents very complex military system which consists of numerous parts. In general there are 3 main pillars.

- Detectors (e.g. radars, visual sensors, etc.)
- Effectors (e.g. missile launchers, cannons, fighters, etc.)
- Command and Control (e.g. command posts, fire distribution centres, etc.)

Furthermore, SBAD units operate in the joint domain of air and land forces and should be able to operate with both of them. This interoperability is essential and due to the different structures of Air and Land forces and its C2 system standards it is challenging to reach it in the full range [2].

1.1 Air Command and Control System Structure

The following design of the possible C2 system implementation to the simulator is based on the main structure of the Air Command and Control System (ACCS), which is used within NATO air forces (see Fig. 1) [3]. The tactical level of ACCS consists of Air Component Headquarters (HQ AIRCOM), Combined Air Operation Center (CAOC), Airspace Control Center (ACC), Recognized Air Picture (RAP) Production

J. Mazal et al. (Eds.): MESAS 2019, LNCS 11995, pp. 351–360, 2020.
https://doi.org/10.1007/978-3-030-43890-6_28

Centre (RPC), Sensor Fusion Post (SFP) with Early Warning Radars (EWR). SBAD part is Surface to Air Missile Operation Centre (SAMOC), Group Operation Center (GOC) both with Air Defence Radars (ADR) and the fighter part is Wing Operation Center (WOC) and Squadron Operation Center (SQOC). Each of these entities has its capability and functionality depending on a mission, delegated authority and mode of the command and control (centralized, decentralized or autonomous).

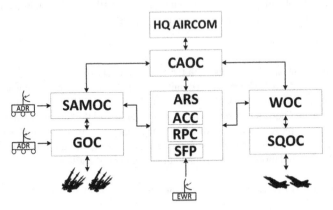

Fig. 1. Air Command and Control System schema

The main goal of this article is to design possible structure and models of C2 systems of SBAD for the tactical simulators. This layout reflects the issue of the capability and authority of particular command posts (operation centres).

1.2 Operation Centres Functions and Authority

According to [4], there are 15 different TBMF, which can be delegated within the operation centres (OC) and SBAD units. Delegation of these functions in the real deployment highly depends on the tactical situation, state of connection and communication security.

For the article purpose let us assume following authority functions.

1. Target identification (ID) authority (the entity usually has a flight plans and has ability to identify friend targets, and provide this information to subordinate operation centres and units, this entity assign the ID of the target – friend, enemy, jammer, etc.).
2. Target engagement (ENG) authority (the entity has the right to issue the engage order).
3. Choice of weapons (WCH) authority (the entity has right to choose a type of weapon).
4. Emission control (EC) authority (the entity has right to control radars and its emission status).
5. Deployment (DEP) authority (the entity determines the units location e.g. launchers, radars, etc.).
6. Readiness state (RS) control authority (the entity has right to change to state of preparedness of the units e.g. ready to fire immediately, in 5 min, in 6 h, etc.).

1.3 State of Air – Simulation Software

Nowadays, number of commercial simulation SW is available on the market. The well-known and most used are Virtual Battlespace by Bohemia Interactive Simulations[1], VT MÄK simulators[2], MASA SWORD[3] or PRESAGIS[4], which are also used for military application, training and wargaming [5]. Example of the implementation of the simulation can be found in [6]. All of them represents very complex solution of M&S, offers a various possibilities of usage and supports High Level Architecture (HLA) and Distributed Interactive Simulation (DIS) standards.

Authors of the article have experience with all of the mentioned simulators, mainly with VT MÄK, VBS and PRESAGIS. The detailed comparison of the simulators transcends the range of the article, nevertheless the way work with these simulators is very similar and can be generally described in these steps, which are also followed for the simulation described in this article.

1. Entity definition in database (with all parameters, DIS code, 3D model, etc.)
2. Simulation setup (implement maps, scenario layout, entity behaviour settings, etc.)
3. Simulation run (live 2D/3D simulation, etc.)
4. Simulation evaluation (results, settings modification, etc.)

Based on authors experience with these SW, the entities (scenarios) and their behaviour are usually simulated as standalone objects, which act independently with minimum cooperation and communication aspects, although the producers of the simulators present, that the simulators includes the possibility of communication, command and control.

Therefore, for the purpose of the SBAD units and C2 system M&S, the more complex structure of communication (chain of command) was modelled and verified.

2 Scenario Layout

For the purpose of this article let us assume three authority delegation layouts[5] [7].

– Autonomous mode of operations (MOO)
– Centralized C2 – variant one
– Centralized C2 – variant two

2.1 Autonomous MOO

This layout reflects the situation where the fire unit (FU) has no connection to the superior level, and all functionality is delegated to the FU. In this situation, all additional

---

[1] https://bisimulations.com/.

[2] https://www.mak.com/.

[3] https://masasim.com/.

[4] https://www.presagis.com/en/.

[5] WOC and SQOC elements are not included (only SBAD part).

procedures according to a weapon control status (WCS), right to self-defence, "lame-duck" procedures, etc. must be precisely followed (Table 1).

Table 1. Autonomous MOO

Entity/Function	ID	ENG	WCH	EC	DEP	RS
HQ AIRCOM	–	–	–	–	–	–
CAOC	–	–	–	–	–	–
ARS	–	–	–	–	–	–
SAMOC	–	–	–	–	–	–
GOC	–	–	–	–	–	–
FU	X	X	X	X	X	X

This is the simplest situation from the C2 point of view, and the FU entity, make its own decisions.

2.2 Centralized C2 – Variant One

In this situation, there is a full connection within all C2 elements and FU. Authority is delegated according to the Table 2. This situation represents optimal state of C2 system where a full chain of command and control is operational. However, due to the number of superior C2 elements (five) information delay may occur, e.g. distribution of RAP from ARS to the FU may take up to 20 s and engage order from HQ AIRCOM must be issued in advance or this authority must be delegated to the lower C2 level (CAOC or SAMOC).

Table 2. Centralized C2 – variant one

Entity/Function	ID	ENG	WCH	EC	DEP	RS
HQ AIRCOM	–	X	–	–	–	–
CAOC	–	–	X	–	X	–
ARS	X	–	–	X	–	–
SAMOC	–	–	–	–	–	X
GOC	–	–	–	–	–	–
FU	–	–	–	–	–	–

2.3 Centralized C2 – Variant Two

This layout represents the situation where C2 elements and FU are partly connected or the authority is delegated to the lower level C2 elements. This variant reflects the situation where is no connection from ARS and SAMOC to the superior levels (CAOC and HQ AIRCOM) and all functions are delegated within these C2 elements, according to a Table 3.

Table 3. Centralized C2 – variant two

Entity/Function	ID	ENG	WCH	EC	DEP	RS
HQ AIRCOM	–	–	–	–	–	–
CAOC	–	–	–	–	–	–
ARS	**X**	**X**	**X**	**X**	–	–
SAMOC	–	–	–	–	**X**	**X**
GOC	–	–	–	–	–	–
FU	–	–	–	–	–	–

3 Simulation Setup

The simulation was realized by simulation SW Presagis STAGE 17. Scenario, Toolkit And Generation Environment (STAGE) is a software for designing complex and intelligent strategic simulation applications [8].

Tools Scenario Editor, Database Editor and Mission Editor were used.

3.1 Scenario Design

In Scenario Editor Tool, two scenarios were created. For the purpose of this article to preserve clarity and for operability evaluation several simplifications were made. Scenario consists of one enemy target (MIG 29), Long Range (LR) Radar (100 km), a Short Range (SH) Radar (20 km), ARS, SAMOC, GOC, Short Range Air Defence (SHORAD) FU with generic missile with an active seeker (30 km) and defined Engagement Zone (EZ) [9]. Scenario one represents the autonomous MOO, where FU operates with its own sensor, provides target ID, evaluation if the target is in EZ and engages the target autonomously. Scenario two or responds with the Centralized C2 – variant two, mission is controlled by the ARS, which has a track and ID information from LR radar (see Fig. 2). To increase simulation authenticity the artificial latency in C2 system was added (10 s at each level). Blue lines represent the radio connection and red lines the radar detection.

Main parameters of entity models:

Enemy Fighter – velocity 550 m/s, flight level 2000 m Above Sea Level (ASL), azimuth 160°.

Generic missile – velocity 980 m/s, active guidance system, effective engagement zone 30 km.

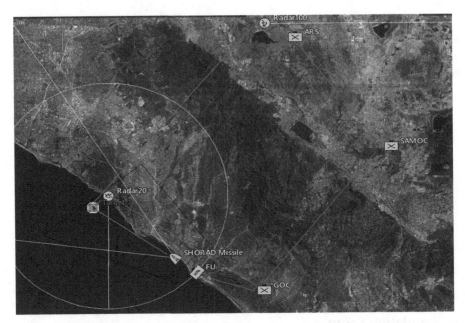

Fig. 2. Scenario design Centralized C2 – variant two (Color figure online)

3.2 Entities Model

In Database Editor, generic models[6] of Missile, FU, GOC, SAMOC, ARS and radars were created. For the evaluation of the C2 systems were created models of Tactical Digital Link (TADIL) radios for the connection of the entities. The block diagram of the models and connection is in Fig. 3. To preserve real conditions, each entity has specific TADIL.

- TADIL 1 LR RADAR - ARS
- TADIL 2 SR RADAR - GOC
- TADIL 3 FU - GOC
- TADIL 4 SAMOC - GOC
- TADIL 5 ARS – SAMOC

This solution ensures the communication within all elements according to the real situation.

3.3 Functionality Model

The Mission Editor allows setting up behaviour of all entities in the scenario and it was used for defining functionalities according a TBMF in each scenario. Because of the very complex and time consuming settings, only fundamental functionality (Detection,

---

[6] Parameters of these models were set up based on authors experience and do not represent any existing system.

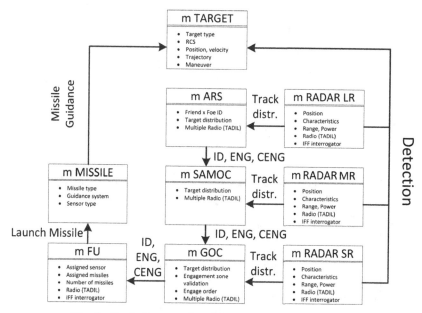

Fig. 3. Block diagram of models and their main parameters

Identification, Orders distribution and Engagement) was realized by the scripts in the Mission editor. The rest of functionalities can be added in the future or it can be provided by a user during the Runtime simulation. Figure 4 represents the functionality schema of the Centralized C2 – variant two. Scripts which define the behaviour in different situations should include all possibilities and entity states (Table 4).

Table 4. Example of Mission Editor script for FU

Task group	Type	Logical oper.	Left term	Oper	Right term	Action
Init	INIT					Activate TADIL3 Frequency setup TADIL 3
Fire	AT		EXTERN EVENT	=	ENGAGE	
	IF		Weapons count	>	0	Weapon launch by type
End	END					

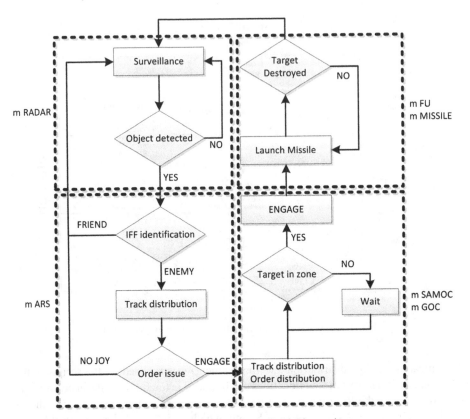

Fig. 4. Functionality schema Centralized C2 – variant two

4 Evaluation and Conclusion

Simulated behaviour of SBAD units and C2 system fulfil the expectations. FU during Autonomous MOO react to the target without any discrepancy and hitting of target depends on calculated probability, based on the defined probability characteristics in models.

In the variant with centralized C2, several entities interoperated according to a set functionality. LR Radar provided the track information; ARS system identifies the target and issues orders, which were distributed via SAMOC and GOC to the FU, which launches the missile.

The run of 60 simulations was realized. The results are presented in Table 5. Hit and Kill probability corresponds with the probability settings (distribution) for hitting and destroying target. Parameter DET – ENG is average time from the first detection from LR radar to the moment of missile launch. Parameter DET – KILL represents the average time from the LR detection to the destroying the target.

Table 5. Simulation results

60 runs of scenario	Autonomous	Centralized variant two
Hit probability [%]	96,5	94,2
Kill probability [%]	89,3	90,5
Time DET – ENG [s]	2,5	33,5
Time DET – KILL [s]	14,8	47,2

TBMF in this variant were simulated as follows:

- ID – was done by Identification Friend or Foe (IFF) interrogator (Radar), IFF transponder (Aircraft), evaluation was done autonomously by mission editor macros at ARS (result – HOSTILE).
- ENG – Issue of engage order was done autonomously by mission editor macros at ARS (result – ENGAGE), Validation of presence target in EZ is provided by GOC.
- WCH - Was done autonomously by mission editor macros at ARS (result – selected SAMOC, GOC and FU).
- EC – Was manually pre-set to full emission in a scenario initialization (INIT) phase (all radars were emitting).
- DEP – Was manually pre-set, all SBAD and C2 entities have fixed position. Enemy had pre-set position, altitude, velocity and flight direction (can be also manually controlled).
- RS – Was manually pre-set, all SBAD and C2 units were ready to react immediately. Artificial latency in C2 system was added (10 s at each level).

This process represents the "real" situation based on the ACCS architecture and TBMF delegation. However, the issue is very wide and complex and requires additional effort to implement all its aspects. The article shows the possible way for simulation and modelling C2 chain not only for SBAD units.

References

1. Prochazka, D., Hodicky, J.: Modelling and simulation as a service and concept development and experimentation. In: Proceedings of the 2017 International Conference on Military Technologies (ICMT), pp. 721–727. Institute of Electrical and Electronics Engineers Inc., Piscataway (2017). ISBN 978-1-5386-1988-9
2. Gerz, M., Mulikita, M., Bau N., Gökgöz, F.: The MIP information model - a semantic reference for command & control. In: 2015 International Conference on Military Communications and Information Systems (ICMCIS), Cracow, pp. 1–11 (2015). https://doi.org/10.1109/icmcis.2015.7158717
3. NATO: Air Command and Control System (ACCS). https://www.ncia.nato.int/NPC/Pages/products/Air-Command-and-Control-System-ACCS.aspx. Accessed 10 Aug 2019

4. UK MoD: JWP 3-63: Joint Air Defence, 2nd edn. https://www.gov.uk/government/publications/joint-warfare-publication-3-63-joint-air-defence-second-edition. Accessed 10 Aug 2019
5. Kacer, J., Kutilek, P., Krivanek, V., Doskocil, R., Smrcka, P., Krupka, Z.: Measurement and modelling of the behavior of military pilots. In: Mazal, J. (ed.) MESAS 2017. LNCS, vol. 10756, pp. 434–449. Springer, Cham (2018). https://doi.org/10.1007/978-3-319-76072-8_32
6. Straus, S.G.: Collective Simulation-Based Training in the U.S. Army: User Interface Fidelity, Costs, and Training Effectiveness. RAND Corporation, Santa Monica (2019). ISBN 978-1-9774-0132-8
7. Biagini, M., Corona, F., Casar, J.: Operational scenario modelling supporting unmanned autonomous systems concept development. In: Mazal, J. (ed.) MESAS 2017. LNCS, vol. 10756, pp. 253–267. Springer, Cham (2018). https://doi.org/10.1007/978-3-319-76072-8_18
8. PRESAGIS: Simulation STAGE. https://www.presagis.com/en/product/stage/. Accessed 10 Aug 2019
9. Farlik, J., Stary, V., Casar, J.: Simplification of missile effective coverage zone in air defence simulations. In: Proceedings of the 2017 International Conference on Military Technologies (ICMT), pp. 733–737. Institute of Electrical and Electronics Engineers Inc., Piscataway (2017). ISBN 978-1-5386-1988-9

Modelling and Simulation Paradigms to Support Autonomous System Operationalization

Jan Hodicky[1]([✉]) and Dalibor Prochazka[2]

[1] Aviation Technology Department at the University of Defense, Brno, Czech Republic
jan.hodicky@unob.cz
[2] Centre for the Security and Military Strategic Studies at the University of Defense, Brno,
Czech Republic
dalibor.prochazka@unob.cz

Abstract. Military Autonomous Systems are one of the critical elements in the current and future operations. System with a level of autonomy is known in the military for more than 50 years. However fully autonomous systems have not been yet fully operationalized. Taken as a military capability, autonomous system must be analyzed, designed and implemented to reflect all Doctrine, Organization, Training, Materiel, Leadership, Personnel, Facilities, Interoperability and Information (DOTMLPFI) aspects. The first part of the paper describes autonomous system current state of the art and challenges following DOTMPLFI classification. Secondly, the modeling and simulation paradigms, Discrete Event Simulation, Agent Based Modelling and System Dynamics are proposed to be the right candidate for each DOTMLPFI aspects of AS capability development. There are two Use Cases, the first one based on Agent Based Modeling paradigm and the second one based on System Dynamics paradigm, both demonstrating advantages and drawbacks of a single modelling and simulation paradigm. The last part of the paper discusses differences, and mutual support of these two paradigms in the context of AS capability development.

Keywords: Autonomous system · Modelling and simulation · Capability development

1 Introduction

Systems with a defined level of autonomy are known in the society for the long time. Even if those are heavily implemented in the civilian domain multiplied by the evidence of a military autonomous system operationalization need [1], there are still opportunities and challenges in this effort [2]. First examples of its implementation date back to the era of remotely controlled torpedo [3]. The system behaviour and its automation were explicitly defined and there was no dispute about the extent of the automation. From that time many examples of autonomous system have been introduced within the given classification where systems vary the level of cooperation between Autonomous System (AS) and human operator when being deployed [4]. From the first category, AS with Human in the Loop (HIL), where the autonomy is limited in the task like local and global

© Springer Nature Switzerland AG 2020
J. Mazal et al. (Eds.): MESAS 2019, LNCS 11995, pp. 361–371, 2020.
https://doi.org/10.1007/978-3-030-43890-6_29

planning and motion planning and optimization [5–9] the teleoperated mobile robots can be taken [10, 11]. The second category, AS and Human on the Loop (HOL), contains applications where only critical decisions are made by human and other activities are fully autonomous [12]. This category may even be represented by complex SW solutions that serves to better decision-making process [13]. The third category, AS and Human out of the Loop (HOUTL), where there is not human being intervention, is now under heavy critic because of moral, ethical and legal consequences [14, 15]. With the current and future AS deployment, the critical element will be its countering as well [16, 17].

Importance and potential of Modeling and Simulation (M&S) in the process of AS design, implementation and operationalization has been declared by many authors [18–23]. However, the role of M&S in the articles has not been classified using the military capability development approach and classification called DOTMLPFI [24].

In the article, after the introduction chapter, challenges in the AS domain are introduced following the DOTMLPFI classification being covered by the second chapter. The third chapter brings in accordance with the previous classification proposed suitable candidates of modelling and simulation paradigms for each category. The fourth chapter shows Use Cases of M&S paradigms being used in the AS domain. The closing chapter compares M&S paradigms each other to specify its benefits and drawbacks in the AS operationalization context.

2   Autonomous System Operationalization and Capability Development Approach

DOTMLPFI classification approach is used in the military as a mnemonic tool to tackle Doctrine, Organization, Training, Materiel, Leadership, Personnel, Facilities, Interoperability aspects in the planning process of the future capability development. Generally, any military planning process at the strategic level should be driven by this acronym not to forget any important planning view on the final product. It helps defining requirements and gaps when specifying a new effort in the military context while bringing thinking outside the box. Further part of the chapter describes current state and main challenges in each DOTMLPFII aspects of AS where M&S is applicable.

Doctrine aspect covers tactics, procedures, best practices and laws enabling to conduct a given task. Current best tactics are available for only for HIL and HOL AS. To design and verify these approaches even with HOUTL AS, the virtual environment is needed. Real battlefield is mission oriented and cannot bring verification opportunities in such extent like virtual testing environment. Therefore, design and implementation of M&S experimental frameworks is a need [25].

Organization aspect covers organic structure, relation and grouping that are used by capability being developed. Finding the ideal composition and the structure of cooperating and collaborating ASs and human beings based on the current and mainly future mission objectives is very demanding effort. Even with the current progress in the Artificial Intelligence it is not successfully implemented. Experiments driven by constructive simulations being able to replicate ASs and human operators and human factors bring a new possibility to these types of tasks [26].

Training aspect includes full spectrum of individual education and training up to the collective one. In the paper, exercises are part of T aspect. Simulation environments now support all forms and types of training. Distributed simulation environments following the current simulation best practices and standards like High Level Architecture, Distributed Interactive Simulation or Data Distribution Service are the core of any training framework. Current trend and challenge are to integrate all types of simulation available into these training frameworks. This approach is called Live, Virtual, Constructive (LVC) integration [27]. Models and life AS assets are not yet fully integrated in this framework. However, the integration of individual simulation assets should be done only if technologically required by Training Objectives, otherwise it might be resources demanding activity without added value to the training event. Training is not just about training with AS, it should be open to the idea of training events for HOUTL AS. It would require designing a new training concept for AS and human being cohabitation.

Materiel aspect covers all technology related components, equipment, systems, capacity and performance. It may be further classified based on the conceptual model of AS composed of blocks of sensors, AS communication with AS and human being, external environment, control mechanisms, effectors, movement, sources of energy and internal signal processing. These building blocks are heavily investigated; however, there are still missing or challenging parts:

- no mature common languages for AS design, development and verification and validation of individual components of AS taken as a system of systems;
- no common languages for HMI following the HIL, HOL, and HOUTL classification;
- missing approaches to enhance AS perception to be closer to the human being;
- no M&S standards for the synthetic environment extended by inclusion of information needed for collaboration among human being, AS and ASs;
- no agreed ontology of AS operationalization;
- no simulation platforms available for AS components composition following the HIL, HOL, and HOUTL philosophy.

Leadership aspect covers the way the capability should be used by leaders that are not a part of the capability. It is related to the philosophy how to prepare the leadership not about execution of training. Promising M&S approach is an immersive training environment for individuals putting leaders into the situation that is replicating the current and the future mission environment with AS HIL, HOL a HOUTL capacity. In this way, the leadership is exercised in the use of the future capability. It should not be mistaken with the UAVs operators' training that is in many cases already available [28].

Personnel aspect includes human beings who operates or support a new capability and their qualification. These aspects do not cover only the operators training mentioned in the previous paragraph [28], but it contains design and optimization of the numbers, structure and methods of theses operators' preparation to get expected quality for deployment. As for the operators' training, a challenging part is to introduce human being factors like stress and post trauma syndromes into the mission preparation.

Facilities aspect covers all infrastructure needed to prepare, accommodate, deploy and sustain a new capability. These types of activities are well known and supported by

M&S, namely by operations research approaches typically represented by optimization tasks. Logistic flows and spare parts distribution are examples of these activities.

Interoperability aspect covers all factors needed to work and collaborate in the coalition that must be added to a new capability. Gaps in the interoperability may be identified from the M&S experimental frameworks where national ASs and national doctrinal procedures are implemented. These experimental frameworks need to comply to M&S related standards; therefore, it should be founded in High Level Architecture, Distributed Interactive Simulation or Data Distribution Service for the internal distribution of information among simulation assets, Military Scenario Definition Language and Coalition Battle Management Language for the orders and reports interoperability and finally, Robot Operating System for the implementation of AS and its components.

3 M&S Paradigms for the AS Capability Classification

Modelling and Simulation is a scientific discipline containing two main activities. The first one, modelling, produces a model that is any meaningful representation of a defined part of a modeled system. The model serves to better understand the structure; however, there is not "big" analytical value from the experimental point of view. To make an experiment over the model, the simulation must be carried out to generate raw data sets that are analyzed. Therefore, in the context of the article, only M&S paradigms that can transform, easy per experience, a model into the simulation are taken into the consideration. These are Discrete Event Simulation (DEVS), Agent Based Modeling (ABM) and System Dynamics (SD). This approach is driven by the idea of simulation-based paradigm [29].

DEVS requires a view on the model like a design of a process that is composed of a flow of operations that are consuming resources. Operations form delays, activities, splits and branches. Operations are competing for limited resources and therefore queues belong to the DEVS paradigm. ABM is the newest paradigm comparing to the DEVS and SD. It is founded in the idea of defining local agent characteristics, behavior and the way they communicate each other while overseeing the whole system looking for its patterns of characteristic and behavior. It can help to find unexpected parameter of the modeled system while knowing the system microstructure. Agents that are represented by people, ideas, systems and organizations form the system microstructure. SD models system as a casually closed structure with internal behavior. It allows to define feedback loops that balance of reinforce the modeled flow. Stocks represents an accumulation and describes the system state. Flows are rates in which the stocks are being changed. For further reading on the use of these M&S paradigms refer to Borshchev's paper [30].

DOTMLPFI classification is primary used for a capability development, however to have AS fully operational, the whole AS life cycle must be taken into the consideration. AS life cycle, generally from the system engineering or any system or system of systems point of view, is composed of the following steps: Design, Development, Verification and Validation and Operational Use. For further reading on AS life cycle refer to Hodicky's paper [31].

Therefore, each aspect of DOTMLPFI is confronted with the each steps of the AS life cycle and proper M&S paradigm is recommended. Table 1 demonstrates what M&S paradigm has potential to be used in the defined step of AS capability life cycle.

Table 1. M&S paradigms supporting AS operationalization

AS	Design	Development	Verification and validation	Operational use
D	ABM, DEVS, SD	ABM, DEVS, SD	ABM, DEVS	
O	ABM, DEVS, SD	ABM, DEVS, SD	ABM, DEVS	ABM, DEVS, SD
T	ABM, DEVS, SD	ABM, DEVS	ABM	ABM, DEVS, SD
M	ABM, DEVS			ABM, DEVS, SD
L	ABM, DEVS	ABM, DEVS	ABM	ABM, DEVS
P	ABM, DEVS	ABM, DEVS	ABM	
F	ABM, DEVS		ABM	ABM, DEVS
I	ABM, DEVS		ABM	

4   Use Cases of M&S Paradigm Used in the AS Domain

This section describes two Use Cases of M&S supporting AS operationalization.

The first Use Case uses ABM paradigm. Development of operations concepts is a critical activity belonging to the Doctrinal aspect of AS capability development. The model of simplified ASs lifecycle and their ability to discover Targets was implemented in Anylogic application to reveal details of needed number of ASs with defined capability related to elapsed time to acquire Targets. Two population of agents were created with defined behavior described by state charts. Figure 1 demonstrates the first population of agents called AS with all states that AS goes through, starting from its Availability for mission, through Mission execution up to Maintenance, if needed.

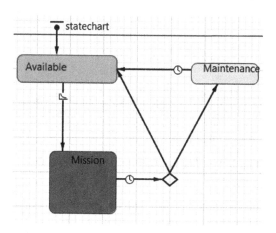

Fig. 1. AS state chart

Figure 2 demonstrates the second population of agents called Targets described by the state chart changing Target status among Detection, Detected and Not Detected states.

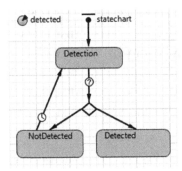

Fig. 2. Target state chart

The two charts in Fig. 3 where populated as the result of simulation runs over the stochastic model.

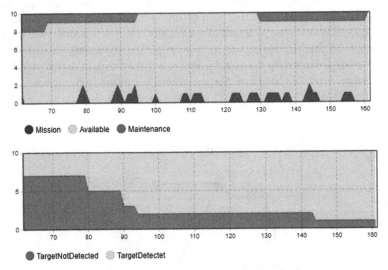

Fig. 3. Populated charts from the model execution

These two charts demonstrate situation with basic setting of 10 agents for both AS and Targets. It reveals that if at least two AS are needed to confirm acquisition of a Target then in the defined pace of ASs deployment, failure and maintenance, the minimum acquired time for all Targets is around 160 h in defined area of operation. Having detailed ABM brings opportunity to run what-if experiments to get estimates of the architecture of the operation and proposed structure and numbers of ASs.

The second Use Case uses System Dynamics paradigm. "System dynamics is a perspective and set of conceptual tools that enable us to understand the structure and dynamics of complex systems. System dynamics is also a rigorous modelling method that enables us to build formal computer simulations of complex systems and use them to design more effective policies and organizations" [32].

To demonstrate System Dynamics approach to AS modelling, we can introduce a qualitative model of an AS capability. In DOTLMPFI qualification, we can define a required capability as:

$$C(t) = \min_i C_i(t), \ i \in I = \{D, O, T, L, M, P, F, I\}, \ C_i(t) \in \langle 0, 1 \rangle. \tag{1}$$

Required capability $C = 1$ if every its component reaches 1. Equation 1 says that the capability quality cannot exceed its limits, i.e. training can be optimized to an optimal level, which means that $C_T (t_S) = 1$ at defined time t_S. On the other hand, overall capability quality is determined by its weakest component and cannot be improved by a better performance of other components. This interpretation is simplified but admissible considering the qualitative approach.

For the use case we limit ourselves by selecting Training, Materiel and Personnel components, see Fig. 4. Each component is modelled by a feedback structure, where rectangle boxes represent accumulations, double arrows with valves represent inflows and outflows and single arrows represent information couplings. The model was created in Vensim application.

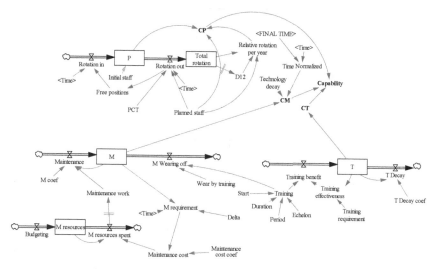

Fig. 4. Capability model with T, M and P component

The personnel model deals with required personnel number and personnel rotation in given period. To be capable of operation, both values must be within limits usually given by doctrines. In this simple case it is supposed that Rotation out takes random values within limits given by PCT ratio (maximum rotation per year in percentage) using uniform distribution.

Training contribution to the overall capability uses periodic training pattern given by a training start, a duration, a period and an echelon.

The Materiel component of the capability is influenced by financial resources available (M resource) which must fulfil requirements (M requirement) to hold the Materiel component at required level. The Maintenance requirement is generated by wearing off caused by utilization in the training process. To incorporate into the model maintenance requirements from an operational engagement would just mean to use a different utilization pattern. The Technology decay is an external factor which can act against the required capability. In case the required capability is detection, it can represent a new technology introduced into opponent equipment preventing or decreasing detection by autonomous systems.

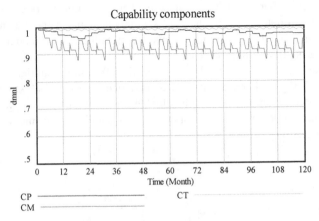

Fig. 5. Capability components function in time

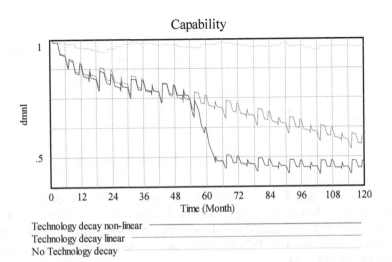

Fig. 6. Influence of Technology decay on Capability

Results of the simulation are given in Figs. 5 and 6. The first figure shows waveforms of Capability components. The second figure demonstrates influence of Technology decay on Capability. All component models can be further decomposed and detailed and dependencies among them can be modelled and analysed.

5 Conclusion

Development of a new capability shouldn't be done in an isolated fashion, using separated DOTMLPFI aspect. This shall be applicable even to the AS operationalization. AS has its own lifecycle and therefore the overall philosophy to the AS capability development should follow the two-dimensional approach. The first dimension covers all DOTMLPFI aspects, their combination and their effects of mutual dependences. The second dimension is bringing system engineering point of view and offers deeper partitioning of DOTMLPFI classification into phases of AS life cycle. This two-dimensional approach to the AS capability development opens a space for the creativity in the process. To evaluate SD approach to AS capabilities, it is necessary to say that this paradigm support high level of abstraction and fits better to strategies evaluation, capability life cycle modelling and seeking from organization structure and composition. It best fits to the Doctrine and Organization aspects of AS capability development. Limitation of the method is given by stocks and flows philosophy, where it is not possible to follow individual entities. AMB can be used to support operationalization of AS through all DOTMLPFI aspects, however not in all phases of AS life cycle. Its main value is seen in the Training and Materiel aspects of DOTMLPFI together with DEVS where SD is not seen as applicable. All in all, using a single modelling and simulation paradigm loses the potential of reveling unexpected features from the simulation that should be the main driver of any experiment. Therefore, if possible, the model should be designed in the open fashion to be extensible by other M&S paradigm. Next phase of the research will be focused on a detailed model of each DOTMLPFI aspect of AS capability development while mixing ABM and DS paradigms.

References

1. Fučík, J., Frank, L., Stojar, R.: Autonomous systems and chinese strategic thinking. In: Mazal, J. (ed.) MESAS 2018. LNCS, vol. 11472, pp. 588–598. Springer, Cham (2019). https://doi.org/10.1007/978-3-030-14984-0_44. ISSN 0302-9743, ISBN 978-3-030-14983-3
2. Stojar, R.: The robotisation of armed conflict. In: 4th International Multidisciplinare Scientific Conference, SGEM 2017, Book 1, Modern Science, pp. 269–276. STEF92, Sofia (2017). ISSN 2367-5659. ISBN 978-619-7408-14-0
3. Vijay, K.: 50 years of robotics. IEEE Robot. Autom. Mag. **17**(3), 8 (2010)
4. Hodicky, J., Prochazka, D., Prochazka, J.: Training with and of autonomous system – modelling and simulation approach. In: Mazal, J. (ed.) MESAS 2017. LNCS, vol. 10756, pp. 383–391. Springer, Cham (2018). https://doi.org/10.1007/978-3-319-76072-8_27. ISBN 978-3-319-76071-1
5. Nohel, J., Stodola, P., Flasar, Z.: Model of the Optimal Maneuver Route. IntechOpen. https://doi.org/10.5772/intechopen.85566. https://www.intechopen.com/online-first/model-of-the-optimal-maneuver-route

6. Stodola, P., Nohel, J., Mazal, J.: Model of optimal maneuver used in tactical decision support system. In: 21st International Conference on Methods and Models in Automation and Robotics, MMAR 2016, pp. 1240–1245 (2016). Article no. 7575316

7. Stodola, P., Mazal, J.: Model of optimal cooperative reconnaissance and its solution using metaheuristic methods. Def. Sci. J. **67**(5), 529–535 (2017). ISSN 0011-748X

8. Hrabec, D., Mazal, J., Stodola, P.: Optimal manoeuvre for two cooperative military elements under uncertain enemy threat. Int. J. Oper. Res. **35**(2), 263–277 (2019). ISSN 1745-7645

9. Mazal, J., Stodola, P., Procházka, D., Kutěj, L., Ščurek, R., Procházka, J.: Modelling of the UAV safety manoeuvre for the air insertion operations. In: Hodicky, J. (ed.) MESAS 2016. LNCS, vol. 9991, pp. 337–346. Springer, Cham (2016). https://doi.org/10.1007/978-3-319-47605-6_27. ISSN 0302-9743, ISBN 978-3-319-47604-9

10. Kot, T., Krys, V., Novak, P.: Simulation system for teleoperated mobile robots. In: Hodicky, J. (ed.) MESAS 2014. LNCS, vol. 8906, pp. 164–172. Springer, Cham (2014). https://doi.org/10.1007/978-3-319-13823-7_15. ISBN 978-3-319-13822-0

11. Doskocil, R., Hosek, J., Krivanek, V., Stefek, A., Bergeon, Y.: Stereo vision for teleoperated robot. In: 16th International Conference on Mechatronics – Mechatronika 2014, Brno, University of Technology, pp. 511–518. IEEE, December 2014

12. Nahavandi, S.: Trusted autonomy between humans and robots: toward human-on-the-loop in robotics and autonomous systems. IEEE Syst. Man Cybern. Mag. **3**(1), 10–17 (2017)

13. Nohel, J.: Possibilities of raster mathematical algorithmic models utilization as an information support of military decision making process. In: Mazal, J. (ed.) MESAS 2018. LNCS, vol. 11472, pp. 553–565. Springer, Cham (2019). https://doi.org/10.1007/978-3-030-14984-0_41. ISSN 0302-9743, ISBN 978-3-030-14984-0

14. Coeckelbergh, M., Funk, M.: Data, speed, and know-how: ethical and philosophical issues in human-autonomous systems cooperation in military contexts. In: Hodicky, J. (ed.) MESAS 2016. LNCS, vol. 9991, pp. 17–24. Springer, Cham (2016). https://doi.org/10.1007/978-3-319-47605-6_2

15. David, W.: The rise of the robotic weapon systems in armed conflicts. In: Proceedings of 7 th Crisis Management and Disaster Response Annual Conference, Sofia, 5–6 June 2019 (2019). https://www.cmdrcoe.org/download.php?id=1434

16. Kratky, M., Farlik, J.: Countering UAVs - the mover of research in military technology. Def. Sci. J. **68**(5), 460–466 (2018). ISSN 0011-748X

17. Farlik, J., Kratky, M., Casar, J., Stary, V.: Multispectral detection of commercial unmanned aerial vehicles. Sensors **19**(7), 1–28 (2019). ISSN 1424-8220

18. Hodicky, J.: Autonomous systems operationalization gaps overcome by modelling and simulation. In: Hodicky, J. (ed.) MESAS 2016. LNCS, vol. 9991, pp. 40–47. Springer, Cham (2016). https://doi.org/10.1007/978-3-319-47605-6_4. ISSN 0302-9743, ISBN 978-3-319-47604-9

19. Hodicky, J.: Modelling and simulation in the autonomous systems' domain – current status and way ahead. In: Hodicky, J. (ed.) MESAS 2015. LNCS, vol. 9055, pp. 17–23. Springer, Cham (2015). https://doi.org/10.1007/978-3-319-22383-4_2. ISSN 03029743, ISBN 978-331922382-7

20. Biagini, M., Corona, F.: M&S-based robot swarms prototype. In: Mazal, J. (ed.) MESAS 2018. LNCS, vol. 11472, pp. 285–301. Springer, Cham (2019). https://doi.org/10.1007/978-3-030-14984-0_22

21. Skrzypecki, S., Pierzchała, D., Tarapata, Z.: Distributed simulation environment of unmanned aerial systems for a search problem. In: Mazal, J. (ed.) MESAS 2018. LNCS, vol. 11472, pp. 65–81. Springer, Cham (2019). https://doi.org/10.1007/978-3-030-14984-0_6

22. Fan, J., Li, D., Li, R., Yang, T., Wang, Q.: Analysis for cooperative combat system of manned-unmanned aerial vehicles and combat simulation. In: Proceedings of 2017 IEEE International Conference on Unmanned Systems, ICUS 2017, January 2018, pp. 204–209 (2018). https://doi.org/10.1109/icus.2017.8278341

23. Stary, V., Krivanek, V., Stefek, A.: Optical detection methods for laser guided unmanned devices. J. Commun. Netw. **20**(5), 464–472 (2018)
24. Spisak, J.: Military concepts – a background for future capabilities development. Econ. Manag. **7**(1), 75–81 (2013)
25. Hodicky, J.: HLA as an experimental backbone for autonomous system integration into operational field. In: Hodicky, J. (ed.) MESAS 2014. LNCS, vol. 8906, pp. 121–126. Springer, Cham (2014). https://doi.org/10.1007/978-3-319-13823-7_11
26. Hodicky, J., Prochazka, D., Prochazka, J.: Automation in experimentation with constructive simulation. In: Mazal, J. (ed.) MESAS 2018. LNCS, vol. 11472, pp. 566–576. Springer, Cham (2019). https://doi.org/10.1007/978-3-030-14984-0_42. ISBN 978-3-030-14984-0
27. Kim, K., et al.: Modeling of complex scenarios using LVC simulation. In: Proceedings - Winter Simulation Conference, January 2015, pp. 2931–2941 (2015). https://doi.org/10.1109/wsc.2014.7020133. Article no. 7020133
28. Postal, G.R., Pavan, W., Rieder, R.A.: Virtual environment for drone pilot training using VR devices. In: Proceedings - 18th Symposium on Virtual and Augmented Reality, SVR 2016, pp. 183–187 (2016). https://doi.org/10.1109/svr.2016.39. Article no. 7517273
29. Ören, T., Mittal, S., Durak, U.: A paradigm shift from model-based to simulation-based: timeliness and usefulness for many disciplines. Int. J. Comput. Softw. Eng. **3**, 125 (2018). https://doi.org/10.15344/2456-4451/2018/126
30. Borshchev, A.: Multi-method modelling: anylogic. Discret Event Simul. Syst. Dyn. Manag. Decis. Mak., 248–279. https://doi.org/10.1002/9781118762745.ch12
31. Hodicky, J.: Standards to support military autonomous system life cycle. In: Březina, T., Jabłoński, R. (eds.) MECHATRONICS 2017. AISC, vol. 644, pp. 671–678. Springer, Cham (2018). https://doi.org/10.1007/978-3-319-65960-2_83
32. Sterman, J.D.: Business Dynamics Systems Thinking and Modeling for a Complex World. Irwin/McGraw-Hill, Boston (2000). ISBN 007238915X

Wars Without Soldiers and Casualties or Victories in Hearts and Minds?

Richard Stojar[⊠], Jakub Fučík, and Libor Frank

Centre for the Security and Military Strategic Studies at the University of Defense,
Brno, Czech Republic
{richard.stojar,jakub.fucik,libor.frank}@unob.cz

Abstract. The text deals with the psychological and ethical aspects of using autonomous weapons. It focuses on controversies associated with the contemporary use of robotic weapons, respectively unmanned weapon systems and the possible use of autonomous weapons in future armed conflicts led by state and non-state actors. These means can achieve significant success at the tactical level while minimizing their own human loss or even the complete absence of their own human element at the point of projection of military force. However, their use may, on the other hand, be in direct contradiction with the long-term strategic objectives of their user and partially delegitimize his intentions. War, as a complex phenomenon, is not limited to direct combat activity, and in relation to a number of non-military factors, the use of autonomous weapons can be problematic from both ethical and psychological points of view. Thus, the military and technological superiority of one party may be partially offset in some conflicts by the ideological superiority of the weaker adversary. The text tries to characterize the main controversies that the deployment of autonomous weapon systems can represent in this respect.

Keywords: Autonomous weapons · Conflict · Psychological aspects

1 Introduction

Although fully armed autonomous systems (AS) are the subject of reflection on the forms of future armed conflicts, rather than reality, the possibilities of the use against human adversaries are already controversial. The deployment of robotic unmanned systems (i.e. the direct predecessor of AS) in the current conflicts has not only demonstrated their effectiveness, but also the negative psychological aspects of their use. Apart from the episodic cases of simultaneous use of these systems by less sophisticated non-state actors, the main deployment is realized in counter-insurgency operations of technologically advanced state actors. A dynamic increase in the use of UAVs can thus be observed in the first two decades of this century in US counter-insurgency operations in Afghanistan or counter-terrorist strikes in the Middle East. The positives that led to this boom are easy to identify. Low economic costs and logistical demands compared to traditional weapon systems with human crew, possibility of keeping human personnel in combat zones in significantly lower numbers, minimizing own human losses. These factors may

© Springer Nature Switzerland AG 2020
J. Mazal et al. (Eds.): MESAS 2019, LNCS 11995, pp. 372–378, 2020.
https://doi.org/10.1007/978-3-030-43890-6_30

lead to the idea of an almost ideal way of waging a war in which political elites and society will not be concerned about deploying their own troops in a hostile environment and confronting their potential losses.

2 Robotic Weapons in Counterinsurgency Operations

Already the current operational deployment of remote controlled/unmanned weapon systems represents a controversial and discussed topic. Fully autonomous weapons would undoubtedly increase the controversy associated with ethical or psychological aspects of their use. However, even the question of practical effectively usability, separate from consideration of the ethical dimension of their deployment, may not have a clear answer. While armed unmanned systems are a suitable means of eliminating the targets, their use may be ineffective in many ways. For example, it does not need to be implemented as part of an overall anti-insurgency strategy (COIN), and it often depends on the territory in which these funds are deployed. In this respect, there can be a great deal of discretion for UAV users in Yemen or Somalia, where there is no in-house power, and a comprehensive approach to stabilizing the region is not realized. However, the situation is different when used in Afghanistan or tribal areas in northern Pakistan. From the perspective that war is a complex phenomenon, which is not limited to direct combat activity but also includes a social dimension and many other non-military factors, the long-term deployment of weapons of this type in rebel regions may seem counterproductive. Here, the main goal is to achieve some regional stability and the sustained threat of a deadly blow from the sky by the unmanned machine, felt by the local population, may contradict the principles defined by current COIN experts such as Ralph Peters or David Kilcullen.

At present, population-centric approach is the predominant approach in counterinsurgency strategies. This approach considers decisive factor in gaining support from the local population as an absolutely key condition for achieving long-term stability and a de facto victory in the ongoing conflict. However, this support can be obtained primarily by persuading the local population. That is, not by lethal blows, however targeted, but by effective action in the information sphere. For this reason, the StratCom - Strategic Communication concept has been developed to play a key role in NATO's counter-insurgency strategy and its operations against the asymmetric adversary [1]. Victory in hearts and minds is thus perceived as a necessary condition for any successful counterinsurgency operation, but this is difficult to achieve in many cases, and the projection of deadly military force may be in direct opposition.

The current doctrinal approaches of the major powers thus increasingly accentuate the information dimension in contemporary conflicts, i.e. a dimension of primarily non-lethal character. Even in the context of considering or implementing the deployment of autonomous weapon systems in conflicts of lower intensity [2]. However, working in the information dimension is primarily a mother of the human element, while most of the existing considerations about the deployment of AS are focused outside of working in this dimension. The tactical benefits and achievements achieved by UAVs today may be in direct conflict with long-term strategic goals. Low costs, the absence of risk for own soldiers and the absence of own human losses can ultimately be a factor that will not lead to a successful end of the conflict, but rather to its prolongation. Not to mention the resistance that armed UAV attacks can trigger not only in the conflict zone population, but also in its allies and partners. For example, the Pakistani government unofficially gave the US permission to use drones in its territory, but over time it began to criticize, in its view, excessive collateral losses between civilians and its own troops and security forces. The disputable number of these losses has been the subject of a sharp dispute between these partners, and in 2012 Pakistan initiated an investigation into these attacks through the UN, although acknowledging at a later date that its collateral loss figures did not correspond to reality and were overstated. The use of combat UAVs arouses strong emotions even in states that are not directly related to their deployment or are not their destination. Also in 2012, allegations have been made in the UK regarding the legality of UAV attacks and the UK's illegal cooperation with the US. This was to provide information by the British Intelligence Service, which was subsequently used in operations in Pakistan and Yemen. In Scotland, in 2013, the University of Edinburgh was forced to stop investment in Ultra Electronics and discontinue cooperation with it under the pressure of student activists and pressure left groups. The company in question also produced components for the US UAV, which was found to be a business that is not socially responsible. Unclear legal aspects of UAV use were highlighted in 2016 by the blockade of Rammstein air force base, where the USAF headquarters are located in Europe. US drones are a controversial topic in Germany due to the fact that the local satellite communication station is reportedly used to transfer information and data between US operators and drones in the deployment area, which, according to the organizers of the protests, contradicts the German constitution [3]. And in these cases, these are still human-driven systems; in the case of fully autonomous systems, social resistance would undoubtedly be significantly stronger. Partial cooperation between AS and human being should also be maintained in this respect in the future. However, this is very difficult to achieve under operating conditions [4]. The currently used technologies allow relatively reliable identification of individuals and will probably be able to realize this identification in the near future even in complicated conditions of the real battlefield. The autonomous system would theoretically already be able to adequately assess the situation, identify enemy activities, assess the risk of collateral damage and minimize it. But it is still a question of whether the human factor can be completely omitted in such an unpredictable environment as the battlefield represents. The fatal failure of artificial intelligence, similar to what has already occurred in attempts to implement AI in the civilian sector, but this time with far more devastating consequences, can not be completely ruled out. The battlefield or operating space in which fully autonomous robotic systems would move is undoubtedly very complex, and features such as trap, surprise friction and uncertainty can not be reliably predicted or programmed with flawless behavioral algorithms. Autonomous robotic systems are designated to be more efficient than humans and prevent emotionally tainted errors through calculations, but they are faster due to machine date analysis, but are still unable to respond adequately to unforeseen circumstances [5]. A potential AS user in combat operations could also be deprived of legal responsibility for their erroneous decision or, on the contrary, be used directly in a manner contrary to the war conventions while at the same time dissociating themselves from their consequences.

On the other hand, AS would not be subject to real psychological stress, prejudice or hatred of opponents and the resulting unwanted behavior or committing war crimes. However, even from an ethical and legal point of view, it is desirable in the future that the human element is not completely excluded from the decision-making process [6].

3   Cultural Dimension of AS Use

With the increasing use of UAVs and potentially Ass for combat operations, and reflections on the increasingly wider range of tasks that they will perform in the future, there are concerns about the implications this development may have for the military and society. There are visions of the gradual degradation of military personnel to operators whose activities will be comparable to those of civilian companies serving prospectively to deliver commercial products. The gradual robotization of military operations could lead to further weakening and de facto extinction of the existing military culture as such. This would, of course, be offset by a significant reduction in the physical and probably psychological demands placed on today´s soldiers and by facilitating the recruitment process. In its consequences, robotization of combat operations may lead to truly revolutionary changes here. Changes in the field of traditional military values not unlike the demise of European knightly culture in confrontation with the democratization of war at the end of the Middle Ages. However, in this context, there may be a sharp difference between opponents on future battlefields. If there is no truly widespread proliferation of AS among the warring parties, there will already be a significant cultural gap between the technologically advanced actors and their adversaries.

Leaving aside the already mentioned ethical dimension, which is not directly reflected in the effectiveness of military and special operations or the deployment of UAVs/ASs within them, there is a problematic cultural and social dimension. This is particularly evident in the conflicts that the West has in a culturally different environment. Although the armed drones currently in use are not autonomous robotic systems and in practical terms, there is little difference in whether the target object is hit by a remote-controlled drone, piloted aircraft or artillery, their perception is significantly different [7]. From the point of view of the adversary and the regional population in the insurgent regions, they are perceived very differently from human or direct manned weapon systems. Contemporary drones are often conceived as an almost robotic weapon, despite its technological advancement, a symbol of cowardice and the decline of the West. Especially because of the perceived unwillingness to risk or deploy the lives of its own soldiers for the values that the West is trying to import into the local environment. There arises an undesirable contradiction between sacrificing martyrs on the one hand and the murderous robotic weapons that these fighters resist and can only fight with unequal combat.

Technical superiority is no longer seen as an expression of the adversary's power and strength, as it may have been in the recent past, but rather a symptom of its weakness. The military inferiority of rebel or terrorist groups may turn into ideological superiority, and the imaginary struggle of values may not sound in favor of the West. The population in the drones' scope, also confronted with the collateral damage that these blows bring, is not becoming the appropriate material for winning hearts and minds. Thus, many critical expertise claims that, despite their effectiveness, UAVs produce more enemies than they eliminate today. Consequently, the current conflicts between state and non-state actors, which is asymmetric in nature, are even more difficult for regular conventional forces to consider whether and how to use the deadly potential at their disposal [8].

However, the negative view is not limited to the population in the target areas, but also affects Western society. Here, drone attacks are often demonized and weaken social support for political efforts and engagement of own or allied forces in conflict regions. Today's controversies about the deployment of armed UAVs are probably not due solely to resistance to external action in conflict zones or the war itself, as was the case with the US anti-war movement during the Vietnam War. Opposition today is based on similar cultural patterns to regional populations. The West, living in post heroic society, is often confronted with images of the struggle between human heroes and murder machines, where the boundary between good and evil is clearly defined, thanks to Hollywood production largely determining the cultural paradigm. In this respect, a member of the Western Civilization Circle formed by this paradigm is no different from a population from other cultures. Man naturally identifies himself with human counterparts and not with artificial intelligence, whether serving his own party or posing a threat. Applying these images to the present reality gives the impression that the current deployment of armed drones or autonomous robotic weapons in the future is not an ideal solution and an ethical response to security threats. Even a post heroic Western society needs its human heroes, and the AS or drone operator killing insurgents from thousands of kilometers away without personally exposing themselves to minimal risk does not meet those needs. From this perspective, it seemed necessary for the specific task of destroying the living symbol of Osama bin Laden's terrorism to be carried out by a human commando. Thus, US soldiers took revenge on September 11, 2001 in a traditional manly manner, and not by an anonymous drone, which is now standard practice for similar US operations.

The aforementioned notional value deficit, which the present adversary does not experience, may become a reason for weakening social or national morality and, conversely, a trigger for the radicalization of religiously or ethnically related individuals in the western environment [9]. Consequently, these individuals may be identified in individual cases with rebel or terrorist group goals and reinforced a sense of moral superiority over Western values for which Western society is not willing to risk the lives of its soldiers despite all technical and military dominance.

Some experts see a greater possibility not to resign from the use of advanced technology while avoiding the consequences of the aforementioned cultural paradigm in a greater involvement of local troops in a counter-insurgency campaign in which their members would be able to complement the Western armies with a personal approach. This consideration, however, runs into the fact that the local units often do not possess the necessary qualities despite all the effort and cost and can be effectively infiltrated by the adversary. The question remains if armed ASs become the main means by which the powers will act against their irregular adversaries in the framework of a long-term or permanent low-intensity military operation and how the insurgents will counteract them [10]. Robert N. Gates has already warned against excessive fascination with modern weapon technologies that could lead to a false idea of a war deprived of the reality of his own losses and sparing the lives of innocent civilians. On the other hand, the emotional debate over the use of armed AS can lead to the disobedience or rejection of these funds by political decision-makers if they are subject to strong social resistance [11].

4 Conclusion

Robotic weapons, the type of UAV (and potentially AS) are now used to target the destruction of enemy in a number of conflicting regions. Such use, however, meets not only with a positive evaluation of their effectiveness, but also with strong criticism. According to critical voices, unmanned lethal weapon systems significantly reduce the threshold of political sensitivity to the use of force. Flexible deployment, efficiency, human crew absenteeism and low cost operation of unmanned or fully autonomous robotic systems can reduce the barriers to political decision making on whether or not to use armed violence and facilitate authorization of problematic kinetic operations. From this point of view, ASs can allow political elites to conduct a near-constant war of low intensity without much cost, and thus without much interest or resistance from society. However, their real effectiveness in conflicts is also questionable, as their deployment may be in direct contradiction with the principles of parallel counter-insurgency strategy. The ethical dimension of deploying such resources is even more complex. The question of what degree of autonomy should be given to these systems, and whether an autonomous decision can be made from an ethical point of view to kill a human being by artificial intelligence, is unlikely to find an unequivocal answer even when ASs become a standard armament of advanced armed forces.

Acknowledgements. The work presented in this paper has been supported by the Ministry of Defence of the Czech Republic (Research Project "STRATAL" No. 907930101023).

References

1. Divišová, V.: Strategic communications in NATO counterinsurgency operations. Obrana a strategie **14**(2), 105–118 (2014). ISSN 1802-7199
2. Fučík, J., Frank, L., Stojar, R.: Autonomous systems and Chinese strategic thinking. In: Mazal, J. (ed.) MESAS 2018. LNCS, vol. 11472, pp. 588–598. Springer, Cham (2019). https://doi.org/10.1007/978-3-030-14984-0_44. ISSN 0302-9743, ISBN 978-3-030-14983-3
3. Stojar, R.: Bezpilotní prostředky a problematika jejich nasazení v soudobých konfliktech. Obrana a strategie **16**(2), 5–18 (2016). https://doi.org/10.3849/1802-7199.16.2016.02.005-018. ISSN 1802-7199
4. Hodicky, J.: Modelling and simulation in the autonomous systems' domain – current status and way ahead. In: Hodicky, J. (ed.) MESAS 2015. LNCS, vol. 9055, pp. 17–23. Springer, Cham (2015). https://doi.org/10.1007/978-3-319-22383-4_2
5. Danet D.: Cartographie l'autonomie des systèmes d'armes, Convention sur Certaines Armes Classiques, Gèneve 11–15 avril 2016, p. 5 (2016)
6. Hodicky, J., Prochazka, D., Prochazka, J.: Training with and of autonomous system – modelling and simulation approach. In: Mazal, J. (ed.) MESAS 2017. LNCS, vol. 10756, pp. 383–391. Springer, Cham (2018). https://doi.org/10.1007/978-3-319-76072-8_27. ISBN 978-3-319-76071-1

7. Boisboissel, G.: De l'autonomie dans les systèmes robotiques militaires et de la place de l'homme. Nouveaux espaces stratégiques. Revue Défense Nationale, 145 (2016). ISBN 978-2-919639-56-4

8. Majchút, I.: Deployability of armed forces in irregular warfare. In: Proceedings of 24th International Scientific Conference KBO, Sibiu, Romania, pp. 133–134 (2018). https://doi.org/10.1515/kbo-2018-0019. ISSN 1843-6722

9. Stojarová, V., Stojar, R.: Balkan regional development: moderate or radical Islam for the Balkans. J. Balk. East. Stud., 1–15 (2018). https://doi.org/10.1080/19448953.2018.1506284. ISSN 1944-8953

10. Gusteron, H.: Drone: Remote Control Warfare. MIT Press, Washington (2016). ISBN 978-0-2623-3437-2

11. Fučík, J., Kříž, Z.: Informační revoluce, vojensko-technická revoluce, nebo revoluce ve vojenských záležitostech? Obrana a strategie **13**(2), 15–24 (2013). https://doi.org/10.3849/1802-7199.13.2013.02.015-024. ISSN 1802-7199

Maneuver Control System CZ

Jan Nohel$^{(\boxtimes)}$ (iD) and Zdeněk Flasar (iD)

University of Defense, Brno, Czech Republic
{jan.nohel,zdenek.flasar}@unob.cz

Abstract. The planning and decision-making process for conducting combat operations must take into account the development of the situation in a number of diverse areas that affect the action of forces and resources on the battlefield. An analysis of their impact can be done through computational programs and mathematical algorithmic models, using a raster representation of geographic and tactical data. Raster data layers in the mathematical model allow for a combination of surface effects, terrain elevation and weather effects as well as the forces and vehicles of both the enemy and friendly units. Mathematical calculations result in a maneuver route, optimized based on predefined criteria, such as speed and safety. The result can have a double use. In case of the maneuver of enemy forces and vehicles, it is possible to simulate their probable future activity. The result of combining all effects of the situation on the battlefield is the optimal route of maneuver of friendly units designed in several seconds. Utilization of such software will provide commanders with substantive independence and speed of decision-making in the course of military operations. Sharing designed maneuver route with all adjacent units and higher headquarters also enables to coordinate the activity of all superior task forces.

Keywords: Decision-making process · Offensive maneuver · Restricted area · Maneuver model · Target enemy

Unexpected attack by an enemy, identifying high-priority objectives and/or a significant change in the situation on the battlefield are cases when it is necessary to make decisions quickly in order to take immediate action. Output of such a decision may be, above all, response of the unit attacked by a weaker or stronger enemy, hasty attack planning and/or forced movement over a greater distance. Any delay or incorrect assessment of the geographic tactical characteristics may lead to casualties or loss of vehicles, or squandering an opportunity to destroy the enemy. A particularly detailed analysis needs to be conducted when using autonomous devices of destroying an identified enemy, which is due to the limited ability to respond. Fast and effective accomplishment of an offensive or defensive maneuver is conditioned by a fast and precise analysis of terrain passability affected by the enemy's combat possibilities. On this basis, every commander or operator/commander of an autonomous device makes a decision as to whether eliminate the attacker and with what type of offensive maneuver, or which way to withdraw from a dangerous area. Spatial expression of the maneuver route is a cue for the movement of allocated forces and devices.

Maneuver represents employment of forces on the battlefield through movement in combination with fire, or fire potential, to achieve a position of advantage in respect

© Springer Nature Switzerland AG 2020
J. Mazal et al. (Eds.): MESAS 2019, LNCS 11995, pp. 379–388, 2020.
https://doi.org/10.1007/978-3-030-43890-6_31

to the enemy in order to accomplish the mission. [1, pp. 78] It is a dynamic combat element, its purpose being elimination of the enemy's ability to conduct effectively combat operations with forces from favorable positions and strike the decisive blow. With a synchronized maneuver, optimally defined in terms of space and time, a sufficient concentration of forces for a decisive attack can be gathered and surprise effect can be taken advantage of. Methods of mathematic algorithm simulation of the maneuver route are also dealt with in [2–5]. Possibilities of planning and modeling maneuver routes for autonomous vehicles are described in [6–10].

Solutions to such situations are offered by Maneuver Control System CZ (MCS CZ), software that performs assessment of battlefield situation factors using predefined criteria. It runs using Tactical Decision Support System (TDSS), a platform that has been developed at University of Defense, the Czech Republic, by associate professor Ing. Petr Stodola, PhD and associate professor Ing. Jan Mazal, PhD since 2006, see [11]. The output of MCS CZ operations is the Model of Optimal Maneuver Route described in [12]. The model was designed by one of the authors of this article in 2015 as part of his PhD studies at University of Defense, the top education institution of the Army of the Czech Republic. The latest addition to MCS CZ is four offensive maneuvers of a unit on a battlefield, described below in the article.[1] The paper reports on the designed capabilities that are further demonstrated in selected scenarios.

1 MCS CZ Models

The Model of the Optimal Maneuver Route assesses and combines the impact of diverse battlefield aspects on space passability. They include influence of the surface and vegetation, terrain elevation, weather, activity of friendly forces and devices and of the enemy. On the basis of TDSS, it subsequently compiles cost surface of passability between the starting and end point. The resulting output of the model is a maneuver route proposal, optimized in terms of time and safety. Other models of MCS CZ maneuver employ calculations of the Model of the Optimal Maneuver Route for spatial specification of each route in the terrain.

After defining the target position of the enemy and friendly (allocated) maneuver unit, one of the predefined offensive maneuvers can be selected, see Fig. 1. MCS CZ operates with basic maneuvers: envelopment, turning movement, frontal attack and attack by fire. Routes of envelopment and turning movements are further defined by an impassable area situated between the friendly unit and the enemy target position. The attack by fire aimed at achieving a fire position utilizes the area of direct visibility of the enemy target position. The defensive maneuver of withdrawal calculates the route to a defined safe position.

The final form of the selected maneuver also depends on the type of the moving element, i.e., infantry unit, wheeled and tracked vehicles. Each type of movement is linked with various possibilities of terrain passability. Before entering the final calculations, a specific type of maneuver devices can be selected together with characteristics of predefined speed on different types of surface.

---

[1] The offensive maneuver models were implemented in MCS CZ by assoc. prof. Ing. Petr Stodola, PhD, on the basis of a proposal by the author of this article.

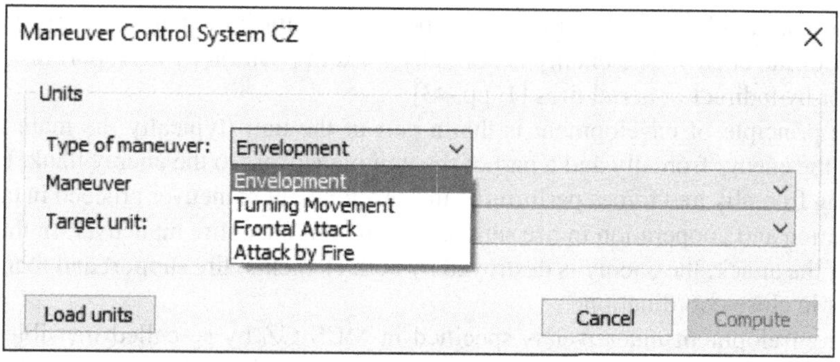

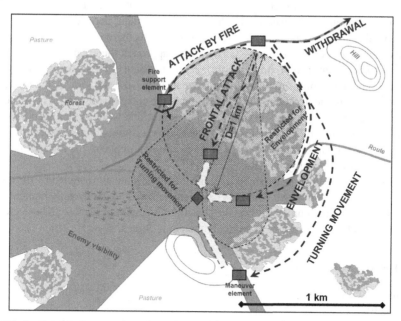

Fig. 1. MCS CZ panel of maneuvers selection implemented in TDSS

None of the abovementioned maneuvers is universal. Their use depends on vegetation and relief as well as on the enemy forces and position. No specific maneuver is prescribed for performing a defensive response in combat with the enemy (withdrawal). For this case, the proven Model of the Optimal Movement Route can be employed, its route leading to a predefined safe space, see Fig. 2.

Fig. 2. Graphical expression of particular maneuver routes computation by MCS CZ

1.1 Envelopment

Envelopment is defined by [1, pp. 48] as an offensive maneuver in which the main attacking force passes around or over the enemy's principal defensive positions to secure objectives to the enemy's rear. Double envelopment is a maneuver executed by forces that move around both flanks of an enemy position to attack the flanks or objectives in the rear of the enemy. The enemy is normally fixed in position by a supporting frontal attack or by indirect or aerial fires [1, pp. 43].

The principle of envelopment is that a part of the unit (typically the main force) attacks the enemy frontally and a part of the unit maneuvers to the enemy flank. Forces attacking frontally and forces performing the envelopment maneuver proceed in tactical cooperation and cooperation in fire support throughout the entire maneuver. In the final stage of the attack, the enemy is destroyed by both elements: fire support and maneuver element in close coordination.

The envelopment maneuver is specified in MCS CZ by so-called invisible layer of the cost surface as an impassable (restricted) area, see Fig. 2. This non-passable area is in the form of a circle with a diameter equaling the distance (D) between the position of the friendly unit and enemy unit, but not more than 1 km. The maximum distance of the envelopment maneuver from the enemy position is derived from many tactical principles and experiences. The first of them is the maximum possible distance of 1 km for the destructive effect of direct fire of hand weapons and devices attacking frontally. The second one takes into account the actual capability of friendly forces and devices to perform an effective maneuver. The fire element of the unit attacking frontally should be able to fire at the identified enemy from a distance of up to 1 km and thus limit the enemy's movement. Subsequently, the attacking element, depending on the terrain, should be able to overcome this semi-circle distance to the enemy positions. In case of a distance of more than 1 km it is advisable to approach the enemy undetected and perform envelopment from a more opportune closer distance. Passing a larger distance could take more time for the moving element during which the situation on the battlefield could change dramatically including the position of the enemy target unit. The maneuver route for envelopment shall be outside the impassable circle with uncalculated influence layer (effective range) of the target enemy. The reason for intentional suppression of the influence of the enemy's effective range is the resulting absence of the fastest safe route for movement to the enemy position.

MCS CZ always designs a maneuver route outside the area threatened by the enemy fire, which is the reason why it could not calculate it. Threat to the friendly maneuvering unit by the enemy target unit's fire and the possibility of counterattack shall be decreased by fire of friendly covering fire of frontally attacking forces.

1.2 Turning Movement

Turning movement is defined by [1, pp. 127] as a variation of envelopment in which the attacking force passes around or over the enemy's principal defensive positions to secure objectives deep in the enemy's rear to force the enemy to abandon its position or divert major forces to meet the threat. It is performed in tactical coordination with frontally attacking forces with the view of limiting the enemy movement. In comparison with envelopment, turning movement is usually a wider and deeper maneuver. In the final stage of the maneuver, the enemy should be again under fire support and maneuver element proceeding in close coordination. Turning movement is specified in MCS CZ by the so-called invisible layer of cost surface of passability and impassable (restricted) area, see Fig. 2. The basis for defining the maneuver route is the distance between the position of friendly forces and devices and the enemy (D). The impassable area consists of two semi-ellipsoids with dimensions of 1.3D (length) and 0.5D (the widest part). They spread from the position of friendly unit to the wider (at both ends) position of the enemy unit with the intersection of the nearer semi-ellipsoids in the position of the enemy unit, within the maximum distance of D = 1 km. The turning movement route shall be designed outside the impassable circle. Its calculation does not include the influence of effective range of the target enemy, which is for the same reason as in the case of envelopment.

1.3   Frontal Attack

The frontal attack is defined by [1, pp. 55] as an offensive maneuver in which the main action is directed against the front of the enemy forces. The maneuver route is calculated in the traditional manner, i.e. the fastest and safest route with respect to the influence of the effective range of enemy forces and devices (except for the target units), see Fig. 2. The influence of its effective range is, again, suppressed, for the same reason as in the previous maneuvers. What is of utmost importance in the case of frontal attack is the coordination between the attacking unit maneuver and the covering fire. This maneuver can be applied when performing an MTC (Move to Contact) task when the assigned unit is searching for the enemy with the view of destroying it.

1.4   Attack by Fire

Attack by fire can represent either single task of enemy destruction, harassing fire or fire support of other maneuver units' activity. The fire support defined by [1, pp. 52] reflects an application of fire, coordinated with the maneuver of forces, to destroy, neutralize or suppress the enemy. When selecting attack by fire, MCS CZ calculates the movement route to the nearest edge of the area of so-called effective fire and direct visibility of the target enemy, see Fig. 2. The final position of the movement is the nearest edge of the enemy effective range, as after achieving it the allocated unit may attack by fire. This maneuver can be employed for the purpose of attacking the enemy by fire from the maximum effective distance. The resulting destructive effect also depends on the effective range of the particular weapon system of the allocated unit, up-to-dateness of the elevation data of MCS CZ and height of the surrounding vegetation in the terrain. It can be presumed that the target enemy returns fire and responds to the attack. However, in case the unit gets under threat, the fire position being on the edge of the enemy effective range allows for fast abandoning of the dangerous area.

1.5   Withdrawal

The withdrawal operation is specified in [1, pp. 132] as a planned operation in which a force in contact disengages from an enemy force. It may be a forced or preventive measure consisting in units threatened by destruction abandoning the area. It is a defensive maneuver for which there is no special model in MCS CZ. The route of withdrawal from a dangerous area is calculated using the Model of the Optimal Maneuver Route, after the final position or checkpoint of withdrawal is specified. MCS CZ finds the fastest safe route toward the final position or checkpoint of withdrawal, see Fig. 2. Withdrawal is a maneuver that can be used, for instance, when a unit is attacked by a stronger enemy when the surrounding terrain does not allow for choosing another option.

2   Testing Maneuver Models

All maneuver models were tested in practice with units solving the identical tactical situation: a maneuvering unit was assigned the task of destroying the identified enemy (SAM, Surface to Air Missile). The enemy position was situated 440 m from the position of the friendly unit. The solution depends on many circumstances, the most important ones being terrain passability in the intermediate area, strength and ability of the identified enemy as well as the friendly unit's abilities. In case of defensive response, i.e., withdrawal, the system designs the fastest safe route back to the selected position of withdrawal. However, if the unit commander decides to attack the enemy, he can choose in MCS CZ from four offensive maneuvers. On the basis of tactical decisions witnessed, it can be said that the attacking unit will be typically divided to a fire support element and a maneuver element. The fire element attacks the enemy with fire, covering the operation of the maneuver element performing frontal attack, envelopment or turning movement. A similar solution will be employed also when a group of Unmanned Ground Vehicles (UGV) is used.

Practical measurement was made in two variants: for infantry and for a cooperating UGV group, simulated by the Yamaha Grizzly four-wheeler. The maneuver routes are shown in Figs. 3, 4, 5 and 6 with the UGV route on the left and the infantry element on the right. The option of using paved as well as soft paths was suppressed for infantry, as these attract enemy's attention. The use of terrain was not adjusted for the UGV maneuver, particularly with respect to its restricted passability through the terrain, as it needs to pass primarily through pathways and open areas. However, UGV usually has a lower silhouette and when it used there is no risk of casualties.

2.1   Turning Movement

The turning movement routes were calculated by MCS CZ in both cases for the northern part of the intermediate area, see Fig. 3. However, the route of the infantry maneuver

Fig. 3. Computation of turning movement maneuver routes by MCS CZ

was calculated to lead through forested terrain, which is why it was designed that UGV primarily uses relatively easily passable paths. The maneuver times are shown in Table 1.

Table 1. Turning movement times of UGV and infantry

Maneuver	MCS CZ time	Real time	Difference
UGV	05:27	06:20	+00:53
Infantry	34:32	36:15	+01:43

2.2 Envelopment

The envelopment routes were calculated by MCS CZ differently, depending on the elements' passability through the terrain. Again, the UGV maneuver was designed to lead through pathways that are relatively easily passable. The first half of the infantry maneuver was designed for forested terrain that provides cover. Nevertheless, further advancement goes through an open area, more or less directly to the enemy target position, as shown in Fig. 4. The maneuver times are shown in Table 2.

Fig. 4. Computation of envelopment maneuver routes by MCS CZ

Table 2. Envelopment maneuver times of UGV and infantry

Maneuver	MCS CZ time	Real time	Difference
UGV	04:09	04:01	−00:08
Infantry	22:56	23:50	+00:54

2.3 Frontal Attack

The frontal attack routes were calculated by MCS CZ in both cases in a similar way, see Fig. 5. The reason was the presence of soft pathways in the shortest direction of the maneuver to the target enemy. The first half of the maneuver route of the infantry led through forested terrain that provides cover from enemy's observation and fire. The maneuver times are shown in Table 3.

Fig. 5. Computation of frontal attack maneuver routes by MCS CZ

Table 3. Frontal attack maneuver times of UGV and infantry

Maneuver	MCS CZ time	Real time	Difference
UGV	01:16	01:12	−00:04
Infantry	08:48	08:43	−00:05

2.4 Attack by Fire

The attack by fire routes were designed by MCS CZ identically, which is due to a very short distance (approximately 60 m) to the nearest edge of an area of direct visibility of the target enemy. The maneuver times are shown in Table 4.

Fig. 6. Computation of attack by fire maneuver routes by MCS CZ

Table 4. Attack by fire maneuver times of UGV and infantry

Maneuver	MCS CZ time	Real time	Difference
UGV	00:54	01:03	+00:09
Infantry	01:05	01:18	+00:13

All routes of offensive maneuvers were calculated by MCS CZ to last 20 s at most, with medium degree of geographic documents accuracy. The weather conditions at the time of measurement can be defined as partly cloudy, no rainfall, temperature 24 °C, humidity 60%, last rainfall 16 mm 1 day ago.

3   Conclusion

The results of the experiments suggest that the implemented models can be used when designing a route of an offensive maneuver. The actual solution of the tactical situation would probably require dividing the unit in two independent elements: a covering fire element and an attacking element. After the necessary preparation, the covering fire element would commence movement to the fire position that should be achieved, according to MCS CZ, by UGV in 00:54 s (infantry 00:65 s). Subsequently, the attacking element of the unit would perform destruction of the target enemy, the calculated time in case of UGV ranging between 01:16 and 05:27 min. It would take between 8:48 and 34:32 min for the infantry element to accomplish the same task, according to MCS CZ.

By actually performing the calculated maneuvers we ascertained the delay, particularly of the infantry element, caused by increased cautiousness when approaching the target enemy. From the enemy position, the elements attacking by fire remained unnoticed. The movement of the attacking elements was only detected from the distance of approximately 220 m and the surprise effect played an important role. However, not a single attacking element was noticed by enemy neighboring units during the movement.

MCS CZ maneuver models can be applied, in particularly, in situations where there is not enough time to plan attack on an enemy priority target and only brief preparation is possible.

The attack maneuver can be simulated using MCS CZ by conducting the maneuver calculation for all variants. Such results can be quickly assessed based on the calculated time needed for achieving the objective. The allocated unit then uses the maneuver route that meets the time requirements for destroying the enemy, while maximizing the surprise effect. Similarly, the sequence of destroying targets can be assessed based on the time needed by the friendly units for performing the maneuver and achieving the enemy targets. The types of maneuvers can be combined in various allocated unit elements in order to achieve the maximum surprise and destructive effect. At the same time, the operation of several maneuvering and firing elements can be coordinated based on detailed knowledge of the progress and duration of the planned maneuvers.

MCS CZ in combination with GPS technology is a suitable tool for a very fast design of maneuver routes for forces and devices optimized in terms of time and safety. Future development and improvement of military operations consists in group employment and combat UGV cooperation when attacking enemy positions. MCS CZ is a tool that enables to follow this trend. Its substantial contribution is the ability to design, almost immediately, solutions to unpredictable situations, which can be a way to gain domination over the battlefield.

References

1. AAP-06 (2018): NATO glossary of terms and definition (English and French). NATO Standardization Office, Brussels (2018)
2. Tarapata, Z.: Military route planning in battlefield simulation: effectiveness problems and potential solutions. J. Telecommun. Inf. Technol. **2003**(4), 47–56 (2003)
3. Delling, D., Sanders, P., Schultes, D., Wagner, D.: Engineering route planning algorithms. In: Lerner, J., Wagner, D., Zweig, K.A. (eds.) Algorithmics of Large and Complex Networks. LNCS, vol. 5515, pp. 117–139. Springer, Heidelberg (2009). https://doi.org/10.1007/978-3-642-02094-0_7
4. Rybanský, M., et al.: Modelling of cross-country transport in raster format. Environ. Earth Sci. **74**(10), 7049–7058 (2015)
5. Rybanský, M.: Modelling of the optimal vehicle route in terrain in emergency situations using GIS data. IOP Conf. Ser. Earth Environ. Sci. **18** (2014). https://doi.org/10.1088/1755-1315/18/1/012131
6. Zhang, X., Duan, H.: An improved constrained differential evolution algorithm for unmanned aerial vehicle global route planning. Appl. Soft Comput. **26**, 270–284 (2015)
7. González, D., Pérez, J., Milanés, V., Nashashibi, F.: A review of motion planning techniques for automated vehicles. IEEE Trans. Intell. Transp. Syst. **17**(4), 1135–1145 (2016)
8. Hamid, U., et al.: A review on threat assessment, path planning and path tracking strategies for collision avoidance systems of autonomous vehicles. Int. J. Veh. Auton. Syst. **14**(2), 134–169 (2018)
9. Hodický, J., Procházky, D.: Challenges in the implementation of autonomous systems into the battlefield. In: Proceedings of the 2017 International Conference on Military Technologies (ICMT), pp. 743–747. Institute of Electrical and Electronics Engineers Inc., Piscataway (2017). https://doi.org/10.1109/miltechs.2017.7988855. ISBN 978-1-5386-1988-9
10. Hodicky, J.: Standards to support military autonomous system life cycle. In: Březina, T., Jabłoński, R. (eds.) MECHATRONICS 2017. AISC, vol. 644, pp. 671–678. Springer, Cham (2018). https://doi.org/10.1007/978-3-319-65960-2_83. ISSN 2194-5357, ISBN 978-3-319-65959-6
11. Stodola, P., Mazal, J.: Tactical decision support system to aid commanders in their decision-making. In: Hodicky, J. (ed.) MESAS 2016. LNCS, vol. 9991, pp. 396–406. Springer, Cham (2016). https://doi.org/10.1007/978-3-319-47605-6_32. ISBN 978-3-319-47605-6
12. Nohel, J.: Possibilities of raster mathematical algorithmic models utilization as an information support of military decision making process. In: Mazal, J. (ed.) MESAS 2018. LNCS, vol. 11472, pp. 553–565. Springer, Cham (2019). https://doi.org/10.1007/978-3-030-14984-0_41. ISBN 978-3-030-14984-0

C2SIM Operationalization Extended to Autonomous Systems

Fabio Corona$^{(\boxtimes)}$ and Marco Biagini

NATO M&S Centre of Excellence, Piazza R. Villoresi 1, 00143 Rome, RM, Italy
{mscoe.cde04,mscoe.cde01}@smd.difesa.it
http://www.mscoe.org

Abstract. Technical Activity in the NATO Modelling and Simulation Group (MSG–145) for operationalization of new Simulation Interoperability Standards Organization (SISO) C2SIM standard is approaching its completion. This second generation of C2SIM standards from SISO for coalitions to interoperate their national command and control (C2) and simulation systems is ready for balloting and being the basis of a STANAG. This standard for synthetic battlespace can have a great impact on the effectiveness of coalition military operations and training. MSG-145 conducted extensive testing to validate this standard. Modelling and Simulation Centre of Excellence participated to these efforts focusing in extending the operationalization of the C2SIM standard to the Autonomous System functional area in the framework of the Research on Robotics for Concept and Capability Development (R2CD2) project. In this paper, at first the rational and goals of the R2CD2 project are illustrated, then the process followed to develop an extension of the C2SIM standard is described. In particular, how was possible to follow the SISO guidelines for developing a simulation scenario for Autonomous Systems and generating the necessary information exchange requirements to build the C2SIM extension is treated. Then, the methodology suggested by SISO to construct the extension is shown as applied in this specific use case. Finally, this paper deals with the design and development of a modular, scalable and distributed architecture demonstrator to run the designed scenario and test the C2SIM extension to Autonomous Systems. Results of the experimentation performed during R2CD2 project testing, the Coalition Warrior Interoperability eXercise (CWIX) and the MSG–145 mini-exercise are reported. This paper can provide complete guidelines to successfully extend the C2SIM standard, with a particular focus on the use of this new standard to automatize the scenario initialization and the C2 messages between humans in a command post and simulated or real robots.

Keywords: C2SIM · Autonomous Systems · M&S COE

1 Introduction

The Simulation Interoperability Standard Organization (SISO) draft of the new standard document [1] states that *Command and Control Systems to Simula-*

© Springer Nature Switzerland AG 2020
J. Mazal et al. (Eds.): MESAS 2019, LNCS 11995, pp. 389–408, 2020.
https://doi.org/10.1007/978-3-030-43890-6_32

tion Systems Interoperation (C2SIM) is a standard for expressing and exchanging Command and Control (C2) information among C2 systems, simulation systems, and robotic and autonomous (RAS) systems in a coalition context. This new standard for interoperability between C2 and simulation systems can have a huge impact on modern military operations and training, where effective interoperation among coalition systems is critical for military needs like force readiness, situation awareness, operational training, information sharing and decision support [2–5]. It is not surprising that North Atlantic Treaty Organization (NATO) is interested into the operationalization of C2SIM in several military areas through its Scientific and Technology Organization (STO). STO NATO Modelling and Simulation Group (NMSG) has been cooperating with SISO C2SIM Product Development Group (PDG) [6] for many years [7–9] and, more recently, the MSG–145 *Operationalization of Command and Control – Simulation Interoperation (C2SIM)* Technical Activity [10] has been working in the last three years for the exploration, experimentation, validation and extension of C2SIM in different areas developed as separated use cases. This paper illustrates how the NATO Modelling and Simulation Centre of Excellence (M&S COE), a COE accredited by NATO Allied Command for Transformation (ACT) to provide to the Alliance expertise in M&S field, contributed to these efforts extending C2SIM to the Autonomous Systems (AS) area. As developed, C2SIM messages exchange for robots answers the requirements for an human–robotic interaction which depends more on level of Autonomy of robots than on the technology maturity of robotic platforms, in accordance to ACT conceptualization of AS.

So, this paper presents at first the M&S COE project for research on robotics to explain the rational behind the interest on C2SIM for AS, therefore the process agreed among MSG–145 group to develop an extension of C2SIM standard is illustrated as applied for AS. Finally, this paper shows the experimental results for C2SIM validation, both in its standard core part and in developed extension. The extension to AS proved to be successfully implemented either in isolation during project testing or in a coalition environment with several different systems during Coalition Warrior Interoperability eXercise (CWIX) and a miniature exercise organized by MSG–145. In conclusions, this paper deals with a complete process to successfully extend the C2SIM standard, with a particular focus on automatization of scenario initialization and C2 messages exchange between humans and simulated or real robots.

2   R2CD2 Project

The C2SIM Autonomous System eXtension (ASX), as it is named according to the three letters SISO convention, has been developed in the wider scope of the "Research on Robotics Concept and Capability Development (R2CD2)" project. The R2CD2 is the M&S COE project on robotics whose aim is to leverage M&S technology in order to perform Concept Development and Experimentation (CD&E) on Unmanned Autonomous Systems (UAxS) employment in the modern urban battlefield. Many studies can be found in literature demonstrating how M&S can be in support of solving military problems concerning autonomous systems employment in different fields, among all [11–21]. The R2CD2 project was designed to support the NATO Transformation with reference to new Autonomous Systems capability, innovative concepts on Autonomy and on countering robotic systems. Moreover M&S COE mission includes both studies and experimentation of interoperability standards in the M&S domain, and supporting technical activity of the STO for this goal is always in its lines of efforts. With these premises, the choice of experimenting the new SISO C2SIM standard for command and control of UAxS, developing an extension of this language tailored for the project, was natural.

The M&S COE level of ambition is to investigate on five main areas relative to near or mid-term future employment of UAxS in urban environment:

- interaction between human troops and robots – military C2 of robotic units;
- Verification and Validation (V&V) of AS;
- Tactics, Techniques and Procedures (TTPs) for UAxS;
- development of functional requirements of new robotic platforms;
- countering UAxS;

The R2CD2 project up to now concentrated into some of these points, dealing with: the interaction between simulated UAxS and real C2 systems; study of UAxS employment in a megacity of the future (for land and air domains); Decision-making support for UAxS—implemented either on an external system or directly on simulated UAxS based on their level of Autonomy. In order to perform experimentation about new UAxS-related concepts and standards, with these objectives in mind, after a first phase of conceptualization [22,23], a prototype of a scalable and modular demonstrator, based on open standards and selected constructive simulators, was built during the R2CD2 project in collaboration with the Industry and Academia. Thanks to the possibility that M&S technology gives to reuse models, proof-of-concept prototypes, systems, studies, saving precious resources, for this demonstrator the followings elements have been re-used: the Level of Autonomy (LoA), concept developed during the Autonomous Systems Countermeasures (C-UAxS) project of the ACT [24], for the robotic behaviour and degree of human–robot interaction; "Archaria" urban model, a model of a mega city of the future built during the ACT Urbanization Project (UP) [25] by the NATO M&S COE, for the terrain generation.

2.1   Level of Autonomy (LoA)

The LoA concept deserves a brief description and some definitions since it is of central importance for the requirements of the C2 messages exchange and of the demonstrator architecture. Firstly, the focus is an Unmanned Autonomous Systems (UAS), which act without human intervention, opposite to the Manned systems, and which are intelligence-based, can behave as self-directed entities in a non-deterministic way. Based on the interaction with humans, it is possible to distinguish systems with: human-in-the-loop, where humans are in full control of a mission; human-on-the-loop, where humans don't control but can still veto on machine actions; human-out-of-the-loop, where machines are completely in control. In the scope of the R2CD2 project these ideas were adopted re-using preliminary results on the Levels of Autonomy (LoA) of the Autonomous Systems Countermeasures (C-UAxS) project of the ACT. Conceptually, these LoAs are more based on the mission and the human-machine interaction than on the real skills/features which technology enables to machines. They were seven levels from 0 to 6. Figure 1 shows how all these ideas are correlated.

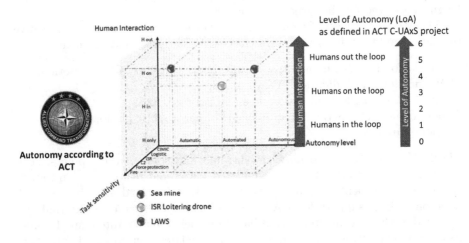

Fig. 1. Levels of Autonomy and human-machine interaction for AS.

Linked to LoA is the idea that Autonomous Functions, which allow to perform a task autonomously, can be separated from platforms. Basically an AS can have autonomous functions and/or automated function (with pre-determined output) as well as a manned system can be characterized by manned, automated and/or autonomous function. According to the LoA of the AS, Autonomous Functions should be assured either by the autonomous platforms or external subsystems. For example in the R2CD2 project, for low LoAs, Autonomy Functions for mission planning are taken over by an external tool, in order to find the best paths for reconnaissance and exfiltration missions, based on information about the terrain and enemy. For this reason a decision making tool was paired with the C2 system in order to generate orders to simulated UAxS. Figure 2 shows LoAs used in the R2CD2 project and their relationship with external decision-making function.

As shown in Fig. 2, in the R2CD2 project the LoAs was grouped into three categories to simplify the UAxS modelling: LOW, MEDIUM and HIGH.

LOW—humans only gather, monitor and analyse data, make decision, while UAxS don't assist. Neither collision avoidance or environment recognition are implemented in the UAxS behaviour, so they need well defined routes from an external system.

MEDIUM—UAxS gather, monitor, analyze data, but humans interpret them. UAxS assist in ranking task, but humans can veto machine actions and decisions. UAxS have good navigation skills in the environment and collision avoidance is implemented, so few waypoints are necessary in the order.

HIGH—UAxS perform a mission gathering, monitoring and analyzing data; humans are informed only at the end of the mission. UAxS have excellent navigation skills in the environment and collision avoidance is implemented. Only final destination is communicated to the UAxS in the order and they decide all.

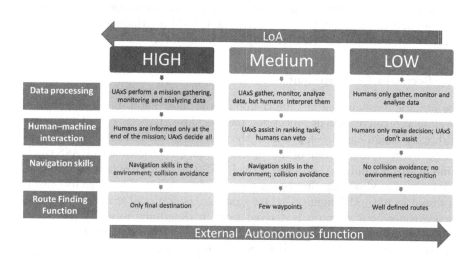

Fig. 2. LoA vs external autonomy function

3   Autonomous Systems eXtension (ASX)

The methodology/process followed to develop the ASX extension, and consequently to define the architecture of the R2CD2 project demonstrator, is here described. The first step is to search for requirements of the message exchange, the Information Exchange Requirements (IER), using a scenario-based methodology delineated in the SISO Guidelines for Scenario Development (GSD) [26]. The SISO GSD is widely accepted among STO MSG-145 group as the preferred methodology to find the IERs through a scenario-driven process. It was applied for the UAxS use case a first time by M&S COE in collaboration with FKIE[1] to extract IERs for C-BML messages [27] for UAxS [28], and subsequently used for the same purpose and to built a first version of the R2CD2 project technology demonstrator [29,30]. This first demonstrator made use of C-BML messages because the C2SIM core was not yet well defined, so it could not be extended.

---

[1] Fraunhofer-Institut für Kommunikation, Informationsverarbeitung und Ergonomie (FKIE), Bonn, Germany.

The IERs are the main source for requirements of new data classes necessary for orders, reports and initialization information to build the ASX. Once the IERs are defined, the ASX can be developed.

The second step is to build an ontology of the C2SIM extension to AS, i.e. the necessary vocabulary and semantic needed to extend the core of the language to add information to messages, suitable for missions of UAxS according to the found IERs. Finally, the C2SIM eXtensible Markup Language (XML) schema of ASX can be obtained applying an eXtensible Stylesheet Language Transformation (XSLT), according to the rules fixed by SISO C2SIM PDG. The XML schema is essential to build orders, reports and initialization files to execute the scenario, and to develop the software for the C2SIM interfaces of all simulators and other elements of the R2CD2 project demonstrator.

3.1 Scenario Development

The scenario development is a multi-step process, starting from the definition of the simulation environment objectives, passing through a conceptual analysis to finish with design and development of the simulation environment. An extended description of an application of this process for an air scenario with UAxS can be found in [31]. Simplifying, as done for the R2CD2 project, an operational scenario is designed based on the simulation objects of a project. This scenario can be expressed in natural language by, for example, operational military personnel. Then a conceptual scenario is derived from it, describing formally the actors, their interactions and flow of actions, making use of the NATO Architectural Framework (NAF). Therefore, IERs for the scenario are derived, describing in a tabular form, the information which are to be conveyed between the logical actors of the scenario. In the following a brief description of the operational and conceptual scenarios are reported.

Operational Scenario. To support the R2CD2 prototype goals the operational scenario is designed with the following simulation objectives:

– Detection and Identification of enemy robotic units utilizing UAxS and sensors;
– Situational Awareness augmented with external decision-making support tool;
– Experiment about defense against UAxS using UAxS;
– UAxS employed in urban environment both in land and air domain;
– Distinguish human–robot interaction according to three LoAs.

Based on the above requirements, the designed operational scenario shows an mission for protecting the troops and populations against hostile UAxS in modern urban environment. A team of unmanned ground vehicles (UGV) escorts a human platoon in a city while a swarm of unmanned air vehicles (UAV) performs a reconnaissance of the area searching for threats. As soon as hostile air drones show up, UAVs generate reports on enemy activity for UGVs which activate a two levels defensive system based on a safety bubble where, according to the proximity of the threat, the countermeasures increase from non-kinetic (jamming or capturing) to kinetic (shooting).

Conceptual Scenario. When the conceptual analysis of the scenario is performed, the logical nodes involved are identified, together with their main interactions. These can be seen as logical roles to be played by actors, which on their side are still logical entities, to be realized physically by real or simulated entities or systems. Figure 3 illustrates this high level logical scenario including: a C2 unit, played by a Command Post or C2 system; a Reconnaissance Autonomous Unit, played by a UAV swarm; a Land Protection Forces Unit, played by a UGV team; others actors, like humans and enemy.

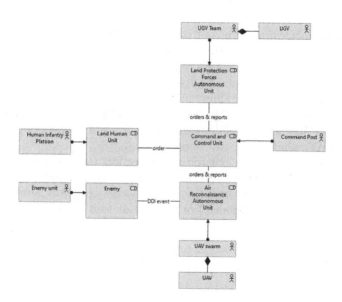

Fig. 3. NAF v4 L2 – Logical scenario.

Each logical actor performs some actions/tasks, which are linked by triggering relationship, if a cause-effect relationship is present, or simply one follow another. Figure 4 specifies tasks performed by which actor and how they are linked to each other. In this scenario the UAV swarm can perform a reconnaissance, return to base, send both a position report, about their location and status, and an observation report, about the detection and/or identification of a hostile unit. UGV team can return to base and send reports as the UAVs, but the main mission is to escort the human unit. This task is performed more or less autonomously according to the LoA: for high LoA they can decide if attack, firing or jamming, or retreat; for medium LoA they wait for confirmation order to attack or return to base, while autonomously use the jammer if the enemy if farther than a fixed distance or fire if the enemy is closer; for low LoA they need very punctual order like move, jamm or fire.

Because of the LoAs, also the Command Post needs to specialize the orders based on the LoA of UAVs or UGVs. As shown in Fig. 2, for lower LoA the Command Post must be assisted by an external decision-making function to find the best route to perform the mission and to provide the necessary waypoints if the navigation skills of the UAxS are not adequate enough to avoid obstacles. Once defined who are the players of the scenario and what they do, the temporal sequence of actions and interaction can be defined by a logical L6 as shown in Fig. 5 per a medium LoA scenario. In verbose mode, the logical sequence can be described as following:

- Command post receives Air and Ground mission orders and send UAV and UGV orders with computed optimized routes for UAV swarm and UGV team respectively;
- UAVs perform reconnaissance of the Area Of Interest (AOI); UGVs escort the human platoon leading the column of vehicles; they have good level of navigation skills to optimize a route between waypoints and avoid crashes, or following roads, open terrain, bridges, tunnels, etc.;
- Reports are generated containing information about general status of UAxS;
- As soon as hostile units are detected and/or identified, observation reports are generated; UAxS suggests following tasks, but waits for human confirmation (order). UAVs send report and suggest action;
- UAVs receive the order to exit the area according to a computed route;
- UGVs receive the order to escort the human platoon out of danger zone according to a computed route; they autonomously perform jamming as soon as enemy enters area of defence 1 or fire as soon as it enters area of defence 2.

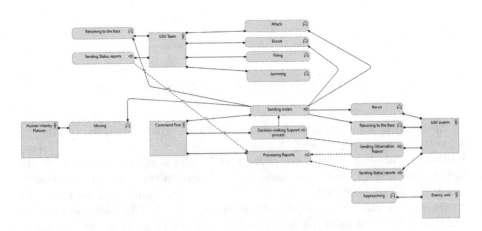

Fig. 4. Logical actors with tasks/actions.

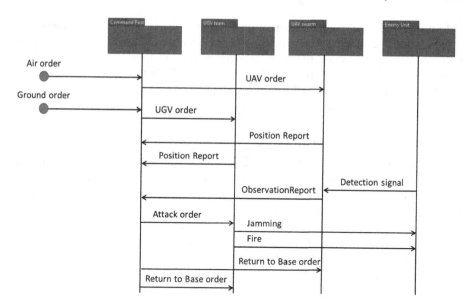

Fig. 5. NAF v4 L6 – Logical sequence.

The actors' activity flow can be isolated, together with the logical data which are accessed in write or read mode to perform each action, as shown in Fig. 6. The logical data, here orders and reports, are to be implemented with real physical messages in XML format according to the C2SIM ASX schema.

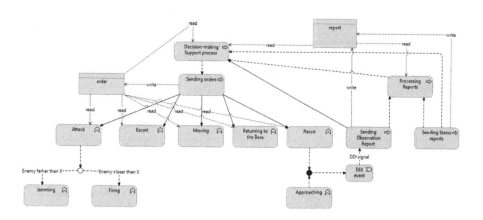

Fig. 6. NAF v4 L4 – Logical activity.

Information Exchange Requirements. According to the identified messages to be exchanged to allow the execution of the scenario, a series of tables can be built with a row for each message, reporting: type of message; producer; consumer; format; frequency; information contained. Table 1 is an example for the first phase of the scenario with the UAV reconnaissance and ground movement. All these tables constitute the Information Exchange Requirements.

3.2 Ontology and XML Schema

As already introduced, to build the C2SIM ASX, the standard C2SIM core for orders, reports and initialization of scenarios, needs to be enriched with new data elements peculiar to Autonomous Systems scenario. So, ASX was developed on top of the core, the Standard Military eXtension (SMX), which is part of the standard, and Land Operation eXtension (LOX), which is considered the first extension developed directly by C2SIM PDG, according to the information exchange requirements for the R2CD2 demonstrator. What was followed is general two-step process, meaning that it can be followed for whichever C2SIM extension. These two steps are building an ontology and generating an XML schema.

Table 1. Information exchange requirements – UAV reconnaissance and ground movement—node interaction (NAV v4 L3)

Supported operational task	Message	Producer	Consumer	Message attributes		
				Format	Frequency	Content
Air reconnaissance mission	Air order	Command post	Decision-making sys	C2SIM XML	Once	n. of UAVs, AOI (polygon), UAV parameters (initial position, average and angular velocity, Flight height, FoV of EO sensor)
Ground mission	Ground order	Command post	Decision-making sys	C2SIM XML	Once	Initial and final position, type of unit
Specify mission for UAV swarm	UAV order	Decision-making sys	UAV swarm	C2SIM XML	Once	<Task> (with TaskNameCode: Recce & List of waypoints), <IssuedTime>, <OrderID>, <RequestingEntity>, <LevelOfAutonomy>, <TTPCode>, <TacticalAttitudeCode>, <UAVFlightFormationCode>. The list of waypoints defines the route for a single UAV, from the point where the Swarm splits
Specify mission for UGV team and human platoon	UGV order	Decision-making support	UGV Team	C2SIM XML	Once	<Task> (with TaskNameCode: Escort & List of waypoints), <IssuedTime>, <OrderID>, <RequestingEntity>, <LevelOfAutonomy>, <TTPCode>, <TacticalAttitudeCode>. The list of waypoints defines the route for all UGV team, which moves as aggregate

Ontology. Building the ASX ontology means to extend the objects and their properties, data and their properties, contained in the basement made by the core+SMX+LOX ontology. For this goal the Protégé [32] software can be employed, as recommended by SISO C2SIM PDG. Their guidelines must be followed, avoiding repetitions and definitions of elements not peculiar to AS domain.

XML Schema. After building an ontology, the XML schema for an extension can be generated applying the standard SISO C2SIM XSLT. This is exactly what was performed to derive the ASX XML schema from ASX ontology. Some refinements could be necessary to avoid useless duplications in the definitions of simple types, elements, complex types and model groups derived from the ontology. It is noteworthy that the described process for schema development is a continuous one: the ASX schema should automatically include any changes in the core+SMX+LOX schema, and also eventual modifications in the ASX ontology, based on the modifications on the scenario requirements. Figure 7 shows these two-step process to generate the ASX XML schema.

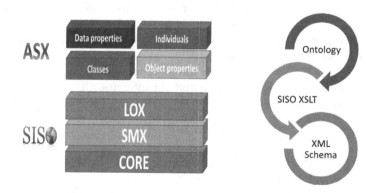

Fig. 7. Extension ontology building and XML schema processing.

4   ASX Experimentation

After being developed, the ASX was tested during the R2CD2 project implementation of the demonstrator and immediately afterwards in the context of a join coalition during NATO Coalition Warrior Interoperability eXercise (CWIX) 2019 and a miniature exercise organized by MSG–145 group. In this section details about this ASX experimentation are reported.

4.1   R2CD2 Demonstrator

The simulation environment to execute the described UAxS scenario was designed and realized. The MSG–145 choice for distributing the C2SIM messages was to adopt a simulation architecture based on Web Services using a client–server solution, with one or more servers and a client for each C2 or simulation system. Each system which participates to the coalition scenario has a C2SIM interface connected as client to the so-named C2SIM Reference Implementation Server [33]. It answers REST [34] requests to receive and store orders and reports, while it makes available C2SIM messages over STOMP[2] to all clients. The R2CD2 demonstrator makes no difference and it represents a little distributed simulation environment. The logical actors are realized with simulation entities with their own coded model. Each model is associated with one or several behaviours to perform requested tasks and interact with the external environment according to the LoA to be implemented. Two different simulators are employed for the two different operational domains of the scenario: air and land. So, one simulator runs models for UAVs and hostile drones and the other those for UGVs and human platoon. All interactions between the two simulators which are out of the scope of C2SIM standard are managed through an HLA [35] federation. The Command Post functions are distributed between two systems: a GUI[3] tool for editing the orders and displaying the report information on a map, like a C2 system, since a real C2 system with a C2SIM interface is not currently available for most of the MSG–145 members; a separate software for decision-making support to UAxS for path computing in case of low LoA according to information about terrain and enemy units. Obviously, all systems share the same urban terrain (piece of Archaria) and geographical coordinate system.

In details, as shown in Fig. 8, the R2CD2 project demonstrator is made of:

- BMLC2GUI of the George Mason University (GMU) as open source C2SIM order editor and displayer of reports [36];
- open source C2SIM Reference Implementation Server, developed by GMU [36] and customized for handling the ASX schema;
- VT MÄK VRForces as simulator of air domain;
- MASA Sword as simulator of land domain;
- C2SIM interface for VRForces simulator for handling the ASX schema to generate tasks of entities and producing position and observation reports;
- C2SIM interface for Sword simulator for handling the ASX schema to generate tasks of entities and producing position and observation reports;
- Tactical Decision Support System (TDSS) of the University of Defence in Brno (CZE) as external software for decision-making support, fully supporting the C2SIM ASX to enrich orders with detailed paths to follow for missions to low LoA UAxS and to read reports produced by UAxS.

---

[2] Simple Text Orientated Messaging Protocol.
[3] Graphical User Interface.

To make clearer how all the systems interact during a simulation, Fig. 9 shows the initialization phase when the *order of battle* (units with their organization, locations and some simulation parameters – ORBAT) is shared among all systems. The BMLC2GUI edits or opens an C2SIM initialization file to push it to the server (through RESTful service), therefore the server can share it to simulators and TDSS (through STOMP service). Figure 10 illustrates the C2SIM messages exchange during the scenario execution for tasking and reporting.

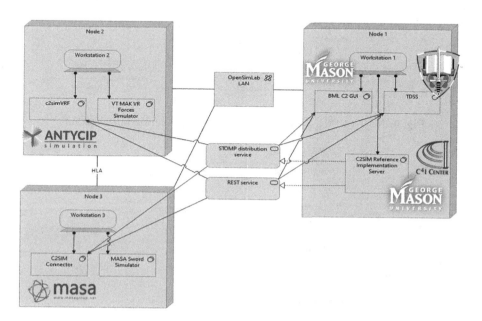

Fig. 8. Technology view reporting resource structure & connectivity (NAF v4 P2-3)

With this demonstrator the ASX was tested successfully in isolation, meaning that only messages formatted according to the ASX schema were exchanged. Actually this experimentation allowed already to test that mixed tasks both for traditional land units (according to LOX) and for UAxS (according to ASX) could coexist in the same order. For tests involving different kinds of systems and messages in a join coalition environment, part of the demonstrator was employed during CWIX and the mini-exercise.

4.2 CWIX 2019

CWIX is the NATO venue focused on interoperability to explore, experiment and examine systems. MSG–145 group participate at the 2019 edition with the intent to test the version 9 of the C2SIM standard core together with SMX and LOX to start the validation process for the SISO balloting process of the

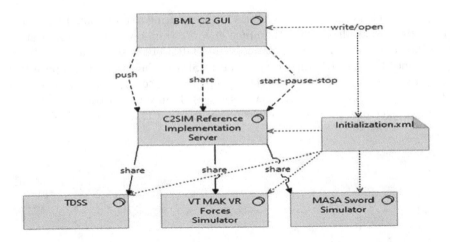

Fig. 9. NAF v4 P6 – Systems message exchange during initialization.

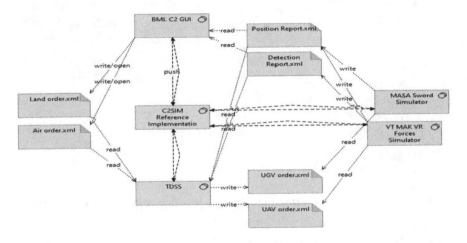

Fig. 10. NAF v4 P6 – Systems message exchange during tasking/reporting.

standard. The ASX was added to the equation. Figure 11 shows the network diagram of the MSG-145 participation to the exercise.

The capabilities (systems) involved were:

- USA – BMLC2GUI of GMU, for simulation control, monitor and dislayer, on site in the CWIX Unclassified Network
- DEU – Kora simulator and BMLC2GUI, on site in the CWIX Unclassified Network;
- Italy – C2SIM server and BMLC2GUI, in Roma (ITA) at NATO M&S COE
- Italy – Sword and VRForces simulators, in Roma (ITA) at NATO M&S COE;
- GBR – JSAF simulator and BMLC2GUI, in Portsdown West, Fareham (UK), at Defence Science and Technology Laboratory (DSTL);

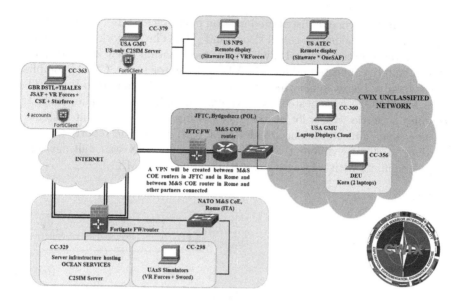

Fig. 11. CWIX 2019 diagram of the C2SIM testing

- USA – C2SIM server, back-to-back connected to the server in Roma to be the front-end of an US-only enclave, in Fairfax, VA (USA);
- USA – SitaWare HQ and VRForces, in an US-only enclave, in Monterey, CA (USA) at Naval Postgraduate School (NPS);
- USA – SitaWare HQ and OneSAF, in an US-only enclave, in Huntsville, AL (USA) at Army Test and Evaluation Command (ATEC);

The US-only enclave was necessary for license issues linked to the US Sitaware HQ C2 system. It is worth mentioning that this system is the first commercial C2 system compliant with C2SIM standard, even if it is able to read reports and not to edit orders. Another peculiarity is that JSAF simulator produced reports in IBML09 format, while it could be initialized and receive orders in C2SIM. The C2SIM server took care of the IBML09/C2SIM translation. The R2CD2 project demonstrator participated as capability CC-298 NATO MSCOE C2SIM R2CD2 EVO 2.0. As for all the tests during CWIX, each trial is basically a message transmission with a producer, one or more consumers and eventually a distributor or mediator. CC-298 did 9 successful tests, as producer or consumer or in both roles. The test successfully proved that ASX can be employed in a coalition environment with a server supporting it and distributing C2SIM messages for all the systems connected and formatted according the C2SIM standard, whose the ASX is a peculiar subset.

4.3   MSG-145 Mini-exercise

During the miniature exercise a more appropriate common coalition scenario was executed with the MSG–145 partners participating. The experimentation was conducted in the form of a distributed mission planning exercise, at brigade-level, supporting a fictional nation called "Bogaland" [37]. The network diagram for the exercise is represented in Fig. 12, where one more nation (New Zealand) participated remotely connected adding the VBS3 simulator to the C2SIM-compliant systems family. The systems which were on site at CWIX moved to Roma (ITA) at the M&S COE, who hosted the activity. The mini-exercise allowed to test a complex scenario with a lot of messages flowing between different systems at the same time. This coexistence of messages, with orders and reports formatted according to slightly different schemas, proved that ASX was well developed, avoiding conflicts with messages supporting only core+SMX+LOX.

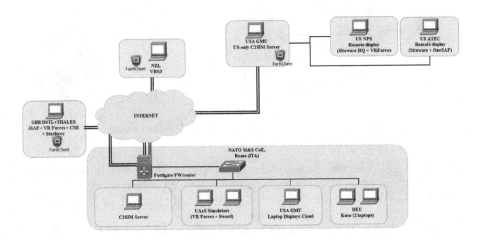

Fig. 12. Mini-exercise diagram of the C2SIM testing

5 Conclusions

In conclusions, this paper illustrated a complete process to successfully extend the C2SIM standard to a specific area. In particular, this paper dealt with the ASX extension and how it can be used to initialize a simulation scenario and to exchange C2 messages between humans and simulated or real robots. In details, the results reported in this paper are summarized here:

1. R2CD2 project
   - ASX successfully implemented with a process compliant with SISO C2SIM PDG guidelines
   - Three C2SIM client interfaces developed and experimented supporting ASX for the following systems:
     • MASA Sword
     • VT MÄK VRForces by Antycip Simulation (two versions supporting both HLA and DIS [38])
     • TDSS by University of Defence, Brno (CZE)

2. CWIX 2019
   - CC-298 NATO MSCOE C2SIM R2CD2 EVO 2.0 did 9 successful tests, as producer or consumer or in both roles
   - VR-Forces and Sword simulators performed as expected exchanging orders and reports with BMLC2GUI through C2SIM server using ASX schema
3. MSG-145 mini-exercise
   - ASX successfully deployed in Coalition Distributed Simulation with VR-Forces and Sword

5.1 Way Ahead

Future improvements are already on their way for realization through collaboration with national industry. In particular:

1. CD&E on UAxS capability and countermeasures (requirements; TTPs)
2. Cyber domain to protect and/or counter UAxS, including a communication and network simulator in the demonstrator architecture, according to the idea in [39]
3. adopting the M&S as a Service paradigm [40], migrating all R2CD2 project demonstrator element in the MSaaS OCEAN infrastructure [41]
4. use of Artificial Intelligence (AI) to support decision making in an operational scenario dominated by robots, for speeding up the choice of the proper countermeasure or secure exfiltration path or attack route, based on near real time information.

Acknowledgements. The authors would like to thank the Prof. Mark Pullen and his staff at GMU for the collaboration and outstanding work with the C2SIM server and support to ASX. All the SISO C2SIM PDG was also of precious help in amending the ASX ontology to produce a clean and usable XML schema. Furthermore, the ASX could not have ever been implemented and experimented without the efforts of Beatriz Garmendia-Doval, MASA Group, and David Kamp and Marco Pelusi, Antycip Simulation, whose work went beyond the contractual obligations. Special mention deserved Lt. Col. Petr Sodola, University of Defence in Brno (CZE), who developed the first C2SIM interface not belonging to a C2 or simulation system, in the context of the Czech partnership with the M&S CoE.

References

1. Pullen, J.M., et al.: Standard for Command and Control Systems – Simulation Systems Interoperation – draft version 11 (2019)
2. Pullen, J.M., Patel, B., Khimeche, L.: C2-simulation interoperability for operational hybrid environments. In: NATO Modelling and Simulation Symposium 2016, Bucharest, Romania (2016)
3. Sudnikovich, W., Pullen, J., Kleiner, M., Carey, S.: Extensible battle management language as a transformation enabler. Simulation **80**, 669–680 (2004)

4. Perme, D., Hieb, M., Pullen, J., Sudnikovich, W., Tolk, A.: Integrating air and ground operations within a common battle management language. In: Spring Simulation Interoperability Workshop, San Diego, CA, USA (2005)
5. Remmersmann, T., Tiderko, A., Schade, U.: Interacting with multi-robot systems using BML. In: 18th International Command and Control Research and Technology Symposium (ICCRTS), Alexandria, VA, USA (2013)
6. Simulation Interoperability Standards Organization: C2SIM PDG/PSG - Command and Control Systems - Simulation Systems Interoperation. https://www.sisostds.org/StandardsActivities/DevelopmentGroups/C2SIMPDGPSG-CommandandControlSystems.aspx. Accessed Oct 2019
7. NATO Collaboration Support Office: RTO-TR-MSG-048 coalition battle management language (C-BML): Technical report, February 2012
8. NATO Collaboration Support Office: MSG-085 standardization for command and control – simulation interoperability: Final report, July 2015
9. Pullen, J.M., Hieg, M.R., Levine, S., Tolk, A., Blais, C.: Joint Battle Management Language (JBML) — US Contribution to the C-BML PDG and NATO MSG-048 TA. The NPS Institutional Archive, Calhoun (2014)
10. NATO Collaboration Support Office: MSG 145 Operationalization of Standardized C2-Simulation Interoperability. https://www.sto.nato.int/Pages/activitieslisting.aspx. Accessed Oct 2019
11. Foltin, P., Vlkovský, M., Mazal, J., Husák, J., Brunclík, M.: Discrete event simulation in future military logistics applications and aspects. In: Mazal, J. (ed.) MESAS 2017. LNCS, vol. 10756, pp. 410–421. Springer, Cham (2018). https://doi.org/10.1007/978-3-319-76072-8_30
12. Foltin, P., Gontarczyk, M., Świderski, A., Zelkowski, J.: Evaluation model of the companies operating within logistic network. Arch. Transp. **32**(4), 21–34 (2015)
13. Brunclík, M., Vogal, L., Foltin, P.: Computer modelling and simulation of the supply chain in military operation. In: Proceedings of the 18th International Scientific Conference — Business Logistics in Modern Management, Josip Juraj Strossmayer University of Osijek, Faculty of Economics, Osijek, Chorvatsko, pp. 671–682 (2018)
14. Mazal, J., Stodola, P., Procházka, D., Kutěj, L., Ščurek, R., Procházka, J.: Modelling of the UAV safety manoeuvre for the air insertion operations. In: Hodicky, J. (ed.) MESAS 2016. LNCS, vol. 9991, pp. 337–346. Springer, Cham (2016). https://doi.org/10.1007/978-3-319-47605-6_27
15. Stodola, P., Mazal, J.: Architecture of the advanced command and control system. In: 6th International Conference Proceedings on Military Technologies, ICMT 2017, pp. 340–343. Institute of Electrical and Electronics Engineers Inc., Piscataway (2017)
16. Stodola, P., Mazal, J.: Model of optimal cooperative reconnaissance and its solution using metaheuristic methods. Def. Sci. J. **67**(5), 529–535 (2017)
17. Hrabec, D., Mazal, J., Stodola, P.: Optimal manoeuvre for two cooperative military elements under uncertain enemy threat. Int. J. Oper. Res. **35**(2), 263–277 (2019)
18. Neubauer, J., Veselý, V.: Detection of multiple changes in mean by sparse parameter estimation. Nonlinear Anal. Model. Control. **18**(2), 177–190 (2013)
19. Neubauer, J., Veselý, V.: Change point detection by sparse parameter estimation. Informatica **22**(1), 149–164 (2011)
20. Neubauer, J.: Selected statistical methods in R. In: XXIX International Colloquium Proceedings on the Management of Educational Process, pp. 239–249. University of Defence, Brno (2011)
21. Odehnal, J., Neubauer, J.: Economic determinants of military spending – causal analysis. Ekonomicky casopis **63**(10), 1019–1032 (2015)

22. Biagini, M., Corona, F.: Modelling & simulation architecture supporting NATO counter unmanned autonomous system concept development. In: Hodicky, J. (ed.) MESAS 2016. LNCS, vol. 9991, pp. 118–127. Springer, Cham (2016). https://doi.org/10.1007/978-3-319-47605-6_9

23. Biagini, M., et al.: Modelling and simulation supporting unmanned autonomous systems (UAxS) concept development and experimentation. In: SPIE Defense and Security Proceedings on Disruptive Technologies in Sensors and Sensor Systems, Anaheim, CA, USA (2017)

24. NATO ACT CEI CAPDEV: Autonomous Systems Countermeasures. https://www.innovationhub-act.org/project/counter-measures. Accessed Oct 2016

25. NATO Allied Command for Transformation: NATO Urbanization Project. http://www.act.nato.int/activities/nato-urbanisation-project. Accessed Oct 2015

26. Simulation Interoperability Standards Organization: Guideline on Scenario Development for Simulation Environments (2018)

27. Simulation Interoperability Standards Organization: SISO-STD-011 Standard for Coalition Battle Management Language Phase 1 (2014)

28. Biagini, M., Corona, F., Wolski, M., Shade, U.: Conceptual scenario supporting extension of C2SIM to autonomous systems. In: 22nd International Command and Control Research and Technology Symposium (ICCRTS), Los Angeles, CA, USA (2017)

29. Biagini, M., Corona, F.: M&S-based robot swarms prototype. In: Mazal, J. (ed.) MESAS 2018. LNCS, vol. 11472, pp. 285–301. Springer, Cham (2019). https://doi.org/10.1007/978-3-030-14984-0_22

30. Biagini, M., Corona, F., Innocenti, F., Marcovaldi, S.: C2SIM Extension to Unmanned Autonomous Systems (UAXS) - Process for Requirements and Implementation. NATO Modelling and Simulation Centre of Excellence, Roma, ITA (2018)

31. Biagini, M., Corona, F., Casar, J.: Operational scenario modelling supporting unmanned autonomous systems concept development. In: Mazal, J. (ed.) MESAS 2017. LNCS, vol. 10756, pp. 253–267. Springer, Cham (2018). https://doi.org/10.1007/978-3-319-76072-8_18

32. Stanford University: Protégé: A free, open-source ontology editor and framework for building intelligent systems. https://protege.stanford.edu. Accessed Oct 2019

33. Pullen, J.: A distributed development environment for a C2SIM system of systems. In: 22nd International Command and Control Research and Technology Symposium, Los Angeles, CA, USA (2017)

34. Fielding, R.T.: Architectural styles and the design of network-based software architectures. Doctoral dissertation, University of California, Irvine, CA, USA (2000)

35. IEEE: 1516-2010 - IEEE Standard for Modeling and Simulation (M&S) High Level Architecture. IEEE Standard Association (2010)

36. George Mason University - Cyber & C4I Center: OpenBML repository. https://netlab.gmu.edu/trac/OpenBML. Accessed Oct 2019

37. Pullen, J.M., Wardman, B., Ruth, J.: Experimental evaluation of a command and control - simulation interoperation standard in a coalition environment. In: International Command and Control Research and Technology Symposium, Baltimore, MD, USA (2019)

38. IEEE: 1278-2012 Standard for Distributed Interactive Simulation (DIS) — Application protocols. IEEE Standard Association (2012)

39. Biagini, M., Forconi, S., Corona, F., Mursia, A., Ganga, L., Battiati, F.: The unmanned autonomous systems cyberspace arena (UCA). A M&S architecture and relevant tools for security issues analysis of autonomous system networks. In: Hodicky, J. (ed.) MESAS 2016. LNCS, vol. 9991, pp. 168–175. Springer, Cham (2016). https://doi.org/10.1007/978-3-319-47605-6_13

40. NATO Collaboration Support Office: Operational Concept Document (OCD) for the Allied Framework for M&S as a Service, ST-TR-MSG-136-Part-III (2019)

41. Biagini, M., La Grotta, M., Corona, F., Forconi, S., Picollo, M., Faillace, C.: NATO MaaS — a comprehensive approach for military operational requirements development. In: Corona, F. (ed.) 2017 Annual Review, vol. 1, pp. 31–47. NATO M&S COE, Roma (2017)

Legality and Legitimacy of the Autonomous Weapon Systems

Jakub Fučík[✉] ⓘ, Libor Frank ⓘ, and Richard Stojar ⓘ

Centre for Security and Military Strategic Studies,
University of Defence, Tučkova 23, 602 00 Brno, Czech Republic
{jakub.fucik,libor.frank,richard.stojar}@unob.cz

Abstract. Nowadays, from the military perspective, development of autonomous weapon systems (AWS) represents opportunity especially for States to enhance their military power and change their status in the system of international relations probably with the presumptions of the new Revolution in Military Affairs (RMA). Not-only the most powerful States such as the U.S., People's Republic of China, or Russian Federation, but practically all State and non-State actors closely scrutinize this process and its implication for the future security environment. On the other hand, implementation of the AWS technologies poses many challenges (for example independence of AWS on the human control and decision-making processes), which are connected with almost completely new nature of these weapon systems and their influence on the relations across the humankind and its general character. The aim of this paper is to analyse one possible set of such challenges focusing on legal and legitimate (ethical) aspects of the AWS and their compliance with the public international law. Analyses will focus on norms of international humanitarian law and their connections with ethical perspective. This paper will provide necessary understanding of the AWS' (non)conformity with the international norms based on the international customs and treaties relevant (and binding) for the NATO members State and their efforts to implement such technologies.

Keywords: Autonomous weapon systems · International law · International humanitarian law · Legal aspects · Ethical aspects

1 Introduction

Nowadays, the Autonomous Weapon Systems (AWS) represent opportunity especially for States to enhance their military power and change their status in the system of international relations probably with the presumptions of the new Revolution in Military Affairs (RMA) [1]. This is mainly related to the expansion of information technology, where many factors make possible to create systems capable of performing enormous amounts of calculations per second. Along with the advancement of robotics and its successor - mechatronics, it is now possible to create robotic systems with capabilities that fell into the science fiction category a decade ago. Individual systems should be able not only to obtain information about the environment but also to process (evaluate) this information and take appropriate decisions on their own [2]. By general definition,

© Springer Nature Switzerland AG 2020
J. Mazal et al. (Eds.): MESAS 2019, LNCS 11995, pp. 409–416, 2020.
https://doi.org/10.1007/978-3-030-43890-6_33

autonomy is the ability of an entity to make conscious, unforced decisions. In order to apply this definition to artificial intelligence or robotic means, it is necessary to express the autonomy of the robotic means in relation to the environment, or better in relation to the human operator. For military purposes, there are already several definitions of the level of control or the level of independence of the system on the human operator. Scharre, for example, five levels of control - automatic, automated, semi-autonomous (Man-In-The-Loop; MIL), autonomous with supervisor (Man-On-The-Loop; MOL), and fully autonomous without supervisor (Man-Out-Of-The-Loop; MOOL) [3].

On the other hand, development and implementation of the AWS' technologies poses many challenges [4–6], which are connected with almost completely new nature of these weapon systems and their influence on the relations across the humankind and its general character. The aim of this paper is to analyse one possible set of such challenges focusing on legal and legitimate (ethical) aspects of the AWS and their compliance with the public international law. Analyses will focus on norms of international humanitarian law and their connections with ethical perspective. Both perspectives and arguments will be represented in two possible "extreme" outcomes – scenarios - of AWS' evaluation, i.e. AWS are legal and legitimate; AWS are illegal and illegitimate. This paper will provide necessary understanding of the AWS' (non)conformity with the international norms based on the international customs and treaties relevant (and binding) for the NATO members State and their efforts to implement such technologies.

2 Legality

In the system of law, legality generally represents key characteristic and condition of every fact or State. Generally, this concept refers to two connected presumptions: (1) legal norms complies with rule of law set by constitutional system; (2) everyone's actions complies with set rule of law defined by legal norms. First presumption, also known as legislative [7], origins in obligation to only publish and enforce such rules which are not in conflict with existing system of law. In the democratic society, this principle demonstrates the fact that the issuance of a legal norm may be carried out only within the limits set by law, by the body stipulated by law and in the form prescribed by law. Second presumption represents application dimension of the legal norm. Everyone is obliged to observe the law and if he fails to do so (breach the law), he will be punished with the foreseen sanction. Both - process of punishment (including pool of authorized public authorities) and character of sanction – are bound by law and reflect such principles as nullum crimen sine lege, nulla poena sine lege (no crime without law, no punishment without law) and State power can be exercised only in cases and within limits prescribed by law [8].

2.1 International Humanitarian Law

International Humanitarian Law (IHL) or also known as *Ius in Bello* represents specific branch of *Law of Armed Conflict* (LOAC) which focuses on character of use of force in terms of means and methods. Legal norms set the regime under which military actions are evaluated in terms of legality (or illegality). This approach generally represents humanitarian philosophical tradition and presumptions about using only necessary amount of (military) force to accomplished set (political) interests and goals and prevention of un-necessary suffering and collateral damage. Historically, roots of modern IHL were created in 19th century. After the Battle of Solferino in 1861, Swiss trader and philanthrope Henri Dunant initiated establishment of International Red Cross Committee. Institution which is till now responsible for propagation and strengthening of this international legal regime.

General framework of IHL is based on two pillars (sets of international treaties) – *Geneva* and *Hague Conventions*. *Geneva Conventions* mainly focus on status of persons in armed conflicts. They mainly distinguish between two categories – combatants and non-combatants. Only combatants (lawful or unlawful) could be legally targeted. On the other hand, only lawful combatants could legally use the force in armed conflicts and have immunity from general prosecution. Under *Geneva Conventions,* use of force against non-combatants is prohibited. This broad category of protected people consists from specific groups which have certain rights, but also obligations. These groups are: Civilians, Wounded and Sick, Medical and Religious Personnel, and Prisoners of War.

Legal regime set by *Hague Conventions* subsumes methods and means of waging armed conflicts. From this point of views, *Conventions* regulate especially land, naval and air warfare. They also focus on certain weapon systems and limitation or prohibition of their deployment. As an example, we can mention obligation for treaties' parties to abstain from using bullets which expand or flatten easily in the human body [9]. This imposes direct bans on soft-points and cross-tipped bullets (known as Dum Dums). Nowadays, this framework is broadened through international treaties such as the Treaty on the Non-Proliferation of Nuclear Weapons, the Biological Weapons Convention and the Chemical Weapons Convention – all concerning weapons of mass destruction – or the Convention on Cluster Munitions and Anti-Personnel Mine Ban Convention – concerning conventional weapons.

All legal norms of the IHL and their application is based on four fundamental principles which also provide criterions for evaluation of certain military actions. These principles are: military necessity, distinction, proportionality, prevention of unnecessary suffering. *Military necessity* means that the attack (military action) must be intended to help in the military defeat of the enemy [10] and this action must not be otherwise forbidden by IHL (for example abuse of protected symbols such as sign of International Red Cross Committee). To fulfil *Distinction*'s criterion attack shall targets only military objectives (which can be persons or objects). This principle was also mentioned earlier in terms of connection with *Geneva Conventions* and their requirements on distinguishing between combatants and non-combatants. *Proportionality* ensures that expected collateral damage is not excessive to the expected military advantage [11]. From this perspective, collateral damage is strictly connected to suffering, injury or destruction of civilians or civilian objects. Military commander must assess distinction obligations, while avoiding actions that are indiscriminate. On the other hand, IHL does not prohibit collateral damage at all, but it imposes limitations on them. They are manifested for example in obligations to establish standards and methods for estimating collateral damage or to weigh their risk against military necessity. Last, but not least, principle - *Unnecessary suffering* - refers to obligation to avoid the infliction of injuries or suffering beyond what is required to achieve the military aim [12]. This limitation subsumes both – character of weapons and tactics of employing weapons or use of force in general. Weapons may be unlawful when per se calculated to cause unnecessary suffering according to "usage of States", or by improper use of otherwise lawful weapons, or by agreement of States through international treaty (the example is the Chemical Weapons Convention and ban on chemicals weapons) [13]. In this term, weapon employment is prohibited when normal or expected use inevitably would cause injury or suffering manifestly disproportionate to its military effectiveness.

3 Legitimacy

Unlike the *legality*, *legitimacy* is much less objective and is often used as a synonym for morality and justice. Fundamental understanding and defining the *legitimacy* is still a matter of debate, where it has to be stressed that no systematic examination or universal approach which would be binding globally is available to this date. For this reason, a number of definitions and interpretations of the term are used in the current practice, ranging from the classical theory of legitimacy, which focus on the relationship between the State and its citizens [14], through the perspective of international organizations and end with the concept of world superpowers, which establish rules to other actors of the international system.

In general, legitimacy always applies to a target group of people, which may be represented, for example, by the local population of the host State, nationals of States sending military contingents to the conflict area, or representatives of sovereign States in the environment of international organizations. Nature of legitimacy implies process of justification of certain activities or standpoints by set of common beliefs, values and cultural aspects [15]. Specific character of this presumption depends on group which was chosen as the focal point and reflects general theoretical, but also practical, struggle between two philosophical standpoints – particularism v. universalism.

The legitimacy of use of force can be understood as the relationship of three interrelated and interacting aspects, which are represented by political consensus, legality and moral authority. Political consensus refers to an agreement, or at least understanding, inside the international community that the use of force is desirable and appropriate in the circumstances. Legality was mainly discussed in previous chapters. Political consensus and legality are generally regarded as determining the justification of mandate to employ power solution. The moral authority of the operation represents the standards of conduct of the deployed forces and weapon systems, to what extent they follow international standards and how they are able to enforce these standards in practice. If one of aforementioned aspects is undermined, it may directly affect the other aspects, thereby limiting the effectiveness of the measures taken, and thus jeopardizing the legitimacy as general [16, 17].

4 Legality and Legitimacy of the Autonomous Weapon Systems

4.1 Legal and Legitimate

This scenario implies compliance of AWS with both - legal and legitimacy – regimes. From the legal perspective such statement is valid when AWS fulfil all obligations and requirements set by IHL. Generally speaking, AWS must withstand the test through four fundamental principles mentioned in Sect. 2.1 - military necessity, distinction, proportionality, unnecessary suffering. Considering character of the first principle, we can presume, that certain armed forces would be able to justify the deployment of the AWS as the necessary tool to accomplish the military objectives [10]. Reasoning may for example stress out the effectiveness AWS or the protection of own human personnel. On the other hand, the distinction principle is much more challenging. AWS need to directly target only military objects and avoid civilian and protected ones. The MIL and even MOL systems would fulfil such requirements through partial control or supervision by operator. This person would be also probably legally responsible in case the breach of law. However, the MOOL systems lack such human element and all decisions are made and carried out independently. Still IHL and the State and court praxis set rules (not only in form of legal norms, but also as rules of engagement) which are binding for military personnel and through which they evaluate the character of possible targets. We could presume, that it depends only on technological development, which would ensure, that these rules will be applied in decision-making process of the MOOL systems. Logic of application of the third principle – proportionality – is much the same as by the second one. Compliance with the IHL depends on capability of AWS to follow set rules and processes which are the same for living personnel by their nature. On the other hand, the fourth principle represents probably the broadest set of conditions which should by fulfilled. AWS should negate all three conditions of prohibition – (a) general attitude of States, or (b) by improper use of otherwise lawful weapons, or (c) by agreement of States through international treaty – which proclaim weapon system/military tactic unlawful. First condition refers to long term and stable factual approach which is so intensive that create international binding norm. In this term, currently, neither States through their international interactions consider AWS as weapons causing unnecessary suffering. Even discussion or proclamations for example in the UN General Assembly meetings themselves do not reach required level of intensity of international legal customs [18]. Also neither international treaty imposes explicit ban on AWS (third condition). Considering second condition we should investigate if such weapon always result in superfluous injury needed to accomplish the military advantage sought. As long as AWS designers do not specifically create AWS that are only capable of operating munitions causing unnecessary suffering or superfluous injury, then such weapon systems would abide by this element [19].

Legitimacy of the AWS is based on two main premises: (1) reduction of casualties on the side which deploy this kind of weapon system; (2) diminish the influence of negative aspects or imperfection in human nature. First premise considers the different perception of casualties by public opinion and society as general. Destruction of machine or let say artificial organism does not create such negative and emotional reaction as death or injury of human personnel, regardless if he was soldier or civilian consultant [20–22]. From the State perspective, first case represents merely financial loss and task or burden for industrial base and logistical capabilities to provide replacement. On the other hand, loss of human persons imposes social pressure on their relatives and also on political elites. Historically, cases such the Vietnam War (1955–1975) or the UN intervention in Somalia (1993–1995) represent situation when such casualties led to public delegitimization of further engagement in these conflicts and inevitably to withdrawal of deployed the US and the UN troops. Second premise points on remove limits resulting from human physiology (such as the need for sleep, impact of fatigue or the influence of stress). From this point of view, AWS could ensure, that decision-making process and use of force itself will not be burdened by mistakes arising from these imperfections. Efficiency, speed and accuracy of information processing should provide necessary conditions to reach a much higher level of objectivity than by same types of human actions.

4.2 Illegal and Illegitimate

This scenario represents completely different standpoint to AWS and implies incompliance with both - legal and legitimacy – regimes. From the legal perspective, key question arising from above mentioned principles (Sect. 2.1) is whether the AWS would function in a way that respects the obligation to distinguish military and civilian objects and persons and also other types of protected people. For autonomous weapon systems intended for use in environment where they are likely to encounter protected persons or objects, there are serious doubts as to whether they would function in a way that respects the obligation to carry out the complex, context-dependent assessments required by the IHL requirements of distinction and proportionality of use of force. We could presume that these assessments are inherently qualitative based in which unique human nature will continue to have undisputable place [23]. This aspect is strongly connected with responsibility of States to ensure that every new weapon would comply with IHL [24]. Yet foreseeing such guaranties may become impossible if autonomous weapon systems were to become more complex and independent in their operations, and therefore become less predictable. Realistically, this situation deeply questions the obligations of commander to credibly control course of actions and thus compliance with law. This issue is closely connected with accountability of examined activities. Generally speaking, to whom the AWS actions could be attributed and who will be responsible for breaches of IHL norms during their deployment. This gap could not be so aggravated by MIL and MOL systems. On the other hand, the limits of control over, or the unpredictability of, even these weapons could make difficult to find individuals involved in deployment or programming responsible for mentioned violations. Should we punish programmer? Or should be responsible commander? And what if the investigation come to conclusion that IHL violation have been caused strictly by AWS and their decision-making process? These are all questions which dispute legal certainty in terms of binding law and its enforceability.

From the perspective of legitimacy, the main criticism of AWS is based on threat of *dehumanization* of use of force [25]. Generally, this is the case when humankind is losing control over lethal actions against its members and rights to decide between life and death pass to other non-human (artificial) actor. This situation could develop to the point where humans are so far removed in time and space from the use of force against the targets that the decision-making will be completely substituted with machine.

On the other hand, some situations are not logically unequivocally solvable e.g. so-called *trolley problems*. In both cases, the question is whether a human being or a robot, based on actual circumstances, is able to make a decision with unintended consequences. Unique character of human being and its development ensure that such decision would come from complex set of factors such as individual experience, norms, physical and psychical features. Ethical gap of AWS comes from the lack of such complex "mind-set" and even from absence of only-one completely right and true set of characteristics which would be universally recognized and requested.

5 Conclusion

Autonomous weapon systems represent challenges both in terms of legal and ethical norms. Legality perspective is based on International humanitarian law and four main principles - military necessity, distinction, proportionality, and prevention of unnecessary suffering. Compliance with the IHL depends on capability of AWS to follow set rules and processes which are the same for living personnel by their nature and will also depend on technological development of these systems. Nowadays, neither international treaty, nor State customs imposes explicit ban on AWS. On the other hand, these weapons also establish legal gaps in process of control and attribution. Arising key question also arising is also whether the AWS would function in a way that respects the obligation to distinguish military and civilian objects and persons and also other types of protected people.

Legitimacy of AWS is based on premises considering reduction of casualties on the side which deploy this kind of weapon system; and diminish the influence of negative aspects or imperfection in human nature. Both aspects bring interesting opportunities not only for armed forces in terms of protection of human beings. On the other hand, AWS also represent threat of *dehumanization* of armed conflict. This situation could develop to the point where humans are so far removed in time and space from the use of force against the targets that the decision-making will be completely substituted with machine. Worst scenarios in this case warn against possible uprising of AWS and conflict their former creators.

Acknowledgements. The work presented in this paper has been supported by the Ministry of Defence of the Czech Republic (Research Project "STRATAL" No. 907930101023).

References

1. Fučík, J., Frank, L., Stojar, R.: Autonomous systems and Chinese strategic thinking. In: Mazal, J. (ed.) MESAS 2018. LNCS, vol. 11472, pp. 588–598. Springer, Cham (2019). https://doi.org/10.1007/978-3-030-14984-0_44
2. Hodický, J.: Modelling and simulation in the autonomous systems' domain – current status and way ahead. In: Hodický, J. (ed.) MESAS 2015. LNCS, vol. 9055, pp. 17–23. Springer, Cham (2015). https://doi.org/10.1007/978-3-319-22383-4_2
3. Scharre, P.: Autonomy, "Killer Robots," and Human Control in the Use of Force – Part I. Just Security, vol. 7, no. 1 (2014). https://www.justsecurity.org/12708/autonomy-killer-robots-human-control-force-part/

4. Hodicky, J., Prochazka, D.: Challenges in the implementation of autonomous systems into the battlefield. In: ICMT 2017 - 6th International Conference on Military Technologies, Brno, pp. 743–744. IEEE (2017). https://doi.org/10.1109/miltechs.2017.7988855

5. Hodický, J.: Použití experimentu ve vojenství (Experiment in the Military Domain). Vojenské rozhledy **27**(2), 19–32 (2018). https://doi.org/10.3849/2336-2995.27.2018.02.19-32

6. Drozd, J.: Experiment of the tactical decision support system within company defensive operation. In: Mazal, J. (ed.) MESAS 2018. LNCS, vol. 11472, pp. 544–552. Springer, Cham (2019). https://doi.org/10.1007/978-3-030-14984-0_40

7. Knapp, V.: Teorie práva (Law Theory), p. 212. C.H.Beck, Prague (2012)

8. von Liszt, F.: The rationale for the nullum crimen principle. J. Int. Crim. Justice **5**(4), 1009–1013 (2007). https://doi.org/10.1093/jicj/mqm054

9. Declaration concerning the Prohibition of the Use of Bullets which can Easily Expand or Change their Form inside the Human Body such as Bullets with a Hard Covering which does not Completely Cover the Core, or containing Indentations

10. Hague Convention IV, Art. 23

11. Additional Protocol to Geneva Conventions I, Art. 51, para. 5(b)

12. Hague Convention IV, art. 23(e) and Additional Protocol to Geneva Conventions I, Art. 35, para. 2

13. Additional Protocol to Geneva Conventions I, Art. 36

14. Especially in terms of so called *social contract* - for further details see Locke, J.: Two Treatises of Government: In the Former, the False Principles, and Foundation of Sir Robert Filmer, and His Followers, are Detected and Overthrown. The Latter is an Essay Concerning the True Original, Extent, and End of Civil Government. Awnsham Churchill, London (1689)

15. Chiuyuki, A.: Legitimacy and the Use of Armed Forces, Stability Missions in the Post-Cold War Era. Routledge, New York (2011)

16. Kolín, V.: The legitimacy of humanitarian intervention: a moral perspective. Obrana a Strategie **7**(1), 5–28 (2007)

17. SIPRI Yearbook 2009: The Legitimacy of Peace Operations. Oxford University Press, Oxford (2009). https://www.sipri.org/sites/default/files/SIPRIYB0903.pdf

18. Wareham, M.: Banning Killer Robots in 2017. The Cipher Brief (2017). https://www.thecipherbrief.com/article/tech/banning-killer-robots-2017-1092

19. Toscano, C.P.: Friend of humans: an argument for developing autonomous weapons systems. J. Nat. Secur. Law Policy **8**(1), 207 (2015)

20. Stojar, R.: Bezpilotní prostředky a problematika jejich nasazení v soudobých konfliktech (the unmanned aerial vehicles and issues connected with their use in contemporary conflicts). Obrana a Strategie **16**(2), 5–18 (2016). https://doi.org/10.3849/1802-7199.16.2016.02.005-018

21. Stojar, R., Frank, L.: Changes in armed forces and their significance for the regular armed forces. In: The 18th International Conference. The Knowledge-Based Organization: Conference Proceedings 1 - Management and Military Sciences, vol. 1, pp. 142–145 (2012)

22. Stodola, P., Kozůbek, J., Drozd, J.: Using unmanned aerial systems in military operations for autonomous reconnaissance. In: Mazal, J. (ed.) MESAS 2018. LNCS, vol. 11472, pp. 514–529. Springer, Cham (2019). https://doi.org/10.1007/978-3-030-14984-0_38

23. ICRC: Autonomous Weapon Systems: Implications of Increasing Autonomy in the Critical Functions of Weapons. Versoix (2016)

24. ICRC: A Guide to the Legal Review of New Weapons, Means and Methods of Warfare: Measures to Implement Article 36 of Additional Protocol I of 1977. Geneva (2006). www.icrc.org/eng/assets/files/other/icrc_002_0902.pdf

25. Wagner, M.: The dehumanization of international humanitarian law: legal, ethical, and political implications of autonomous weapon systems. Vanderbilt J. Transnational Law **47**(15–1), 1371–1424 (2014)

ASAT Weapons: Enhancing NATO's Operational Capabilities in the Emerging Space Dependent Era

Antonio Carlo[1](✉) and Nikolaos Veazoglou[2]

[1] Sapienza University of Rome, Piazzale Aldo Moro 5, Rome, Italy
antonio.carlo@pec.it
[2] National and Kapodistrian University of Athens, Solonos 104, Athens, Greece
nickveazoglou@gmail.com

Abstract. After more than 60 years of human activities in outer space, society is highly dependent on space based technologies.

A State that aims to enhance its capacities in the sectors of defence, communication, Earth monitoring and emergency management needs to invest in the Space sector. This instigated enormous investments by private and public entities in order to develop Space programmes and deploy satellites in orbit.

Satellites are used for both military and civilian purposes and are developed in order to establish a state of security. The military applications of satellites vary from reconnaissance, early warning and telecommunications to meteorology and geodesy.

States, recognising these strategic advantages space based assets provide and their importance in the modern theatre of operations, sought the development of technologies capable of neutralising them, in order to deprive the adversary of these advantages. This introduced a new type of weapons, the Anti-Satellite Weapons (ASAT), which can be both hard-kill (kinetic energy weapons, explosions) and soft-kill (jamming, cyber attacks) in nature. The US, Russia, China and now India have developed and tested these weapons which can drastically change the established Space ecosystem.

The paper will demonstrate that, the development and use of ASAT creates a new field where NATO and its member States can enhance their operational capabilities in order to safeguard their security and defence. Additionally, given the ultra-hazardous nature of Outer Space, security concepts should extend beyond cyber security to cyber defence and eventually also cyber resilience.

Keywords: ASAT weapons · NATO · Space · Cyber security

1 Introduction

Space has always been considered as the final and unreachable frontier. However, this border was conquered on 4 October 1957, in the middle of the Cold War, with the launch of the USSR satellite "Sputnik I", marking the beginning of the Space Age [1].

© Springer Nature Switzerland AG 2020
J. Mazal et al. (Eds.): MESAS 2019, LNCS 11995, pp. 417–426, 2020.
https://doi.org/10.1007/978-3-030-43890-6_34

In that historical moment the aim of the space conquest was for the two superpowers of the time, the USA and the USSR, to demonstrate their technological and military superiority.

Space became the new field of competition between the two world powers. The USSR and the USA were committed with high investments in developing the most advanced and aggressive technologies, with the aim of becoming the one country that would dictate the new rules at World level in terms of armaments. The driving forces motivating these economic and intellectual efforts were national prestige and security.

With the development and advancement of technology, today the space sector witnesses a change with the undertaking of space activities by a multitude of both public and private actors. The goal is no longer just to reach outer Space, but to exploit it for strategic and economic purposes. This conquest is taking place on a global scale by sending satellites to Earth's orbits and through the realization of exploration missions. Nevertheless only few players have the technological capabilities to impose themselves by threatening the spatial security of other actors and secure their own, with the development of weapons capable of momentarily or permanently damaging the pre-established equilibrium. These weapons are called Anti-Satellite Weapons (ASAT) due to the fact that they target satellites.

2   The Applications of Space Platforms

Since the dawn of the space age, outer space has been regarded as the ultimate high ground, which could provide a decisive military advantage to the State that retains superiority over it [2]. In the context of NATO operations space-based assets play an essential role, providing a multitude of services for more than 35 years. Some of the most advanced space-faring States are part of the alliance [3]. It is highly anticipated that in the next leaders' summit taking place in London NATO will recognize space as a domain of warfare [4].

Since NATO does not own any satellites in orbit, it relys on services provided by governments, military, civilian and commercial entities. NATO has terrestrial SATCOM capabilities and units (terrestrial SATCOM anchor stations, transportable satellite ground terminals and equipment). The C2 for SATCOM is managed by NATO Communication and Information Agency (NCIA) and operated by NATO CIS Group (NCISG) [5].

Space-based assets function as force multipliers, providing support and crucial information during the strategic, operational and tactical levels of war. According to the Allied Joint Doctrine for Air and Space Operations, space capabilities provide a wide range of applications such as: global, strategic and intra-theatre satellite communications (SATCOM); positioning, navigation, and timing (PNT) services; terrestrial and space environmental monitoring; space situational awareness (SSA); intelligence, surveillance, and reconnaissance (ISR); NATO Shared Early Warning [6].

1. Satellite Communications (SATCOM): One of the most widespread functions of satellites, either civilian or military, is telecommunications. SATCOM provides support to C2 through its multiple applications, such as the establishment of communications in regions with minimal or even non existent infrastructure; transmission of intelligence; relay of messages and control of UVs.

2. Position, Navigation and Timing (PNT): The PNT data provided by space-based assets are essential for the prosecution of NATO operations, since they are used for precision targeting; tracking of friendly and enemy forces; provision of precise timing which is also vital for the function of networks and accurate navigation of troops.

3. Environmental Monitoring: Meteorological and oceanographic data collected by satellites are crucial to NATO forces since they play an important role in the planning of missions and the selection of the optimal weapons system to be deployed based on weather conditions. Also the knowledge of the conditions on the theater of operations allows forces to take advantage of them, for example the prediction of flooding based on maps developed in Afghanistan was used enhancing military operations and provide humanitarian support [7].

4. Space Situational Awareness (SSA): Space situational awareness is the knowledge regarding the outer space environment, natural and operational, and its effects on NATO operations. SSA applications includes knowledge regarding the operational capabilities and limitations of both allied and adversary space platforms; tracking of space debris; observation of space weather; tracking of adversary activities in outer space and detecting attacks against space based assets. SSA is essential for the function of satellites and the conducting of their missions.

5. Intelligence, Surveillance and Reconnaissance (ISR): Space based assets equipped with sophisticated sensors provide a host of services, such as intelligence gathering, including Signal Intelligence (SIGNIT); target information and damage assessment; warning of attacks and situational awareness.

6. NATO Shared Early Warning (SEW): Dedicated sensors onboard satellites can detect the launch of ballistic missiles and track their trajectory. Satellites also provide NATO with the capacity to detect nuclear explosions (Nuclear Detonation Detection System) which is essential for identifying any violations of international treaties banning nuclear detonations (e.g. the Partial Test Ban Treaty).

Satellites are divided into two main categories of use, military and civilian. At the dawn of the space age, satellites were predominantly used for military purposes but with the passing of time and the advancement of technology satellites have also become of civil use. The main difference between the two systems is the end user. Dual Use technology addresses both military and commercial markets. In the US sector dual use satellites serve both the federal government and the civilian market.

A historical case example of Dual Use technologies can be traced in the context of the Space race that saw the US and the USSR in competition to rule outer space. This race was carried out with military and civilian personnel to develop technologies that could carry satellites in outer space for scientific, as well as military purposes. The re-entry of the launcher with scientific data was used by the military for the potential deployment of multiple independently targetable re-entry vehicles. This is exactly what has also been experienced at national level in the EU and in the US where there is a strong tendency to look for synergies.

In the early 1990s the US Agency DARPA started a Dual Use collaboration in the Global Mobile Information Systems (GloMo) programme. This programme aimed to accelerate the development of mobile computing and looked at Dual Use technologies for digitising military and civilian communications.

In late 1993, DARPA was managing the Dual Use programme "Technology Reinvestment Program" [8] (TRP), with the goal of forging stronger collaborations between the military and commercial R&D sectors. This collaboration granted security investment for this field. The synergies between the military and the Civilian intertwined with the R&D is still carried out with the development of technologies that are used by both the field for security and defence.

The driver for both American and Soviet space programmes was the acquisition of military capabilities: in terms of capacity of delivering nuclear weapons as well as placing satellites in orbit for strategic communications and acquisition of information on the adversary's territory [9]. Another contribution that highlights the role of outer space as a geopolitical variable meant to enhance state power is Everett Dolman's Astropolitik which "encompass[es] the social and cultural effects of new technologies, in this case space technologies, on the subsequent evolution of political institutions" [10].

3 Asat

Bearing in mind the host of services that satellites provide, it is a natural consequence that, parallelly with the development of satellite technology, the space powers sought ways to deny their adversaries such services by neutralising their space platforms. This led to the development of Anti-Satellite weapons (ASAT). These weapons function by Denying, Disrupting, Disabling, Destroying or Deceiving their targets (5Ds) [11]. Denying and disrupting have temporary effects, while disabling may be of permanent nature. The kinetic destruction of satellites has permanent and irreversible effects. Except for the targeting [12] of space based assets, their supporting ground facilities can be the targets of an attack as well.

3.1 Hard-Kill and Soft-Kill ASAT Weapons

ASAT weapon systems are divided in two categories, hard-kill and soft-kill.

- Hard-kill ASAT weapons are based on the use of a projectile or other methods in order to achieve the kinetic destruction of the target. Due to the predictability of satellite orbits and their restricted maneuverability, satellites are particularly susceptible to such attacks [13].
- Soft-kill ASAT attacks, on the other hand, rely on interfering with the satellite's sensors (via jamming, spoofing or blinding through the use of powerful lasers), or with the satellite's software (via cyber attack). These attacks can render a satellite defunct without destroying it.

3.2 ASAT Testings

USA

The United States, along with Russia, were the precursors of ASAT weapons and have carried out a number of successful testings. The most recent ASAT testing was Operation Burnt Frost, entailing the interception of the reconnaissance satellite USA-193, which failed one month after its launch and was decaying from orbit. The interception was carried out on 20 February 2008 from the USS Lake Erie using a RIM-161 Standard Missile 3 [14].

Russia

Russia tested five ASAT experiments between November 2015 and December 2018. The testings were carried out with the russian anti-ballistic/anti-satellite missiles A-235 PL-19 Nudol, without intercepting any targets.

Russian R&D continue to improve on-orbit capabilities that could serve dual-use purposes and that can be deployed anywhere. Since 2010, Russia stated that the "weaponization of information is a key aspect of this strategy and is employed in times of peace, crisis, and war. Russia considers the information sphere to be strategically decisive and has taken steps to modernize its military's information attack and defense organizations and capabilities". Moreover Russia's President Vladimir Putin stated that the laser weapon system is a "new type of strategic weapons" [15].

China

On 11 January 2007, China targeted and destroyed the aging weather satellite Feng Yun 1C in LEO with a single ballistic missile launched from the Xichang Space Center. This ASAT testing led to the creation of more than 2000 pieces of trackable space debris [16, 17].

China put a great focus on the development of launchers such as the Long March 11 (LM-11) defined as quick response, which can support military operations in a conflict or civilian in the event of a disaster. Unlike other launchers, these can be transported by wheeled vehicles or railroad in unmarked containers. On 5 June 2019, a LM-11 was launched from a floating platform from the chinese Yellow Sea. This operation demonstrated the deployment capabilities of stealthy ballistic missiles and Anti-Satellite Weapons (ASATs). This operation had previously only been completed by Russia.

By 2020 China's military is expected to deploy a laser weapon (ASAT) capable of damaging satellites in low earth orbit. This is a development of the 2006 chinese test from a ground based laser that dazzle an orbiting satellite [18]. Moreover China "probably intends to pursue additional ASAT weapons capable of destroying satellites up to GEO" [19].

India

On 27 March 2019, India intercepted and destroyed Microsat-R Earth observation satellite on Low Earth Orbit with an Prithvi Defence Vehicle (PDV) Mark-II interceptor [20]. This test proved that India has the necessary capabilities to perform an anti-satellite operation. Moreover India is performing a large number of launches of nano and small satellites. India is providing the necessary equipment to other nations that have no launch capabilities, mitigating the monopoly that the US and Russia have established in the last years.

3.3 Future Threats

Nations with a space objective, such as North Korea, are increasingly getting to the point of developing technologies that would allow them to reach space. The numerous missile test that the nation is carrying out is the proof of a strong interest and a potential threat to the space ecosystem. A militaristic nation such as North Korea may develop and implement their technologies in ASAT weapons due to the high rewards with little investments.

4 The Legal Approach of ASAT Weapons

The legal implications of using ASAT weapons should be examined under international space law as well as international humanitarian law.

4.1 Space Law

Article IV OST

As far as it concerns international space law, the military uses of outer space are regulated by Article IV of the Treaty on Principles Governing the Activities of States in the Exploration and Use of Outer Space, including the Moon and other Celestial Bodies [21] of 1967. Article IV dictates that "States Parties to the Treaty undertake not to place in orbit around the Earth any objects carrying nuclear weapons or any other kinds of weapons of mass destruction, install such weapons on celestial bodies, or station such weapons in outer space in any other manner". Only the "placement" of WMDs in outer space is forbidden, while on the other hand, the use of direct ascent systems loaded with WMDs and their detonation in outer space is not restricted by the OST (but the detonation of a nuclear warhead would violate the 1963 Treaty Banning Nuclear Weapon Tests in the Atmosphere, in Outer Space and Under Water (Partial Test Ban Treaty, PTBT) [22]. Hence the deployment and use of ASAT weapons in Earth's orbit as well as in the void of Outer Space is permitted as long as they do not constitute WMDs.

The same is not true regarding the placement of ASAT weapons on celestial bodies, like the Moon. Article IV dictates that "the Moon and other celestial bodies shall be used by all States Parties to the Treaty exclusively for peaceful purposes". Hence the deployment and use of ASAT weapons on celestial bodies is prohibited by the OST, since it constitutes an aggressive use of said bodies.

Article IX OST

Article IX OST imposes on States Parties the responsibility to undertake international consultations before proceeding with an activity or experiment that the State has reason to believe could potentially cause harmful interference with the activities of other States

Parties in the peaceful exploration and use of Outer Space. The kinetic destruction of a satellite generates a large number of space debris that could hinder the activities of other States, hence the State that has planned the attack is obligated to undertake consultations with any State that could be affected, prior to the attack [23]. This is why the Chinese FY-1C ASAT test was criticized by the international community, since there was no prior notice.

4.2 International Humanitarian Law

Customary international humanitarian law dictates that attacks must be fulfil the criteria of discrimination, proportionality and necessity [24].

- Discrimiation: Articles 48 and 52(2) of the Additional Protocol I to the 1949 Geneva Conventions [25] dictate that only military objectives can be the targets of an attack, with military objectives being assets which "by their nature, location, purpose, or use make an effective contribution to military action and whose total or partial destruction, capture or neutralisation, in the circumstances ruling at the time, offers a definite military advantage". Hence civilian satellites can only be targeted if they provide a military advantage to the adversary.
- Proportionality: The damage caused by the planned attack must not be excessive in proportion to the military advantage gained from it.
- Necessity: The attack must be necessary in order to overcome the enemy.

This is why an ASAT attack based on the electromagnetic pulse created by a nuclear detonation in outer space would violate the regulations of international humanitarian law, since it is by nature indiscriminate and the damage caused would not be proportional to the advantage gained [26]. The same issues appear regarding the kinetic destruction of a space object which results in the creation of a large amount of space debris. On the other hand by using soft kill methods like jamming or cyber attack no issues of proportionality or discrimination arise if the target is a legitimate military objective.

5 Actions that Can Be Taken to Contrast ASAT Weapons

In order to protect its space-based assets from adversary ASAT attacks, NATO needs to take certain countermeasures. These countermeasures can be either passive or active. Passive countermeasures are practices such as stationing decoy satellites, increasing the maneuverability of satellites, so as to be able to avoid kinetic attacks, and hardening their components, such as their remote sensors, in order to withstand an attack. Active countermeasures would entail equipping satellites with defence mechanisms or non destructive countermeasures such as jamming [27].

The increase and the wide range of ASAT has ensured that resilience was used to safeguard activities in Space. There has been an increase in the number of cybernetic systems with defence and security strategies.

Cyber security should reduce the risk of a cyber-attack and protect the satellite. This would reduce the risk but would not eliminate it because there is always the possibility of the satellite being hacked. The only activity that can be done is to work on the capacity of cyber resilience because this allows the continuity of the satellite's operation in such a way as not to influence the activities of the system.

The US Department of Defence considered the occurrence of an attack on a single or multiple satellites. On this end, there has been an increase in the number of satellites in order to have a continuous coverage even with the failure of some units of the system.

With the increase of nano-satellites and mega-constellations an attack would be able to stop an entire system because a single satellite is interconnected with others for sharing information. For this reason not only the number of satellites should be higher but there should be several constellations isolated from each other so that the operation of the constellation or satellite continues even after an attack. This would be considered as a redundancy that prevents data and activity loss.

Good practices that support the creation and sustainability of effective national capacities in order to provide system resilience are those that can prevent and what can be "emergency plans" that should provide "an overview of national incident response mechanisms; in addition to highlight how cybersecurity incidents are classified, based on their impact on critical goods and services".

Information sharing is another key point because during an attack accurate and appropriate communication can eventually lead to the identification of the attackers. Many organisations in the World, such as NATO, are conducting exercises in this field. Periodically NATO implements exercises and simulations of war and cyber attack (CMX) [28].

These international computer security simulations help to strengthen the responsiveness and resilience of states and strengthen trust between countries and improve overall international resilience and preparedness levels. Resilience should focus on two topics: "Critical Infrastructure" and "Critical Information Infrastructures". The first is essential for the functioning and security of a company and an economy while the second is the system that manages the key functions of the critical infrastructure. These two must be protected in accordance with the principle of risk management and resilience.

6 Conclusion

With the military and economic importance of space-based assets increasing so does the need to develop systems that could target and neutralize these assets. This led to the development of Anti-Satellite weapons that can temporarily or permanently damage the adversary's satellites.

The development and use of ASAT created a new field were NATO and its member States can enhance their offensive operational capabilities in order to safeguard their security. NATO already embraced this domain with the implementation of personnel and infrastructure. The fast development of technologies and threats should be faced with the formation and information of NATO and non-NATO personnel.

NATO should also take into consideration the threat adversary ASAT weapons pose to its own space-based assets and take the necessary defensive measures. Such measures would be the enhancement of its cyber-security and the deployment of resilient systems.

ASAT testings have been carried out by single nations, however they have to be done on a more united front. This can be ensured and carried out only by NATO, which aims to maintain a stable balance of power.

The current legal framework for the use and testing of ASAT Weapons does not create any legal implications however the proliferation of these Weapons may create the requirement of its revision on an international level.

The development and deployment of ASAT Weapon systems, would give NATO the capacity to deny its adversaries the multiple services that space platforms provide. ASAT weapons will play a major role in the future of warfare, bearing in mind the increasing reliance on satellites and their applications. It is critical that the Organisation will maintain its superiority as a military force on Earth and in outer space.

References

1. Tronchetti, F.: Fundamentals of Space Law and Policy. Springer Briefs in Space Development, p. 4 (2013)
2. Pike, J.: The military uses of outer space. In: Armaments, Disarmaments and International Security, Stockholm International Peace Research Institute (SIPRI), pp. 613–664 (2003)
3. Lieutenant General Panato, S.: Space and Air Power in NATO. Air & Space Power in NATO-Future Vector Part II, pp. 117–126 (2014)
4. Financial Times: Nato prepares first outer space strategy to deal with new threats. https://www.ft.com/content/08bb833c-9439-11e9-aea1-2b1d33ac3271. Reuters: NATO aims to make space new frontier in defense. https://www.reuters.com/article/us-nato-space-exclusive/exclusive-nato-aims-to-make-space-new-frontier-in-defense-idUSKCN1TM1AD
5. AJP-3.3: Allied Joint Doctrine for Air and Space Operations, Ed. B, Version 1, 5-4 (2016)
6. AJP-3.3: Allied Joint Doctrine for Air and Space Operations, Ed. B, Version 1, 5-1 (2016)
7. Unal, B.: Cybersecurity of NATO's Space-based Strategic Assets. Chatham House, The Royal Institute of International Affairs. The International Security Department (2019)
8. The Technology Reinvestment Project: Integrating Military and Civilian Industries. https://www.cbo.gov/publication/16584
9. Sheehan, M.J.: The International Politics of Space. Routledge, London (2007)
10. Dolman, E.C.: Astropolitik: Classical Geopolitics in the Space Age. School of Advance Airpower Studies, Maxwell Air Force Base, p. 4 (2002)
11. Bourbonniere, M., Lee, R.J.: Jus ad Bellum and Jus in Bello Considerations on the Targeting of Satellites: The Targeting of Post-Modern Military Space Assets, 44 ISR. Y.B. HUM. RTS. 167, p. 218 (2014)
12. Solis, G.D.: The Law of Armed Conflict: International Humanitarian Law in War, p. 519. Cambridge University Press, Cambridge (2010)
13. Lieutenant General Panato, S.: Space and Air Power in NATO. Air & Space Power in NATO-Future Vector Part II, p. 120 (2014)
14. Missle Defence Agency, U.S. Department of Defence. https://web.archive.org/web/20120214031001/http://www.mda.mil/system/aegis_one_time_mission.html
15. Defense Intelligence Agency: Challenges to Security in Space, p. 29 (2019)
16. Chinese ASAT Test. https://celestrak.com/events/asat.php
17. Rosanelli, R.: Le Attività Spaziali nelle Politiche di Sicurezza e Difesa. Istituto Affari Internazionali IAI, p. 38 (2011)
18. Defense Aerospace: China to Deploy ASAT Laser by 2020; China, Russia also set to use anti-satellite missiles. http://www.defense-aerospace.com/articles-view/release/3/200104/dia%3A-china-to-deploy-asat-laser-by-2020.html

19. Defense Intelligence Agency: Challenges to Security in Space, p. 21 (2019)
20. India's A-SAT test and what it tell about the country's capability to shoot down Ballistic Missiles. https://www.drdo.gov.in/drdo/pub/npc/2019/May/din-03may2019.pdf
21. Treaty on Principles Governing the Activities of States in the Exploration and Use of Outer Space, including the Moon and other Celestial Bodies, entered into force Oct. 10, 1967 18 U.S.T. 2410, 610 U.N.T.S. 205 [hereinafter OST]
22. Treaty Banning Nuclear Weapon Tests in the Atmosphere, in Outer Space, and Under Water of 5 August 1963, in force 10 October 1963, 480 UNTS 43, 1964 2 I.L.M. 889 et seq
23. Kyriakopoulos, G.D.: The Current Legal Regulation, in International Law and in Space Law, of the Use of ASAT Weapons
24. Koplow, D.A.: Asat-isfaction - customary international law and the regulation of anti-satellite weapons. Mich. J. Int. Law **30**(4), 1187–1272 (2009)
25. Protocol Additional to the Geneva Conventions of 12 August 1949, and relating to the Protection of Victims of International Armed Conflicts (Protocol I), 8 June 1977
26. See the effects of the Starfish Prime experiment of 1962
27. U.S. Congress, Office of Technology Assessment, Anti-Satellite Weapons, Countermeasures, and Arms Control, OTA- 1.S 281 (Washington, 1) C: (U. S. Government Printing Office, September 1985)
28. North Atlantic Treaty Organization: Crisis Management Exercise 2019. https://www.nato.int/cps/en/natohq/news_165844.htm

Persistence Through Collaboration at Sea for Off-Shore and Coastal Operations

Agostino Bruzzone[1(✉)], Marina Massei[1], Kirill Sinelshchikov[2], Leonardo Baviera[2], Giuliano Fabbrini[2], Marco Gotelli[2], Josef Procházka[3], Libor Kutěj[3], and Radomir Scurek[4]

[1] DIME Genoa University, 16145 Genoa, Italy
{agostino,massei}@itim.unige.it
[2] Simulation Team, Delfino Building, 17100 Savona, Italy
{kirill,baviera,fabbrini,gotelli}@simulationteam.com
[3] University of Defence, Brno, Czech Republic
{josef.prochazka,libor.kutej}@unob.cz
[4] WSB University Dąbrowa Górnicza, Dąbrowa Górnicza, Poland
radomir.scurek@gmail.com

Abstract. Collaboration (Bruzzone et al. 2013a, b, c, d, e, f) is often mentioned as an opportunity to develop new capabilities for autonomous systems; indeed this paper proposes a practical application where use this approach to enhance the autonomy of the systems during operations in coastal areas or around offshore platforms. The proposed case deals with developing a collaborative approach (Bruzzone et al. 2013a, b, c, d, e, f) among an USV (Unmanned Surface Vehicle) with several AUV (Autonomous Underwater Vehicles) to guarantee persistent surveillance over a marine area (Shkurti et al. 2012). Obviously, the proposed solution could be adopted also for defense and homeland security (Bruzzone et al. 2011a, b, 2010) as well as for archeological site protection in consistence with related cost analysis. The authors propose a technological solution as well as a simulation framework to validate and demonstrate the capabilities of this new approach as well as to quantify expected improvements.

Keywords: Simulation · AUV · USV · Autonomous systems · Collaboration

1 Introduction

The increase of marine traffic and growth of marine activities creates many issues related to protect and reduce vulnerabilities by using new technologies, such as those based on autonomous system (Bhatta et al. 2005). Therefore, this field is challenging (Bruzzone 2013) and often it is necessary to develop computer simulation (Bruzzone et al. 2011a, b) to investigate different alternatives related to their use and the technological and engineering solutions to be adopted. Their operational effectiveness and efficiency (Bruzzone 2016). In addition, nowadays, it is possible to develop these new solutions for supporting

© Springer Nature Switzerland AG 2020
J. Mazal et al. (Eds.): MESAS 2019, LNCS 11995, pp. 427–438, 2020.
https://doi.org/10.1007/978-3-030-43890-6_35

regular operations, carrying out inspections and assistance activities in order to maximize their use as well as to improve the overall performance. This is very interesting for cases such as those related to offshore platforms (Bruzzone et al. 2013a, b, c, d, e, f) or critical infrastructures and industrial plants located within ports (Bruzzone et al. 2012). It requires to consider the necessity to transform marine autonomous systems in reliable solutions integrated with other assets and systems operating within this framework (Kalra et al. 2007) as well as to guarantee continuous services to the operations (Martins et al. 2011). The authors in this paper propose a solution devoted to enhance persistence on surveillance and operation within the marine domain by adopting a new engineering solution that support collaboration among different robotic systems (Feddema et al. 2002). The case is described in terms of solution and it is proposed a combined use of simulation to test the engineering solution and detailed configuration as well as to evaluate the operational performance respect a scenario. This research further develops previous activities carried out on the combined use of USV (Unmanned Surface Vehicle) and AUV (Autonomous Underwater Vehicle) out in C++ and Vega Prime. In addition, it specifies them respect new simulation framework based on C# and Unity 3D as well as respect a new scenario of interoperability (Massei and Tremori 2010) with other assets such as ROV and human divers (Tanner and Christodoulakis 2007).

2 Marine Domain and Protection of Critical Infrastructures

Protecting Critical Infrastructures in coastal areas (Bruzzone et al. 2013a, b, c, d, e, f) as well as facing open sea such as offshore platform, is a critical issue for Industrial Development and should address a wide spectrum of potential threats. Therefore, also important outline could result critical to improve performances. For instance, the use of AUV for Off-Shore Platform is growing and it is providing great support to inspections in deep sea as well as supervision to divers on middle range operations (50–300 m) with the big advantage respect ROV (Remote Operated Vehicles) that operating without cables guarantees much more agility, mobility and accessibility over the different underwater areas. These considerations make potentially convenient to adopt solutions that use intensively these systems despite their limitations in terms of autonomy that usually correspond to few hours or maximum one day for propelled systems. Similar considerations could be adopted for operations related to screening or patrolling an area as well an archeological site, to conduct intensive mine hunting or other kinds of missions (Bruzzone et al. 2004).

A classical approach to speed up these process is add additional autonomous systems operating in parallel by subdividing areas and possibly, by collaborative approach, calling support from others into a specific zone when something critical emerge (e.g. suspect image coming from side scanner sonar to be checked by another point of view). However, the limited speed of most AUV (usually less equal to 4 knots) is a hard limit in redeploying the assets around based on emerging needs.

In addition, the single AUV autonomy is still limited despite the availability of multiple assets (Medeiros et al. 2010). Finally, the use of AUV at sea refers to R&D, with limited capability to deploy and recover the vehicle at sea in real operations. Usually these activities are carried out by RHIB (Rigid Hull Inflatable Boat) with humans operating manually and resulting into hard limitations respect usual sea conditions in oceans and open sea (Shafer et al. 2008; Sujit et al. 2009).

Due to this sum of reasons, the authors propose an automated release and recovery system that rely on a flexible solution involving a "catcher" and a "revolver". The catcher is a special AUV connected with a "base" by a cable designed to finalize the final search of an AUV and the docking operations, so the catcher could collect AUV at sea, download data, recharge them and/or simply pull them back to the base (Stilwell et al. 2004). The base include the revolver, which is an automated mechanism able to hold different AUV (e.g. 3 middle size AUV) ready to be re-deployed and/or restored. Indeed a special winch with a basic robotic arm allows to pull back the catcher with its prey and to put the captured AUV in the revolver that block it by special adaptable jaws (Ferrandez et al. 2013; Vail and Veloso 2003). In the proposed case, the revolver is mounted over a special USV, based on a SWATH (Small-waterplane-area twin hull). It is a special boat characterized by extreme capabilities in terms of sea keeping as well as a good configuration to hold the revolver into a central bay. In addition, SWATH speed guarantees the capability to react promptly to requests and to deploy and recover quickly the AUV even in challenging weather conditions. The authors developed an engineering solution for this system and simulated it to check the convenience over operations.

The simulation consider the necessity to maintain a persistent surveillance over underwater operation around an Off-Shor Platform and measure the responsiveness, persistence, costs (Magrassi 2013) and redundancies respect a traditional approach. It results evident the improvement based on this collaborative approach among the AUVs, the catcher and the SWATH, as well as the importance to properly design the logic of these cooperation and the autonomous capabilities of each system by an effective AI solution.

It is evident that the proposed solution is dealing with quite sophisticated systems and complex case to justify costs; therefore, the authors are even considering operating on smaller AUV and SWATH to create flexible solutions to be used in coastal areas in flexible way that could be intensively used over multiple applications thanks to their readiness.

3   Collaborative Operations Based on the Revolver

This innovative system was conceived in order to automate and speed up the recovery and release of AUV systems into the sea.

The author has taken into account different general scenarios. The two main different scenarios are the military one and the civil one (Bruzzone and Massei 2017). AUV and ROV system are used in various military operations, such as: inspection and identification of ports and infrastructures (Bruzzone et al. 2013a, b, c, d, e, f) mine sweeping (cut mines from the minefield), mine hunting (through a sonar identifies and inspects the mine, and then sends the divers to neutralize it) mine breaking (using a ship difficult to sink sent into a minefield in order to explode all the mines) coastal patrolling, long-distance missions (Bui et al. 2017). These systems AUV and ROV are also widely used in the civil with different purposes: background mapping, underwater archeology, wreck search.

AUV and ROV system are widely used because of their multiple vantages. AUV is equipped with a battery compartment so it does not have to be attached to the electricity, wireless technology in order to use the Data transfer unit and the Data receiving unit.

Usually are made in Torpedo shape and, finally yet importantly, AUV can make decisions with AI using data of the GPS. ROV are equipped with fiber optic cable for data transfer to control and command Unit that is on the ship that released the ROV, it has not a battery compartment so it needs a Power Supply cable (Richards et al. 2002).

In order to ensure that the operator that controls ROV can monitor it is equipped with cameras (Tuan Bui et al. 2018) and in some circumstances even with mechanical arms.

To support collaborative models we designed the release system taking into account the customer's precise requests (Bruzzone et al. 2013a, b, c, d, e, f). The loading system with AUVs must be transportable both on board a SWATH catamaran and on board an SH-60 helicopter. In order to respect these specifics we minimize the weight of the system. Originally, the structure was a cylinder with 4 housing for the AUV. Its weight without the AUVs was over 5000 kg that was not good because the maximum load transportable by the SH-60 is 3400 kg. Then, it was decided that 3 housing were enough; indeed the structure was still too much heavy. In a second moment, we also proceeded to lighten the structure passing from a full form to an empty one by over-dimensioning the most stressed areas that were spotted through a FEM analysis. In facts, we inserted an axial-symmetric cylinder to uniform the distribution of pressure. Total weight of the structure without the AUV is now only 633 kg, a good optimization.

Lightening the structure has also made it necessary to design a system of pliers and housings where to hinge them. There are 3 pliers for each AUV in order to make it stable. We can see below the structure data extrapolated from the modeling program PTC CREO PARAMETRIC.

VOLUME = 8.0147249e + 07 MM ^ 3
AREA SURFACE = 9.9802928e + 06 MM ^ 2
DENSITY = 7.9000000e-09 TONNE / MM ^ 3
MASS = 6.3316327e-01 TONNE

BARICENTRO compared to coordinate system _TAMB:
X Y Z 1.6707669e-01 2.5000000e + 03 -6.8959770e + 01 MM

INERTIA TENSOR:
Ixx Ixy Ixz 5.2086376e + 06 -2.6446706e + 02 -1.1614802e + 00
Iyx Iyy Iyz -2.6446706e + 02 7.9650937e + 03 1.0915698e + 05
Izx Izy Izz -1.1614802e + 00 1.0915698e + 05 5.2056357e + 06

BARBELD INERTIA with respect to the _TAMB coordinate system (TONNE * MM ^ 2)

INERTIA TENSOR:
Ixx Ixy Ixz 1.2483562e + 06 0.0000000e + 00 -8.4565151e + 00
Iyx Iyy Iyz 0.0000000e + 00 4.9540998e + 03 0.0000000e + 00
Izx Izy Izz -8.4565151e + 00 0.0000000e + 00 1.2483652e + 06

KEY MOMENTS OF INERTIA: (TONNE * MM ^ 2)
I1 I2 I3 4.9540998e + 03 1.2483512e + 06 1.2483703e + 06

ROTATION MATRIX from orientation _TAMB to MAIN AXES:
0.00000 0.00000 1.00000
1.00000 0.00000 0.00000
0.00000 1.00000 0.00000

ROTATION CORNERS from orientation _TAMB to MAIN AXES (degrees):
angles around x y z 0.000 90.000 90.000

ROTATION RAYS compared to MAIN AXES:
R1 R2 R3 8.8455435e + 01 1.4041404e + 03 1.4041512e + 03 MM

The material chosen for the construction of the structure is martensitic steel and the production process is stamped in the sand, at least for the prototype. The movement of the structure is entrusted to an electric motor in C.C.ad with high braking torque chosen from the AEG catalog with efficiency class IE1 IE2 with protection degree IP54, IP55, IP56 and power of 35 kW. The sensor chosen is very practical and economical, a phonic wheel with proximity sensor. The cylinders were chosen from the Enerpac catalog. We opted for double-acting cylinders of the RR series and we chose a RR-20024 for the front, that is, those with longer strokes and one RR-20018 for the one with the shortest run.

We also proceeded to realize a simulation on Unity where it was necessary to create a various script in C#.

The first was the buoyancy model (Oddone et al. 2017) to be able to position the catamaran SWATH with other boats and ships to demonstrate the potential of a second script, which, in fact, is an AI that makes the catamaran able to conduct itself and avoid the obstacles that are interposed. The AI was also applied to the SH-60 because the specifications required a completely autonomous application with a good degree of interoperability (Bruzzone et al. 2015; Weiss 2011).

The concept of interoperability comes to the fore when the interaction between the helicopter or catamaran controller and the engine that drives the release structure is necessary. In fact, under certain conditions of proximity to a Waypoint, the script starts to activate the engine of the structure providing for the release of the AUVs.

There were many other scripts used for controlling the ship and the helicopter remotely and even one in the case that we want to simulate the AUV. We fixed 3 independent variables and we provided an RSM analysis (Figs. 1, 2 and 3).

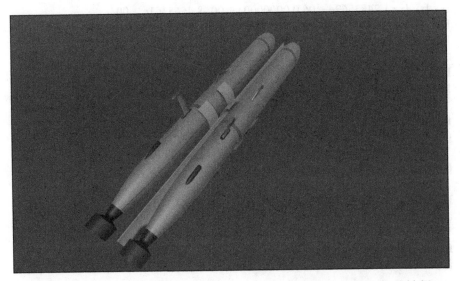

Fig. 1. Automated Revolver able to deploy 3 AUV (Autonomous Underwater Vehicle)

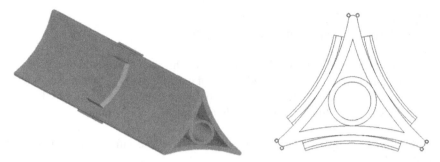

Fig. 2. Body of the Revolver designed to hold the 3 AUV within the SWATH (Small-waterplane-area twin hull) bay and Section of the Revolver able to hold the 3 AUV within the SWATH bay

Fig. 3. Example of Helicopter holding device for deploy and recovery AUV

4 Mission Models and Scenario Description

In order to evaluate the effectiveness and efficiency of proposed solutions and to improve collaboration capabilities among USV and AUV (Stary et al. 2018), it was decided to define specific missions respect the scenario related to operations around an offshore Platform. In this case, it is supposed to operate respect a permanent offshore tension-leg oil platform (TLP) operating in open sea by considering possibility to use Divers up to 300 m for operations as well as ROV and AUV in supporting roles. The main activities are summarized as following:

1. Intensive Operation up to 300 m underwater
2. Underwater Operation between 300 and 2000 m underwater

3. Main Inspection/Support up to 2000 m underwater
4. Minor Inspection/Support up to 2000 m underwater

The activity 1 requires use of Humans or ROV, while activity 2 could operate just by ROV. Other mission could be addressed by any of the different available resources based on the most convenient and effective result also respect dynamic availabilities, location, autonomy level, capability and efficiency. In particular:

- Human Divers with hyperbaric chambers and all related infrastructures (Bruzzone et al. 2017)
- ROV operating from support boats
- AUV using Revolver Solution from the platform
- AUV using Revolver Solution operating from SWATH

The simulator developed to reproduce the detail of the operations is integrated with a scenario generator based on Stochastic Discrete Event Simulation that generate the mission over a time frame that in our case was based over 12 months of operations even considering the different sea conditions and impact on operations. The generation activities is summarized in following figure that present the mapping of operations, while in the table is proposed an extract from the inspections and operations created by the simulator to be addressed by different system (Figs. 4 and 5).

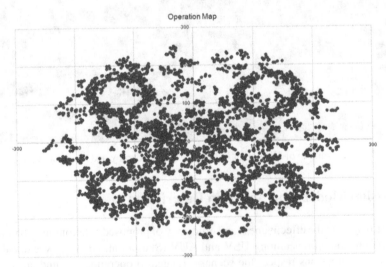

Fig. 4. Operation mapping around oil platform

During the dynamic simulation, at each request for a mission, the simulator identify the most suitable asset based on its capability to address the request, the time required for it to respond, its efficiency on this task, its cost and its residual autonomy. The simulation does not provide directly the optimal configuration, therefore the authors introduced some simplified meta-model that estimate impacts on cost of different high

Time	ID	Mission Code	Workload [h]	X [m]	Y [m]	Depth [m]	Solution	Asset Tag	Time to Finish[h]	Responsiveness [min]
203.12	1690	4	13.91	-26.3	5.9	1'761	Swath & AUV	1	13.97	14
203.45	1691	4	14.21	-21.3	3.3	1'749	Swath & AUV	1	14.26	14
203.79	1692	4	14.58	-32.4	-1.8	1'749	Swath & AUV	1	14.62	15
204.13	1693	4	14.16	-20.8	1.6	1'743	Swath & AUV	1	14.25	14
204.59	27	1	223.06	65.4	-128.4	96	Human Team	3	258.58	48
205.23	1694	4	14.31	-41.3	-13.8	1'227	Swath & AUV	2	14.36	15
205.57	1695	4	14.86	-33.4	-9.6	1'224	Swath & AUV	2	14.95	15
205.92	1696	4	13.92	-42.1	-3.9	1'227	Swath & AUV	2	13.97	14
206.25	1697	4	14.82	-35.6	-4.8	1'225	Swath & AUV	2	14.90	15
206.30	1131	2	13.91	76.6	116.0	1'636	ROV	1	13.94	61

Fig. 5. Inspections and operations

level characteristics of AUV, Swath, ROV adopted on the proposed configuration, in order to estimate also economic relevance of each solutions. These meta-models have been developed based on available data on different assets, correlating costs of operations, acquisition and speed, autonomy, etc. In this way, it was possible to define a Central Composite Design able to investigate the different configurations and to identify most promising combined solutions (Montgomery 2000).

The independent variables considered for this case are summarized in the following table (Fig. 6).

Table: Ind.	ROV	Human Teams	Swath	Swath	Swath Autonomy	AUV	AUV	AUV	Catcher	Catcher
Variables Ranges	Number	Number	Number	Speed [knots]	Autonomy [h]	Number	Speed [knots]	Autonomy [h]	Cable [m]	Speed [knots]
Min	0	1	0	10	12	0	3	8	25	2
Central	2	2	1	18	24	3	4	16	50	3
Maximum	4	3	2	26	36	6	5	24	100	4

Fig. 6. Independent variables

The Human Teams are composed by 8 people operating all around the clock, able to support redundancies related to preparations and just deal with the missions generated by the simulator and does not consider all other activities. Swath number considers having a Vehicle with a Catcher and a Revolver with 3 AUV, while number of AUVs represents the number of AUV supported directly by the platform. Mean Square pure

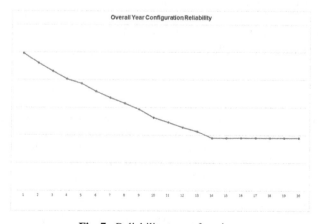

Fig. 7. Reliability target functions

Error analysis was used to validate and verify the model while (Kleijnen 2007) Experimental Results obtained by applying Central Composite Design allowed to create a meta-model to support configuration optimization achieving the improvement proposed by following figure in terms of responsiveness and costs. Some data have been altered due to confidentiality reasons (Figs. 7 and 8).

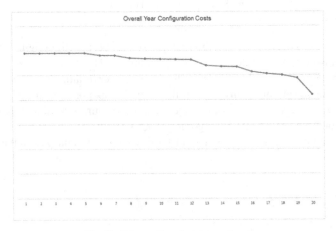

Fig. 8. Fitness function respect cost

5   Conclusions

The proposed research represent an integrated approach to support design, engineering and operations within collaborative use of autonomous systems; the models resulted interesting to support decisions about the configuration as well as how to integrate the new systems with pre-existing assets and how to coordinate their operations (Balci 1998; Telford 2012). This is just a preliminary and synthetic result of the research, therefore the author are currently working on further detailing the models and the simulation experimentation to support decisions in this specific scenario as well as in developing other mission environments (Tether et al. 2009).

References

Balci, O.: Verification, validation and testing. In: Handbook of Simulation: Principles, Advances, Applications, and Practice, pp. 335–393. Wiley (1998)

Bhatta, P., et al.: Coordination of an underwater glider feet for adaptive sampling. In: International Workshop on Underwater Robotics, Genova, Italy, pp. 61–69 (2005)

Bruzzone, A.G., Agresta, M., Sinelshchikov, K.: Hyperbaric plant simulation for industrial applications. In: Proceedings of IWISH, Barcelona, September (2017)

Bruzzone, A.G., Massei, M.: Simulation-based military training. In: Mittal, S., Durak, U., Ören, T. (eds.) Guide to Simulation-Based Disciplines. SFMA, pp. 315–361. Springer, Cham (2017). https://doi.org/10.1007/978-3-319-61264-5_14

Oddone, M., Bruzzone, A.G., Coelho, E., Cecchi, D., Garau, B.: An underwater buoyancy-driven glider simulator with modelling & simulation as a service architecture. In: Proceedings of Defense and Homeland Security Simulation Workshop, Barcelona, September (2017)

Bruzzone A.G.: Simulation and intelligent agents for joint naval training. In: Invited Speech at Naval Training Simulation Conference, London, UK (2016)

Bruzzone, A.G., et al.: Guidelines for developing interoperable simulation focused on maritime operations combining autonomous systems and traditional assets. In: Proceedings of International Defence and Homeland Security Workshop, Bergeggi, September (2015)

Bruzzone A.G., et al.: Virtual framework for testing/experiencing potential of collaborative autonomous systems. In: Proceedings of I/ITSEC, Orlando, FL, USA (2013a)

Bruzzone, A.G., Merani, D., Massei, M., Tremori, A., Bartolucci, C., Ferrando, A.: Modeling cyber warfare in heterogeneous networks for protection of infrastructures and operations. In: Proceedings of I3M2013, Athens, Greece, September (2013b)

Bruzzone, A.G.: New challenges for modelling & simulation in maritime domain. In: Keynote Speech at SpringSim, San Diego, CA, April (2013)

Bruzzone, A.G., et al.: Serious game for multiuser crew collaborative procedural training and education. In: Proceedings of I/ITSEC, Orlando, FL (2013c)

Bruzzone, A.G., Massei, M., Solis, A., Poggi, S., Bartolucci, C., Capponi, L.: Serious games as enablers for training and education on operations over off-shore platforms and ships. In: Proceedings of Summer Computer Simulation Conference, Toronto, Canada (2013d)

Bruzzone, A.G., Longo, F., Tremori, A.: An interoperable simulation framework for protecting port as critical infrastructures. Int. J. Syst. Syst. Eng. **4**, 243–260 (2013e)

Bruzzone A.G., et al.: Simulating the marine domain as an extended framework for joint collaboration and competition among autonomous systems. In: Proceedings of DHSS, Athens, Greece, September (2013f)

Bruzzone, A.G., Tremori, A., Longo, F.: Interoperable simulation for protecting port as critical infrastructures. In: Proceedings of HMS2012, Wien, 19–21 September (2012)

Bruzzone, A.G., Massei, M., Tremori, A., Longo, F., Madeo, F., Tarone, F.: Maritime security: emerging technologies for asymmetric threats. In: Proceedings of EMSS, Rome, Italy, September (2011a)

Bruzzone, A.G., Tremori, A., Massei, M.: Adding smart to the mix. Model. Simul. Training Int. Def. Training J. **3**, 25–27 (2011b)

Bruzzone, A.G., Tremori, A., Bocca, E.: Security & safety training and assessment in ports based on interoperable simulation. In: Proceedings of HMS2010, Fes, Morocco, 13–15 October (2010)

Bruzzone, A.G., Cunha, G.G., Landau, L., Merkuryev, Y.: Harbour and Maritime Simulation. LAMCE Press, Rio de Janeiro, (2004). ISBN 85-89459-04-7, 230 pp.

Bui, M.T., Doskocil, R., Krivanek, V., Ha, T.H., Bergeon, Y.T., Kutilek, P.: Indirect method to estimate distance measurement based on single visual cameras. In: International Conference on Military Technologies (ICMT) 2017, pp. 696–700, May 2017. https://doi.org/10.1109/MILTECHS.2017.7988846

Feddema, J.T., Lewis, C., Schoenwald, D.A.: Decentralized control of cooperative robotic vehicles: theory and application. IEEE Trans. Robot. Autom. **18**(5), 852–864 (2002)

Ferrandez, J.M., De Lope, H., De la Paz, F.: Social and collaborative robotic. Int. J. Robot. Auton. Syst. **61**, 659–660 (2013)

Kalra, N., Ferguson, D., Stentz, A.: A generalized framework for solving tightly-coupled multi-robot planning problems. In: Proceedings of the IEEE International Conference on Robotics and Automation, April, pp. 3359–3364 (2007)

Kleijnen, J.P.C.: Design and Analysis of Simulation Experiments (International Series in Operations Research & Management Science) (2007)

Magrassi, C.: Education and training: delivering cost effective readiness for tomorrow's operations. In: Keynote Speech at ITEC2013, Rome, 22–24 May (2013)

Martins, R., de Sousa, J.B., Afonso, C.C., Incze, M.L.: REP10 AUV: shallow water operations with heterogeneous autonomous vehicles. In: Oceans, IEEE - Spain, pp. 1–6, 6–9 June (2011)

Massei M., Tremori, A.: Mobile training solutions based on ST_VP: an HLA virtual simulation for training and virtual prototyping within ports. In: Proceedings of International Workshop on Applied Modeling and Simulation, St. Petersburg, Russia, May (2010)

Medeiros, F.L.L., da Silva, J.D.S.: Computational modeling for automatic path planning based on evaluations of the effects of impacts of UAVs on the ground. J. Intell. Rob. Syst. 61(1–4), 181–202 (2010). https://doi.org/10.1007/s10846-010-9471-2

Montgomery, D.C.: Design and Analysis of Experiments. Wiley, New York (2000)

Richards, A., Bellingham, J., Tillerson, M., How, J.: Coordination and control of multiple UAVs (2002). http://acl.mit.edu/papers/2002_4588.pdf. Accessed 28 July 2015

Shafer, A.J., Benjamin, M.R., Leonard, J.J., Curcio, J.: Autonomous cooperation of heterogeneous platforms for sea-based search tasks. In: Oceans, pp. 1–10, 15–18 September (2008)

Stary, V., Krivanek, V., Stefek, A.: Optical detection methods for laser guided unmanned devices. J. Commun. Netw. 20(2), 464–472 (2018). https://doi.org/10.1109/JCN.2018.000071

Stilwell, D.J., Gadre, A.S., Sylvester, C.A., Cannell, C.J.: Design elements of a small low-cost autonomous underwater vehicle for field experiments in multi-vehicle coordination. In: Proceedings of the IEEE/OES Autonomous Underwater Vehicles, June, pp. 1–6 (2004)

Shkurti, F., et al.: Multi-domain monitoring of marine environments using a heterogeneous robot team. In: IEEE/RSJ International Conference on Intelligent Robots and Systems (IROS), pp. 1747–1753, 7–12 October (2012)

Sujit, P.B., Sousa, J., Pereira, F.L.: UAV and AUVs coordination for ocean exploration. In: Oceans - EUROPE, pp. 1–7, 11–14 May (2009)

Tanner, H.G., Christodoulakis, D.K.: Decentralized cooperative control of heterogeneous vehicle groups. Robot. Auton. Syst. 55, 811–823 (2007)

Telford, B.: Marine Corps Verification, Validation, and Accreditation (VV & A) Best Practices Guide (2012)

Tether, T.: Darpa strategic plan. Technical report DARPA, May (2009)

Tuan Bui, M., Doskocil, R., Krivanek, V., Hien Ha, T., Bergeon, Y., Kutilek, P.: Indirect method usage of distance and error measurement by single optical cameras. Adv. Mil. Technol. 13(2), 209–221 (2018). https://doi.org/10.3849/aimt.01221

Vail, D., Veloso, M.: Dynamic multi-robot coordination. In: Multi-Robot Systems: From Swarms to Intelligent Automata, vol. II, pp. 87–100 (2003)

Weiss, L.G.: Autonomous robots in the fog of war. IEEE Spectrum 48(8), 30–34+56–57 (2011). art. no. 596 0163

Author Index

Printed in the United States
By Bookmasters